THE BEST PLAYS OF 1968-1969

○ ○○
○ ○○
○ ○○ **THE**
○ ○○
○ ○○ **BURNS MANTLE**
○ ○○
○ ○○ **YEARBOOK**

THE
BEST PLAYS
OF 1968-1969

EDITED BY OTIS L. GUERNSEY JR.

*Illustrated with photographs and
with drawings by* HIRSCHFELD

○○○○○○

DODD, MEAD & COMPANY

NEW YORK • TORONTO

To the American playwright,
with admiration and thanks,
this 50th volume in the *Best Plays* series
is most respectfully dedicated

EDITOR'S NOTE

FIFTY NEW YORK theater seasons ago, reflecting on the 1919-20 theater season in his introduction to the first *Best Plays* volume, Burns Mantle told his readers: "The theater season . . . . . for all its regularity and its admitted commercialism, still plays an important part in the lives of the people. The purpose of this volume, therefore . . . . . has been to cover, as completely and accurately as possible, the activities of the theatrical season in New York, the theory being that by doing so we cover at least the physical source of supply of the drama in America. . . . . It is a compilation, we believe, that has not previously been attempted in so complete a form, and it is hoped in succeeding volumes to amplify and improve upon it."

Fifty *Best Plays* volumes and five editors later, our purpose is still to report and record a complete theater season, amplifying the coverage as needed. And in the half-century meantime, we have added another major purpose: continuity. The work so well begun by Burns Mantle in the first 28 *Best Plays* volumes and carried on by John Chapman for 5 volumes, by Louis Kronenberger for 9 volumes, by Henry Hewes for 3 volumes and by the present editor for 5 volumes including this one, is a comprehensive and *unbroken* record of the living theater in fifty yearbooks published by Dodd, Mead & Company whose dedication to this project has been the equal of any editor's. To mark the half century of this unique chronicle of a major art form, we include in the present volume a special 50th anniversary section with articles by Walter Kerr, the most perceptive drama critic since George Bernard Shaw, evaluating our theater in the perspective of the decades; and by W.A. Darlington, dean emeritus of London drama critics (his final review on Oct. 1, 1968 after 48 years with the London *Daily Telegraph* was of *Hair*) on the influence of the American theater abroad from 1919 to 1969. For this special 50-year section, Al Hirschfeld has selected a gallery of performances he has especially admired (and caricatured) over the years, and the 500 Best Plays from the 50 volumes are presented in a special chronological listing. We are most grateful to our "guest stars" for helping us celebrate the continuity of the *Best Plays* series—the beginning of the next half-century as well as the completion of the first.

Introducing the first volume, Burns Mantle also outlined the standards by which he made his selection of the Best Plays: "They represent the best judgment of the editor, variously confirmed by the public's endorsement. The intention frankly has been to compromise between the popular success, as representing the choice of the people who support the theater, and the success with sufficient claim to literary distinction of text or theme to justify its publication. As frequently has been pointed out, there are many plays that read well which do not 'act,' as the players phrase the description, and many a success that 'acts,' usually by reason of the popularity and skill of the players engaged, becomes the sheerest piffle when submitted to the test of type." John Chapman, introducing *his* first volume (1947-48), quoted from Mantle's statement and declared that his standards of selection would be similar. The Messrs. Kronenberger and Hewes made no formal statement of modus operandi. The present editor stated in *his* first volume (1964-65) that "the play-script is not only the quintessence of the theater's present, it is also most of what endures into the future. It is most of what we all mean when we say the word 'play,' and so it is most of what 'Best Play' should mean in this volume." Under the present editorship, the Best Plays are chosen largely on the basis of the script, giving as little weight as is humanly possible to performance and other production embellishments.

And let none of us forget that there are many fine scripts and productions which do *not* make the Best Plays list. The number 10 is convenient for the formal record, but it is not necessarily a unit of measurement of a whole theater season; so, in our anniversary listing of the 500 Best Plays we have added under each season's heading the titles of plays which didn't make the list but which went on to receive public acclaim in runs of a year or longer. In these volumes we do not list the Best Play titles in the order of preference, but of course there *is* an order of preference—and year after year the shade of preference between number 10 and number 11 which must be left out is very, very slight indeed.

Down through the years, volumes and editors *Best Plays* has striven to obey the Mantle dictum of "amplify and improve," to meet the expanding significance of theater in the life of America, to follow its shifting centers of interest. The complete picture of a New York theater season in 1968-69 must necessarily include complete coverage of off-Broadway production and a close look at "off off Broadway," along with the play-by-play account of Broadway activity with which the first *Best Plays* volume was preoccupied. The current volume contains articles and comprehensive listings on the seasons in London, Paris and elsewhere in Europe, and in dozens of regional theaters from coast to coast.

Such expanded coverage is made possible only by adding together the work of many devoted contributors. In his first introduction, Burns Mantle acknowledged the invaluable aid of two people. *The Best Plays of 1968-69* owes the same heartfelt thanks to more than twenty, including the abovementioned authors of the anniversary articles and Al Hirschfeld for his uniquely fascinating drawings, past and present. Jonathan Dodd of Dodd, Mead is a never-failing source of energetic help and cogent advice. The present editor's assistant-in-residence has long since taken her place in the gallant line of *Best Plays* editors' wives who have backed their husbands with moral support as the deadline approaches and the volume itself with efficient professional attention. The

European Editor of *Best Plays,* Ossia Trilling, brings both distinction and expertise to the volume, as does R.J. Schroeder in the sections devoted to New York's experimental theater. Rue Canvin (off-Broadway listings, publications and necrology), Ella A. Malin (Directory of Professional Regional Theater), Dale Olson (Los Angeles highlights), Bernard Simon (bus-truck tour information), Mimi Horowitz of *Playbill,* Hobe Morrison of *Variety* and Ralph Newman of the Drama Book Shop have made their perennial, invaluable contributions. Our sincerest thanks go out to them, as well as to Henry Hewes for his continuing help, to the authors of the volume's special articles, Leo Brady and John Bowen, to the photographers who cover the theater so well, to the scene and costume designers who contributed their drawings and to the playwrights who chose to write introductions to the synopses of their Best Plays. Did we say twenty? The true figure is nearer 100, as every theater press agent and production assistant knows who has laboriously and meticulously answered the *Best Plays* editors' questions of fact, year in and year out.

Last and most, we owe our deepest admiration and gratitude to the playwrights—not only those whose work is chosen and synopsized in the Best Plays section (one in pictures, to record the "look" of a 1968-69 show), but to all playwrights, the worst as well as the best, past and present. They are the theater's men for all seasons who perform an original act of faith that brings the art into being. They make the down payment of effort and imagination in the far from certain expectation that they will ever derive the slightest satisfaction, let alone benefit, from the enormous expenditure of themselves. Year after year for the five decades recorded by the *Best Plays* series of yearbooks, there has been a theater season in New York largely of *new* play production, all of it an act of a playwright's faith, always some of it good and often some of it memorable. That in itself is a brilliant accomplishment. We salute the American playwright with all the hurrahs there are, and most respectfully we dedicate to him and sometimes her this 50th volume in the *Best Plays* series.

OTIS L. GUERNSEY Jr.

June 1, 1969

CONTENTS

Drawings by HIRSCHFELD

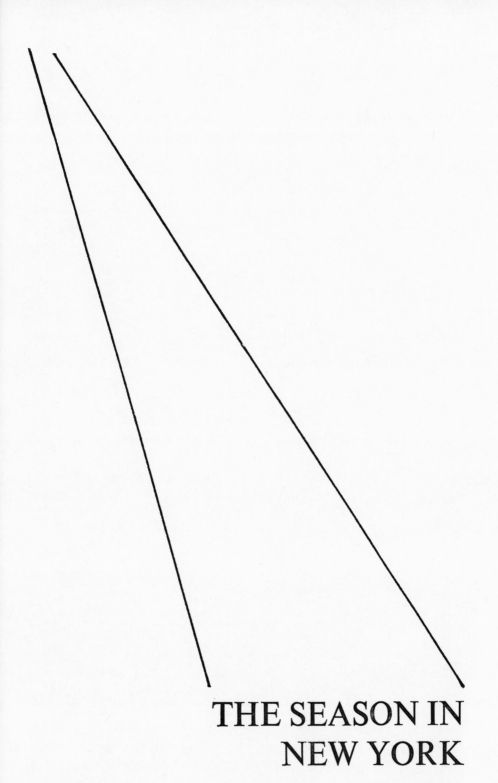

THE SEASON IN
NEW YORK

THE SEASON IN NEW YORK

O *By Otis L. Guernsey Jr.*

O

O

CALL IT A SEASON of transition, of strange new theater forms and strange new plays and playwrights from the hinterlands—but don't insist on burying Neil Simon and overpraising Julian Beck. In 1968-69, at last, you could see plainly that an old theater tradition was dying and a new one was being born; but the process was still in its early stages. The moribund retained most of his signs of vigor, while the new life was in the embryonic state. A swinging good old-fashioned comedy like *Forty Carats* still held the field against the way-out efforts of a *We Bombed in New Haven,* even though it was perfectly clear to the New York theatergoer which one represented the past and which the inevitable future.

As a season of transition, 1968-69 provided an ideal opportunity to look back over the decades of the American theater and reflect on where we have been, as we do elsewhere in this, the 50th volume in the series of *Best Plays* yearbooks started by Burns Mantle in 1919-20. At the same time, this was a season in which the vague outlines of what our theater is to become (perhaps) became clearly perceptible at last, after several seasons of groping and experimentation with new theater forms, like a seed trying to find out what kind of a tree it is going to be. On page 8 of last year's *Best Plays* volume we noted: "In an effort to move closer to their audiences, to penetrate deeper into their minds and hearts, many playwrights have pushed their characters all the way to the apron of the stage to address the audience directly." This characteristic became a trend in 1968-69, and the trend became almost an obsession. Actors were not only speaking to audiences directly, but stepping right down into the auditorium and coaxing spectators to take their clothes off. It now seems certain that the theater of the future will be a theater of more direct contact between play and audience, with the audience not just a group of passive observers like movie or TV watchers, isolated by the convention of an invisible fourth wall, but instead taking on an active relationship with the play.

This was a season, moreover, of experimentation with nakedness onstage, not so much on Broadway as in the smaller playhouses. Males and females in various combinations peeled, groped and pressed against one another. Very little came of it all except publicity, and not much of that. There was hardly even a sense of shock. Theatrically speaking, the nudity and mimed fornication accomplished so little, at the cost of so much effort, that perhaps we have got *that* notion out of the way at last, once and for all.

3

The 1968-69 Season on Broadway

PLAYS (24)

Lovers and Other Strangers
The Cuban Thing
Woman Is My Idea
Box-Mao-Box
THE GREAT WHITE HOPE
We Bombed in New Haven
A Cry of Players
Morning, Noon and Night
The Goodbye People
Jimmy Shine
The Sudden and Accidental Re-education of Horse Johnson
FORTY CARATS
Fire!
The Mother Lover
Play It Again, Sam
Does a Tiger Wear a Necktie?
But, Seriously . . .
The Wrong Way Light Bulb
Zelda
The Watering Place
The Dozens
Cop-Out
The Gingham Dog
My Daughter, Your Son

SPECIALTIES (5)

Marlene Dietrich
Gilbert Becaud Sings Love
The National Theater of the Deaf
Trumpets of the Lord
The World's a Stage

MUSICALS (12)

Her First Roman
Maggie Flynn
Zorbá
Promises, Promises
The Fig Leaves Are Falling
CELEBRATION
Red, White and Maddox
Canterbury Tales
Dear World
1776
Come Summer
Billy

REVUE (1)

Noel Coward's Sweet Potato

REVIVALS (23)

My Fair Lady
West Side Story
APA-Phoenix '68:
Pantagleize
The Show-Off
Theater 1969:
The Death of Bessie Smith and The American Dream
Krapp's Last Tape and The Zoo Story
Happy Days
APA-Phoenix '69:
The Cocktail Party
The Misanthrope
Cock-A-Doodle Dandy
Hamlet
D'Oyly Carte:
H.M.S. Pinafore
Patience
The Mikado
The Pirates of Penzance
Iolanthe
Lincoln Center Rep:
King Lear
The Miser
Carnival!
Minnesota Theater:
The House of Atreus
The Resistible Rise of Arturo Ui
Hamlet
The Front Page

FOREIGN PLAYS IN ENGLISH (6)

LOVERS
THE MAN IN THE GLASS BOOTH
The Flip Side
Rockefeller and the Red Indians
IN THE MATTER OF J. ROBERT OPPENHEIMER
HADRIAN VII

FOREIGN-LANGUAGE PRODUCTIONS (5)

Compagnie Villeurbanne:
The Three Musketeers
George Dandin
Tartuffe
The Megilla of Itzik Manger
Fiesta in Madrid

HOLDOVER SHOW WHICH BECAME HIT DURING 1968-69

Hair

Categorized above are all the plays listed in the "Plays Produced on Broadway" section of this volume.

Plays listed in CAPITAL LETTERS have been designated Best Plays of 1968-69.

Plays listed in **bold face type** were classified as hits in *Variety's* annual list of hits and flops published in midsummer 1969.

Plays listed in *italics* were still running on June 1, 1969.

There was much dramatizing of headlines in the year's best work—not today's headlines, yesterday's, in *The Great White Hope, 1776, The Man in the Glass Booth* and *In the Matter of J. Robert Oppenheimer*. Rising from last season's absolute nadir, the Broadway musical skyrocketed back into prominence with two boldly original shows—*1776* and *Celebration*—with *Zorbá* and *Promises, Promises* also helping to restore the reputation of this uniquely American theater form. And this was a season in which America's playwrights came up with the best drama—Howard Sackler's *The Great White Hope*—and the best comedy—*Adaptation/Next* by Elaine May and Terrence McNally—thus breaking the chain of dominance by overseas playwriting, which was nevertheless well represented on the Best Plays list with four distinguished scripts: Peter Luke's *Hadrian VII* and Robert Shaw's *The Man in the Glass Booth* from England, Heinar Kipphardt's *In the Matter of J. Robert Oppenheimer* from Germany and Brian Friel's *Lovers* from Ireland.

And speaking of sources, the year's best script was developed, not in the New York atmosphere, but in Washington, D.C. *The Great White Hope* had its premiere at the Arena Stage during the 1967-68 season, with James Earl Jones as the boxer Jack Jefferson and Jane Alexander as his mistress, directed by Edwin Sherin. Thus it was literally a play produced in regional theater and sent "on the road" to Broadway, where it topped everything around. *Oppenheimer*, too, had its American premiere in regional theater last year, in the Center Theater Group production in Los Angeles, and came to New York with the leading players and director. Broadway "created" only three of its top ten shows this year: *1776, Celebration* and *Forty Carats*, which Jay Allen adapted from a French script. Of the three foreign Best Plays in English, two—*Hadrian* and *Glass Booth*—came over here with their original stars, and the third, *Lovers*, had an American star joining the Dublin Gate Theater production. The two remaining Best Plays—*Adaptation/Next* and *No Place To Be Somebody*—originated off Broadway. So the 1968-69 proportion of origin in the top ten was 3 (Broadway)—3 (foreign)—2 (regional)—2 (off Broadway).

These scripts represent considerable new growth. Peter Luke, Robert Shaw and Charles Gordone are making their playwriting debuts with *Hadrian, Glass Booth* and *No Place*, as is Sherman Edwards with the co-authorship of *1776*. Howard Sackler's *White Hope* and Heinar Kipphardt's *Oppenheimer* are Broadway debuts.

Statistically, the season was about average. There were 76 programs produced on Broadway in 1968-69 (see the one-page summary accompanying this article), as compared with 84 last season, 78 the year before, 76 the year before that and 81 the year before that. The important figure—the volume of new American work—has remained reassuringly steady except for that alarming drop-off in 1966-67. This season there were 24 new American plays and 12 new musicals produced on Broadway, compared with 25-10 last year, 19-8 in the alarming year before that, 25-11 the year before that and 25-10 the year before that.

The slight decline from last year in overall volume of play production is accounted for by the sharp drop in the number of foreign plays in English—only 6 as compared with last year's 17. There was a corresponding rise in the number of revival programs from 16 last year to 23 this year, which helped keep production activity at a level normal for the 1960s.

There was also a small decline in the Broadway theater's combined gross and activity (as per *Variety's* annual estimate). For the fifth straight year Broadway's total gross topped the $50 million mark, but for the first time in five years it fell short of a record. Broadway took in a handsome $57,743,416 during the season of 1968-69, as compared with last year's record high of almost $59 million. Its additional gross of $42,601,016 for Broadway road companies in 1968-69 made the Broadway theater a better than $100 million dollar proposition overall for the second year in a row.

In the matter of playing weeks (if 10 shows play 10 weeks that's 100 playing weeks) there was also a dropoff. There were 1,209 Broadway playing weeks in 1968-69 (including 101 weeks of previews), continuing the slight but steady decline in previous seasons, from 1,295 in 1965-66, 1,269 in 1966-67 and 1,257 in 1967-68. On the bright side of this statistic, *any* playing week total in the 1,200s is exceptionally high (the record was 1,325 in 1947-48), so that in 1968-69 Broadway was still going strong with a $57 million gross that is the second-highest in its history.

To establish, briefly, a context for these production figures, let us note that 1968-69 was the season in which the box office price for the hottest weekend musical ticket leapt to $15 (for *Promises, Promises* and *Zorbá*), with tickets at the $12.50 level a commonplace. The straight-play top rose to $9.50 (for *White Hope*), and off-Broadway producers found that the traffic would bear $10 a seat at the leading small-house hits *(Dames at Sea, Adaptation/Next* and last season's *The Boys in the Band).*

Half a million bucks was the going rate for mounting a Broadway musical. The total tab for six conspicuous 1968-69 musical flops *(A Mother's Kisses, Her First Roman, Maggie Flynn, The Fig Leaves Are Falling, Billy* and *Come Summer)* amounted to $3,300,500. Straight Broadway plays were being capitalized around $100-150,000. At the same time, rising *net* profit totals had reached at least the following levels by last spring for this sampling of shows: *Hello, Dolly!* $5,886,150, *Man of La Mancha* $4,000,000, *Mame* $1,289,554, *You Know I Can't Hear You When the Water's Running* $564,763 (on an investment of $135,000), *The Price* $70,000 (on an investment of $100,000), *The Boys in the Band* $210,000 (on an off-Broadway investment of $20,000).

So much for numbers. It was actors who made the season, in a way; excellent as many of the scripts may have been, the 1968-69 show was stolen by its noteworthy performances. James Earl Jones's Jack Jefferson . . . Alec McCowen's Hadrian . . . Al Pacino's drug addict, Bickham . . . William Daniels' John Adams . . . Donald Pleasence's Jew posing as a Nazi . . . Milton Berle's brave old man in *The Goodbye People* . . . Bernadette Peters as Ruby Keeler in *Dames at Sea* . . . Julie Harris in *Forty Carats* . . . Jerry Orbach's rising young executive with an apartment key . . . these were the standouts in stiff competition with such as Art Carney, George Grizzard, William Devane, Jane

Alexander, Keith Charles, Maria Karnilova, Dustin Hoffman, Angela Lansbury, Jay Garner, Nicol Williamson, Brenda Vaccaro, Lorraine Serabian, Joseph Wiseman, Marco St. John, Woody Allen, Anthony Roberts, Hal Holbrook, Howard Da Silva, Lee J. Cobb and many others.

For directors, 1968-69 was a year in which they heard from informed sources that they were on the verge of inheriting the earth—or at least that part of it which is merely a stage—via the growth of improvisational or "collaborative" theater in which the play is not so much written as invented by everybody during rehearsal. Nevertheless, 1968-69 was not a directors' year (in the professional theater, at least; I am not speaking of off off Broadway), but an actors' and writers' year. Producers? Three of David Merrick's 4 shows were hits: *Promises, Promises, Forty Carats* and *Play It Again, Sam.* Harold Prince added a third musical, *Zorbá,* to his simultaneously long-running *Cabaret* and *Fiddler on the Roof.* Alexander H. Cohen struggled for much of the season to get *Dear World* off the ground (it flew about as far as the Wright Brothers crate at Kitty Hawk); but at the same time he was opening a London office for transatlantic play production and had three shows running there in the month of April. The roster of impresarios who enjoyed exceptional success of one kind or another this season includes Morton Gottlieb, Herman Levin, Jules Irving, Lester Osterman, Cheryl Crawford and Stuart Ostrow.

Of course, 1968-69 brought disappointment to some, often those of whom we have the highest expectations. Aeschylus for one, and Edward Albee for another, bombed at the Billy Rose. Esthetically, this was a season of so many plays about sex that one wished for a sexy play to come along—but none ever happened. It has been said that the realistic theater reached its full bloom when, in a restaurant scene, David Belasco caused to be placed onstage a fully operative steam table. In this season of 1968-69 the realistic theater of David Belasco seemed to be giving way to newer, more dynamic, more imaginative forms—but before the old theater vanished it was trying to get in all the nakedness and fornication omitted during the decorous Ibsen-Chekhov-Belasco decades. Like an aged roue trying everything once before the end comes, the theater in 1968-69 dallied in the copulatory antics of men and women, men and men, women and women, men and animals. Belasco can rest in peace— it was all done, all literally represented, and with real steam coming up. The only thing was, the truly sexy play never arrived.*

A less conspicuous but probably more vital development in the theater esthetic was this business of direct playwright-to-audience and actor-to-audience communication in the theater. The living stage is trying to make the most

* As the season ended, the off-Broadway show *Oh! Calcutta!* devised by Kenneth Tynan, with erotic sketches by Samuel Beckett, Jules Feiffer, John Lennon and other major talents, was in previews and opened in mid-June. Its clinkers of unredeemed vulgarity in a couple of unfortunate sketches were somewhat redeemed by the gracefulness of the dancers, in groups and pairs, in poetic movements of the naked and well-formed male and female bodies. The show had a point of view (blithely hetero) and found some humor in the image of a man and a woman, stark naked and fully lit, copulating. But sexy? Not very.

of the unique characteristic that sets it apart from movies and TV: the audience and the play are physically present *together* in the theater, *living*. Instead of pretending that an invisible fourth wall separates the two, the theater of 1968-69 was pulling down not only the invisible wall but the other three walls of the setting as well, binding the play and the audience into a single intense unit of experience within the four walls of the playhouse.

Thus the script of *The Great White Hope* contains passage after passage, line after line of dialogue underlined by the playwright with the general direction that all such lines are to be spoken *directly* by the actor to the audience— no pretense that the play is to take place independently of its witnesses. Thus Joseph Heller's *We Bombed in New Haven* is constructed as a "rehearsal" of a "play" at which the "actors" frequently appeal directly to the audience; in fact, the irony of the audience reaction, or lack of it, to the events onstage is the whole point of the script. Thus, off Broadway, *The People vs. Ranchman* broke the auditorium into blocks of seats and stages, laid out irregularly like sections of a Mondrian painting. Thus, even farther off Broadway at the Brooklyn Academy of Music, The Living Theater issued its gentle summons to the *Paradise Now* audience to shed its inhibitions (and its clothes) and enter into a whole new, anarchic but meaningful relationship of actors and audience. During the show performers and observers were gradually homogenized into one group of people, indivisible.

The transition from the theater of the uniformed maid dusting the furniture behind the invisible fourth wall, to the new theater of naked actors sitting in the audience's lap, is of course far from complete. The shining new theatrical form of our Columbus-like dreams is still far over the horizon; but in 1968-69, at least there were signs of new life floating past us in the waters of play production. It is a major disadvantage in this season of passage that the division of styles onstage tended to divide the audience. In previous 20th century decades, with a stable theatrical form, everyone knew approximately what to anticipate in a musical, comedic or dramatic evening on Broadway, and therefore each show of quality had a satisfactorily broad-based audience potential. In the theater of 1968-69, almost any individual production worth naming (*Forty Carats; Adaptation/Next*) was calculated either to entrance or offend either Aunt Hattie from Scarsdale or her hippie niece, but seldom both the same at the same production. As tastes begin to fragment, so does the size of the potential audience for any one show, forward-looking or backward-reaching. In a transition season like this, playgoers were warier than ever of finding themselves in the wrong theater. The New York *Times* drama reviewer, with his virtual monopoly on directing audience traffic because of the paper's position in the New York area, had an ever weightier *negative* influence than ever on the success factor of each production. (His *positive* influence was less certain; for example, his enthusiasm could not drive the Broadway theatergoer to Theater 1969's repertory of Albee and Beckett revivals, nor to the sex-play one-acters *Lovers and Other Strangers*.)

As a result of taste fragmentation, of *Times*-watching and of other factors this season, several inventive and richly endowed shows failed to attract the attention that they might deserve in the healthiest of all possible theatrical environments. Herb Gardner's *The Goodbye People,* for example, though handicapped with a slow-starting first half, built into one of the most poignant experiences of the season, not only in its writing but also in Milton Berle's portrayal of an aged Coney Island concessionaire determined to do or die in making a comeback with the grand opening on the beach—in February—of a hot dog stand. *The Goodbye People* was edged off the Best Plays list by work of more consistent strength. But in my opinion Gardner's work reached the year's playwriting pinnacle in the following speech by the Berle character, Max. Max has been phoning his former business associates to buy the inventory of hot dogs, rolls, furnishings, etc, he needs, on credit. But instead of his associates who are "busy being dead" Max is reaching the sons who have inherited the businesses—a new generation of "cold voices, people born for telephones." They will extend Max no credit like their hustler fathers who sometimes sold Max second-rate products but at least were willing to talk business. The sons hedge, they will make no commitment. Max is complaining to his own (unsympathetic) son, but in reality, of course, his words are addressed to us, the audience, in a comment * about the times in which we live:

MAX: . . . . . A dozen numbers I dialed and each place the *same fellah* answered. . . . . You couldn't tell who, what, which one? Could be they all got together, hired a fellah to make a record? O.K., their fathers had accents, but they got no sound at all! Billy Gallino, he repeated a bread order, you could tango to it! We had a fight once on Canal Street. He hit me. I hit him. *(Points to a mark over his eye.)* Here's a scar from Gallino. He hit me and I miss him. We did business. Junior with his micey voice, he nibbles, he nibbles, he noshes on my soul. His father I knew what he was. Him, he could be anything; a sea captain, a potato-chip, a corn-muffin, what? *(Very quietly.)* I'll tell you the truth, buddy, the old days wasn't so terrific . . . but God help me from the new ones . . . *(Suddenly, shouting.)* Ah-*hah!* But at the end of the conversation, these sweethearts'll do a goodbye for you—oh, *boy,* it's beautiful! "Hello," they don't do so good; and after "Hello," nervous and rotten . . . but "Goodbye," will *they* do a job for you on "Goodbye!" *(Max blows a goodbye kiss into the air.)* "Goodbye . . . keep in touch . . . so long . . ." All of a sudden warm and personal and terrific . . . *(Waving goodbye.)* "Goodbye to ya . . . alla best to ya . . . see ya around . . ." All of a sudden, it's happiness, it's sweetness, it's their best number, it's the goodbye people and they're feelin' terrific; they got through a whole phone call without promising anything, without owing, they lived another day without getting into trouble . . . *(Max takes off his hat and waves it in the air.)* "Goodbye . . . goodbye . . . we're rootin' for ya . . . goodbye . . ." *(He puts his hat back on, adjusts the brim.)* Go look for Prometheus. He's outa town.

In many cases where the footprints of Prometheus clearly showed, as in

* Reprinted by permission of the author.

The Goodbye People, the public failed to get excited. Don Petersen's excellent play *Does a Tiger Wear a Necktie?* deserved a much longer run than the 39 performances it received. So did Lanford Wilson's 5-performance *The Gingham Dog,* with George Grizzard's shattering portrayal of a Southerner in despair at the failure of his marriage to a Harlem Negro. Perhaps the greatest loss to the 1968-69 Broadway theatergoer was his failure to find out in time that the Tom Jones-Harvey Schmidt *Celebration* was one of the rare new experiences of the Broadway musical's rapidly developing art/entertainment form. The book of *Celebration* is a fable about a lad who wants permission to plant a garden in the yard of a demolished church, of which he has been able to rescue only the Eye of God (a symbol of the sun) from the heap of shattered stained glass. A rich roue competes with the boy for the attention of a venal young dancer who wants it all no matter what she has to do to get it. This triangle is compressed on all its sides by the schemes of a vagrant philosopher, played by Keith Charles. *Celebration's* lyrics are strongly poetic. It suffers its moments of cynicism and despair, even of ugliness, but its theme of regeneration always finds the upbeat ("beneath the snow/there's a tiny seed/ and it's gonna grow!"). Vernon Lusby's choreography illustrated each sardonic turn of the fable, and the design was a visual marvel of symbolic scenery, costumes and gargoyle masks by Ed Wittstein.

Like *Man of La Mancha* in its early weeks, which it somewhat resembles in mood, *Celebration* struggled forward in an effort to find its audience. It was urged on by the enthusiasm of a few major critics and it also basked in loud and joyful applause from the members of the public who half-filled its auditorium—but it could survive no more than 109 performances. Lack of public information and/or appreciation of a worthwhile show is the worst that can happen in any theater season. Underneath all the affluent statistics and eager esthetic hopes and dreams of 1968-69, there was a mushy layer of doubt, of unwarranted skepticism. Playgoers lacked the spirit of adventure in a rather adventurous season, and this cost the theater the full appreciation of some of its best work.

The Hits

In the purely technical sense a "hit" is a show that pays off its production cost by means of popularity at the box office or a movie sale and begins to show a profit. Listed below are the 1968-69 shows which, according to *Variety's* annual estimate, can be placed in the hit column. We add to *Variety's* list the probable hits: shows which are almost certainly destined to pay off (we believe) as they run past June 1, 1969 into the new season. There were 11 hits and probables this year, as compared with 13 last and 11 in 1966-67. Here they are (titles listed in CAPITAL LETTERS were also Best Plays):

Hits (*Variety* estimate)

LOVERS   *Jimmy Shine*
Marlene Dietrich   FORTY CARATS
THE GREAT WHITE HOPE   *The Front Page*
Promises, Promises   *Play It Again, Sam*
                                          HADRIAN VII

Probable Hits

1776   *Zorbá*

Marlene Dietrich is the title of a one-woman show and the name of a one-of-a-kind star who made the hit list last season in her Broadway debut and returns to the hit list this season in a return engagement. *The Front Page* is a revival described further along in this article in the section on revivals.

Exactly half the Best Plays made the hit list. Irish playwright Brian Friel made it early with his second Best Play in three seasons: *Lovers* in the Dublin Gate Theater production, with Art Carney added to the cast, which had its American premiere at the Vivian Beaumont during the summer festivities and then moved downtown to the Music Box. *Lovers* was billed as "A Play in Two Parts," but it was more like a pair of one-acters with separate characters, joined by the same Commentator. In the first playlet, *Winners,* two young lovers appear on a sunny Irish hilltop the day before their wedding in an idyll of schoolboy and schoolgirl youth on the very threshold of maturity and eager to begin the future. Meanwhile the Commentator (Carney) is reading from his newspaper that in some way, no one knows exactly, the two lovers (played in exuberant high spirits by Dublin Gate's own Fionnuala Flanagan and Eamon Morrissey) were drowned on the lake that perfect afternoon. They are "Winners" drowned at their moment of greatest joy, in a skillful mood piece which participates in the newest stylistic trend in expressing the sorrowful events *directly to the audience* in the words of an observer.

In Friel's second playlet, *Losers,* the Commentator tells us of his own courtship, marriage and war of wills with his wife's invalid mother. It is a hilarious struggle for command of the household in which the devout old woman recruits the very saints to her cause. The husband can win a battle or two, but inevitably he cannot win the war against this subtle woman. In this playlet the Commentator is more than just a link between the audience and events. He is up to his neck in the play, but he keeps coming "outside" the house to report to the audience on how he thinks he is doing. The two halves of *Lovers* show Friel exercising his previously established (in *Philadelphia, Here I Come!*) ability to draw accurate sketches of vulnerable human beings, both comic and poignant.

The second hit from abroad was *Hadrian VII,* another outstanding British play with a like performance by Alec McCowen as a penniless misfit whose many efforts to enter the priesthood have been frustrated. He imagines himself the first British Pope in hundreds of years—and what a pontiff he makes of himself, a veritable John XXIII, in his efforts to pull the vainglorious princes of the church back to the first principles of their shepherd's duty. Peter Luke's play is based on the life and works of a debatable turn-of-the-century literary figure named Frederick Rolfe (alias Baron Corvo) who wrote the original version of this daydream as a novel, *Hadrian the Seventh,* and who appears as the leading character of the play. Rolfe was indeed rejected for the priesthood several times, and *Hadrian VII* represents a breakout of frustrated dedication, a dream in compensation for the reality of failure. The final irony of the play is that even in his imaginings Rolfe's enemies penetrate the Vatican and destroy him. *Hadrian* is a playwriting debut and a most successful one, an almost noble dramatic treatment of spirituality.

The most conspicuous success of the year, however, was not foreign but American: the Critics, Pulitzer and Tony Award-winning *The Great White Hope,* the Broadway debut of its author Howard Sackler and the vehicle for a magnificent performance—that of James Earl Jones as Jack Jefferson, a Negro heavyweight boxer who reaches the fistic heights of the world championship, only to be pulled inexorably down by the unanswerable gravity of American racial prejudice. Both play and performance were polished in a regional theater production last season at the Arena Stage in Washington, D.C., and they reached Broadway in gleaming condition. Sackler's script (which, as previously noted, addresses itself to the audience frequently in single lines of dialogue or elaborate setpieces) is written mostly in blank verse rhythm and has a narrative flow through nineteen scenes in the United States, Europe, Mexico and Cuba. Its events were suggested by the real-life career of the black heavyweight Jack Johnson in America's extrovert period before and during World War I. The role of Jack Jefferson is written in colorful dialect and is spoken boldly by the actor Jones as though language like ring challengers were something to be conquered by force. What the New York boxing crowd, chagrined at finding a black man wearing the champion's belt, does about the situation is the story told in this play: how they hound the champion out of the country with trumped-up charges—he has accompanied his white mistress across a state line. They plunge him into poverty, despair and spiritual depletion, to the point at which he quarrels with his love and drives her to suicide. With all love and pride gone, he agrees to throw a fight to the newest White Hope. The black champion bloodies his white challenger savagely in the Havana ring in one last gesture of animal defiance before taking the arranged dive and accepting his ignoble fate, made to seem all the more piercingly unfair in contrast to Jones's noble, larger-than-life portrayal. Jane Alexander's performance of the loving and faithful-unto-death companion was also one of the season's best. The play spoke to 1968-69 audiences directly, not only in the dialogue directed outward by the playwright, but also in its deepest dramatic voice: it is not somebody else's prejudice which is an object of terror here, making the fighter an object of pity, but *our* prejudice, deep rooted in the past and hard as ever to kill in the present. It wasn't only one of our heroes, but our own villainy too that came under dramatic examination in *The Great White Hope,* the year's outstanding play.

Another Best Play on the hit list was *Forty Carats,* a finely-honed comedy adapted by Jay Allen from a French script by Pierre Barillet and Jean-Pierre Gredy, whose *Cactus Flower* was a Broadway hit three seasons ago. In this new one, Julie Harris plays a divorcee of 40 who at first enjoys, then resists, then finally succumbs to the attentions of a handsome, knowledgeable and persistent young man in his 20s. Every possibility of this May-August wooing is developed with a smooth interworking of script, performance and direction, the latter by Abe Burrows who also wrote and directed *Cactus Flower* and whose name is a very synonym of comedic skill.

It is said that few critics are able to observe and separate with any great percentage of accuracy the nuances of direction from the other elements of production; and this is probably true, present company no exception. Admitting that I have no secret means of determining what should be credited to the director and what to the playwright (except for my own instinct which is no better than it should be), I nevertheless confidently name a best straight-play director for the 1968-69 season. The top contenders are Harold Pinter for *The Man in the Glass Booth,* Elaine May for *Adaptation/Next,* Peter Dews for *Hadrian VII,* Edwin Sherin for *The Great White Hope* and Abe Burrows for *Forty Carats.* Choosing among these excellent candidates, I pick the comedy man. It is taking nothing away from Jay Allen's excellent adaptation to say that it benefits from the added inspiration of Burrows's staging. Likewise, in a final narrowing-down for best female performance among various convincing dramatic portrayals and Julie Harris's sharply-timed, play-sustaining performance in *Forty Carats,* I pick the comedy girl.

The two other comedies on the hit list, *Jimmy Shine* and *Play It Again, Sam* were one-man shows of performance and personality. The man in *Jimmy Shine* was The Graduate, Dustin Hoffman, playing a born loser who accepts his status as an unsuccessful abstract painter with good humor and only slightly tarnished hope. This Murray Schisgal script is a series of episodes in which the loser goes back over his life remembering its major emotional crises, and there are times when mere words are inadequate for Jimmy Shine—he must express himself in songs (written for the play by John Sebastian). Like The Graduate, Jimmy is a generally inexpert but eager lover, and of course Dustin Hoffman made the most of this characteristic on the stage, as he did on the screen in the Mike Nichols movie.

The man in *Play It Again, Sam* was Woody Allen, also playing a loser-lover, in a script of his own fabrication. The role Allen cut out for himself was that of a movie critic whose wife has left him and who imagines that he is coached by an embodiment of Humphrey Bogart into seducing his best friend's wife. Romantically speaking, he is a mouse that finally roars. The mild-mannered antihero personified by Hoffman and Allen, the Jimmy-Sam figure of a shuffle-footed, daydreaming lover may be a kind of comic backlash from the wham-bam-thank-you-mam lover in most fiction of this James Bond era. At any rate, in two versions he was instantly popular on Broadway this season.

Broadway's musical writers came out of the 1967-68 inertia with a glorious fanfare of musical successes in 1968-69, one of them a Best Play. This was *1776,* the year's happiest surprise, a successful musicalization of the debate in the Second Continental Congress that led to signing of the Declaration of Independence (I know this sounds theatrically implausible but it's a fact). This wonderful show, with book by Peter Stone and music and lyrics by Sherman Edwards, is like no other before it, demonstrating again that the musical form developed on Broadway in the past 50 years is only beginning to realize its full potential. *1776* is no song-and-dance show, it is a drama of ideas with the interplay of characters and events leading toward a climax in which John Adams, Benjamin Franklin and Thomas Jefferson sacrifice their deepest beliefs about equality in order to gain the necessary unanimous vote for independence. When the political maneuvering becomes too emotionally intense for mere words, *1776* breaks into song—as when a young soldier of Washington's army tries to explain what it was like at Lexington and Concord. William Daniels's portrayal of the waspish John Adams was the best musical performance of the year, and many other *1776* contributions were outstanding including Jo Mielziner's single thrust-stage set representing the Congress but adjustable for moving the action out into Philadelphia occasionally; Patricia Zipprodt's costumes; Peter Hunt's direction, and so many of the performances that it seems almost unfair to single out Howard Da Silva's Franklin as the best of a uniformly interesting group. The emotional heat generated by this musical about a political debate is amazing—all the more so because when you entered the theater you knew how it was going to come out. After half an hour of *1776,* however, you weren't so sure. And finally you were made to understand that it didn't come out quite as red, white and blue as you thought it did.

Finally on the list of hits and probable hits were the season's two blockbuster expense-account ($15 a ticket at the box office for weekend evenings) musicals, both with subject matter fresh in the minds of movie fans: *Promises, Promises* based on the script of the Jack Lemmon comedy *The Apartment,* and *Zorbá* based on the same novel as the movie *Zorba the Greek.* Both shows were superbly produced, the first by David Merrick and the second by Harold Prince; both were imaginatively directed, the first by Robert Moore and the second by its producer; and each package contained elements of theater artistry that ranked among the top achievements of the season: the Burt Bacharach-Hal David score of *Promises* and its leading performance by Jerry Orbach, the Boris Aronson setting for *Zorbá* and the supporting performances of Maria Karnilova and Lorraine Serabian. Neil Simon salted *Promises* with the cool humor of the 1960s and Joseph Stein colored *Zorbá* red with primitive passion and motivation. In Miss Serabian's function as a Greek chorus leader cynically warning lovers to love fiercely because death comes early, *Zorbá* reached its emotional peak on exactly the same mountain *Cabaret* climbed with a male counterpart, the skull-faced emcee played by Joel Grey. In *Promises,* the Orbach performance of a Neil Simon character can't be denied its full measure of humor and style, yet the comic despair of business

CARMEN ALVAREZ, HERSCHEL BERNARDI, LORRAINE SERABIAN
(REAR), MARIA KARNILOVA AND JOHN CUNNINGHAM IN
"ZORBA"

executives lacking a place for a 4 p.m. assignation seems somewhat pale in a
season which has freely offered us (in Terrence McNally's *Sweet Eros*) the
vision of a man tying a woman to a chair and stripping her preparatory to
rape. The trouble with *Promises* and *Zorbá* is that they are deja vu in subject
matter, specifically and generically, and in concept of what a Broadway musical should be.

This is not to quarrel with their success. Consider how dismal the theater
season often seemed last year, when there was no handsome *Promises, Promises* or *Zorbá* to glamorize Broadway. Our theater needs all of its ingredients
for a season of full, rich flavor; it needs the expense-account musicals as well
as the dynamically original Best Plays and the way-out off-Broadway hits. The

producers of these big 1968-69 musicals, David Merrick and Harold Prince, have contributed enormously to the most subtle progress of their art form in past years, and they will both do so again; maybe next year. Meanwhile they also make important contributions to the New York theater and its audiences by providing such entertainments as *Promises, Promises* and *Zorbá*. As a fitting end to this chapter on the 1968-69 hits, we bow deeply in their direction and voice our congratulations on the popularity of their shows, our admiration for the consistency of their effort and our best wishes for ever more brilliant achievement in the shining future.

New on Broadway

The ultimate insignia of New York professional theater achievement (we insist) is not the instant popularity of the hit list, but selection as a Best Play in these volumes. Such selection is made with the script itself as the primary consideration, for the reason (as we have stated in previous volumes) that the script is the very spirit of the theater, the soul in its physical body. The script is not only the quintessence of the present, it is most of what endures into the future.

So the Best Plays are the best scripts. As little weight as humanly possible is given to comparative production values. The choice is made without any regard whatever to a play's type—musical, comedy or drama—or origin on or off Broadway, or popularity at the box office or lack of same.

The Best Plays of 1968-69 were the following, listed in the order in which they opened (an asterisk * with the performance number signifies the play was still running on June 1, 1969):

Lovers
(hit; 148 perfs.)

Celebration
(109 perfs.)

The Man in the Glass Booth
(hit; 268 perfs.)

Adaptation/Next
(off Broadway; 126* perfs.)

The Great White Hope
(hit; 276* perfs.)

J. Robert Oppenheimer
(repertory; 64 perfs.)

Forty Carats
(hit; 180* perfs.)

1776
(hit; 89* perfs.)

Hadrian VII
(hit; 166* perfs.)

No Place To Be Somebody
(off Broadway; 30* perfs.)

One of the Best Plays from regional theater was *In the Matter of J. Robert Oppenheimer,* which marks the return of the Repertory Theater of Lincoln Center to this particular winner's circle for the first time since the Kazan-Whitehead era. This documentary play about Oppenheimer's security-clearance hearing during the McCarthy era of accusation and mistrust was written by a German playwright, Heinar Kipphardt, translated by Ruth Speirs and mounted in an American premiere by Center Theater Group in Los Angeles under the direction of Gordon Davidson, with Joseph Wiseman in the title role. Davidson directed the play in New York, with Wiseman repeating his portrayal of the angular, enigmatic physicist "Father of the Atom Bomb," so that Lincoln Center was playing host to the West Coast production. It proved a most distinguished guest; a tangle of intellectual positions and at the same time a taut courtroom-like drama echoing to the distant thunder of Alamogordo and Eniwetok.

Kipphardt's countryman, Rolf Hochhuth, has attracted much attention in recent years with his "documentary" plays in which the facts of history are rearranged, or juxtaposed, so as to form a propagandistic cop-out for Nazi guilt. Kipphardt's play is nothing of *that* sort. His search for some kind of truth within the weedy testimony of the Oppenheimer hearing seems inspired by curiosity rather than preconviction. Kipphardt is not trying so much to point a moral as to dramatize a conflict of moral values, and he has succeeded in this play. Certainly it is limited in scope, even with newsreel and other footage projected on screens behind its confining hearing-room setting. But in this modern theater where plays are being aimed more directly at the audience, the direct-testimony method of courtroom drama does not seem as static as it might once have seemed—particularly when expressed in the carefully-reasoned form of *In the Matter of J. Robert Oppenheimer.*

One last backward glance over the list of Best Plays reminds us that the scarcity of so-called "serious" drama, deplored by so many observers of New York theater in the earlier 1960s, seems to have ended. *Oppenheimer* may not be tragedy in the classical sense, but it is totally serious-minded as it addresses its audience. Half of *Lovers* is a tragic idyll (the sheer high spirits of the lovers on this day of days will make them careless with a rowboat and bring them to destruction). And different kinds of semi-tragic heroes are victimized in the losing struggles of *The Great White Hope, Hadrian VII, The Man in the Glass Booth* and *No Place To Be Somebody.* A serious Best Play from abroad was *The Man in the Glass Booth,* with which the well-known stage and screen actor Robert Shaw made his debut as a playwright with the drama of a rich and powerful German-born American Jewish millionaire who for reasons of his own decides to pose as an Eichmann-like ex-Nazi. Played with ferocity and a twist of irony by Donald Pleasence, this onetime concentration camp victim frames himself as a Nazi war criminal and permits himself to be kidnaped to Israel for trial, for the most noble of reasons: he wants to honor the memory of the Nazis' victims with the sacrifice of himself. Posing as a Nazi who is unregenerate, remorseless, even boastful of his viciousness, he is giving his fellow Jewish victims the ideal villain of their most horrible nightmares, the villain they need to exorcise their hatred, instead of the apologists and buck-passers that they have seen in the courtrooms. His disguise is penetrated before the sacrifice can be consummated, but not before many powerfully prodding reminders not only of Nazi villainy but also of the need for continuing vigilance against any kind of repetition.

Another important drama this season was *Does a Tiger Wear a Necktie?,* a series of episodes presenting the hang-ups of juvenile drug addicts in detention "on an island in a river bordering on a large industrial city"—and the painted skyline behind the setting had the Gothic-arched look of New York Hospital viewed from Welfare Island. The episodes were tied together in Don Petersen's play (his first full-length work) by the character of an English teacher, played by Hal Holbrook, trying to offer his teen-aged pupils adult help without increasing their tensions. He even manages to establish a form of communication with an unregenerate tough-guy addict named Bickham—a name worth remembering because it is the role that provided the Broadway acting debut of Al Pacino (just as Sage McRae is the name of the character Marlon Brando was portraying when he walked onto the Broadway stage in *Truckline Cafe* in 1946). We have seen Pacino before—last year for example as the bully in *The Indian Wants the Bronx*—but in *Tiger* we saw him clearly as an electrifying acting talent. He was authentic in the ultimate degree in the play's most demanding scene, a virtual monologue, in which Bickham describes his great expectations of a first meeting with his long-gone father and his emotionally devastating shock and disappointment when the meeting actually took place. The scene itself is worthy of Pacino's performance and vice versa. Petersen's *Tiger* can be faulted on grounds of continuity, but never in regard to insight or empathy. The great majority of the theater audience which failed to attend one of *Tiger's* scant 39 performances missed what may be one of the most memorable playwriting-acting Broadway debuts of this era.

Other noteworthy efforts at dramatizing "serious" matters were the aforementioned *The Goodbye People* and *The Gingham Dog;* Leonard Spigelgass's *The Wrong Way Light Bulb* which dramatized today's slum-area frictions in the example of an apartment dwelling, formerly in an upper middle class Jewish neighborhood, now being taken over by upward-striving blacks and Puerto Ricans, another play that deserved wider attention than it received; and William Gibson's *A Cry of Players,* viewing a young Elizabethan named "Will" in growing revolt against his squire's authority and his wife's emotional possessiveness, until finally he breaks away and runs off with a group of strolling players, dropping out of life and into the theater. Jack Gelber's *The Cuban Thing* was an effort to come to terms on the stage with the Castro movement. It attracted more attention in the streets than in the theater, stirring up anti-Castro agitators but closing after only one performance. John Roc's *Fire!* was an allegorical drama which searched the human spirit and sometimes found itself gazing into hell. Jerome Weidman's *The Mother Lover* also explored the darker areas of the human spirit in a triangular arrangement of mother, son and call girl; so did Lyle Kessler's *The Watering Place* in presenting the impact of a returning Vietnam War veteran on a dead friend's neurotic family; both the latter plays for only one performance each. Laird Koenig's *The Dozens* attempted a comment on the black link between Africa and America in the incident of a night club singer, her ineffectual husband and a fugitive African leader spending a night together. Julius J. Epstein's *But Seriously . . .* concerned itself with the marital and character tensions of a Hollywood writer —on the edge of comedy, except that the writer wept often. And finally, a musical based on Herman Melville's dire Billy Budd story, *Billy,* was the fourth of this season's Broadway shows to last only a single performance.

Of the season's 30 new plays in English, only eight billed themselves in the program as comedy. As an identifying label, this word "comedy" is like the little girl with the curl in the middle of her forehead in the nursery rhyme. *Forty Carats* was very, very good, and toward the end of the season Phoebe and Henry Ephron's *My Daughter, Your Son* invented a pleasant fancy about the planning of a full-scale wedding for the daughter of a screen writer and the son of a mid-Western dentist (and of course the happy couple has been living together in New York for months), with Robert Alda, Vivian Vance, Dody Goodman and Bill McCutcheon having a TV situation-comedy field day with the roles of the quivering parents. But the other six 1968-69 comedies were something else: *Lovers and Other Strangers,* an assortment of one-acters about married or soon-to-be-married couples' emotional hang-ups; *Woman Is My Idea,* about love among the Salt Lake City Mormons of the Brigham Young era; *The Sudden and Accidental Re-Education of Horse Johnson,* in which an average guy tries to study up on how to change the world; *Zelda,* about a world-ending hurricane of the same name (that's what we call *comedy*); and two British imports, *The Flip Side* about wife-swapping and *Rockefeller and the Red Indians,* a spoof of Westerns.

Where the theater has exerted its most vital energy in recent seasons has been in that mysterious area between nominal drama and nominal comedy— the area of *Rosencrantz and Guildenstern Are Dead* and *A Day in the Death of Joe Egg* and *Marat/Sade* and *A Delicate Balance* and this season the area of Joseph Heller's *We Bombed in New Haven* and Edward Albee's *Box* and *Quotations from Chairman Mao Tse-Tung (Box-Mao-Box).* Neither of these two new works was nearly as effective as the best of this genre in recent seasons; 1968-69 was not a vintage year for greyish comedy. Albee's newest work was incomprehensible (to me); not only because it failed to communicate during the time it played in the theater, but also because I cannot sense its creative purpose; I touch the wire and am convinced that it is cold. *Box-Mao-Box's* curtain went up on an empty stage, set with the open frame of a boxlike cube. A recorded voice (Ruth White's in this production) made a protracted philosophical statement while the stage remained empty. Then four characters came on: an actor in a fixed-smile Mao mask who walked the aisles reciting chosen sayings of the Chinese leader, an emotionally disturbed woman (Nancy Kelly) in a deck chair who told a silent clergyman the most intimate secrets of her unfortunate marriage, and behind them a gaunt, elderly woman who recited the poem "Over the Hill to the Poorhouse"—and meanwhile, segments of the recorded voice were repeated. There was a kind of orchestration to this, of voices that differed in timbre, and a literary orchestration in styles of language that were as different as the tonality of instruments. But as far as I can determine there is no theme and (let's remember where we are) no theatrical gratification of any kind.

Joseph Heller's *We Bombed in New Haven* communicated more clearly; in fact, it is one of those plays in the newly-developing form. It not only made its appeal directly to the audience but also cast the audience in a major role. The spectators are the fall guys of this piece. The jokes in this comedy are not on the characters, but on *you*. The characters aren't supposed to be real, anyway, they are actors rehearsing a play about an American bombing squadron that goes on absurd missions like the bombing of Minneapolis. The squadron commander (Jason Robards) keeps stepping out of character to reassure the audience that the actors aren't really being killed on these missions, just "written out" of the story. The events of the play are *only* a story (Robards keeps reassuring us). This should be obvious—because (the squadron commander points out) if these events were real, if young Americans were *really* being sent off on bombing missions to kill or be killed, you, the audience, would rise up out of your seats to stop it, *wouldn't you?* That's the irony of *We Bombed in New Haven,* so that the presence of the audience to be reassured and not to act is absolutely essential to the point and performance of the play. If that isn't playing an active part in an evening of theater, I don't know what is. Heller's play is one-joke irony, and its incidents are repetitive, but it was one of the season's noteworthy events simply because of its contemporary style and highly relevant subject matter.

A couple of programs of dark-comedy one-acters provided noteworthy high spots. Within *Morning, Noon and Night,* a trio of one-acters, Terrence McNally's *Noon* was a joke at the expense of sex deviates. In it, a group of weirdos with totally different hang-ups have been summoned to the same rendezvouz, under the false pretenses of a mysterious caller, just for the mischief of placing lions and tigers and bears in the same cage to see what happens. John Guare's *Cop-Out* presented a pair of saw-toothed sketches. The first was a post-World War I skit about the generations of a German family in various stages of "passing" as Americans in America. The second was a series of two-character sketches of the violence and neurosis of the day, ending up with the man shooting the woman "dead" in the aisle of the theater. There she remained, so that the audience had to step across the "dead" actress on the way home.

In the elephant graveyard of Broadway production where the massive no-hit musicals go to die, there is left behind the occasional lingering memory of a tune, a performance or a design to show that the great beasts existed. *Dear World,* for example, can be remembered for Angela Lansbury's performance of Giradoux's Madwoman of Chaillot in musical version, and also for the title number, a standout show tune by Jerry Herman. The British musical *Canterbury Tales* was handsomely designed in lively colors by Loudon Sainthill. Underneath the fine feathers, though, was a jade of bawdy affectation, often in doubtful taste. Only one of the also-ran musicals left Broadway wishing it had stayed longer. This was *Red, White and Maddox,* a political satire which had been mounted in Atlanta, but, when Theater Atlanta lost its playhouse, became homeless and wandered north to Broadway. The show took direct aim at Georgia's onetime Pickrick Restaurant celebrity, now governor of the state, in an engaging performance by Jay Garner as Lester Maddox. Among the other mammoths (as previously noted, they cost their producers $3,300,500 in their aggregate of failure), one, *A Mother's Kisses,* folded out of town. Four others—*Her First Roman* (17), *The Fig Leaves Are Falling* (4), *Come Summer* (7) and *Billy* (1)—played a total of 29 performances. A sixth, *Maggie Flynn,* struggled for 81 performances through a story about a New York City orphanage in the Draft Riot days of the Civil War. The songs of *Maggie Flynn* linger in memory, however: "The Thank You Song," "Mr. Clown" and the title number from an admirable score.

The season's single revue, *Noel Coward's Sweet Potato,* compiled songs, sketches and play scenes from the work of the master. It seemed thin-blooded. The year's specialty shows included, besides Miss Dietrich, two unusual musical opportunities: Gilbert Becaud from France in a solo appearance, and a staged revival meeting called *Trumpets of the Lord,* with soaring gospel hymns. Then there was a silent show, the sign-language theater of The National Theater of the Deaf, which visited Broadway. A hypnotist, Sam Vine, appeared in a Broadway house for 7 performances of an audience-participation show called *The World's a Stage.*

Among the season's foreign-language exhibits the standout was the Compagnie du Théâtre de la Cité de Villeurbanne's camp version of *The Three Musketeers,* with antic stagecraft and performances adding tart modern flavors to the smooth old tale of d'Artagnan and Anne of Austria's diamonds. René Allio's kinetic scenery, including a stormy English Channel devised out of blue gauze, was a delightful and integral part of the action. The Compagnie also revived *George Dandin* and *Tartuffe.* An Israeli musical, *The Megilla of Itzik Manger,* which transposed the Bible story of the Book of Esther to a modern Middle European village, came around twice—once for its premiere and again for a return engagement. Finally, there was the lively Spanish zarzuela production *Fiesta in Madrid* at City Center.

Individual contributions are the sparkle of any theater season, and it remains to list a Best Plays selection of the very best work of 1968-69 in New York. In the category of so-called "supporting" performances, clear distinctions cannot possibly be made on the basis of official billing, in which an actor's agent may get him a contract as a "star" ahead of the title, or following the title (which is not true star billing), or as an "also starring" star, or any of the other contractual typographical gimmicks. Thus, billing is not a reliable means of distinguishing between leading and supporting performances. Take the case of *1776.* The billing reads *"1776* starring William Daniels, Paul Hecht, Clifford David, Roy Poole, also starring Howard Da Silva." What rubbish. It gives rise to the kind of confusion in which William Daniels (billed here as a star in non-star billing) found himself nominated in the Tony Awards category of best featured or supporting performance and withdrew his name for fear of injuring his professional standing.

Not in *Best Plays,* thank you. In our list of bests we divide the acting into "primary" and "secondary" roles. A primary role in our book is one which carries a major responsibility for the play; *one which might some day cause a star to inspire a revival just to appear in that role.* All others, be they vivid as Mercutio, are classed as secondary in our consideration. Might an actor revive

1776 some day in order to play John Adams? Certainly—and so Daniels's role is a primary one. None of the other *1776* roles, however memorably performed or illustriously billed, pass this test.

Here, then, are the *Best Plays* bests of 1968-69:

Plays

BEST PLAY: *The Great White Hope* by Howard Sackler

ACTOR IN A PRIMARY ROLE: James Earl Jones as Jack Jefferson in *The Great White Hope*

ACTRESS IN A PRIMARY ROLE: Julie Harris as Ann Stanley in *Forty Carats*

ACTOR IN A SECONDARY ROLE: Al Pacino as Bickham in *Does a Tiger Wear a Necktie?*

ACTRESS IN A SECONDARY ROLE: Jane Alexander as Eleanor Bachman in *The Great White Hope*

DIRECTOR: Abe Burrows for *Forty Carats*

SCENERY: René Allio for *The Three Musketeers*

COSTUMES: Robert Fletcher for *Hadrian VII*

Musicals

BEST MUSICAL: *1776* by Peter Stone and Sherman Edwards

ACTOR IN A PRIMARY ROLE: William Daniels as John Adams in *1776*

ACTRESS IN A PRIMARY ROLE: Bernadette Peters as Ruby in *Dames at Sea*

ACTOR IN A SECONDARY ROLE: Keith Charles as Potemkin in *Celebration*

ACTRESS IN A SECONDARY ROLE: Maria Karnilova as Hortense in *Zorbá*

DIRECTOR: Peter Hunt for *1776*

SCENERY: Boris Aronson for *Zorbá*

COSTUMES: Ed Wittstein for *Celebration*

CHOREOGRAPHY: Vernon Lusby for *Celebration*

SCORE: Burt Bacharach and Hal David for *Promises, Promises*

Revivals

It was an outstanding revival season in the large number of plays brought out of the library and in the expertise of their airing. Perversely, it was also a season which found many partly subsidized producing organizations in deep trouble from insufficient support.

Among 1968-69's 23 revival programs (as compared with 16 last year and 32 the year before) there crackled the electric presence of an all-star production of *The Front Page* and an angry-young-man *Hamlet*. This year it wasn't all Gilbert and Sullivan (though we enjoyed our biennial visit from the incomparable D'Oyly Carte), it wasn't all Molière (though we had outstanding productions of *The Miser* by Lincoln Center Repertory and *The Misanthrope* by APA-Phoenix). This season we had Beckett too, and Albee, and T.S. Eliot; we had *West Side Story* at Lincoln Center's New York State Theater and *My Fair Lady* and *Carnival* at City Center.

This year, as last, Hamlet was very much a presence on New York stages, no doubt because the hung-up young Prince of Denmark relates in some way to today's hung-up youth. The under-30s of 1969 may or may not be confused, threatened, overprivileged, underloved, etc., but there is no doubt that they dig Shakespeare. During the past two New York seasons, while Zeffirelli's movie *Romeo and Juliet* was packing in the youngsters, Prince Hamlet was under continuous stage scrutiny, exposed to camp in the Joseph Papp production and portrayed eerily as a member of a hostile Establishment in *Rosencrantz and Guildenstern Are Dead*. This year we had Ellis Rabb emphasizing the paralizing effect of the Prince's inner conflict in the APA-Phoenix production, and we had Nicol Williamson's much-discussed *Hamlet* played as though John Osborne had both written and directed the tragedy, with the Prince as a nasal whiner, a lip-curler, shouting in accents strange to American ears but clearly not acquired at Elsinore or even Wittenberg. Played as a used-car salesman with a real grievance against the loan company (and played thus with brilliant accuracy by Williamson, who is one of our most accomplished actors), Hamlet descends to a level at which his emotional equipment is too flimsy for grand passion. The most understandable element of this production was the confusion of Ophelia, Gertrude, Polonius and Claudius as to what could possibly ail this sulky stranger-in-their-midst. The angry-young-man *Hamlet* didn't work onstage, but the season was more interesting because it was tried by so gifted an artist as Nicol Williamson.

The revival hit of the season was Harold J. Kennedy's staging of the Ben Hecht-Charles MacArthur 1928 newspaper play *The Front Page* with an all-star cast that included Robert Ryan as the managing editor, Bert Convy as Hildy Johnson, Katharine Houghton as Hildy's fiancee, John McGiver as Chicago's mayor and the selfsame Mr. Kennedy as Bensinger, the Chicago *Tribune* reporter. Kennedy's performance as well as his direction left us wishing he would visit Broadway more often than each decade or so. Kennedy put on *The Front Page* as though every nuance of political chicanery, every sharp tilt of a reporter's sarcasm was right out of today's headlines and press room instead of the 1920s. Two seasons ago APA-Phoenix proved you don't have to have a depression to appreciate the quixotic essence of *You Can't Take It With You,* and the same held true for *The Front Page*. The Hecht-MacArthur kind of reporter who would trade his mother-in-law for a good story and his fiancee for a page one byline went out long ago with the advent of the suburban-living wage and the public relations handout. But *The Front Page* remains insistently alive, and played on its own terms it was a delight.

The Hecht-MacArthur play was produced by Theater 1969 (Richard Barr, Edward Albee and Charles Woodward) as a kind of fund-raiser for the group's program of developing new playwriting talent. Previously in the season, Theater 1969 tried to mount repertory on Broadway (at the Billy Rose) without

BERT CONVY AND ROBERT RYAN IN THE
REVIVAL OF "THE FRONT PAGE"

success. Their schedule began with Albee's new work *Box-Mao-Box* and then went on to revivals of some of the most distinguished works of the new theater: Albee's *The Death of Bessie Smith, The Zoo Story* and *The American Dream* and Samuel Beckett's *Happy Days* and *Krapp's Last Tape*. The presence of such scripts as these on Broadway might cause some future historian of the theater to guess that in 1968-69 we were enjoying a period of cultural sophistication. He would be wrong. Despite an encouraging press, Theater 1969 Playwrights Repertory found no audience and closed early, leaving the Broadway scene the richer for its presence on the record and the poorer for its departure from the stage.

It was an economically troublesome year. Both subsidies and audiences were coming tough. The clamor from the ghettos for the attention and support of Congress and the private foundations was drowning out the rational and continuing need of the performing arts for some kind of subsidy. In competition with other, more urgent human needs, the arts as a whole and the theater in particular suffered a cutting-off of funds—that's as it should be, probably, but it made for long faces in the Green Room. For example, APA-Phoenix lost an expected $250,000 from the National Endowment owing to Congressional cutbacks, and this automatically deprived the troupe of another

$250,000 in matching grants from the Ford Foundation. At the same time, the expected massive response of supposedly culturally-oriented America to good retrospective theater never materialized—not in New York, anyway. In New York, the culturally-oriented theater audience wants the same thing the tired business man wants: hits.

Thus, for want of a 1968-69 hit the APA-Phoenix was lost to Broadway in April, possibly permanently. In the past two seasons the popularity of *You Can't Take It With You* and then of *The Show-Off* had helped keep them going. This year APA-Phoenix brought back *The Show-Off* with *Pantagleize* for a brief fall engagement in repertory, but later in the season it could not find a hit among its four new productions. Personally, I looked forward to seeing Eliot's *The Cocktail Party* again; but I can't say that the APA's production was equal to the high-tension inferences of the script. Equally, *Cock-A-Doodle Dandy, Hamlet* and a well-executed *The Misanthrope* failed to stir the interest of the town. With no outside help in sight after a losing season, the APA-Phoenix now plans to split at the hyphen. The APA (Association of Producing Artists under Rabb's direction) will return to the University of Michigan. The Phoenix will go its own way, possibly as an adjunct to a university theater and/or an off-Broadway operation.

The Repertory Theater of Lincoln Center was also reported to be in financial difficulty, in a season in which it took great strides esthetically. Members of its company worked in both the showcase Vivian Beaumont Theater and its experimental basement Forum Theater (classified in these pages as an off-Broadway house). Each theater opened its season with two productions alternating in repertory: the Beaumont with *King Lear* and William Gibson's new *A Cry of Players,* and the Forum with John White's *Bananas,* which used reminiscences of burlesque as a vehicle for satire, and Charles Dizenzo's one-act play program *An Evening for Merlin Finch.* The outstanding element of these shows was Lee J. Cobb's performance of Lear, but they certainly opened Lincoln's Center's season with a bang of progressive programming. The memorable evening came later, with *In the Matter of J. Robert Oppenheimer.* The fourth and final production in the big theater was a very well-received staging of *The Miser,* ending the year with a classical flourish.

At the Forum, too, the season progressed from strength to strength. Following its two-play repertory, the Forum offered the American premiere of James Hanley's *The Inner Journey,* a dark study of tensions within a family of vaudevillians whose son is a dwarf. Finally there was the powerful drama by John Ford Noonan, *The Year Boston Won the Pennant,* using the baseball world and a baseball hero to symbolize Everyman as a wounded hero, ringed round with hostility and crippled little by little in mind and body until he is ripe for the kill. It was one of the best offerings of the off-Broadway year, tightly directed by Tim Ward and grimly acted by Roy R. Scheider, who resembles George C. Scott in both appearance and ability, in the role of the pitcher who has lost an arm. While all of this was going on under the artistic guidance of Jules Irving and Robert Symonds, the business leadership of Lincoln Center Rep passed into the hands of Robert Montgomery, who was elected to the presidency of the company's board of directors. There are problems, but Lincoln Center's immediate future is almost certainly secure. This year, at least, the organization seemed to have struck a proper balance in programming: a new American play, a new European play, a Shakespeare and a Molière in the big theater and four new-play programs in the small one. Lincoln Center Rep is now much nearer to the goal which, in recent seasons, the APA-Phoenix approached so closely: the establishment of an exciting, versatile, permanent *American* repertory ensemble.

Broadway was also offered a glimpse of how the grass grows on the other side of the repertory fence. The Minneapolis Theater Company from the Tyrone Guthrie Theater paid a visit with *The House of Atreus,* an adaptation of Aeschylus' trilogy about Agamemnon's homecoming and its aftermath, and Bertolt Brecht's *The Resistible Rise of Arturo Ui.* They were competent revivals whose impact on Broadway was slight—but any kind of evaluation in Broadway context is meaningless. Clearly, the Guthrie troupe is a great success in its own environment, and it has no added responsibility to electrify New York audiences to whom the APA-Phoenix, Lincoln Center, City Center and all the off-Broadway organizations have been readily available.

And speaking of City Center, it too curtailed its play-producing activity this season, in which Richard Clurman was selected to fill the chairmanship of the board left vacant by the death of Morton Baum. The City Center Light Opera Company mounted two musicals with their usual flair under Jean Dalrymple's supervision, but there was no season of American play revivals and no spring season of musicals. The City Center is in a transitional period, with plans to vacate their present theater, the old Mecca Temple, and move into new, more elaborate quarters.

To sum up, revivals and repertory tend to be classified in the public mind as "culture," and culture does not sell especially well in today's New York commercial theater environment. But this year with the Albee plays, *The Front Page,* the musicals, the Molière revivals and even the oddball *Hamlet,* the enjoyment of "our cultural heritage" was often indistinguishable from the enjoyment of pure theater.

Off Broadway

If you haven't seen everything yet, you didn't get around off Broadway much this season, because they tried just about everything. Nudity was commonplace, heterosexuality was square. In Rochelle Owens's *Futz!* it was man and pig; in *Geese* it was man and man in the first one-acter, woman and woman in the second. In Terrence McNally's *Sweet Eros,* a man tied a woman to a chair and then raped her. He was only pretending, but in at least one off-off-Broadway show, *Che!,* the actors were determined to do the real thing if they found they could (at least that's what the show's publicity led us to believe). *Triple Play* and *The Grab Bag* were programs of one-acters with a variety of sex deviation, and in the full-length *Spitting Image,* imported from England,

The 1968-69 Season off Broadway

PLAYS (55)

Daddy Goodness
Futz!
An Ordinary Man
Another City, Another Land
Before I Wake
American Place:
  The Cannibals
  Trainer, Dean, Liepolt & Co.
  Boy on Straight-Backed Chair
Papp
Don't Shoot Mable
People vs. Ranchman
The David Show
Triple Play
The Grab Bag
Public Theater:
  Huui, Huui
  Cities in Bezique
  Invitation to a Beheading
  NO PLACE TO BE SOMEBODY
Sweet Eros & Witness
Papers
Possibilities
Forum Theater:
  Bananas
  An Evening for Merlin Finch
  The Year Boston Won the Pennant
Big Time Buck White
Americana Pastorale
Lemonade & The Autograph Hound
Belch
Negro Ensemble:
  "God Is a (Guess What?)"
  Ceremonies in Dark Old Men (2 productions)
  An Evening of One Acts
Yes Yes No No
Geese
Shoot Anything with Hair
ADAPTATION/NEXT
Open 24 Hours
Corner of the Bed
Frank Gagliano's City Scene
Stop, You're Killing Me
The Perfect Party
World War 2½
Lime Green Khaki Blue
God Bless You, Harold Fineberg
Someone's Comin' Hungry
War Games
The Honest-to God Schnozzola
A Home Away From
The Triumph of Robert Emmet
In the Bar of a Tokyo Hotel
De Sade Illustrated
Pets
Exhibition
Spiro Who?
The Transgressor Rides Again
Arf & The Great Airplane Snatch

SPECIALTIES (7)

The Fourth Wall
Walk Together Children
Chad Mitchell
The Wizard of Oz
To Be Young, Gifted and Black
An Evening with Max Morath
Make Me Disappear

MUSICALS (11)

Frere Jacques
The Happy Hypocrite
Month of Sundays
How To Steal an Election
Just for Love
Up Eden
Ballad for a Firing Squad
Dames at Sea
Horseman, Pass By
Get Thee to Canterbury
Peace

REVUES (2)

Now
Walk Down Mah Street!

FOREIGN PLAYS IN ENGLISH (7)

The Empire Builders
Tea Party and The Basement
The Inner Journey
Tango
Spitting Image
Man with the Flower in His Mouth
Philosophy in the Boudoir

REVIVALS (11)

Song of the Lusitanian Bogey (return eng.)
N.Y. Shakespeare:
  Henry IV, Part 1
  Henry IV, Part 2
  Romeo and Juliet
A Moon for the Misbegotten
In Circles (return eng.)
The Firebugs
Winnie the Pooh
Little Murders
The Millionairess
Of Thee I Sing

FOREIGN-LANGUAGE PRODUCTIONS (10)

Atelje 212:
  The Progress of Bora
  Ubu Roi
  Who's Afraid of Virginia Woolf?
  Victor
Die Brücke:
  Minna von Barnhelm
  Das Schloss
Piraikon Theatron:
  Iphigenia in Aulis
  Hippolytus
Tréteau de Paris:
  Quoat-Quoat
  Pique-Nique and Guernica

Categorized above are all the plays listed in the "Plays Produced off Broadway" section of this volume.
Plays listed in CAPITAL LETTERS have been designated Best Plays of 1968-69.
Plays listed in *italics* were still running June 1, 1969.

two "married" male homosexuals have a baby. In Miss Owens' *Beclch,* sadism rules as queen of the jungle, and in *Pets*—let's see, in the three one-acters of *Pets,* a female painter intimidates her model with a palette knife, an old man is tied up, robbed and teased by a couple of young women, and a woman in a cage is attacked by a man with a whip. And speaking of sadism, de Sade's own *Philosophy in the Boudoir* (a series of bedroom incidents in the education of a young girl by libertines into the purpler forms of passion) was the subject of *two* stage adaptations, one under its own name and one called *De Sade Illustrated*—illustrated with slides, that is.

In *Winnie the Pooh* as done by the Baird marionettes, the animals are all cute and the jokes all pure—but then of course this show was a *return* engagement, a throwback to the dim, distant, innocent, pre-*Hair* era of a year ago.

Once you have mentioned what these plays *do,* you have just about said it all. The naked deviates made little impression on the theater art or audiences, despite their large numbers and uninhibited nature. This year they tried almost everything, but little of it worked theatrically.

By off Broadway we mean, as usual, that formal area of play production of non-Broadway shows which 1) were performed by professional Equity casts, (2) offered themselves for review by the critics and (3) planned a regular weekly schedule of public performances (visiting foreign troupes are exempt from these qualifications, however). The less formal, farther-out area of experimental production in New York is generally referred to as off off Broadway and is covered elsewhere in this volume in an article and listing prepared by R.J. Schroeder.

Together with the outburst of sex off Broadway in 1968-69 there was an outburst of production: 103 productions of record compared with 72 last year and 69, 66 and 75 in recent seasons (see the one-page summary accompanying this article). This total included 55 new American play programs, more than double the 24 produced on Broadway this year and the 27 produced off Broadway last year. Had it accomplished nothing else, the 1968-69 off-Broadway season distinguished itself in this large number of American playwrights given a hearing, both in individual productions and on the schedules of the various permanent groups—American Place, the Public Theater, the Negro Ensemble Company, the Forum.

But the off-Broadway season *did* boast many other accomplishments, including two Best Plays. One of these was *Adaptation/Next,* a program of two one-acters, one by Elaine May and one by Terrence McNally (surely the most-produced playwright as well as one of the best on, off and off off Broadway this season). One-acters have been named Best Plays, but never before a program of one-acters by two different authors. It is appropriate to do so with this one, both because of the high quality of the scripts and because they seem made for each other in a dual comment on our homogenized, computerized times. In Elaine May's *Adaptation,* life is a bewildering TV game. The contestant, being alive, must perforce compete and try to move forward on the game board's squares. But inevitably in the struggle to raise a family and find the "security square" there are penalty cards to set the player back. "This is a hard game!"

gasps exhausted Gabriel Dell as the contestant, after he suffers a humiliating reverse (he's a Hilton hotel man in Chicago during the Democratic convention), his son grows up to be a long-haired hippie and his wife orders him to move to one side and not block her view of the TV screen. Don't we know that it is a hard game—but in Miss May's capsule version it ends swiftly enough for the player when he is ordered by the grinning master of ceremonies to have a heart attack right there in the appropriate square.

Terrence McNally's *Next* is played in exactly the same key, with James Coco in the role of a middle-aged movie theater manager who for some utterly unexplained and unexplainable reason has been ordered to take an Army physical exam. The broad-beamed lady technician who is to give him the exam (Elaine Shore) is not at all sensitive to his feelings of humiliation and anxiety —her job is to examine him, and she means to do it. Miss May staged McNally's playlet as well as her own to reach out as far as possible with the farcical situations, without losing a balance of sardonic comment on man as the victim of his own monstrous system, in which he must not ask "Why?" because the machine issuing the instructions isn't programmed to answer that question.

In the second of 1968-69's off-Broadway Best Plays, *No Place To Be Somebody,* as in *Adaptation/Next,* the time is Now. *No Place* came along late in the season as a sort of afterthought of Joseph Papp's New York Shakespeare Festival. After the group had tried it out during their experimental Other Stage activities, it was decided to add it to the regular indoor season as a full-scale off-Broadway presentation at the Public Theater.

This decision was on the order of Papp's decision last season to produce *Hair.* The first playwriting work of the actor-director Charles Gordone, *No Place To Be Somebody* is a stinging account of an ambitious, aggressive, ruthless—and black—owner of a bar in a West Village neighborhood controlled by white hoodlums. Characterized by its author as "a black black comedy," it is an outcry of a play, with its black characters including a poet, a thief, a ballet dancer and a whore, set in abrasive action against white characters including a busboy, an idealistic college girl, a judge, an assortment of killers and a whore. This is an uproar of a play, with explosions of violence knocking over furniture and people and explosions of language to match. The script is unique in that 90 per cent of the dialogue is punctuated with exclamation points; apparently Gordone wrote his play to be shouted. Yet this is not an angry play. The black poet addresses the audience directly, several times, on the subject of blackness and prejudice, but his mood like that of the play is more arrogant than angry; it lacks the ingredient of fear. *No Place* is acted by the most successful ensemble since last year's *The Boys in the Band,* headed by Nathan George as the bar owner, Ronnie Thompson as the seedy white busboy and Ron O'Neal as the poet, and blended so carefully that the performance of one actor who doesn't seem to know the first thing about his craft is turned into an asset of naivete. Of several good plays this year about the contemporary black condition, *No Place To Be Somebody* was clearly the most relevant and most powerful.

Another relevant, powerful drama on much this same subject was *Ceremonies in Dark Old Men,* the professional playwriting debut of Lonne Elder III with a script about an ex-vaudeville dancer, now an unsuccessful Harlem barber, whose family is inexorably pushed toward dishonest means of earning an adequate living. *Ceremonies in Dark Old Men* was produced by the Negro Ensemble Company under the artistic directorship of Douglas Turner Ward— who, under his acting name of Douglas Turner, played the barber in *Ceremonies* at the head of an ever more cohesive Negro Ensemble troupe. Other standouts in this production were David Downing as Bob; the barber's youngest, most cynical and most vulnerable son, and Samual Blue Jr. as Blue Haven, an emissary from the underworld. The barber is a man who makes mistakes but is unfailingly decent and often courageous, retaining some hope even as he moves closer and closer to tragedy. The script, written by Elder more than three years ago, is more compassionate, more direct than most of the angry-young-black-man writing of 1969. That the mood has darkened and the complexity of the problem increased in the past three years is no reflection on the play, which was staged by Edmund Cambridge to take advantage of its simplicity of construction and clarity of expression. *Ceremonies* was produced twice off Broadway this season: first in the Negro Ensemble Company's regularly-scheduled limited engagement, and again by Michael Ellis for an indefinite run in an off-Broadway house.

This season, off Broadway was developing a hit pattern of its own for those very few productions which attained the apex of the popularity pyramid. A show like last year's *The Boys in the Band* or this year's *Adaptation/Next* could raise its top price (applicable to most of the seats in the small houses) from an off-Broadway norm of $5-$7 to $10, which evidently the traffic will now bear. *Dames at Sea* entered the winner's circle with its hilarious take-off of Dick Powell-Ruby Keeler movie musicals. Like all good parodies, this George Haimsohn-Robin Miller-Jim Wise baby extravaganza paid homage to the lovable old format in the very observance of its cliches—and each and every cliche was minutely and delightfully observed in *Dames at Sea,* from the heroine's wrinkled-forehead emoting and machine-gun ferocity with the taps, to the show-biz slang and slant of the plot, with most of the action taking place "in rehearsal" and finally, lacking a theater, playing the opening performances on the deck of a convenient battleship in New York harbor. The performances were good parody, too, including those of Bernadette Peters as "Ruby" and Sally Stark standing hands on hips and tossing bleached-blonde curls and sarcasms as "Joan." The director of *Dames at Sea,* Neal Kenyon, got all his ducks in a row with their tails up, in this year's logical successor to such off-Broadway musical hits as *Your Own Thing* and *You're a Good Man Charlie Brown.*

Among the other off-Broadway musicals, a minstrel-show format based on Aristophanes' *Peace,* a campy version in which a nobleman rescues the goddess Peace from heaven and brings her home, has enjoyed a long run, owing in large part to the Al Carmines score (and the Carmines musicalization of Gertrude Stein's *In Circles* played a return engagement). *Horseman, Pass By,* a musical arrangement by Rocco Bufano and John Duffy of writings of W.B. Yeats, also attracted the attention of connoisseurs, albeit in a limited run. There was a *Canterbury Tales* musical off Broadway as well as on in 1968-69, *Get Thee to Canterbury,* but it fared not even as well as its Broadway cousin. The Mata Hari musical dropped by David Merrick out of town last year turned up this season off Broadway under the title *Ballad for a Firing Squad,* but it didn't make it in this league either.

One of the season's most effective plays in the new genre was Megan Terry's *The People vs. Ranchman,* loosely based on the Caryl Chessman case, a farcical treatment of the punishment impulse in society. Ranchman, an admitted and almost boastful rapist, looks down from the Olympian height of his jail cell upon the conflict raging below between those who agitate to free him because there isn't enough evidence against him (his victims may have been more willing than they can admit to themselves) and those who agitate to hang, electrocute and/or shoot him. The characters seethe from one part of the theater to another—the action was staged by Robert Greenwald in various parts of the auditorium, with the audience seated in blocks among the stages—everyone had at least one scene take place in his lap. In the pro-Ranchman contingent were two blacks and three hippies; anti-Ranchmanites were a soldier, a baseball player and the Girl Next Door. William Devane's performance of the grinning, unrepentant Ranchman was one of the season's standouts, as he was executed over and over again until society's urge to violence seemed far more evil than any trivial crime Ranchman might have committed.

Off Broadway also received Tennessee Williams's latest work, *In the Bar of a Tokyo Hotel,* about a painter (Donald Madden) in the final stages of failing artistic powers, and the selfish wife (Anne Meacham) who refuses to sympathize with his bewilderment. A fair amount of the Williams fire burned hotly under the surface of this play, which might have blazed into a real conflagration if the painter's suffering had been more clearly exposed to the audience's view. Instead, the wife monopolized the attention with her hang-ups, in a play that seemed wrongly balanced.

Other highlights included an outstanding revival of Jules Feiffer's *Little Murders,* a 7-performance Broadway flop two seasons back, a limited-run hit in repertory in London, and now a palpable off-Broadway hit and the standout of the year's list of 11 revivals. Somewhat rewritten for this new production, *Little Murders* found the means of communicating its farcical, bitterly ironic attitudes toward violence to New York audiences. Also present in the limelight were a pair of Harold Pinter one-acters, *Tea Party* and *The Basement,* sketches of a tired business man, and of a pair of friends conniving for the attentions of a woman; based on TV plays and providing a kind of between-meals snack of Pinter until his next swinging new play comes along. There was a program of semi-biographical writing collected from the late Lorraine Hansberry's work and presented under the title *To Be Young, Gifted and Black.* There was a popular one-man show by Max Morath accompanying himself on the piano in turn-of-the-century song numbers. There was Slawomir Mrozek's *Tango* in translation, the noted Polish playwright's comment on the nature of totalitarianism, in the form of a play about a conservative son who disapproves of his parents' extravagant behavior and tries to impose his will on them. There was a successful and popular group called *The Fourth Wall* which offered improvisations at each performance.

Of the major producers of a schedule of off-Broadway plays on a subscription basis, Joseph Papp's New York Shakespeare Festival was the most active, with a summer season of revivals outdoors in Central Park (the two *Henry IVs* and *Romeo and Juliet*) and a busy winter season indoors at the Public Theater. Papp's schedule of four new American plays included, besides *No Place To Be Somebody,* Russell McGrath's adaptation of Vladimir Nabokov's *Invitation to a Beheading,* the black comedy of a man awaiting execution by he knows not whom for he knows not what, providing yet another in the long list of Kafkaesque plays on and off Broadway this season. In his first two seasons of theater indoors, Papp has certainly distinguished himself, last year with *Hair* and a pair of interesting European scripts, this year with four new American scripts including a Best Play. Papp has steadfastly insisted on reaching out with every indoor production, instead of once in a while playing it safe. He ended his season in financial difficulty like every other enterpreneur, facing curtailment of the 1969 summer program. Nevertheless his is a highly creative performing-arts group which must be sustained somehow, even in hard and distracting times, if we are to maintain any pretense at all to culture as a spinoff of affluence.

Another of our cherished off-Broadway subscription organizations, Th. American Place Theater, presented a 1968-69 schedule of four new-play programs, of which Ronald Tavel's *Boy on the Straight-Back Chair* attracted the most attention with a study of the character and motives of a young man who has committed mass murder. American Place's final production, Kenneth Cameron's *Papp* (no connection with Shakespeare Joe), was an imaginative play about religion changed into a primitive, barely recognizable form in the post-holocaust future. Still another group, Lincoln Center Repertory, as previously noted, ran a four-play schedule in its small Forum Theater, with good results.

The Negro Ensemble Company was going from strength to strength in its second year of operation. It ran through most of the summer with the late Richard Wright's adaptation of a French play about a religious charlatan, *Daddy Goodness,* presented in repertory with a return engagement of last season's *Song of the Lusitanian Bogey,* about Portuguese policies in Africa. For the new season, Negro Ensemble mounted a three-play schedule which included *Ceremonies in Dark Old Men,* plus a program of one-acters, and Ray McIver's *"God Is a (Guess What?)"*—you guessed it, in this manifestation He is black. All these works had themes of and attitudes toward blackness, as the Negro Ensemble continued to work toward the creation of a permanent black ensemble for the performance of black-oriented plays.

Elsewhere in the off-Broadway pot-pourri there was, among the new American plays, an effort to express the new generation's goals and discontents in the mouths of three college-student characters in *Spiro Who?* Among specialties, there was a cheerful and imaginative new Baird marionette show, *The*

Wizard of Oz. Among revivals, there was a creditable re-staging of Eugene O'Neill's *A Moon for the Misbegotten* which ran for 199 performances; and an effort was made to bring back *Of Thee I Sing,* the 1931 Gershwin musical which won the Pulitzer Prize and was the first musical to be named a Best Play, but the production was short-lived. Among new foreign plays presented in English were two American premieres of Luigi Pirandello one-acters in translation on the program *The Man with the Flower in His Mouth.* Distinguished foreign visitors were the Yugoslav troupe Atelje 212 with a program that included Edward Albee's *Who's Afraid of Virginia Woolf?* in Serbo-Croat, plus the German Die Brücke, the Greek Piraikon Theatron and France's Le Tréteau de Paris.

To sum up, 1968-69 was a big year off Broadway in volume of activity, in the impetus of the top hits and in the quality of individual achievement (and, it goes without saying, in the cost of production). In looking back on an off-Broadway year, however, we should ask ourselves whether it functioned merely as a junior Broadway or whether it continued to serve its own unique purpose. The latter was clearly the case in 1968-69. The best of its new work —*Adaptation/Next, No Place To Be Somebody, Dames at Sea, Ceremonies in Dark Old Men, The People vs. Ranchman*—resembled the style, shape and content of Broadway hardly at all. The program of one-act plays is a frequently-recurring form off Broadway, where it serves more than an entertainment function; it is a sampler for playwrights and plays. There were 20 programs of one-acters presented off Broadway this season, 17 of them one-man shows displaying for better or for better-luck-next-time the work of Israel Horovitz, Harold Pinter, Adrienne Kennedy, Terrence McNally, Charles Dizenzo, James Prideaux, Frank Gagliano, James Leo Herlihy, Ben Piazza and others.

Finally, off Broadway found the handle for *Little Murders,* thus adding still another to the list of Broadway scripts *(Summer and Smoke, The Crucible, The Iceman Cometh,* etc.) which proved their full capacity when reaching off-Broadway revival. Certainly the tributary theater has continued to serve its unique theatrical purposes in 1968-69, affording many the opportunity to try —even to try nakedness as a form of frankness, perversion as a form of passion—and some the opportunity to find fulfillment not attainable elsewhere.

Offstage

Outside the theaters, the Broadway sound of 1968-69 was the sound of the jackhammer, as the office-building boom crept over westward and penetrated the theater district like the prongs of an exercise in military strategy. The Playhouse went the way of the Astor, Capitol, Paramount and Roxy, with office towers mushrooming on the sites. True, the city authorities have bargained with the developers for new theaters: zoning laws limiting the size and shape of new office buildings are to be relaxed slightly in exchange for the inclusion of new theaters within the construction. Many "official spokesmen" for various branches of the theater think this is an adequate safeguard for the legit stage's physical future. Others do not, citing two reasons why new theaters-within-offices are not true replacements for the old: 1) any change in the size and shape of the playhouses will influence the form of the plays, with the intimate type of production finding less and less lebensraum and 2) dispersal of theaters into office buildings, some of them placed above street level, will cost the Broadway area its compact, show-biz-flavored theater district. While the arguments continue a theater vanishes—and at least a half dozen of the old legit playhouses, maybe as many as a dozen, face the imminent and deadly threat of progress. The issue will almost certainly be decided, by militant action or by default, by the end of 1970.

Two established theater organizations were wheeling and dealing in playhouses. ANTA transferred ownership of its Broadway house to the National Arts Council, which presumably will operate it as a New York showcase for drama and dance groups from around the country. City Center plans to move from its 3,000-seat 55th Street house into a new facility to be built on the old Madison Square Garden site. It will include a 1,200-seat drama theater, a 2,000-seat dance theater and a 400-600-seat experimental theater.

Along with steadily rising production costs and ticket prices, there were steadily increasing efforts made to develop new ways of getting the tickets to the customers by means of a computer connected to remote sales outlets in department stores, etc., in New York and in other cities. Wherever you are, the computer sells you a numbered slip to be exchanged for the actual ticket at the theater. In one of the earliest experiments in this method, the machine began selling the same pair of tickets to Jack Gelber's *The Cuban Thing* to all the play's customers. Luckily for the machine, these were few. The play closed after its opening night performance, taking the machine off the hook. Further experiments during the season were more successful, selling Broadway theater tickets as far away as Los Angeles.

This was the season that the Theater Development Fund began to function in aid of selected productions on and off Broadway by means of subsidized ticket purchases. The Fund operated in 1968-69 with an endowment of about $400,000, some of it Federal and some private foundation money. The Fund comes into the picture *after* a play is in production (so that it has no influence on which plays are to be produced). Before the chosen play opens, the Fund may buy a block of tickets to increase the advance sale and tide the show over the first few weeks, as it did this season, $10,000 worth, in the case of *The Great White Hope*. Or the Fund may circularize a special segment of the public, offering cut-rate theater tickets and paying the difference on the box office price, to broaden the base of the theater's audience generally and an individual play's in particular as it did, $25,000 worth, for *We Bombed in New Haven*. The Fund also assisted *Big Time Buck White* and *Little Murders* off Broadway. The Fund is an ingenious method of subsidy which can operate effectively within the context of the commercial theater, without usurping any independent prerogatives of taste and risk. Its play selector is Harold Clurman and its executive secretary is Hugh Sothern, who describes the Fund's aims as "to lower, to a degree, the worsening odds against worthwhile plays" and to build "audiences for the future by promoting the playgoing habit among students, teachers, union members and others who might not otherwise be able to afford it."

Among other organized theater activity in 1968-69 was the Equity strike June 17-19, whose events and settlements took place just before last year's *Best Plays* volume went to press and were fully reported in it. In the past year the actors' organization also negotiated a new three-year agreement for stock production, by which actors' minimums were raised from $115 to $130, directors (represented by Equity in stock) from $250 to $275 and stage managers $135-$160 to $150-$180. At mid-season, an Equity statement about employment in general opined that even in the most favorable circumstances it seemed unlikely that more than 25 per cent of available actors would be employed at any one time.

At the Dramatists Guild, the playwrights' organization, Sidney Kingsley declined to run for a fifth term as president, and Frank D. Gilroy was elected to take his place. In May it was decided by the Guild Council and active membership to alter the organization's constitution so as to offer off-Broadway playwrights the same full membership rights (and duties) as their Broadway colleagues. Until this action was taken, off-Broadway authors had been "associate members" of the Dramatists Guild and could not vote or serve on its Council. Now they can, in a step which may ultimately have a very important effect on the status and even the art of playwriting.

As though in response to this move, shortly after the season ended the various producing organizations formed a coalition called the Organization of Legitimate Theaters whose stated purpose is to promote the theater as a whole. Its members include the League of New York Theaters (Broadway producers), the League of off-Broadway Theaters, the League of Resident Theaters, Lincoln Center Rep, City Center and various other musical and stock establishments. Officers elected at the first meeting were Jules Irving of Lincoln Center, president; Whitfield Connor of the Council of Stock Theaters, vice president; and Richard Barr, president of the League of New York Theaters, secretary-treasurer. Also shortly after the end of the season, Mr. Barr's League revived the old suggestion that New York, like London, should raise its curtain early, at 7:30 instead of 8:30 p.m., to permit the commuter to get home early and the city-dweller to plan a leisurely supper after the show instead of a hasty dinner before. At press time, the League Council had voted to experiment with the early curtain in 1969-70, if details of implementation (union contracts, etc.) could be worked out.

The drama critics had an active year in the rough-and-tumble of industrial relations with David Merrick, Alexander H. Cohen and others. Clive Barnes of the New York *Times* was a frequent target because of his paper's make-or-break influence on the Broadway box office. After the Equity strike last June, Merrick stated facetiously that he would desist from hiring foreign actors if the *Times* would do the same with its English-born drama critic. During the Tony Awards warm-up before the ceremony went on TV, Cohen, the master of ceremonies, introduced "Clive Barnes," and onto the stage came a man dressed in a gorilla suit. The producers of *The Flip Side* requested that Barnes *not* cover the opening of their show, so Dan Sullivan did and reported unfavorably on it as did a majority of critics (Sullivan has since transferred to the Los Angeles *Times* as its drama critic). The New York *Times* Sunday critic, Walter Kerr, drew fire from Julian Beck, who blamed Kerr's denigration of his show *Paradise Now* on Kerr's "loneliness," his non-participation in the performance, his refusal to accept the actors' invitation to all members of the audience to come up on the stage and take their clothes off.

David Goldman of WCBS ran afoul of Cohen, who had a grudge against him for his reportage of the 1968 Tony Awards program and withheld Goldman's review tickets for *Dear World* (Goldman went with another critic and panned the show anyway). The newspaper *Variety* noted in its March 5 issue that John Chapman and the *Daily News* have evidently developed an "aversion" to plays with homosexual themes and did not review *Geese, Spitting Image, The Boys in the Band* or *Fortune and Men's Eyes*. Personnel changes among the critics this season saw Emory Lewis depart from *Cue* and Allan Jefferys from ABC-TV; and Ross Wetzsteon replaced Michael Smith as the first-string drama critic of *The Village Voice*. Walter Winchell hung up his typewriter after several decades of prominence as a general columnist who covered the theater regularly and liked to refer to himself as his paper's drama critic.

The question of whether and when foreign actors are to be employed in Broadway shows has been one of the running controversies within the theater. Certainly it had much to do with the Equity strike in June. As part of the strike settlement, it was decided to set up an arbitration procedure to mediate cases in which a producer insists on hiring a foreign actor over Equity's objection. Norman Nadel served as the abitrator in at least one case this season (he decided against the producer), but a major confrontation between Equity and Merrick on this issue, over the all-British cast of *Rockefeller and the Red Indians,* was avoided at the 11th hour after Equity O.K.'d the employment of the English personnel. Like most controversies in the theater, therefore, this one has not entirely cooled off and continues to simmer on the back burner.

Ditto the running dispute with the Union of South Africa over production rights to American playscripts. Most American playwrights object to the production of their works for segregated audiences, but the copyright tribunal in that country ruled that it can overrule authors in this matter and grant compulsory licenses for production. This was done in the cases of *West Side Story, Man of La Mancha* and *Fiddler on the Roof.* Appropriate protests were filed through available channels, but the dispute still seethes.

One that seems to have been settled was the flare-up between the authors and producers of *Hair.* Gerome Ragni and James Rado, stars as well as authors of the Broadway musical, were experimenting onstage with new material. Rado and Ragni were replaced in their roles and barred from the theater by the producer, Michael Butler. After a few days and several meetings, all parties finally reached an understanding about a procedure for introducing new material, the boys returned to their roles and everything returned to smash-hit normal at the popular rock musical.

In a season in which almost every imagineable sex act was mimed onstage, with actors appearing in various degrees of the nude from suggestive to total, there was surprisingly little censorship activity. The New York theater cannot be said to be suffering the pangs of censorship in the way, say, the London theater did before the historic office of play censor (Lord Chamberlain) was abolished by act of Parliament, taking effect on Sept. 26, 1968 (the opening date of *Hair* in London was deliberately scheduled after that date); or the Paris theater did last September when Andre Malraux, France's minister of culture, dismissed Jean-Louis Barrault from the Odeon following a dispute arising from events during the student rebellion. Nevertheless there seems to be a limit to what even the New York authorities will tolerate, and this limit seems to have been reached finally with the off-off-Broadway production of *Che!,* a symbolic drama of modern ideologies in which nudity, explicit sex acts (both straight and kinky) and the characters of Che Guevara, the President of the United States and a nymphomaniac nun are all stirred together in a kind of sociological-political metaphor. After *Che's* opening performance the police arrested the cast, the producers and other personnel on charges which included obscenity and consentual sodomy. All were later released on bail and subsequent performances of *Che!* were held in the East Village. Still, it was not the facts of the case but its implications that must be given some attention in any review of the 1968-69 season.

This is the problem: the pre-opening publicity had included the boast that actors playing Che and the nun would not only mime the sex act called for in the play, they would *do* it in reality, if they were able to at any given performance. Whether this is to be taken with a grain or mountain of salt is beside the controversial point. It raises a question even for those who take the extreme, purist anti-censorship position. Even those who make it an article of faith that the theater should be able to mime *anything* must pause to ask themselves whether it is also permissible to *do* anything—or is there a borderline between art and reality, and, if so, where does this border lie? Obviously, only Nero himself would consider it a curtailment of artistic freedom to insist that murders on the stage must be mimed, not performed. The fact that an overt sex act might offend some people is no reason for banning it from the stage (those people who might be offended can stay home). But is it a curtailment of artistic freedom to insist that this act be mimed, not actually performed? As this 1968-69 season of transition ended, no truly satisfactory answer had been found to this question raised by the *Che!* case.

In November 1968, in France's Chamber of Deputies, a legislator attacked Andre Malraux's proposal to establish cultural centers throughout France, on the ground that the contemporary theater had little to offer but "unrelieved metaphysical anguish." Malraux replied: "Don't you know the two greatest

French poets aside from Victor Hugo—Baudelaire and Rimbaud? Are they not bitterness incarnate? And is our civilization not dominated by gloom?"

In May 1969, Angus Duncan, executive secretary of Actors Equity Association, issued a policy statement: "It is not the policy of Actors Equity to be guided by considerations of morality, literary merit or artistic value. . . . . (But) when a performer is required to disrobe as the sole prerequisite for a job, then both his dignity and his artistic integrity are under attack."

The theater season of 1968-69 was not entirely dominated by gloom and/or nudity, though there were times when it might have seemed that way. But this was a season in which environment took on a special importance; in which the theater was as continuously aware of its environment as a violin teacher with a parade going by. The plays and musicals of 1968-69 existed not in a mere social, political or artistic "climate," but in a savage weather of events. The theater year had just begun last June when the second of two horrible assassinations rocked the world. This was followed by the shameful happening at the Democratic convention in Chicago. Then there was the Presidential election (in which theater folk took a less conspicuous part than usual) and a change of government. During the Christmas Season, as *Forty Carats* opened on Broadway, man at last reached and orbited the moon; and along with the Christmas carols on the radio there was the booming poetry of Genesis coming down through the quarter-million miles of space between Apollo 9 and the earth, and suddenly after all these earthbound millenia there was an incredible new perspective on our planet in the photos of an earthrise as seen from the moon's surface.

And as if this weren't enough environment for one year, there was the continuing tragedy of the Vietnam War and the painful efforts toward peace. There were the campus rebellions; the have vs. have-not tensions; the increasing computerization of society; the polarizing race troubles.

The theater responded to this heavy 1968-69 environmental presence with renewed effort at finding new forms and ideas. After the environmental shocks of 1968-69, it is unlikely that human beings will settle for the same world they lived in before—or the same theater they enjoyed before. The world, we know, is going to the moon and stars. The theater's destination isn't that clear yet, but at least the art form was aroused and on the move in a season that, taken as a whole in retrospect, must be judged a pretty good one. Like the world, the theater is going *somewhere,* and for the time being we must settle for enjoyment of the adventure for its own sake, maintain our faith in survival and even in progress, and await results.

THE 1968-69 OFF-OFF-BROADWAY SEASON

By R.J. Schroeder

Editor, *The New Underground Theater* (Bantam Books)

The 1968-69 off-off-Broadway season saw the experimental theater's major trends evolve into definitive focus. One set of innovators had been exploring the theatrical possibilities of onstage nudity and sexual confrontation. Another group had been searching for a modern equivalent to tribal ritual.

The nudity-sex act people came up with shows that quickly went commercial, either by moving from their off-off-Broadway point of origin into a commercial theater under commercial auspices (as did, for example, *De Sade Illustrated*), or by exacting *Hair*-level prices for admittance into the original off-off-Broadway theater (as Ed Wode did with his production of Lennox Raphael's *Che!*). Prolonged full-front nudity having been exploited last season, this year's entrepreneurs advanced upon the only remaining fronts—prolonged group nudity, and simulations of the sex act in pairs and in groups.

While it was initially announced by the several producers of this genre of show that the sex acts would be genuine "when the performers felt like it," practical experience proved that they did not, during public performances, actually "feel like it." Simulations became the order of the day, and, by the spring of 1969, undulating choruses of stripped actors were copping out on copulation during seeming hours of denatured Dionysian revelry in a growing number of off-off-Broadway grind houses—theaters that were coming to rival the 42nd Street grind movie houses not only in show content, but also in audience composition.

I would like to have been an appreciative observer of the off-off-Broadway innovations in onstage nudity and sexuality, but I was forced by the artistic ineptitude of the perpetrators into the role of voyeur. This season's output could only be labeled exploitative—I saw no intellectually intriguing or emotionally absorbing (or even erotically stimulating) use of onstage nudity or sexuality in the off-off-Broadway theater. In contrast, I felt that the nude dances Ann Halprin's San Francisco Dance Workshop displayed in last season's New York appearance, and some of the similar dances incorporated into current Broadway and off-Broadway shows constituted an actual extension of the theater's horizons. It will be to off off Broadway's everlasting discredit that while it was first to undress, and first to pretend that it went "all the way," it will have been last to approach a sensual aesthetic.

The other principal movement in the off-off-Broadway theater—that reaching toward a sense of theater as ritual that might contribute a rediscovered feeling of community, as exemplified by the work of The Performance Group, The Living Theater, and The Open Theater—achieved a greater total expression than it had in the immediately preceding seasons, because 1968-69 was the first season in which these major proponents of ritual theater played concurrent New York engagements.

The Living Theater's return from its self-imposed European "exile" promised to be the big event in 1968-69 non-commercial theater in New York. For several years, many of those theatrical reporters and commentators who, whatever their other differences, could conscientously subscribe to the slogan "I hate Broadway" had made pilgrimages to whatever European city Julian Beck and Judith Malina had converted into temporary Meccas in order to send back glowing endorsements of The Living Theater's development of what was extolled as "a new theater language."

First to find the "new language" for the most part incommunicative was the redoubtable Robert Brustein, theater critic for *The New Republic* and dean of the theater department at Yale, where The Living Theater had been invited to give its pre-New York performances. His subsequently published bewilderment at the non-viability of The Living Theater was soon shared by many New Yorkers, when the group came to the Brooklyn Academy of Music to perform an adaptation of Brecht's adaptation of *Antigone,* and three original works, *Frankenstein, Mysteries and Smaller Pieces,* and *Paradise Now.*

The consensus of non-apostolic opinion was that each of the four-to-five-hour performances contained passages of interest and of artistic merit, but that the audience was made to endure almost unendurable lengths of desert for each transient oasis. It was the consensus also that, for all of the troupe's protests that it was illustrating love, never had so much unrelieved hate been focused on a New York audience for such protracted periods of time. There was much actor-roaming amongst the audience, with shouted insults, physical molestation, near-miss kicks and swipes, and other manifestations not ordinarily associated with the concept of love.

When the performances were interesting, which was seldom and only for short periods of time, the interest derived from the kind of group choreography that one associates with the work of the Berliner Ensemble, or with the more literal interpolations by modern dance groups. But even in the areas where the work of The Living Theater was at its best, it was only doing second-rate Joffrey, second-rate Graham, second-rate Halprin, or third-rate Berliner Ensemble.

The Open Theater, which grew out of a nucleus of Living Theater members who had not joined the Becks in "exile," performed two major works this season, Jean-Claude van Itallie's *The Serpent: A Ceremony* and a version of Alfred Jarry's *Ubu Cocu.* In performance, their work proved to be a cross between The Living Theater's choreography, and Jerzy Grotowski's Polish Laboratory Theater's use-of-entire-body miming with supplemental—almost sub-title—verbalization.

The Performance Group's version of Euripides' *The Bacchae,* retitled *Dionysus in '69,* has changed considerably during this season's series of weekend performances. But despite the variations in dress and undress, expansions and contractions of dialogue, and greater and lesser encouragement of audience participation, the work has remained sub-Grotowski. The group's effort grew out of a class Grotowski had conducted at NYU the previous season, and can best be described as an attempt to achieve an American ritual in Grotowski's partially Catholic-derived and partially Karl Jung-derived sense of unconscious communal awareness.

A third branch of off-off-Broadway endeavor is a reaching for the far-out for the sake of "mind-blowing." Theater Genesis continues as the chief expositor of this vein of theater, its stable of authors made to seem united in purpose largely through the dominating influence of Ralph Cook, head of the project and director of most of its shows. But this season, a foreign invader succeeded for several weeks in splattering its brains to farther reaches than have yet been grey-mattered by the Genesis crowd. The invaders were a French troupe calling themselves Le Grand Panic Circus, who performed first at Brandeis University, and then at off off Broadway's The Extension. Disciples of the Spanish-French playwright Arrabal, the troupe described itself as consisting of "hermaphrodites and sad-eyed animals", and performed what Olsen and Johnson of *Hellzapoppin'* fame might have performed had they been, one night, tripping on LSD. Arrabal's theory is that it is the contemporary artist's job to help our current society into its "deserved grave" by "accelerating its disorientation." Le Grand Panic Circus seemed to be doing its part.

Not included in what has previously been thought of as off off Broadway, but a growing element of non-commercial theater in New York, is black theater. The Afro-American Studio, the James Weldon Johnson Theater Arts Center and the New Lafayette Theater, all in Harlem, presented season-long programs of plays and musicals intended as black point of view expression by blacks. The Chelsea Theater Center and the New York Shakespeare Festival's Public Theater also presented significant expressions of new black voices this season.

The OM Theater Workshop of Boston staged a New York season with its production of *Riot,* a mock-debate ending in holocaust which highlighted aspects of the contemporary urban crisis.

The established off-off-Broadway repertory groups, CSC Repertory, Thresholds, and the Roundabout Theater, continued to present works from the classis and contemporary literature. The Universalist Theater and the Workshop of the Players' Art initiated bids to play a similarly important role in such stagings.

A personal listing of off off Broadway's 1968-69 "bests": Afro-American Studio's *Black Nativity* by Langston Hughes, the Cooper Square Arts Theater's *Georgie-Porgie* by George Birimisa, The Extension's *Leonce and Lena* by Georg Büchner, the James Weldon Johnson Theater Arts Center's *A Raisin in the Sun* by Lorraine Hansberry, the New Lafayette Theater's *Who's Got His Own* by Ronald Milner, the Roundabout Theater's *King Lear,* Threshold's adaptation of *Finnegans Wake* and the Workshop of the Players' Art's staging of Ugo Betti's *The Gambler.*

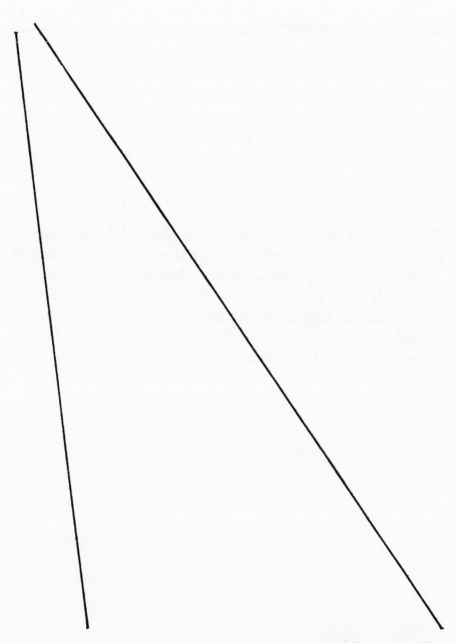

1919-1969:
A HALF CENTURY OF
AMERICAN THEATER

This 1968-69 volume of Best Plays *is the 50th in the series of theater yearbooks started by Burns Mantle for the season of 1919-20 and published annually through five decades by Dodd, Mead & Company. On the occasion of this Golden Anniversary of* Best Plays, *we offer on the following pages a special reflection upon the half century of American theater covered in the first 50 volumes.*

O
O
O
1919-1969:
A REVIEW OF THE HALF CENTURY
OF AMERICAN THEATER

BY WALTER KERR

Sunday drama critic of the New York *Times*

O
O
O

I THINK we must take some pains to develop a nostalgia for the present.

Going back over all forty-nine earlier volumes in the *Best Plays* series—and I have reread all forty-nine descriptions of seasons past, if not all 490 shining plays—is illuminating in at least one way. The seasons we admire most are those we never saw.

Pick up almost any volume between 1919 and 1930 and you will be staggered not perhaps by the absolute quality of the plays selected but by a feeling of theatrical robustness that seems to leap from the Table of Contents page. The New York theater had almost too much energy. In 1921 alone it managed to produce 196 plays, *Anna Christie, A Bill of Divorcement, Dulcy, He Who Gets Slapped* and *The Circle* among them.

How do you think you'd have felt about being in on a season that led off with *What Price Glory?, They Knew What They Wanted* and *Desire Under the Elms,* and found time thereafter for Philip Barry's first play? There's a vigor in those first three titles that may simply come from the sound of the words (you need only hear the phrase "What Price Glory?" to imagine an uproar in the playhouse) or that may suggest to us the exuberant freedoms that were being born, willy nilly, in 1924, but a vigor it is and its bristle is contagious.

What of a season that included *Broadway, Chicago, The Constant Wife, The Play's the Thing, The Road to Rome, The Silver Cord* and *Cradle Song?* Doesn't that sound a tumble of treasures—of legends, even? *The Silver Cord,* after all, was definitive with us, a watershed play that meant mother-love would never be the same again while Freud would become a casual playgoing companion.

But notice that, for all its "modernity" and its introspection, *The Silver Cord* comes directly alongside a couple of blockbusting melodramas, *Broadway* and

45

Chicago, with hoofers and gangsters and acquitted murderesses everywhere. The very existence of such melodrama cheers us as we look back on it. Too bad we were born so late, too bad we're no longer innocent enough to enjoy unabashed melodrama's special pleasures. Melodrama could be even more unabashed than *Broadway* and *Chicago* and still find a place in Burns Mantle's early lists: think of *On Trial, Seven Keys to Baldpate, The Green Goddess* and *The Bad Man.* Editing the series, Mr. Mantle could be charmingly unruffled in dealing with such plays. Making no particular claim for literary merit, not even supposing the issue entirely relevant, he could drop something like Channing Pollock's *The Sign on the Door* into the hallowed ten with the offhand remark that it was to be "accepted as the most stirring of the season's melodramas." *Stirring* is the evocative word here. As late as 1926, the *Silver Cord-Chicago* year, playgoers could go to the theater to be both harried *and* stirred. Our consciences hadn't narrowed yet, we hadn't thrown out the lively in our search for the literary, there was a range to what was going on on Broadway that still seems attractively animated. The theater had an appetite.

I'll mention one more season and then stop tormenting you. The season that began in 1927 included *Strange Interlude, The Royal Family, Burlesque, Coquette, Porgy, Paris Bound,* John Galsworthy's *Escape* (I mention the author because I think you may have forgotten that one) and *The Plough and the Stars.* The fact of the matter is that for quite a long while in the 1920s Mr. Mantle had an embarrassment of apparent riches on his hands. We really don't seem to be faced with such hard choices any more.

As *I* run my finger down the Burns Mantle years, the very type seems to dance until—well, about 1930-31. There my hand hesitates a little, I go back to see if I have really read aright, my heart grows just a shade heavy. Glamor and yearning seem suddenly to have dimmed, as though some of the light bulbs in the marquee had burnt out and not been replaced. A creative pressure has weakened; I find myself less jealous. True, there were plays that are still remembered, *Elizabeth the Queen, Once in a Lifetime, The Barretts of Wimpole Street.* There is even a single melodrama, just for old time's sake, a yellow-journalism exposé called *Five Star Final.* Add a big showpiece, *Grand Hotel.* But in and around these still teasing titles on the Best Plays list are softer, less assertive, inclusions: *Alison's House, As Husbands Go, Overture.* What, in heaven's name, can *Overture* have been? During the following season, and in spite of *Mourning Becomes Electra,* there are more: *Another Language, The Devil Passes, Cynara.* Not bad plays—just quieter ones, tamer ones. The theater had been jumping up and down. In the two seasons 1930-32 it sat down and sighed, rather.

Historically speaking, things had been happening to it. The matter can be explained, or explained away, rationally, objectively. A depression had happened. Fewer theaters were open, fewer plays being produced. Talking pictures had happened. A great many stars who had formerly kept vehicles alive on the strength of their personal followings had gone to speak in Hollywood. Worse, many, many playwrights had gone, in dire need of the money available there. A part of the playwriting range had been usurped by Hollywood; certainly melodrama, and *Grand Hotel* showpieces, were now the property of Warner Brothers and M-G-M. The theater lost some crackle because a soundtrack could crackle louder. It became more reflective, having little else to do. And it had, along with the country, lost the brash confidence that had sustained it joyfully, jazzily, since the end of World War I. The go-getting American of the 1920s was dead, killed by what he had got. The go-getting theater of the 1920s, the theater of appetite and ardor, of course had to leave the scene with him.

Indeed, indeed. If that were all. But it wasn't all, not really. Something else had intervened to halt my urgent finger and delay my racing heart. In 1931 or 1932 nostalgia had lost its force, I realized with a start, because it was approximately at that time that I began seeing the plays.

This sounds as though I were going to say that the theater's magic is essentially spurious and cannot survive direct acquaintance, that it only functions by hearsay or at discreet distances. I am going to try to say something else, though of course we must take a moment to admit that *some* of the yearning we all feel for glories past is mightily helped along by our imaginations. I had always loved George S. Kaufman's *The Butter and Egg Man* until I saw it off Broadway recently. There are funny things in it, but not enough of them to warrant continuing the affair. I don't know what *What Price Glory?* would look like now. I have an idea that I'd like to see it—in fact, I have an idea that I'd like to see it in a repertory house with Moses Gunn and Godfrey Cambridge in the principal roles—but I haven't quite had the nerve to take it down off the shelf for a many-years-after reading. It might bite me. Has anyone seen *Elizabeth the Queen* lately? Don't.

Some few plays have kept their glow, some will keep it. *Anna Christie* will be done again, whether *Strange Interlude* is or not. *The Front Page* still has good skin tone. *The Constant Wife* has been successfully revived, as I'm sure *The Circle* could be. *The Plough and the Stars* has by no means vanished—no more than the slighted *Juno and the Paycock* has—and *Liliom* and *Saint Joan* do seem to be with us. Occasionally, with a sufficiently sensitive production, a work felt to be lost can be made to display its special virtues, as the APA's tender production of *The Show-Off*—one of the Best Plays of 1923-24—emphatically demonstrated. With skill and patience, the colors of a time can be renewed.

But most will not be. We know that we must surrender the halos that hover, ever so faintly now, over a thousand plays we never saw. The age did not belong to Pericles, or to *Elizabeth the Queen*. It belonged to Harding and Coolidge and to the playwrights they begat. All right. We can stifle our sniffles and become cagier about the unremembered memories we revere.

But what about the thousand plays we actually saw? Need we be so very, very cagey about them?

We are cagier about them. We are *sure* they are destined for oblivion, certain they represent a falling-off from some vague earlier excellence, ever ready to proclaim the new season we have just sat through as "undoubtedly the worst within the memory of living man." Why are we so sure?

Of course our conviction is part common sense: Pericles and his writers didn't put in an appearance in 1931, or 1969, either. We live, generally speaking, in a time of second-rank theater, theater at less than masterpiece heat, and we know it. Truly great periods come infrequently and it just hasn't been our luck to have stumbled at birth into one of them. Our conviction is also, no doubt, part self-protection. It is always safest to say that the plays one is seeing aren't masterpieces, or aren't even likely to be recognized by the children we are presumably educating. (My children occasionally come to me with the news that they have just discovered a fascinating piece of material on television. As likely as not, they have just come upon an old movie version of *Arsenic and Old Lace* or *The Petrified Forest*. They are invariably surprised to realize that I know the material and that it once had something to do with that alien and vanishing rumor, the theater.) One doesn't like to be caught overpraising something that falls to dust in a year or two, and overpraise can be avoided by maintaining a sufficiently skeptical attitude toward everything that happens between 8:30 and 11 on a post-midcentury evening. You can't go wrong saying no. Ninety-nine times out of a hundred no is prophetic.

But there is at least one more factor, I think, to be taken into account in accounting for the diminished enthusiasm we feel for the immediate. I started to say a few paragraphs ago that something of the tarnished lustre that attaches to everything *I* saw beginning about 1931 or 1932 has less to do with the plays I saw than it has to do with me. I play a part in the changed attitude, the refusal to wax nostalgic, the reluctance to praise (and not because I happened to become a reviewer, either, it is nothing so personal or so accidental as that). The thing is, I belong to the play, I am in and of it because I happened to be there when it spoke, I participate in it directly—and nothing that I belong to or have participated in can ever be regarded as quite perfect.

You see, all of us bring *ourselves* into the act of judging any play we actually see and when we do we must necessarily be more severe. This play is our play because we literally helped to make it: sitting in the theater, we sent a response up to the actors and author, which means that we played a vital part in the shape it took, we played what was actually a determining part in its continued existence. The actors heard our laughter or silence, our applause or surly departures. Because of the way we behaved in the theater, they altered some of what they did. So, at least in his next play, did the author. We were more than the author's contemporaries. We lived as his collaborators.

Being on such intimate terms with the author, we were much more aware of him than we can ever hope to be, say, of Shakespeare. Above all, as playwatchers we are tremendously aware of possible danger, of the risk that the play may very well fall apart before it comes together, we can sense the holes in it. We are intensely aware of potential shortcomings because the author is there before us, alive, imperfect, vulnerable, never secure. He is a duplicate of each of us. We were born to the same lawns, grew up in the same apartment buildings, studied under the same teachers, went roller-skating on the same sidewalks, stole into the same movies, suffered the same politicians, endured the same war (whichever it may have been), for all practical purposes married the same girl and had all the same children. We know that playwright, we can check the truth of the report he is giving us. Indeed we are in a contest with him—for truth. Has he got that inflection exactly right, has he misremembered the August weather of our adolescence, has he found out how we feel and shown it back to us exactly? Has he honored our self-knowledge or is he in the business of making fakes? We do more than check. We challenge upon the instant, supposing a false note to have been sounded. Some notes are bound to be false. We won't miss a one of them. This play, however fine, however entertaining, however true, is honeycombed with minute error—or at least it may be, it may relax its grip upon exactness, if we do not watch it with extremely critical eyes. We assume that it is not perfect and we spend a good bit of our time proving ourselves right.

There is nothing despicable in this, not even really anything captious in it. It is necessary and inevitable. A play is not only about a contest, it always *is* a contest between author and audience. Truth-seeking needs checks and balances, even delight needs a devil's advocate. Indeed, without just this sort of contention there would be no excitement in theater at all. Excitement is the result of risk, it comes of trying out the new knowing that the new may crash in flames, it thrives on the suspense of waiting to see whether this rather reckless dramatist will get away with all the chances he is taking. Opening nights are always cliff-hangers. Who will surrender—the audience or the poor fellow who's dared to put his eyesight on the line? At a good play there is a delicious moment when the audience finally gives in. At a bad play there is a shamefaced moment when the author does. Not to have this uncertainty would be fatal to the fun of theatergoing. Sitting only through secure plays, in which the worst could not possibly happen, would be like seeing *Macbeth* five times a week for the rest of our natural lives.

Awareness that the project before us, in which we are directly and vitally engaged, may very well be defective—will in all probability be to some degree defective—is perfectly natural in an audience when the audience is dealing with the new. It is the only responsible attitude an audience can take.

But it does destroy nostalgia, or whatever nostalgia might be called if it were ever applied to the here, now, and nervous. The apprehensively critical frame of mind that is essential to any experience of the immediate takes one color out of the spectrum. Rosiness, I suppose. A degree of glamor is forsworn, sentiment is suppressed for fear of sentimentality, we do not allow ourselves the luxury of loving unequivocally. We are hedgers, and it hurts a little. We do not take *all* of the pleasure we might take if our consciences were altogether clear.

Can we take a little more, can we permit ourselves to kick our heels *slightly* higher when we like something without confusing ourselves about what is actually there, without corrupting the standards we need to get home by? I would like to think so, if only to get us all past that faintly querulous tone that accompanies the enthusiasms we have. So often we apologize, and even temper an enthusiasm we actually feel, for fear of being caught out enjoying the ephemeral—as though the ephemeral weren't something that might be enjoyed. All too often we preface our praise with a waiver: "Of course, it's nothing, I know that," "Well, it's only trivia," "I suppose a lot of people aren't going to like it, but—" *But* constructions are commonplace enough in the theater to have become a joke; when we cannot do better, we cushion our praise of a play with an indictment of the season as a whole. With a little sigh of relaxation, Burns Mantle called the 1922-23 season "the first season in a generation not to have been described as the 'worst in years.' " The phrase is familiar to us, the exception to it is not.

Could we try it *this* way? Face the fact that most of what we see is certainly ephemeral. (The Best Plays of 1941-42, to move up a little, were *In Time to Come, The Moon Is Down, Junior Miss, Candle in the Wind, Letters to Lucerne, Jason, Angel Street, Uncle Harry, Hope for a Harvest* and *Blithe Spirit*.) Then consider that we are ephemeral, too, and that if a man is going to have to dance with the girl he came with, he might as well take pleasure in the dance.

It is good to be strict where matters of quality are at stake. It is good to try to sharpen standards over those of a generation ago and to pass on to the next generation a select body of work for it to be mean about. But it is also good to exhale now and again, to embrace what is available because it and only it is available. You can put your arms around a girl you know to be less than perfect. In fact, you'd better.

Can we restore a little color to our pleasures by telling ourselves that they *are* our pleasures, that neither they nor we will happen this way again, that no matter how ill-made we think them they are in fact the fit for us, that a star danced and both of us were born? After all, sometime, somewhere, someone will be nostalgic about *A Streetcar Named Desire* and *The Waltz of the Toreadors* and *The Collection* (look it up, 1962-63) and *Who's Afraid of Virginia Woolf?* and *The Odd Couple* and *America Hurrah,* wishing they'd been there on opening nights. Why not get the jump on them?

To speak for myself, I've decided to try. I know that *The Rose Tattoo* has faults. I'm sure the author thinks I've gone on endlessly about them. No matter. It's a nice thing, and I'm glad I was in New York to see Maureen Stapleton and Eli Wallach play it. I know that the double bill *The Typists* and *The Tiger* is slight. I would not have been happier if it had been heavier. I saw a lost Chekhov play salvaged *(A Country Scandal);* I am determined to be grateful. Joseph Chaikin and Jean-Claude van Itallie have not yet perfected their work at The Open Theater. It may come to nothing. I'm going to keep certain fragments of *The Serpent* tucked away in my head and take them out now and then for my remembered pleasure anyway. I'm happy to have heard George C. Scott say "I want to do it all over again" in *Plaza Suite.* It's not "Hey, Flagg, wait for baby!" perhaps; but it's a good line.

I could go on. I won't. Those are random choices and I'm not going to add to them because adding would make a list and making a list always seems to close the books. I suppose I'm trying to say that as long as the books are open, and our eyes are open, our arms might as well be open, too. Think severely, as all living men must. But thank God and Tennessee Williams and Edward Albee and Jean Anouilh and Harold Pinter and Murray Schisgal between thoughts.

○
○
○

1919-1969:
A REVIEW OF
THE HALF-CENTURY INFLUENCE
OF AMERICAN THEATER
ABROAD

BY W.A. DARLINGTON

Former drama critic of the London *Daily Telegraph*

○
○
○

FIFTY YEARS AGO, with World War I just over and very little of the mess cleared up, the serious theater in London was at its lowest state within living memory. The English capital, lying as it did close behind the battlefront yet immune from any attack except occasional Zeppelin raids, had been the most sought-after center for warriors on leave, American as well as British; and its theater managers had had little incentive to look for plays of quality. "Stuff to give the troops" was all the producers wanted; and the troops, traditionally, had no ideas beyond glitter, gaiety and girls. Consequently, in 1919, when I made my first tentative approach to drama criticism, I found London's show business going strong. But there was little sign of anything that could be called serious theater.

In New York, the war years had had a very different effect. So far from bringing the serious theater to the brink of ruin, they had acted as a stimulant. It is hardly too fanciful to suggest that it was the shock of war's outbreak that acted as a signal to the American theater that a long, pleasant and in many ways brilliant adolescence was now over, and that it must come of age.

When 1914 arrived, I had been for 6 years a devoted and rather serious-minded London playgoer, who had made the theater a subject of special study in school holidays and college vacations, and had stayed on at Cambridge for a year after graduation, nominally to pass an examination in English Literature, but actually—since I was working without supervision—to throw the official specification out of the window, and devise another of my own dealing with drama and the theater. I crashed heavily in the examination, of course, since the man who set the papers wasn't aware of the theater's existence; but I got the knowledge I was after, and very useful it proved when, 6 years later, I was hired as a drama critic.

During this year of study, the various influences that had been brought to bear on British drama during its four centuries or so of recorded history revealed themselves clearly. Ancient Greece and Rome, Renaissance Italy, Germany, Spain, Austria-Hungary, Russia, Scandinavia and of course our nearest neighbor, France, had all made—and most of them were still making—important contributions to the work of our own native playwrights. But so far as my memory serves, it never crossed my mind that any such contribution had so far been made by America.

It must not be deduced from this that I knew nothing of the American theater, or that I did not respect what I knew. For good and all the lesson had come home that, for me at least, the academic approach to the drama was the wrong one; and I was well aware that on its lighter side the American theater was brilliantly efficient, and brilliantly served by its actors. But I took it for granted that if an impresario in New York wished to present his star players in something which went deeper than entertainment, he would send to Europe for it. Charles Frohman, the American impresario of whose activity I was most sharply aware, seemed to be ceaselessly engaged in this traffic; and if there was any similar traffic coming the other way, I never heard of it. The American plays I saw were near-farces of the order of *Brewster's Millions* or *Broadway Jones*.

It was, then, with no feeling of surprise that in 1919, having at last got free of the Army, I came back to a theatrical London full of light comedies and farces imported from America. The situation was natural enough. The London producers, faced with a public at once disillusioned and overexcited, and in no mood for the classics or anything solemn, looked about them for gaiety and glitter and found it in New York. I had intended to take up my study of the serious stage at the point where I had laid it down, but for the moment there was nothing doing in my line.

I was not too badly placed, however. I had got myself a precarious job on a once-famous but now moribund weekly, of which every issue seemed certain to be the last but one. Its appeal to me was that the drama critic, who also owned the paper, was a lazy man who always sent in short measure and was pleased to let me fill up for him. I was able to serve a rough apprenticeship to my hope of becoming a drama critic on my own account.

In 1920 my apprenticeship was brought to a sudden end. I was appointed chief drama critic of the London *Daily Telegraph,* a post which, as things turned out, I was to occupy for nearly 49 years; and a close study of the furious theatrical activity in America became no longer a spare time hobby but a professional duty.

The situation was confused. So strong was the demand for brightly-written, light-textured American pieces that some of the importers lost their sense of discrimination and accepted for presentation in London a number of pieces so peculiarly American in situation, sentiment and solution that they meant nothing to English audiences. In my first two years as critic I found myself writing article after article designed to help straighten out the mechanics of this situation.

Meanwhile, two things were happening. The first was that English playgoers were being steadily conditioned to American customs. At the prosperous middle-income level with which light comedy mainly dealt, the American and British ways of life were not markedly different; and when any such comedies had successful London runs (as a good few did) the English public was made familiar with American scenes, American idioms or the pungent American slang. This conditioning process was made more complete by the swift rise to popularity of the movies. All over the country, now that the retarding effects of the war had worn off, cinemas were being opened; and, with the British film-industry not fully re-established, the majority of the films shown came from America.

The second thing that happened during this early postwar period was the gradual realization in London that behind the facade of successful show business which New York displayed, people were deeply engaged with that almost forgotten entity, the art of the theater.

There seemed, for instance, to be some people called the Provincetown Players who were making quite a stir. There was a man called Stark Young who must be looked into, and a woman called Susan Glaspell. Above all, there was a man called O'Neill who seemed to be writing plays that were causing great excitement, though so far only one short play of his had been seen, at an outlying theater in a London suburb.

About 1922, the situation began to change. A new postwar generation of British dramatists was beginning to make its appearance with the infant prodigy Noel Coward as its brilliant leader; and London producers began to find that they need not import American light entertainment in quite such bulk as hitherto. But with the drop in quantity there came a marked improvement in quality. Elmer Rice's *The Adding Machine,* for instance, was seen in London in 1924, though only in a special Stage Society performance, and some of the early work of George S. Kaufman and Marc Connelly was put on for runs.

Meanwhile, quite other influences were making themselves felt. The work of Professor George Pierce Baker's famous school for dramatists at Harvard, the 47 Workshop, had made a deep impression in England, and while neither Oxford nor Cambridge was inclined to admit that the study of drama was anything more than a branch of English Literature, certain theater-minded scholars in the newer universities were ready to follow where Baker had led. In 1926 Professor Allardyce Nicoll of London University founded a school on Baker's model. This failed for lack of funds, but Nicoll's effort had not gone unremarked: seven years later he was invited to carry on similar work at Yale.

It was in the middle 1920s, too, that the effect of American drama criticism began to be felt in England. Up until about 1925 this had not happened. The very able journalists who wrote day-to-day notices for the leading American papers seemed to be concerned more closely with the theater as a business than as an art, and their shrewd and pungent commentaries (and even their names) were known to few English readers except those whose job it was to keep in touch. Criticism of a more serious order seemed to be left to college professors who were apt to write learned books of what came to be known as "undramatic criticism" because it dealt with plays from printed texts rather than stage performances. The one writer internationally known and respected was Brander Matthews, a practising dramatist as well as a professor; and he had little to say in praise of his academically minded colleagues.

This state of affairs was brought to an end by the emergence of a new generation of American drama critics capable of emulating the journalists at their own game and of beating the professors at theirs. This new movement might be signalized by the appointment of Stark Young to the New York *Times* in 1924. He did the job for a year, and was succeeded by Brooks Atkinson, whose name very soon became familiar in London, accompanied by those of George Jean Nathan, John Mason Brown, Alexander Woollcott and others.

All these separate currents, coalescing into one stream, operated strongly during the latter half of the 1920s to make London playgoers more conscious and respectful of the goings-on in theatrical New York.

The influence grew steadily stronger, and the quality of the imports from America steadily more impressive. Writers of high comedy like S. N. Behrman (whose *The Second Man* had a run of over 100 performances, which in those days spelt success) and Robert Sherwood made their bows; and in 1928 the arrival of *Show Boat* began that long succession of admirable new-pattern musicals which were collectively to rank as America's most popular contribution to the English scene. Eugene O'Neill's plays, too, were gaining ground, though not until the next decade could they be said to have attracted any but specialized audiences.

The 1930s, indeed, brought a general change in the situation. One reason for this was the arrival of the talkies which had the double effect of increasing the familiarity of the British public with American conditions of life, and of opening up to British actors and dramatists a vast new field of operations. Now that actors on the films were expected to be able to speak, Broadway and Hollywood found themselves in competition for the services not only of stage actors but of writers of dialogue. And as the rates of pay both in New York and Hollywood were much higher than British theater managers or film makers could offer, the United States became a sort of El Dorado, on either coast of which fortunes could be picked up by those who had the skill.

The effect on some British writers was very noticeable; what they wrote from now on was intended as much for the American as for the home market. Noel Coward gives the best example of the trend. Up till 1930, though he had had success in New York both as actor and as dramatist, he had written nothing that was not intended for London. But in 1930, with *Private Lives,* he broke new ground. He arranged for the play to be given a limited season in London, after which he and his leading lady, Gertrude Lawrence, were to take it to New York. His next play, *Design for Living,* was given a New York setting. He did not appear in it in London, but when he and the Lunts produced it in New York in 1933, he played Leo.

His next play, *Point Valaine* (1934) was also produced by the Lunts in New York; but it was a failure and has never been seen in the West End of London at all.

Another example of a British dramatist whose plays became more and more slanted towards America was John van Druten. In his case, however, the process went so far that he changed his nationality and continued his career as an American dramatist whose plays were not much liked in London.

The fact was that from the 1930s for a period of 20-25 years the back-and-forth influence exercised upon one another by the theaters of London and New York was so nearly equal that it defies close analysis. During the whole of this time, except for those years of World War II when actors in London had to dodge the bombs as best they might, the two organizations were so closely linked that sometimes they seemed to have coalesced into a single entity, the English-speaking Theater.

So far as plays were concerned, the exchange was pretty well equal. It could be taken for granted that any play which succeeded in one city would be examined very carefully for its chances in the other.

New York had plenty to bring to the exchange. A number of its dramatic craftsmen (George Abbott, George S. Kaufman, Moss Hart are names that come easily to the memory) had developed a high degree of skill in the manufacture of the lighter kind of straight comedy, and a good many of their products were successfully transformed to the London stage.

The word "manufacture" is properly used here, for the methods of these practitioners were the methods of engineering rather than art. Kaufman was nothing out of the ordinary as a dramatist on his own account, but he had a genius for taking other men's plays to pieces, trying them out on provincial audiences and reconstituting them by a process of trial and error.

In one sense his influence on the British stage was nonexistent; no artificer set himself up in London as a homegrown Kaufman. But it may perhaps be owing to his influence that London producers got into the habit of sending out their plays for provincial runs to give them a chance to settle down before facing the ordeal of a West End first night.

The great American triumph in London of the 1930s, however, was the final full acceptance of O'Neill's work, the production of his major plays in the West End and a general critical acknowledgement of his position as one of the few contemporary dramatists of undoubted genius. One of the finest compliments that could be paid to any author by his leading lady came from Laura Cowie, who played the Clytemnestra part in *Mourning Becomes Electra*. Shortly afterward, she had to leave the stage in order to nurse her sick husband, thus cutting short a fine career. She said she had no regrets; acting that part for O'Neill had given her a satisfaction she could never hope to feel again.

World War II brought an interruption, but when it was over the British theater, though battered, was in surprisingly good shape. A new young audience had grown up and, unlike its counterpart after the first war, was not ready to be put off with rubbish. Surrounded as they were with wartime debris, what they yearned for was brightness, gaiety and vigor, and they found all of these, and a new art form into the bargain, in the current American musicals. No more heartwarming experience could come a playgoer's way than the first night of *Oklahoma!* at Drury Lane in 1947. Others followed; the old liaison was as close as ever and remained so for another 10 years.

Then, in 1956, an event occurred which, unregarded at first, had the ultimate effect of loosening the bond and, indeed, of reducing almost to nothing the influence of New York on London drama. John Osborne's first play, *Look Back in Anger,* was produced at a small outlying theater for a limited season. That play was the first dramatic expression of the point of view of a rebellious young postwar generation, and it acted like the breaking of a dam to let loose a flood. What came to be known as the New Wave of English drama was upon us, and its relevance to the subject of this article is that the writers of these new plays, mostly with working-class sympathies and backgrounds, were not merely uninfluenced by America—they were unconscious that any such influence could exist.

This development caused some consternation on Broadway, and I well remember the horror with which Sol Hurok, paying his customary visit to London in search of exportable material, surveyed the changed scene. There was no sign in sight of the well-made play, either on the O'Neill or the Kaufman model. All was chaotic, obscure and messy. Inevitably, Broadway and the West End drew apart, and have remained slightly apart ever since.

Today, however, a new American influence is making itself felt and is closing the gap. The welcome given in London to Albee's plays is a strong sign of rapprochement; but perhaps an even stronger one is the constant flow to us of off-Broadway products. When a deeply American piece like *Hair* can be one of Shaftesbury Avenue's smash hits, the age of miracles is not past.

O
O
O

1919-1969:
THE 500 BEST PLAYS
OF THE HALF CENTURY
AS SELECTED
IN THE 50 VOLUMES

O
O
O

FIRST and foremost, it was the theater of Maxwell Anderson (19 citations) and of George S. Kaufman (18 citations). The plays of Eugene O'Neill spanned most of it with 12 citations, the first in the season of 1919-20 and the last in 1958-59. Among its 500 remarkable works of the professional New York theater, 10 a year for 50 years, *Life with Father* recorded the longest run (3,224 performances starting in 1939) and the aptly-named *A Very Special Baby* the shortest (5 performances in 1956).

The theater we are speaking of is, of course, the half-century of Best Play selections in the series of theater yearbooks of which this one, *The Best Plays of 1968-69,* is the fiftieth, the golden anniversary volume. The series was started by Burns Mantle in the season of 1919-20 and edited by him yearly through 1946-47; then by John Chapman from 1947-48 through 1951-52; then by Louis Kronenberger from 1952-53 through 1960-61; then by Henry Hewes from 1961-62 through 1963-64; then by the present editor starting with the 1964-65 volume.

At the end of the 1968-69 season when the grand total of Best Plays has reached exactly 500, we pause to consider some of the statistics of the half-century. Maxwell Anderson turns out to be the editors' favorite playwright with a career of 19 citations as author or co-author of a Best Play, the first in 1924-25 and the last in 1954-55. George S. Kaufman was runner-up with 18, Eugene O'Neill was third with 12, Moss Hart fourth with 11, Philip Barry fifth with 10. But the four contenders achieved what the champion Anderson did not. They each managed *two* citations for different works in the *same* season, the *Best Plays* equivalent of the hat trick: Kaufman for *Stage Door* and *You Can't Take It With You* in 1936-37; O'Neill for *Long Day's Journey into Night* and *A Moon for the Misbegotten* in 1956-57; Hart for *George Wash-*

ington Slept Here and *Lady in the Dark* in 1940-41, and Barry for *Here Come the Clowns* and *The Philadelphia Story* in 1938-39. The only other hat-trick playwrights of the half century were Sidney Howard for *The Late Christopher Bean* and *Alien Corn* in 1932-33 and John Osborne for *Look Back in Anger* and *The Entertainer* in 1957-58.

Lillian Hellman was the most-cited of women playwrights, with 9 Best Plays in the seasons from 1934-35 to 1959-60. Rachel Crothers was second with 6 citations.

No musical was named a Best Play until 1931-32 *(Of Thee I Sing),* and it was unusual for musicals to be found on the lists until recent seasons. Consequently, no single musical author or team has piled up a number of citations comparable to those of the straight playwrights. The musical leaders are Jerry Bock and Sheldon Harnick with 4 citations and Kurt Weill with three. The following authors have been cited twice in the Best Plays lists for musicals: Richard Rodgers and Oscar Hammerstein II, Alan Jay Lerner and Frederick Loewe, Leonard Bernstein, Abe Burrows, Ira Gershwin, John Latouche, Frank Loesser and Joe Masteroff.

Here is a list of those who have received 4 citations or more as author, co-author, adapter, etc., in the list of 500 Best Plays.

AUTHOR	NO. OF CITATIONS	AUTHOR	NO. OF CITATIONS
Maxwell Anderson	19	Joseph Fields	5
George S. Kaufman	18	Jean Giraudoux	5
Eugene O'Neill	12	Clifford Odets	5
Moss Hart	11	Paul Osborn	5
Philip Barry	10	John Osborne	5
S.N. Behrman	9	Elmer Rice	5
Lillian Hellman	9	Jerome Chodorov	4
Robert E. Sherwood	9	Rose Franken	4
Tennessee Williams	9	Christopher Fry	4
Jean Anouilh	7	Paul Green	4
Arthur Miller	7	Lucienne Hill	4
John van Druten	7	William Inge	4
Marc Connelly	6	George Kelly	4
Rachel Crothers	6	Howard Lindsay &	
Sidney Howard	6	Russel Crouse	4
Sidney Kingsley	6	Thornton Wilder	4

In making their selections, the editors of the 50 *Best Plays* volumes sometimes ignored an extremely popular show, or even a distinguished prizewinner. Broadway's longest-run play *Life with Father* and longest-run musical *My Fair Lady* (2,717 performances) were named Best Plays, but not *Tobacco Road* (3,182 performances) or *Abie's Irish Rose* (2,327) or *South Pacific*

(1,694 performances *and* a Pulitzer Prize). The only other Pulitzer Prize winner passed over in Best Play selection was *Miss Lulu Bett* in 1919-20, the first volume in the series. New York Drama Critics Circle Award-winning musicals were passed over more often than not, including such as *Pal Joey, The Consul* and *The Music Man.* The only Critics Award straight plays that failed to make the Best Plays list were *No Exit, The Lady's Not for Burning* and *Ondine.*

On the other hand, sometimes the Best Plays designation was given to works which were ignored by the theatergoing public. The under-20-performances Best Plays, besides *A Very Special Baby,* were *The Egg* (8 performances in 1961-62), *Andorra* (9 performances in 1962-63), *The Story of Mary Surratt* (11 performances in 1946-47), *Daughters of Atreus* (13 performances in 1936-37), *The Emperor's New Clothes* (16 performances in 1952-53) and *Poor Bitos* (17 performances in 1964-65).

Vintage years of Best Plays? How about 1935-36: *Winterset, Dead End, Pride and Prejudice, First Lady, Boy Meets Girl, Victoria Regina, Ethan Frome, Call It a Day, End of Summer* and *Idiot's Delight.* Or sample 1955-56: *A View from the Bridge, Tiger at the Gates, The Diary of Anne Frank, No Time for Sergeants, The Chalk Garden, The Lark, The Matchmaker, The Ponder Heart, My Fair Lady, Waiting for Godot.*

In our profound admiration of each and every one of the golden 500 Best Plays of the half century, we present them here in a special date-order listing, season by season, the 10 from each of the 50 volumes (they have appeared in alphabetical order in recent *Best Plays* volumes and will do so again after this special anniversary listing). Here are the titles of each work in **bold-face type** followed by its number of performances (in parentheses with an asterisk * signifying that the show was still running as of June 1, 1969), with its authorship, opening date and major awards.

And as a footnote to each season we add *(in italics)* the titles of the plays of that year which didn't make the Best Plays list but won major prizes or popular support in runs of about a year or longer.

THE EDITOR

1919–1920

Adam and Eva (312)
     By Guy Bolton and George Middleton. September 13, 1919.
The Jest (197)
     By Sem Benelli; adapted by Edward Sheldon. (Opened April 19, 1919; suspended June 14, 1919.) Reopened September 19, 1919.
Clarence (306)
     By Booth Tarkington. September 20, 1919.
Déclassée (257)
     By Zoë Akins. October 6, 1919.
Wedding Bells (168)
     By Salisbury Field. November 12, 1919.

Abraham Lincoln (193)
> By John Drinkwater. December 15, 1919.

The Famous Mrs. Fair (344)
> By James Forbes. December 22, 1919.

Mamma's Affair (98)
> By Rachel Barton Butler. January 29, 1920.

Beyond the Horizon (160)
> By Eugene O'Neill. February 2, 1920. Pulitzer Prize.

Jane Clegg (158)
> By St. John Ervine. February 23, 1920.

Irene (670), The Gold Diggers (720).

1920–1921

Enter Madame (350)
> By Gilda Varesi and Dolly Byrne. August 16, 1920.

The Bad Man (350)
> By Porter Emerson Browne. August 30, 1920.

The First Year (760)
> By Frank Craven. October 20, 1920.

The Skin Game (176)
> By John Galsworthy. October 20, 1920.

The Emperor Jones (204)
> By Eugene O'Neill. November 1, 1920.

Mary Rose (127)
> By James M. Barrie. December 22, 1920.

Deburau (189)
> By Sacha Guitry; adapted by H. Granville Barker. December 23, 1920.

The Green Goddess (440)
> By William Archer. January 18, 1921.

Nice People (247)
> By Rachel Crothers. March 2, 1921.

Liliom (300)
> By Ferenc Molnar; adapted by Benjamin Glazer. April 20, 1921.

The Bat (867), Miss Lulu Bett (200+; Pulitzer Prize), Ladies' Night (360+), Sally (570), Shuffle Along (504).

1921–1922

Dulcy (246)
> By George S. Kaufman and Marc Connelly. August 13, 1921.

Six Cylinder Love (430)
> By William Anthony McGuire. August 25, 1921.

The Hero (80)

 By Gilbert Emery. September 5, 1921.

The Circle (175)

 By W. Somerset Maugham. September 12, 1921.

Ambush (98)

 By Arthur Richman. October 10, 1921.

A Bill of Divorcement (173)

 By Clemence Dane. October 10, 1921.

Anna Christie (177)

 By Eugene O'Neill. November 2, 1921. Pulitzer Prize.

The Dover Road (324)

 By A.A. Milne. December 23, 1921.

He Who Gets Slapped (308)

 By Leonid Andreyev; adapted by Gregory Zilboorg. January 9, 1922.

The Nest (152)

 By Paul Geraldy; adapted by Grace George. January 28, 1922.

Abie's Irish Rose (2,327), Blossom Time (592), Kiki (600), Chauve-Souris (520).

1922–1923

The Old Soak (423)

 By Don Marquis. August 22, 1922.

Loyalties (220)

 By John Galsworthy. September 27, 1922.

R.U.R. (184)

 By Karel Capek. October 9, 1922.

The Fool (373)

 By Channing Pollock. October 23, 1922.

Rain (648)

 By John Colton and Clemence Randolph; based on the story by W. Somerset Maugham. November 7, 1922.

Merton of the Movies (381)

 By George S. Kaufman and Marc Connelly; based on Harry Leon Wilson's novel. November 13, 1922.

Why Not? (120)

 By Jesse Lynch Williams. December 25, 1922.

Mary the 3rd (162)

 By Rachel Crothers. February 5, 1923.

Icebound (171)

 By Owen Davis. February 10, 1923. Pulitzer Prize.

You and I (178)

 By Philip Barry. February 19, 1923.

The Gingham Girl (422), Seventh Heaven (704).

1923–1924

Sun-Up (356)
> By Lula Vollmer. May 25, 1923. (Entry appears in 1922-23 *Best Plays* volume, but was named a Best Play of 1923-24.)

The Changelings (128)
> By Lee Wilson Dodd. September 17, 1923.

Chicken Feed (144)
> By Guy Bolton. September 24, 1923.

Tarnish (248)
> By Gilbert Emery. October 1, 1923.

The Swan (255)
> By Ferenc Molnar; translated by Melville Baker. October 23, 1923.

Hell-Bent fer Heaven (122)
> By Hatcher Hughes. January 4, 1924. Pulitzer Prize.

Outward Bound (144)
> By Sutton Vane. January 7, 1924.

The Goose Hangs High (183)
> By Lewis Beach. January 29, 1924.

The Show-Off (571)
> By George Kelly. February 5, 1924.

Beggar on Horseback (224)
> By George S. Kaufman and Marc Connelly. February 12, 1924.

Little Jessie James (453+), White Cargo (686).

1924–1925

Dancing Mothers (312)
> By Edgar Selwyn and Edmund Goulding. August 11, 1924.

What Price Glory? (433)
> By Maxwell Anderson and Laurence Stallings. September 3, 1924.

Minick (141)
> By George S. Kaufman and Edna Ferber. September 24, 1924.

The Firebrand (269)
> By Edwin Justus Mayer. October 15, 1924.

Desire Under the Elms (208)
> By Eugene O'Neill. November 11, 1924.

They Knew What They Wanted (414)
> By Sidney Howard. November 24, 1924. Pulitzer Prize.

The Youngest (104)
> By Philip Barry. December 22, 1924.

Mrs. Partridge Presents (144)
> By Mary Kennedy and Ruth Hawthorne. January 5, 1925.

The Fall Guy (176)
> By James Gleason and George Abbott. March 10, 1925.

Wild Birds (44)
> By Dan Totheroh. April 9, 1925.

Is Zat So? (618), The Student Prince (608), Rose Marie (557).

1925–1926

The Green Hat (231)
> By Michael Arlen. September 15, 1925.

The Butter and Egg Man (243)
> By George S. Kaufman. September 23, 1925.

Craig's Wife (360)
> By George Kelly. October 12, 1925. Pulitzer Prize.

The Enemy (203)
> By Channing Pollock. October 20, 1925.

Young Woodley (260)
> By John van Druten. November 2, 1925.

The Last of Mrs. Cheyney (385)
> By Frederick Lonsdale. November 9, 1925.

The Dybbuk (120)
> By S. Ansky; adapted by Henry G. Alsberg. December 15, 1925.

The Great God Brown (271)
> By Eugene O'Neill. January 23, 1926.

The Wisdom Tooth (160)
> By Marc Connelly. February 15, 1926.

Bride of the Lamb (109)
> By William Hurlbut. March 30, 1926.

The Cradle Snatchers (478), Earl Carroll's Vanities (440), George White's Scandals (424), The Girl Friend (409), Lulu Belle (461), Sunny (517), The Vagabond King (511).

1926–1927

Broadway (603)
> By Philip Dunning and George Abbott. September 16, 1926.

Daisy Mayme (112)
> By George Kelly. October 25, 1926.

The Play's the Thing (326)
> By Ferenc Molnar; adapted by P.G. Wodehouse. November 3, 1926.

The Constant Wife (295)
> By W. Somerset Maugham. November 29, 1926.

The Silver Cord (112)
> By Sidney Howard. December 20, 1926.

Chicago (172)
> By Maurice Watkins. December 30, 1926.

In Abraham's Bosom (200)
>By Paul Green. December 30, 1926. Pulitzer Prize.

The Cradle Song (57)
>By Gregorio and Maria Martinez Sierra; translated by John Garrett Underhill. January 24, 1927.

Saturday's Children (310)
>By Maxwell Anderson. January 26, 1927.

The Road to Rome (392)
>By Robert E. Sherwood. January 31, 1927.

The Desert Song (471), The Ladder (789), Rio Rita (494), The Squall (444).

1927–1928

Burlesque (372)
>By George Manker Watters and Arthur Hopkins. September 1, 1927.

Porgy (367)
>By Dorothy and DuBose Heyward. October 10, 1927.

Escape (173)
>By John Galsworthy. October 26, 1927.

Coquette (366)
>By George Abbott and Ann Preston Bridgers. November 8, 1927.

The Racket (119)
>By Bartlett Cormack. November 22, 1927.

The Plough and the Stars (32)
>By Sean O'Casey. November 28, 1927.

Behold the Bridegroom (88)
>By George Kelly. December 26, 1927.

Paris Bound (234)
>By Philip Barry. December 27, 1927.

The Royal Family (345)
>By George S. Kaufman and Edna Ferber. December 28, 1927.

Strange Interlude (426)
>By Eugene O'Neill. January 30, 1928. Pulitzer Prize.

Blackbirds of 1928 (518), A Connecticut Yankee (418), Good News (551), Show Boat (572), Skidding (472), The Trial of Mary Dugan (437).

1928–1929

The Front Page (276)
>By Ben Hecht and Charles MacArthur. August 14, 1928.

Machinal (91)
>By Sophie Treadwell. September 7, 1928.

Little Accident (303)
>By Floyd Dell and Thomas Mitchell. October 9, 1928.

Holiday (229)
    By Philip Barry. November 26, 1928.
Wings Over Europe (90)
    By Robert Nichols and Maurice Browne. December 10, 1928.
The Kingdom of God (92)
    By Gregorio Martinez Sierra; adapted by Helen and Harley Granville-
    Barker. December 20, 1928.
Street Scene (601)
    By Elmer Rice. January 10, 1929. Pulitzer Prize.
Gypsy (64)
    By Maxwell Anderson. January 14, 1929.
Let Us Be Gay (353)
    By Rachel Crothers. February 19, 1929.
Journey's End (485)
    By R.C. Sherriff. March 22, 1929.

   *Bird in Hand (500), Follow Thru (403), Hold Everything (413), The New
Moon (509).*

1929–1930

Strictly Dishonorable (557)
    By Preston Sturges. September 18, 1929.
The Criminal Code (173)
    By Martin Flavin. October 2, 1929.
June Moon (273)
    By Ring W. Lardner and George S. Kaufman. October 9, 1929.
Berkeley Square (229)
    By John L. Balderston. November 4, 1929.
Michael and Mary (246)
    By A.A. Milne. December 13, 1929.
Death Takes a Holiday (180)
    By Alberto Casella; adapted by Walter Ferris. December 26, 1929.
The First Mrs. Fraser (352)
    By St. John Ervine. December 28, 1929.
Rebound (114)
    By Donald Ogden Stewart. February 3, 1930.
The Last Mile (289)
    By John Wexley. February 13, 1930.
The Green Pastures (640)
    By Marc Connelly; based on Roark Bradford's *Ol Man Adam and His
    Chillun.* February 26, 1930. Pulitzer Prize.

1930–1931

Once in a Lifetime (406)
    By Moss Hart and George S. Kaufman. September 24, 1930.

Elizabeth the Queen (147)
>By Maxwell Anderson. November 3, 1930.

Grand Hotel (459)
>By Vicki Baum; adapted by W.A. Drake. November 13, 1930.

Alison's House (41)
>By Susan Glaspell. December 1, 1930. Pulitzer Prize.

Overture (41)
>By William Bolitho. December 5, 1930.

Five-Star Final (175)
>By Louis Weitzenkorn. December 30, 1930.

Tomorrow and Tomorrow (206)
>By Philip Barry. January 13, 1931.

Green Grow the Lilacs (64)
>By Lynn Riggs. January 26, 1931.

The Barretts of Wimpole Street (370)
>By Rudolph Besier. February 9, 1931.

As Husbands Go (148)
>By Rachel Crothers. March 5, 1931.

1931–1932

The House of Connelly (91)
>By Paul Green. September 28, 1931.

The Left Bank (242)
>By Elmer Rice. October 5, 1931.

Mourning Becomes Electra (150)
>By Eugene O'Neill. October 26, 1931.

Cynara (210)
>By H.M. Harwood and R.F. Gore-Browne. November 2, 1931.

Brief Moment (129)
>By S.N. Behrman. November 9, 1931.

Reunion in Vienna (264)
>By Robert E. Sherwood. November 16, 1931.

Of Thee I Sing (441)
>Musical with book by George S. Kaufman and Morrie Ryskind; music by George Gershwin; lyrics by Ira Gershwin. December 26, 1931. Pulitzer Prize.

The Devil Passes (96)
>By Benn W. Levy. January 4, 1932.

The Animal Kingdom (183)
>By Philip Barry. January 12, 1932.

Another Language (344)
>By Rose Franken. April 25, 1932.

1932–1933

When Ladies Meet (191)
    By Rachel Crothers. October 6, 1932.
Dinner at Eight (232)
    By George S. Kaufman and Edna Ferber. October 22, 1932.
The Late Christopher Bean (224)
    By René Fauchois; adapted by Sidney Howard. October 31, 1932.
Biography (267)
    By S.N. Behrman. December 12, 1932.
Pigeons and People (70)
    By George M. Cohan. January 16, 1933.
We, the People (49)
    By Elmer Rice. January 21, 1933.
Design for Living (135)
    By Noel Coward. January 24, 1933.
One Sunday Afternoon (322)
    By James Hagan. February 15, 1933.
Alien Corn (98)
    By Sidney Howard. February 20, 1933.
Both Your Houses (72)
    By Maxwell Anderson. March 6, 1933. Pulitzer Prize.

1933–1934

Men in White (351)
    By Sidney Kingsley. September 26, 1933. Pulitzer Prize.
Ah, Wilderness! (289)
    By Eugene O'Neill. October 2, 1933.
The Green Bay Tree (166)
    By Mordaunt Shairp. October 20, 1933.
Her Master's Voice (224)
    By Clare Kummer. October 23, 1933.
Mary of Scotland (248)
    By Maxwell Anderson. November 27, 1933.
Wednesday's Child (56)
    By Leopold Atlas. January 16, 1934.
No More Ladies (162)
    By A.E. Thomas. January 23, 1934.
The Shining Hour (121)
    By Keith Winter. February 13, 1934.
They Shall Not Die (62)
    By John Wexley. February 21, 1934.

Dodsworth (315)
>   By Sidney Howard; based on the novel by Sinclair Lewis. February 24, 1934.

Tobacco Road (3,182), Sailor, Beware! (500), As Thousands Cheer (400).

1934–1935

The Distaff Side (177)
>   By John van Druten. September 25, 1934.

Merrily We Roll Along (155)
>   By George S. Kaufman and Moss Hart. September 29, 1934.

Lost Horizons (56)
>   By Harry Segall; revised by John Hayden. October 15, 1934.

The Farmer Takes a Wife (104)
>   By Frank B. Elser and Marc Connelly; based on the novel *Rome Haul* by Walter Edmonds. October 30, 1934.

The Children's Hour (691)
>   By Lillian Hellman. November 20, 1934.

Valley Forge (58)
>   By Maxwell Anderson. December 10, 1934.

Accent on Youth (229)
>   By Samson Raphaelson. December 25, 1934.

The Old Maid (305)
>   By Zoë Akins; based on the novel by Edith Wharton. January 7, 1935. Pulitzer Prize.

The Petrified Forest (197)
>   By Robert E. Sherwood. January 7, 1935.

Awake and Sing (209)
>   By Clifford Odets. February 19, 1935.

Anything Goes (420), Personal Appearance (501), Three Men on a Horse (835).

1935–1936

Winterset (195)
>   By Maxwell Anderson. September 25, 1935. Critics Award (American play).

Dead End (687)
>   By Sidney Kingsley. October 28, 1935.

Pride and Prejudice (219)
>   By Helen Jerome; based on the novel by Jane Austen. November 5, 1935.

First Lady (246)
>   By Katharine Dayton and George S. Kaufman. November 26, 1935.

Boy Meets Girl (669)
>   By Bella and Samuel Spewack. November 27, 1935.

Victoria Regina (517)
> By Laurence Housman. December 26, 1935.

Ethan Frome (120)
> By Owen and Donald Davis; based on the novel by Edith Wharton. January 21, 1936.

Call It a Day (194)
> By Dodie Smith. January 28, 1936.

End of Summer (153)
> By S.N. Behrman. February 17, 1936.

Idiot's Delight (300)
> By Robert E. Sherwood. March 24, 1936. Pulitzer Prize.

1936–1937

St. Helena (63)
> By R.C. Sherriff and Jeanne de Casalis. October 6, 1936.

Daughters of Atreus (13)
> By Robert Turney. October 14, 1936.

Tovarich (356)
> By Jacques Deval; translated by Robert E. Sherwood. October 15, 1936.

Stage Door (169)
> By George S. Kaufman and Edna Ferber. October 22, 1936.

Johnny Johnson (68)
> By Paul Green; incidental music by Kurt Weill; lyrics by Paul Green. November 19, 1936.

You Can't Take It With You (837)
> By Moss Hart and George S. Kaufman. December 14, 1936. Pulitzer Prize.

The Women (657)
> By Clare Boothe. December 26, 1936.

High Tor (171)
> By Maxwell Anderson. January 9, 1937. Critics Award (American play).

Yes, My Darling Daughter (405)
> By Mark Reed. February 9, 1937.

Excursion (116)
> By Victor Wolfson. April 9, 1937.

Brother Rat (577), Room Service (500).

1937–1938

The Star-Wagon (223)
> By Maxwell Anderson. September 29, 1937.

Susan and God (288)
> By Rachel Crothers. October 7, 1937.

Amphitryon 38 (153)

> By Jean Giraudoux; adapted by S.N. Behrman. November 1, 1937.

Golden Boy (250)

> By Clifford Odets. November 4, 1937.

Of Mice and Men (207)

> By John Steinbeck. November 23, 1937. Critics Award (American play).

Shadow and Substance (274)

> By Paul Vincent Carroll. January 26, 1938. Critics Award (foreign play).

On Borrowed Time (321)

> By Paul Osborn; based on a novel by Lawrence E. Watkin. February 3, 1938.

Our Town (336)

> By Thornton Wilder. February 4, 1938. Pulitzer Prize.

Prologue to Glory (70)

> By E.P. Conkle. March 17, 1938.

What a Life (538)

> By Clifford Goldsmith. April 13, 1938.

Bachelor Born (400), Pins and Needles (1,108).

1938–1939

Kiss the Boys Good-bye (286)

> By Clare Boothe. September 28, 1938.

Abe Lincoln in Illinois (472)

> By Robert E. Sherwood. October 15, 1938. Pulitzer Prize.

Rocket to the Moon (131)

> By Clifford Odets. November 24, 1938.

Here Come the Clowns (88)

> By Philip Barry. December 7, 1938.

The White Steed (136)

> By Paul Vincent Carroll. January 10, 1939. Critics Award (foreign play).

The American Way (164)

> By George S. Kaufman and Moss Hart. January 21, 1939.

The Little Foxes (410)

> By Lillian Hellman. February 15, 1939.

The Philadelphia Story (417)

> By Philip Barry. March 28, 1939.

No Time for Comedy (185)

> By S.N. Behrman. April 17, 1939.

Family Portrait (111)

> By Lenore Coffee and William Joyce Cowen. May 8, 1939.

Hellzapoppin (1,404).

1939–1940

Skylark (256)
> By Samson Raphaelson. October 11, 1939.

The Man Who Came to Dinner (739)
> By Moss Hart and George S. Kaufman. October 16, 1939.

The Time of Your Life (185)
> By William Saroyan. October 25, 1939. Pulitzer Prize and Critics Award (American play).

Margin for Error (264)
> By Clare Boothe. November 3, 1939.

Life With Father (3,224)
> By Howard Lindsay and Russel Crouse; based on the book by Clarence Day. November 8, 1939. Broadway's longest-running play.

The World We Make (80)
> By Sidney Kingsley; based on the novel *The Outward Room* by Millen Brand. November 20, 1939.

Key Largo (105)
> By Maxwell Anderson. November 27, 1939.

Morning's at Seven (44)
> By Paul Osborn. November 30, 1939.

The Male Animal (243)
> By James Thurber and Elliott Nugent. January 9, 1940.

There Shall Be No Night (181)
> By Robert E. Sherwood. April 29, 1940. Pulitzer Prize (for 1940-41).

Du Barry Was a Lady (408), Louisiana Purchase (444), Separate Rooms (613).

1940–1941

George Washington Slept Here (173)
> By George S. Kaufman and Moss Hart. October 18, 1940.

The Corn Is Green (477)
> By Emlyn Williams. November 26, 1940. Critics Award (foreign play).

My Sister Eileen (864)
> By Joseph Fields and Jerome Chodorov; based on Ruth McKenney's stories. December 26, 1940.

Flight to the West (136)
> By Elmer Rice. December 30, 1940.

Arsenic and Old Lace (1,444)
> By Joseph Kesselring. January 10, 1941.

Mr. and Mrs. North (163)
> By Owen Davis; based on Frances and Richard Lockridge's stories. January 12, 1941.

Lady in the Dark (162)
> Musical with book by Moss Hart; music by Kurt Weill; lyrics by Ira Gershwin. January 23, 1941.

Claudia (722)
> By Rose Franken. February 12, 1941.

Native Son (114)
> By Paul Green and Richard Wright; based on Richard Wright's novel. March 24, 1941.

Watch on the Rhine (378)
> By Lillian Hellman. April 1, 1941. Critics Award (American play).

Panama Hattie (501).

1941–1942

Candle in the Wind (95)
> By Maxwell Anderson. October 22, 1941.

Blithe Spirit (657)
> By Noel Coward. November 5, 1941. Critics Award (foreign play).

Junior Miss (710)
> By Jerome Chodorov and Joseph Fields. November 18, 1941.

Hope for a Harvest (38)
> By Sophie Treadwell. November 26, 1941.

Angel Street (1,295)
> By Patrick Hamilton. December 5, 1941.

Letters to Lucerne (23)
> By Fritz Rotter and Allen Vincent. December 23, 1941.

In Time to Come (40)
> By Howard Koch and John Huston. December 28, 1941.

Jason (125)
> By Samson Raphaelson. January 21, 1942.

The Moon Is Down (71)
> By John Steinbeck. April 7, 1942.

Uncle Harry (430)
> By Thomas Job. May 20, 1942.

By Jupiter (427), Let's Face It (547), Sons o' Fun (742).

1942–1943

The Eve of St. Mark (307)
> By Maxwell Anderson. October 7, 1942.

The Damask Cheek (93)
> By John van Druten and Lloyd Morris. October 22, 1942.

The Skin of Our Teeth (359)
> By Thornton Wilder. November 18, 1942. Pulitzer Prize.

Winter Soldiers (25)
> By Daniel Lewis James. November 29, 1942.

The Doughgirls (671)
> By Joseph Fields. December 30, 1942.

The Patriots (173)
> By Sidney Kingsley. January 29, 1943. Critics Award (American play).

Harriet (377)
> By Florence Ryerson and Colin Clements. March 3, 1943.

Kiss and Tell (956)
> By F. Hugh Herbert. March 17, 1943.

Oklahoma! (2,212)
> Musical with book and lyrics by Oscar Hammerstein II; music by Richard Rodgers; based on the play *Green Grow the Lilacs* by Lynn Riggs. March 31, 1943.

Tomorrow the World (500)
> By James Gow and Arnaud d'Usseau. April 14, 1943.

Janie (642), Rosalinda (521), Something for the Boys (422), Star and Garter (609), Stars on Ice (830), Three's a Family (497), Ziegfeld Follies (553).

1943–1944

Outrageous Fortune (77)
> By Rose Franken. November 3, 1943.

The Innocent Voyage (40)
> By Paul Osborn; based on the novel *A High Wind in Jamaica* by Richard Hughes. November 15, 1943.

Winged Victory (212)
> By Moss Hart; music by David Rose. November 20, 1943.

The Voice of the Turtle (1,557)
> By John van Druten. December 8, 1943.

Over 21 (221)
> By Ruth Gordon. January 3, 1944.

Storm Operation (23)
> By Maxwell Anderson. January 11, 1944.

Decision (160)
> By Edward Chodorov. February 2, 1944.

Jacobowsky and the Colonel (417)
> By S.N. Behrman; based on Franz Werfel's play. March 14, 1944. Critics Award (foreign play).

The Searching Wind (318)
> By Lillian Hellman. April 12, 1944.

Pick-up Girl (198)
> By Elsa Shelley. May 3, 1944.

Carmen Jones (503), Mexican Hayride (481), One Touch of Venus (567), The Two Mrs. Carrolls (585), Follow the Girls (882).

1944-1945

Anna Lucasta (957)
> By Philip Yordan. August 30, 1944.

Soldier's Wife (253)
> By Rose Franken. October 4, 1944.

I Remember Mama (714)
> By John van Druten; based on the book *Mama's Bank Account* by Kathryn Forbes. October 19, 1944.

Harvey (1,775)
> By Mary Chase. November 1, 1944. Pulitzer Prize.

The Late George Apley (385)
> By John P. Marquand and George S. Kaufman; based on John P. Marquand's novel. November 23, 1944.

A Bell for Adano (304)
> By Paul Osborn; based on John Hersey's novel. December 6, 1944.

Dear Ruth (683)
> By Norman Krasna. December 13, 1944.

The Hasty Heart (207)
> By John Patrick. January 3, 1945.

Foolish Notion (104)
> By Philip Barry. March 3, 1945.

The Glass Menagerie (561)
> By Tennessee Williams. March 31, 1945. Critics Award (American play).

Bloomer Girl (654), Hats Off to Ice (889), On the Town (463), Ten Little Indians (426), Up in Central Park (504), Song of Norway (860), Carousel (890; opened April 19, 1945 and won the 1945-46 Critics Award for best musical).

1945-1946

Deep Are the Roots (477)
> By Arnaud d'Usseau and James Gow. September 26, 1945.

The Rugged Path (81)
> By Robert E. Sherwood. November 10, 1945.

State of the Union (765)
> By Howard Lindsay and Russel Crouse. November 14, 1965. Pulitzer Prize.

Dream Girl (348)
> By Elmer Rice. December 14, 1945.

Home of the Brave (69)
> By Arthur Laurents. December 27, 1945.

The Magnificent Yankee (160)
> By Emmet Lavery. January 22, 1946.

O Mistress Mine (452)
> By Terence Rattigan. January 23, 1946.

Born Yesterday (1,642)
>   By Garson Kanin. February 4, 1946.

Lute Song (385)
>   Musical with book by Sidney Howard and Will Irwin; music by Raymond Scott; lyrics by Bernard Hanighen; based on the Chinese classic *Pi-Pa-Ki*. February 6, 1946.

Antigone (64)
>   By Jean Anouilh; adapted by Lewis Galantière. February 18, 1946.

Show Boat (418; revival), The Red Mill (531; revival), Call Me Mister (734), Annie Get Your Gun (1,147).

1946-1947

The Iceman Cometh (136)
>   By Eugene O'Neill. October 9, 1946.

Joan of Lorraine (199)
>   By Maxwell Anderson. November 18, 1946.

The Fatal Weakness (119)
>   By George Kelly. November 19, 1946.

Another Part of the Forest (182)
>   By Lillian Hellman. November 20, 1946.

Christopher Blake (114)
>   By Moss Hart. November 30, 1946.

Years Ago (206)
>   By Ruth Gordon. December 3, 1946.

All My Sons (328)
>   By Arthur Miller. January 29, 1947. Critics Award (American play).

John Loves Mary (423)
>   By Norman Krasna. February 4, 1947.

The Story of Mary Surratt (11)
>   By John Patrick. February 8, 1947.

Brigadoon (581)
>   Musical with book and lyrics by Alan Jay Lerner; music by Frederick Loewe. March 13, 1947. Critics Award (musical).

No Exit (31; Critics Award for best foreign play), Burlesque (439; revival), Happy Birthday (564), Icetime of 1948 (422), Finian's Rainbow (725).

1947-1948

The Heiress (410)
>   By Ruth and Augustus Goetz; suggested by the novel *Washington Square* by Henry James. September 29, 1947.

Command Decision (408)
>   By William Wister Haines. October 1, 1947.

Allegro (315)
>Musical with book and lyrics by Oscar Hammerstein II; music by Richard Rodgers. October 10, 1947.

An Inspector Calls (95)
>By J.B. Priestley. October 21, 1947.

The Winslow Boy (215)
>By Terence Rattigan. October 29, 1947. Critics Award (foreign play).

Eastward in Eden (15)
>By Dorothy Gardner. November 18, 1947.

A Streetcar Named Desire (855)
>By Tennessee Williams. December 3, 1947. Pulitzer Prize. Critics Award (American play).

Skipper Next to God (93)
>By Jan de Hartog. January 4, 1948.

Mister Roberts (1,157)
>By Thomas Heggen and Joshua Logan; based on Thomas Heggen's novel. February 18, 1948.

Me and Molly (156)
>By Gertrude Berg. February 26, 1948.

Make Mine Manhattan (429), High Button Shoes (727).

1948–1949

Edward, My Son (260)
>By Robert Morley and Noel Langley. September 30, 1948.

Life With Mother (265)
>By Howard Lindsay and Russel Crouse; based on Clarence Day's book. October 20, 1948.

Goodbye, My Fancy (446)
>By Fay Kanin. November 17, 1948.

Light Up the Sky (216)
>By Moss Hart. November 18, 1948.

The Silver Whistle (219)
>By Robert E. McEnroe. November 24, 1948.

Anne of the Thousand Days (286)
>By Maxwell Anderson. December 8, 1948.

The Madwoman of Chaillot (368)
>By Jean Giraudoux; adapted by Maurice Valency. December 27, 1948. Critics Award (foreign play).

Death of a Salesman (742)
>By Arthur Miller. February 10, 1949. Pulitzer Prize. Critics Award (American play).

Two Blind Mice (157)
>By Samuel Spewack. March 2, 1949.

Detective Story (581)

    By Sidney Kingsley. March 23, 1949.

South Pacific (1,925; Critics Award for best musical and Pulitzer Prize for 1949-50), As the Girls Go (420), Howdy, Mr. Ice (406 for 1949 version; 430 for 1950 version), Lend an Ear (460), Where's Charley? (792), Kiss Me, Kate (1,077).

1949–1950

Lost in the Stars (273)

    Musical with book and lyrics by Maxwell Anderson; music by Kurt Weill; based on the novel *Cry, the Beloved Country* by Alan Paton. October 30, 1949.

I Know My Love (246)

    By S.N. Behrman; adapted from *Auprès de Ma Blonde* by Marcel Achard. November 2, 1949.

Clutterbuck (218)

    By Benn W. Levy. December 3, 1949.

The Member of the Wedding (501)

    By Carson McCullers; adapted from her novel. January 5, 1950. Critics Award (American play).

The Enchanted (45)

    By Maurice Valency; adapted from the play *Intermezzo* by Jean Giraudoux. January 18, 1950.

The Cocktail Party (409)

    By T.S. Eliot. January 21, 1950. Critics Award (foreign play).

The Happy Time (614)

    By Samuel Taylor; based on Robert Fontaine's book. January 24, 1950.

The Innocents (141)

    By William Archibald; based on *The Turn of the Screw* by Henry James. February 1, 1950.

Come Back, Little Sheba (191)

    By William Inge. February 15, 1950.

The Wisteria Trees (165)

    By Joshua Logan; based on *The Cherry Orchard* by Anton Chekhov. March 29, 1950.

The Consul (269; Critics Award for best musical), Gentlemen Prefer Blondes (740).

1950–1951

Affairs of State (610)

    By Louis Verneuil. September 25, 1950.

Season in the Sun (367)

    By Wolcott Gibbs. September 28, 1950.

The Country Girl (235)
> By Clifford Odets. November 10, 1950.

Bell, Book and Candle (233)
> By John van Druten. November 14, 1950.

Guys and Dolls (1,200)
> Musical with book by Jo Swerling and Abe Burrows; music and lyrics by Frank Loesser; based on a story and characters by Damon Runyon. November 24, 1950. Critics Award (musical).

Second Threshold (126)
> By Philip Barry; revisions by Robert E. Sherwood. January 2, 1951.

Darkness at Noon (186)
> By Sidney Kingsley; based on Arthur Koestler's novel. January 13, 1951. Critics Award (American play).

The Rose Tattoo (306)
> By Tennessee Williams. February 3, 1951.

Billy Budd (105)
> By Louis O. Coxe and Robert Chapman; based on Herman Melville's novel. February 10, 1951.

The Autumn Garden (101)
> By Lillian Hellman. March 7, 1951.

The Lady's Not for Burning (151; Critics Award for best foreign play), Call Me Madam (644), The Moon Is Blue (924), Stalag 17 (472), The King and I (1,246).

1951–1952

Remains to Be Seen (199)
> By Howard Lindsay and Russel Crouse. October 3, 1951.

The Fourposter (632)
> By Jan de Hartog. October 24, 1951.

Barefoot in Athens (30)
> By Maxwell Anderson. October 31, 1951.

Gigi (219)
> By Anita Loos; based on Colette's novel. November 24, 1951.

I Am a Camera (214)
> By John van Druten; based on Christopher Isherwood's Berlin stories. November 28, 1951. Critics Award (American play).

Point of No Return (364)
> By Paul Osborn; based on J.P. Marquand's novel. December 13, 1951.

The Shrike (161)
> By Joseph Kramm. January 15, 1952. Pulitzer Prize.

Jane (100)
> By S.N. Behrman; suggested by W. Somerset Maugham's story. February 1, 1952.

Venus Observed (86)
> By Christopher Fry. February 13, 1952. Critics Award (foreign play).

Mrs. McThing (350)
>By Mary Chase. February 20, 1952.

Pal Joey (540; revival; Critics Award for best musical), Don Juan in Hell (105; special Critics citation).

1952-1953

The Time of the Cuckoo (263)
>By Arthur Laurents. October 15, 1952.

Bernardine (157)
>By Mary Chase. October 16, 1952.

Dial "M" for Murder (552)
>By Frederick Knott. October 29, 1952.

The Climate of Eden (20)
>By Moss Hart; based on the novel *Shadows Move Among Them* by Edgar Mittleholzer. November 13, 1952.

The Love of Four Colonels (141)
>By Peter Ustinov. January 15, 1953. Critics Award (foreign play).

The Crucible (197)
>By Arthur Miller. January 22, 1953.

The Emperor's Clothes (16)
>By George Tabori. February 9, 1953.

Picnic (477)
>By William Inge. February 19, 1953. Pulitzer Prize. Critics Award (American play).

Wonderful Town (559)
>Musical with book by Joseph Fields and Jerome Chodorov; based on their play *My Sister Eileen* and Ruth McKenney's stories; music by Leonard Bernstein; lyrics by Betty Comden and Adolph Green. February 25, 1953. Critics Award (musical).

My 3 Angels (344)
>By Samuel and Bella Spewack; based on the play *La Cuisine des Anges* by Albert Husson. March 11, 1953.

Wish You Were Here (598), The Fifth Season (654), Can-Can (892), The Seven Year Itch (1,141).

1953-1954

Take a Giant Step (76)
>By Louis Peterson. September 24, 1953.

Tea and Sympathy (712)
>By Robert Anderson. September 30, 1953.

The Teahouse of the August Moon (1,027)
>By John Patrick; based on Vern Sneider's novel. October 15, 1953. Pulitzer Prize. Critics Award (American play).

In the Summer House (55)
> By Jane Bowles. December 29, 1953.

The Caine Mutiny Court Martial (415)
> By Herman Wouk; based on his novel. January 20, 1954.

The Immoralist (96)
> By Ruth and Augustus Goetz; based on Andre Gide's novel. February 8, 1954.

The Girl on the Via Flaminia (111)
> By Alfred Hayes; based on his novel. February 9, 1954.

The Confidential Clerk (117)
> By T.S. Eliot. February 11, 1954.

The Magic and the Loss (27)
> By Julian Funt. April 9, 1954.

The Golden Apple (125)
> Musical with book and lyrics by John Latouche; music by Jerome Moross. April 20, 1954. Critics Award (musical).

Ondine (157; Critics Award for best foreign play); Kismet (583), The Solid Gold Cadillac (526), Anniversary Waltz (615), Comedy in Music (849), The Pajama Game (1,063).

1954–1955

The Boy Friend (485)
> Musical with book, music and lyrics by Sandy Wilson. September 30, 1954.

The Living Room (22)
> By Graham Greene. November 17, 1954.

Bad Seed (332)
> By Maxwell Anderson; adapted from William March's novel. December 8, 1954.

Witness for the Prosecution (645)
> By Agatha Christie. December 16, 1954. Critics Award (foreign play).

The Flowering Peach (135)
> By Clifford Odets. December 28, 1954.

The Desperate Hours (212)
> By Joseph Hayes; based on his novel. February 10, 1955.

The Dark is Light Enough (69)
> By Christopher Fry. February 23, 1955.

Bus Stop (478)
> By William Inge. March 2, 1955.

Cat on a Hot Tin Roof (694)
> By Tennessee Williams. March 24, 1955. Pulitzer Prize. Critics Award (American play).

Inherit the Wind (806)
> By Jerome Lawrence and Robert E. Lee. April 21, 1955.

The Saint of Bleeker Street (92; Critics Award for best musical), Plain and Fancy (461), Silk Stockings (478), Fanny (888), Damn Yankees (1,019).

1955–1956

A View From the Bridge (149)
> By Arthur Miller. September 29, 1955.

Tiger at the Gates (217)
> By Jean Giraudoux; translated from his *La Guerre de Troi n'Aura Pas Lieu* by Christopher Fry. October 3, 1955. Critics Award (foreign play).

The Diary of Anne Frank (717)
> By Frances Goodrich and Albert Hackett; based on Anne Frank's *The Diary of a Young Girl*. October 5, 1955. Pulitzer Prize. Critics Award (American play).

No Time for Sergeants (796)
> By Ira Levin; adapted from Mac Hyman's novel. October 20, 1955.

The Chalk Garden (182)
> By Enid Bagnold. October 26, 1955.

The Lark (229)
> By Jean Anouilh; adapted by Lillian Hellman. November 17, 1955.

The Matchmaker (486)
> By Thornton Wilder; based on Johann Nestroy's *Einen Jux Will Er Sich Machen*. December 5, 1955.

The Ponder Heart (149)
> By Joseph Fields and Jerome Chodorov; adapted from Eudora Welty's story. February 16, 1956.

My Fair Lady (2,717)
> Musical with book and lyrics by Alan Jay Lerner; music by Frederick Loewe; based on George Bernard Shaw's play *Pygmalion*. March 15, 1956. Critics Award (musical). Broadway's longest-running musical.

Waiting for Godot (59)
> By Samuel Beckett. April 19, 1956.

Middle of the Night (477), Will Success Spoil Rock Hunter? (444), The Most Happy Fella (676; 1956-57 Critics Award for best musical), The Three-penny Opera (2,611), The Iceman Cometh (565; revival).

1956–1957

Separate Tables (332)
> By Terence Rattigan. October 25, 1956.

Long Day's Journey Into Night (390)
> By Eugene O'Neill. November 7, 1956. Pulitzer Prize. Critics Award (American play).

A Very Special Baby (5)
>By Robert Alan Aurthur. November 14, 1956.

Candide (73)
>Musical with book by Lillian Hellman; music by Leonard Bernstein; lyrics by Richard Wilbur, John Latouche and Dorothy Parker; based on Voltaire's satire. December 1, 1956.

A Clearing in the Woods (36)
>By Arthur Laurents. January 10, 1957.

The Waltz of the Toreadors (132)
>By Jean Anouilh; translated by Lucienne Hill. January 17, 1957. Critics Award (foreign play).

The Potting Shed (143)
>By Graham Greene. January 29, 1957.

Visit to a Small Planet (388)
>By Gore Vidal. February 7, 1957.

Orpheus Descending (68)
>By Tennessee Williams. March 21, 1957.

A Moon for the Misbegotten (68)
>By Eugene O'Neill. May 2, 1957.

Happy Hunting (412), The Tunnel of Love (417), New Girl in Town (431), Auntie Mame (639), L'il Abner (693), Bells Are Ringing (924).

1957–1958

Look Back in Anger (407)
>By John Osborne. October 1, 1957. Critics Award (foreign play).

Under Milk Wood (39)
>By Dylan Thomas. October 15, 1957.

Time Remembered (248)
>By Jean Anouilh; adapted from his *Leocadia* by Patricia Moyes. November 12, 1957.

The Rope Dancers (189)
>By Morton Wishengrad. November 20, 1957.

Look Homeward, Angel (564)
>By Ketti Frings; based on Thomas Wolfe's novel. November 28, 1957. Pulitzer Prize. Critics Award (American play).

The Dark at the Top of the Stairs (468)
>By William Inge. December 5, 1957.

Summer of the 17th Doll (29)
>By Ray Lawler. January 22, 1958.

Sunrise at Campobello (556)
>By Dore Schary. January 30, 1958.

The Entertainer (97)
>By John Osborne. February 12, 1958.

The Visit (189)

> By Friedrich Duerrenmatt; adapted by Maurice Valency. May 5, 1958.
> 1958-69 Critics Award (foreign play).

The Music Man (1,375; Critics Award for best musical), Jamaica (555), West Side Story (732), Two for the Seesaw (750), The Boy Friend (763; revival), The Crucible (571; revival).

1958-1959

A Touch of the Poet (284)

> By Eugene O'Neill. October 2, 1958.

The Pleasure of His Company (474)

> By Samuel Taylor and Cornelia Otis Skinner. October 22, 1958.

Epitaph for George Dillon (23)

> By John Osborne and Anthony Creighton. November 4, 1958.

The Disenchanted (189)

> By Budd Schulberg and Harvey Breit; based on Budd Schulberg's novel. December 3, 1958.

The Cold Wind and the Warm (120)

> By S.N. Behrman. December 8, 1958.

J.B. (364)

> By Archibald MacLeish. December 11, 1958. Pulitzer Prize.

Requieum for a Nun (43)

> By Ruth Ford and William Faulkner; adapted from William Faulkner's novel. January 30, 1959.

Sweet Bird of Youth (375)

> By Tennessee Williams. March 10, 1959.

A Raisin in the Sun (530)

> By Lorraine Hansberry. March 11, 1959. Critics Award (American play).

Kataki (20)

> By Shimon Wincelberg. April 9, 1959.

La Plume de Ma Tante (835; Critics Award for best musical), The World of Suzie Wong (508), The Marriage-Go-Round (431), Redhead (452), Flower Drum Song (600), Destry Rides Again (472), A Majority of One (556), Once Upon a Mattress (460), Gypsy (702).

1959-1960

The Tenth Man (623)

> By Paddy Chayefsky. November 5, 1959.

Fiorello! (795)

> Musical with book by Jerome Weidman and George Abbott; music by Jerry Bock; lyrics by Sheldon Harnick. November 23, 1959. Pulitzer Prize. Critics Award (musical).

Five Finger Exercise (337)
> By Peter Shaffer. December 2, 1959. Critics Award (foreign play).

The Andersonville Trial (179)
> By Saul Levitt. December 29, 1959.

The Deadly Game (39)
> By James Yaffe; based on Friedrich Duerrenmatt's novel. February 2, 1960.

Caligula (38)
> By Albert Camus; adapted by Justin O'Brien. February 16, 1960.

Toys in the Attic (556)
> By Lillian Hellman. February 25, 1960. Critics Award (American play).

A Thurber Carnival (127)
> By James Thurber. February 26, 1960.

The Best Man (520)
> By Gore Vidal. March 31, 1960.

Duel of Angels (51)
> By Jean Giraudoux; adapted from his *Pour Lucrèce* by Christopher Fry. April 19, 1960.

Take Me Along (448), The Miracle Worker (700), Bye Bye Birdie (607), The Sound of Music (1,443), The Fantasticks (3,800*; longest off-Broadway musical run and longest run on record in the American theater), The Balcony (672), Krapp's Last Tape and The Zoo Story (582), Little Mary Sunshine (1,143), Leave It to Jane (928; revival), The Connection (722).

1960–1961

The Hostage (127)
> By Brendan Behan. September 20, 1960.

A Taste of Honey (376)
> By Shelagh Delaney. October 4, 1960. Critics Award (foreign play).

Becket (193)
> By Jean Anouilh; translated by Lucienne Hill. October 5, 1960.

Period of Adjustment (132)
> By Tennessee Williams. November 10, 1960.

All the Way Home (333)
> By Tad Mosel; based on the novel *A Death in the Family* by James Agee. November 30, 1960. Pulitzer Prize. Critics Award (American play).

Rhinoceros (240)
> By Eugene Ionesco; translated by Derek Prouse. January 9, 1961.

Mary, Mary (1,572)
> By Jean Kerr. March 8, 1961.

The Devil's Advocate (116)
> By Dore Schary; based on Morris L. West's novel. March 9, 1961.

Big Fish, Little Fish (101)
>By Hugh Wheeler. March 15, 1961.

A Far Country (271)
>By Henry Denker. April 4, 1961.

Carnival (719; Critics Award for best musical), Irma La Douce (524), Do Re Mi (400), The Unsinkable Molly Brown (532), Come Blow Your Horn (677), Camelot (873), The Blacks (1,408; longest run for an off-Broadway play).

1961-1962

The Caretaker (165)
>By Harold Pinter. October 4, 1961.

How To Succeed in Business Without Really Trying (1,417)
>Musical with book by Abe Burrows, Jack Weinstock and Willie Gilbert; music and lyrics by Frank Loesser; based on Shepherd Mead's novel. October 14, 1961. Pulitzer Prize. Critics Award (musical).

The Complaisant Lover (101)
>By Graham Greene. November 1, 1961.

Gideon (236)
>By Paddy Chayefsky. November 9, 1961.

A Man for All Seasons (637)
>By Robert Bolt. November 22, 1961. Critics Award (foreign play).

Stone and Star (also called **Shadow of Heroes**) (20)
>By Robert Ardrey. December 5, 1961.

The Night of the Iguana (316)
>By Tennessee Williams. December 28, 1961. Critics Award (American play).

The Egg (8)
>By Felicien Marceau; adapted by Robert Schlitt. January 8, 1962.

Oh Dad, Poor Dad, Mamma's Hung You in the Closet and I'm Feelin' So Sad (454)
>By Arthur L. Kopit. February 26, 1962.

A Thousand Clowns (428)
>By Herb Gardner. April 5, 1962.

Take Her, She's Mine (404), Milk and Honey (543), Brecht on Brecht (424), The Hostage (545; revival), No Strings (580), A Funny Thing Happened on the Way to the Forum (964).

1962-1963

Stop the World—I Want to Get Off (555)
>Musical with book, music and lyrics by Leslie Bricusse and Anthony Newley. October 3, 1962.

Who's Afraid of Virginia Woolf? (664)
> By Edward Albee. October 13, 1962. Critics Award.

Tchin-Tchin (222)
> By Sidney Michaels; based on François Billetdoux's play. October 25, 1962.

P.S. 193 (48)
> By David Rayfiel. October 30, 1962.

The Collection (578)
> By Harold Pinter. November 26, 1962.

The Milk Train Doesn't Stop Here Anymore (69)
> By Tennessee Williams. January 16, 1963.

Andorra (9)
> By Max Frisch; adapted by George Tabori. February 9, 1963.

Mother Courage and Her Children (52)
> By Bertolt Brecht; adapted by Eric Bentley. March 28, 1963.

Rattle of a Simple Man (94)
> By Charles Dyer. April 17, 1963.

She Loves Me (301)
> Musical with book by Joe Masteroff; music by Jerry Bock; lyrics by Sheldon Harnick; based on the play *Parfumerie* by Miklos Laszlo. April 23, 1963.

Beyond the Fringe (667; special Critics citation), Never Too Late (1,007), Oliver (774), Enter Laughing (419), Six Characters in Search of an Author (529; revival), The Boys from Syracuse (500; revival).

1963–1964

The Rehearsal (110)
> By Jean Anouilh; adapted by Pamela Hansford Johnson and Kitty Black. September 23, 1963.

Luther (211)
> By John Osborne. September 25, 1963. Critics Award.

Chips With Everything (149)
> By Arnold Wesker. October 1, 1963.

Barefoot in the Park (1,530)
> By Neil Simon. October 23, 1963.

Next Time I'll Sing to You (23)
> By James Saunders. November 27, 1963.

Hello, Dolly! (2,210*)
> Musical with book by Michael Stewart; music and lyrics by Jerry Herman; based on the play *The Matchmaker* by Thornton Wilder. January 16, 1964.

Dylan (153)
> By Sidney Michaels. January 18, 1964.

After the Fall (208)

    By Arthur Miller. January 23, 1964.

The Passion of Josef D. (15)

    By Paddy Chayefsky. February 11, 1964.

The Deputy (109)

    By Rolf Hochhuth; adapted by Jerome Rothenberg. February 26, 1964.

The Trojan Women (600; revival; special Critics citation), Any Wednesday (982), What Makes Sammy Run? (540), Funny Girl (1,348), The Knack (685).

1964–1965

The Subject Was Roses (832)

    By Frank D. Gilroy. May 25, 1964. (Entry appears in 1963-64 *Best Plays* volume but was chosen a Best Play of 1964-65). Pulitzer Prize. Critics Award.

Fiddler on the Roof (1,956*)

    Musical with book by Joseph Stein; music by Jerry Bock; lyrics by Sheldon Harnick; based on Sholom Aleichem's stories. September 22, 1964. Critics Award (musical).

The Physicists (55)

    By Friedrich Duerrenmatt; adapted by James Kirkup. October 13, 1964.

Luv (901)

    By Murray Schisgal. November 11, 1964.

Poor Bitos (17)

    By Jean Anouilh; translated by Lucienne Hill. November 14, 1964.

Slow Dance on the Killing Ground (88)

    By William Hanley. November 30, 1964.

Incident at Vichy (99)

    By Arthur Miller. December 3, 1964.

The Toilet (151)

    By LeRoi Jones. December 16, 1964.

Tiny Alice (167)

    By Edward Albee. December 29, 1964.

The Odd Couple (964)

    By Neil Simon. March 10, 1965.

Golden Boy (568), The Owl and the Pussycat (427), Half a Sixpence (511), A View from the Bridge (780; revival).

1965-1966

Generation (299)
By William Goodhart. October 6, 1965.
The Royal Hunt of the Sun (261)
By Peter Shaffer. October 26, 1965.
Hogan's Goat (607)
By William Alfred. November 11, 1965.
Man of La Mancha (1,467*)
Musical with book by Dale Wasserman; music by Mitch Leigh; lyrics by Joe Darion; suggested by the life and works of Miguel de Cervantes y Saavedra. November 22, 1965. Critics Award (musical).
Inadmissible Evidence (166)
By John Osborne. November 30, 1965.
Cactus Flower (1,234)
By Abe Burrows; based on a play by Pierre Barillet and Jean-Pierre Gredy. December 8, 1965.
The Persecution and Assassination of Marat as Performed by the Inmates of the Asylum of Charenton Under the Direction of the Marquis de Sade (144)
By Peter Weiss; English version by Geoffrey Skelton; verse adaptation by Adrian Mitchell. December 27, 1965. Critics Award.
Philadelphia, Here I Come! (326)
By Brian Friel. February 16, 1966.
The Lion in Winter (92)
By James Goldman. March 3, 1966.
"It's a Bird   It's a Plane   It's Superman" (129)
Musical with book by David Newman and Robert Benton; music by Charles Strouse; lyrics by Lee Adams; based on the comic strip "Superman." March 29, 1966.

The Impossible Years (670), Sweet Charity (608), Mame (1,260), Happy Ending and Day of Absence (504), The Pocket Watch (725), The Mad Show (871).*

1966-1967

A Delicate Balance (132)
By Edward Albee. September 22, 1966. Pulitzer Prize.
The Killing of Sister George (205)
By Frank Marcus. October 5, 1966.
The Apple Tree (463)
Musical with book and lyrics by Sheldon Harnick; music by Jerry Bock; additional book material by Jerome Coopersmith; based on stories by Mark Twain, Frank R. Stockton and Jules Feiffer. October 18, 1966.
America Hurrah (634)
By Jean-Claude van Itallie. November 6, 1966.

Cabaret (1,153*)

    Musical with book by Joe Masteroff; music by John Kander; lyrics by Fred Ebb; based on the play *I Am a Camera* by John van Druten and stories by Christopher Isherwood. November 20, 1966. Critics Award (musical).

The Homecoming (324)

    By Harold Pinter. January 5, 1967. Critics Award.

Black Comedy (337)

    By Peter Shaffer. February 12, 1967.

You're a Good Man Charlie Brown (895*)

    Musical with book, music and lyrics by Clark Gesner; based on the comic strip "Peanuts" by Charles M. Schulz. March 7, 1967.

Hamp (101)

    By John Wilson; based on an episode from a novel by J.L. Hodson. March 9, 1967.

You Know I Can't Hear You When the Water's Running (755)

    By Robert Anderson. March 13, 1967.

Don't Drink the Water (598), I Do! I Do! (560).

1967–1968

After The Rain (64)

    By John Bowen. October 9, 1967.

Scuba Duba (674*)

    By Bruce Jay Friedman. October 10, 1967.

Rosencrantz and Guildenstern Are Dead (420)

    By Tom Stoppard. October 16, 1967. Critics Award.

Staircase (61)

    By Charles Dyer. January 10, 1968.

Your Own Thing (580*)

    Musical with book by Donald Driver; music and lyrics by Hal Hester and Danny Apolinar; suggested by William Shakespeare's *Twelfth Night*. Opened January 13, 1968. Critics Award (musical).

I Never Sang for My Father (124)

    By Robert Anderson. January 25, 1968.

A Day in the Death of Joe Egg (154)

    By Peter Nichols. February 1, 1968.

The Price (429)

    By Arthur Miller. February 7, 1968.

Plaza Suite (537*)

    By Neil Simon. February 14, 1968.

The Boys in the Band (471*)

    By Mart Crowley. April 15, 1968.

George M! (427), Hair (455), Curley McDimple (647*).*

1968–1969

Lovers (148)
> By Brian Friel. July 25, 1968.

The Man in the Glass Booth (268)
> By Robert Shaw. September 26, 1968.

The Great White Hope (276*)
> By Howard Sackler. October 3, 1968. Pulitzer Prize. Critics Award.

Forty Carats (180*)
> By Jay Allen; adapted from a play by Pierre Barillet and Jean-Pierre Gredy. December 26, 1968.

Hadrian VII (166*)
> By Peter Luke; based on *Hadrian the Seventh* and other works by Fr. Rolfe (Baron Corvo). January 8, 1969.

Celebration (109)
> Musical with book and lyrics by Tom Jones; music by Harvey Schmidt. January 22, 1969.

Adaptation/Next (126*)
> Two one-act plays: *Adaptation* by Elaine May and *Next* by Terrence McNally. February 10, 1969.

In the Matter of J. Robert Oppenheimer (64)
> By Heinar Kipphardt; translated by Ruth Speirs. March 6, 1969.

1776 (89*)
> Musical with book by Peter Stone; music and lyrics by Sherman Edwards. March 16, 1969.

No Place To Be Somebody (30*)
> By Charles Gordone. May 4, 1969.

1968-1969

1919-1969: SOME OUTSTANDING PERFORMANCES

BY AL HIRSCHFELD

These are some of the performances Mr. Hirschfeld has admired most during his years of covering the New York theater. He has selected the drawings from his published work, and they appear in their original form.

ELIZABETH BERGNER
IN "ESCAPE ME NEVER" (1935)

ALFRED LUNT AND LYNN FONTANNE
IN "THE TAMING OF THE SHREW" (1935)

KATHARINE CORNELL
IN "SAINT JOAN" (1936)

RUTH GORDON IN "THE COUNTRY WIFE" (1936)

ORSON WELLES IN "DR. FAUSTUS" (1937)

HELEN HAYES IN "VICTORIA REGINA" (1937)

RAYMOND MASSEY IN
"ABE LINCOLN IN ILLINOIS" (1938)

VICTOR MOORE
IN "LOUISIANA PURCHASE" (1940)

ED WYNN IN "BOYS AND GIRLS TOGETHER" (1940)

SARA ALLGOOD AND BARRY
FITZGERALD IN "JUNO AND
THE PAYCOCK" (1940)

LAURETTE TAYLOR IN
"THE GLASS MENAGERIE" (1945)

DOLLY HAAS IN "LUTE SONG" (1946)

BOBBY CLARK IN "AS THE GIRLS GO" (1948)

JOSE FERRER IN "THE SILVER WHISTLE" (1949)

CAROL CHANNING IN "GENTLEMEN PREFER BLONDES" (1949)

ETHEL WATERS IN
"THE MEMBER OF THE WEDDING" (1950)

MAUREEN STAPLETON IN
"THE ROSE TATTOO" (1951)

JULIE HARRIS IN "I AM A CAMERA" (1951)

JOSEPHINE HULL
IN "THE SOLID GOLD CADILLAC" (1953)

MARY MARTIN IN "PETER PAN" (1954)

BERT LAHR IN "WAITING FOR GODOT" (1956)

ZERO MOSTEL IN "ULYSSES IN NIGHTTOWN" (1958)

LAURENCE OLIVIER AND ANTHONY QUINN IN "BECKETT" (1960)

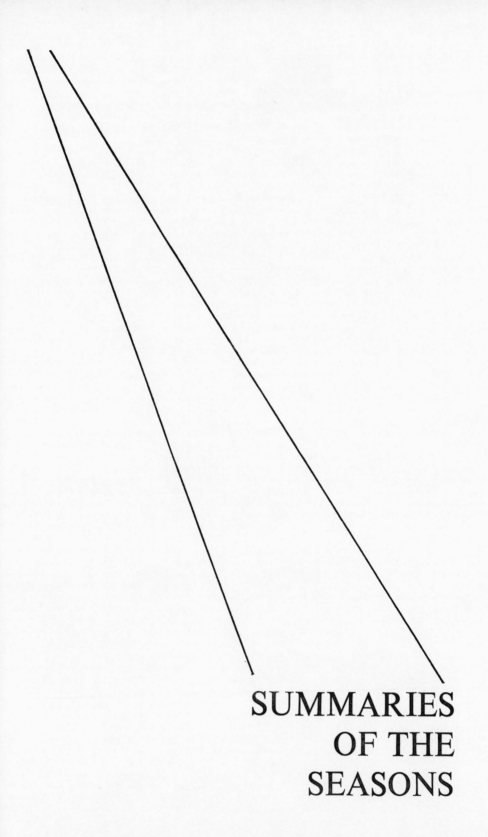

SUMMARIES
OF THE
SEASONS

O
O
O

THE SEASON AROUND THE UNITED STATES

with

A DIRECTORY OF PROFESSIONAL REGIONAL THEATER

O
O
O

INTRODUCTION

By Leo Brady

Professor, Department of Speech and Drama, Catholic University

WHEN ROGER STEVENS went before a House Public Works Committee last May to get more money to finish building the John F. Kennedy Center for the Performing Arts, Apollo 10 was making its way back to earth from the moon, and the front pages were occupied. Stevens got the money but not much encouragement for the future; the reluctance of legislators to support this and other projects was symptomatic of how things were between the government and the arts in 1969. The Center continued to rise, somewhat uncertainly, on the banks of the Potomac, but it was clear that art was playing second fiddle to the music of the spheres, and other utilitarian noises.

The Nixon administration, cautious even in its statements about front-page stuff like the war and poverty, was practically tongue-tied when it came to the arts. Daughter Patricia helped decorate a board fence around a landscaping job opposite 1600 Pennsylvania Avenue, and the new Chief Justice of the Supreme Court was revealed as a part-time sculptor, but otherwise the new regime distinguished itself by showing *The Sound of Music* in the executive projection room. During the Johnson administration, artists were as common around the White House as pickets, but 1969 was a year in which the subject of art was getting harder and harder to bring up, and even when broached, set off a discussion of deficits. Even under President Johnson, the Congress had trimmed the appropriation for the National Arts Endowment. A direct casualty of this economic slash was the Association of Producing Artists (APA-Phoenix) in New York, which was forced to surrender its three-year-old home in the Lyceum Theater. Whether the recipient was depending on local support or national, the picture was pretty much the same all around. The Atlanta Municipal Theater went off like a skyrocket in the fall of 1968 but four months later had spluttered out in a flare of red ink. In San Francisco, the American Conservatory Theater continued to add to both a record repertory and a record deficit; it was clear that William Ball, its artistic director, was as good at mounting costs as he is at mounting masterpieces. Critical acclaim was everywhere being drowned out by lugubrious treasurers' reports. Somebody estimated that of the 200 million Americans now crowding the continent, only 5 per cent had any sort of constant interest in the performing arts. It looked all too discouragingly accurate.

Actually, the record of artistic accomplishment in many of the subsidized theaters was impressive, and it was especially so in the city of Washington. Three miles down the Potomac from the burgeoning marble of the Kennedy Center squats a theater called Arena Stage which might remind students of early American history of a cheese-box on a raft. Guided by Zelda and Tom Fichandler, Arena has managed to flourish for close to two decades on a mixed grill of grit, luck, talent and the kind of high-sounding pronouncements that persuade foundations. The company has benefited from National Endowment grants, Ford Foundation money, strong local support, and a big subscription. It plays to 90 per cent of 700-seat capacity and still has money troubles. For a couple of years after the construction of their new theater, the Fichandlers were preoccupied with housekeeping and with rearranging the furniture, and the productions palled. Then, last season, they broke out to national prominence with the first performances of Howard Sackler's *The Great White Hope,* a sweaty, poetic, Elizabethan-sprawling play based on the life of prizefighter Jack Johnson—a play that had some of the grandeur and the gore of Greek tragedy, that managed to create a flawed protagonist at the same time it made clear our national tragedy in dealing with racial problems. Jefferson (as Johnson is thinly disguised in the play) is enraged by a system that is not so much corrupt as obtuse and becomes himself corrupted.

Probably no other regional theater in the country—even with the help of patrons—could have brought this play to the stage, since it demands some twenty scenes and more than sixty black and white actors. But Arena did it, and created national interest in both itself and the play. Transferred to a Broadway house, along with its star James Earl Jones and director Edwin Sherin, *The Great White Hope* was the outstanding theatrical event of the 1968-69 season in America. Money came into the picture here in a surprising way. Zelda Fichandler had got interested in Sackler's play when it consisted of one act and an outline. Convinced of its merit, she wheedled $25,000 from the Arts Endowment to help finance its completion and production. Seventy-five hundred of this went to the playwright and enabled him (with the producer's prodding) to finish the script . . . one year later than scheduled.

Arena's books showed a $50,000 loss on the project, but after Herman Levin optioned the play for Broadway, the Fichandlers looked forward to a share in the rewards. Alas, in defiance of Sam Goldwyn's aphorism about verbal contracts not being worth the paper they are written on, nothing had been put in writing. Arena, despite its clearly significant contribution to the genesis of the play, received nothing from the Broadway grosses or from the lucrative movie sale which followed. Irony reared its brassy head here: at a time when everyone (or at least that art-loving 5 per cent) was agreed that artists couldn't be expected to support themselves, Arena was on the brink of proving that it might be possible—and then lost out on a share of the money, as in old melodrama.

But also as in old melodrama, the Marines arrived. In the spring of 1969, Arena presented the American premiere (it had been done in London) of Arthur Kopit's swirling, dark-comic *Indians,* another tragedy with a social conscience. Here the almost-unidentifiable author of *Poor Dad* employs the framework of the old Wild West Show to comment on the wild East show staged by Presidents and the Congress in the late 19th century which outdid the Jameses and the Hickoks when it came to outrageous thievery and official shots in the back. One of the devices Kopit uses to spin his tall tale is a hearing before a Congressional delegation which took place in 1868. The senators are portrayed as moderate Claghorns, in accord with the poster style of the play, and one might have expected some show of protest from Congress and some—at least token—defense of the federal treatment of the Indian. But not a word has been heard from government public relations departments. Now it's possible that this unwonted silence can be explained by our devotion to freedom of speech (though this principle usually supposes instant rebuttal); or because we have gallantly forgiven ourselves for our transgressions against the redskins; or perhaps there are so many current scandals that it was too much to expect *Indians* to out-Fortinbras Fortas. But the play is haunting and ought to catch the conscience of somebody, especially since we are in the process of reviving at the moment almost the same historical error with the Negro. In the sombre half-light of Arena's square stage, the actors stand in their motley garb, topped by totem animal heads, and spookily survey the audience, and the past seems suddenly not disposed of and the future ominous. Stacy Keach gives an astonishing performance—shambling and crazy-optimistic—as Buffalo Bill Cody, and Manu Topou is like a malefic elemental force as Sitting Bull. But there has been no protest—not even from the Bureau of Indian Affairs—except from the father of a family who complained about Wild Bill Hickok's vulgar speech. Maybe the disheartening explanation is that the theater affects so small a portion of our population that even Congressmen don't care how they are maligned by it, and hence are not willing to put money into something they can't even get mad at.

The Department of the Interior got into the theater business a year ago when it shined up Ford's Theater and turned it over to the National Repertory Theater. Producer Michael Dewell conceived the idea of presenting plays that might have been done in the history-haunted house when it was in its heyday and set up a repertory of *The Comedy of Errors, John Brown's Body* and *She Stoops to Conquer.* Unfortunately, the productions had something of a century-old air about them, and after a public and fairly sordid hassle about money (again!) NRT was replaced by the Circle in the Square in the fall of 1968. *A Moon for the Misbegotten,* their first attempt, didn't quite fit on a stage congenial to *Our American Cousin,* but *Trumpets of the Lord* was a great success, and Ted Mann's arrangements, financial as well as artistic, were pleasing enough to his bureaucratic patrons to insure his being invited back for another season.

In May, Ford's Theater, with its high-polished floors, its uncomfortable chairs, and the bunting hung on Lincoln's box provided part of the locale for the American College Theater Festival, a covey of ten plays done by university drama departments. The productions were selected by representatives of American Educational Theater Association (AETA) and American National Theater and Academy (ANTA)—Miss Peggy Wood, guiding light and chief organizer. Additional sponsorship was provided by the Kennedy Center and the Smithsonian Institution, and the money ($100,000) was put up by American Airlines. Five plays were done at Ford's and five in a tent theater staked out on the Mall, not far from where the Poor Peoples' March had flopped in the mud a year before. The results were uneven. Minnesota, Yale, Catholic, and Northwestern, among the old-line drama schools, were not represented—though Brandeis had the courage to do a new play (not very good) and Wayne State's classic rep company, somewhat unfairly semi-professional, did a bang-up version of Feydeau's *A Flea in Her Ear.* This sort of venture, combining sightseeing and amateur art, was thought to be the kind of thing the Kennedy Center would devote itself to once it got roofed and equipped, since there has been an official announcement that it will not house a resident acting company.

The Washington Theater Club, the city's other year-round Equity company, this year received the Margo Jones award as "the theater most active in the development of new plays in America." In four seasons, Davey Marlin-Jones, WTC's artistic director, had given sixty-three writers a shot at the spotlight, admittedly counting sketch-writers who contributed to the annual political revue, *Spread Eagle.* Marlin-Jones is an inventive and adventurous director, and the staging of Lance Wilson's *The Gingham Dog* was the high point of the season. It was no particular comment on the director's work or the playwright's when the play was done later in New York and failed—though it might be a comment on the competence of regional theater as compared to Broadway. In 1969-70, WTC will be able to carry its trophy to a new building on the edge of Georgetown, with a thrust stage and 370 seats, a capacity which will give the company a fighting chance to be solvent as well as admirable.

Olney Theater, which has a unique niche locally because it carts Culture out to the cornstalks at a location midway between Washington and Baltimore for the summer with such works as Duerrenmatt's *The Physicists* and Synge's *The Playboy of the Western World,* last year stitched together the classical past and the quivering present with a rock musical version of *Lysistrata* called *The Coldest War of All.* James Waring's mixed media production with slides, tapes, films, and an ear-wounding teen-age combo made the costs soar as high as the intown temperatures.

In sum, the arts were in trouble in 1969, suffering from short-sightedness and short-change. The cast of *1776,* on its way to fame and fortune in New York, waited in vain for President Nixon to drop in at the National Theater during its local run. The Washington *Post,* which once boasted the most influential drama page in town, suddenly made the eminent Richard L. Coe an occasional writer and lumped its entertainment coverage into a section called *"Style:* Women/The Arts/Classified"—an equation that baffled its readers— which features gossip, architecture, and hot stories on pornography from the hippie front. But there were still a lot of brave hearts backstage in the Nation's Capital, all with the hope that as time went on, those who make the nation's laws might be willing to pay the piper, urged by the memory that life is short, art is long, and both are expensive.

Highlights of the Season in Los Angeles

By Dale Olson

A curious paradox has developed in the growth pattern of Los Angeles theater, but one that in the long run may prove to be healthy. Several of the organizations that shot up with great vigor and promise have begun to subside, but in their stead has developed a series of substantial companies and theaters that are attracting wider appeal and gaining stronger support than has been shown in the community's theater history.

Certainly, we mourn the demise of the Inner City Cultural Center, which for the most part has fallen short of the lofty purposes for which it was organized. Similarly, this season saw a breakdown in the Actors Studio West-UCLA Plays in Progress series that started so impressively. The Pasadena Playhouse has finally given up the ghost as a professional production company of any stature, and an attempt to reinstitute the Lindy as a major legitimate house failed when only second-rate companies were brought in—with the exception of the superb Circle in the Square production of *A Moon for the Misbegotten,* directed handsomely by Theodore Mann and featuring a memorable performance by Salome Jens.

On the other hand, there has been impressive support for new, experimental theater, particularly evidenced by the increased attendance for the Gordon Davidson-Edward Parone New Theater For Now series at the Forum. By the end of its second season, it had brought the work of twenty-six new playwrights in 28 plays to Los Angeles, marking a record that cannot be matched by any other theater in the country. The plays are new, fresh, alive. Some are woefully undeveloped, some excellent, but the important point is that they are being presented and audiences are eagerly supporting them. I think, for instance, that A. R. Gurney Jr.'s *The Golden Fleece* is an excellent new play that indicates promise for a new writer.

Perhaps the most significant event to herald the growing influence of theater here this year was the banding together of the city's drama critics to form a Los Angeles Drama Critics Circle, indicating that those who write about theater feel there is now sufficient important Los Angeles activity to merit their concentrated interest and attention. Dedicated to encouraging the level of production and rewarding excellence with public recognition, the Circle began its first year with James Powers as President and myself as secretary-treasurer.

With the decline of some theaters, there was established a certain strength for others. For instance, James Doolittle courageously stepped out and established the first major open-end booking at the Huntington Hartford Theater with the Mike Nichols production of *Plaza Suite,* starring Lee Grant and Dan Dailey, followed by a similar open-end booking of *The Boys in the Band.* Until this season, no one believed long runs here were possible.

Michael Butler erupted in Los Angeles, spent a great deal of money remodeling the old Earl Carroll Theater as the Aquarius and set the town on its ear with a sensational production of *Hair,* which may prove to be the most spectacular success in Los Angeles theater history. And a small but good production of *You're a Good Man Charlie Brown* shows no sign of ending a run after more than a year at the Ivar, while Sal Mineo's *Fortune and Men's Eyes* seems to be enjoying similar success.

Of course, the season enjoyed the usual highly popular productions of Edwin Lester's Civic Light Opera Association, including Angela Lansbury's re-creation of *Mame* and a lovely revival of *My Fair Lady* starring Douglas Fairbanks Jr. and Margot Moser. And there were superb presentations of *Rosencrantz and Guildenstern Are Dead* and the Minnesota Theater Company's *The House of Atreus* and *The Resistible Rise of Arturo Ui,* as well as a return of the Royal Shakespeare Company with lavish productions of *Dr. Faustus* and *Much Ado About Nothing.* A revival of Tennessee Williams' *Camino Real* was colorful and exciting (and highly praised by the author), and there also was a devastating flop musical called *Love Match,* beautifully presented, excitingly directed and choreographed by Danny Daniels and liltingly performed by Patricia Routledge, but sadly heavy and awkward as a whole.

Just when a new attitude of freedom and honesty was beginning to form in Los Angeles, news suddenly was made with the sudden eviction of The Living Theater in the middle of its run at the University of Southern California. Still, it became apparent this is the kind of theater that is attaracting most audiences. It received wider attention with the sudden boom of Steve Kent's Company Theater production of the James Joyce Liquid Theater. Kent's direction was outstanding, and so were the performances of Candace Laughlin and Wiley Renaldi, when the new kind of "feel" theater was presented.

Generally, the importance of the showcase theater which has been a large activity in this movie-conscious town, has dwindled. There are still the groups doing sporadic performances hoping to catch the eye of film people, but only

Jane Alexander as Eleanor Bachman and James Earl Jones as Jack Jefferson in *The Great White Hope*

Julie Harris as Ann Stanley in *Forty Carats*

Al Pacino as Bickham in *Does a Tiger Wear a Necktie?* (FAR RIGHT)

William Daniels as John Adams in *1776* (FAR LEFT)

Keith Charles as Potemkin in *Celebration*

Bernadette Peters as Ruby in *Dames at Sea*

George Grizzard as Vincent in *The Gingham Dog* (FAR RIGHT)

Jay Garner as Lester Maddox in *Red, White and Maddox* (FAR LEFT)

Dustin Hoffman as Jimmy in *Jimmy Shine*

Maria Karnilova as Hortense in *Zorbá*

Milton Berle as Max in *The Goodbye People* (FAR RIGHT)

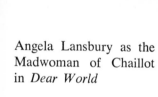

Ron O'Neal as Gabe in *No Place To Be Somebody* (FAR LEFT)

Nicol Williamson as Hamlet in *Hamlet*

Angela Lansbury as the Madwoman of Chaillot in *Dear World*

Alec McCowen as Haddrian in *Hadrian VII* (FAR RIGHT)

Jerry Orbach as Chuck Baxter in *Promises, Promises* (FAR LEFT)

Donald Pleasence as Arthur Goldman in *The Man in the Glass Booth*

The three generations of *Forty Carats:* daughter (Gretchen Corbett), mother (Julie Harris), grandmother (Glenda Farrell)

Alec McCowen as Frederick William Rolfe in his fantasy of sitting on the throne of St. Peter in *Hadrian VII*

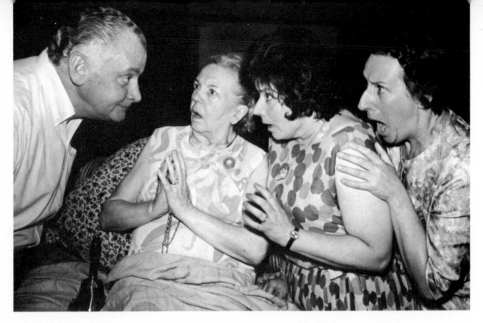

Art Carney, the fox in the henhouse of the *Losers* segment of *Lovers,*
with Grania O'Malley, Anna Manahan and Beulah Garrick

Philip Bosco, Eduard Franz, Harry Townes, Whitfield Connor and
Joseph Wiseman (as the physicist) in Lincoln Center Repertory's *In
the Matter of J. Robert Oppenheimer*

Donald Pleasence *(left)* as the defendant in a war crimes trial in Israel confronts an accuser in *The Man in the Glass Booth*

Bob Dishy and Milton Berle on the beach in *The Goodbye People*

Hal Holbrook *(second from right, rear)* as an English teacher with his class of teen-aged drug addicts in a correctional institution, in *Does a Tiger Wear a Necktie?*

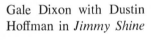

Gale Dixon with Dustin Hoffman in *Jimmy Shine*

Diane Keaton, Woody Allen and Jerry Lacy (as a fantasy image of Humphrey Bogart) in *Play It Again, Sam*

Frank Langella (as "Will"), Stephen Elliott and Anne Bancroft (as "Anne") in the Lincoln Center Repertory production of *A Cry of Players* about a stage-struck Elizabethan country boy

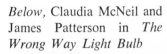

Above, Nancy Kelly, Sudie Bond and Wyman Pendleton (as Mao Tse-Tung) in *Box-Mao-Box*

Right, Gerald S. O'Lough and Renee Taylor in *Love and Other Strangers*

Left, Sorrell Booke and Charlotte Rae in the *Noon* portion of *Morning, Noon and Night*

Above, Vivian Vance, Robert Alda, Lee Lawson, Gene Lindsey, Dody Goodman, Bill McCutcheon in *My Daughter, Your Son*

Right, Jason Robards and Diana Sands in *We Bombed in New Haven*

1776—Members of the Second Continental Congress watch John Adams of Massachusetts (William Daniels, *right foreground*) demand the signature of Edward Rutledge of South Carolina (David Cryer, who took over this role early in the run). *Below,* Jo Mielziner's design for the Congressional Chamber in the musical about the Declaration of Independence

MUSICALS

1776—Costume designs by Patricia Zipprodt for Thomas Jefferson *(above)* and Benjamin Franklin *(below)*

RED, WHITE AND MADDOX—Jay Garner *(top)* as Lester Maddox in political satire

ZORBÁ — A Boris Aronson sketch for the scenery, which won the Tony and other awards. *Left,* Herschel Bernardi as Zorba lifted on the shoulders of Greek villagers in the mine-opening celebration scene of the musical

MAGGIE FLYNN — Shirley Jones *(left)* aloft in the title role of the Civil War-era musical

PROMISES, PROMISES— *Below,* cocktail time in show based on *The Apartment,* with *(foreground)* Baayork Lee, Donna McKechnie and Margo Sappington

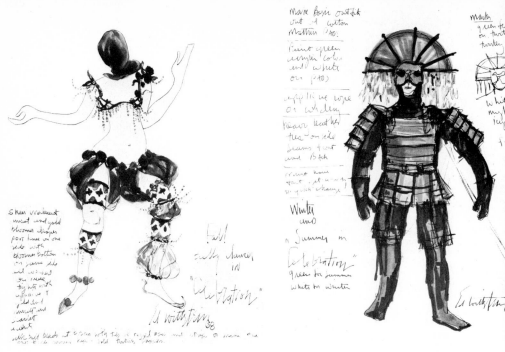

CELEBRATION—Pictured on this page are four of Ed Wittstein's costume sketches for the musical's gargoyle-masked figures. *Top left,* a belly dancer symbolizes Fall; *top right* is the dual personality of Winter and Summer; *bottom left* is a tattered Reveler; *bottom right,* another expression of Winter. Special photo section on *Celebration* appears elsewhere in this volume

CANTERBURY TALES—*Above,* the pilgrims enjoy a refreshing pause on their journey to Canterbury. Loudon Sainthill costume sketches pictured *at right* are *(top)* the Wife of Bath and *(bottom)* the Queen of Fairyland in the Merchant's Tale

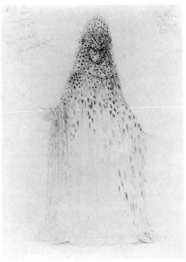

DEAR WORLD—*Above,* the Madwomen of Montmartre (Jean Connell), Chaillot (Angela Lansbury) and the Flea Market (Carmen Matthews) in tea party scene

THE *HAMLETS* — *Above,* the death scene in the British production, with Gordon Jackson as Horatio holding Nicol Williamson as the dying prince. *Below,* Ellis Rabb as Hamlet in the APA-Phoenix production of the tragedy

At right, another of the 1968-69 APA-Phoenix revivals: *The Misanthrope* with Brian Bedford, Richard Easton *(in background)* and Christine Pickles

Above, Lee J. Cobb in the title role of the Lincoln Center Repertory revival of *King Lear* at the Vivian Beaumont

Left, Sada Thompson in *Happy Days;* and *below,* Stephen McHattie and Sudie Bond in *The American Dream,* as presented in Theater 1969 Playwrights Repertory

Left, Robin Gammell as Arturo Ui *(above)* and Charles Keating as his henchman in the visiting Minnesota Theater Company production of *The Resistible Rise of Arturo Ui*

AT CITY CENTER—*Above*, Inga Swenson and Fritz Weaver as Eliza Doolittle and Henry Higgins in *My Fair Lady; below*, Pierre Olaf *(center, in cap and glasses)* and the chorus line of *Carnival*

Above, Carole Morley, Gabriel Dell and Paul Dooley in *Adaptation; right,* Elaine Shore and James Coco in *Next,* on the one-act play program entitled *Adaptation/Next*

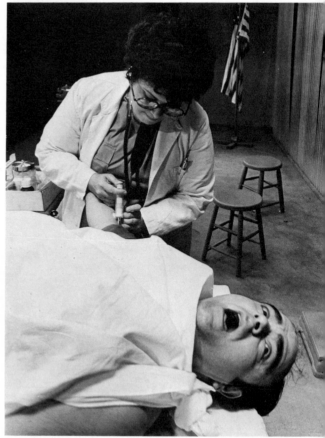

Above, Sally Stark, Steve Elmore, David Christmas (holding flag), Bernadette Peters, Tamara Long and Joseph R. Sicari in *Dames at Sea*

Left, Vincent Gardenia and Carole Shelly in the revival of *Little Murders.*

ON THESE
TWO PAGES:
NEW YORK
SHAKESPEARE
FESTIVAL
PUBLIC THEATER

Closeups from *No Place To Be Somebody: above,* Ron O'Neal *(left)* and Nathan George with bread; *right,* Marge Eliot and Ronnie Thompson with grass

Left, Barry Primus and Sharon Laughlin in *Huui, Huui*

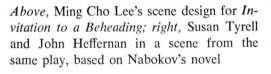

Above, Ming Cho Lee's scene design for *Invitation to a Beheading; right,* Susan Tyrell and John Heffernan in a scene from the same play, based on Nabokov's novel

Left, Joan Harris and Cynthia Belgrave in *Cities in Bezique*

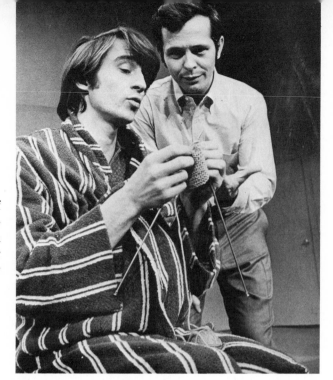

In *Spitting Image,* one of a pair of "married" homosexuals *(right,* Sam Waterston and Walter McGinn) expects a baby

Jean David and Monty Montgomery in *Beclch (left)* and Ted Daniels and Linda Justin Barret in *Futz! (above),* two plays by Rochelle Owens

LIKE IT WAS

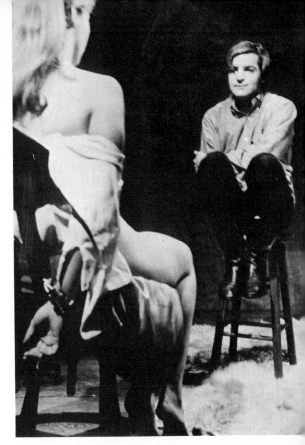

Right, Sally Kirkland and Robert Drivas in *Sweet Eros*

Below, a scene from *Geese*

A has-been vaudeville dancer (Douglas Turner) shows off for his son (David Downing) in the Negro Ensemble Company production of *Ceremonies in Dark Old Men,* the first of two 1968-69 productions of this play

LINCOLN CENTER REP-
ERTORY IN THE FOR-
UM THEATER — *Above*,
Patricia Roe and Larry
Robinson in *Bananas. Be-
low*, Roy R. Scheider and
Paul Benjamin in *The Year
Boston Won the Pennant*

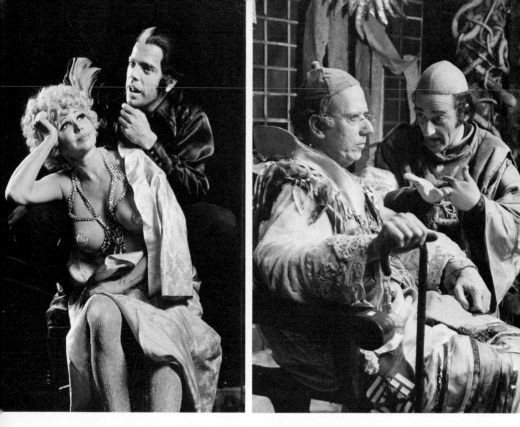

TWO 1968-69 PRODUCTIONS AT AMERICAN PLACE THEATER—
Left, Gloria LeRoy and Kevin O'Connor in *Boy on the Straight-Back Chair;*
right, Albert Paulsen and Arnold Soboloff in *Papp*

Elizabeth Swain, Da
Margolies and Lily
Wilder in Slawomir M
zek's *Tango*

Below, Trygaeus (Reathel Bean) with the beetle he rides to heaven in *Peace,* the minstrel musical based on Aristophanes

Above, Max Morath in his one-man show *An Evening with Max Morath at the Turn of the Century*

Below, the team of improvisers in *The Fourth Wall:* Kent Broadhurst, Bette-Jane Raphael, Jeremy Stevens, Marcia Wallace, James Manis

As the 1968-69 New York theater season ended, this undressed off-Broadway revue, devised by Kenneth Tynan, was in previews for a June opening. Pictured on this page is the show's highlight, the Margo Sappington-George Welbes pas de deux. The choreography is Miss Sappington's a few of them like Paul Kent's Melrose Workshop, The Showcase and Lawrence Parke's organization continue to operate with regularity and generally with solid professionalism. The professional theater as a whole, however, is taking a good hold here and looking toward a very bright future.

1968-69 programs of the Center Theater Group and the New Theater for Now are listed in the Los Angeles entry of the Directory of Professional Regional Theater.

A DIRECTORY OF
PROFESSIONAL REGIONAL THEATER

Professional 1968-69 programs and repertory productions by leading resident companies around the United States, plus selected Shakespeare festivals including that of Stratford, Ontario (Canada), are grouped in alphabetical order of their locations and listed in date order from June 1, 1968 through May 31, 1969. This list does not include Broadway, off-Broadway or touring New York shows, summer theaters, single productions by commercial producers or college or other non-professional productions. The directory was compiled by Ella A. Malin for *The Best Plays of 1968-69* from information provided by the resident producing organizations at Miss Malin's request. Figures in parentheses following titles give number of performances and date given is opening date, whenever a record of these facts was available from the producing managements.

Summary

This Directory lists 279 plays (including one-acters and workshop productions) produced by 37 groups in 49 theaters in 35 cities during the 1968-69 season. Of these, 153 were American plays in 118 full productions and 35 workshop productions. 32 programs were world premieres and 9 others were American premieres.

Frequency of production of individual scripts was as follows:

 1 play received 7 productions (*The Homecoming*)
 1 play received 5 productions (*Hamlet*)
 2 plays received 4 productions (*Arms and the Man, The Lion in Winter*)
 10 plays received 3 productions (*As You Like It, A Midsummer Night's Dream, Three Sisters, The Seagull, The Misanthrope, Muzeeka, Summertree, Six Characters in Search of an Author, The Birthday Party, Macbeth*)
 41 plays received 2 productions
224 plays received 1 production

Listed below are the playwrights who received the greatest number of productions. The first figure is the number of productions; the second figure (in parentheses) is the number of plays produced, including one-acters:

Shakespeare	24	(19)	Chekhov	6	(3)
Shaw	14	(10)	Ibsen	5	(5)
Molière	11	(7)	Anouilh	5	(4)
Pinter	9	(4)	Beckett	5	(3)
Albee	8	(8)	Brecht	5	(3)
Williams	7	(4)	Miller	4	(4)
			Wilder	4	(2)

ABINGDON, VA.

Barter Theater

FAIR HARVARD by Sam Brattle; based on stories by Charles Macomb Flandrau (world premiere). Director, Pierrino Mascarino; scenery, Michael Stauffer; lighting, John Baker; costumes, Linda Rogers. With Gloria Shott, Charles Matlock, Thomas Hughes.

A GIFT FOR CATHY by Ronald Alexander (world premiere). Director, Robert Brink; scenery, Michael Stauffer; lighting, John Baker; costumes, Linda Rogers. With Joann Chalfont, George Mathews, Dale Carter Cooper.

THE IMPOSSIBLE YEARS by Bob Fisher and Arthur Marx. Director, Owen Phillips; scenery, Michael Stauffer; lighting, John Baker; costumes, Linda Rogers. With Jay Bell, Anna Stuart, Diane Hill, Jerry Hardin.

CATCH ME IF YOU CAN by Jack Weinstock and Willie Gilbert. Director, Owen Phillips; scenery, Michael Stauffer; lighting, John Baker; costumes, Linda Rogers. With Jay Bell, Robert Foley, Tom Hughes.

CACTUS FLOWER by Abe Burrows. Direc-

tor, Owen Phillips; scenery, Michael Stauffer; lighting, John Baker; costumes, Linda Rogers. With Naomi Robin, Jack Cowles.

BLACK COMEDY by Peter Shaffer. Director, Owen Phillips; scenery, Michael Stauffer; lighting, John Baker; costumes, Walter Williamson. With Jay Bell, Dorothy Marie, Tom Hughes, Kay Carroll.

PRESENT LAUGHTER by Noel Coward. Director, Robert Brink; scenery, Michael Stauffer; lighting, John Baker; costumes, Linda Rogers. With Jerry Hardin, Diane Hill, Robert Foley, Jay Bell.

WAIT UNTIL DARK by Frederick Knott. Director, Robert Brink; scenery, Michael Stauffer; lighting, John Baker; costumes, Linda Rogers. With Jack Cowles, Roger Omar Serbagi, Dorothy Marie.

THE CARETAKER by Harold Pinter. Director, Pierrino Mascarino; lighting; John Baker; costumes, Linda Rogers. With Roger Omar Serbagi, Dan A. Yount, Thomas Hughes.

ANN ARBOR, MICH.

University of Michigan Professional Theater Program: Association of Producing Artists (APA-Phoenix) Repertory

THE MISANTHROPE (12). By Molière; translated and adapted by Richard Wilbur. September 17, 1968. Director, Stephen Porter; scenery and lighting, James Tilton; costumes, Nancy Potts. With Richard Easton, Patricia Conolly, Christine Pickles, Brian Bedford, Sydney Walker, Keene Curtis.

HAMLET (12). By William Shakespeare. October 1, 1968. Director, Ellis Rabb; scenery and lighting, James Tilton; costumes, Nancy

Potts. With Ellis Rabb, Amy Levitt, Katherine Helmond, Richard Woods, Donald Moffat, Marco St. John, Richard Easton.

COCK-A-DOODLE DANDY (12). By Sean O'Casey. October 15, 1968. Director, Jack O'Brien; scenery and lighting, James Tilton; costumes, Nancy Potts. With Donald Moffat, Katherine Helmond, Amy Levitt, Richard Woods, Philip Minor.

University of Michigan Professional Theater Program: New Play Project

THE CASTLE (5). By Ivan Klima. December 3, 1968 (American premiere). Director, Marcella Cisney; scenery and lighting reproduced from Prague production. With Nancy Wickwire, Henderson Forsythe, Edgar Daniels, William Glover.

University of Michigan Professional Theater Program: Stratford Festival Company of Canada

THE ALCHEMIST by Ben Jonson. Director, Jean Gascon; scenery, James Hart Stearns; lighting, John Gleason. With Powys Thomas, Jane Casson, Bernard Behrens, William Hutt.

HAMLET by William Shakespeare. Director, John Hirsch; scenery, Sam Kirkpatrick; lighting, John Gleason. With Kenneth Nelson, Leo Ciceri, Angela Wood, Anne Anglin, Kenneth Pogue.

Note: These programs were presented in repertory March 25 through April 6, 1969, prior to the Stratford Festival Company's summer 1969 Ontario season (see entry elsewhere in this listing).

ASHLAND, ORE.

The Oregon Shakespearean Festival

CYMBELINE (13). By William Shakespeare. July 20, 1968. Director, James Sandoe; scenery, Clayton L. Karkosh; lighting, Steven A. Maze; costumes, Jack A. Byers. With Philip Davidson, Cindy Veazey, Dennis Higgins, Carrillo Gantner.

HAMLET (13). By William Shakespeare. July 21, 1968. Director, Patrick Hines; scenery, Clayton L. Karkosh; lighting, Steven A. Maze; costumes, Jack A. Byers. With Richard Risso, Shirley Patton, Carrillo Gantner, Ann Kinsolving, Patrick McNamara.

AS YOU LIKE IT (13). By William Shakespeare. July 22, 1968. Director, William Kinsolving; scenery, Clayton L. Karkosh; lighting, Steven A. Maze; costumes, Jack A. Byers.

With Ann Kinsolving, Cindy Veazey, Scott Porter.

HENRY VIII (12). By William Shakespeare. July 23, 1968. Director, Richard Risso; scenery, Clayton L. Karkosh; lighting, Steven A. Maze; costumes, Jack A. Byers. With Patrick Hines, Amanda McBroom, Danny Davis, Ann Kinsolving.

LOCK UP YOUR DAUGHTERS (12). By Bernard Miles; adapted from *Rape Upon Rape* by Henry Fielding; music by Laurie Johnson; lyrics by Lionel Bart. August 14, 1968. Director, Carl Ritchie; scenery, Clayton L. Karkosh; lighting, Steven A. Maze; costumes, Jack A. Byers. With Karen Sue Boettcher, Danny Davis, Amanda McBroom, Scott Wagoner.

BALTIMORE

Center Stage

BOY MEETS GIRL (33). By Bella and Samuel Spewack. September 27, 1968. Director, Ruth White; scenery and lighting, Robert T. Williams; costumes, Ritchie M. Spencer. With Kathryn Baumann, Gerald E. McGonagill, Lenny Baker, William Pardue.

THE JOURNEY OF THE FIFTH HORSE (33). By Ronald Ribman. November 1, 1968. Director, John Stix; scenery and lighting, Kert Lundell; costumes, Ritchie M. Spencer. With Bruce Kornbluth, Colgate Salsbury.

THE HOMECOMING (29). By Harold Pinter. December 6, 1968. Director, Kent Paul; scenery and lighting, Robert T. Williams; costumes, Ritchie M. Spencer. With Larry Gates, Colgate Salsbury, Guy Boyd, Gerald E. McGonagill, Ann Whiteside.

THE MERCHANT OF VENICE (36). By William Shakespeare. January 10, 1969. Director, John Olon-Scrymgeour; scenery and lighting, Robert T. Williams; costumes, Ritchie

M. Spencer. With Larry Gates, Maury Cooper, DeVeren Bookwalter, Ann Whiteside.

BONUS MARCH (26). By Wallace Hamilton. February 14, 1969 (world premiere). Director, Dennis Rosa; scenery and lighting, Roger Morgan; costumes, Ritchie M. Spencer. With Bruce Kornbluth, Colgate Salsbury, David Huddleston.

THE SKIN OF OUR TEETH (28). By

Thornton Wilder. March 14, 1969. Director, John Olon-Scrymgeour; scenery and lighting, Robert T. Williams; costumes, Ritchie M. Spencer. With Cynthia Harris, Mary Hara, Maury Cooper.

A DOLL'S HOUSE (28). By Henrik Ibsen. April 11, 1969. Director, John Stix; scenery and lighting, Robert T. Williams; costumes, Ritchie M. Spencer. With Dorothy Tristan, Colgate Salsbury.

BOSTON

Charles Playhouse

LOOK BACK IN ANGER (40). By John Osborne. September 26, 1968. Director, Jon Jory; designer, Richard W. Kerry. With Marion Killinger, Karen Grassle.

THE BACCHAE (40). By Euripides; adapted from the translation by William Arrowsmith. Director, Timothy S. Mayer; designer, Richard W. Kerry. With Yolande Bavan, Patricia Cutts, Edward Finnegan, Donald Marye, Kevin O'Connor.

THE MILLIONAIRESS (40). By George Bernard Shaw. December 5, 1968. Director; Philip Minor; designer, Richard W. Kerry. With Robert Moberly, Barbara Caruso, Peter Coffeen, Joy Mills, Nicholas Kepros.

EVERYTHING IN THE GARDEN (40). By Edward Albee. January 9, 1969. Director,

Louis Criss; designer, Richard W. Kerry. With Jane Cronin, Robert Foxworth, Paddy Croft, Jack Simons.

THE REHEARSAL (40). By Jean Anouilh; translated by Lucienne Hill. February 9, 1969. Director, Michael Murray; designer, Victor C. DiNapoli. With John-Michael King, Anne Murray, Meg Myles, Gwyllum Evans.

ANYTHING GOES (40). Music and Lyrics by Cole Porter; book by Guy Bolton, P.G. Wodehouse, Howard Lindsay, Russel Crouse. March 20, 1969. Director and choreographer, Frank Westbrook; musical director, Mack Schlefer; designer, Victor C. DiNapoli. With Don Liberto, Fiddle Viracola, Kenneth McMillan, Jeanne Shea, Leslie Franzos, Richard Kinter, Helen Noyes, Edward Stevlingson.

Theater Company of Boston, Inc.

BENITO CERENO (22). By Robert Lowell. October 17, 1968. Directors, David Wheeler, Frank Cassidy; scenery, Robert Allen; lighting, Richard Lee; costumes, Penelope Belknap. With William Young, James Spruill, Larry Bryggman, Arthur Merrow.

BRECHT ON BRECHT (22). By George Tabori; from the works of Bertolt Brecht. November 7, 1968. Directors, David Wheeler, Frank Cassidy; scenery, Robert Allen; lighting, Richard Lee; costumes, Penelope Belknap. With Larry Bryggman, Janet Lee Parker, Penelope Allen, Arthur Merrow, Gilbert Lewis.

MORE STATELY MANSIONS (20). By Eugene O'Neill. November 27, 1968. Director, David Wheeler; scenery, Robert Allen; lighting, Richard Lee; costumes, Penelope Belknap. With Penelope Allen, Jane Hoffman, Larry Bryggman, Frank Cassidy.

THE BLOOD KNOT (29). By Athol Fugard. March 18, 1969. Director, Barney Simon; scenery, Robert Allen; lighting, Richard Lee; costumes, Penelope Belknap. With James Spruill, John Dullaghan.

THE DEER PARK (20). By Norman Mailer. April 10, 1969. Director, David Wheeler; scenery, Robert Allen; lighting, Lance Crocker; costumes, Penelope Belknap. With Ralph Waite, Paul J. Speyser, Aida Berlyn, Linda Selman, Frank Savino.

AFTER THE FALL (22). By Arthur Miller. May 1, 1969. Director, William Young; scenery, Robert Allen; lighting, Lance Crocker; costumes, Penelope Belknap. With Ralph Waite, Elizabeth Farley, Frank Savino, Audrey Ward.

HOW DO YOU DO, IT HAS NO CHOICE and THE CORNER by Ed Bullins. THE GAME OF ADAM AND EVE by Ed Bullins; written with Shirley Tarbell. (14) May 22, 1969 (American premiere). Directors, James Spruill, Ralph Waite, David Wheeler, Timothy Affleck; scenery, Robert Allen; lighting, Lance Crocker; costumes, Jean O'Hara. With Gustave Johnson, Novella Nelson, Dennis Tait, Robert Collinge, James Spruill, Naomi Thornton, Stockard Channing, Addie Brown, William Adell Stevenson III.

NOTE: Theater Company of Boston's Monday night staged workshop readings of new plays were *The Eagle of the Cordilleras* by W.E. Wilson (March 10, 1969), director Timothy Affleck; *June 5, 1968, Interludes* and *Dionysius X* by Geoffrey Bush (March 24, 1969), director Timothy Affleck; *O Family Bliss* by Mark Mirsky, director Timothy Affleck, and *The Corner* by Ed Bullins, director James Spruill (May 5, 1969); and *Happiness* by Arthur Pittman (May 26, 1969).

BUFFALO

Studio Arena Theater

THE DEATH OF BESSIE SMITH and THE AMERICAN DREAM (5). By Edward Albee. September 10, 1968. Directors Michael Kahn, Edward Albee; scenery, William Ritman; lighting, David Zierk. With Rosemary Murphy, Carolyn Coates, Ben Piazza, Sada Thompson, Donald Davis, Sudie Bond.

BOX and QUOTATIONS FROM CHAIRMAN MAO TSE-TUNG (1). By Edward Albee. September 15, 1968. Director, Alan Schneider; scenery, William Ritman; lighting, David Zierk. With Ruth White, Wyman Pendleton, Nancy Kelly, Sudie Bond, George Bartenieff.

KRAPP'S LAST TAPE by Samuel Beckett and THE ZOO STORY by Edward Albee (3). September 17, 1968. Directors, Alan Schneider, Richard Barr; scenery, William Ritman; lighting, David Zierk. With Donald Davis, Ben Piazza.

HAPPY DAYS (2). By Samuel Beckett. September 20, 1968. Director, Alan Schneider; scenery, William Ritman; lighting, David Zierk. With Sada Thompson, Wyman Pendleton.

YOU'RE A GOOD MAN CHARLIE BROWN (40). Book, music and lyrics by Clark Gesner; based on the comic strip "Peanuts" by Charles M. Schulz. September 24, 1968. Director, Joseph Hardy; scenery and costumes, Alan Kimmel; lighting, Jules Fisher; musical supervision, Joseph Raposo. With Grant Cowan, Alan Lofft, Derek McGrath, Marylu Moyer, Blaine Parker, Cathy Wallace.

THE LION IN WINTER (36). By James Goldman. October 31, 1968. Director, Nikos Psacharopoulos; scenery, Stephen J. Hendrickson; lighting, David Zierk; costumes, Carrie Fishbein. With Carolyn Coates, Donald Davis, Robert Foxworth, Carrie Nye.

BLITHE SPIRIT (28). By Noel Coward. December 5, 1968. Director, Warren Enters; scenery, Neal Du Brock; lighting, David Zierk; costumes, Duane Andersen. With Margaret Phillips, Michael Lipton, Edith Meiser.

THE KILLING OF SISTER GEORGE (28). By Frank Marcus. January 8, 1969. Director, Warren Enters; scenery, Mike English; lighting, David Zierk, costumes, Duane Andersen. With Betty Leighton, Patricia Cutts, Suzanne Osborne.

THE HOMECOMING (28). By Harold Pinter. February 6, 1969. Director, Warren Enters; scenery, Mike English; lighting, David Zierk; costumes, Pearl Smith. With William Roerick, Joan Bassie, David Snell.

THE STAR-SPANGLED GIRL (35). By Neil Simon. March 6, 1969. Director, Tom Sawyer; scenery, Russell Drisch; lighting, David Zierk. With Arthur Roberts, Barbette Tweed, Gene Nye.

THE SCHOOL FOR WIVES (23). By Molière. April 8, 1969. Director, Warren Enters; scenery and costumes, Stephen J. Hendrickson; lighting, David Zierk. With Harris Yulin, Diana Davila, Michael Enserro, Donald Ewer.

LOST IN THE STARS (37). Book and lyrics by Maxwell Anderson; music by Kurt Weill; based on Alan Paton's novel *Cry, the Beloved Country.* May 1, 1969. Director, Neal Du Brock; scenery and costumes, Duane Andersen; lighting, David Zierk; musical director, Stuart Hamilton. With Beatrice Mackin, Jeff Jeffrey, Clarke Salonis, Mabel E. Wyatt, Donald Dennis.

Studio Arena Theater: Black Monday Series (new play workshop)

Three One-Act Reader's Plays (1). April 21, 1969. ON THE ROAD by Tony Preston. Director, Ed Smith. With Laverne Clay, Ed Smith. HOW DO YOU DO by Ed Bullins. Director, Ed Smith. With Jo Ann Jones, Roosevelt Wardlaw, William E. Watkins. JOHNNAS by Bill Gunn. Director, Charlotte Huey. With Alfred C. Brown, William C. Brown, Charles Huey, Elsie Rellinger.

BURLINGTON, VT.

Champlain Shakespeare Festival

MACBETH (17). By William Shakespeare. July 21, 1968. Director, Edward J. Feidner; scenery and lighting, W. M. Schenk; costumes, Fran Brassard. With J. J. Sullivan, Carol Gutenberg, Wayne Grace, Ronald B. Parady.

HENRY IV, PART 2 (12). By William Shakespeare. July 26, 1968. Director, James J. Thesing; scenery and lighting, W. M. Schenk; costumes, Fran Brassard. With John H. Fields, Jo Anne Jameson, Ronald DiMartile, Emily Feffer, Earl McCarroll.

ALL'S WELL THAT ENDS WELL (12). By William Shakespeare. July 24, 1968. Director, Earl McCarroll; scenery and lighting, W. M. Schenk; costumes, Fran Brassard. With Jo Anne Jameson, Carol Gutenberg, Con Roche, Wayne Grace, Ronald B. Parady.

WAITING FOR GODOT (8). By Samuel Beckett. July 29, 1968. Director, Gerard E. Moses; scenery and lighting, W. M. Schenk; costumes, Fran Brassard. With Ronald B. Parady, John H. Fields, Earl McCarroll, Wayne Grace.

CHICAGO

Goodman Memorial Theater

THE SALZBURG GREAT THEATER OF THE WORLD (30). By Hugo von Hofmannsthal; metrical translation by Lisel Mueller and John Reich. October 4, 1968 (world premiere in English). Director, John Reich; scenery, James Maronek; lighting; G. E. Naselius; costumes, Alicia Finkel; music, Robert Lombardo; choreography, Thomas Jaremba. With Edgar Daniels, Dina Halpern, Maurice Copeland.

THE DEATH AND LIFE OF SNEAKY FITCH (29). By James L. Rosenberg. November 15, 1968 (world premiere). Director, Joseph Slowik; scenery, Marc Cohen; lighting, G. E. Naselius; costumes, E. Oliver Olsen. With Jerry Harper, Win Stracke.

RED ROSES FOR ME (29). By Sean

O'Casey. January 3, 1969. Director, John O'Shaughnessy; scenery, James Maronek; lighting, Jerrold Gorrell; costumes, E. Oliver Olsen. With Pauline Flanagan, Harry Townes, Marie Brady.

MEASURE FOR MEASURE (30). By William Shakespeare. February 14, 1969. Director, Charles McGaw; scenery, Marc Cohen; lighting, G. E. Naselius; costumes, Alicia Finkel. With Donald Harron, Clayton Corzatte, Haskell Gordon.

TOM PAINE (29). By Paul Foster. March 28, 1969. Director, Patrick Henry; scenery, Joseph Nieminski; lighting, Jerrold Gorrell; costumes, Virgil Johnson. With Michael Higgins, Ellen Travolta.

CINCINNATI

Playhouse in the Park: Main Theater

THE MISER (37). By Molière. June 13, 1968. Director, scenery, Ed Wittstein; lighting, Joe Pacitti. With Ronald Bishop, David Hooks, Laurie Brooks-Jefferson.

CAMINO REAL (22). By Tennessee Williams. July 18, 1968. Director, Michael Kahn; scenery; Douglas Schmidt; lighting, Joe Pacitti; costumes, Caley Summers. With Al

Freeman Jr., Michael Enserro, Edward Zang, Michael Lipton, Lynn Milgrim.

CRIME ON GOAT ISLAND (22). By Ugo Betti. August 8, 1968. Director, David Hooks; scenery and lighting, Joe Pacitti; costumes, Martha Braun. With Michael Enserro, Ellen Holly, Tom Klunis, Julie Bovasso, Lynn Milgrim.

THE MADWOMAN OF CHAILLOT (22). By Jean Giraudoux; translated by Maurice Valency. August 29, 1968. With Anne Meacham, Ronald Bishop.

VOLPONE (31). By Ben Jonson. April 3, 1969. Director, Byron Ringland; scenery, Ed Wittstein; lighting, Joe Pacitti; costumes, Caley Summers. With Jake Dengel, Ronald Bishop, Patricia McAneny.

THE BALCONY by Jean Genet; translated by Bernard Frechtman. May 1, 1969. Director, Brooks Jones; scenery, John Scheffler; lighting, Joe Pacitti; costumes, Caley Summers. With Ronald Bishop, Eve Collyer, Patricia McAneny, Leonardo Cimino.

THREE MEN ON A HORSE by George Abbott and John Cecil Holm. May 29, 1969.

Note: The balance of the 1969 spring-summer season will include *The Good Woman of Setzuan* by Bertolt Brecht (June 26), *Lady Audley's Secret*, musical adaptation by Douglas Seale (July 24), and *Six Characters in Search of an Author* (August 21).

Playhouse in the Park: Shelterhouse Theater

WHAT TIME IS IT? OR THE HINDU ROPE TRICK (1). By George Thompson. July 29, 1968. END OF THE WORLD (3). By Keith Nielson. August 14, 1968. THE YEAR OF THE GURU (1). By Pauline Smolin. August 19, 1968. New Plays Program workshop; director, Robert Stevenson.

HONOUR AND OFFER (23). By Henry Livings. November 21, 1968 (world premiere).

Director, Melvin Bernhardt; scenery, Ed Wittstein; lighting, Joe Pacitti; costumes, Caley Summers. With Ronald Bishop, Estelle Parsons, Dick Latessa, Paul Milikin.

FOUR MEN AND A MONSTER (16). By Maryat Lee. December 11, 1968. Director, Brooks Jones; scenery and lighting, Joe Pacitti; costumes, Happy Yancey. With Dick Latessa, Ronald Bishop, Paul Milikin.

CLEVELAND

Cleveland Play House: Euclid-77th Theater

DEAR LIAR (14). By Jerome Kilty; adapted from correspondence by George Bernard Shaw and Mrs. Patrick Campbell. September 20, 1968. Director, Richard Oberlin; costumes, Carol Margolis. With Edith Owen, Mario Siletti.

THE DAY OF THE LION (20). By Joel Wyman; adapted from the novel *A Dance in the Sun* by Dan Jacobson. October 11, 1968 (American premiere). Director, John Marley; scenery and lighting, Paul Rodgers; costumes, Carol Margolis. With Vaughn McBride, Jane Gibbons, Allen Leatherman.

THE JEALOUS HUSBAND and THE DOCTOR IN SPITE OF HIMSELF (26). By Molière; adapted by the Play House Theater Lab ensemble. November 8, 1968 (world premiere). Director, William Greene; scenery, Paul Rodgers; costumes, Myrna Kaye. With Jonathan Bolt, Richard Halverson, Myrna Kaye, Bob Moak, Ross Morgan.

AH, WILDERNESS! (26). By Eugene

O'Neill. December 13, 1968. Director, Robert Snook; scenery, Paul Rodgers; costumes, Carol Margolis. With Robert Snook, Richard Quinn, Richard Oberlin, Edith Owen.

THIEVES' CARNIVAL (32). By Jean Anouilh; English version by Lucienne Hill. January 17, 1969. Director, Mario Siletti; scenery and lighting, Paul Rodgers; costumes, Carol Margolis. With Richard Oberlin, David Frazier, Gregory Abels, Robert Allman, Edith Owen.

THE PLAY'S THE THING (32). By Ferenc Molnar; adapted by P. G. Wodehouse. February 28, 1969. Director, Mario Siletti; scenery and lighting, Paul Rodgers. With Robert Snook, Nancy Barrett, William Greene.

THE MALE ANIMAL (28). By James Thurber and Elliott Nugent. April 11, 1969. Director, William Greene; scenery and lighting, Marla Nedelman; costumes, Carol Margolis. With Dorothy Quinn, Richard Oberlin, Robert Allman.

Cleveland Play House: Drury Theater

SUMMERTREE (26). By Ron Cowen. October 18, 1968. Director, Mario Siletti; scenery and lighting, Maria Nedelman. With Greg-

ory Abels, Vivienne Stotter, Richard Oberlin, Janet Kapral.

THE BIRTHDAY PARTY (20). By Harold Pinter. November 22, 1968. Director, Richard Oberlin; scenery and lighting, Paul Rodgers. With Nick Devlin, June Gibbons, Mario Siletti, Gregory Abels.

A FLEA IN HER EAR (32). By Georges Feydeau; translated by John Mortimer. December 20, 1968. Director, William Greene; scenery, Paul Rodgers; costumes, Carol Margolis. With Myrna Kaye, Bob Moak, Richard Halverson, Nancy Barrett.

AFTER THE RAIN (26). By John Bowen. January 31, 1969. Director, William Greene; scenery and lighting, Maria Nedelman; costumes, Carol Margolis. With Bob Moak, Ross Morgan, Margaret Christopher, Jean Morris.

MONEY (28). Book and lyrics by David Axelrod and Tom Whedon; music by Sam Pottle; additional material by Dorothy Paxton. March 2, 1969. Director, Richard Oberlin; musical director, Donna Renton; scenery and lighting, Paul Rodgers; costumes, Carol Margolis. With Richard Halverson, Marcia Ross, David Frazier, Bob Moak.

IPHIGENIA IN AULIS (30). By Euripides. April 9, 1969. Director, Mario Siletti; scenery and lighting, Paul Rodgers; costumes, Carol Margolis. With Mario Siletti, Janet Kapral, Evie McElroy, Larry Tarrant.

Cleveland Play House: Brooks Theater

MRS. LINCOLN (14). By Thomas Cullinan. November 1, 1968 (world premiere). Director, Robert Snook; costumes, Carol Margolis. With Evie McElroy, Donald Chodos, Keith Mackey, Nancy Barrett.

THE UNITED STATES VS. JULIUS AND

ETHEL ROSENBERG (52). By Donald Freed. March 14, 1969 (world premiere). Director, Larry Tarrant; scenery and lighting, Paul Rodgers; costumes, Charlotte Hare; filmed sequences, Gregory Abels. With Stuart Levin, Elizabeth Lowry, Nolan D. Bell, Vaughn McBride, Allen Leatherman.

DALLAS

Dallas Theater Center: Kalita Humphreys Theater

THE GIRL OF THE GOLDEN WEST (25). By David Belasco. June 11, 1968. Director, Ken Latimer; scenery, Pauline Diskey; lighting, Robyn Baker Flatt, Carleton Tanner; costumes, Kathleen Latimer. With Anna Paul Marsh-Neame, Matt Tracy, Preston Jones.

UNDER THE YUM-YUM TREE (23). By Lawrence Roman. July 18, 1968. Director, Preston Jones; scenery, Bob Baca; lighting, Bob Baca, Evangelos Voutsinas; costumes, Pat Baca. With Robyn Baker Flatt, John Figlmiller, Matt Tracy, Jane Milburn Tracy.

MACBETH (34). By William Shakespeare. October 24, 1968. Director, Paul Baker; scenery, Mary Sue Jones; lighting, Randy Moore; projections, John Figlmiller. With Ken Latimer, Randy Moore, Mona Pursley, Gene Leggett.

HIPPOLYTUS and IPHIGENIA IN AULIS by Euripides (6). November 5, 1968. Director, Dimitrios Rondiris. Performed by the Piraikon Theatron in a guest appearance of the Greek company.

H.M.S. PINAFORE (27). By W. S. Gilbert and Arthur Sullivan. December 10, 1968. Director, Glenn Allen Smith; musical director, Raymond Allen; scenery and costumes, Archie Andrus; lighting, Kathleen Latimer. With Linda Mann, Campbell Thomas, Steven Mackenroth, Louise Mosley.

JOURNEY TO JEFFERSON (12). By Robert L. Flynn, adapted from the novel As I Lay Dying by William Faulkner. January 18, 1969. Director, Paul Baker; scenery, Virgil Beavers; lighting, Robyn Baker Flatt, Randy Moore; costumes, Mary Sue Jones. With James Nelson Harrell, Mary Sue Jones, Drexel H. Riley, Ken Latimer.

THE TAMING OF THE SHREW (24). By William Shakespeare. February 6, 1969. Director, Mike Dendy; scenery and costumes, Fernando Colina; lighting, Frank Schaefer. With Randy Moore, Synthia Rogers, John Figlmiller, Steven Mackenroth.

RAGS TO RICHES (11). By Aurand Harris, based on two stories of Horatio Alger. March 12, 1969. Director, Frank Schaefer; musical director, Raymond Allen; lyrics, Aurand Harris and Eva Franklin; music, Eva Franklin; choreography, Honey Hobson; scenery and costumes, Kathleen Latimer; lighting, Robyn Baker Flatt. With Alex Burton, Richard Cohen, Stephanie Rich.

THE STAR-SPANGLED GIRL (27). By Neil Simon. April 1, 1969. Director, Anna Paul Marsh-Neame; scenery, Archie Andrus;

lighting, Paul John Smith. With Christopher Hendrie, Steven Mackenroth, Deanna Dunagan.

A GOWN FOR HIS MISTRESS (25). By Georges Feydeau; translated by Barnett Shaw.

Dallas Theater Center: Down Center Stage

CRIME ON GOAT ISLAND (20). By Ugo Betti; translated by Henry Reed. July 9, 1968. Director, John Logan; scenery, Jere Broussard; lighting, Rene Assa; costumes, Gene Leggett. With Lynn Trammell, Ken Latimer, Kathleen Latimer, Claudette Gardner.

THE KILLING OF SISTER GEORGE (28). By Frank Marcus. September 28, 1968. Director, Frank Schaefer; scenery, Jere Broussard; lighting, Frank Schaefer. With Ella-Mae Brainard, Patricia Pearcy, Reta La Force, Jacque Thomas.

WAR by Jean-Claude van Itallie and MUZEEKA by John Guare (13). December 19, 1968. Director-designer, Fernando Colina;

May 13, 1969 (American premiere). Director, Preston Jones; scenery and costumes, David Pursley; lighting, Steven Mackenroth. With Robyn Baker Flatt, Preston Jones, Ken Latimer.

lighting, Arthur Jensen Rogers. With Don Davlin, Robyn Baker Flatt, Preston Jones, Gene Leggett, John Figlmiller, Jacque Thomas.

A TASTE OF HONEY (21). By Shelagh Delaney. January 23, 1969. Director, Rebecca Logan; scenery, Anne Butler; lighting, John Fish. With Roberta Rude, Jacque Thomas, John Shepherd.

SUMMERTREE (22). By Ron Cowen. March 20, 1969. Director, Irene Lewis; scenery, Charles Jarrell; lighting, Don Davlin; costumes, John Fish. With John Hancock, Ronald Wilcox, Claudette Gardner, Candy Couillard, Gene Wheeler.

HARTFORD, CONN.

The Hartford Stage Company

THE SEAGULL (44). By Anton Chekhov; translated by Eva Le Gallienne. October 11, 1968. Director, Paul Weidner; scenery, Wolfgang Roth; lighting, Peter Hunt; costumes, Caley Summers. With Anne Meacham, Henry Thomas, Louise Shaffer, Anthony Heald.

THE ROSE TATTOO (44). By Tennessee Williams. November 22, 1968. Director, Arthur Storch; scenery, Santo Loquasto; lighting, William Mintzer; costumes, Kate Vachon. With Vera Lockwood, John Seitz, Tana Hicken.

THE WALTZ INVENTION (44). By Vladimir Nabokov. January 3, 1969 (professional world premiere). Director, Paul Weidner; scenery, Santo Loquasto; lighting, Atlee Stephan; costumes, Kate Vachon. With Roland Hewgill, Henry Thomas, Ed Preble.

THE HOMECOMING (44). By Harold

Pinter. February 14, 1969. Director, Melvin Bernhardt; scenery, Santo Loquasto; lighting, Atlee Stephan; costumes, Kate Vachon. With Jeremiah Sullivan, Alan Gifford, Charlotte Moore.

THE TRIAL (44). By Andre Gide and Jean-Louis Barrault, based on the novel by Franz Kafka; translated by Leon and Joseph Katz. March 28, 1969. Director, Paul Weidner; scenery and projections, Wolfgang Roth; lighting, Peter Hunt; costumes, A. Christina Giannini. With Henry Thomas, Louis Beachner, Katherine Helmond, Darthy Blair.

LIFE WITH FATHER (44). By Howard Lindsay and Russel Crouse. May 9, 1969. Director, Louis Beachner; scenery, Ray Perry; lighting, Atlee Stephan; costumes, A. Christina Giannini. With Katherine Helmond, Anthony Heald, Richard Kneeland.

Monday Night Workshops: *Next Time I'll Sing to You* by James Saunders, *Spoon River Anthology* by Edgar Lee Masters, *The Flying Fish* by Glen Graves, *An Evening With Ogden Nash* by Ogden Nash, *The Cocktail Party* by T. S. Eliot.

HOUSTON

Alley Theater: Large Stage

GALILEO (45). By Bertolt Brecht; translated by Charles Laughton. November 26, 1968. Director, Nina Vance; scenery and lighting, Grady Larkins; costumes, Paul Owen;

music, Hanns Eisler. With Tony van Bridge, Joseph Ruskin, John Wylie, Jeannette Clift, Michael Scanlon.

SAINT JOAN (38). By George Bernard Shaw. January 9, 1969. Director, Michael Meacham; scenery, lighting, costumes, Paul Owen. With Alexandra Berlin, Trent Jenkins, William Hardy, Carl Bensen, Dale Helward.

DON JUAN IN HELL (3). By George Bernard Shaw. February 27, 1969. Director, Joseph Ruskin. With Jeannette Clift, Joseph Ruskin, Jay Sheffield, John Wylie.

WAR AND PEACE (38). By Erwin Piscator; adapted from the novel by Leo Tolstoy; English adaptation by Robert David MacDonald. April 3, 1969. Director, Robert David MacDonald; scenery and costumes, Paul Owen; lighting, Richard D. Cortright. With Joseph Ruskin, Dale Helward, Nancy Evans Leonard, Ted D'Arms.

LIGHT UP THE SKY (38). By Moss Hart. May 8, 1969. Director, Sherman Marks; scenery, Joe Lunday; lighting and costumes, Paul Owen. With Jeannette Clift, Joseph Ruskin, John Wylie, Dale Helward.

Note: The Alley Theater's 1968-69 season will conclude with *All the Way Home* by Tad Mosel, June 12, 1969.

Alley Theater: Arena Stage

BILLY LIAR (54). By Keith Waterhouse and Willis Hall. February 13, 1969. Director, Beth Sanford; scenery, Dan Bolen; lighting, Paul Owen; costumes, Charles Batte. With Dale Helward, Virginia Payne, I. M. Hobson, Lillian Evans.

CHARLIE and OUT AT SEA (54). By Slawomir Mrozek; translated by Nicholas Bethell. April 17, 1969. Director, Louis Criss; scenery and lighting, Paul Owen. With Sidney Armus, Clarence Felder, Milton Selzer.

KANSAS CITY, MO.

Missouri Repertory Theater

OEDIPUS REX (17). By Sophocles. July 2, 1968. Director, Alexis Minotis; scenery, J. Morton Walker; lighting, Suellen Childs; costumes, Vincent Scassellati. With Alvah Stanley, Curt Williams, Patricia Trescott Ripley, Cathy Clark, Robin League.

THE MISER (15). By Molière; adapted by Miles Malleson. July 11, 1968. Director, J. Morton Walker; lighting, Suellen Childs; costumes, Vincent Scassellati, Richard Hieronymus. With Curt Williams, Cherie Shuck, Richard Calvin, Richard Halverson, Peter Bartlett.

AEGINA (15). By James Costin. July 18, 1968 (world premiere). Director, Alvah Stanley; scenery, Frederic James; lighting, Suellen Childs; costumes, Vincent Scassellati. With Patricia Trescott Ripley, Peter Bartlett, Cherie Shuck, Irwin Atkins, Robert Elliott, Catherine Wolf, Holly Villaire, Richard Halverson.

PHILADELPHIA, HERE I COME! (15). By Brian Friel. July 25, 1968. Director, Patricia McIlrath; scenery, Jim Blackwood; lighting, Suellen Childs; costumes, Vincent Scassellati. With Sylvia Spencer, Curt Williams, Richard Halverson, Irwin Atkins.

LAFAYETTE, IND.

Purdue University Professional Theater Program

THE SCHOOL FOR WIVES (14). By Molière; translated by Miles Malleson. June 19, 1968. Director, Joseph Stockdale; scenery and costumes, Jerry Williams; lighting, Randy Earle. With John Newton, Andrew Jarkowsky, Stuart Howard, Janet Hayes.

BUS STOP (14). By William Inge. July 3, 1968. Director, Stuart Howard; scenery and costumes, Jerry Williams; lighting, Randy Earle. With Marie Louise, Peter Simon, Connie Heaver, Reid Shelton.

THE HOMECOMING (14). By Harold Pinter. July 17, 1968. Director, Joseph Stockdale; scenery and costumes, Jerry Williams; lighting, Randy Earle. With Reid Shelton, Stuart Howard, John LeGrand, Peter Simon, John Newton, Janet Hayes.

NIGHT MUST FALL (13). By Emlyn Williams. July 31, 1968. Director, Joseph Stockdale; scenery and costumes, Jerry Williams; lighting, Randy Earle. With Dorothy Harlan, Reid Shelton, Peter Simon.

BORN YESTERDAY (24). By Garson Kanin. September 17, 1968. Director, Joseph Stockdale; scenery, Jerry Williams; lighting, Randy Earle; costumes, Lyn Carroll. With Lee Kirk, John Carces, Thomas Connolly.

ALL MY SONS (23). By Arthur Miller. October 9, 1968. Director, Joseph Stockdale; scenery, Jerry Williams; lighting, Randy Earle; costumes, Lyn Carroll. With Louis Girard, Thomas Connolly, Mary Hara, Connie Heaver.

YOU NEVER CAN TELL (24). Book by Joseph Stockdale, based on the play by George Bernard Shaw; music by Roz Aronson; lyrics by Stuart Howard. February 11, 1969 (world premiere). Director, Joseph Stockdale; musical direction and choreography, Wayne Lamb; scenery, Jerry Williams; lighting, Randy Earle; costumes, Lyn Carroll. With Candy Coles, Jay Stuart, Michael Stoddard, Mary Nettum, Connie Heaver.

THE LITTLE FOXES (23). By Lillian Hellman. March 5, 1969. Director, Joseph Stockdale; scenery and costumes, Jerry Williams; lighting, Randy Earle. With Connie Heaver, Angelo Mango, Robert Donley, David C. Jones, Louis Girard.

LAKEWOOD, OHIO

Great Lakes Shakespeare Festival

THE TEMPEST (19). By William Shakespeare. July 5, 1968. Director, Lawrence Carra; scenery, Milton Howarth; lighting, David Jager; costumes, Tom Rasmussen; music, Arthur Sullivan; choreography, Marguerite Duncan. With Tom Gorman, Norma Joseph, Jeremiah Sullivan, Josef Warlik.

ARMS AND THE MAN (17). By George Bernard Shaw. July 10, 1968. Director, Allen R. Belknap; scenery, Milton Howarth; lighting, David Jager; costumes, Tom Rasmussen. With Marian Clarke, Evan Williams, Marie Geist, Don Bishop, Richard Bowden.

HAMLET (20). By William Shakespeare. July 24, 1968. Director, Lawrence Carra; scenery, Milton Howarth; lighting, David Jager; costumes, Tom Rasmussen; music, David Amram. With Jeremiah Sullivan, Norma Joseph, Richard Fancy, Marie Geist, Tom Gorman, Evan Williams.

THE BEAUX' STRATAGEM (10). By George Farquhar. August 7, 1968. Director, Lawrence Carra; scenery, Milton Howarth; lighting, David Jager; costumes, Tom Rasmussen. With Keith Mackey, Norma Joseph, Eve Collyer, Kermit Brown, Marie Geist.

CYMBELINE (7). By William Shakespeare. August 21, 1968. Director, Lawrence Carra; scenery, Milton Howarth; lighting, David Jager; costumes, Tom Rasmussen. With Charles Smith, Eve Collyer, Marian Clarke, Josef Warlik, Tom Gorman.

LOS ANGELES

Center Theater Group of the Mark Taper Forum

CAMINO REAL (61). By Tennessee Williams. August 21, 1968. Director, Milton Katselas; scenery and lighting, Peter Wexler; costumes, Peter J. Hall. With Frank Schofield, John Baragrey, Earl Holliman, Nancy Wickwire, Clifford David, Karen Black.

THE GOLDEN FLEECE by A. R. Gurney Jr. (world premiere) and MUZEEKA by John Guare (61). October 11, 1968. Directors, Jered Barclay, Edward Parone. With Helen Westcott, Tim O'Connor; Philip Proctor, Gwynne Clifford, Barrie Chase.

THE HOUSE OF ATREUS by John Lewin; adapted from the *Oresteia* of Aeschylus. Director, Tyrone Guthrie; designer, Tanya Moiseiwitsch. And THE RESISTIBLE RISE OF ARTURO UI by Bertolt Brecht; translated by George Tabori (45). January 17, 1969. Director, Edward Payson Call; scenery and costumes, Richard L. Hay. Performed in two-play repertory by the Minnesota Theater Company in a guest appearance.

THE ADVENTURES OF THE BLACK GIRL IN HER SEARCH FOR GOD (54). By George Bernard Shaw; adapted by Christopher Isherwood. March 20, 1969 (world premiere). Director, Lamont Johnson; scenery, costumes and masks, Jeremy Railton; lighting, Gilbert V. Hemsley Jr. With Susan Batson, Douglas Campbell, Ed Flanders, Arthur Malet, J. Walter Smith, Olive Dunbar.

Note: Center Theater Group's 1969 season at the Mark Taper Forum also will include the American premiere of Feydeau's *Chemin de Fer* June 5, 1969, directed by Stephen Porter, and Chekhov's *Uncle Vanya* August 20, 1969, directed by Harold Clurman.

New Theater for Now Workshop of the Mark Taper Forum

THE GOLDEN FLEECE by A. R. Gurney Jr. and PRIVATE PRIVATE by Douglas Wedel (2) June 3, 1968. Directors, Jered Barclay, Robert Calhoun; scenery, Raymond Jens Klausen; lighting, Ken Fryer; costumes, Jered Green. With Helen Westcott, Tim O'Connor, Edward Binns, Joseph Reale, John Ragin.

THE MOTHS (2). By Raffi Arzoomanian. June 17, 1968. Director, Edward Parone; scenery, Raymond Jens Klausen; lighting, Ken Fryer; costumes, Gymno. With Simon Oakland, Lesley Woods.

WITNESSES (2). By William Murray. July 1, 1968. Director, Stephen Strimpell; lighting, Ken Fryer. With Robert Guidi, Paul E. Winfield, Phyllis Raphael, Morris Erby.

NIAGARA FALLS (2). By Leonard Melfi. October 14, 1968. Director, James Bridges; scenery, Edward Flesh; lighting, Ken Fryer. With Kathleen Nolan, John Beck, Barbara Minkus, Al Alu.

MOVIE, MOVIE ON THE WALL by Sally Ordway, PICTURE by Oliver Hailey, CLICK by Stan Hart (2). October 28, 1968. Directors, Robert Calhoun, Morgan Sterne. With Gwynne Gilford, Joe Reale; John Rubinstein, John Garfield Jr., Robert Pratt, Howard Caine, Helen Page Camp, Al Checco, Herbert Voland.

WELCOME TO SERENITY FARMS (2). By Garry White. November 11, 1968. Director, Edward Parone; scenery, Ed Flesh; lighting, Ken Fryer; costumes, Pete Menefee. With Anthony Zerbe, Joan Van Ark, Ed Flanders, DeAnn Mears, Scott Thomas, Ben Hammer.

SISTER SADIE AND THE SONS OF SAM (2). By Clifford Mason. November 25, 1968. Director, Ben Shaktman; scenery, Ed Flesh; lighting, Ken Fryer; costumes, Jered Green. With Virginia Capers, Cal Wilson, Clyde Houston.

TILT (FORMERLY UNTILTED) (6). By Joel Schwartz. May 13, 1969. Director, Robert Calhoun; scenery, Jeremy Railton; lighting, Ken Fryer; costumes, Al Lehmann. With Glynn Turnman, Alan Bergmann, Philip Proctor, Karen Black.

SLIVOVITZ by Joel Schwartz and A^3 by James Bridges (6). May 15, 1969. Director, Edward Parone; scenery, Jeremy Railton; lighting, Ken Fryer; costumes, Al Lehmann. With Pippa Scott, Paul Carr, Marge Champion, John Beck, Hal England, T. J. Escott.

LOUISVILLE, KY.

Actors Theater of Louisville

THE MEMBER OF THE WEDDING (20). By Carson McCullers. November 14, 1968. Director, Tom Gruenewald; scenery, Brooke Karzen; lighting, Richard Mix; costumes, James Larsen. With Beatrice Winde, Jane Buchanan, Timothy Jansing, Mitzi Friedlander.

THE BIRTHDAY PARTY (20). By Harold Pinter. December 5, 1968. Director, Richard Block; scenery, Brooke Karzen; lighting, Tom Hanson; costumes, James Larsen. With Fred Morsell, Dale Carter Cooper, Gardner Hays, David Zirlin.

THE CRESTA RUN (20). By N. F. Simpson. December 26, 1968 (American premiere). Director, Pirie MacDonald; scenery, Brooke Karzen; lighting, Richard Dunham; costumes, James Larsen. With Kathryn Grody, Robert Milton, Dale Carter Cooper, Gardner Hays.

AFTER THE FALL (20). By Arthur Miller. January 16, 1969. Director, Richard Block; scenery, Brooke Karzen; lighting, Tom Hanson; costumes, James Larsen. With Aida Berlyn, Frank Savine, Jane Welch, Rand Bridges.

RHINOCEROS (20). By Eugene Ionesco. February 6, 1969. Director, Jacques Cartier; scenery, Brooke Karzen; lighting, Richard Dunham; costumes, James Larsen. With J. S. Johnson, Mitzi Friedlander, Fred Morsell, Marguerite Davis.

UNCLE VANYA (20). By Anton Chekhov. February 27, 1969. Director, Richard Block; scenery, Joe Pacitti; lighting, Tom Hanson; costumes, James Larsen. With Rand Bridges, David Zirlin, Kathryn Grody, Robert Milton.

SUMMER AND SMOKE (20). By Tennessee Williams. March 20, 1969. Director, Louis Criss; scenery, David Gano; lighting, Richard Dunham; costumes, James Larsen. With Jane Welch, Kathryn Grody, Fred Morsell, Dale Carter Cooper.

THE IMAGINARY INVALID (23). By Molière; adapted by Miles Malleson. April 10, 1969. Director, Richard Block; scenery, David Gano; lighting, Richard Dunham; costumes, James Larsen. With J. S. Johnson, Reedy Gibbs, Robert Brink, Harriet Dean Richards, Robert Milton.

MILWAUKEE

Milwaukee Repertory Theater Company: Robert E. Gard Theater

MARY STUART (15). By Friedrich von Schiller; translated by Sophie Wilkins. Director, Eugene Lesser; scenery, William James Wall; lighting, William Mintzer; costumes, Cara Z. Shubin. With Penelope Reed, Marc Alaimo, William McKereghan, Erika Slezak, Charles Kimbrough.

AMPHITRYON 38 (14). By Jean Giraudoux; adapted by S. N. Behrman. Director, Tunc Yalman; scenery and costumes, William James Wall; lighting, William Mintzer. With Charles Kimbrough, Jeff Chandler, Frank Borgman, Michael Fairman, Erika Slezak, Rhoda B. Carrol.

A STREETCAR NAMED DESIRE (14). By Tennessee Williams. Director, Eugene Lesser; scenery and costumes, William James Wall; lighting, William Mintzer. With Penelope Reed, Michael Fairman, Rhoda B. Carrol, Charles Kimbrough.

Note: The above plays were presented in repertory June 12, 1968 through July 28, 1968.

Milwaukee Repertory Theater Company: Milwaukee Repertory Theater

THE SKIN OF OUR TEETH (36). By Thornton Wilder. October 11, 1968. Director, Tunc Yalman; scenery and costumes, William James Wall; lighting, William Mintzer. With Erika Slezak, Penelope Reed, Michael Fairman.

DULCY (36). By George S. Kaufman and Marc Connelly. November 15, 1968. Director, Tunc Yalman; scenery and costumes, William James Wall; lighting, William Mintzer. With Erika Slezak, Michael Fairman, E. Daniel Mooney.

THE IMAGINARY INVALID (36). By Molière; adapted by Miles Malleson. December 20, 1968. Director, Anthony Perkins; scenery and costumes, William James Wall; lighting, William Mintzer. With Charles Kimbrough, Penelope Reed, Mary Jane Kimbrough, William McKereghan, Michael Tucker.

THREE SISTERS (36). By Anton Chekhov; translated by Tyrone Guthrie and Leonid Kipnis. January 31, 1969. Director, Boris Tumarin; scenery, William James Wall; lighting, William Mintzer; costumes, Janet C. Warren. With Judy Mueller, Mary Jane Kimbrough, Erika Slezak, Michael Tucker, Michael Fairman.

MARAT/SADE (36). By Peter Weiss; translated by Geoffrey Skelton, verse adaptation by Adrian Mitchell. March 7, 1969. Director, Eugene Lesser; scenery, Kenneth W. Mueller; lighting, William Mintzer; costumes, Janet C. Warren. With William McKereghan, Robert Jackson, Rhoda B. Carrol, Erika Slezak.

DANGEROUS CORNER (36). By J. B. Priestley. April 25, 1969. Director, Tunc Yalman; scenery and costumes, William James Wall; lighting, William Mintzer. With Diana Kirkwood, Mary Jane Kimbrough, William Lafe, R. Daniel Mooney.

Milwaukee Repertory Theater Company: Theater for Tomorrow

THAT'S THE GAME, JACK (12). By Douglas Taylor. April 11, 1969 (world premiere). Director, Wayne Grice; scenery, William James Wall; lighting, William Mintzer; costumes, Deborah M. Mitchell. With Hazel Bryant, Michael Fairman, D'Urville Martin, Gerald McKinney, Carl Thoma.

NEW HAVEN, CONN.

Long Wharf Theater

THE LION IN WINTER (25). By James Goldman. October 18, 1968. Director, Arvin Brown; scenery and costumes, Will Steven Armstrong; lighting, Ronald Wallace. With Ralph Waite, Joyce Ebert.

THE PLAY'S THE THING (25). By Ferenc Molnar; adapted by P. G. Wodehouse. November 15, 1968. Director, Meredith Dallas; scenery, Will Steven Armstrong; lighting, Ronald Wallace, costumes, Alec Sutherland. With William Swetland, Ellen Tovatt, John Braden, Tom Atkins.

EPITAPH FOR GEORGE DILLON (25). By John Osborne and Anthony Creighton. December 13, 1968. Director, Maurice Breslow; scenery, Vanessa James, lighting, Ronald Wallace; costumes, Margaret Mahoney. With Ken Jenkins, Laurie Kennedy, Joyce Ebert, James Valentine.

AMERICA HURRAH (25). By Jean-Claude van Itallie. January 10, 1969. Director, Michael Youngfellow; scenery, Will Steven Armstrong; lighting, Ronald Wallace; costumes, Alec Sutherland. With Tom Atkins, Joyce Ebert, Ken Jenkins, Laurie Kennedy, Stephen

Kyprianides, Ruth Maynard, Chris Sarandon, William Swetland, Ellen Tovatt.

THE INDIAN WANTS THE BRONX and IT'S CALLED THE SUGAR PLUM (25). By Israel Horovitz. March 7, 1969. Director, Arvin Brown; scenery and lighting, Elmon Webb and Virginia Daney; costumes, Alec Sutherland. With Henry Bal, Harvey Keitel, Chris Sarandon, Ellen Tovatt.

UNDER MILK WOOD (25). By Dylan Thomas. April 4, 1969. Director, Jon Jory; scenery and lighting, Ronald Wallace; costumes, Alec Sutherland. With members of the company and Jerome Raphel, Eric Tavares, Jean Weigel.

GHOSTS (25). By Henrik Ibsen; translated by Peter Watts. May 2, 1969. Director, Arvin Brown; scenery, Will Steven Armstrong; lighting, Ronald Wallace; costumes, Alec Sutherland. With Mildred Dunnock, William Hansen, Joyce Ebert.

NEW ORLEANS

Repertory Theater of New Orleans

ARMS AND THE MAN (15). By George Bernard Shaw. November 22, 1968. Director, Stuart Vaughan; scenery, Lloyd Burlingame; lighting, Fred Allison; costumes, Matthew Ryan. With Anne Thompson, Donald Perkins, Richard Lupino, Nina Polan, Barbara McMahon.

TWELFTH NIGHT (15). By William Shakespeare. January 10, 1969. Director, Stuart Vaughan; scenery, Lloyd Burlingame; lighting, Fred Allison; costumes, Matthew Ryan. With Jenneth Webster, Richard Lupino, Nina Polan, Robert Benson, Donald Perkins.

AN ENEMY OF THE PEOPLE (15). By Henrik Ibsen; new English version by David Scanlan. February 28, 1969 (world premiere). Director, David Scanlan; scenery, Lloyd Bur-

lingame; lighting, Fred Allison; costumes, Matthew Ryan. With Stuart Vaughan, Herbert Nelson, Jenneth Webster.

THE BALD SOPRANO and THE CHAIRS (15). By Eugene Ionesco. April 11, 1969. Directors, Stuart Vaughan, David Scanlan; scenery, Lloyd Burlingame; lighting, Fred Allison; costumes, Matthew Ryan. With Anne Thompson, Robert Benson, Barbara McMahon, Nina Polan, Don Perkins, Jane Rose, Dillon Evans.

PRIVATE LIVES (17). By Noel Coward. May 19, 1969. Director, Dillon Evans; scenery, Lloyd Burlingame; lighting, Fred Allison; costumes, Matthew Ryan. With Stuart Vaughan, Barbara McMahon, Robert Benson, Anne Thompson.

OKLAHOMA CITY

Mummers Theater

HEDDA GABLER by Henrik Ibsen. Director, Andrew Way; scenery and lighting, Robert Steinberg; costumes, Jean E. McFaddin. With Anne Ault, Grant Sheehan, Jeri Walker, Raymond Allen.

BIG FISH, LITTLE FISH by Hugh Wheeler. Director, Jean E. McFaddin; scenery and lighting, Robert Steinberg; costumes, Jeri

Walker. With Raymond Allen, Grant Sheehan, Anne Ault, Tom Kroutil.

THE SEAGULL by Anton Chekhov; translated by Anya Lachman and Mack Scism. Director, Mack Scism; scenery and lighting, Robert Steinberg; costumes, Jean E. McFaddin. With Kate Webster, Laurie Hutchinson, Carter Mullaly Jr.

OUR TOWN by Thornton Wilder. Director, Andrew Way; scenery and lighting, Robert Steinberg and Gary Stevens; costumes, Jean E. McFaddin, Jeri Walker. With Grant Sheehan, John Milligan, Alice Elliott.

STATE OF THE UNION by Howard Lindsay and Russel Crouse; new adaptation by Jeannette Edmondson. Director, Mack Scism; scenery and lighting, Robert Steinberg; costumes, Jean E. McFaddin. With Grant Sheehan, Kate Webster.

MISALLIANCE by George Bernard Shaw. Director, Jean E. McFaddin; scenery and lighting, Robert Steinberg; costumes, Jean E. McFaddin, Helene Wilkinson. With Tom Kroutil, Sean Griffin, Anne Ault, Raymond Allen.

A THOUSAND CLOWNS by Herb Gardner. Director, Jean E. McFaddin; scenery and lighting, Robert Steinberg; costumes, Helene Wilkinson. With Grant Sheehan, Mark Shanker, Pamela Muench.

PHILADELPHIA

Theater of the Living Arts: Guest Productions

THE TALE OF KASANE by Tsuruya Namboku; TYGER! TYGER! AND OTHER BURNINGS (poems) adapted by Eric Malzkuhn; THE CRITIC by Richard Brinsley Sheridan; THE LOVE OF DON PERLIMPIN and BELISA IN THE GARDEN by Federico Garcia Lorca; BLUEPRINTS (poems) adapted by Bernard Bragg and Lou Fant; GIANNI SCHICCHI, adapted by Robert F. Panara and Eric Malzkuhn (8), October 1, 1968. Presented by National Theater of the Deaf Company. THE CONCEPT (16), October 8, 1968, Daytop Theater Company. JACQUES BREL IS ALIVE AND WELL AND LIVING IN PARIS (24), October 29, 1968. THE HAPPINESS BENCH by Thomas Bellin (16), November 19, 1968 (world premiere). AMERICA HURRAH by Jean-Claude van Itallie (24), December 3, 1968. WALK TOGETHER CHILDREN by Vinie Burrows (21), May 21, 1969.

Theater of the Living Arts: Resident Company

SIX CHARACTERS IN SEARCH OF AN AUTHOR (30). By Luigi Pirandello; English version by Eric Bentley. January 2, 1969. Director and designer, James D. Waring. With Gloria Maddox, William Countryman, Vivienne Shub, Benjamin Slack.

LITTLE MURDERS (28). By Jules Feiffer. January 30, 1969. Director, Gene Lasko; scenery and costumes, Fred Voelpel; lighting, Don Earl. With Susan Barrister, Brendan Hanlon, Jeremiah Morris, Kate Wilkinson.

THE COLLECTION by Harold Pinter, directed by Dennis Rosa, and MUZEEKA by John Guare, directed by Ronald Roston (28). February 27, 1969. Scenery and costumes,

Holly Haas; lighting, Don Earl. With Marilyn Coleman, Brendan Hanlon, Gloria Maddox, Michael Procaccino, Ronald Roston.

LA TURISTA (28). By Sam Shepard. March 27, 1969. Director, Tom Bissinger; scenery and costumes, Holly Haas; lighting, Don Earl. With Lee Kissman, Gloria Maddox, Michael Procaccino, Benjamin Slack.

THE HOSTAGE (28). By Brendan Behan. April 24, 1969. Director, Gennaro Montanino; scenery and costumes, Holly Haas; lighting, John Bos. With Dermot McNamara, Paddy Croft, James Glenn, Janice Mars, Bruce Heighley.

PRINCETON, N.J.

McCarter Theater

THE VILLAGE: A PARTY (7). By Charles H. Fuller. October 18, 1968 (world premiere). Director, Arthur W. Lithgow; scenery, Robert Edmonds; lighting, Clyde Blakeley; costumes, Charles Blackburn. With Anne Murray, Ed Bernard, Susan Koslow, Rudy Adams, Will Hicks.

THE GLASS MENAGERIE (8). By Tennessee Williams. October 25, 1968. Director, Gordon Phillips; scenery, Robert Edmonds; light-

ing, Marshall Williams; costumes, Charles Blackburn. With Donegan Smith, Eve Johnson, Holly Villaire, Martin Oliver.

AS YOU LIKE IT (8). By William Shakespeare. November 15, 1968. Director, John Lithgow; scenery, John Lithgow; lighting, Clyde Blakeley; costumes, Charles Blackburn. With Kathryn Walker, Holly Villaire, Tom Tarpey, Brendan Burke, Robert Blackburn, Susan Koslow.

CHARLEY'S AUNT (8). By Brandon Thomas. December 27, 1968. Director, Robert Blackburn; scenery, Robert Edmonds; lighting, Clyde Blakeley; costumes, Charles Blackburn. With Brendan Burke, Tom Tarpey, Donegan Smith, Susan Koslow.

KRAPP'S LAST TAPE by Samuel Beckett. With Frederic O'Brady. OEDIPUS THE KING by Sophocles; adapted by W. B. Yeats (8). January 24, 1969. Directors, Arthur W. Lithgow and Gordon Phillips; scenery, Robert Edmonds; lighting, Clyde Blakeley; costumes, Charles Blackburn. With Ed Bernard, Eve Johnson, Donegan Smith, Robert Blackburn.

THREE SISTERS (8). By Anton Chekhov. January 31, 1969. Director, Tom Brennan;

lighting, Clyde Blakeley; costumes, Charles Blackburn. With Kathryn Walker, Susan Koslow, Beth Dixon, Robert Blackburn, Richard Mathews.

THE SCARECROW (7). By Percy MacKaye. February 21, 1969. Director, Robert Blackburn; scenery, Robert Edmonds; lighting, Clyde Blakeley; costumes, Charles Blackburn. With Kathryn Walker, Donegan Smith, Richard Mathews, Max Gulack.

THE PLOUGH AND THE STARS (7). By Sean O'Casey. March 21, 1969. Director, Brendan Burke; scenery, Robert Edmonds; lighting, Clyde Blakeley; costumes, Charles Blackburn. With Brendan Burke, Richard Mathews, Holly Villaire, Beth Dixon.

PROVIDENCE, R.I.

The Trinity Square Repertory Company

RED ROSES FOR ME (51). By Sean O'Casey. October 6, 1968. Director, Adrian Hall; scenery, Robert D. Soule; lighting, Roger Morgan; costumes, John Lehmeyer. With Nancy Acly, Martyn Green, Marguerite Lenert, Terry Lomax.

BROTHER TO DRAGONS (28). By Robert Penn Warren. November 21, 1968. Director, Adrian Hall; scenery, Eugene Lee; lighting, Roger Morgan; costumes, John Lehmeyer. With William Cain, Ronald Frazier, Ed Hall, Richard Kneeland, Barbara Meek.

MACBETH (51). By William Shakespeare. January 2, 1969. Director, Adrian Hall; scenery, Eugene Lee; lighting, Roger Morgan; costumes, James Lehmeyer. With William Cain, James Gallery, Katherine Helmond, Richard Kneeland.

THE HOMECOMING (28). By Harold

Pinter. February 13, 1969. Director, Pirie MacDonald; scenery, Eugene Lee; lighting, Roger Morgan; costumes, John Lehmeyer. With Clinton Anderson, William Cain, Paul Collins, James Gallery, Katherine Helmond, Patrick Hines.

BILLY BUDD (51). By Herman Melville; adapted from the novel by the Trinity Square Repertory Company. March 3, 1969 (world premiere). Director, Adrian Hall; scenery, Eugene Lee; lighting, Roger Morgan; costumes, John Lehmeyer. With Clinton Anderson, James Gallery, Martin Molson, Brad Sullivan, Timothy Taylor.

EXILES (28). By James Joyce. April 24, 1969. Director, Adrian Hall; scenery, Eugene Lee; lighting, Roger Morgan; costumes, John Lehmeyer. With Nancy Acly, James Broderick, William Cain, Elizabeth Eis, Marguerite Lenert.

ROCHESTER, MICH.

John Fernald Company

THE APPLE CART (28). By George Bernard Shaw. October 24, 1968. Director, Richard Curnock; scenery, Frank Masi; lighting, Pat Simmons; costumes, Elizabeth Penn. Eric Berry, Elisabeth Orion, Mary Savidge, Douglas Seale, Joseph Shaw.

THE MAGISTRATE (28). By Sir Arthur Wing Pinero. November 28, 1968. Director, Douglas Seale; scenery, Chris Tree; costumes, Elizabeth Penn; lighting, Pat Simmons. With

Eric Berry, Max Howard, J. Michael Bloom, Ronald Chudley, Mary Savidge, Virginia North, Bonnie Hurren.

THE SECOND COMING OF BERT (28). By Ronald Chudley. January 2, 1969 (world premiere). Director, John Fernald; scenery, Anna Gisle; lighting, Pat Simmons; costumes, Elizabeth Penn. With Ronald Chudley, Marshall Borden, Richard Curnock, Diane Stapley.

LONG DAY'S JOURNEY INTO NIGHT (28). By Eugene O'Neill. February 6, 1969. Director, Johan Fillinger; scenery, Anna Gisle; lighting, Pat Simmons; costumes, Elizabeth Penn. With Eric Berry, Jenny Laird, Jeremy Rowe, Victor Holchak.

TROILUS AND CRESSIDA (28). By William Shakespeare. April 17, 1969. Director, John Fernald; scenery, Anna Gisle; lighting, Pat Simmons; costumes, Ross Young. With

Eric Berry, Jeremy Rowe, Ronald Chudley, Bonnie Hurren.

AMPHITRYON 38 (28). By Jean Giraudoux, adapted by S. N. Behrman. March 13, 1969. Director, Douglas Seale; scenery and costumes, Anna Gisle; lighting, Pat Simmons. With Marshall Borden, Jeremy Rowe, Mikel Lambert, Jenny Laird.

SAINT JOAN by George Bernard Shaw. May 22, 1969. (No further information available at press time.)

SAN FRANCISCO

American Conservatory Theater (ACT): Geary Theater

THE MISANTHROPE by Molière; translated by Richard Wilbur. In repertory, April 23-August 18, 1968. Director, David William; scenery, Stuart Wurtzel; lighting, John McLain; costumes, Patrizia von Brandenstein. With Barry MacGregor, John Schuck, Kitty Winn, Carol Mayo Jenkins; Mark Bramhall.

TARTUFFE by Molière; translated by Richard Wilbur. In repertory, May 10-August 18, 1968. Director, William Ball; scenery, Stuart Wurtzel; lighting, John McLain; costumes, Jane Greenwood. With Patrick Tovatt, Ann Weldon, Michael Learned, Robert Gerringer, Philip Kerr.

TWELFTH NIGHT by William Shakespeare. In repertory, May 22-August 18, 1968. Director, William Ball; scenery, Stuart Wurtzel; lighting, John McLain; costumes, Nagle Jackson. With John Schuck, Ellen Geer, William Paterson, Harry Frazier, Angela Paton, Ken Ruta.

A STREETCAR NAMED DESIRE by Tennessee Williams. In repertory, June 9-August 18, 1968. Director, Robert Goldsby; scenery, Stuart Wurtzel; lighting, John McLain; costumes, Walter Watson. With DeAnn Mears, Ray Reinhardt, Dana Larson, John Schuck.

LONG DAY'S JOURNEY INTO NIGHT by Eugene O'Neill. In repertory, July 5-August 4, 1968. Director, Robert Goldsby; scenery, Stuart Wurtzel and Paul Staheli; lighting, John McLain; costumes, Walter Watson. With William Paterson, Josephine Nichols, John Schuck, David Dukes, Kitty Winn.

TINY ALICE by Edward Albee. In repertory, July 12-August 2, 1968. Director, William Ball; scenery, Stuart Wurtzel; lighting, John McLain; costumes, Robert Joyce. With Harry Frazier, Ray Reinhardt, Paul Shenar, Scott Hylands, DeAnn Mears.

THE CRUCIBLE by Arthur Miller. In repertory, October 21-December 7, 1968. Directors, Allen Fletcher and William Ball; scenery, Stuart Wurtzel; lighting, John McLain; costumes, Lewis Brown. With Ramon Bieri, Angela Paton, Kitty Winn, Ken Ruta, Jay Doyle, Carol Mayo Jenkins.

HAMLET by William Shakespeare. In repertory, October 25-February 27, 1969. Director, William Ball; scenery, Stuart Wurtzel; lighting, John McLain; costumes, Robert Fletcher. With Ray Reinhardt, Paul Shenar, Angela Paton, Harry Frazier, Izetta Smith.

A FLEA IN HER EAR by Georges Feydeau, translated by Barnett Shaw. December 10, 1968 (in 1969 repertory). Director, Gower Champion; scenery, Stuart Wurtzel; lighting, John McLain; costumes, Lewis Brown. With Michael O'Sullivan, Ann Weldon, Carol Teitel, Robert Gerringer, Philip Kerr.

THE DEVIL'S DISCIPLE by George Bernard Shaw. In repertory, December 31, 1968-April 29, 1969. Director, Edward Hastings; scenery, Paul Staheli; lighting, John McClain; costumes, Patrizia von Brandenstein. With James Milton, William Paterson, Carol Mayo Jenkins, Paul Shenar, Jay Doyle.

THREE SISTERS by Anton Chekhov. February 19, 1969 (in 1969 repertory). Director, William Ball; scenery, Paul Staheli; lighting, John McLain; costumes, Ann Roth. With Angela Paton, Michael Learned, Kitty Winn, Paul Shenar, Ken Ruta.

ROSENCRANTZ AND GUILDENSTERN ARE DEAD by Tom Stoppard. April 22, 1969 (in 1969 repertory). Director, William Ball; scenery, Stuart Wurtzel; costumes, Robert Fletcher. With James Milton, Philip Kerr, Ken Ruta, Kenneth Julian, Paul Shenar.

GLORY! HALLELUJAH! by Anna Marie Barlow. May 21, 1969 (world premiere; in 1969 repertory). Director, Edward Sherin; scenery, Stuart Wurtzel; lighting, John Mc-Clain; costumes, Walter Watson. With Mark Bramhall, Philip Kerr, Kitty Winn, Michael Learned, David Dukes.

ACT: Marines' Memorial Theater

LONG LIVE LIFE by Jerome Kilty; adapted from the correspondence of Anton Chekhov as edited by M. Malyugin. In repertory, April 26-June 28, 1968 (world premiere). Director, Jerome Kilty; scenery, Paul Staheli; lighting, Michael Clivner; costumes, Lewis Brown. With Ken Ruta, Ellen Geer, George Ede, Ramon Bieri, DeAnn Mears.

CAUGHT IN THE ACT, a revue devised by Nagle Jackson. In repertory, May 15-August 18, 1968 (world premiere). Sketches and lyrics, Nagle Jackson; music, Jerry Cournoyer; director, Nagle Jackson; scenery, Stuart Wurtzel; lighting, John McLain. With Mark Bramhall, Ruth Kobart, Barry MacGregor, Deborah Sussel, Ann Weldon, Tony Williams.

UNDER MILK WOOD by Dylan Thomas. In repertory, May 26-August 18, 1968. Director, William Ball; scenery, Stuart Wurtzel; lighting, John McLain; costumes, Walter Watson. With Ray Reinhardt, Mark Bramhall, Peter Donat, Barry MacGregor, Ellen Geer, Barbara Colby, Izetta Smith, DeAnn Mears, David Dukes, Philip Kerr.

DEEDLE, DEEDLE DUMPLING, MY SON GOD by Brian McKinney. In repertory, June 16-29, 1968 (world premiere). Director, Patrick Tovatt; scenery and costumes, Paul Staheli; lighting, Michael Clivner. With David Dukes, Michael Learned, Peter Donat.

YOUR OWN THING by Hal Hester and Danny Apolinar; book by Donald Driver; adapted freely from *Twelfth Night*. In repertory, July 2-December 10, 1968. Director, Donald Driver; scenery, Robert Guerra; lighting, Tom Skelton; costumes, Albert Wolsky; musical director, Charles Gustafson. With Peter Jason, Renata Vaselle, Bonnie Franklin, Gerry Glasier, Nagle Jackson.

LITTLE MURDERS by Jules Feiffer. January 1, 1969 (in 1969 repertory). Director, Nagle Jackson; scenery, Stuart Wurtzel; lighting, Michael Clivner; costumes, Walter Watson. With Angela Paton, Mark Bramhall, G. Wood, Michael Learned, John Schuck.

STAIRCASE by Charles Dyer. In repertory, January 2-May 18, 1969. Director, Robert Goldsby; scenery, Paul Staheli; lighting, Michael Clivner; costumes, Patrizia von Brandenstein. With Peter Donat, Ramon Bieri.

IN WHITE AMERICA by Martin Duberman. January 25, 1969 (in 1969 repertory). Director, Nagle Jackson; scenery, Stuart Wurtzel; lighting, Michael Clivner; costumes, Walter Watson. With Christopher Payne, Jerry Franken, John Hancock, Eileen Ramsey, Jennifer MacNish, James Watson, Joel Rudnick.

A DELICATE BALANCE by Edward Albee. In repertory, January 29-February 6, 1969. Director, Edward Hastings; scenery, Paul Staheli; lighting, Michael Clivner; costumes, Walter Watson. With Josephine Nichols, Robert Gerringer, Michael Learned, Patricia Falkenhain.

THE PROMISE by Aleksei Arbuzov; translated by Edward Hastings and Dwight Stevens. February 26, 1969 (in 1969 repertory). Director, Edward Hastings; scenery, Paul Staheli; lighting, Michael Clivner; costumes, Patrizia von Brandenstein. With Dana Larson, David Dukes, Mark Bramhall.

THE ARCHITECT AND THE EMPEROR OF ASSYRIA by Fernando Arrabal; translated by Everard d'Harnoncourt and Adele Shank. March 26, 1969 (American premiere; in 1969 repertory). Director, Robert Goldsby; scenery, Paul Staheli; lighting, John McLain; costumes, Patrizia von Brandenstein. With Peter Donat, Michael O'Sullivan.

ROOM SERVICE by John Murray and Allen Boretz. May 28, 1969 (in 1969 repertory). Director, Nagle Jackson; scenery, Paul Staheli; lighting, Michael Clivner; costumes, Julie Staheli. With Paul Shenar, Ray Reinhardt, Deborah Sussel, James Milton, Izetta Smith.

Note: The time period of this listing, June 1, 1968-May 31, 1969 overlaps seasons of ACT repertory in the above entries. In neither case was a record of performance numbers available at press time.

SARASOTA, FLA.

Asolo Theater Festival

A MIDSUMMER NIGHT'S DREAM (25). By William Shakespeare. June 20, 1968. Director, Keith Fowler; scenery, Keith Fowler; lighting, Richard C. Evans; costumes, Joy Breckenridge. With Janet Bell, C. David Colson, Anthony Heald, Donald C. Hoepner, Margaret Kaler, M'ichael Reynolds, Isa Thomas, Albert L. Smelko.

ANTIGONE (27). By Jean Anouilh; adapted by Lewis Galantière. June 22, 1968. Director, Richard D. Meyer; scenery, Larry Riddle; lighting, Richard C. Evans; costumes, W. Harlan Shaw. With Marti Maraden, David Petersen, Robert Strane, Karen Zenker.

THE ALCHEMIST (25). By Fred Gaines; based on the play by Ben Jonson. June 28, 1968 (world premiere). Director, Eberle Thomas; scenery, Ray Perry; lighting, Richard C. Evans; costumes, Joy Breckenridge; music, Stephen W. Smith; lyrics; Fred Gaines. With Bradford Wallace, Robert Britton, Albert L. Smelko, Margaret Kaler, Keith Fowler.

THE VISIT (22). By Friedrich Duerrenmatt; adapted by Maurice Valency. July 5, 1968. Director, Robert Strane; scenery, Ray Perry; lighting, Richard C. Evans; costumes, Sylvia Hillyard, Dan Ater, Joy Breckenridge. With Isa Thomas, Macon McCalman, Albert L. Smelko.

WILDE! (10). By Fred Gaines. July 26, 1968 (world premiere). Director, Eberle Thomas; scenery, Ray Perry; lighting, Richard C. Evans; costumes, Sylvia Hillyard. With Albert L. Smelko, Margaret Kaler, Donald C. Hoepner, Janet Bell.

THE CARETAKER (9). By Harold Pinter. August 9, 1968. Director, Robert Strane; scenery, Ray Perry; lighting, Richard C. Evans. With Anthony Heald; David Petersen, Macon McCalman.

ARMS AND THE MAN (22). By George Bernard Shaw. February 21, 1969. Director, Eberle Thomas; scenery and costumes, Holmes Easley; lighting, John Gowans. With Sharon Spelman, Robert Britton, Bradford Wallace, Barbara Redmond.

THE MISANTHROPE (18). By Molière; translated by Eberle Thomas and Robert Strane. February 22, 1969. Director, Robert Strane; scenery and costumes, Holmes Easley; lighting, John Gowans. With C. David Colson, Macon McCalman, Bradford Wallace, Barbara Redmond.

OH WHAT A LOVELY WAR (20). Musical revue by Joan Littlewood and Ted Allan. February 28, 1969. Director, Robert Strane; music and dance staging, Jim Hoskins; musical director, Joyce Millman; scenery and costumes, Holmes Easley; lighting, John Gowans. With the Asolo Theater Company.

THE LION IN WINTER (19). By James Goldman; March 7, 1969. Director, Howard J. Millman; scenery, Holmes Easley; lighting, John Gowans; costumes, Joyce Millman. With Robert Strane, Isa Thomas, Sharon Spelman.

THE HOMECOMING (18). By Harold Pinter. March 14, 1969. Director, Jon Spelman; scenery, Holmes Easley; lighting, John Gowans; costumes, Cherrill Colson. With Macon McCalman, Eberle Thomas, Carlton Berry, William Perley, Bradford Wallace, Stephanie Moss.

TWO GENTS (16). By Eberle Thomas, adapted from Two Gentlemen of Verona by William Shakespeare. April 4, 1969 (world premiere). Director, Eberle Thomas; scenery and costumes, Holmes Easley; lighting, John Gowans; choreography, Jim Hoskins. With Robert Britton, C. David Colson, Macon McCalman, Stephanie Moss.

SEATTLE

Seattle Repertory Theater: Center Playhouse

OUR TOWN (30). By Thornton Wilder. October 23, 1968. Director, Allen Fletcher; scenery and costumes, Peter Wingate; lighting, John McLain. With Jacqueline Coslow, Kay Doubleday, Ken Parker, Archie Smith.

JUNO AND THE PAYCOCK (29). By Sean O'Casey. October 31, 1968. Director, Byron Ringland; scenery and costumes, Peter Wingate; lighting, John McLain. With Bernard

Frawley, Patrick Hines, Patrick Gorman, Marjorie Nelson.

A MIDSUMMER NIGHT'S DREAM (30). By William Shakespeare. December 4, 1968. Director, Allen Fletcher; scenery and costumes, Peter Wingate; lighting, Peter O'Rourke. With Beverly Atkinson, Jason Bernard, Jacqueline Coslow, Jeffery Craggs; Kay Doubleday, Patrick Hines.

LYSISTRATA (31). By Aristophanes; adapted by John Lewin. January 15, 1969. Director, William Francisco; scenery and costumes, William Roberts. With Eve Roberts, Maureen Quinn, Richard Kavanaugh, Ken Parker.

SERJEANT MUSGRAVE'S DANCE (29). By John Arden. February 5, 1969. Director, Allen Fletcher; scenery and costumes, Peter Wingate; lighting, John McLain. With Josef

Sommer, Jonathan Farwell, Theodore Sorel, Marjorie Nelson.

A VIEW FROM THE BRIDGE (30). By Arthur Miller. March 12, 1969. Director, Allen Fletcher; scenery and costumes, Peter Wingate; lighting, Steven A. Maze. With Laurie Brooks-Jefferson, Marjorie Nelson, Josef Sommer, Jonathan Farwell, Jeffery Craggs.

Seattle Repertory Theater: Off Center Theater

MOURNING BECOMES ELECTRA (9). By Eugene O'Neill. November 7, 1968. Director, Allen Fletcher; scenery and costumes, Peter Horne; lighting, John McLain. With Eve Roberts, Jacqueline Coslow, Theodore Sorel, Josef Sommer.

THREE CHEERS FOR WHAT'S-ITS-NAME! (11). Three one-act plays by Jon Swan. November 14, 1968 (world premiere). Director, Josef Sommer; scenery, Peter Horne; lighting, Mark S. Krause; costumes, Linda Martin. With Robert Loper, Maureen Quinn, Bernard Frawley, Jason Bernard, Stanley Anderson, John Odegard.

LOOK BACK IN ANGER (12). By John Osborne. December 12, 1968. Director, Archie Smith; scenery and lighting, Phil Schermer; costumes, Linda Martin. With Theodore Sorel, Laurie Brooks-Jefferson, Judith Long.

THE BLOOD KNOT (12). By Athol Fugard. January 23, 1969. Director, Robert Loper. With Stanley Anderson and Jason Bernard.

BIG NOSE MARY IS DEAD by Barry Pritchard and THE QUICKIES (11 one-act plays, previously produced as *Collision Course*) by Leonard Melfi, Lanford Wilson, Adrienne Kennedy, Rosalyn Drexler, Jack Larson, Jean-Claude van Itallie and Sharon Thie, Harvey Perr, Robert Patrick, Jules Feiffer, John Rechy, Sam Shepard (12). February 13, 1969. Director, Archie Smith; scenery, Peter Horne; lighting, Kent Bishop; costumes, Linda Martin. With members of the company.

THE BLACKS (12). By Jean Genet. March 20, 1969. Director, Jason Bernard; scenery and costumes, Peter Horne; lighting, Mark S. Krause. With Jason Bernard, Beverly Atkinson, Beatrice Winde, Daniel Putman.

SPRINGFIELD, MASS.

The Springfield Theater Company

BAREFOOT IN THE PARK (21). By Neil Simon. November 1, 1968. Director, Jon Jory; scenery, John Jacobson; lighting, Ronald Wallace; costumes, Margaret Mahoney. With Barrie Charles, Michael Youngfellow, Leslie Cass, Robert Baines.

THE GLASS MENAGERIE (21). By Tennessee Williams. November 29, 1968. Director, Michael Youngfellow; scenery, Richard Montfort Cary; lighting, Ronald Wallace; costumes, Margaret Mahoney. With Leslie Cass, Wayne Maxwell, Barrie Charles, Mike Henisse.

HAY FEVER (21). By Noel Coward. December 29, 1968. Director, Jon Jory; scenery, Richard Montfort Cary; lighting, Robert W. Perkins; costumes, Alec Sutherland. With Leslie Cass, Robert Baines, Barrie Charles, Wayne Maxwell, Mara Lane.

THE BIRTHDAY PARTY (21). By Harold Pinter. January 24, 1969. Director, James Cromwell; scenery, Richard Montfort Cary; lighting, Ronald Wallace; costumes, Alec Sutherland. With Eric Tavaris, Leslie Cass, Robert Baines, Mike Henisse.

ARMS AND THE MAN (21). By George Bernard Shaw. February 21, 1969. Director, Jon Jory; scenery, Adam Sage; lighting, Ronald Wallace; costumes, Margaret Mahoney. With Barrie Charles, Eric Tavaris, Robert Baines, Jean Barker.

WHO'S AFRAID OF VIRGINIA WOOLF? (21). By Edward Albee. March 21, 1969. Director, Michael Youngfellow, scenery, Will Steven Armstrong; lighting, Ronald Wallace; costumes, Alec Sutherland. With Leslie Cass, George Hearn, Roland Hewgill, Barrie Charles.

STRATFORD, CONN.

American Shakespeare Festival Theater

RICHARD II by William Shakespeare. June 22, 1968. Director, Michael Kahn; scenery, Ed Wittstein; lighting, Jennifer Tipton; costumes, Ray Diffen. With Donald Madden, Charles Cioffi, Richard Mathews, Denise Huot.

AS YOU LIKE IT by William Shakespeare. June 23, 1968. Director, Stephen Porter; scenery and costumes, Ed Wittstein; lighting, Tharon Musser. With Diana Van Der Vlis, Marian Hailey, Thomas Ruisinger, Lawrence Pressman, Stefan Gierasch.

ANDROCLES AND THE LION by George

Bernard Shaw. June 25, 1968. Director, Nikos Psacharopoulos; scenery, Will Steven Armstrong; lighting, Tharon Musser; costumes, Jane Greenwood. With Gene Troobnick, Jan Miner, Kathleen Dabney, Josef Sommer, Ted Graeber, Jane Farnol.

LOVE'S LABOUR'S LOST by William Shakespeare. June 26, 1968. Director, Michael Kahn; scenery, Will Steven Armstrong; lighting, Jennifer Tipton; costumes, Jane Greenwood. With Charles Siebert, Lawrence Pressman, Diana Van Der Vlis, Denise Huot, Stefan Gierasch.

Note: The above programs were presented in repertory June 22, 1968 through September 15, 1968. No record of the number of performances is available.

STRATFORD, ONT. (CANADA)

Stratford Festival

ROMEO AND JULIET by William Shakespeare. June 10, 1968. Director, Douglas Campbell; designer, Carolyn Parker; music, Louis Applebaum. With Christopher Walken, Louise Marleau, Leo Ciceri, Amelia Hall.

TARTUFFE by Molière; translated by Richard Wilbur. June 11, 1968. Director, Jean Gascon; designer, Robert Prevost; music, Gabriel Charpentier. With William Hutt, Barbara Bryne, Martha Henry, Douglas Rain, Leo Ciceri.

A MIDSUMMER NIGHT'S DREAM by William Shakespeare. June 12, 1968. Director, John Hirsch; designer, Leslie Hurry; music, Stanley Silverman. With Martha Henry, Douglas Rain, Christopher Newton, Jane Casson, Tedde Moore, Christopher Walken, Neil Dainard.

THE THREE MUSKETEERS by Alexandre Dumas; adapted by Peter Raby. July 22, 1968. Director, John Hirsch; designer, Desmond Heeley; music, Raymond Pannell. With Douglas Rain, James Blendick, Christopher Newton, Powys Thomas, Mia Anderson, Anne Anglin.

THE SEAGULL by Anton Chekhov. July 23, 1968. Director, Jean Gascon; designer, Brian Jackson. With Denise Pelletier, William Hutt, Louise Marleau, Marilyn Lightstone, Patrick Crean.

WAITING FOR GODOT by Samuel Beckett. August 12, 1968. Director, William Hutt; designer, Brian Jackson. With James Blendick, Eric Donkin, Adrian Pecknold, Powys Thomas.

Note: The above programs were presented in repertory June 10, 1968 through October 12, 1968. No record of the number of performances is available.

SYRACUSE, N.Y.

Syracuse Repertory Theater

THE THREEPENNY OPERA (12). By Bertolt Brecht and Kurt Weill; English version by Marc Blitzstein. February 26, 1969. Director, Rex Henriot; musical director, Arthur Shaffer; scenery, Leonard Dryansky; costumes, Ruth Frank. With Michael Norell, Edgar

Daniels, Zoaunne Henriot, Alice Cannon, Adale O'Brien, Erica Yohn.

SIX CHARACTERS IN SEARCH OF AN AUTHOR (11). By Luigi Pirandello; English version by Paul Avila Mayer. March 13, 1969.

Director, Rex Henriot. With Edgar Daniels, Shirley Ann Fenner, Colin Hamilton, Joyce Krempel, George Wyner, Sam Henriot.

THE HOMECOMING (11). By Harold Pinter. March 27, 1969. Director, G. F. Reidenbaugh; scenery, Leonard Dryansky. With Erica Yohn, John Eames, Colin Hamilton, Dan Hogan, George Wyner, Edgar Daniels.

THE LADY'S NOT FOR BURNING (11).

By Christopher Fry. April 10, 1969. Director, Rex Henriot; scenery, Robert Lewis Smith; costumes, Rex Henriot. With William Shust, Zoaunne Henriot, Gary Gage, Adale O'Brien.

SUMMERTREE (11). By Ron Cowen. April 24, 1969. Director, G. F. Reidenbaugh; scenery, Leonard Dryansky; costumes, Ruth Frank. With Darryl Wells, Gail Oliver, Nancy Reardon, Dan Hogan.

WALTHAM, MASS.

Brandeis University: Spingold Theater

THE DUCHESS OF MALFI (9). By John Webster. October 30, 1968. Director, Charles Werner Moore; scenery, Chris Idoine; lighting, Hinda Sklar; costumes, Richard Keshishian. With Bronia Stefan, Howland Chamberlain, Peter MacLean, Charles Conwell.

EH? (9). By Henry Livings. December 4, 1968. Director, Howard Bay; scenery, John Kavelin; lighting, John B. Gordon; costumes, Maura Smolover. With David S. Howard, Peter Battis, Bronia Stefan.

THE PHYSICISTS (9). By Friedrich Duerrenmatt. February 5, 1969. Director, Peter M. Sander; scenery, John B. Gordon; lighting, Richard Kashishian; costumes, John Kavelin.

With Bronia Stefan, Matt Conley, Mervyn Williams.

AN ITALIAN STRAW HAT (9). By Eugene Labiche. March 19, 1969. Director, James H. Clay; scenery, Anthony Sabatino; lighting, Wayne Chouinard; costumes, Madeleine Graneto. With Mervyn Williams, Matt Conley, Howland Chamberlain, Bronia Stefan.

HOME MONSTER (9). By Stan Thomas. April 30, 1969 (world premiere). Director, Charles Werner Moore; scenery, Eric Levenson; lighting, Chris Idoine; costumes, Mabel Astarlos. With Laurance Angelo, William A. Cortes, Jane Paley.

Note: New plays presented in workshop productions at the Laurie Premiere Theater were *Four: A Rock Musical* by Stan Thomas; *An Evening of Fast Ones* by Stan Thomas, Dennis Kostyk and Daniel Estow; *Apostle of the Idiot* by Richard Goldberg; *Edward II* by Henry C. Timm; *The Criminals* by Jose Triana (American premiere), translated by Pablo Armando Fernandez and Michael Kustow, adapted by Adrian Mitchell.

WASHINGTON, D.C.

Washington Theater Club

THE GINGHAM DOG (38). By Lanford Wilson. September 26, 1968 (world premiere). Director, Davey Marlin-Jones; scenery, James Parker; lighting, William Eggleston. With Robert Darnell, Micki Grant, Diane Gardner, Bob Spencer.

THE LION IN WINTER (38). By James Goldman. October 31, 1968. Director, Davey Marlin-Jones; scenery, Susan Tuohy; lighting, Robert Darnell; costumes, James Parker. With Ralph Strait, Anne Chodoff, Diane Gardner, John Hillerman.

LOCK UP YOUR DAUGHTERS (38). By Henry Fielding; adapted by Bernard Miles; music by Laurie Johnson, lyrics by Lionel Bart. December 5, 1968. Director and chore-

ographer, Darwin Knight; musical director, Harrison Fisher; scenery, James Parker; lighting, Miles Circo; costumes, Susan Tuohy. With Bryan Clark, Anne Chodoff, John Hillerman, Janet McCall, Joneal Joplin.

MR. TAMBO, MR. BONES (38). By Alexander Panas; music, William Goldstein. January 9, 1969 (world premiere). Director, Davey Marlin-Jones; musical director, Harrison Fisher; production designers, James Parker, Susan Tuohy, Michael R. Oberndorf, Joneal Joplin. With Bob Spencer, Bryan Clark, John Hillerman, Anne Chodoff.

WHO'S HAPPY NOW? (38). By Oliver Hailey. February 13, 1969. Director, Davey Marlin-Jones; scenery, James Parker; lighting,

Miles Circo; costumes, Susan Tuohy; songs, Dion McGregor, Michael Barr. With Robert Darnell, Jo Deodato, John Hillerman, Jane Singer, Bob Spencer.

THREE ONE-ACT PLAYS (38). March 20, 1969. *The Indian Wants the Bronx* by Israel Horovitz; director, Herb Sufrin. *And Other Caged Birds* (world premiere) by Richard O'Donnell; director, Davey Marlin-Jones. *Odds and Ends* (world premiere) by Milton Wisoff; director, Ralph Strait. Scenery, Susan

Tuohy; costumes, James Parker. With Ralph Cosham, Robert Darnell, John Hillerman, Fredric Lee, Jane Singer, Bob Spencer, Ralph Strait.

BREAD AND BUTTER (38). By Cecil Taylor. April 24, 1969 (American premiere). Director, Herb Sufrin; scenery, James Parker; lighting, Ralph Strait; visuals, Susan Tuohy. With Gisela Caldwell, Ralph Cosham, Robert Darnell, Carol Emshoff.

Washington Theater Club: Monday Night Series (New Plays)

AND OTHER CAGED BIRDS by Richard O'Donnell, and WILLYUM by Philip Balestrino (1). November 18, 1968. Director, Davey Marlin-Jones. With Tim Rice, Carol Glasgow, Brenda Hagert, Mark Rodger, Harriet Warnock, Ralph Strait, Robert Darnell, Ralph Cosham.

THE GOAT (1). By Milton Wisoff. December 16, 1968. Director, Ralph Strait. With Bob Spencer, Robert Darnell, Eda Zahl.

SOME WINTER GAMES (1). By Richard

Koesis. January 20, 1969. Director, Ralph Strait. With Anne Chodoff, Ed Beller, Ralph Cosham.

CHAMBER COMEDY (1). By David Starkweather. February 24, 1969. Director, Robert H. Leonard. With Ralph Strait, Angela Schreiber, Susan Swope, Ed Beller.

THE NOTE and THE PROJECTION ROOM (1). By Robert Somerfeld. May 5, 1969. Director, Ralph Strait. With Bob Spencer, Gisela Caldwell, Ed Beller, Ralph Cosham.

Arena Stage

THE THREEPENNY OPERA (40). By Bertolt Brecht; music by Kurt Weill, English version by Marc Blitzstein. November 26, 1968. Directors, Donald Moreland, Zelda Fichandler; musical director, Richard W. Dirksen; scenery, John Conklin; lighting, William Eggleston; costumes, Marjorie Slaiman. With Richard Bauer, Hugh Hurd, Marcie Hubert, Laura Campbell, Dimitra Arliss.

SIX CHARACTERS IN SEARCH OF AN AUTHOR (40). By Luigi Pirandello; translated by Paul Avila Mayer. November 27, 1968. Director, Zelda Fichandler; scenery, John Conklin; lighting, William Eggleston; costumes, Marjorie Slaiman. With Richard Venture, Grayce Grant, Richard Bauer, Olivia Cole, Ned Beatty, Dimitra Arliss.

KING LEAR (38). By William Shakespeare.

January 21, 1969. Director, Edwin Sherin; scenery and costumes, John Conklin; lighting, William Eggleston. With Frank Silvera, Mary Alice, Robert Prosky, Barton Heyman.

MARAT/SADE (40). By Peter Weiss; translated by Geoffrey Skelton; verse adaptation by Adrian Mitchell. March 25, 1969. Director, Alfred Ryder; scenery, John Conklin; lighting, William Eggleston; costumes, Marjorie Slaiman. With Richard Venture, Barton Heyman, Grayce Grant, Melinda Dillon.

INDIANS (40). By Arthur Kopit. May 6, 1969 (American premiere). Director, Gene Frankel; scenery, Kert Lundell; lighting, William Eggleston; costumes, Marjorie Slaiman. With Stacy Keach, Manu Tupou, Barry Primus, Raul Julia.

NOTE: The first three plays were presented in repertory through March 16, 1969. The balance of the Arena Stage's season will include *Jacques Brel Is Alive and Well and Living in Paris* June 17, 1969.

THE SEASON IN LONDON

By John Bowen

Author of the 1967-68 Best Play *After the Rain* and other playscripts

"IT WAS the best of seasons; it was the worst of seasons," as a short-lived British musical based on *A Tale of Two Cities* might well have had it. The best ideologically, the worst practically.

Ideologically because at last the power of the Lord Chamberlain to censor plays was abolished, and words and parts of the body hitherto unknown in the London theater were introduced to the public. Bliss was it in that false dawn to be alive. Paul Scofield, as Laurie in John Osborne's *The Hotel in Amsterdam,* had been forced to say "extra-bloody-curricular" at the Royal Court Theater. When the play transferred (after the abolition) to the New Theater, he said "extra-fuckin-curricular." An artistic shackle had fallen away. As for nudity, while the commercial theater didn't see all that much of it, except in *Hair* and *Fortune and Men's Eyes,* in the uncommercial theaters everywhere one looked there were goose pimples.

And practically, in terms of the plays to be enjoyed, it was, as I have suggested, a terrible season. During it, I myself accepted the invitation of *The London Magazine* to write a monthly column on the theater. I have believed that there should be at least a few among the drama critics who can bring a practical knowledge of how plays are written and directed and acted to their criticism, and I was proud to follow Frank Marcus and the late John Whiting in the magazine's tradition of employing a playwright-critic. Seven months later, disgusted and despairing and in the grave danger for a playwright of growing to hate the theater, I asked to be released.

Why? Because the Lord Chamberlain never had been more than a paper tiger. "The drama's laws the drama's patrons give," and with rising costs the people who could afford to pay for stalls in a theater were of the kind which did not, in general, want honesty, insights, theatrical experiments, or to be purged by pity and terror. They were prepared to go for "culture" to the subsidised National Theater Company and to the Royal Shakespeare Company or even to the H.M. Tennent repertory season at the Haymarket, and by "culture" they meant established classics or at least fancy dress: they did not want to see new plays on contemporary themes, even at the "cultural" theaters. Consequently, as I write, many producers have accepted the principle that "serious plays won't pay" and only Arthur Miller's *The Price* (an excellent play, indifferently acted) remains as an honorable exception.

136

It is easy for dramatists to blame producers, but producers might as easily blame dramatists and critics. Once it is accepted that "serious plays don't pay," then, by a little logical jump, it can come to be believed that plays which don't pay are probably serious. Then: that for a play to be serious it has to be un-workmanlike. More: it can't be truly "serious" unless an audience is positively bored. This season has seen extravagant praise piled on a long farrago of old jokes and social philosophy called *The Ruling Class* (the "in" adjective for the season was "Jacobean") and a "re-valuation" of Edward Bond's cannibalistic phantasmagoria, *Early Morning.*

However, first to musicals. The British producers' dependence on revivals extended this season to reviving an American musical (how safe can you play?), the Gershwin *Lady Be Good,* but it did only moderately well, as did another "sure-fire" bet, *The Student Prince.* A Novello revival, *The Dancing Years,* did positively badly, and, by the end of the season, a thoroughly tatty revival of *The Merry Widow* closed so swiftly that it might have been a new play. So it may be that the boom that began with *The Desert Song* is over.

New musicals did little better. Swift closures for *Viva! Viva!,* adapted from Machiavelli, and *Man with a Load of Mischief,* adapted from Ashley Dukes. Almost as swift for *Mr. and Mrs.,* made out of two Noel Coward one-acters *(Fumed Oak* and *Still Life)* with two principals, Honor Blackman and John Neville, better known as actors than singers. Two more adaptations did little better, but not much. *Two Cities* was distinguished by a bravura performance as Sydney Carton by Edward Woodward and the unobtrusively excellent direction of Vivian Matalon, but the book was flat and the music derivative, and it made way for the American import, *Belle Starr,* with Betty Grable. *The Young Visiters* (sic) was a musical adaptation of the book Daisy Ashford wrote when she was 9 years old. It was charmingly done, with delightful and ingenious sets by Peter Rice, and a singing and acting performance of great distinction by Alfred Marks as Mr. Salteena who was "not quite a gentleman," but it was essentially a miniature and could not survive in the great barn of the Piccadilly Theater (where *Man of La Mancha* had lasted a mere 115 performances). Nor was its public large enough to pay for such a large-scale musical production. Played to two pianos and with no chorus of dancers and singers, it might have run a year in a small house, but one mustn't expect common sense from producers. As matters were, it lasted a couple of months. *Ann Veronica* (adapted from H.G. Wells) did no better. The musical surprise of the season was Canadian, *Anne of Green Gables,* to which the critics went determined to scoff and from which they all staggered wet-eyed. Heaven send, however, that *this* doesn't launch a new fashion.

American imports were, if you'll allow the play on words, crowned by *Hair,* with the famous nude scene discreetly backlit so that members of our Royal Family were able to see it (and indeed dance on stage afterwards) without making any very shocking discoveries about the shape of the human body. Once again, *Hair* proved that it's the music which makes a musical. Leave aside Mr. O'Horgan's gift for making dramatic pictures and burying a text, leave aside the undoubted attraction of youthful high spirits and amateurishness (we had something of the same in *Salad Days* long ago), the music in *Hair* sold LPs in quantity, cropped up again and again in the Gramophone Record Charts, and kept the public coming. Lacking music of the same quality, another rock musical *Your Own Thing* arrived and died, and *Golden Boy*, though its limited run was extended and it could not be called a failure, attracted nothing like the same popularity, Sammy Davis Jr. notwithstanding. Of *Mame* I cannot speak. Though I greatly admired Angela Lansbury's personality performance when I saw it in New York, it did seem to conform to the new rule for American musicals that nothing must happen in the second half except that money must be seen to have been spent. In the British production everything has been subordinated to selling, not so much *Mame* as Ginger Rogers; and when to that distortion effect is added the second, that one of the attractions of an evening at the Theater Royal, Drury Lane, is the theater itself, so that the coachloads kept coming even for such a witless, tuneless affair as *The Four Musketeers*, "hit" is not a meaningful word. Lastly a word about another off-Broadway import, *Jacques Brel Is Alive and Well and Living in Paris*. This was neither a revue nor a musical, but a succession of songs, which might have done well enough in cabaret, but was clearly unsuited to a proscenium-arch theater.

Two other entertainments, both British, were also musical, though not musicals. One was mildly successful, the second hugely so. The first was Alan Plater's *Close the Coalhouse Door*, a piece of regional history about North Country miners, acted out with songs and pieces of caricature, and set in a framework of a present festivity: the silver wedding party of an old miner and his wife. The interior charade was moving, rousing, often funny; the framework was sentimental. This was a successful piece of regional theater, brought to London and finding a small, but probably just sufficient, audience. Alan Bennett's *Forty Years On*, with Sir John Gielgud leading the cast, was an exactly similar piece. Again, history was set in the framework of a festivity. This time it was the end-of-term play given by a run-down private boarding school (symbolising England) and the history was of England just before the 1914 war and during the 1939-1945 war. The theme in both pieces was the decline of greatness. In both, the good days were the old days. *Forty Years On* featured the world of the upper middle classes and *Close the Coalhouse Door* the world of often unemployed miners, and this explains the difference in the size of their respective publics; but both were well played ("played" is a better word than "acted" here: they *were* well acted, of course, but "played" gives you more of a sense of the high spirits involved) and very efficiently directed.

Back to American imports. We must put into a special section the Royal Shakespeare Company's decision, under their new managing director Trevor Nunn, who this year replaced Peter Hall in that office, to mount a little American season. In it each play until the last was a worse play, worse acted and worse directed than the one before. Arthur Kopit's *Indians* was a sub-Brechtian strip-cartoon, Paddy Chayefsky's *The Latent Heterosexual* a good idea about the logical extremes of tax evasion, stretched to an inordinate length and tarted up (perhaps by the director) with a little Christ-symbolism, and Jules

Feiffer's *God Bless* was sub-late-Shaw, and you can't get more sub than that. Then the season ended with a skillful, though a little Anglo-flavored production by Peter Hall of Edward Albee's *A Delicate Balance,* and the theatrical reputations of the U.S.A. and the Royal Shakespeare Company were precariously retrieved. It is significant, however, that the cast of the Albee, headed by Peggy Ashcroft and Michael Hordern, was recruited largely outside the company, as was Lee Montague, who gave the only good performance in the Chayefsky. Companies do go through periods of doldrums. The National Theater did so some years ago, though nowadays it has almost more good actors than it has parts for. Recently the Royal Shakespeare Company has been both overextended and over-loyal.

Other American imports fared better. Though *You Know I Can't Hear You When the Water's Running* failed because of very vulgar acting (except from Rosemary Murphy) *Plaza Suite,* with Rosemary Harris and Paul Rogers, was well received, and so was an Anglicized version of *Absence of a Cello,* rechristened *Out of the Question,* which appeared to cater exactly to every prejudice held by the middle-aged middle classes. *The Price* has rightly received general respect, and *The Boys in the Band,* after a slightly shaky start, found the same success as it did off Broadway; I think deservedly. It is not only a skillfully confected piece, but it has a strongly voyeuristic appeal and is sentimental with it. Skill in the playwright was complemented by some equally skillful ensemble acting, and, if I pick out Laurence Luckinbill and Reuben Greene as particularly moving, that may be no more than a personal preference or an accident of the evening.

Britain is not very European these days. The International Theater Club mounted a series of translations and imported the French Grand Théâtre Panique in an entertainment loosely based on Arrabal's *The Labyrinth.* But the larger theatrical public generally ignored Europe, with the exception of those who attended Peter Daubeny's fifth World Theater Season, presented by the Royal Shakespeare Company's governors at the Aldwych Theater. Romain Weingarten's *Summer* appeared briefly at the Fortune Theater with Jane Asher, the National Theater mounted Natalia Ginzburg's *The Advertisement,* a near-monologue from the Italian, superbly played by Joan Plowright, and the biggest non-event of the year was Hochhuth's *Soldiers* (with the original Toronto and New York cast and production). First there had been the refusal of Lord Chandos—chairman of the board—to allow the National Theater to present it, then the Lord Chamberlain's refusal to allow Kenneth Tynan to present it privately outside the National Theater, then (with the abolition of theatrical censorship) it was presented anyway jointly by British and American producers at the New Theater amid a froth of leading articles, letters to the *Times,* and angry confrontations on television. But all this whipped-up excitement could not induce many of the public to go to it, since the public is largely bored by both Sir Winston Churchill and dialectical debates.

The beginnings of a proliferation of off-Broadway-type theaters is worth noting. In addition to the International Theater Club, housed in Dame Marie Rambert's old Mercury Theater at Notting Hill, there is the American Edward

D. Berman's Ambiance Theater, operating at lunch time in a coffee shop in Bayswater, the American Charles Marowitz's Open Space in a basement in Soho, the Jeanetta Cochrane Theater in Holborn, the Americans Jim Haynes' and Jack Moore's Arts Laboratory in Covent Garden, the Theater Upstairs (a room above the Royal Court), and the Roundhouse, a converted engine shed at Chalk Farm. All except the Jeanetta Cochrane and the Mercury are open-stage—a welcome development!—and all except the Roundhouse are very small so that they cannot afford to pay their actors a living wage, which is usual but not so welcome.

The "Arts Lab," the home of London's hippies, is addicted mainly to anti-literary and participatory theater and staged the world premieres of Tulli Kupferberg's *Fucknam* and Jane Arden's *Vagina Rex and the Gas Oven,* starring the talented comedian Victor Spinetti and Sheila Allen, who appeared for more than half the length of the play in the clothes her Maker had given her. The Ambiance is also participatory, though not anti-literary, but Ed Berman's word is "environmental." He involves the audience passively: they do not change the play by interfering but are part of its environment. This applied to John Arden's *The True History of Squire Jonathan and His Unfortunate Treasure,* in which a comely actress called Jenny Lee (not to be confused with the British minister responsible for the arts of the same name) willingly stripped before everybody's eyes. Berman's most interesting offering was *The Window* by Frank Marcus, finely acted by Richard Pascoe and David Cook. In this play, originally written for and screened by the B.B.C. television service, a blind man, in love with the girl in an apartment opposite his, employs a young homosexual to watch with binoculars her sexual encounters, and to describe them in detail. Since the girl left some time ago, the descriptions have to be invented. Berman put his audience behind a muslin curtain, making voyeurs of them as they watched the voyeurs.

The Jeanetta Cochrane Theater has no policy as such. It is owned by an art school and can be hired, as this season the National Theater did hire it (using the designs made by the students) for a short experimental season of first plays. Two of these, *Rites* by Maureen Duffy and *Macrune's Guevara* by John Spurling, were revived in the company's regular repertory in a double bill. The Royal Court's Theater Upstairs uses actors and dramatists already familiar to Royal Court audiences. It began with a play by David Cregan, whose earlier plays had already been seen at what we may now call the Theater Downstairs. The Roundhouse was originally bought as a theater by Arnold Wesker's Center 42 several years ago. A project that aimed to popularize the arts, it ran out of money and into apathy and the Roundhouse was used mainly for psychedelic rave-ups until, in consequence of the students' revolt in Paris, the international group of actors rehearsing in Paris with Peter Brook and Jean-Louis Barrault moved to London and used it to undertake an experiment in actor-audience relationships. Like many of Mr. Brook's ventures, this was marked by a degree of disrespect for the text (in this case *The Tempest*), but it brought theatrical attention back to the Roundhouse. John Arden presented his new musical play about Nelson there, and then Tony Richardson mounted *Hamlet* with Nicol Williamson and a distinguished supporting cast.

The Open Space began inauspiciously and (it was thought) unexperimentally with a sentimental Canadian prison-drama, *Fortune and Men's Eyes,* earlier seen off Broadway. This made the transfer to the Comedy Theater but did not last long there. The policy became more adventurous—work by van Itallie was seen—but it was clear from such conventional material as Paul Ableman's double-bill *Blue Comedy* that the Open Space still has its sights fixed on the West End. Mr. Marowitz pleads lack of money and his off-beat *Macbeth* was paid for by, and saw the light of day at, a German theater festival before reaching London. The other club theater to provide transfers was Hampstead. A disastrously slipshod play about a male homosexual marriage in which one of the partners gives birth, *Spitting Image,* was booed at its West End opening and soon closed. A program of short playlets about marriage by various authors *, called *We Who Are About To . . .* and retitled *Mixed Doubles* for the West End, did a great deal better.

Two other plays were booed by the Gallery on opening nights; that is, by members of the Gallery first nighters who invariably express their views of a play's merits in a vocal way. Both were by authors of reputation. Ann Jellicoe's *The Giveaway* might be thought to have deserved it. This was a farce without structural ingenuity, wit, humor or characterization, and the mystery was that it should ever have appeared in London at all. But the late Joe Orton's *What the Butler Saw* was another matter: there was evidence for believing that the gesture (particularly ludicrous against a dead man) was against the author's moral views more than against his play. *What the Butler Saw,* in which Sir Ralph Richardson, Coral Browne and Stanley Baxter headed a talented cast, had weaknesses, since Orton died before he could fully revise it. But it *was* witty, it *was* ingenious, and it showed that both in style and attitude Orton came closer to Oscar Wilde than to any of his contemporaries. And it makes me happy to report that the play survived its first reception and settled down to a run.

The Giveaway came in from Edinburgh, as *Close the Coalhouse Door* had done from Newcastle, *The Ruling Class* from Nottingham, *Narrow Road to the Deep North* from Coventry, and a revival of *She Stoops to Conquer,* with Tom Courtenay, from Theater 69 in Manchester. This illustrates the second development of the season—an acceleration of the process by which the old touring circuit is falling in. Nowadays the cost of sending plays out on tour is prohibitive. Instead, a play may begin at one of the better provincial repertory theaters: the Bristol Old Vic and the Glasgow Citizens may be added to those already mentioned. (I myself had my new play, *The Disorderly Women,* mounted at the Stables Theater Club which had just opened in Manchester, built and subsidized by a television company). The danger of trying out a play at a first class provincial theater within reach of London is that the London

* Editor's note: In the West End, this program contained the world premiere of Harold Pinter's *Night* and John Bowen's *Silver Wedding,* adjudged the two best of an excellent bunch.

critics will come to it and may not wish to re-review it in depth when it opens again in London. English producers are therefore borrowing the preview from New York and may use a fortnight to run the play in before the official opening. It is early yet, however, to know how the public are responding.

Among established dramatists, Pinter gave us one of the playlets in *Mixed Doubles:* it was like a pebble dropped into a pool, making ripples far greater than its size. James Saunders, Alun Owen and Alan Ayckbourn (of *Relatively Speaking*) also contributed to this program. At the Criterion, Tom Stoppard showed a kind of extended revue sketch, *The Real Inspector Hound:* it was glossily done, but singularly un-nourishing. John Osborne dominated the season, and at one time it seemed likely that he would have three plays in the West End at once, but in fact *Time Present* closed at the Duke of York's before a revival of *Look Back in Anger* had moved in from the Royal Court to the Criterion.

Of *Time Present* Frank Marcus wrote in last year's *Best Plays* volume. It and *The Hotel in Amsterdam* form a group to which Osborne has given the title *In the Mean Time*. The plays are clearly of a piece, both with one of those central monsters whose monologues on the topics of the day form the flesh of the play—in which all too often the bones appear to have sunk without trace. Both plays are dominated by offstage characters, and by the end of both plays those characters are dead. The actors talk and talk and somewhere somebody is dying: it is an image of England. Of all English dramatists, Osborne, who so often seems to be writing about himself, is most usually writing about his country.

The other dramatist to consolidate a critical reputation was Edward Bond, when the Royal Court mounted a season of his three plays so far, *Saved, The Narrow Road to the Deep North* and *Early Morning* (which ran into trouble with the censor last year). Bond is a most erratic dramatist, obsessed with images of mutilation, but there could be no doubt, even in the rather messy production the Court gave it, that the second of the three is a most accomplished play. The Royal Court also appointed a resident dramatist, Christopher Hampton, whose second play, *Total Eclipse,* about Rimbaud and Verlaine, confirmed the promise of *When Did You Last See My Mother?*. New plays there by David Cregan and John Antrobus didn't do very well, and one of the finest plays of the season, John Hopkins' *The Story of Yours,* in spite of very good acting by Michael Bryant and Gordon Jackson, did downright badly, perhaps because of its subject. It was about a policeman who kills a child-molester, finding in himself the same desires as he interrogates the man. David Storey's new play, *In Celebration,* though it seemed more like an early play in the autobiographical vein of *This Sporting Life,* showed once again his intelligence, his feeling for family relationships and his talent for the display of naked emotion, but also his inexperience in construction and the Royal Court's fatal inability to cut the work of their favored playwrights. It was compellingly acted by Bill Owen and Alan Bates.

The National Theater and the Royal Shakespeare Company each also offered a new play by a British dramatist. At the Aldwych, *Dutch Uncle* by

Simon Gray (who wrote *Wise Child*) was another farce which wasn't funny. At the National, Charles Wood's *H* was concerned once again with the author's favorite topic, the British Army, this time during the Indian Mutiny of 1857. It was an episodic play with flashes of power, but no sustained force, and it was movingly acted by Robert Lang as General Havelock, by Frank Wylie and by Gerald James. There was fine acting also by Ronald Pickup in the National's other new play, John Lennon's one-acter *In His Own Write* (I say John Lennon, though the authorship of the piece was something under dispute but it was at least adapted from John Lennon's work). Of the National's comparatively young entry, I should choose Pickup as undisputed star in 7 years' time.

The National Theater also mounted a beautiful but slow *Love's Labour's Lost* and a brisk and funny revival of W. Somerset Maugham's comedy *Home and Beauty* (director: Frank Dunlop) in which Sir Laurence Olivier made a brief appearance in a minor role toward the end of the season. There was also a singularly flat production of Congreve's *The Way of the World,* directed by Michael Langham and enlivened by Hazel Hughes' balefully eccentric Lady Wishfort.

Other revivals elsewhere were *The Cocktail Party,* brought in from the Chichester Festival, in which only Eileen Atkins survived the general sanctimoniousness; a slightly shoddy *Ring Round the Moon* mounted by H.M. Tennent at the Haymarket, and *Dear Charles,* designed, like the 1967 revival of *Dear Octopus,* as a vehicle for Cecily Courtneidge, but it had no engine and did not run. Since many producers exist by trying to jump on bandwagons, there was an attempt by H.M. Tennent to copy one of the National's biggest hits, the Feydeau farce *A Flea in Her Ear,* translated by John Mortimer and directed by Jacques Charon of the Comédie Française. In this case the same team rode again with *Cat Among the Pigeons,* from *Un Fil à la Patte,* and the general view was that it did well enough, but not *as* well.

Other successes of new works in the commercial theater were *Queen Passionella,* a pantomime starring Danny La Rue, the female impersonator; *Oh, Clarence!* and *A Boston Story,* adaptations of P.G. Wodehouse and Henry James respectively; two comedies, *The Secretary Bird* and *The Man Most Likely To . . . ,* and a farce, *Not Now, Darling. The Mousetrap* (in its "17th inexorable year"), *There's a Girl in My Soup, Charlie Girl, Canterbury Tales, The Black and White Minstrel Show, Hadrian VII* (transferred from the Mermaid to the West End) and *Fiddler on the Roof* continued to run. Perhaps it was just a season like any other.

Highlights of the London Season

Selected and compiled by Ossia Trilling

OUTSTANDING PERFORMANCES

PAUL SCOFIELD
as Laurie in
The Hotel in Amsterdam

AL MANCINI
as Queenie in
Fortune and Men's Eyes

JOAN PLOWRIGHT
as Teresa in
The Advertisement

JOHN GIELGUD
as Headmaster in
Forty Years On

ROY DOTRICE
as William Clark Brackman in
God Bless

MICHAEL BRYANT
as Johnson in
This Story of Yours

PEGGY ASHCROFT
as Agnes in
A Delicate Balance

ROSEMARY HARRIS
as three characters in
Plaza Suite

OLIVER TOBIAS
as Berger in
Hair

LAURENCE OLIVIER
as Mr. A.B. Raham in
Home and Beauty

VICTOR HENRY
as Jimmy Porter in
Look Back in Anger

ALAN BATES
as Andrew Shaw in
In Celebration

HAROLD GARY
as Solomon in
The Price

NICOL WILLIAMSON
as Hamlet in
Hamlet

TREVOR PEACOCK
as Tony Lumpkin in
She Stoops to Conquer

OUTSTANDING DIRECTORS

WILLIAM GASKILL
Early Morning

LAURENCE OLIVIER
Love's Labour's Lost

STUART BURGE
The Ruling Class

OUTSTANDING DESIGNERS

CARL TOMS
Love's Labour's Lost

RALPH KOLTAI
Soldiers

SEAN KENNY
Gulliver's Travels

OUTSTANDING NEW BRITISH PLAYS

(D)—Playwright's London debut. Figure in parentheses is number of performances;
plus sign (+) indicates play was still running on June 1, 1969.

THE HA-HA by Jennifer Dawson; adapted by Richard Eyre. (D) Dramatization of novel of a mental patient's heartaches. With Angela Pleasence, June Watson, James Lawrenson. (25)

THE TRUE HISTORY OF SQUIRE JONATHAN AND HIS UNFORTUNATE TREASURE by John Arden. One-act comedy of rival allurements of wealth and sex. With Ian Trigger, Jennie Lee. (39)

THE REAL INSPECTOR HOUND by Tom Stoppard. Two drama critics fall victim to their own foul fantasies. With Richard Briers, Ronnie Barker. (200)

THE HOTEL IN AMSTERDAM by John Osborne. Offstage film mogul controls the lives of an escapist screen writer and his cronies. With Paul Scofield, Judy Parfitt, Joss Ackland, Susan Engel. (131)

SPITTING IMAGE by Colin Spencer. Two homosexuals scandalize society by producing a baby. With Julian Holloway, Derek Fowlds. (50)

BLUE COMEDY (*Hank's Night* and *Madly in Love*) by Paul Ableman. (D) Two one-acters about the odd behavior of ordinary folk driven by sexual urges. With Jonathan Burn, Jonathan Lynn, Gordon Whiting. (36)

WORKING TITLE by Rio Fanning. (D) An investigation into authority, with racial undertones. With Tony Doyle, John Lyons, Nigel Hawthorne. (72)

H, OR MONOLOGUES AT FRONT OF BURNING CITIES by Charles Wood. The Indian Mutiny seen as a Victorian melodrama. With Robert Lang, Frank Wylie, Jane Wenham, Gerald James. (24+ in repertory)

VAGINA REX AND THE GAS OVEN by Jane Arden. The weaker sex uses unorthodox arts to assert its equality. With Sheila Allen, Victor Spinetti. (30)

NARROW ROAD TO THE DEEP NORTH by Edward Bond. Brechtian parable of man's ambivalent attitude to violence and the call of brotherhood. With Peter Needham, Gillian Martell. (15 in repertory)

THE RULING CLASS by Peter Barnes. A scabrous satire on the establishment and its bids for self-perpetuation. With Derek God- frey, Moira Redmond, Dudley Jones, David Dodimead. (85)

ALTERNATIVES by Nancy Meckler. (D) One-act fantasy comedy about human contact over a life's span. With the Freehold Company. (36)

IN CELEBRATION by David Storey. The suppressed memories and desires of a miner's family come into the open with distressing results. With Alan Bates, Bill Owen, Constance Chapman. (41+)

LIMITED RUNS OF INTERESTING NEW BRITISH PLAYS

THE PLAY OF THE ROYAL ASTROLO-GERS by Willis Hall. Adventures with pirates in the East. With Henry Manning, Ursula Jones. (28)

HENRY MOUSE by Roberta Dolby. (D) How the Mouse family and Freddie Frog controlled Freddie's delight in tail-treading. With Ursula Jones, Peter Corey. (6)

HAROLD MUGGINS IS A MARTYR by John Arden, Cartoon Archetypical Slogan Theater and Margaretta D'Arcy. A private caterer's business is taken over by gangster capitalists. With the authors. (23)

IN HIS OWN WRITE by John Lennon, Adrienne Kennedy and Victor Spinetti. A working class boy's autobiography, a one-acter based on the Beatle book. With Ronald Pickup. (17 in repertory)

HELLO, GOODBYE SEBASTIAN by John Grillo. (D) The impotence of youth and a graveyard encounter. With the Brighton Combination Company. (18)

THE NUDIST CAMPERS GROW AND GROW by Ed.B. The embarrassments of going native. With Marie Adams, Bill Bailey. (24)

DOUBTFUL HAUNTS (The Ghost and No Principals) by Christopher Guinee. (D) Two actorish one-acters about a returning ghost and an aging pair of retainers. With Annette Crosbie, George Cole. (20)

SHOUTS AND MURMURS devised by Jim Haynes. (D) Dramatization of an interview in The Observer between Kenneth Tynan and John Osborne. With Mark Long, Sid Palmer. (36)

CHANGING LINES by Nicholas Wright. (D) The performance of a corny thriller is disrupted. With Susan Williamson. (1)

THE RASPUTIN SHOW by Michael Almaz. (D) A hotch-potch on the life and times of Rasputin. With John Grillo, Katie Heyland. (12)

TRIXIE AND BABA by John Antrobus. A nightmare view of a middle class marriage. With Gillian Martell, Joe Melia. (19)

THE POPE AND THE PILL devised by Alan Seymour. Dramatization of the Papal encyclical. With Will Spoor. (12)

TOTAL ECLIPSE by Christopher Hampton. The Verlaine-Rimbaud affaire. With Victor Henry, John Grillo. (19)

PARAFINALIA by Ken Campbell. (D) A crazy comedy about two eccentric private eyes. With Clive Elliott, Matyelock Gibbs. (28)

THE PROTAGONIST by Pip Simmons. (D) Drama based on Georg Kaiser's play of that name. With the Pip Simmons Group. (18)

RAILINGS IN THE PARK by Jeff Nuttal. A play on the theme of birth. With the People Show Company. (18)

WHY BOURNEMOUTH? by John Antrobus. One-act surrealist comedy of family relations. With Margaret Nolan, Michael Da Costa, Maurice Good, Phyllis Morris. (24)

THE HOUSES BY THE GREEN by David Cregan. Satire of English mores based on the rivalries of two old gentlemen. With John Normington, Bob Grant. (19)

FUNNY SUNDAY *(Funny People* and *Come Sunday)* by Roy Minton. Two one-acters about frustrations of two women, and of a newly-married oldster. With Hazel Hughes, Jimmy Gardner. (29)

IT'S ALL IN THE MIND by John Hale. A liberal married woman learns the truth about herself. With Zena Walker, John Harvey. (21)

TIMES ARE GETTING HARD, BOYS by Keith Darvill. Documentary of the 1930s. With Tom Conti. (10)

INSIDE OUT by David Hare. (D) Based on Kafka's diaries. With the Portable Theater Company. (24)

JOHNNY SO LONG by Vivienne C. Welburn. (D) Communication between a group of youngsters. With Jack Chissick, Naomi Sharron. (1)

CAN'T HELP LOVING YOU and HENRY by Neil Hornick. (D) Double-bill about computerized love, and a missing friend. With Sandy Macdonald. (16)

THE GOBLET GAME by Rex Edwards. (D) Life in London's East End symbolized by a children's game. With Hilda Fennemore, Colin Bell, Tommy Godfrey. (10)

THE STRANGE CASE OF MARTIN RICHTER by Stanley Eveling. (D) A comic critique of neo-Nazi racialism. With Leonard Rossiter, Tony Steedman. (21)

THE HERO RISES UP by John Arden and Margaretta D'Arcy. Musical about Lord Nelson. With Henry Woolf, Bettina Jonic. (5)

JOHNNY MOONBEAM AND THE SILVER ARROW by Joseph Golden. (D) Red Indian boy battles with the elements to win the Silver Arrow. With Laurence Keane, Henry Manning. (8)

SHOP? MRS. BUTTERWORTH by the People Show Company. Collective nightmare fantasy. With the People Show Company. (18)

I WONDER by Michael Kustow & Adrian Henry. (D) Anthology of the life of Guillaume Apollinaire. With Tom Kempinski, Wendy Giffard. (9)

THERE WAS A MAN by Tom Wright. (D) One-man play (with voices) on the life of Robert Burns. With John Cairney. (17)

THE PUPPET PRINCE by Alan Cullen. The breaking of a spell to make a prince into a puppet. With Rosemary Blake, Peter Bourne. (7)

THE LUNATIC, THE SECRET SPORTSMAN AND THE WOMAN NEXT DOOR by Stanley Eveling. Surrealist philosophical drama of communication. With Pamela Moiseiwitsch, Derrick O'Connor. (12)

SAGITTARIUS and VIRGO by Ed.B. Two experiments in split speech or polyphonic dialogue. With Marie Adams, Bill Bailey, Bob Hoskins. (17)

THIS STORY OF YOURS by John Hopkins. (D) A killer policeman discovers hidden impulses in himself. With Michael Bryant, Gordon Jackson, John Phillips. (25)

THE PRINCE, THE WOLF AND THE FIREBIRD by Jackson Lacey. (D) Children's play based on the Russian folk fable. With Matyelock Gibbs, Laurence Keane. (22)

COME AND BE KILLED by Stanley Eveling. Four duologues in comic vein on the theme of abortion. With Malcolm Tierney, Irene Hamilton. (24)

SUPER SANTA by Ed.B. A Yuletide surrealist jeu d'esprit. With Jim Hiley, Margaret Nolan. (10)

THE WRONG SIDE OF THE MOON by Nicholas Stuart Grey. The Rapunzel story updated. With Eileen Pollock. (15)

LIFE PRICE by Michael O'Neill and Jeremy Seabrook. (D) A sexual child-murder in a working class community. With Anthony Douse, Yvonne Antrobus. (25)

THE WINDOW by Frank Marcus. A case of voyeurism, with observations reported to a blind man. With Richard Pasco, David Cook, Warwick Stuart. (16)

THE MUSICIANS by Garry O'Connor. (D) Events in the life of a frustrated family. With Margaret Drabble, Clive Swift, Richard Marquand. (6)

MACRUNE'S GUEVARA (AS REALIZED BY EDWARD HOTEL) by John Spurling. (D) The romantic myth of Che Guevara seen from a new perspective. With Jeremy Brett, Ronald Pickup, Robert Stephens. (8) See NOTE below.

AN EVASION OF WOMEN—*Nurse Macateer* by Shena Mackay, (D) a nurse's campaign for euthanasia; *Pursuit* by Gillian Freeman, (D) a married couple revealingly play out their public life in private; *Bird of Paradise* by Margaret Drabble, (D) the private failures of a successful businesswoman (5). And *Rites* by Maureen Duffy, (D) The Bacchantes legend updated and re-sited in the powder room (8). With Sheila Reed, Gillian Barge, Louise Purnell, Geraldine McEwan. See NOTE in next item below.

SCRABBLE devised by Claude Chagrin and written with Oliver Cotton and Richard Mangan. A mime, with speech, music and dance. With Edward Petherbridge, Charles Kay, Philip Locke, Alan Adams. (4) NOTE: This and the previous two entries made up a three-week experimental season staged by the National Theater, to which *Guevara* and *Rites* transferred in a double bill.

INTRO by Jeremy Gibson. (D) One-act variant of the eternal triangle in an eternal circle. With Larry Aubrey, Errol Bolger, Vivien Brooks. (12)

THE KING'S THINGS by Diana Wynne-Jones. A king sells the Crown Jewels to keep going. With Henry Manning, Ursula Jones. (10)

THE FALL OF SAMSON MOROCCO by John Grillo. One-acter about the violent end of a frustrated violinist. With Roger Cartland, Sarah Rivington. (16)

A COMEDY OF THE CHANGING YEARS by David Cregan. The rise of Hitlerism in British experience. With Jonathan Lynn, Judith Paris. (18)

VARIABLE LENGTHS AND LONGER (*Variable Lengths, Does It Make Your Cheeks Ache?*, and *The Reasons for Flying*) by Henry Livings. Three sketches about a man with anatomical oddities, a put-upon ventriloquist, and a would-be aeronaut. With Victor Henry, David Baxter. (16)

HAVE YOU ANY DIRTY WASHING, MOTHER DEAR? by Clive Exton. (D) Slanted send-up of British parliamentarianism. With Roddy Maude-Roxby, Glynn Edwards, Anthony Nicholls. (21)

EARLY MORNING by Edward Bond. Anti-imperialist satire ranging from lesbianism to cannibalism. With Moira Redmond, Shirley Anne Field, Nigel Hawthorne, Henry Woolf. (13 in repertory)

DUTCH UNCLE by Simon Gray. The farci-

cal bungling of a would-be wife-murderer. With Warren Mitchell, Megs Jenkins, Patrick Magee. (12 in repertory)

CHICKEN CURRY AND POPPADOMS by Richard Nugget. A racialist love-affair. With Dino Shafeek. (24)

URBANE TATTERS by Gransha Rainy. (D) Dream-fantasy of sex in suburbia. With Jenny Lee, Christopher Heywood. (3)

THE MAN WHO ALMOST KNEW EAMON ANDREWS by John Heilpern. (D) A moving monologue of a man smitten with cancer. With John Pine. (18)

EROGENOUS ZONES by Mike Stott. (D) The American way of life satirized in a series of sketches. With John Grillo, Tom Kempinski, Henry Woolf. (18)

THE POBBLE WHO LOST HIS TOES by Wilf Harvey. A play based on Edward Lear's nonsense. With Matyelock Gibbs, Brian Sheehy. (12)

ANNA LUSA by David Mowat. One-acter about the plight of two blind girls. With Philippa de Gobeo, Rosamund Nelson. (6)

THE GIVEAWAY by Ann Jellicoe. Farcical send-up of acquisitive society. With Rita Tushingham, Roy Hudd, Dandy Nichols. (15)

THE BLACK SWAN WINTER by John Hale. Retired Army sergeant tells his muddled son some home truths. With Eric Thompson, Esmond Knight. (21)

HONOUR AND OFFER by Henry Livings. Farcical treatment of the eternal triangle with a happy (?) ending. With Ken Wynne, Ray Mort, John Sharp, Ursula Smith. (26+)

LOVE PLAY by Lee Harris. Lyrical fantasy of deadbeats in London's Soho today. With Clive Colin-Bower, Jenny Harrington. (10)

THE DRAGON'S GRANDMOTHER and SWINDLE by Marged Smith. Double-bill, comprising a fantasy with audience participation, and a tale of London in 1851. With Ursula Jones, Brian Sheehy. (7+)

PARTY by Robert Walker. (D) One-act study of loneliness, premiered at the Berlin Experimental Festival 1969 before its London premiere. With Ann Mitchell, Barry Houghton. (3+)

POPULAR ATTRACTIONS

HADRIAN VII by Peter Luke. The title role was successfully taken over by Douglas Rain during its continued run and transfer. (466+)

THE MERRY WIVES OF WINDSOR by William Shakespeare. New production at the Open-air Theater. With James Cossins, Charmian Eyre. (62)

THE FOUNDATIONS by John Galsworthy. Revival of World War I drama of social criticism. With Janet Hargreaves, Emrys Jones. (18)

THE DANCING YEARS by Ivor Novello. Revival of British pre-war operetta. With June Bronhill, Robert Crewdson. (44)

LIGHTS UP! devised by Josephine Wilson from scientific data. Education through drama. With the Molecule Company. (44)

NOT NOW, DARLING by Ray Cooney and John Chapman. The misadventures of an erring furrier. With Donald Sinden, Bernard Gribbins, Jill Melford. (408+)

MY GIDDY AUNT by Ray Cooney and John Chapman. Suburban cleaning woman impersonates a murdered elderly eccentric. With Irene Handl, Manning Wilson. (118)

THE MAN MOST LIKELY TO . . . by Joyce Raeburn. A father and son (if it *is* his son) cast eyes on the same girl. With Leslie Phillips, Ciaran Madden, Trevor Kent. (412+)

THE MERRY WIVES OF WINDSOR by William Shakespeare. Transfer to London of Terry Hands' Stratford production. With Brewster Mason, Ian Richardson, Elizabeth Spriggs, Brenda Bruce. (54 in repertory)

TWO GENTLEMEN OF VERONA by William Shakespeare. New production at the Open-air Theater. With Bernard Bresslaw, Gemma Jones, John Quentin. (42)

THE RELAPSE by John Vanbrugh. Re-cast revival of Trevor Nunn's 1967 Stratford production. With Barrie Ingham, Emrys James, Toby Robins, Lynn Farleigh, Michael Jayston, Jeffery Dench. (45 in repertory)

OH, CLARENCE! by John Chapman; adapted from P.G. Wodehouse stories. With Naunton Wayne, Agnes Lauchlan, James Hayter, Peggy Mount, Robertson Hare, Tamara Ustinov. (189)

THE BEGGAR'S OPERA by John Gay; edited by David Turner. Edinburgh Festival production transfer. With Frances Cuka, Peter Gilmore, Jan Waters, James Cossins, Hy Hazell. (68)

A BOSTON STORY by Ronald Gow; dramatization of Henry James's *Watch and Ward*. With Tony Britton, Dinah Sheridan, Basil Hoskins, Rosamund Burne. (220)

THE DAUGHTER-IN-LAW by D.H. Lawrence. Pre-European-tour revival of 1968 success. With Elizabeth Bell, Michael Coles. (8)

HOME AND BEAUTY by W. Somerset Maugham. Revival of farcical comedy of a supposed World War I widow's remarriage. With Geraldine McEwan, Robert Stephens, Robert Lang, Arthur Lowe (later Laurence Olivier). (37+ in repertory)

THE SECRETARY BIRD by William Douglas Home. The eternal triangle quadrilaterally resolved. With Kenneth More, Jane Downs, Judith Arty, Terence Longdon. (231+)

CLOSE THE COALHOUSE DOOR by Alan Plater. Story of miners based on Sid Chaplin's stories. With John Woodvine, Bryan Pringle, Caroline Hunt. (135)

LOOK BACK IN ANGER by John Osborne. Re-cast revival of dramatic milestone. With Victor Henry, Jane Asher, Martin Shaw, Caroline Mortimer, Edward Jewesbury. (127)

RING ROUND THE MOON by Christopher Fry. Revival of famous Anouilh adaptation. With John Standing, Flora Robson, Robert Eddison, Angela Thorne, Isabel Jeans, Moyra Fraser, Bill Fraser. (101)

FORTY YEARS ON by Alan Bennett. A satirical pageant of British history (1900-1968) staged by schoolboys. With the author, John Gielgud, Dorothy Reynolds. (244+)

THE COCKTAIL PARTY by T.S. Eliot. Chichester Festival production transfer. With Alec Guinness, Eileen Atkins, Michael Aldridge, Pauline Jameson. (149)

THEATERGOROUND seasons included *Room for Company* devised by Gareth Morgan, an anthology of London for the Festival of London. (5) At the Royal Shakespeare Company's London home, a three-week season: *Pleasure and Repentance* devised by John Barton and Gareth Morgan, a lighthearted look at love; *Waiting for Godot* by

THE SEASON IN LONDON

Samuel Beckett; *The Fox and the Fly* adapted from Ben Jonson's *Volpone;* revival of *The Hollow Crown* devised by John Barton; *Eve and After* devised by Sheila Allen, a feminist point of view; *Alarums and Excursions* devised by Guy Woolfenden, sound and music in the theater; *Men at Arms* devised by Michael Rudman, peace and war in fact and fiction; *All the World's a Stage,* a symposium of Elizabethan writing and song. With the Royal Shakespeare Company's "Theatergoround" travelling company. (18)

O.K. FOR SOUND devised by Gerald Frow and Powell Jones from scientific data. Education through drama. With the Molecule Company. (43)

JULIUS CAESAR by William Shakespeare. Transfer to London of John Barton's Stratford production. With Barrie Ingham, Ian Richardson, Brewster Mason, Geoffrey Hutchings, Charles Thomas. (34 in repertory)

THEY DON'T GROW ON TREES by Ronald Millar. A farce with nine roles for a single comedienne. With Dora Bryan. (132)

MR. AND MRS. by Ross Taylor; musical adapted from two Noel Coward playlets. With John Neville, Honor Blackman. (53)

GULLIVER'S TRAVELS by Gerald Frow and Sean Kenny; adapted from Jonathan Swift. With Michael D'Abo, William Rushton, Brian Murphy. (108)

TONS OF MONEY by Will Evans and Valentine. Revival of a famous 1920s Aldwych farce. With Richard Murdoch, William Kendall, Joe Shelton, Chili Bouchier. (28)

LOVE'S LABOUR'S LOST by William Shakespeare. National Theater's revival of the comedy. With Joan Plowright, Jeremy Brett, Derek Jacobi, Richard Kay, Louise Purnell, Ronald Pickup, John McEnery. (41 in repertory)

QUEEN PASSIONELLA AND THE SLEEPING BEAUTY by Bryan Blackburn and Freddie Carpenter. A high camp romp for a famous female impersonator. With Danny La Rue, Alan Haynes. (185+)

THE YOUNG VISITORS by Michael Ashton; musical adaptation of Daisy Ashford's book. With Alfred Marks, Jill Riddick. (63)

SAVED by Edward Bond. Re-cast revival of former banned drama. With Kenneth Cranham, Adrienne Posta. (27 in repertory)

WE WHO ARE ABOUT TO . . . by James Saunders, Lyndon Brook, Alun Owen, Julia Jones, Fay Weldon, Alan Ayckbourn, John Bowen, David Compton, George Melly. An entertainment on marriage comprising 8 playlets and a linking commentary. Transferred, with *Night* by Harold Pinter replacing Julia Jones's playlet, and retitled *Mixed Doubles.* With Oscar Quitak, Andrée Melly, Nigel Stock, Vivien Merchant. (79+)

HAMLET by William Shakespeare. Openstage revival at the Roundhouse. With Nicol Williamson, Marianne Faithfull, Mark Dignam. (70)

THE MERRY WIDOW by Franz Lehar. Revival of operetta. With Lizbeth Webb, John Rhys Evans. (63)

BRIEF LIVES by Patrick Garland; adapted from John Aubrey's book. With Roy Dotrice. (113+)

TWO CITIES by Constance Cox; musical of Dickens novel *A Tale of Two Cities.* With Edward Woodward, Kevin Colson, Elizabeth Power. (36)

WHAT THE BUTLER SAW by Joe Orton. Posthumous farce of strange goings-on in a psychiatrist's clinic. With Ralph Richardson, Coral Browne, Stanley Baxter, Julia Foster. (101)

JUST A SHOW by Barry Humphries. A oneman revue. With the author. (42)

DEAD SILENCE by Monte Doyle. A detective is implicated in a crime. With Alfred Marks. (85+)

LOCK UP YOUR DAUGHTERS by Bernard Miles and others. Re-cast revival of musical of Fielding's *Rape upon Rape.* With Russell Hunter, Veronica Clifford. (108+)

THE ENOCH SHOW by various authors. Anti-racialist political documentary. With Malcolm Tierney, Henry Woolf, Deborah Norton. (39)

ANN VERONICA by Frank Wells and Ronald Gow; musical adapted from the novel by H.G. Wells. With Mary Millar, Arthur Lowe, Hy Hazell. (45)

THE AU PAIR MAN by Hugh Leonard. Grass widow instructs a caller in the niceties of breeding. With Joan Greenwood, Donal McCann. (45+)

THE WAY OF THE WORLD by John Wycherley. Revival marking Michael Langham's directorial debut with the National Theater. With Geraldine McEwan, Robert Lang, Hazel Hughes. (15+ in repertory)

SHE STOOPS TO CONQUER by Oliver Goldsmith. Transfer of Theater 69's Man-

chester production. With Tom Courtenay, Trevor Peacock, Ciaran Madden. (29+)

SHAKESPEARE'S MACBETH adapted by Charles Marowitz. Transfer of Open Space production from Wiesbaden 1969 Festival. With Nikolas Simmonds, Thelma Holt. (11+)

SOME AMERICAN PLAYS PRODUCED IN LONDON

GOLDEN BOY by Clifford Odets and Clifford Gibson. With Sammy Davis Jr., Gloria De Haven. (136)

YOU KNOW I CAN'T HEAR YOU WHEN THE WATER'S RUNNING by Robert Anderson. With Tom Ewell, Nicole Shelby. (37)

INDIANS by Arthur Kopit. World premiere of an historical tale of genocide set in a circus ring. With Barrie Ingham, Emrys James, Michael Jayston, Gaye Brown. (34 in repertory)

LADY BE GOOD (musical) by George Gershwin. With Aimi Macdonald, Lionel Blair. (156)

JANIE JACKSON by Robert P. Hillier. With Marlene Warfield, Earl Cameron. (24)

THE ELECTRONIC NIGGER by Ed Bullins. With Michael Da Costa, Stefan Kalipha. (24)

KEEP TIGHTLY CLOSED IN A COOL DRY PLACE by Megan Terry. With Roger Hendricks Simon. (18)

THE LATENT HETEROSEXUAL by Paddy Chayefsky. With Roy Dotrice, Lee Montague, Toby Robins, Ian Hogg. (36 in repertory)

HAIR (musical) by Gerome Ragni and James Rado. With Oliver Tobias, Paul Nicholas, Annabel Leventon. (231+)

ABSENCE OF A CELLO (British title: Out of the Question) by Ira Wallach. With Gladys Cooper, Dulcie Gray, Michael Denison. (262+)

GOD BLESS by Jules Feiffer. With Roy Dotrice, Pauline Munro, Robert Lloyd, Barry Stanton, Ian Hogg. (19 in repertory)

SAND by Murray Mednic. With the Pip Simmons Group. (12)

THE BEARD by Michael McClure. With Billie Dixon, Richard Bright. (50)

A MINOR SCENE and IT HAS NO CHOICE by Ed Bullins. With Stefan Kalipha, Margaret Nolan. (24)

HOMO by Rochelle Owens. With Margaret Nolan, Sandy Macdonald. (16)

FUCKNAM by Tuli Kupferberg. World premiere of anti-militaristic drama relating violence to sexual deprivation, transferred from Lund, Sweden. With the Lund University Theater Group. (15)

A DELICATE BALANCE by Edward Albee. With Peggy Ashcroft, Elizabeth Spriggs, Patience Collier, Sheila Hancock, John Welsh, Michael Hordern. (48 in repertory)

WAR by Jean-Claude van Itallie. With Lesley Ward, Michael Elphick, Richard Howard. (6)

YOUR OWN THING (musical) by Donald Driver. With the original U.S. cast. (59)

THE BOYS IN THE BAND by Mart Crowley. With an American cast (later replaced by all-British cast). (167+)

PLAZA SUITE by Neil Simon. With Paul Rogers, Rosemary Harris. (119+)

MAME (musical) by Jerome Lawrence and Robert E. Lee. With Ginger Rogers. (114+)

THE FUN WAR by Geoffrey Bush and MUZEEKA by John Guare. With Clive Cazes, Paul Jones, Al Mancini. (12)

MR. JELLO by George Birimisa. With Tony Sibbald, Dinah Stabb, Maurice Colbourne. (6)

THE GENTLEMAN CALLER and HOW DO YOU DO by Ed Bullins. With Stan Chaman, Sheila Scott-Wilkinson. (16)

LA TURISTA by Sam Shepard. With Barry Dennen, Al Mancini, Leila Goldoni. (11)

TATTOO PARLOR by Tom LeBarr. With David Liddy, Julian Brett. (12)

THE PRICE by Arthur Miller. With Shepperd Strudwick, Albert Salmi, Kate Reid, Harold Gary. (102+)

A WHITMAN PORTRAIT by Paul Shire. With Alexander Crosbie. (12)

AND THESE IS NOT ALL by James Paul Dey. World premiere of drama of cross-section of U.S. life on the Pacific Coast of Mexico. With Marie Adams, Bill Bailey, Kathleen Moffatt. (24)

SOME FOREIGN PLAYS PRODUCED IN LONDON

THE LABYRINTH by Arrabal and Barbara Wright. With Jérome Savary and the Paris Grand Théâtre Panique Company. (23)

SUMMER by Romain Weingarten. With Jane Asher, Brian Murphy, Bryan Pringle. (22)

JACQUES BREL IS ALIVE AND WELL AND LIVING IN PARIS by Jacques Brel. With Elly Stone, Mort Shuman, Shawn Elliott, June Gable. (22)

FORTUNE AND MEN'S EYES by John Herbert. With Al Mancini, Peter Marinker, Louis Negin. (149)

ENCARNACION IN THE SQUARE by Frank Castillo. (D) World premiere of Venezuelan play about a young girl's frustrations. With Anne Freud. (12)

TOMORROW MORNING and PICNIC by Yossi Allfi. With Aaron Daniel, David Saxon, Celia Quick, Helen Sirocco. (2)

VIVI VIVA! by Ian Lindsay; adapted from Machiavelli's Clizia. With Serena Harington. (12)

THE ADVERTISEMENT by Natalia Ginzburg. World premiere of 1968 Marzotto prize-winning drama of a selfish wife driven by desperation to a dreadful deed. With Joan Plowright, Derek Jacobi, Louise Purnell. (35 in repertory)

THE TUTOR by Jakob Lenz. With Oliver Cotton, Jill Allen. (1)

LISTEN HERE NOW by Leopoldo Mahler; Argentinian play based on Leon Ferrari's Palabras Ajenas. World premiere, contrasts America today with Germany in the 1930s. With four B.B.C. announcers. (6)

THE TROUBLEMAKER by Franco Brusati; translated by Henry Reed from La Fastidiosa. With Patrick Waddington, Margaret Vines. (18)

ONE AUTUMN EVENING by Friedrich Duerrenmatt. With Kenneth J. Warren. (3)

DEAR CHARLES by Alan Melville; adapted from Treize à Table by Marc-Gilbert Sauvajon and Frederick Jackson. With Cecily Courtneidge, Jack Hulbert. (13)

THE STRONG BREED by Wole Soyinka. With Keefe West, Uwa Hunwick, Ilario Pedro, Liza Monroe. (11)

SONATA FOR THREE GENTLEMEN and CONVERSATION SINFONIETTA by Jean Tardieu. With the Pip Simmons Group. (36)

SOLDIERS by Rolf Hochhuth. With John Colicos, Raymond Huntley, Basil Langton, George Coulouris, Alec Clunes. (116)

THE SERVANT OF TWO MASTERS by Carlo Goldoni, adapted by David Turner. With Tommy Steele. (61)

CIRKUS by Haakon Strangberg. With Theater Fem Company of Gothenburg. (12)

NARCOLEPSY by Momoko Hosokawa. With Mara Llewellyn, Nathaniel Norward. (24)

SQUASH THEM FLAT (Maman J'Ai Peur) by Rufus, Bernard Higelin, and Briggitte Fontaine. With Marie Adams, Tim Thomas, Christopher Heywood. (21)

FROM THE ASHES OF THEBES by Moris Farhi. World premiere of Turkish poetic drama on present day dilemmas in antique garb. With Pamela Ann Davy, Glynn Jones. (17)

BEFORE YOU GO by Lawrence Holofcener. With Toby Robins, Dinsdale Landen. (21)

WORLD THEATER SEASON with the Roger Planchon company in Bérénice and George Dandin (8 each); the Prague Theater Behind the Gate in Three Sisters (4), The Single-Ended Rope (2) and The Green Cockatoo and An Hour of Love (2); the New York Negro Ensemble Company in Song of the Lusitanian Bogey (12) and "God is a (Guess What?)" (4); the Athens Art Theater in Lysistrata and Oedipus Rex (8 each); the Anna Magnani Company in The She-Wolf (8).

THE METAMORPHOSIS by Franz Kafka, adapted by Steven Berkoff. With the adapter. (4)

ANNE OF GREEN GABLES by L.M. Montgomery; adapted by Donald Harron. With Polly James, Barbara Hamilton, Hiram Sherman. (53+)

CAT AMONG THE PIGEONS (Un Fil à la Patte) by Georges Feydeau; adapted by John Mortimer. With Elizabeth Seal, Richard Briers, Murray Melvin, Victor Spinetti. (54+)

JUMP by Myles Murchison. With the Western Canada Youth Theater. (1)

O
O
O

THE SEASON ELSEWHERE
IN EUROPE

By Ossia Trilling

O
O
O

AS ALWAYS, the German-speaking theater takes pride of place in any review of the year's work, if only because of its numerical strength. This year's
European harvest has yielded an unusual number of theatrical scandals of one
sort or another: the departure, unexpected or long awaited, premature or long
delayed, of this or that institution, manager or artist; government interference,
foreign interference, civic protest, student protest and objections by literary
agents and even—God save the mark!—by authors themselves to what a director may be doing to their original scripts. The season began controversially
with the early removal from the management of the Hamburg City Theater of
Oscar Fritz Schuh's successor, Egon Monk, a pupil of Brecht who set off on
the wrong foot by contributing a disproportionate amount of original text and
other innovatory matter into his first productions. It was never explained why
a director might not also write his own plays, but he fell quickly under the
pressure of an unyielding press campaign, headed by the Hamburg-based *Die
Welt*. He returned to his former job in North Germany's TV-drama department, where he was able to continue to spread his brand of political philosophy
via the drama undisturbed. The appointment of the inventive Heinz Lietzau
as his successor dealt a blow to the Munich State Dramatic Theater which
Lietzau had only recently taken over. It also provoked yet another clash of
personalities when Ivan Nagel, literary adviser to the neighboring Kammerspiele in Munich, invited by Lietzau to join him in Hamburg, at first accepted
and then resigned before assuming office, following mutual public accusations
of dishonesty.

During Nagel's tenure of office at the Kammerspiele, an injunction against
Hans Neuenfels's production of Edward Albee's *Everything in the Garden*
was granted to the author's literary agents in Germany (notwithstanding the
peaceful passage of Albee's *Box-Mao-Box* there earlier in the season), to fore-
stall the director's distortion of the dramatist's intentions. Neuenfels thereupon stole from Peter Zadek his reputation as the year's *enfant terrible* with
near-blasphemous stage business which he introduced into Peter Terson's *Zigger-Zagger* at Heidelberg. Provocatively staged throughout, this noisy production of social protest in the British provinces was marred by walk-outs by

153

offended Catholics that nearly led to the dismissal of the newly-appointed manager, Piscator's former assistant, Peter Stoltzenberg. *Zigger-Zagger* was taken by Heidelberg to the annual review in Berlin of the season's best productions to compete with several other daunting contenders for the title. The two highlights of the Munich State Dramatic Theater (the so-called Residenztheater) were both staged by Lietzau and broke the record for curtain calls when taken to the Berlin review. They were *Philoctetes* by the East German Heiner Müller, a world premiere of a new work inspired by Sophocles but using a wholly modern theatrical idiom—that of the theater of cruelty—on an asymmetrical wooden space-stage, with stylized costumes and changeable masks borrowed from the Italian comedy convention; and Schiller's *The Brigands,* in which the company succeeded, miraculously, in creating almost as many decibels of unbearable noise through sheer shouting as did the raucous productions of *Hair* that covered the theatrical face of Europe throughout the year, from Stockholm to Belgrade.

With Harry Buckwitz gone from Frankfurt, the City Theater settled down to a less adventurous regime under Ulrich Ehrfurt, who inaugurated a series of new Shakespearean translations (by Hartmut Lange) over the coming years. The first, directed with epic coolness by Dieter Reible on an open-timbered, Elizabethan-type octagonal thrust stage surmounted by a metal gallery and modernistic reflected ceiling lighting, was *Richard II*. Peter Kollek's petulant monarch made an interesting contrast with Rüdiger Bahr's more reticent Richard in Erich Fried's rival version at Braunschweig, now under Heidelberg's former chief, Hans Peter Doll, and Fried's staunchest champion as Shakespeare translator. The Shakespeare cult begun by Jörg Wehmeier and Peter Palitzsch at Stuttgart took on a new shape in their adaptation of *Richard III,* intentionally renamed *The Third Richard.* In Wilfried Minks's neon-lighted architectural set, Hans-Christian Blech gave a subtle, Arturo-Ui-like interpretation of the title role and Palitzsch again displayed his debt to his former teacher, Brecht, in his epic handling of the chronicle. This special talent was further evidenced in two world premieres: Tankred Dorst's semi-documentary of the abortive Bavarian Soviet Republic of 1919, entitled *Toller,* after the poet-dramatist who chaired the revolutionary committee, and *Thief and Monarch,* a witty send-up of German militarism by the East German Rolf Schneider, each play imaginatively set by Minks. Having two actresses play the Prussian Emperor Frederick the Great and his favorite *en travesti* set the seal on the director's impudence. *Toller* won golden opinions at the Berlin review, though left wingers objected to the equating (in the newsreel commentaries) of the Nazi and Russian invasions of Czechoslovakia. The untimely death of Teo Otto robbed the German-speaking theater of its outstanding scene designer, but not before he had completed the settings for *Artur Anonymus* in his native Wuppertal. This was the late Else Lasker's 37-year-old dramatic plea for reconciliation between Jew and gentile, staged by Hans Bauer in the author's birthplace and taken at the year's end to the Berlin review—where, to the eternal shame of Berlin, its sentimentality provoked reactions of racial rather than esthetic prejudice.

West Berlin

The highlights of theatrical life in West Berlin were concentrated in and around the Schiller Theater, with its two ancillary stages, the Schlosspark and the Studio Theaters. All the same, Hans-Jörg Utzerath's second year of office at the Free People's Theater had two resounding successes to chalk up: an ingeniously mirrored setting (by Heinz Balthes) for the German premiere of Jean-Paul Sartre's *Kean* (with Uwe Friedrichsen) and a lustily bawdy-cum-hippie production of *Much Ado About Nothing,* using a long-forgotten Swiss 17th century translation that came much nearer the Renaissance spirit of Shakespeare's original text than the more usual, romanticized versions of later years. The climax of the 1968 Berlin festival was *Macbeth,* closely modeled by Romanian guest-director Liviu Ciulei on his Bucharest production (see page 122 of the 1967-68 *Best Plays* volume), with the electrifying Hans-Dieter Zeidler as Macbeth and Eva Katharina Schultz as his sadistically insatiable lady. It was followed by his perceptive version of *The Seagull.* Hans Schwei-kart was entrusted by Boleslaw Barlog with the European premiere of Joseph Heller's *We Bombed in New Haven* weeks before its New York opening, with Ernst Schröder as the bland U.S. Air Force officer in charge of the play within the play. Fritz Kortner's Shakespearean ventures, always a pleasure to watch, proved less inspiring in the case of *Antony and Cleopatra* (with Carl Raddatz stealing the show as Enobarbus), the work of a palpably tired director.

The one major artistic defeat (though a box office hit) proved to be *Before-hand,* Günter Grass's first play since the controversial *Plebians Rehearse the Uprising.* Inspired by the shooting of a student by the Berlin police, *Before-hand* was mainly concerned with motives and disclaimed interest in events. This was at once its appeal and its weakness. Though the five players were carefully organized by Heintz Lietzau throughout two hours of static debate on a pentagonal simultaneous space-stage (and among them was the brilliant Martin Held in the role of Olympian string-puller), the foreign visitor failed to be swept off his feet by the problem of student protest seen from a parochi-ally German viewpoint, despite some tantalizing dialogue that included a re-minder that the German chancellor had been a Nazi. Grass, true to his con-victions, took successful legal action to prevent the later producer of the play in Münster from cutting the incriminating line.

East Berlin

In East Berlin, controversy, as always, took on an ideological tone. The masterly production by Wolfgang Heinz of *Faust I* at the Deutsches Theater was attacked by supporters of official party policy who took inspired issue with the portrayal of Faust as a nincompoop and Mefisto as a clown, so soon after the cultural minister had held Germany's literary hero up as an exemplar of humanism. The dispute was clouded by the departure of Heinz's best di-rectorial staff member, the Swiss-born Benno Besson, after artistic disagreements. Besson was thereupon appointed to the East Berlin People's Theater. After a reconciliation with Helene Weigel and the Berliner Ensemble after an absence of 15 years, he promised to stage Brecht's *Turandot or the Washerwoman's Congress* there, as soon as commitments allowed—an invitation given and accepted after staging the world premiere of the play as guest director in Zurich. A surprising resignation was that of Manfred Wekwerth from the Berliner Ensemble, where he had kept Brecht's torch alit as his prime disciple since 1956. His decision was partly occasioned by illness. All the same, two disappointing productions by Wekwerth (Brecht's *Saint Joan of the Stockyards,* with Miss Weigel and Brecht's daughter by his first marriage, Hanna Hiob; and Helmut Baierl's *Joan of Döbel,* starring Renate Richter, who is Mrs. Wekwerth) may have added their weight to it.

Both the Deutches and the Ensemble lost some of their best players, who left to join Besson at the rival playhouse; but the Ensemble were lucky with the youthful team of Manfred Karge and Mathias Langhoff, if their breathtakingly modern handling of *Seven Against Thebes,* adapted from Aeschylus by Heiner Müller, was anything to go by. Artistic differences and illness of the star had caused Brecht's anti-capitalist tragedy, set in the Chicago stockyards, to be postponed. Despite Karl von Appen's monumental sets and a sterling Brechtian performance from Hilmar Thate, to name only one name, both *Joan* and her interpreter (who normally resides in Switzerland and created the role 10 years back) were quickly dropped. Had the role been given, in the first place, to Miss Richter, the production could certainly have been saved; but her stage presence was not striking enough to rescue from banality Baierl's companion piece about a peasant girl from a state farm who causes havoc in a state-run factory by taking Communist slogans literally. Its best feature was its occasional humor, a quality sorely lacking in modern German drama, both East and West. Humor was the most welcome feature of Günther Rücker's first play, at the Deutsches Theater—a political satire that punctured the balloon of class-conscious foes of Marxism. *Mr. Schmidt* (as it was called after a notorious 19th century police spy) allowed Friedo Solter's witty direction to tap an unseen vein of richly comic talent in the company. Klaus Piontek was the eponymous red-baiter.

Switzerland

In Switzerland, too, there were changes. The retirement of Leopold Lindtberg from the Zurich Schauspielhaus, after last year's scandal over Frisch's *Biography,* led to an interregnum, during which his obvious successor, Werner Düggelin, switched his allegiance to the rival city of Basle, where he was joined by the playwright Friedrich Duerrenmatt as co-manager and resident dramatist. A production of note in Zurich was Besson's of the Brecht play, in an eye-catching decor (by Horst Sagert of East Berlin) that recalled something of the panache of a Joan Littlewood musical. *Turandot* is a modern political variant on an ancient theme, and a pretext for ridiculing the compromising intellectuals who sell their souls even to the tyrants who will behead them, in a vain attempt to keep their bodies. Though aimed at Weimar Germany and then directed at Nazi totalitarianism, the political satire proved double-edged, since, as Brecht's later writings revealed, he was as critical of Stalinism. Still, it was as an anti-capitalist dramatic tract that Besson viewed it, and its enthusiastic reception by the well-to-do fellow citizens of Zurich's internationally famed bankers, in the audience on opening nights, must have rung hollow in his ears.

Duerrenmatt's first two entries for the Basle-Zurich stakes won the coveted plaudits of local audiences and of the international press. His *King John,* loosely based on Shakespeare, took a macabre view of power politics and blended melodrama and impishness into a reformist thesis for the present day, with Horst Christian Beckmann as the unruly ruler leading Duerrenmatt's theatrical army of blaspheming and flattering rogues and harridans into unbounded carnage and violence. *Play Strindberg* was the punningly voguish title he gave to his macabre "game for three performers," a 90-minute concentrate (arrived at in collaboration with the actors) of *The Dance of Death,* from which all psychologizing has been cut and the sexual battle trimmed to bare essentials. Beckmann (supported by Regine Lutz as the soured Alice and Klaus Höring as the villainous Kurt) played the tormented and sadistically impotent Captain. Inside a claustrophobic boxing-ring type of stage the three players, manipulating props and furniture themselves, delivered the pungent dialogue with the crispness of pistol shots.

An engrossing production by Iwo Moszkowicz at the Theater an der Josefstadt in Vienna of the Hungarian Julius Hay's latest drama, *The Grand Inquisitor,* served as a reminder that a number of East European dramatists are still proscribed or else have to seek an outlet for their work in the West. Hay, in his 70th year, was one such. His cautionary fable about the self-devouring evils of usurped worldly power, as told by a heretical though unrepentant Marxist, used Pirandellian devices to introduce the dilemma of a disgruntled literary lion of an unnamed People's Republic faced by the dogmatic spokesman of the proletarian dictatorship with the uncomfortable message that power dearly bought would not be lightly shed. Staged, as it was, within miles of the Czech frontier, then being manned by Soviet troops to guard against a mythical threat from without and a real threat from within, it acquired tragically ironic overtones. Another banned dramatist was the Pole, Slawomir Mrozek, no longer published in the noted Warsaw theatrical publication *Dialog,* since Adam Tan, its septuagenarian editor, was turned out of a job and followed Ida Kaminska, former head of the Jewish State Theater, into transatlantic exile. It was left to Karl Heinz Stroux, in Dusseldorf, to stage the West European premieres of Mrozek's latest one-acters, *Out of the Frying-Pan* and *Testarium,* in symbolical settings by Czech guest designer Zbynek Kolar. Each deals with the theme of dictatorship in an allegorical manner, the former recalling *Tango* in its mesmeric horror, the latter some clownishly scabrous medieval Morality. Before leaving the German-speaking theater, mention should be made, for the record, of Eugene Ionesco's directorial debut with his own *Victims of Duty* in a small Zurich playhouse; and the world premieres of two new English plays in Germany, made possible by funds provided by the Berlin Experimental Festival to the Arts Laboratory, and by the Wiesbaden Festival to the Open Space Theater, both of London, the former with Robert Walker's *Party* and the latter with Charles Marowitz's *Macbeth* collage.

France

Scandal and controversy also dogged the poor French theater, hit by the student riots and general strike of May and June 1968. After six weeks' closure and the abandonment of numerous projects, theatrical producers and festival organizers could do little but lick their wounds. Some paid for their loyalty to their audiences and their democratic principles by being repudiated by the employing city authorities. One notable case was that of Maurice Sarrazin, founder and for 23 years head of the Toulouse Capitol Theater. Another that met with worldwide publicity and indignant protests (including those of Harold Hobson, drama critic of the *Sunday Times* of London, who returned his Legion d'Honneur to the French state in disgust) was the case of Jean-Louis Barrault, peremptorily dismissed as head of both the Théâtre de l'Odéon and the Theater of the Nations, in Paris, by an ungrateful government. Roger Planchon's tender to take over the newly re-built Théâtre de la Ville (re-fitted as an ultra-modern funnel-shaped amphitheater inside the walls of the old Sarah Bernhardt) was rejected in favour of Jean Mercure, an older man but with less managerial experience. Planchon's own future, despite two stimulating productions, a satire on the works of Corneille in the light of present-day events, and his own *The Wretch,* based on an actual case of a cruel sexual murder by a Catholic priest, was left in the balance at the season's end. The Avignon Festival had to drop all its French drama programs, leaving The Living Theater in possession of the field. This, however, was abandoned after three performances of *Paradise Now,* out of solidarity with the prevailing anti-Gaullist sentiment, and as a protest against the Philistinism, not of Jean Vilar who kept faith with them, but of the city fathers who objected, though not without some reason, to the ear-piercing sorties of the Beck-Malina company into the sleeping streets of Avignon at dead of night.

The Théâtre National Populaire was obliged, midway through its season, to stop its production of Armand Gatti's *The Passion of General Franco,* as a result of pressure from the Spanish embassy, though the play had already been staged in Germany and dealt with the fate of the exiled victims of fascism rather than with that of their persecutors. And, at a performance of his *Lucifer and the Lord* at the height of the controversy, Sartre made an impassioned plea for liberty of thought and condemned the supine attitude of the French government and its cultural minister, who had once "fought against fascism" in the very land to which he was now kowtowing. Gatti's play was dropped and Georges Wilson put on nothing in its place, as a protest. His revival of Brecht's *The Resistible Rise of Arturo Ui* followed, with the ineffable Robert Hirsch (on loan from the Comédie Française) in the lead, and it acquired a new and unexpected topicality. While Madeleine Renaud made her debut at the Théâtre Gémier (the small stage of the T.N.P.) in Marguerite Duras's latest stream-of-consciousness drama, with the untranslatably punning title of *L'Amante Anglaise,* about an unmotivated murderess, Miss Renaud's husband, Barrault, launched into a private venture that paid off handsomely, both financially and artistically, and won him invitations to several foreign festivals and to London's National Theater in the months to come. This entertainment, called *Rabelais,* was staged arena-fashion in a wrestling ring, as the hippiest, noisiest, gayest, most colorful and exciting theatrical experience in town.

By contrast, the established theaters had little that was adventurous to show, though Jacques Charon's new production of *Tartuffe* at the Comédie Française, with Robert Hirsch as the posturing, effeminate scoundrel of the title, had many good moments. To Guy Rétoré's bold attempt to translate Sean O'Casey's *The Silver Tassie* into terms acceptable to French audiences at the Théâtre de l'Est Parisien, should be added the inauguration of a counterpart playhouse in Boulogne-sur-Seine, called the Théâtre de l'Ouest Parisien (TOP, as against TEP, as Parisians came to know them), with Strindberg's *Charles XII* and a memorable French premiere, that of Wesker's *Roots.* Among other outlying theaters, Aubervilliers fared better with Arthur Adamov's latest drama, the anti-American *Off Limits,* than the producers at the Theatre de Mathurins did with his penultimate *Mr. Moderate.* At the Paris City Theater, which Jean Mercure opened with a somber *Six Characters in Search of an Author* (which won Anne Doat the Year's Best Actress award for her strident performance of the daughter-in-law), the unbridled imagination of Jorge Lavelli played havoc with *Much Ado About Nothing.* At the Lyons Théâtre des Celestins, the new managerial incumbent, Jean Meyer, dividing his time between Paris and Lyons, began well by offering his patrons the French premiere of Peter Ustinov's *The Unknown Soldier and His Wife* and the world premiere of René de Obaldia's *In the Beginning Was the Bang,* whose title speaks for itself.

The unchallenged highlight of the Paris season was Oskar Panizza's "celestial tragedy" *The Council of Love.* Written by its late German author 80 years ago, it was not only banned but scorned by all producers until Lars Schmidt (who had originally planned it for the abortive Avignon Festival) had the imagination to get Lavelli to stage it, with resplendent decors and even more resplendent costumes (topless for courtesans of the 16th century Papal court), at the Théâtre de Paris, a private theater. Offensive to orthodox Catholic opinion, which the author anathematized, but defended by leading Catholics who urged that "its filth lay solely in the beholder's eye and in his mind," this play purported to lay the ghost of the immoral tradition that attributed the scourge of syphilis to the wrath of the Almighty at man's sexual depravity. The sheer artistry and taste of the production helped to give a rightful emphasis to Panizza's scurrilous, not to say blasphemous, dramatic pamphlet.

Among the remaining offerings in the private sector, only a handful rate honorable mention. Pierre Barillet and Jean-Pierre Gredy were among commercial boulevard authors who turned in hits, but Anouilh's *The Baker, the*

Baker's Wife, and the Baker's Apprentice (an allusive historical reference
that only deepens the marital tragi-comedy's structural confusion), failed to
repair the impression that this theatrical past master's hand had lost its cunning. The four next best performances were all by foreigners. The first,
Brecht's *Mother Courage* (with Maria Casarès), was staged in a disputably
ambivalent manner by Jean Tasso. Two of the other three were world premieres. Remo Forlani's *War and Peace at the Cafe Sneffle* was a black comedy
in Alexandrines, by a French writer of Italian descent, that dragged at times
but showed unusual promise. *The Nuns,* by the Cuban writer Eduardo Manet,
was a cross between Arrabal and Triana, but had original virtues of its own.
The other was Istvan Orkény's absurdist drama of violence and revolt, *The
Tot Family,* that was also still running in Budapest after three years, and
could be seen in several West European cities this season. The outstanding
presentation at the French-speaking National Theater in Brussels was guest-
director's Dario Fo's production of his own comedy *Take the Lady Away,*
with the insuppressibly funny André Debaar in the main role of the Clown
Dario.

Italy

The threatened resignation of Giorgio Strehler from the Milan Piccolo finally took effect, and his old theater struggled on as best it could without him,
beginning with two plays by foreign authors, Bulgakov's *The Purple Island*
and Adamov's *Off Limits.* Strehler began a new career as head of an experimental group called "Theater and Action" and late in the season launched
out with a radically adapted version of Weiss's *Song of the Lusitanian Bogey,*
with pop-decors by Ezio Frigerio and Carlo Tomasi, and a new score by
Fiorenzo Carpi and Bruno Nicolai. Much of the effectiveness of the company's
plastic movement was due to the work of Marisa Flach, formerly of the Piccolo. Giorgio De Lullo's third venture into new Pirandello ground, *The Wives'
Friend,* had two astonishingly stylized performances by Rossella Falk and
Romolo Valli and a characteristically claustrophobic decor by Pierluigi Pizzi.
Among the season's highlights were Moravia's poetic anti-Nazi drama *God
Kurt,* set in a murder camp, with Alida Valli, Rossella Falk's *Hedda Gabler*
(directed by De Lullo), Anna Proclemer's triple bill, culminating in Cocteau's
The Human Voice, Armand Gatti's *The Rebirth,* a tragedy of partisan strug-
gle in Guatemala which had its world premiere in its original French at the
Venice Festival before moving via Berlin to its native land, and Luchino Vis-
conti's production of Natalia Ginzburg's *The Advertisement,* with Adriana
Asti in the role created in London by Joan Plowright.

Sweden

All eyes in Sweden were turned to Stockholm for Ingmar Bergman's return
to direct a play at the Royal Dramatic Theater after a three-year absence. His
choice fell on Büchner's *Woyzeck,* which he staged in unorthodox fashion "in

the round" of the adapted baroque playhouse, by placing part of his audience on stage, screening off the top circles, introducing uniform low prices, abolishing compulsory cloak rooms and inviting interested persons (including critics) to free attendance of preliminary rehearsals twice daily until the opening. That this gave him a chance to revenge himself and his affronted fellow-artists on the hated critic of a leading Stockholm daily paper by assaulting him (a publicity gesture that cost him a fine of $1,000) only shows what a versatile man of the theater Bergman is. Tommy Berggren, Sigge Fürst, Gunnel Lindbloom and Lars Amble took the leading roles in a production as unforgettable as it was ingenious, both on account of its persuasively intimate nature and the skillful transfer of the locale to turn-of-the-century Sweden. The Finnish-born Ralph Langbacka made his debut at this theater with a fetchingly comic version of Strehler's adaptation of Goldoni's *Village Trilogy*. Alf Sjöberg capped his previous efforts with a revealingly psychological production of *The Father,* starring Georg Rydeberg, and a colorful *The Threepenny Opera* whose main originality lay in its four hours' playing time. Inga Tinblad made a welcome return as Mrs. Alving in Stig Torsslow's revival of *Ghosts*. Geoffrey Reeves paid a return visit to stage Edward Bond's *Early Morning,* banned in England and virtually a world premiere (with Birgitta Valberg as Queen Victoria), while among new plays of note was Arne Törnqvist's biographical study of the painter-genius Ernst Josephson, entitled *Carl Joseph XVI* and acted with aplomb by Ernst-Hugo Järegard.

In other Scandinavian theaters, notable novelties were Klaus Rifbjerg's re-examination of bourgeois morality (in Copenhagen's New Theater) entitled *Where Did Nora Go When She Slammed the Door?;* Johan Falck's rediscovery, in Gothenberg, of Nikolai Erdman's banned anti-Stalinist satire of 1928, *The Suicide,* claimed as the world premiere of a play by a man Gorki described as "our new Gogol"; and, in Stockholm's City Theater, Johan Bergenstrahle's streamlined, open-stage production of *Saint Joan of the Stockyards,* adorned by films of police brutality in Chicago and elsewhere, posters of the American labor movement in the 1920s and 1930s, and the lovely Lena Granhagen in the title role. Gothenberg also followed up their earlier collective production of *The Old People's Home* (which they showed at the Florence Drama Festival with singular success) and with a third social satire called *The Sandbox,* one of several collective productions that set a new trend in Scandinavian dramaturgy. The Finnish premiere of the former play on the flexible small stage of the City Theater's magnificent new home was nicely adapted to local conditions; while Kalle Holmberg was responsible, on the same stage, for an anti-Stalinist drama, masquerading as a historical tragedy of 16th century Finland, a first play by the poet Paavo Haavikko entitled *Agricola and the Fox*. On the large stage (where *Fiddler on the Roof* in a wholly original production owing nothing to its U.S.A. model broke all local records by exceeding 300 performances in 2 years), he mounted an updated revival, with political overtones, on a timbered open-stage setting, of Artturi Järviluoma's popular folk-tragedy *The Ostrobothnians.*

Eastern Europe

Sackings and the displacement of artists are less common in state-controlled theaters in the east, except, of course, on ideological grounds or during periods of political upheaval. When Czechoslovakia was invaded by the armies of the Warsaw Pact powers, many theatrical artists went on indefinite leave of absence, some like Alfred Radok and Eugen Drmola to Sweden, others to Western Germany and elsewhere. Those who stayed expressed their disapproval in other ways. For the first six months not a single Russian play (or film) could be seen in the land, though Krejca's Theater Behind the Gate capitalized on his marvellous production of *Three Sisters* during a prolonged West European tour. Jan Grossman left the Theater on the Balustrade, moving to another playhouse in the provinces. In Bratislava, the Slovakian National Theater, on the eve of cultural independence consequent upon formal federalisation, abandoned its projected production of the Pavlicek adaptation of Babel's tales of the Red Cavalry, entitled *The Resurrection of Sashka Krista:* a pity, since the late Leopold Lahola's *Sunspots,* a tragedy of a misjudged revenge by a victim of fascism, made little impression as its replacement, despite the powerful playing of its three principals. The Prague Players Theater (the so-called Cinoherni Klub) revived its grotesque two-year-old production of Gogol's *The Inspector-General* (directed by Jan Kacer) after the boycott of Russian plays was lifted, and drew many more ironic laughs from the audience than before the invasion, without changing a word of text or altering the emphasis of the playing—an experience that was curiously repeated in front of non-Czech audiences at the Florence Festival. Their latest new play, *The Night-Time Hotelier* directed by film-maker Ewald Schorm, about a seedy old man and his roommate who rent out their solitary room overnight to a couple on the brink of separation, revealed a new psychological dramatist of undoubted power in Pavel Landovsky, who gave a hilariously macabre performance as the guilt-laden Burgomaster in the Gogol.

One production above all others, at the Budapest National Theater, pointed to a new direction being taken by the Hungarian theater after years in the doldrums. Madách's little-known, philosophical, 120-year-old drama *Moses* not only has acquired political innuendoes in 1968 that recall the national struggle for independence in 1848, but also found in Endre Marton a director and in Matyas Varga a designer of uncommon suggestivity and in Imre Sinkovits an expressive interpreter of immense range. By contrast with Warsaw, where Kazimierz Dejmek was sacked from the National Theater, and which lost some of its best writers and artists to the rival city of Wroclawl, generally acknowledged as the new theatrical capital of Poland, the Bucharest theater forged ahead. Two highlights were Ionesco's *The Killer* at the Comedy Theater (which earned its manager and principal actor, Radu Beligan, the post of head of the National Theater) and *Jonah,* an allegorical verse drama of the human condition, by Marin Sorescu, at the Little Theater. In Yugoslavia the Year's Best Play award went to Djordje Lebovic's *Viktoria* staged at the Novi Sad Theater. This moving human document, which examines the motives of the survivors and the persecutors of a Nazi death camp, reaches awkward conclusions that come surprisingly from a Jewish writer.

Russia

The Moscow Art Theater celebrated its 70th anniversary by staging a new production of its celebrated emblematic comedy *The Seagull*. Boris Livanov cut and adapted the original text, adding lines from Chekhov's works to underline the egotism of the characters, and generally treating it more like a film than a play, with short scenes and several changes of setting. Opinions differed about this alleged sacrilege, but the film star Oleg Strizhanov played Konstantin in a touching manner that was widely admired. At the Mossoviet Theater, Evgeni Zavadski revived Gorki's forgotten 55-year-old drama *The Judge,* about the former inmate of a labor camp who hounds an innocent man to death. A parallel production at the Maly Theater won veteran actor Mikhail Tsaryov the Year's Best Actor award in the same leading role. Evgeni Simonov was promoted to the Vakhtangov Theater to replace his father, the late Ruben Simonov, as its titular head. The award of the first scene-design prize at the Prague Quadriennale to Josif Sumbatashvili's spare decor for Leonid Heifits's three-year-old production of Aleksei Tolstoy's *The Death of Ivan the Terrible* crowned this team's fruitful period of work at the Central Army Theater. The year's hit at the Sovremennik Theater was Galina Volchok's stylized handling of Gorki's *Lower Depths* (with Lyudmila Tolmasheva as Nastya). Never were so many western plays to be seen in Soviet theaters. Even long neglected authors, like the late Mikhail Bulgakov, were more widely performed than before. The absence of western plays of "bourgeois decadence" (e.g. Beckett, Ionesco, Pinter) was partly made up for by their Soviet equivalent. Arbuzov's latest drama, *Happy Days of an Unhappy Man,* staged simultaneously by Anatoli Efros at Moscow's Malaya Bronnaya and by Georgi Tovstogonov at the Leningrad Gorki Theater (where Miller's *The Price* was yet another of the hits), had a dissident "negative" hero for protagonist.

Efros's *Three Sisters* from the previous season was finally stopped by party censorship, which also stepped in and aborted the latest production by Yuri Lyubimov at the popular Taganka Theater of his own adaptation of Boris Mozhayev's widely acclaimed short story about the superhuman struggles of a stubborn farmer against even more stubborn officialdom, called *The Life of Fyodor Kuzkin.* As though in protest against this uncomprehending act of repression, Lyubimov staged *Tartuffe* in a manner reminiscent of early Meyerhold as a plea against royal and clerical (and, by analogy, party) censorship. Dramas that dealt with failure and disillusionment in contemporary Soviet society continued to come up against official disapproval, but not every new play saw life through rosy spectacles. An interesting development was the Mossoviet's program of late-night tryout dramas in the foyer, including a dramatization of the Kirghizian novelist Mar Badzhiyev's *The Duel,* about three youngsters who make a mess of their lives. It was enthusiastically welcomed by a largely youthful audience.

Highlights of the Paris Season

Selected and compiled by Ossia Trilling

OUTSTANDING PERFORMANCES

JACQUELINE MAILLAN as Noëlle in *The Invoice*	JEAN MARAIS as Richard Dudgeon in *The Devil's Disciple*	FRANÇOIS PÉRIER as Goetz in *Lucifer and the Lord*
CLAUDE RICHE as Alain in *The Four Seasons*	DELPHINE SEYRIG as Suzanne in *The Aide-Memoire*	YVES RENIER as Tony in *The Servant*
GABRIEL JABBOUR as Commanding Officer in *The Tot Family*	HENRI VIRLOGEUX as Panurge in *Rabelais*	PAUL TABARD as Gregor in *The Metamorphosis*
MADELEINE RENAUD as Claire Lannes in *The English Mistress*	JULIETTE VILLARD as The Woman in *The Council of Love*	JEAN-PIERRE MARIELLE as Le Babo in *War and Peace at the Cafe Sneffle*
ROBERT HIRSCH as Arturo Ui in *The Resistible Rise of Arturo Ui*	MARIA CASARÈS as Mother Courage in *Mother Courage and her Children*	JACQUES VEBER as Vincent in *Tchao!*

OUTSTANDING DIRECTORS

JEAN-LOUIS BARRAULT *Rabelais*	JACQUES CHARON *Tartuffe*	JORGE LAVELLI *The Council of Love*

OUTSTANDING DESIGNERS

MICHEL RAFFAELLI *The Silver Tassie*	MATIAS *Rabelais*	LILA DE NOBILI *The Council of Love*

OUTSTANDING NEW FRENCH PLAYS
(D)—Playwright's Paris Debut

LE BOULANGER, LA BOULANGÈRE, ET LE PETIT MITRON (The Baker, the Baker's Wife, and the Baker's Apprentice) by Jean Anouilh. The picaresque daydreams of a boy and his soured parents. With Sophie Daumier, Michel Bouquet, Jean Paradès.

JE NE VEUX PAS MOURIR IDIOT (I Don't Want to Die an Idiot) by Georges Wolinski. (D) Wolinski's famous cartoons of the 1968 "May Events" dramatized with song. With Georges Bellea, Hermine Karageuz, Philippe Ogouz.

RABELAIS by Jean-Louis Barrault. Hippie dramatization of the works of Rabelais. With the author, Dora Doll, Henri Virlogeux, Pierre Bertin.

L'AMANTE ANGLAISE (The English Mistress/English Mint) by Marguerite Duras. The punning title refers to an item in the cross-examination of a wanton murderess. With Madeleine Renaud, Claude Dauphin, Michael Lonsdale.

LES ROSENBERG NE DOIVENT PAS MOURIR (The Rosenbergs Shall Not Die) by Alain Decaux. (D) A documentary tragedy arguing the innocence of the executed American spies. With Sylvia Monfort, Bernard Rousselet, Jacques Charby.

UNE TORTUE NOMMÉE DOSTOIEVSKI (A Turtle Called Dostoyevski) and BESTIALITÉ ÉROTIQUE (Erotic Bestiality) by Arrabal. A young man, eaten by a turtle, is as happy as Dostoyevski's politician devoured by a crocodile, and a sado-masochistic symbolical one-acter about the torments of mankind. With Roland Bertin, Christian Bouillette, Hazel Carr.

LE JARDIN DE BETTERAVES (The Beet Patch) by Roland Dubillard. Absurdist drama about four punningly Beethoven-playing musicians adumbrated in typical Dubillard fashion. With the author, Roger Blin, Maria Machado.

L'ENGRENAGE (Clockwork) by Jean-Paul Sartre. A stage version of Sartre's famous wartime screen play. With Raymond Pellerin, Marie Dubois, Maurice Teynac.

GUERRE ET PAIX AU CAFÉ SNEFFLE

(War and Peace at the Cafe Sneffle) by Remo Forlani. A wry, symbolic verse tragedy of race prejudice and hatreds in occupied Paris. With Jean-Pierre Marielle, Micheline Luccioni, Pierre Leproux.

CIEL! OU SONT PASSÉES LES DATES DE TES OASES? (Heavens! Where Are the Dates of Thy Oases Now?) by Roger Hanin. (D) What price liberalism, in an age where intolerance and self-interest pay? With the author, Odile Versois, Lyne Chardonnet.

LIMITED RUNS OF INTERESTING NEW FRENCH PLAYS

CHANSONS-BÊTES (Silly Songs) by Jean Anouilh. Short animal fables in song, set to music. With Simone Bartel, Marguerite Cassan.

LE TABLEAU (The Picture) by Eugène Ionesco and GUERNICA by Arrabal. A satire of a nouveau riche art-collector, and a revival of playlet of the Spanish Civil War. With Arlette Thomas, Henri Virlogeux.

M. LE MODÉRÉ (Mr. Moderate) by Arthur Adamov. Political satire of a dictator driven into inglorious exile. With Jacques Debary, Marguerite Cassan, Max Vialle.

LA NUIT (Night) by Jeannine Worms. A wife's three-way view of her husband. With Edith Scob, Gilberte Geniat, François Perrot, Jean-Pierre Miquel.

CHARLES VII by Claude Cyriaque. (D) A 14th century king protests his reluctant duties. With the author, Tatiana Moukhine.

LUCKY LUKE by Giorda. (D) A musical parody of Westerns and comics. With the Falguières company.

LA MOITIÉ DU PLAISIR (Half the Pleasure) by Stève Passeur, Robert Chazal and Jean Serge. Murder at a well-known critic's dinner-party. With Gérard Buhr, Evelyne Dandry, Robert Hossein.

LA RUE OBALDIA (Obaldia Street) by René de Obaldia. Obaldian sketches, verses and songs. With Jacques Achédian, France Dany.

LE MYSTÈRE DE L'OFFICE DES MORTS (The Mystery of the Funeral Service) by Michel Cazenave. (D) The way to God through spiritual experience. With Edith Garraud, Robert Dadies.

EN PASSANT PAR LA LORRAINE (Passing Through Lorraine) by Philippe Adrien. The human condition in two monologues and three duologues. With the Bourges National Drama Center Company.

LA TOUR D'EINSTEIN (Einstein's Tower) by Christian Liger. (D) Albert Einstein's philosophy in duologue form. With Pierre Fresnay, Julien Bertheau.

MATHIEU LEGROS by Jean-Claude Grumberg. The tale of a Napoleonic deserter. With Yves Gasc, Francis Lemaire, Harry-Max, Angelo Bardi.

LA PAILLE HUMIDE (Damp Straw) by Albert Husson. Comedy of a prison escape. With Michel Roux, Jacqueline Jehanneuf, Jacque Morel.

OMBRE ET SOLEIL (Shadow and Sun) by Jean Le Marois. (D) Historical drama of Spanish heretics. With Nadia Taleb, Robert Bazil.

LES DIALOGUES DU SIEUR DE LA BRUYÈRE (La Bruyère Dialogues). Dramatized excerpts from his writings. With Liliane Patrick, Michel Paulin.

SPECTACLE OBALDIA-JARRY. Playlet and verses (set to music) by Rene de Obaldia, and dramatized excerpts from Alfred Jarry's writings. With the Annie Deguay company.

POPULAR ATTRACTIONS

QUE LES HOMMES SONT BÊTES (How Silly Men Are) by Marc Mays and Lancelot. The love affairs of a willing grass widower. With Suzy Delair, Annette Poivre, Eric Martell.

L'ENLÈVEMENT (The Abduction) by Francis Veber. (D) The comic complications of a businessman's wife's kidnapping. With Yvonne Clech, Pierre Mondy, Jacques Fabbri.

GUGUSSE by Marcel Achard. Triangular sex drama in occupied France and after. With Michel Serrault, Mylène Demongeot, Georges Marchal.

L'AIDE-MÉMOIRE (The Aide-Memoire) by Jean-Claude Carrière. (D) A bachelor's futile efforts to resist an unwanted visitor's charms. With Delphine Seyrig, Henri Garcin.

LA DAME DE CHICAGO (The Lady from Chicago) by Frédéric Dard. The troubles of a 1929 bootlegger and his female rival. With Elvire Popesco, Robert Vattier, Olivier Hussenot.

LA FACTURE (The Invoice) by Françoise Dorin. In a series of sketches, a woman beautician tries to settle life's accounts too quickly. With Jacqueline Maillan, Bernard Noel.

LES FOURBERIES DE SCAPIN (Scapin's Pranks) by Molière. Revival of timeless comedy. With Edmond Tamiz.

ATHALIE by Racine. Imposing Comédie Française revival. With Annie Ducaux, Claude Winter, Michel Etcheverry.

SEULS LES TILLEULS MENTENT (Only the Limes Lie) by Michel André and Jean Le Poulain. Mr. and Mrs. Lime lie to save face with Auntie. With Roger Nicolas, Pierre Doris.

LORENZACCIO by de Musset. Revival of famous drama. With Roger Hanin, Corinne Marchand, Jacques Ardouin.

LE DIABLE ET LE BON DIEU (Lucifer and the Lord) by Jean-Paul Sartre. Revival of historical drama at the T.N.P. With François Périer, Alain Mottet, Judith Magre.

L'AMOUR PROPRE (Self-Love) by Marc Camoletti. Love conquers all, even self-love. With Gaby Sylvia, Philippe Nicaud.

FREDDY by Robert Thomas. To get his circus going again, a famous clown accuses himself of murder. With Fernandel, Rellys.

TARTUFFE by Molière. Notable revival at the Comédie Française, designed by Robert Hirsch. With the designer, Jacques Charon, Françoise Seigner, Denise Gence.

LUNDI, MONSIEUR, VOUS SEREZ RICHE (Monday, You'll Be Rich, Sir) by Remo Forlani. (D) Musical about the thwarted hopes of a night-club's inmates.

QUATRE PIÈCES SUR JARDIN (Four Rooms—or Plays—Overlooking the Garden) by Pierre Barillet and Jean-Pierre Gredy. Two players play four couples in four playlets in four rooms, linked by various sentimental bonds. With Sophie Desmarets, Jean Richard.

S.O.S. HOMME SEUL! (S.O.S. Man Alone!) by Jacques Vilfrid. (D) Two grass widowers on the loose in Paris. With Daniel Gélin, Jacques Jouanneau.

FANNY by Marcel Pagnol. Revival of the Marseilles waterfront drama. With Cathérine Rouvel, Henri Vilbert, Lucien Barjou.

TCHAO! By Marc-Gilbert Sauvajon. Comedy of contemporary values and the generation gap. With Jacques Weber, Elisabeth Wiener, Pierre Brasseur, Gérard Séty, France Delahalle.

VOYAGE À TROIS (Journey for Three) by Jean de Letraz. Revival of 30-year-old sexual triangle comedy. With Jacqueline Noëlle, Jacques Morel, Jean-Paul Coquelin, Frederica Layne.

SOME AMERICAN PLAYS PRODUCED IN PARIS

THE CONNECTION by Jack Gelber. With Aldo Romano, Gordon Heath, Anne-Marie Coffinet.

THE CHINESE and FRAGMENTS by Murray Schisgal. With Laurent Terzieff, Pascale de Boysson.

MAN OF LA MANCHA (musical) by Dale Wasserman. With Jacques Brel, Joan Diener.

THE VERDICT by James Carter. With Mary Grant, Jacques Harden.

THREE MEN ON A HORSE by John Cecil Holm and George Abbott. With Robert Dhéry, Colette Brosset.

THE GLASS MENAGERIE by Tennessee Williams. With Sibyl Sorel, Maud Rayer, Jacques Portet.

THE INDIAN WANTS THE BRONX and RATS by Israel Horovitz. With Michael McVay, Manuel de Morias.

THE PRICE by Arthur Miller. With Claude Dauphin, Pierre Mondy, Jean Rochefort, Yvette Etiévant.

HOME FREE by Lanford Wilson. With Marpessa Dawn, Daniel Kamwa.

THE BEARD by Michael McClure. With Billie Dixon, Richard Bright.

HAIR (musical) by Gerome Ragni and James Rado. With Julien Clerc, Herve Wattine, Vanina Michel.

SOME OTHER FOREIGN PLAYS PRODUCED IN PARIS

THEATER OF THE NATIONS SEASON included, in 1968, the Prague Theater Beyond the Gate's production of *Three Sisters* and three other plays; and, in 1969, the Dublin Abbey Theater's *She Stoops to Conquer* and *Borstal Boy;* the Bratislava Slovakan National Theater's *Dancing Tears* by Peter Zvon; the Bucharest Lucia Sturdza Bulandra City Theater's Caragiale's *Carnival Scenes;* the Turin City Theater's *Murad III* by Habib Boulares.

RIGHT YOU ARE! by Luigi Pirandello. With Michel Vitold, François Darbon, Orane Demazis.

THE FOUR SEASONS by Arnold Wesker. With Claude Riche, Nicole Courcel.

STRANGER IN MY BED by Muriel and Sidney Box. With Maria Mauban, Guy Bedos, Lucien Raimbourg.

NEIGHBOURS and THE TRIANGLE by James Saunders. With Pascale de Boysson, Gordon Heath, Laurent Terzieff.

LET SLEEPING WIVES LIE by Harold Brooke and Kay Bannerman. With Claude Nicot, Claire Maurier.

THE DEVIL'S DISCIPLE by George Bernard Shaw; adapted by Jean Cocteau. With Jean Marais, Jean Servais, Anne Carrère.

THE SERVANT by Robin Maugham. With Raymond Gérome, Yves Renier.

THE MYSTERY OF RIVER LODGE by Reginald Long. With Jacques Harden, Dominique Valensi.

THE TOT FAMILY by Istvan Orkény. With Gabriel Jabbour, Michel Galabru, Dominique Blanchard.

THE GOOD SOLDIER SCHWEIK by Jaroslav Hasek; adapted by Milan Kepel. With Claude Legros, Gérard Boucaron.

THE METAMORPHOSIS by Franz Kafka; adapted by Maria Ley Piscator. With Pierre Tabard, Daniel Emilfork.

A NIGHTINGALE TO SUPPER by Josef Topol. With Olivier Hussenot, Nadia Taleb.

THE MEEK ONE by Fyodor Dostoyevski; adapted by Gabriel Blondé. With Nadia Taleb, François Perrot.

REFUGEE CONVERSATIONS by Bertolt

Brecht. With Raymond Rouleau, Bernard Fresson.

STILL LIFE and WE WERE DANCING by Noel Coward. With Jean Desailly, Simone Valère, Michel de Ré.

THE SILVER TASSIE by Sean O'Casey. With Arlette Téphany, Dominique Vilar, Victor Garrivier.

THE BLACK SWAN by Martin Walser. With Sacha Pitoëff, Richard Leduc.

SIX CHARACTERS IN SEARCH OF AN AUTHOR by Luigi Pirandello. With Jean Mercure, Anne Doat.

GOAT ISLAND by Ugo Betti. With Sylvie Artel, Fabiène Mai, Henri Marteau.

MUCH ADO ABOUT NOTHING by William Shakespeare. With Michel Auclair, Danièle Lebrun.

THE UNKNOWN SOLDIER AND HIS WIFE by Peter Ustinov. With Jean-François Prévand, Michèle Grellier.

THE MAGNIFICENT CUCKOLD by Fernand Crommelynck. With Gaelle Romande, Le Royer, Claude Brosset.

THE GIRL FROM STOCKHOLM by Alfonso Leto. With Rosy Varte, Christian Alers.

THE COUNCIL OF LOVE by Oskar Panizza. (D) World premiere of banned anti-Catholic dramatic pamphlet. With Henri Martin, François Maistre, Juliette Villard.

BLACKMAIL IN THE THEATER by Dacia Maraini. With Bulle Ogier, Bernadette Lafont, Michèle Moretti.

SWEET METROGLODYTES by Claude Feraldo. With Bernard Fresson, Huguette Hue.

THE BATTLE OF LOBOSITZ by Peter Hacks. With Gérard Desarthe, Pierre Hatet.

BLOOD WEDDING by Federico Garcia Lorca. With Renée Faure.

THE PLEASURES OF HONESTY by Luigi Pirandello. With Jacques Toja, Geneviève Casile, Denise Noël, Michel Etcheverry, François Chaumette; with, as curtain-raiser, *An Imbecile* by Pirandello. With Michel Aumont, Jacques Eyser.

THE KILLING OF SISTER GEORGE by Frank Marcus. With Katarina Renn, Evelyne Ker, Anne Carrère, Colette Lecourt.

NOT NOW, DARLING by Ray Cooney and John Chapman. With Jean Poiret, Michel Serrault, Karin Petersen.

MY MOCKING HAPPINESS by Leonid Maliugin. With Giani Esposito, Sophie Marin, Hélène Vallier.

MR. KARL by Helmut Qualtinger. With Bruno Balp.

FOR KARIN by Ari Chen. With Christian Alers, Danielle Evenon.

WHITE NIGHTS by Fyodor Dostoyevski. With Dominique MacAvoy, Thierry Labey.

MOTHER COURAGE AND HER CHILDREN by Bertolt Brecht. With Maria Casarès, Françoise Brion.

THE TOURNIQUET by Josef Sandor. With Marc Cassot.

PLATONOV by Anton Chekhov. With Michel Vitold, Helène Sauvaneix, Nathalie Nerval.

THE RESISTIBLE RISE OF ARTURO UI by Bertolt Brecht. With Robert Hirsch, Georges Wilson.

FANDO AND LIS by Arrabal. With Danny Arkro, Robert Benoit.

THE UNEXPECTED GUEST by Agatha Christie; adapted by Robert Thomas. With Simone Valère, Jean Desailly, Roland Piétri.

THE NUNS by Eduardo Manet. (D) World premiere of Cuban baroque drama of greed and violence in 19th century Haiti. With Etienne Berry, Suzel Goffre.

LE QUADRILLÉ (The Graph) by Jacques Duchesne. With the Théâtre du Quebec company.

DRACULA by Alfredo Rodriguez Arias and GODDESS by Javier Arroyuelo. With the Argentinian T.S.E. troupe.

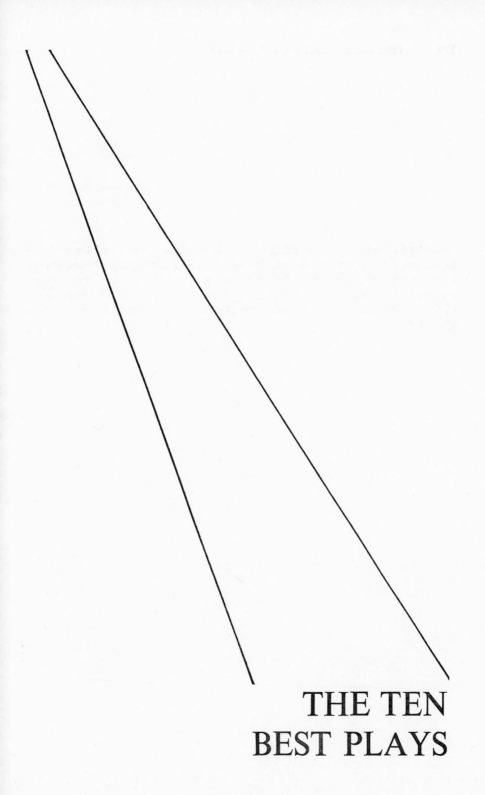

THE TEN
BEST PLAYS

In the following synopses of 1968-69's Best Plays, scenes and lines of dialogue, stage direction and description quoted from the scripts appear *exactly* as in the stage version of the play unless (in a very few instances, for technical reasons) an abridgement is indicated by five dots (. . . . .). The appearance of three dots (. . .) is the script's own punctuation to denote the timing of a spoken line.

 # LOVERS

A Program of Two One-Act Plays

BY BRIAN FRIEL

Cast and credits appear on page 375

BRIAN FRIEL was born in 1929 in Derry City, Northern Ireland. He became a school teacher but since 1960 has devoted himself to writing. His short stories have appeared in The New Yorker *and have been collected in two volumes,* The Saucer of Larks *and* The Gold in the Sea.

In more recent years Friel has concentrated on playwriting. His This Doubtful Paradise, The Enemy Within *and* The Blind Mice *were produced in Dublin, Belfast and London. His* Philadelphia, Here I Come! *was produced in Dublin in September 1964 then moved to Broadway February 16, 1966 for 326 performances. It was named a Best Play of its season and was runner-up, by one point, to* Marat/Sade, *for the Critics Award. His* The Loves of Cass McGuire *made its world debut in a Broadway engagement October 6, 1966.*

Friel's Lovers *is a program of two one-act plays—*Winners *and* Losers*— connected by time, place and the leading character of the Commentator, presented in New York in the Dublin Gate Theater production, first as part of the Lincoln Center summer festival and then at the Music Box. His* Crystal and Fox *and* The Mundy Scheme *have been produced abroad and are expected in New York next season.*

Friel now lives in the Republic (in Donegal). He is married and has four daughters.

Time: The present

*Place: The town of Ballymore, County Tyrone,
Northern Ireland*

I. WINNERS

SYNOPSIS: At the center of the stage is a gently-sloping height of land named Ardnageeha, overlooking the town of Ballymore. A Commentator enters (in one version of *Lovers* this role is shared by two persons, a man and a woman; but in the New York version the Commentator was the single character who will be Andy Tracey in the second playlet). In manner he is *"impersonal, completely without emotion; his function is to give information. At no time must he reveal an attitude toward his material."*

The Commentator is reading an account in the *Irish Times*. He reads aloud from the newspaper: "At approximately 9:45 on the morning of Saturday, June 4, 1966 Margaret Mary Enright set out from her home, a detached red brick house on the outskirts of the town of Ballymore, County Tyrone, Northern Ireland. Before she left she brought breakfast to her mother who was still in bed; and as she passed her father's surgery, which is built as an annex to the house, she tapped with the back of her fingers on the frosted glass panel of the door. In a small attache case she had her schoolbooks and sandwiches for lunch. She cycled through the town and at High Street she met two friends and stopped to talk to them: Joan O'Hara, a classmate, and Philip Moran. They told her they planned to go boating on Lough Gorm that afternoon and asked her to join them. She said perhaps she would. Then she cycled out the Mill Road until she came to Whelan's Brae. There she left the road and pushed her bicycle. . . . . ."

As the Commentator continues reading aloud, Mag enters. *"She is 17, bubbling with life. Although she is not really very beautiful, her vivacity gives her a distinct attraction."*

Mag reaches the top of the hill, looks around, lights a cigarette and waits. The Commentator explains that at this same time Joseph Michael Brennan left his home (his father was asleep, his mother at work) carrying his schoolbooks. Joe enters—*"He is 17 and a half, a serious boy and a good student, interested in books."* Joe and Mag are pupils at different grammar schools, but both have final exams the coming Wednesday. And they are to be married in three weeks' time, because Mag is pregnant.

Playfully, Mag hides herself from Joe. Joe sits down to study and Mag jumps out at him. He continues to study—or tries to—as she prattles on. She is beginning to have morning sickness, and she is happy that Joe doesn't feel "sympathetic sickness" like some expectant fathers.

MAG: . . . . . I love this view of Ballymore: the town and the fields and the lake; and the people. When I'm up here and look down on them, I want to run down and hug them all and kiss them. But then when I'm down among them I feel like doing that—
She cocks a snook into Joe's face.
—into their faces. I bet you that's how God feels at times, too. Wouldn't you think so?

JOE: I don't know how God feels.

MAG: Why not?

JOE: Because I'm not God.

MAG: Oh, you're so clever! Well, I'll tell you something: there are occasions in my life when *I* know how God feels.

JOE: Good for you.

MAG: And one of those occasions is now.
Puffing her cigarette regally.
At this moment God feels . . . expansive . . . and benificent . . . and philanthropy.

JOE: Philanthropic.

MAG *(after a momentary setback):* And we will not be put into bad humor by grubby little pedants.

JOE: Look, Mag: we came up here to study. . . . .

They discuss their subjects—French, literature, mathematics—Joe is concentrating on math. Mag will be "scootrified" if they ask her about the volume of a cone. They are school children fearful of the coming exams—and then, abruptly, Mag changes the subject: "Joe, last night again Papa asked me to let him get the flat painted for us before we move in."

JOE *(doggedly):* I said I'll paint the flat.

MAG: That's what I told him. And I was thinking, Joe . . .

JOE: What?

MAG: If we put a lace curtain across the kitchen windows we wouldn't actually *see* down into the slaughterhouse yard.

JOE: And if we wore ear-plugs all the time we wouldn't actually *hear* the mooing and the shooting.

MAG *(softly to herself):* And even if a curtain did make the room darker, it'll still be lovely.

JOE: I signed the lease yesterday evening.

MAG *(absolutely thrilled):* It's ours now? We own it?

JOE: Old Kerrigan was so busy working he wouldn't take time off to go into the office; so we put the document on the back of a cow that was about to be shot and that's where we signed it. . . . .

Joe describes the slaughterhouse scene with the blood and the dying animals, and suddenly they are children again, thrilled by the horror of it, then turning it into a game and pretending that they are shooting all the people in Bally-more they don't happen to like.

Finally Joe returns to his books, muttering in answer to Mag's question that he would *not* prefer to live on the top floor of Mag's father's house (Mag wouldn't either). Mag tells Joe how much she likes his parents.

The Commentator describes Joe's and Mag's backgrounds. Joe's father Mick hasn't worked in 20 years because of asthma. He lives on his unemploy-ment benefits and his wife's wages as a charwoman. Mag is the daughter of a dentist whose wife Beth has never been well since Mag's twin brother, Peter, died in infancy, smothered by the pillow in his cot.

Mag looks down at the town and describes the scene to Joe, who is not really listening. She rambles on about her likes and dislikes; about her coming child ("I hope it's a boy, and that it'll be like you—with a great big bursting brain"). Perhaps she will have twins. Mag herself and her twin brother were five weeks premature and born by Caesarean (Joe pretends he knows what this word means, though he has never heard it before).

Mag announces that she found a gray hair in her comb that morning. She decides: "If I had to choose between a young face and black hair and an old face and silver hair I think I'd prefer the young face. *(Gently.)* You have a young face. You're only a boy. You're a baby, really. I'll have two babies to take care of. *(She touches his shoe.)* Joe, we'll be happy. Joe, won't we? It's such a beautiful morning. So still; I think this is the most important moment in my life. And I think—*(She laughs with embarrassment.)* I think sometimes that happiness, real happiness, was never discovered until we discovered it. Isn't that silly? And I want to share it with everyone—everywhere."

They argue playfully; then Mag throws Joe into a panic by clutching her stomach and moaning—false pains, she finally tells him, and he is much re-lieved. Joe tries to reassure her that he will take care of her, but he can't find the words. He goes back to his books. She decides that the pain was hunger pangs and eats some sandwiches she has brought.

Mag tells Joe a story she heard about a girl who was kidnaped at the movies. Joe complains that she is interrupting his study of integration in mathematics. Mag counters with a complaint of her own.

MAG: You haven't *asked* me to marry you.
JOE: What are you raving about?
MAG: Propose to me.
JOE: God!
MAG: Now.
JOE: You really are—
MAG: Ask me.
JOE: Will-you-marry-me. Now!
MAG: Thank you, Joseph, I will.
     He goes back to his books.
JOE: Bats! Raving bloody bats!
MAG: The children will want to know. Especially the girls. And I'll tell

them it was a beautiful morning in June, a Saturday, four days before the exams began, on top of Ardnageeha, the Hill of the Wind. And everything was still. And their father said, "Maggie," very shyly, "Maggie Enright, will you make me the proudest and happiest man in the whole world? Will you be my spouse?" And I said, "Joe"—nothing more. And I think that was the most important moment in my life.

> *She looks at Joe, sees him engrossed in his work, has a sudden stab of anxiety, and grabs a book.*

I really am scootrified this time! Integration—that's on my course, too—I think. What in the name of God does it mean?

> *She buries her head in her hands and studies furiously.*

The Commentator continues reading from his newspaper: Joe and Maggie were seen later, going in the direction of Lough Gorm. A fisherman named William Anthony Clerkin had left his boat unattended on the shore with oars and rowlocks. "When he returned an hour and twenty minutes later the boat was gone; and a girl's bicycle was lying at the edge of the water."

Maggie cannot study for long in Joe's presence without breaking the silence. She tells him the way to succeed on an exam is to set down everything you know, regardless of what the question asks for. She begins to recite everything she knows—then, suddenly, she feels lonely, nervous, frightened.

The Commentator states matter-of-factly that the bicycle was later identified as Mag's, and the fisherman sighted his boat, upturned, "floating about fifty yards west of the biggest island, Oilean Na Gcrann."

Mag tries to study but begins to ramble again: pregnant women, she declares, have particularly important intuitions. She imagines that the baby is going to be late, she imagines the trouble she will have with it. Joe shushes her and goes on studying.

Mag reminds Joe that his parents sleep in the same bed. She wants theirs to be that kind of a marriage.

MAG: . . . . . When I look around me at Papa and Mother and the O'Haras —I think: my God we'll never become like that because—don't laugh at me, Joe—because I think we're unique! Is that how you feel, too?

> *Joe flings his book from him in exasperation.*

JOE *(very articulately):* You-are-a-bloody-pain-in-the-neck! *(Quickly.)* You haven't shut up for five consecutive minutes since we got here! You have done no work yourself and you have wasted my morning, too! And if anyone should be working, it's you, because you haven't a clue about anything! In fact you're the stupidest person I ever met!

MAG: Stewbag!

JOE: Sticks and stones—go ahead!

MAG: And you can't kick a football the length of yourself!

JOE: What has that got to do with it?

MAG: That's what everybody calls you 'cause that's all you can do is stew— stew—stew!

JOE: Born stupid.

MAG *(crying):* Stewbag! Stewbag!

JOE: Bawl away. Bawl your head off. But if you think I'm going to waste my life in Skinny Skeehan's smelly office, that's where you're mistaken. You trapped me into marrying you—that's all right—I'll marry you. But I'll lead my own life. And somehow—somehow I'll get a degree and be a maths teacher. And nobody, neither you nor your precious baby nor anyone else, is going to stop me! So put that in your pipe and smoke it!

He opens his book and pretends to work, but he is too agitated. Mag covers her face and cries.

COMMENTATOR: The search was continued without interruption for three days. An S.O.S. was broadcast, and ports and airports were watched. It was reported to the police that a young couple answering to the description were seen in Liverpool and later in the Waterford area. But an investigation proved both reports to be false. Margaret Mary Enright and Joseph Michael Brennan had disappeared. On Wednesday, June 8, the search was called off.

Now it's Joe who is talking and Mag who is silent. Finished math and about to spend some time on French and history, Joe takes time out to tell Mag of his meeting with Skinny Skeehan and the offer of a clerk's job. Joe wishes he could have turned the offer down, arrogantly. He hopes to take a correspondence course toward getting his B.S.

Mag does not answer him—she is still thinking over what he told her previously, the names he called her "with hate in his eyes." Joe tries to joke her out of her mood, and finally succeeds with mimicry of various village characters. After they roll on the ground in their hilarity, Mag warns Joe that for every five minutes you laugh you cry for ten. Joe disappears to dispose of some old papers. Mag closes her eyes.

COMMENTATOR: On Tuesday, June 21 a local boy was driving his father's cows down to the edge of Lough Gorm for a drink when he saw what he described as "bundles of clothes" floating just off the north shore. He ran home and told his mother. The police were informed, and Sergeant Finlay accompanied by two constables went to investigate. The "bundles" were the bodies of Margaret Mary Enright and Joseph Michael Brennan. They were floating, fully clothed, face down in twenty-seven inches of water.

Returning to the hilltop, Joe confesses to Maggie that he has saved more than 23 pounds in a post office account and means to spend it on new clothes and an electric razor. He outlines their finances to his future wife who, he discovers on further examination, is sound asleep and therefore not hearing any of this.

Joe takes this opportunity to look up the word "Caesarean" in the dictionary. When he discovers what it means, he is alarmed for Maggie. He covers her with his blazer, he tells her she can have his 23 pounds to spend on frivolities. Joe tells sleeping Mag: "I'm not half good enough for you. I'm jealous and mean and spiteful and cruel. But I'll try to be tender to you and good to you; and that won't be hard because even when I'm not with you—just when I think of you—I go all sort of silly and I say to myself over and over again: *I'm crazy about Maggie Enright;* and so I am—crazy about you. You're a thousand times too good for me. But I'll try to be good to you; honest to God, I'll try."

He tells his sleeping bride-to-be he hopes the child will be a girl. He is amused to notice that he has adopted her habit of thinking out loud, skipping from thought to thought. He reflects on the close similarities and relationships that develop between couples married a long time.

Mag begins to wake up. Joe warns her she'd better study; if he should die and leave her with a dozen kids, she'd need her education. Mag wonders where the dozen kids came from, warns Joe that she doesn't intend to waste all her life bearing children, maybe developing "pernicious micropia." Joe accuses her of inventing this disease.

JOE: Pernicious what?

MAG: You're too ignorant to have heard of it. My father came across frequent cases of it. I don't suppose your parents ever heard of it.

> *As soon as she has said this, she regrets it. But she cannot retract now. Joe's banter is suddenly ended. He is quietly furious.*

JOE: Just what do you mean by that?

MAG: What I say.

JOE: I said, what do you mean by that remark?

MAG: You heard me.

JOE: You insulted my parents—deliberately.

MAG: I was talking about a disease.

JOE: You think they're nobody, don't you?

MAG: You were mocking me.

JOE: And you think your parents are somebody, don't you?

> *Mag picks up a book, opens it at random, turns her back to him and begins to read.*

MAG: I have revision to do.

JOE: Well, let me tell you, madam, that my father may be temporarily unemployed, but he pays his bills; and *my* mother may be a charwoman but she isn't running out to the mental hospital for treatment every couple of months. And if you think the Brennans aren't swanky enough for you, then, by God, you shouldn't be in such a hurry to marry one of them!

> *As soon as he has said this, he regrets it. But he cannot retract now.* You dragged that out of me. But it happens to be the truth. And it's better that it should come out now than *after* we're married. At least we know where we stand . . . *(His anger is dead.)* Margaret? . . . Maggie? . . . *(Stiff again.)* Well, it was you that started it. And if you're going into another of your huffs, I swear to you I'm not going to be the first to speak this time.

> *He picks a book, opens it at random, turns his back to her and begins to read.*

COMMENTATOR: At the post-mortem on the evening of June 21 evidence of identification was given by Walter Enright. He said that the body recovered from Lough Gorm was the body of his daughter, Margaret Mary Enright. Michael Brennan identified the male body as that of his son, Joseph Michael Brennan. Doctor Watson said that he examined the bodies of both the deceased. There were no marks of violence on either, he said. And in his opinion—which, he submitted, was given after a hasty examination—death in both cases was due to asphyxiation. Mr. Skeehan, the coroner, asked was there any evidence as to how both deceased fell into the water. Sergeant Finlay replied that there was no evidence. A verdict in accordance with the medical evidence was returned. Mr. Skeehan and Sergeant Finlay expressed their grief and the grief of the community to the parents. And it was agreed that the inquest should be held as soon as possible because the coroner took his annual vacation in the month of July.

Joe tries to break the awkward silence between himself and Mag by commenting on the countryside and on the weather. Finally, he apologizes to her, but she is weeping and means to continue. He jokes and sings, eliciting no response. He perseveres, on another tangent of mockery.

JOE: When Father Kelly sent for me last Friday fortnight, I knew I was done for, and I pretended I was so frightened I had a stammer—did I tell you that part of it? (Pompous.) You know, of course, Brennan, that we are going to expel you. (Abject.) Yes, F-f-f-father. (Pompous.) Because of your mother's pleading on your behalf, however, we have decided to allow you to return to sit for your examinations. But in the meantime I must insist that you remove all your belongings from the college and that you don't set foot within the grounds until the morning of the first examination. (Abject.) T-t-t-thank you, Father. (Pompous.) I will not talk again about the dishonor you have brought to your school, your family, and yourself. And I trust you have made your peace with God. Goodbye, Brennan. (Abject.) Goodbye, Father. (Pompous.) Incidentally, Brennan, when did you develop the stammer? (Abject.) W-w-w-when Maggie told me she was in trouble, Father.
> Mag began chuckling silently—and unnoticed by Joe—at the beginning of this interview. Now she can contain her laughter no longer. At last she screams her delight and throws herself at him, and they roll on the ground.
MAG: God forgive you!

As their wrestling match ends in a kiss, the Commentator goes on with his story: an inquest was held, at which it was decided that the pair met their death by drowning: "There was no evidence as to how the deceased got into the water. William Anthony Clerkin's boat was perfectly sound. Sergeant Finlay stated that the temperature on that afternoon was seventy-seven degrees. And there was no wind."

The following Sunday, the Commentator continues, there was a large turnout for a solemn requiem mass. "The bodies were buried in the local cemetery, each in the family plot."

Mag imagines what it'll be like, living married in their flat—she thinks of many homey details. They will even have a dog. In the valley below she sees girls from her school on their way to church, and for a moment she feels a pang of regret at the loss of the security of being a schoolgirl. But she finally decides she wouldn't go back if she had the chance. Neither would Joe. Furthermore, he tells her, maybe he should forget about taking a correspondence course.

MAG: If that's what you want.

JOE: It's maybe not what I want. But that's the way things have turned out. A married man with a family has more important things to occupy his mind besides bloody books.

> *She gives him a brief squeeze. But she has not heard what he has said. Pause.*

Ballymore.

MAG: Home.

JOE: See the sun glinting on the headstones beside the chapel.

MAG: Some day we'll be buried together.

JOE: You're great company.

MAG: I can't wait for the future, Joe.

JOE: What's that supposed to mean?

> *Maggie suddenly leaps to her feet. Her face is animated, her movements quick and vital, her voice ringing.*

MAG: The past's over! And I hate this waiting time! I want the future to happen—I want to be in it—I want to be in it with you!

JOE: You've got sunstroke.

> *She throws her belongings into her case.*

MAG: Come on, Joe! Let's begin the future now!

> *Not comprehending, but infected by her mood, he gets to his feet.*

JOE: You're nuts.

MAG: Where'll we go? What'll we do? Let's do something crazy!

JOE: Mad as a hatter.

MAG: The lake! We'll dance on every island! We'll stay out all night and sing and shout at the moon!

> *Joe does a wolf-howl up at the sky.*

Come on, Joe! While the sun's still hot!

They have no boat (says Joe), but they will find and take one (says Mag). Mag takes Joe's hand and leads him to run down the hill toward the lake, despite his worry about her exerting herself in her condition. At the bottom of the hill Joe takes Mag's bicycle and they move out of sight.

COMMENTATOR: Beth Enright's health has improved greatly. She has not had a relapse for almost seven months. And every evening, if the weather is good, Walter and she go for a walk together out the length of Whelan's Brae. Mick Brennan never mentions his son's name. . . . . Nora Brennan has had to limit the amount of work she does because her varicose veins turned septic. . . . . In the past eight months the population of Ballymore has risen from thirteen thousand five hundred twenty-seven to thirteen thousand five hundred sixty-nine. Life there goes on as usual. As if nothing had ever happened.

The Commentator closes his paper and exits. Curtain.

II. LOSERS

SYNOPSIS: The Commentator, Andy Tracey, is sitting upstage center in the backyard area of the Wilson house. He is *"a man of 50, a joiner by trade, heavily built."*

Behind Andy at left is the living room and kitchen of the house. On a level above, at right, is a bedroom furnished with *"a big iron double bed, a chest of drawers with a statue of St. Philomena on top of it (the 'altar') and a few chairs."* At present, the bedroom is hidden behind a large screen.

Through a pair of binoculars, Andy is looking idly at nothing in particular until he spots the audience. He lowers the glasses and confides: his wife Hanna never disturbs him when he comes out here to sit in the yard. Andy started courting Hanna Wilson four years previously, shortly before her father died in this very yard. A heart attack it was, and Mrs. Wilson, Hanna's mother, was so upset that she took to her bed and stayed there.

ANDY: . . . . . Hanna and me, as I say, we were only started going at the time; and then with the aul fella dying and the aul woman taking to the bed, like we couldn't go out to the pictures nor dances nor nothing like any other couple; so I started coming here every evening. And this is where we done our courting, in there, on the couch. *(Chuckles briefly.)* By God, we were lively enough, too. Eh? I mean to say, people think that when you're . . . well, when you're over the forty mark, that you're passified. But aul Hanna, by God, I'll say that for her, she was keen as a terrier in those days. *(Chuckles at the memory.)* If that couch could write a book—Shakespeare, how are you!

Andy describes how he used to come calling on Hanna after work. He steps from the backyard area into the house as Hanna enters—*"a woman in her late 40s . . . . . dressed in a gray skirt and blue jumper"*—and they act out Andy's memory. Andy brings her the usual "quarter of a pound of clove rock," a small present of candy.

ANDY: How's the mother?
HANNA *(sharp):* Living. And praying.
ANDY: Terrible sore thing, the heart, all the same.
HANNA: I come home from my work beat out and before I get a bit in my

mouth she says, "Run out like a good child and get us a sprig of fresh flowers for St. Philomena's altar."

ANDY: Did you go?

Hanna points to the flowers wrapped in paper lying on the kitchen table.

HANNA: But she can wait for them.

ANDY: She'll miss you when you leave, Hanna.

HANNA: Hasn't she Cissy Cassidy next door? And if she hadn't a slavey like me to wait hand and foot on her, her heart mightn't be just as fluttery!

The sound of a brass bell being rung behind the screen causes Hanna to exit upstairs with the flowers. Andy turns to the audience and explains that Hanna's mother Mrs. Wilson in her bed upstairs would use this bell to summon Hanna. When Andy was courting Hanna the bell was rung frequently, on any pretext, to keep the couple from enjoying themselves.

But, Andy reveals, he and Hanna "got cute to her." It was the silences that made Mrs. Wilson suspicious—as long as she could hear talking she wouldn't ring her bell. So "It was the brave Hanna that hit on the poetry idea. Whenever we started the courting, she made me recite the poetry—you know there, just to make a bit of a noise. And the only poetry I ever learned at school was a thing called 'Elegy Written in a Country Churchyard' by Thomas Gray, 1716-1771, if you ever heard of it. And I used to recite that over and over again. And Hanna she would throw an odd word in there to make it sound natural."

As Andy describes how they deceived the old woman by reciting Gray's "Elegy" while making love, Hanna returns to report that as usual her mother has told her, "The pair of you'll be up later for the Rosary, won't you?" They sit on the sofa together, and soon they are caressing each other.

ANDY: Very nice . . .

Very suddenly, almost violently, Hanna flings herself on him so that he falls back and she buries her face in his neck and kisses and caresses him with astonishing passion. He is momentarily at a loss. But this has happened before, many times, and he knows that this is his cue to begin his poem. His recitation is strained and too high and too loud—like a child in school memorizing meaningless facts. Throughout his recital, they court feverishly.

ANDY:

"The curfew tolls the knell of parting day,
The lowing herd winds slowly o'er the lea,
The plowman homeward plods his weary way,
And leaves the world to darkness and to me.
Now fades the glimmering landscape on the sight—"

HANNA *(to ceiling):* It's a small world, isn't it?

BEULAH GARRICK, GRANIA O'MALLEY, ANNA MANAHAN
AND ART CARNEY IN "LOVERS"

Andy continues reciting Gray's "Elegy" and Hanna continues to make meaningless remarks to deceive Mrs. Wilson upstairs, while they continue to make love. They forget themselves in a kiss, and remain silent a beat too long —and the bell upstairs clangs. Hanna adjusts her jumper and runs out of the room.

Andy tells the audience that Hanna "had spunk in those days," but right before his eyes she turned into a younger version of her mother—though that is not the story he's here to tell. Every night (Andy informs the audience) at 10 o'clock, Mrs. Wilson's friend Cissy Cassidy would come over and they'd all be invited upstairs where, amid flowers and candles and the big statue of St. Philomena, they would join in the Rosary. Andy always felt that the whole ritual was some sort of hidden plot, "Like I knew damn well what the aul woman was up to; if she couldn't break it up between Hanna and me, at least she was going to make damn sure that I wasn't going to take Hanna away from her. And *she* knew that *I* knew what she was up to with her wee sermons about Father Peyton and all the stuff about the family that prays together stays together. And there was the pair of us, watching and smiling, each of us knowing that the other knew, and none of us giving away anything. By God, it was strange. Eh? 'Cause she thought that every time I got down on my knees in that bedroom to join in the Rosary I was cutting my own throat. But because I knew what she was up to, I was safe—or at least I thought I was. She's crafty, that aul woman . . . . ."

Hanna comes down with the invalid's tray, as Andy goes to the door to let in Cissy, *"a small, frail wisp of a woman in her late 60s."* Cissy greets the lovers politely, then goes upstairs to her friend Mrs. Wilson's room.

Andy and Hanna sit on the couch again, Hanna is depressed; she vows that the day she marries she is "getting shot" of her mother for good. But in the meantime, Mrs. Wilson is not sick enough to be transferred to a hospital and refuses to sell the house and enter a home. There is a kind of unspoken suggestion that maybe Andy would move in here with them all, but Andy will have none of that—he means to take his bride to Riverview.

Hanna weeps at their problem, but Andy comforts her, and soon they are making love again, with Andy frantically trying to remember all the "Elegy" verses. Once again they kiss in silence, and once again the bell rings. They are both furious.

HANNA *(evenly):* One of these days I'm going to strangle that woman—with her Rosary beads.

       She marches off. Andy grabs a paper and tries to read it. We now see Hanna enter the bedroom and we hear Mrs. Wilson's voice.

MRS. WILSON *(behind screen):* We're going to say the Rosary a bit earlier tonight, dear. Cissy has a bit of a headache.

       Hanna removes the screen and puts it to the right. In the large iron bed, propped up against the pillows, lies Mrs. Wilson. Like Cissy, she is a tiny woman, with a sweet, patient invalid's smile. Her voice is soft and commanding. Her silver hair is drawn back from her face and tied with a blue ribbon behind her head. She looks angelic. Cissy, her understudy, is sitting beside her, watching her with devotion. Directly facing Mrs. Wilson is a chest of drawers, on which sits a white cloth, two candles, a large statue of a saint and a vase of flowers—a miniature altar. Mrs. Wilson frequently nods and smiles to the statue and mouths "Thank you, thank you." Hanna clumps around the room, doing her chores with an ungracious vigor and with obvious ill will.

HANNA: Whatever suits Cissy suits me!

CISSY: She's looking lovely tonight, Hanna, isn't she? It must be the good care you're taking of her.

MRS. WILSON: I'm blessed, Cissy dear, and I know it. A good daughter is a gift of God. *(To the statue.)* Thank you.

Cissy opines that "Invalids is all saints." Then she summons Andy upstairs —their nightly ceremony is about to begin. Mrs. Wilson, holding her beads, gives thanks to the statue for this gathering of family and friends. Hanna, prodded, begins to recite the prayers and everybody, including Andy, devoutly follows the words, kneeling and facing the "altar." As the prayer continues, Andy rises and replaces the screen while the lights black out.

When the lights come up, Andy has returned to the back yard of the Wilson house. He is telling the audience how he made the big mistake of returning to the Wilson house with Hanna after their honeymoon, just for a short temporary stay of two weeks, while the Riverview place was being painted.

Funny thing about Hanna, too (Andy noticed), after they were married, the fire seemed to go out of her resentment of her mother's demands. And now the bell no longer rang when they were silent, but whenever they started talking.

Andy put his foot down about the Rosary—he refused to join the ceremony after his marriage but remained downstairs to say his own "mouthful of prayers" by himself. And as for the "crafty aul woman," Andy recalls: "I got her! By God I got her! . . . Or, I damn near got her." At work one day, a Protestant handed him a newspaper while making a gibe about the Pope not being infallible. "And true as Christ, when I seen it, you could have tipped me over, I was that weak. Like, for five seconds I couldn't even speak with excitement; only the heart thumping like bloody hell in my chest. For there it was in black and white before my very eyes—THE SAINT THAT NEVER WAS. 'Official Vatican sources today announced—' I know it by heart—'that the devotion of all Roman Catholics to St. Philomena must be discontinued at once because there is little or no evidence that such a person ever existed.' Like I never knew I was a spiteful man until that minute; and then, by God, my only thought was to stick that paper down the aul woman's throat. . . . ."

But Andy made a mistake: he went to the pub first, to celebrate. By closing time he was reeling drunk. Back home, Hanna pulls aside the screen to reveal a scene of "feminine solidarity and suffering womanhood," as the three women wonder anxiously where Andy can be.

They pray for his safe return. But their anxiety turns to shock and outrage when they hear him coming in raucously singing "God Save Ireland." Andy weaves into the house and flings his coat on the couch. Cissy is horrified: "A drunk man!" Hanna is bewildered. Mrs. Wilson takes charge.

MRS. WILSON: Don't worry. I'll settle him. And stop whining!
        Andy enters and surveys the three alarmed faces. He has the newspaper in his hand.
ANDY: By God, if it's not the Dolly Sisters!
        He gives them a grand bow.
And Saint Philomena!
        Grand bow to the statue.
All we need now is Father Peyton . . . Where's Father Peyton? . . . I'll tell you something; The family that drinks together sinks together.
MRS. WILSON: Andrew!
ANDY: "The cock's shrill clarion, or the echoing horn—"
CISSY: Dirty animal!
ANDY:
        "No more shall rouse them from their lowly bed.
        For them no more the blazing hearth shall burn,
        Or busy housewife ply her evening care—"
Thomas Gray, 1716-1771.
HANNA: Mother, please!
MRS. WILSON: Listen to me, Andrew!
ANDY: She *(Hanna)* knows what I'm talking about 'cause she's my wife.

MRS. WILSON: If you don't behave yourself—

ANDY: As for prissy Cissy here—

CISSY: All for Thee, all for Thee—

ANDY: You'll go down with the white bobbins. Know what that means, prissy Cissy? The white bobbins? It means you'll never know your ass from your elbow.

HANNA: Andy!

MRS. WILSON: I'll give you one minute to get out of this house!

ANDY: News for you, old mammy—here in this paper. *(To the statue.)* And news for you, darling, too.

MRS. WILSON: Get out!

ANDY *(to statue):* You've been sacked.

MRS. WILSON: I said get out!

ANDY *(to statue):* You and me—both sacked.

He comes over to the bed with the paper.

HANNA: Stop it, Andrew! Stop it!

ANDY: In black and white . . . Read it . . . It says, we don't stay together—that's what it says. Father Peyton, it says, your head's a marley. That's what it says.

Instead of looking at the newspaper, Mrs. Wilson clutches her heart. Cissy and Hanna are alarmed, but Andy merely walks over to the statue of Philomena, picks it up and waltzes with it.

Horrified at this sacrilege, Cissy and Hanna take the statue from Andy while Mrs. Wilson actually gets out of bed. The women gather up the "altar" things. Cissy helps Mrs. Wilson from the room—they are all fleeing to Cissy's house. Hanna informs her husband angrily, "You'll regret this day, Andrew Tracey! You'll regret this day as long as you live!" Then Hanna follows her mother and helps Cissy lead Mrs. Wilson out of the house with the sacred objects.

Andy goes downstairs and disappears, then soon reappears sober, dressed in cardigan and house slippers, carrying the binoculars into the backyard area. He tells the audience about the fine tenant he now has over in Riverview—pays the rent regularly. Sometimes Andy walks over there and looks at the house which might have been his and Hanna's home.

Usually, though, when Andy gets home from work he's so tired he doesn't feel much like going anywhere.

ANDY *(to audience):* . . . . . I usually sleep at the fire for a while and then come out here for a breath of air. Kills an hour or two. And then when the bell rings I go up to the aul woman's room for prayers. Well, I mean to say, anything for a quiet life. Hanna sleeps there now, as a matter of fact, just in case the aul woman should get an attack during the night. Not that that's likely. The doctor says she'll go on forever. And a funny thing, you know, nothing much has changed up there. Philomena's gone, of course. But she still has the altar and she still lights the candles and has the flowers in the middle and she still faces it when she's praying and mouths away to it. I says to Cissy one night I says, "Who's she supposed to be praying to?" "A saint," says she very quick. "What saint?" says I, "Sure there's no statue there." "I'm not blind," says she. "Well, I mean to say," says I, "what does she think she's at?" "True enough, there's no statue there," says Cissy, "but we have a saint in our mind when we're praying even though we have no figure for it." "What saint?" says I. "Aha," says she, "that's something you'll never know. Wild horses wouldn't drag that out of us. You robbed her of Saint Philomena but you'll never be told who it is!" Crafty, eh? And when I go into the bedroom she smiles and nods at me and you can see her lips saying "Thank you thank you" to the altar. And when we kneel down, she says, "It's so nice for me to have you all gathered around my bed. As a certain American cleric says, 'The family that prays together stays together.' " By God, you've got to admire the aul bitch. She could handle a regiment.

> He lifts the binoculars, puts them in front of his eyes and stares at the wall in front of him. The lights go down slowly until the stage is totally black. Curtain.

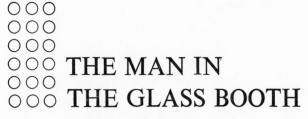

THE MAN IN
THE GLASS BOOTH

A Play in Two Acts

BY ROBERT SHAW

Cast and credits appear on page 378

ROBERT SHAW was born in Lancashire in 1927, studied for the stage at the Royal Academy of Dramatic Art and, in 1948, embarked upon a successful career as an actor. After a year's repertory experience he joined the acting company at Stratford-on-Avon and remained with them in 1949 and 1950. In 1951 Shaw joined the Old Vic and played Cassio in Othello *and Lysander in* A Midsummer Night's Dream. *His acting career continued on the London stage in* Tiger at the Gates, Shadow of Heroes *and the Laurence Olivier production of* Lodging for a Bride; *on Broadway as Aston in* The Caretaker *in the 1961-62 season and in the leading role of Möbius in* The Physicists *in the 1964-65 season; and on the screen in* A Man for All Seasons *(for which he won an Academy Award nomination),* From Russia with Love *and* The Royal Hunt of the Sun.

As a writer, Shaw produced his first novel The Hiding Place *in 1959. It was given an American television production with Trevor Howard, Richard Basehart and James Mason. His second novel,* The Sun Doctor, *won the Hawthenden Award for literature. His third was* The Flag *and his fourth* The Man in the Glass Booth *upon which he based this, his first play. He has also written a screen play and many book reviews and articles. Shaw lives in England and is married to Mary Ure, the actress.*

Time: 1964-65

Place: New York and Israel

ACT I

Scene 1

SYNOPSIS: The Verdi requiem is heard, and a bald-headed man in a silk dressing gown (Arthur Goldman) is seen praying beside an urn. When he is finished praying he dusts the urn and goes to his chair. Gradually we notice details of this combined living-and-office eyrie of a very rich man, high above most New York City penthouses:

> *A masterpiece rests upon an easel. A glass elevator rises into one side of the room; doors and a hallway lead off—one of the doors is locked. French windows open onto a roof garden full of statues, artificial flowers, and artificial trees. Beyond the garden rise the peaks of Manhattan. . . . .*

It is eight o'clock on a fine autumn morning. Two servants, Sam and Jack, first change the masterpiece on the easel for another one, a Rembrandt; then they turn their solicitous attention to Goldman, taking away his dressing gown, valeting him, bringing his coffee and a stock ticker.

Charlie Cohn, Goldman's secretary, comes in with all the day's newspapers. Goldman notices the Rembrandt and is bored with it—Jack whisks it out.

Charlie wishes Goldman a happy birthday, reminding him that he is 52 years old today. Sam goes to the kitchen, leaving Goldman and Charlie alone to discuss business. The temperature outside is 41.5 degrees centigrade.

GOLDMAN: Forty-one and a half. (*Pause.*) If I wasn't so old I'd don my vicuna. Matilda always adored me in my vicuna. (*Pause.*) It's a house without a woman, Charlie. (*Pause.*) I ought to get a new wife.

CHARLIE: Yes, Mr. Goldman.

GOLDMAN: I should bring in naked servants. Naked black female servants.

CHARLIE: That would be very delightful, Mr. Goldman.

GOLDMAN: Miss America. Miss America 1964. That's what I need. I'd knock her up in no time. (*Waving his hand.*) It's all these empty closets that's getting me down. All those coathangers with no frocks on 'em. A man without a woman . . . a man without a woman . . . (*He sighs.*) Maybe I got to go for intelligence . . . maybe I need one of those reporters . . . one of those *Time* and *Life*—long-legged—Washington *Posts* . . . one of those articulates. (*He sighs again.*) When are we due at the banks?

CHARLIE: 11:05 at the Irving Trust. 11:22 the Bank of Montreal. 11:47 the Trade and 12:35 the Chase Manhattan.

GOLDMAN: When do I see Levinsky?

CHARLIE: He's coming from Boston this afternoon, Mr. Goldman.

GOLDMAN: Call Schwab—tell him I'm in.

CHARLIE: For how much, Mr. Goldman?

GOLDMAN: All the way, all the way. He's my blood brother, Charlie. Charlie, the thing about a wife is . . . Where do I go tonight?

CHARLIE: The opera tonight, Mr. Goldman. You're escorting the duchess. And there's twenty-two begging letters this morning.

GOLDMAN: Give 'em all somethin' but not too much. *(Pause.)* Listen, when you call Schwab tell him my limit's a hundred thousand: I think you're right there, I think you made a substantial point. . . . .

Goldman gives an order for white-curtained walls on the new Lexington Avenue building, but gold on the penthouse floors. Goldman is taking a group of men to the Stadium for a game the next day and he wants Charlie to invite some beautiful women to keep them company.

CHARLIE: If I may say so, it will be cold out there in the Stadium, Mr. Goldman—the forecast . . .

GOLDMAN: So get me some sables with interior electric currents—build in some cabinets of champagne and put a few scent sprays in the collars. I gotta have somebody to look at, Charlie! And nothin' common! I gotta have somebody with a face. Somebody with bones. Somebody aristocratic. Charlie! See if Garbo's in town.

At Goldman's request, Charlie reads aloud from a brochure he is writing for Goldman's organization, about the beginnings of his boss's climb to power and wealth. Meanwhile, Goldman is scanning the newspapers and discovers, first, that an old friend has died and, second: "Jesus! The Pope's forgiven the Jews. Jesus. The Pope has forgiven the Jews." His old friend never lived to know it.

Sam and Jack come in carrying Poussin's "Arcadia," but Goldman directs them to take it away and leave an empty easel in memory of his friend who didn't live long enough to hear of the Pope's momentous decision. Impulsively, Goldman orders Charlie to "Get the Pope on television. . . . . We have fourteen channels—he has to be on one of them."

While Charlie fiddles with the dial, the house phone rings. Goldman answers it, and the elevator starts down to pick up a visitor.

Meanwhile, Charlie *does* find the TV broadcast from Rome—in color. A Commentator is describing the Pope's entourage and ceremony.

GOLDMAN: Turn down the sound. I make my own comments from now on. Let's cut out all this shtick.

As Charlie Cohn turns down the sound so that it becomes indistinguishable, the elevator slides into the room and a man of Goldman's weight and age, dressed in a smart suit and loaded with artificial flower plants, steps out of it. Charlie hurries to help and leads him to the roof garden but Goldman does not turn around. He sits absorbed, making his comments.

Hey, he's giving the Virgin Mary a new title—I can see that. Monsignor Dante's fumbling for his handkerchief—Monsignor Dante's bustin' into tears . . . The Arabs must be . . . bustin' into tears . . . The Fuehrer said: "Es darf nunmehr für die Welt Kein Fuehrer oder ein Mann sprechen, jetzt spricht das deutsche Volk . . ." The Fuehrer said: . . . "no longer speaks one man but the German people" . . . The Fuehrer said: "Your Holiness, in order to carry on his existence as a parasite on other peoples, the Jüdlein is forced to deny his inner nature. The more intelligent the individual Jew is, the more . . . the more he will succeed in this deception."

Turning around to Charlie.

God bless America, we got him in color, Charlie.

As he turns, Goldman sees Charlie and the man who brought the flowers coming back from the roof garden. Something about this flower man startles him.

I know you.

FLOWER MAN: Sir?

GOLDMAN: I know you. *(Pause.)* You know I know you.

FLOWER MAN: I've delivered here before.

Pause.

GOLDMAN: My mistake, then.

The flower man leaves but Goldman, puzzled, sits and thinks about him. The flower man returns, pretending to look for his hat. Goldman comments to him: "You've lost weight," but the flower man merely smiles and departs once again.

Goldman orders Charlie to check up on the flower man, have him watched. Goldman decides against going out today, to the banks or anywhere else. He will stay here safely in his tower. And from now on, Charlie is to sleep here.

The elevator starts back up. Goldman wonders: "Who's this? My cousin again?"

Goldman goes to the locked door, opens the various locks and disappears into a vault. He comes out carrying a Luger. The elevator arrives and the visitor steps out—it is only Dr. Kessel come to give Goldman his Vitamin B-12 shot. Like a nervous Borgia, Goldman orders the doctor to give the shot to Charlie. He does so; it is harmless.

Goldman, who has been drinking his coffee laced with brandy, summons Jack and orders bourbon with beer chasers all around. Charlie had an appointment to visit his tailor this morning, but Goldman orders him to stay in, to have the tailor come up here.

Goldman tells them that the flower man's real name is Dorff, Cousin Adolf Dorff. While Charlie talks on the phone to his tailor, and Jack fixes the drinks, Goldman tells Dr. Kessel: "You see, Doc, I can't go out. I'm under observation. They're on to me. I've got to stay here with you guys and work somethin' out. Don't think I'm fevered. . . . ."

Goldman dismisses Jack and hands around the drinks himself. Suddenly he shouts "Remember me!" to the doctor and disappears into the locked room.

Charlie and Dr. Kessel discuss Goldman. He has never neglected to make the rounds of the banks before, never brought out a gun. No one has ever seen what Goldman keeps in the locked vault—he even cleans the place himself.

Goldman comes back and warns Charlie that if his tailor is coming here, he must be checked at the door: "I want no more flower guys up here."

Goldman proceeds to harangue his listeners with extravagant anecdotes about himself and the F. Scott Fitzgeralds. The doctor observes that perhaps Goldman is a bit feverish today.

GOLDMAN: . . . . . I'm seeking both to inspire and distract myself.

KESSEL: From what?

GOLDMAN: From the arbeit-macht-frei gray stone edifices . . . the innumerable three-floor-high-identical-edifices. Charlie, you call this a metropolis . . . that place . . . that place . . . was boundless. Being an athlete stood me in good stead. Sing me the "Internationale," Charlie, move me, render me, rape my senses. From the dead, Doc, from the dead. It's my birthday, you see.

KESSEL: Oh. Many happy returns.

CHARLIE: I'm sorry. I don't know that song, Mr. Goldman.

GOLDMAN: Then you're in neglect. It's the living who are in neglect. It's not ended, you know. What can we do for the living? *(Very quietly.)* The last time I saw Dorff . . . the last time but one I saw my cousin, Dorff, he was goin' from bed to bed, from litter to litter, from place to place . . . with his pistol. He was tappin' them on their domes with the barrel, he was testin' their brains out, he was listenin' to see what was hollow. One, two, three, not another sound but the echo. Bang, bang, bang and I bring up the trolley.

The phone rings. Charlie goes and picks it up.

Check the voice!

CHARLIE: Hello. What? No. No. You must have the wrong number. This is Mr. Arthur Goldman's residence.

GOLDMAN *(exploding)*: What you tell him that for? Idiot. You don't tell nobody nothin' from now on.

CHARLIE: I'm sorry.

GOLDMAN: A foreign voice?

CHARLIE: No, an American voice.

GOLDMAN: That wasn't no wrong number. And that was a foreign voice. *(Pause.)* The *first* time I saw that Dorff was early . . . wanted to knock up my sister. He was thirteen years old at the time . . . I do believe he made it.

Silence. Then house phone rings. . . . .

Charlie answers; it's the tailor, Rudin, who comes up in the elevator. Goldman puts away the gun and greets Rudin, "the Levite tailor," warmly. He orders suits for himself as well as for Charlie and asks that his measurements be taken. Meanwhile he rambles on, monopolizing the conversation like a voluble drunk, with obscure anecdotes (such as a description of Y.A. Tittle's final intercepted pass in his last game with the Giants) and odd personal references like, "On this day we get loaded. I was . . . chosen . . . you follow? This is the day I was born."

Goldman goes on: "Gentlemen, my Will is in my treasure house. A Hebrew, your Highnesses, can't get converted because how can he bring himself to believe in the divinity of another Hebrew . . . German fellow citizens, I . . . In German law . . . there is a time limit . . . As a zoologist there are no villains . . . no villains and no heroes . . . Gentlemen, once I was passionate. I WAS PASSIONATE." Goldman screams, and everybody rises. Then: "Sit down. Be seated, Doc, I don't need you. Just an old wound opening up . . . I'll close it. I'll close it when I work it out . . . you follow?"

Sam and Jack, alarmed by the scream, come running in. They are given the day off and sent away.

Goldman continues to harangue Rudin and declares his own position: "I spit on all these Cardinals and all these Rabbis." He waves his pistol at his guests and orders them out, frightening them (but he is only joking). He describes himself as "almost there . . . it's a matter of cunning from here on in."

Goldman dismisses Kessel and Rudin in a friendly, half-drunken manner. Alone with Charlie, he reminds him that he pays him $400 a week; then Goldman smiles.

GOLDMAN: You see, Charlie . . . it don't matter whether that flower guy was my cousin Dorff or not.
        He takes off his jacket.
Shut the louvres.
        Charlie does so.
CHARLIE: Shall I put on a light?
GOLDMAN: Yes, a soft light. Did you buy me a birthday present?
CHARLIE: Yes, Mr. Goldman.
GOLDMAN: You did?
CHARLIE: Of course, Mr. Goldman. Shall I get it?
GOLDMAN: No. Later. Later. Thank you, Charlie. Thank you. Go to the study, get a new line on that phone, a new number. Keep it to yourself and when you've got it—call me overseas. Let's have a breeze. Put on the fan.
        Charlie does as asked.
Not freezin', young Charlie. None of your high winds of Asia blowin' over the face of the earth—no whip to it, you see. I was great at tennis, Charlie. Could have been a pro.
        He takes off his waistcoat and tie.
CHARLIE: Yes?
GOLDMAN: Keep loyal to me and I change my Will. You follow?

CHARLIE: Yes, Mr. Goldman.

GOLDMAN *(gently placing his hand on Charlie's shoulder):* A man who has no shoes is a fool. I won't involve you . . . I need you, Charlie. Bear with me and I'll not put you down. Okay? I'll be wantin' the Vatican, Cairo and Jerusalem. Okay, dear Charlie.

> *Charlie leaves the room. Goldman calls after him.*

Nothin' for half of an hour.

> *He takes off his shirt, lights a cigar with a table lighter, and sings softly:*

what bells will ring for those who died
like sheep?
dies irae, dies illa
solvet saeclum in favilla,
what bells will ring for those who died
defiled?
for those who died in excrement?
rest eternal grant them
light eternal shine upon them.

> *He holds up the cigar, draws deeply on it and holds the lighted end under his left armpit. Blackout.*

Scene 2

Goldman's voice is heard. When the lights come up, Charlie Cohn is sitting at Goldman's desk, listening to a tape recording of his employer's voice instructing him on various matters of business.

The phone rings—it is Charlie's mother. Charlie explains to her that Goldman has given all the servants a holiday and gone away to Buenos Aires on an unknown errand, leaving Charlie in sole charge.

The tape recorder tells Charlie that if Goldman fails to return he can open the Will. Charlie goes to unlock the vault door. The tape recorder begins to give out one of Hitler's speeches which Goldman had put on "for inspiration."

Charlie opens the door and disappears into the vault, just as the elevator arrives and Goldman steps into the room. Goldman goes to the desk and turns up the sound of the Fuehrer's voice. Charlie comes out of the vault, embarrassed and apologetic at having been caught prying. Goldman reprimands him gently, then instructs Charlie to call him "Colonel."

Goldman tells Charlie that "it's a condition in my Will that everything you leave goes to the first Jewish Pope." The money is to be held for this in perpetuity, if necessary.

Abruptly, Goldman changes the subject.

GOLDMAN: . . . . . Of course, this guy Dorff might just be eliminated. That's my worry. You see . . . I've done all my research. I've got my case. *(Pause.)* They say the word's around town I'm thinkin' of suicide.

CHARLIE *(astonished):* I've certainly not heard that, Mr. Goldman.

GOLDMAN: Colonel, Charlie. Colonel. Yeah, they say I carry poison. They got a great museum in Prague—seventy thousand dead names painted on the walls . . . couple of hundred years and my . . . effort . . . might be in vain. Only Israel left.

CHARLIE: How'd you mean, Colonel?

GOLDMAN: The final assimilation. What the council said, Charlie . . . what the Pope's council said was: "The Jewish people should never be presented as one rejected, cursed or guilty of deicide, and the council deplores and condemns hatred and persecution of Jews whether they arose in former or in our own days." Overwhelming majority! Ain't that ironic?

The house phone rings. Charlie answers it.

CHARLIE: What? All right, I'll tell him.

He puts down the phone.

Mr. Goldman, Pete says two men are sitting across the street in a Cadillac and like you said he was to tell you if he thought anyone was watching the apartment.

Goldman asks for a description of the men. They are both young, one blond—they are probably not Arabs. They could be Germans.

Goldman forbids Charlie to call the police; he doesn't want anyone hurt. He rambles on about different kinds of inconsistent Jewish behavior. He comments cryptically: "Yeah, put me in one of my own incinerators. Can't make any difference. However . . . however, that matter may soon be out of my hands. *(Pause.)* I don't know if they're enemies or friends. *(Pause.)* I hope I'm right to do this. . . . ."

Finally, Goldman orders Charlie to go downstairs and invite the watchers up. Charlie is frightened, but Goldman insists: "Tell 'em I have to find peace with my former enemies. They'll believe that. Tell 'em it's for the youth of Germany. They'll believe that too. Until I offer them the cash! I got the cash, I *got* the cash, I got the loot."

Charlie departs on the elevator. Goldman drops his pistol into the fish tank and sits waiting.

Two young men with drawn guns—Steiger and Durer—step off the elevator, followed by Charlie and a stocky, purposeful woman who is holding a gun pressed to Charlie's back. The woman is immediately recognized by Goldman as "Rosy" Rosen, an American who emigrated to Tel Aviv. Steiger searches the apartment to make sure no one else is there. Durer searches the vault.

Mrs. Rosen presses the button of the tape recorder. The Hitler recording comes on. Durer comes out of the locked room.

MRS. ROSEN: What's in there?

Pause.

DURER: A stool. A table. Cartons of chocolate bars. And a copy of *Mein Kampf.*

GOLDMAN *(quickly):* How much?

MRS. ROSEN: What?

GOLDMAN: How much?

MRS. ROSEN: What for?

GOLDMAN: For my life.

MRS. ROSEN *(smiling):* Not Christ's blood would buy it. Not from me. I can't think what you heard.

GOLDMAN *(slowly):* But I understood . . . one million dollars . . . one million dollars cash. Three. Three million dollars cash. Give me a few days and I'll make it seven. Seven million dollars hard cash.

> *A pause.*

There's been a mistake.

> *The two young men search Goldman. They take off his shirt and trousers. They examine, they poke.*

STEIGER: Peh! Peh!

> *He takes something out of Goldman's mouth.*

Phial of poison.

MRS. ROSEN: Lift up his left arm.

STEIGER: Scar.

MRS. ROSEN: Insignia and blood type tattooed under that scar, Mr. Cohn.

CHARLIE: Insignia of what?

MRS. ROSEN: S.S. insignia.

> *Steiger runs his fingers over Goldman's collar bone and left kneecap.*

STEIGER: Two old fractures—same places as the X-rays.

> *Mrs. Rosen takes a photograph out of the briefcase, studies it and nods her head.*

There are a few more items of evidence which cause Mrs. Rosen to decide: "Goldman" is Adolf Karl Dorff, a former colonel in the S.S.'s mobile killing unit. Mrs. Rosen and her helpers are Israelis, and they mean to take Goldman-Dorff to Israel for trial as a war criminal. Goldman falls on his knees, raises his offer to eight million. Mrs. Rosen refuses.

GOLDMAN: I am a citizen of the United States.

MRS. ROSEN: We have discussed that.

GOLDMAN: The United States will not permit the violation of its sovereignty.

> *He rises.*

MRS. ROSEN: There's already been a precedent.

GOLDMAN: That was different. That wasn't in the United States.

MRS. ROSEN: So you want to be shot?

GOLDMAN: Murderer.

MRS. ROSEN: I have my orders.

GOLDMAN: Orders! Orders! I had my orders!

> *He draws himself up and thunders.*

What are the demands of Justice? What are the demands of Law? *(Pause.)* Who are my Judges? And by what right? *(Pause. Calmly.)* I will go with you.

I will go with you, sheep. Yes, I'll tell you a joke, Rosy Rosen, I'll tell you a couple of jokes and I'll bleed you that blood you're talkin' about.
Curtain.

ACT II

Goldman is in a cell, dressed in prison clothes and being interrogated by Mrs. Rosen, while Durer listens and a guard is on duty outside the peephole.

MRS. ROSEN: Why did you pretend to be Jewish?
Silence.
In the reports of the Einsatzgruppen I notice plain words do not occur: we have "final solution," "evacuation" and "special treatment." On the other hand, in *your* reports you always stated "extermination" or "killing." Why is that?
GOLDMAN: Always call a spade a spade. Those euphemisms you speak of were best for keepin' order—they didn't want the typists to get the message . . . you follow? But in my case I'm not here to tell you I didn't enjoy it—I'm here to tell you I did. *(He laughs.)* No clerk, Rosen! Issued my own orders, plotted my own plots, had a ball, you follow?
MRS. ROSEN: Why did you pretend to be Jewish?
GOLDMAN: Have you noticed I'm losin' weight? Much fitter. It was all that rich food done me in. And I am sleepin' great. I *am* sleepin' great. You should come in here and join me. Come in here and diet. Come in here and lay yourself down and diet.
MRS. ROSEN: Why did you pretend to be Jewish?
GOLDMAN: I'm not here to plead I took orders. I had initiative. First honest man who's stood in your dock. Like you got the Fuehrer himself in here. . . . .

Mrs. Rosen continues to wonder why Goldman pretended to be Jewish. Goldman replies by making playful sexual overtures to his businesslike questioner. Goldman declares to her, "I ain't got guilt. I'm not riddled and weary" and warns her, "I'm still an American. To keep me here you'll need my help."
The lights indicate the passage of time to the next day, and Mrs. Rosen is again questioning Goldman about his motives (this time with Steiger accompanying her), calling him "Colonel Dorff." Maybe Goldman gave false information in becoming an American citizen.

GOLDMAN: . . . . . I pretended to be Jewish because I made the acquaintance of old-American-Jewish-Uncle-Hymie's nephew, Arthur Goldman. Got to know him in Deutschland. Got to know Arthur so well I called him "Cousin." Perhaps he was, Cousin.
MRS. ROSEN: He's dead?
GOLDMAN: Don't you know that?
MRS. ROSEN: Who killed Arthur Goldman?

GOLDMAN: Between you and me, the question is who didn't kill Arthur Goldman. You know somethin' . . . you got great teeth.

MRS. ROSEN: Did you kill Arthur Goldman?

GOLDMAN: I have brooded on that. I have pondered on that. *(Pause.)* Get this while you can, Sexy: I the undersigned . . . Yeah, that's it. I the undersigned, Adolf Karl Dorff, declared of my own free will, dear President Johnson, and dear people and government of the United States, that it has become clear to me there is no point in hiding any more. I declare I came to Israel of my own free will and am willing to stay here and face an authorized court. I understand I will be given legal aid but I am going to decline it because I want to present such a case as will interest the new generation. I make this statement without threats of any kind. Since I cannot always remember details I hereby ask to be assisted by having access to certain documents. Finally, I reserve the right to know what witnesses the State of Israel will call, to defend myself, and to wear my uniform—Colonel, S.S.—in the court.

MRS. ROSEN: I shall have to consult my superiors.

GOLDMAN: Not to be signed unless all the conditions fulfilled. I shall want my uniform brushed and pressed. And my jackboots gleaming.

Mrs. Rosen and Steiger leave the cell. Goldman sunbathes in the shaft of light from the window and tells his guard about his wife Matilda—his second wife, a gentile, for whom he bought all the art treasures he could find; whom he loved, and for whom he wept. Goldman hardly mentions his first wife, except to tell the guard that she bore him a brood of children.

At dawn the next day, Mrs. Rosen and Durer come in with the necessary papers—Goldman's conditions are accepted, and Goldman dresses himself in his S.S. Colonel's uniform.

Mrs. Rosen still wonders: is Colonel Dorff perhaps *partly* Jewish, with Jewish cousins? In answer to her question, while dressing, Goldman tells her his father was Hindenburg's cousin, and his mother—well, they kept her out of sight. Meanwhile, he shot his quota of Jews with a clear conscience, "gaining confidence at every pull." He describes at length the stacking, shooting and burning of hundreds of Jews of all ages from babies to grandmothers in a mass grave, one incredible day—"Just a day in my life. Just a clear day to enjoy forever. Am I Jewish? I don't know about my mother, but my father was pureblood Aryan. That I'm proud of."

Mrs. Rosen raises the subject of Colonel Dorff's first wife and children, but Goldman is evasive—he has lost touch with his children, and the memory of them brings him pain. Goldman taunts his questioner: "I got such cooperation from your folks. Your folks always made up the transport lists. The chosen, was chosen, and well they chose!"

A visitor has arrived to see Goldman. It is Charlie Cohn, the only person who has volunteered to testify for the defense. Left alone with Goldman in the cell, Charlie brings him up to date on New York happenings: the electricity blackout, the new mayor and all. Charlie has left his mother's apartment and has moved to Goldman's penthouse, where he can keep a close and continuous eye on things.

Charlie has told no one about the Will and intends telling no one about it, not even on the witness stand. Charlie has come here to tell the court "how good you've been to me, Mr. Goldman—and to everybody." Goldman is satisfied that Charlie was the right man to carry on in his absence.

> CHARLIE: Mr. Goldman . . . why have you left *me* your money?
> > *Silence.*
> I mean, why have you left all your money to a Jew, Mr. Goldman?
> > *Pause.*
> GOLDMAN: Because I love you, Charlie—you know that.
> > *He stares at Charlie.*
> Come here.
> > *Charlie goes to Goldman, who waits until he gets close, then whacks him across the face. Charlie staggers back and bursts into tears. Goldman speaks very quietly.*
> Stay out of the court. Don't come in there and ball me up.
> > *He goes over to Charlie.*
> There's more to this than my future. There's more to this than my palaces.
> > *He steps back and calls to Durer.*
> My boots.

The boots are brought. As Goldman puts them on and leaves the cell with a guard, the lights black out and then come up on a courtroom scene with Goldman in a bullet-proof glass booth, the Judge at one table, the Prosecutor at another and Mrs. Rosen, Steiger and Durer at another.

The Prosecutor tells the court that "This monster has only murdered Jews! And when I look at this monster, *I* am only concerned with Jews." He will picture the whole calamity of Jewish suffering in his case against the defendant.

Goldman interrupts: he has seen Mrs. Dorff in the audience; he had thought she was dead. The Judge reprimands Goldman for greeting her, for digressing. Goldman counters with the complaint that his own guilt, not the general subject of the Jewish tragedy, should be the focus of this trial. The Judge assures Goldman it will be.

Goldman argues that he could have had Mrs. Rosen and her two aides killed when they invaded his New York premises, but he spared their lives. The Judge warns him against further digression.

Mrs. Levi takes the witness stand to describe how Dorff killed forty people one day from overwork in a quarry.

> GOLDMAN: Yes, I remember that, but *you* did great—remarkable constitution. 'Course some of you might be wonderin' why Mrs. Levi and her dead friends got on the train in the first place—got on the train to the quarry. There was only three guards as I recall—Kirlewanger's got a villa in Cairo, I'm here, and Pohse's drawing a pension in Hamburg. Anyway, why did all those

DONALD PLEASENCE IN
"THE MAN IN THE GLASS BOOTH"

people keep gettin' on cattle trains and goin' to quarries and such like? Might I enlighten you on that, Your Honor?

JUDGE: No, I know why. Their fate was beyond their knowledge. Every conjecture was arbitrary. They had no foundation.

GOLDMAN: Yes, that's it. I always confused 'em. Everything was done so simple. Ask for your suitcase, I said: "Sure, later!" Ask for your baby, I said: "Sure, stick with the kid." All very peaceful, all very calm. Of course, if I had to make an example I'd use my imagination—stuff your genitals in your mouth, burn your feet off . . . somethin' like that. Couldn't allow any precedents. Couldn't allow any heroes . . . you follow?

Silence. Mrs. Levi leaves the stand. . . . .

What I don't get, Your Honor, is why the Prosecutor does not demand the exposure of all the German authorities who permitted me to get on with my German work, and all those Jews who helped me? I got West German names here of civil servants, businessmen, ministers, priests, doctors, lawyers, generals, whores and haus-fraus . . . Here we are in alphabetical order: Mr. I.G. Braun, former ministerialrat . . .

PROSECUTOR: I object. Not admissible evidence.

JUDGE: Sustained.

Goldman is not permitted to introduce his names into the trial. As he looks around the audience, he can no longer see Mrs. Dorff. He is told that she has decided to return home and will not testify. Goldman claps his hands happily.

In his booth, he continues to clap his hands—but in contempt for the next prosecution witness, a young Jew living well in Johannesburg, South Africa.

A witness named Landau takes the stand.

LANDAU: . . . . . To be truthful, on the journey when Dorff and his men transferred us from Dachau to Buchenwald, although the journey lasted just as long as the one when I went to Dachau—a journey on which many were murdered—on this journey under Dorff no one actually was murdered.

GOLDMAN: This man's an idiot.

PROSECUTOR: This is intolerable.

JUDGE: Dorff—I will only allow you to speak if you are respectful.

GOLDMAN: Excuse me, Your Honor, but the point is, of course, nobody was murdered on that second journey. No need for it. The method! Can't you follow the method? That first journey was an initiation and an initiation's a project. An initiation's a defilement. Make 'em kick each other, make 'em accuse each other, make 'em curse their god, make 'em speak of their wives' intercourse and their own. Make 'em do it with their wives, make 'em do it with other wives, make 'em do it with children. After that they'll do anythin'— no need to waste your energy twice. And I always swore in the anal sphere. They always had to get permission to defecate. "Jewish prisoner number six million and a half most obediently prays to be permitted to defecate." What I was always looking out for, what I was always looking for when I was in the camps . . . were the survivors. What I sought was those not walking dead, those degraded and defiled but still human. I sought 'em with my pistol. And they were always different. They was cunning and tenacious. But I had an eye for 'em. I could smell 'em. They smelled of freedom. And I sought 'em out and I shot them because I could not let them live.

JUDGE: Thank you, Colonel Dorff.
    Landau exits.

But Goldman is wound up now, and he continues his diatribe: in the camps many victims came to believe in their torturers' doctrine of superiority, of Nazism. The Pope, he points out, can and probably will "go back on all this dispensin'." And the Prosecutor drives a Volkswagon. And there are other strange signs, "anti-Semitic daubings" in London, Chicago, Cologne, Stockholm.

Goldman gets on to the subject of the Fuehrer. Goldman describes how Hitler, not even a German, won the love of the people and began to pull them from the depths of their post-World War I despair. The cheers which greeted his speeches were "calls of love from the people." Starving, defeated, bombed at the end of the war, still the people loved Hitler.

GOLDMAN: ". . . . . He never deserted us. All but he! He, only, loved to the end. While he lived, Germany lived. And the people demanded it. We never denied him. People of Israel, we never denied him. And those who tell you different . . . lie. Those who tell you anything else lie in their hearts. And if,

if he were able to rise from the dead, he would prove it to you now. All over again. If only . . . if only we had someone to rise to . . . throw out our arms to . . . love . . . and stamp our feet for. Someone . . . someone to lead.
>   *Pause. Then calculatedly.*
People of Israel . . . people of Israel, if he had chosen you . . . if he had chosen *you . . . you* also would have followed where he led.
>   *Pause. An old woman in the front of the audience rises and speaks quietly.*
>
> OLD WOMAN: This man is not Dorff.
> JUDGE: What's that?
> OLD WOMAN: This man is not Dorff.

The Judge is acquainted with this woman—her name is Mrs. Lehmann—and he asks her to step forward. She does so and informs the court that the defendant is not the German Dorff but a German Jew named Arthur Goldman.

> OLD WOMAN: . . . . . I knew him. I knew his cousin . . . Dorff. And I knew his wife and children. Mr. Goldman had three children. Teresa died on the train. Arthur and Jacob in the first year. Mrs. Goldman in the second. Christina . . . When Dorff came to our camp . . .
> JUDGE: Mrs. Lehmann, enter the stand.
> OLD WOMAN: When Dorff came to our camp he would talk to this man and call him "Cousin . . . , Cousin Arthur." Dorff would smile at this man, pat this man, give him food . . . so all could see. There was a likeness. A family likeness. I think Dorff must have been part Jewish or all Jewish. Dorff would come on Holy Days, give Mr. Goldman food, and laugh. Goldman would wait till Dorff had gone, then give away the food. People followed Mr. Goldman. He never had enough food to give them. People lay on the ground for him. The food was too rich. Bars of chocolate. People cursed Mr. Goldman. People died because of the food. People died because they wanted it too much. And Dorff would come back and sit watching, and laugh and tell the German band to play "Rosamunda." Dorff would sit there sniffing in the sweet brown smoke from the chimneys, and laughing at Mr. Goldman, and calling him Cousin Arthur. It was a game. *(Pause.)* And sometimes he would speak in memory of Mr. Goldman's children. . . . .

The old woman finishes her story: near the end of the war, Dorff remained behind after the other concentration camp personnel had fled. Dorff continued to taunt Goldman as he set about shooting the prisoners methodically, one by one, in the nape of the neck.

Four Russian soldiers arrived in camp, on horseback. They threw Dorff onto the barbed wire, where the inmates killed him by tearing him to pieces. Goldman did not join the others in this act of vengeance.

Mrs. Rosen opens the door to the glass booth and re-examines the left-armpit cigar burn scar of the now silent Goldman. Apparently Goldman burned himself, not to hide an S.S. insignia, but to hide the fact that there never had been one. The concentration camp number on his forearm has been grafted over. Goldman (Mrs. Rosen deduces) must have bribed Israeli agents to accept photographs and X-rays of himself as those of the war criminal Dorff, so that Goldman seemed to match all the details of Dorff's physical description and appearance.

The old woman comments that the Jews would *not* have followed Hitler, and Goldman smiles at her.

The Judge wonders aloud why, why did Goldman perpetrate this hoax: "I understand his need to put a case. I understand a concern for justice . . . a concern for law. I understand his need to put a German in the dock—a German who would say what no German has said in the dock. I understand that. . . . ."

Still, the Judge doesn't understand why Goldman went through with his scheme. It's even possible that Goldman has now done the Jews more harm than good. He has made derogatory comments which are likely to be remembered. But—the Judge finally admits—perhaps Goldman has the right.

No, Mrs. Rosen insists, Goldman does *not* have the right. The Jews have suffered so tragically that now no one has the right to cause them more suffering, for any reason. She calls Goldman "an anti-Semitic Jew" and accuses him of the masochistic desire to be scourged and crucified. Goldman laughs at her.

> *Goldman . . . . . comes out of the booth and goes to the old woman and embraces her.*

GOLDMAN (*to the old woman, very gently*): Sweetheart, you did me. Where's your brains? You're senile. You should never have spoke. Wanted to make some offering for them—something they'd understand. Wanted to let him take me up and swing me north, south, east and west. I wanted when the life was gone, they'd kiss my ass, kiss the turning cheeks of my swingin' ass, kiss my ass and call me sexy. Could I help my own dimensions? Best thing I ever did was break my glasses. Lost my contacts in a urinal. Should've stayed down there in the toilets.

JUDGE: Take him out gently.

GOLDMAN (*grinning*): Was I bein' too hard on ya, sweetheart?

> *He wheels around to the audience. He looks at them.*

I chose ya because I knew ya. I chose ya because you're smart. I chose ya because you're Jewish. I chose ya because you're the chosen. I chose ya for remembrance.

> *He begins to take off his shirt.*

OLD WOMAN (*desperately*): You chose us because you love us.

GOLDMAN (*throwing out his arms to the audience*): Battened down as we were, my brothers, my cousins, shunted from siding to siding, there was time. But after the wire, I rode. I rode on Russian horses, on great black Russian horses. Every lamppost in Danzig a gallows. I clawed out their dead German eyes with my nails. Look at me, my brothers, I did that. I rode on Russian horses and we battered Polish castles, we looted museums, we broke, we burned, we raped and we drank. We draped ourselves with golden tapestries, we covered our fingers with golden rings, we arrayed our horses with golden armor and we ate the German boys. We picked them up and ate them. We crushed them, we trampled them, we ravaged them in the snow—the snow that kept on falling. We kicked in their golden heads. We who were German and Jewish. We did that.

>*Pause.*

JUDGE: You can leave the court.

>*But now Goldman goes to the glass booth. He takes the key and locks himself inside. He takes off the rest of his clothes. The guards beat on the door. The Judge descends from the bench and walks slowly to the naked man in the both. Goldman is silent. The old woman cries in anguish. Silence. Silence. Silence.*

Take him out of the court.

>*The court officials join them. For the moment they do not know how to get the man out. The lights fade. Curtain.*

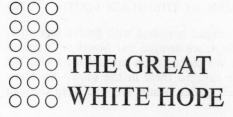

THE GREAT WHITE HOPE

A Play in Three Acts

BY HOWARD SACKLER

Cast and credits appear on page 380

HOWARD SACKLER was born in 1929 in New York City and received his B.A. degree from Brooklyn College in 1950. His many-faceted show business career has included the direction of about 200 records for Caedmon, including Shakespearean plays with the voices of Paul Scofield, Ralph Richardson, Rex Harrison, Margaret Leighton and Flora Robson. Sackler has written and directed for TV and for the movies—two of his screen plays were produced by Stanley Kubrick. His poems have been published in Poetry Magazine, Commentary, The Hudson Review *and* New Directions *and collected in the volume* Want My Shepherd.

In the theater, Sackler is the author of several scripts produced abroad and in the regional theater prior to The Great White Hope. *His play credits include* The Pastime of Monsieur Robert, Uriel Acosta *(for which he won the Maxwell Anderson Award),* The Man Who Stammered, The Yellow Loves *and* Mr. Welk and Jersey Jim. The Great White Hope, *which was previously produced at the Arena Stage in Washington (see the 1967-68* Best Plays *volume) is Sackler's Broadway debut.*

With his wife and two children, Sackler now divides his time between London and the island of Ibiza off the Mediterranean coast of Spain.

Time: The years before and during World War I

Place: North America and Europe

ACT I

Scene 1: Parchment, Ohio, Brady's farm

SYNOPSIS: The Ohio farm of Frank Brady, the reigning heavyweight boxing champion, is suggested by a railed porch and a wooden bench. Brady enters with Cap'n Dan, a heavyweight champion of former years. Their entourage includes Brady's manager Fred, a sportswriter named Smitty and other reporters, photographers, trainers.

Goldie, another manager, stands apart from this group, watching.

(In addition to four formal monologues, the spoken lines of this script are sometimes addressed directly to the audience. In such cases they will appear in parentheses. *Italic* lines in parentheses are stage directions, as usual.)

BRADY *(leads):*
Get Burke, or Kid Foster. Big Bill Brain!
I ain't gonna fight no dinge.
FRED *(coming downstage):* Now Frank—
CAP'N DAN: Listen here to me, Franklin—
BRADY: You wouldn't fight one when you had the belt!
CAP'N DAN:
Well let's say none of them came up to it then.
It wasn't that I wouldn't, I didn't have to.
FRED: He didn't have to, Frank, but you do.
BRADY:
In your hat I do! I know what retired means,
and that's what I am. All I have to do
is dip the sheep and pay taxes.
CAP'N DAN: Hear that, boys? It's old Farmer Brown!
FRED: (Sure looks retired, don't he! Look at the arms on him.)

Three months' training is all Brady needs to get back in shape for a fight, they reassure him. But Brady is adamant—he refuses to fight a black man.

CAP'N DAN:
Now, Franklin,
When you retired with that gold belt last summer
nobody thought it would work out like this.
Everybody just thought that Sweeney'd fight Woods
and whoever won that would be new Number One, right?

So when the nigger asked could he fight Woods first
we figured what the hell, it'll keep up the interest—
nobody, least of all Woods, thought he would lick him.
(And then when he said he wants to try out Sweeney too,
why Sweeney never puts the gloves on with a nigger,
everybody knew that—besides, he was in Australia.)
   Brady breaks downstage. Cap'n Dan follows.
Nobody thought the nigger would go all that way to him,
and even when he did, who would have thought
he could needle old Tommy into taking him on?

SMITTY:
   I was down in Melbourne for the paper, Mr. Brady,
   and let me tell you,
   no paper here could print how bad it really was.
   He'd say, Hit me now, Tommy, and then he'd let him,
   grinning all the time,
   and then cuffing him, jabbing him,
   making smart-ass remarks to the crowd—wouldn't
   be a man and just knock him out, no,
   and then when they stopped it,
   with Tommy there bleeding,
   he's still got that big banjo smile on him—Jesus.

PRESS 1 *(breaks downstage):* You're the White Hope, Mr. Brady!

BRADY: I'm the what?

PRESS 2: The White Hope. Every paper in the country is calling you that.

Brady can't decide. Cap'n Dan discloses that he brought Brady a letter from Washington, D.C. He orders Brady inside the house to read it, although "it'll make you so big-headed you won't be fit to talk to."

Goldie steps forward—he is the black fighter's manager. Goldie assumes that the match is now made and he is willing to accept any terms, so long as Brady will fight his man. They tell Goldie that Brady is to get 80 per cent of the proceeds, and Cap'n Dan is to be the referee. The site is to be Reno, Nevada, in the Rockies, "a white man's country" where the fight will not draw large crowds of Negro spectators.

Brady enters, bringing his gold belt, symbolic of the championship. He has decided: he is ready to fight the black opponent.

BRADY:
   You tell Mr. Black Boy to give me that smile
   when he's inside those ropes—

TRAINER *(to press):* Get it down, get it down—

BRADY:
   I'll appreciate it, tell him—
   (my eyes ain't too good these days, you understand,

I like something nice and shiny to aim at)—
>   *Puts on belt.*
OK, boys?
PRESS 1: Ah!
PHOTO 1: There's the champ—
PHOTO 2: Stance please!
>   *Brady takes stance. Photographers' magnesium flares till end of*
>   *scene.*
FRED *(to Goldie):* Don't let your boy take this nigger stuff to heart, huh?
Explain how it's going to pack 'em in, that's all.
GOLDIE: He knows how it is.

Goldie exits. Cap'n Dan is disturbed by the word "Hope" tagged onto
Brady; it has overtones of doubt. He poses for the photographers.

Scene 2: San Francisco, a small gym

The gym clutter includes a maroon robe, training gloves, a body bag hanging from the ceiling. The black fighter Jack Jefferson is shadow boxing under
the instructions of his trainer, Tick. Jack's white mistress, Eleanor Bachman,
enters and sits on a stool, watching Jack work out.
Jack stops his shadow boxing to speak to Ellie.

JACK *(crosses to Ellie):*
>   Now honey you just know you tired of sittin here,
>   whyn't you go buy yourself a pretty or somethin—
ELLIE *(rises):* No, let me stay. Unless you mind me here, Jack.
JACK: You my Lady Luck! I don mind you nowhere—
TICK: (Oh long as you lookin at him, he don mind—)
JACK: But ain't this too much rough-house for you, honey?
ELLIE: Well—I try not to listen.
TICK: Much obliged!
ELLIE: Oh Tick, I'm sorry—
JACK *(goes to Tick, then returns to Ellie):* She somethin, ain't she!
TICK: Darlin you keep sittin there any way you like it, cause he sure
workin happy. OK?
ELLIE: OK!
>   *Jack kisses her.*

Goldie joins them and receives Tick's report that Jack is working well. The
fight is to take place in Reno July 4 and is already being called the Fight of
the Century. Special trains from St. Louis and Chicago are scheduled.
Jack introduces Goldie to Ellie—Jack and Ellie met on the boat coming
back from Australia. Goldie isn't pleased that Jack has a girl for company in
training. He wants her out of the way at least temporarily, because the press
is due to arrive any minute. But Jack wants Ellie to stay.

JACK: Ain't nobody's business!

GOLDIE *(to Jack):* Grow up, for God's sake—

ELLIE: Let me go, it doesn't matter—

GOLDIE: No—please, one second—Tick, go lock the door.

> *Tick goes off, returns. Goldie goes to Jack.*

So you don't know the score, huh?

Well I'll tell you the score, right now I'll tell you.

And you should listen too, Miss.

> *Takes Ellie to chair. She sits.*

I can see you're a fine serious girl, not a bum,

better you should know, so there's no hard feelings here.

> *Goes to Jack.*

First, Jack, they hate your guts a little bit—OK!

You don't put on gloves everybody should like you.

Then they hate your guts some more—still OK!

That makes you wanna fight, some kinda pep it gives you.

And then they hate you so much they're payin through the nose.

to see a white boy maybe knock you on your can—

well that's more than OK, cash in, after all,

it's so nice to be colored you shouldn't have a bonus?

But Sonny when they start in to hate you more than that,

you gotta watch out. And that means now—

oh I got ears

I get told things—

guys who want to put dope in your food there,

a guy who wants to watch the fight behind a rifle.

OK, cops we'll get, dogs, that we can handle.

> *Goes to Ellie.*

But this on top of it, a white girl, Jack

what, do I have to spell it on the wall for you,

you wanna drive them crazy, you don't hear what happens—

JACK:

What I suppose to do!

Stash her in a iddy biddy hole someplace in niggertown

an go sneakin over there twelve o'clock at night,

carry her roun with me inside a box

like a pet bunny-rabbit or somethin—

ELLIE *(rises):* Jack—

JACK:

Or maybe she just put black on her face,

an puff her mouth up, so's nobody notice

I took nothin from 'em—

> *Knock at door.*

Let 'em wait!

You know I done fool roun plenty, Goldie.

> *Crosses to Ellie. Goldie breaks downstage.*

she know it too, she know it all,
but I ain't foolin round now, unnerstand—
        Points to Tick.
(and if he say "That what you said lass time"
I bust his nappy head—)
TICK: I ain't sayin nothin!
        Knocking.
GOLDIE:

Hold on, I'm comin—
Jack, I swear, I'll help you,
Just you shouldn't throw it in their face, Jack,
I'm beggin you.
JACK: See? This what you fell into, darlin.
ELLIE: Do what he says.
JACK: You go long with him?
ELLIE: Along with you, any way I can.

Goldie capitulates—Ellie can sit there while the press interview takes place.
When the newspapermen come in, Jack exudes confidence. He knows he can
take Brady. The only question is, which round?

"If I lets it go too long in there,
just sorta blockin, and keepin him offa me,
then evvybody say 'Now ain't that one shif'less nigger,
why they always so lazy?' An if I chop him down quick,
third or fourth roun, all at once
then they holler 'No, tain't fair,
that poor man up there fightin a gorilla.' "

Smitty notices Ellie. Goldie pretends she's his secretary, hired in Australia.
One reporter asks Jack: if Brady is the White Hope, does that make Jack
the Black Hope? Most black people want him to win, Jack guesses, but some
don't because "they gonna pay a little high for that belt, if I take it." But Jack
is fighting as an individual, not on behalf of his race.

Clara, a black woman, breaks into the press conference. With scarcely a
word of warning, she attacks Ellie in a jealous rage. In front of the press, Clara
claims to be Jack's common-law wife, but Jack disavows her: "I quit on you
when you cleared outa De-troit with Willie the Pimp." Clara wants to come
back to Jack, but Jack will have none of her. Clara is ushered out by Tick,
still threatening Ellie.

Goldie begs the newspapermen not to write about Jack and Ellie, and they
promise not to.

Scene 3: Reno, Nevada, the fight

Outside a tent, white spectators are shooting craps, listening to a blackface
entertainer, making bets on the fight. There are background sounds of fireworks and a band. A bookie announces he can accept no more Brady money.

The entertainer keeps the crowd laughing with a series of racial slurs against Jack Jefferson and his people. Colonel Cox and Nevada Rangers make the rounds, confiscating all firearms.

Brady arrives for the weigh-in, accompanied by Cap'n Dan and Fred. He is roundly cheered as he steps onto the scale at 204 pounds and then assures his fans he will do his best.

Jack comes in with Goldie and Tick. There are no cheers. Jack mocks Cap'n Dan. The white crowd jeers Jack as he weighs in at 191 pounds. In his words to the crowd, Jack says that after all the mean talk that's been going around, "Ah glad it come down to a plain ole scuffle." A small group of Negroes enters just in time to applaud.

Brady and his friends depart, followed by the white crowd shouting such encouragements as "Kill the coon!" Jack goes to greet the little band of black spectators, led by a Deacon. They have come all the way from Chicago to stand outside the tent (it would be inadvisable for them to go inside) and pray that Jack will "win fo us cullud."

JACK (to young Negro): Hey man. What my winnin gonna do for you!
YOUNG NEGRO: Huh? Oh . . . er . . .
DEACON: Give him self-respeck, that's what!
ALL NEGROES: Amen!
NEGRO 1: Tell it, brother!
YOUNG NEGRO: Yeah—I be proud to be a cullud man tomorrow!
NEGROES (general response): Amen, that's it.
JACK:
     Uh huh.
     Well country boy if you ain't there already
     all the boxin and nigger-prayin in the world
     ain't gonna get you there—
TICK: Jack, let's go—
DEACON: You look cullud son, but you ain't thinkin cullud.
JACK:
     Oh I thinkin cullud, cullud and then cullud,
          "Star Spangled Banner" in the distance.
     I so busy thinkin cullud I can't see nothin else sometime,
     but I ain't thinkin cullud-us, like you.
     An when you come on with it you know what I see, man?
     That ole cullud-us? Just a basketfulla crabs!
     Crabs in a basket—
DEACON: God send you light, son.
          Goldie goes to Jack, takes his arm.
GOLDIE: Time to go, Jack—
          Jack shakes Goldie off.
JACK:
     Tell me you prayin here! And speck I gonto say
     Oh thankya Revren! You ain't prayin for me!

It ain't Lawd don let that peck break his nose,
or Lawd let him get outa town and not get shot at—
I ain nothin in it but a ugly black fiss here!
(They don even push on in to see it workin!)

Colonel Cox comes to get Jack for the fight, and Goldie and Tick follow them off to the arena. The Negroes pray and sing, while the roar of the crowd is heard in the background. Blackout.

Monologue: Cap'n Dan

Cap'n Dan is alone onstage in shirt sleeves and suspenders, lighting a cigar, commenting that the pictures of the fight should be confiscated to avoid the constant reminder of "the biggest calamity to hit this country since the San Francisco earthquake." Cap'n Dan, as referee, had to hold up Jack's hand and declare him champion (Cap'n Dan tells the audience). The calamity is the idea of a black man being champion; not just the "world's biggest genius at making things from peanuts," but *champion*.

CAP'N DAN:
> (. . . . . Heavyweight Champion of the World, well,
> it feels like the world's got a shadow across it.
> Everything's—no joke intended—kind of darker,
> and different, like it's shrinking, it's all
> huddled down somehow, and you with it, you want to holler
> What's he doin up there,
> but you can't because you know . . . that shadow's on you,
> and you feel that smile . . .
> Well, so what do we do!
> Wet our pants, cry in our beer about it?
> No sir, I'll tell you what we do.
> We beat those bushes for another White Hope,
> and if he's no good we'll find another White Hope,
> we'll find them and we'll boost them up till one stays—
> what the hell is this country, Ethiopia?)
> *Blackout; music—"Sweet Georgia Brown."*

Scene 4: Chicago, Cafe de Champion

Negroes are thronging the street in front of Jack Jefferson's Cafe de Champion in Chicago. A policeman holds back the crowds as Jack enters with Ellie, Tick and Goldie. He tells the crowd that he intends to settle here in Chicago, where he can meet all his friends at the cafe.

Jack introduces Ellie to the crowd as his fiancee. Tick holds up the gold championship belt for the crowd to admire. Jack invites everyone inside for an open house, and, cakewalking with Ellie, leads the way into the cafe off-stage.

Goldie confides to Tick his worry that Jack is flaunting Ellie publicly: "Why can't he give them a chance to boil down?"

A crowd of Temperance marchers comes in singing "Woe unto those whose delight is born of evil!" The black folks resent their presence—Division Street is out of bounds for anti-saloon activity. Jack comes out to see what is happening. A woman marcher demands that he shut down his cafe.

A policeman advises Jack that these marchers have a permit to demonstrate. Meanwhile, Smitty, the newspaperman, is observing from the sidelines.

Marchers and Negroes exchange insults. A tussle begins, but Jack restores order. Attempting to make peace, Jack suggests that the Temperance marchers and Negroes join in a song. He wants no trouble that would bring down the law on his cafe. Jack orders folding chairs brought out for the marchers, and some fruit punch, thereby confusing and intimidating them.

Two white men and a woman enter. One of the men announces himself as a Tacoma attorney named Donnelly and tells Jack that his woman companion is Mrs. Bachman, Ellie's mother.

Jack invites Mrs. Bachman inside, as Donnelly enters the cafe looking for Ellie. Mrs. Bachman ignores Jack. Donnelly returns and announces that Ellie insists on staying here with Jack.

Jack promises to send Ellie to see her mother at her Chicago hotel. The white people depart after Donnelly tells Jack and Goldie, "I strongly advise you to send that girl home."

Scene 5: Chicago, District Attorney's office

A meeting is in progress in District Attorney Cameron's office, attended by various civic leaders (one of them a Negro), Smitty, a detective and Dixon, who was the man accompanying Donnelly and Mrs. Bachman the previous evening.

Cameron is explaining to the protesting group that he has no grounds on which to arrest Jack or close his cafe.

MAN 1: Why isn't action taken about the Bachman girl!
CAMERON: She's over the age of consent, Mr. Hewlett—
MAN 2:
    This—
    (To the Negro.) Forgive me, Doctor, but I must speak my mind—
    This connection between them is repulsive
        Rises.
    to every decent Caucasian in America.
    Perhaps he thinks his victories entitled him to it,
    as part of the spoils—
MAN 1: (You know how niggers are!)

MAN 2: Mr. Hewlett!
       Sits.
MAN 1 *(to Negro):* Oh, I'm sorry, Doctor . . .
NEGRO:
> We can't pretend that race is not the main issue here.
> And as you imply, sir, the deportment of this man
> does harm to his race. It confirms certain views of it
> you may already hold: that does us harm.
> But also it confirms in many Negroes the belief
> that his life is the desirable life: and that
> does us even greater harm. (For a Negro today,
> the opportunity to earn a dollar in a factory
> should appear to be worth infinitely more
> than the opportunity of spending that dollar in emulation
> of Mr. Jack Jefferson.)
>   *Steps up on platform.*
> But this I assert: the majority of Negroes
> do not approve of this man or of his doings.
> He personifies all that should be suppressed by law,
> and I trust that such suppression is forthcoming.
>   *General agreement.*

Before departing, the civic leaders warn Cameron that he must take action to correct the situation.

Dixon brings Ellie in for questioning about how and why she went to Australia to obtain a divorce from her former husband; how she was introduced to Jack (at her request) on the boat coming home; how she began to live with him.

Cameron tries to trap Ellie into saying that Jack plied her with drugs—or even bought her a railroad ticket. But the district attorney cannot hurt Jack through Ellie in this way, because the simple truth is, none of those things took place. Nor is Ellie ashamed of her physical relations with Jack. She is proud that Jack loves her, and he makes her very happy. Cameron leads her on—Jack has perhaps influenced her to practices that seemed unnatural? Outraged at such a suggestion; furious and disgusted, Ellie leaves the office.

Cameron admits to Dixon that they have nothing on Ellie—perhaps something might be made of the purchase of train tickets. Dixon suggests they try for a Mann Act violation: "transporting a person across a state line for immoral purposes."

Donnelly comes in and is warned that his client's daughter, Ellie, and Jack are to be kept under surveillance day and night.

Scene 6: Beau Rivage, Wisconsin, a cabin

Furnishings of Jack's cabin hideaway include a chair draped with Ellie's dress and Jack's sweater, a wood box, a table with kerosine lamp and a bed.

Ellie is sitting up in bed wrapped in a sheet. Jack enters draped in a towel, fresh from a cold swim.

Both are sunburned, and Jack pats champagne on Ellie's back to soothe it. He sings a verse to her; they are content with each other's company.

ELLIE:
> Lying in the sun I was, you know, daydreaming . . .
> how maybe I'd stay there . . . and it would keep on burning me . . .
> day after day . . . oh, right through September . . .
> And I'd get darker and darker . . . I really get dark, you know . . .
> and then I'd dye my hair . . . and I'd change my name . . .
> and I'd come to you in Chicago . . . like somebody new . . .
> a colored woman, or a Creole maybe . . .
> and nobody but you would ever guess . . .

JACK: Won't work, honey.

ELLIE: Hm?

JACK: Evvybody know I gone off cullud women.

ELLIE: Oh Jack don't tease . . .

JACK: (I has, too, 'cept for my momma.)

ELLIE: Maybe if I . . .

JACK: Ssh.

ELLIE: What will we do . . .

JACK: Ssh . . . try an sleep, honey.
> *Kisses her. Then turning the lamp down further.*
> Creepin up on me a little too—
> *(Darkness. Sings.)* For how long, how long, I sayin . . .
> Always callin you honey . . . ain't I.

ELLIE: Mm.

JACK:
> Don remember I call no woman by that.
> Call em by their name . . . or jus baby, you know . . .
> Don ever call you by you name.

ELLIE: Oh . . . I don't care about my name . . .

JACK: Honey . . . honey from the bees . . .

ELLIE: Yes.

JACK:
> Nothin like that stuff . . .
> Used to sit . . . Oh, long time ago, in Texas . . .
> we'all ud have a lil honey-treat sometime . . .
> whole yellah mugful . . . used to set there with it
> . . . foolin with it, you know . . .
> liff up a spoonful . . . tip it a lil bit . . .
> watch it start to curve up . . . start in
> to sli-i-i-de ovuh . . . oh, takin its time . . . slow . . . slow . . .
> hundred years up there . . . then down . . . stringing down . . .
> tiny lil dent where it touch . . . and then . . .

Suddenly embracing her.

Oh my sweet sweet baby I want to have it all—

ELLIE: Yes—

Sound of six men—one with a lantern—bursting in. Confusion of light and bodies.

MAN 1: On your feet, Jefferson.

There is the sound of a fight, and when the lamp is lit Ellie is seen huddled at the head of the bed while Jack, grasping a piece of firewood, is holding the intruders at bay. Dixon shows his federal marshal's badge. Jack is under arrest for the Mann Act violation of driving Ellie across the Illinois-Wisconsin state line and then "having done so you proceeded to have relations with her." Ellie is frightened. Jack's first thought is of her—is she also under arrest? No, Dixon assures him, "just you." Jack thanks the marshal and prepares to accompany him without resistance. Blackout.

Monologue: Scipio

Soft woeful singing in the darkness which continues through the following. A bizarre-looking colored man comes from up right: Scipio. He wears a shabby purple cloak clasped with a gold clasp over a shabby dark suit, a bowler hat with a long plume hanging from it, fawn shoes and several large totemic-looking rings. His manner is feverish.

SCIPIO *(speaking over his shoulder into the darkness):*

Start it up, thassit brothers, singin and moanin!
White man just drag him another away here
so all you black flies you light down together
an hum pretty please to white man's Jesus—
Yes, Lawd!

Spits.

Waste a my times . . . (an I don care to talk to you neither!
But I sees two-three out there the same blood is me,
so I says good-evenin to em, then I askin em this:
How much white you up to? How much you done took on?
How much white you pinin for? How white you wanna be?
Oh mebbe you done school youself away frum White Jesus—
but how long you evah turn you heart away frum WHITE!
How you lookin, how you movin, how you wishin an
figgerin—
how white you wanna be, that what I asking!
How white you gaunta get—you tell me!
You watchin that boy? Nothin white-y bout him, huh?
But what he hustle after? White man's sportin prize!
What he gotta itch for? White man's poontang!

What his rich livin like? White man's nigger!
Thinks he walkin and talkin like a natchul man,
don know how he's swimmin half drownded in the whitewash,
like they is, like you is, nevah done diffrunt,
gulpin it in evvy day, pickled in it, right at home there—
Oh year you sayin but what kin we do
what kin us or that boy or them gospellers do,
we passin our days in de white man's world—well,
make you own, brothers!
Don try an join em an don try an beat em,
leave em all at once, all together,
pack up!
Colleck you wages, grab whatevah here gonna come in handy
an sluff off de ress! Time to get it goin!
Time again to make us
a big new wise proud dark man's world—
again! I says again! I tellin what we had once!
Nevah mine that singin—
Learn, brothers learn!
Ee-gyp!!—Tambuctoo! Ethiopya!
Red 'n' goldin cities older than Jeruslem,
temples an prayin to sperrits what stuck with us,
black men carvin ivory, workin up laws!
chartin em maps for the moon an the sun,
refine cultured cullud people hansome as statues there
when Europe an all was juss woods fulla hairy cannibals—)
        A laugh is heard.
(that laughin don harm us none!
Five hundrid million of us not all together,
not matchin up to em, that's what's harmin us!
Dream bout it, brothers—
Five hundrid million on they own part of de earth,
an not a one there evah askin another
how much white you up to
how white you wanna be . . .)
        Glaring, he makes his exit as the lights fade out.

Scene 7: Chicago, Mrs. Jefferson's house

Momma Tiny (Mrs. Jefferson), Jack's mother, sits in her rocking chair, a
shawl over her shoulders. The Pastor is with her, and a group of Brothers and
Sisters singing behind the Pastor's prayers for leniency in Jack's punishment.
Clara, who claims to be Jack's common-law wife, is also present. She now
appears sober in dress and deportment.

Momma Tiny tells her friends, "Fum when he was chile I knowed this day comin." Jack was the kind of a boy who would plead, "why cain't I Momma, lemme lone Momma," refusing to accept the place assigned to him.

MRS. JEFFERSON:
 . . . . . Tried to learn it to him meaner—
(Mo chile you got the meaner you go to
if you lovin you chile. That plain cullud sense.)
Hit him with my han, he say So what.
Hit him with my shoe, he look up an smile.
Took a razor-strop to him, that made him squint
but then he do a funny dance an ask me fo a nickel. . . . .

Mrs. Jefferson asks the Lord's forgiveness for not hitting Jack hard enough to teach him to stay out of trouble.

To Mrs. Jefferson's surprise, three uniformed professional Negro baseball players come to call, carrying their gear in small valises. They explain that they are friends of Jack, who asked them to stop by.

Tick comes in to report that for the Mann Act violation Jack has been sentenced to a $20,000 fine and three years in Joliet. His mother takes the news badly: "I die they lock him up!" Jack is out on bail, but only for the week.

Clara explodes in anger, blaming the mess on Ellie. Jack once brought Ellie to visit his mother, and Mrs. Jefferson found her not "too bad."

In company with Goldie, Jack enters, greets everybody and kneels down beside his mother, reassuring her that everything is going to be all right.

Jack notices Clara and gives her a count of ten to get out, even though his mother pleads that Clara has been a great help to her. Before Jack can throw Clara out, Tick warns him to leave her alone for now. Tick has been watching an automobile through the window, and all at once everyone notices that some sort of plan is being carried out by Jack's friends.

Tick orders Jack to stand near the window so that the detectives in the auto can see him. Jack does so and appears to be undressing. Then he moves away from the window and begins to exchange clothing with Rudy, one of the baseball players. Rudy goes over and stands by the window in Jack's clothes, and Jack, disguised in a baseball uniform, prepares to walk right past the detectives in company with the other two players ("You hear that sayin how all niggers look alike!") on their way to the Montreal train. As soon as possible, Jack plans to take a boat for England.

Jack voices his determination not to rot in prison, but to live his life as Champion of the World, wherever he has to go to do it. The Pastor warns him that it is unwise to flout the law like this, but his mother praises the Lord for setting Jack free.

Clara asks Jack to take her, and when he refuses she tries to betray him to the detectives. But Momma Tiny's friends hold her back. They sing a gospel song to drown out the sounds of Clara's struggle.

Jack says an affectionate goodbye to his mother, then leaves with the baseball players, as the rest remain to sing in full chorus. Blackout.

ACT II

Scene 1: London, the Home Office

A group of middle-aged, soberly-dressed citizens are seated facing a large desk. Jack, Ellie, Goldie and Tick enter while Eubanks, an assistant to the Undersecretary, Sir William Griswold, enters chatting with Treacher, who is Jack's solicitor.

Jack tries to greet the seated group in friendly fashion, but they freeze. Goldie warns Jack to let Treacher do the talking.

Sir William enters and sits at his desk, and a hearing begins. It has been alleged that Jack, a convicted criminal in his own country, is an undesirable alien. A man named Coates directs the attack.

Jack and Ellie's landlady testifies that they have been giving wild dancing parties and damaged the premises (the damage has been paid). A policeman bears witness to a public disturbance and assault (but the charges have been dropped). In fact, all the problems seem to have been settled quietly.

Jack testifies that he has been "fussin" in London because no one would give him a match. Now that Lord Lonsdale has booked him for a fight, however, things will be different. He promises to go into training immediately and "no mo rumpus."

Sir William makes his decision: Jack has broken no law.

SIR WILLIAM:
> Well, Mr. Coates, as I see this at the moment,
> the American legalities are none of our concern,
> the breaches of the peace you've cited are trivial,
> the man's moral character deficient perhaps
> by Queen Victoria's standards, (but she of course is gone now),
> and as to the palaver in the press and the music-halls, these are liberties
> we simply have to bear—
> think of them as part of the White Man's Burden!

But Coates is not to be denied. The London County Council has refused a license for Jack's fight, so he no longer has occupational reasons for remaining in England.

Ellie protests the unfairness; Sir William assures Jack he can stay anyhow, but Jack stalks out angrily.

Scene 2: Le Havre, a customs shed

A crowd and band are on hand to greet Klossowski, a Polish heavyweight who is to fight Jack. Klossowski boasts (in French) that he has fought large black men before and will knock Jack out easily.

Scene 3: Paris, Vel d'Hiver

In the dressing room, Tick is taping Jack's hands. Ellie and a French handler are watching. Jack's championship belt and dinner jacket and pants are draped on the dressing-room furnishings.

Tick and Goldie show signs of nervousness, but Jack is cool. He hasn't bothered to train much for this bout with a "fith-rate geechee." Jack doesn't want Ellie to see the fight and persuades her to remain in the dressing room.

As Jack and his entourage exit to the arena they are greeted by the roar of the crowd—and Smitty comes in to join Ellie. Smitty guesses that the reason Ellie looks pale and tired is that she is going to have a baby. But Smitty is wrong, and the suggestion upsets Ellie even more than she is already upset by each rising decibel of the crowd's roar in the background.

The roar changes to jeers and catcalls, and Jack rushes in, bloodstained, followed by his hurrying manager and handler. Goldie echoes the crowd's anger: "God, why'd you keep on hitting him?" In his frustration, Jack has used his opponent as a punching bag and may have hurt him badly.

The French fight promoter comes in and urges them to hurry. Jack can dress in the car, but they must get out of the crowd's reach. They leave, with Jack apologizing to a silent Ellie.

Scene 4: New York, Pop Weaver's office

In the office of Pop Weaver, a sports promoter, Fred (who formerly managed Brady) and Cap'n Dan are singing the praises of a new White Hope: a big, young farm boy who has performed well in a couple of fights. Weaver is ready to promote the fight, but Cap'n Dan hesitates. They can't afford another victory for Jack. This time they must make sure, Cap'n Dan insists:

"The next White Hope is the one who gets the belt back
Not means to, or almost does, or gets half-killed trying like the Polack.
He takes it, he finishes right on his feet with a big
horizontal nigger down for good there."

Cap'n Dan wants something extra going for them this time. He brings in Dixon, the government agent. The government has the Jack Jefferson case on its mind, too.

DIXON:
When a man beats us out like this, we—the law, that is—
suffer in prestige, and that's pretty serious.
How people regard the law is part of its effectiveness,
it can't afford to look foolish, and this applies
especially now to our Negro population.
Though you may not be aware of it yet,
a very large, very black migration is in progress.
They're coming from the fields down there and filling up the slums—

trouble's starting in Europe, and our mills and factories
have work for them now. And I'm talking of hundreds
of thousands, maybe millions soon—
(millions of ignorant Negroes, rapidly massing together,
their leanings, their mood, their outlook, suddenly
no longer regulated by the little places they come from—
situations have arisen already).
We cannot allow the image of this man
to go on impressing and exciting these people.

POP: I'm only a sports promoter, Mr. Dixon.

CAP'N DAN: He read the writing on the door, Pop. Go on.

DIXON:

If this position he enjoys were to be lost,
through the outcome of his next engagement, let's say,
the effect of this would be so much in our interest
that we would be disposed to reconsider his sentence.

POP: You'd make it worth his while not to win the fight, you mean.

DIXON: I think I've said what I mean, Mr. Weaver.

CAP'N DAN *(to Dixon):* What's the furthest you can go?

DIXON:

We'd reduce it to a year, of which he'd serve six months.
(We're willing to make this as attractive as possible.)

FRED: I say my kid can beat him fair and square!

POP: Don't ride it, Fred.

Fixing the fight goes against Fred's grain, and Weaver's—and Cap'n Dan's,
too, for that matter. But, Cap'n Dan reminds them, they have a situation on
their hands, they may have to bend a little. They must fix the fight—and Jack's
opponent, the Kid, need never know.

Jack is already under pressure in Europe, where nobody will fight him any
more except in minor exhibitions. And Jack's mother hasn't been too well—
maybe he'd like to see her once more before she dies.

POP:

What the hell, Fred.
We'll balance it out on the one after this.
Everything back on the Gold Standard, right?

FRED: OK. OK.

DIXON *(rising):* Well, thank you gentlemen—

CAP'N DAN: And we thank you!

POP: I wouldn't count on results straight off, though.

DIXON:

Oh, I think the country
can hold up a little while.

> *They laugh. Dixon waves them silent and goes down right to audience.*

Excuse me—
(You seem to be indignant, sir. Yes, I heard you.
We have that all the time from people like you,
that old Machiavelli crap. Look into it further, sir.
But not in here, or at home. Give it some thought
next time you're alone on the streets late at night.)
(To Cap'n Dan) I'll be in touch with you.
          Blackout.

Scene 5: Berlin, an outdoor cafe

Jack and Tick are sitting with four drunken German officers, Jack Indian-wrestling with one of them. To the Germans' rising admiration, Jack wins. The officers go off to find Jack "a suitable memento."

Ellie comes in with Ragosy, an impresario, and they sit at the table. Ragosy buys them all champagne. He is one of many promoters who seek to exploit Jack as a vaudeville attraction. Bitterly, Jack leaps up and goes into a buck-and-wing.

ELLIE: Jack, please stop it.
JACK: What?
ELLIE: Can't you just tell him no and—
JACK: I tell him what I wants to hon—
ELLIE: Jack we're in the street—
JACK: An where I wants to an how, hear?
TICK: Baby all she sayin—
JACK: Who ass you!
          (To Ellie.) Talk to me bout streets.
          If you so godam tetchy bout people lookin
          you ain even oughta be here.
ELLIE *(rises):* I don't like them looking when you're this way—
JACK:
          No? Well me neither! But I's stuck with it
          an you ain't, so any time you wanna—where you goin!
                    Ellie goes right.
          (To Ellie.) Git you ass back on there! Man bought champagne—

Ragosy is embarrassed, but Jack keeps on taking his frustrations out on El-lie, who ignores him and calmly departs for the hotel, accompanied by Tick.

The German officers return; they have found a German-speaking African black man in the street and have hustled him, bewildered, to meet Jack.

Jack gets rid of the soldiers, invites the black man to join him at the table. The guest explains in broken English that he is here in Berlin to study and learn so that he can return to his native Africa to use the white man's skills when the right time comes. Jack warns his friend that the white man "ain leavin go, man. No place."

The black African admires Jack for being the Champ, and before leaving he gives Jack his good luck amulet.

Goldie comes in with the news that he has finally made a match. Jack, sensing the truth, asks immediately: "How much I get for losing it?" Smitty has acted as the go-between making Jack the offer from Pop Weaver, Cap'n Dan and the government agent Dixon: throw a fight to the Kid and come home to a sentence reduced to six months.

Jack won't even consider such an offer. Goldie protests that they need a fight, they need money. But Jack still refuses and offers Goldie the money to go home if he wants to. Jack will make out somehow, find something to do.

Scene 6: Budapest, a cabaret

A juggler finishes his act and Ragosy, now in evening dress, introduces the next number. It is a capsule version of *Uncle Tom's Cabin* with Ellie playing Little Eva and Jack as Uncle Tom.

ELLIE *(sits on grass mat):* Here, Uncle Tom, do come and sit beside me.
JACK *(sits):* Deed Ah will Miss Eva. On dis lubly ole grassy bank.
ELLIE: See how beautiful the clouds are Tom. And the water too.
JACK: An you right widdem, Miss Eva, you de byootifluss uf all.
ELLIE: But friend, why do you seem sad this evening?
JACK:
  Oh Miss Eva, you and de massah so kine ter ole Tom
  he juss gotta cry out bout it now and den.
ELLIE: Yes. We are happy here.
JACK:
  It like a plantation fum de Good Book, yessum.
  You de brightest lil sperrit Ah evah seed, Miss Eva.
ELLIE: Oh Tom, sing about the Spirits Bright, would you?
JACK *(rises):* Juss gittin set to.
    Piano gives him a chord and accompanies him as he sings.
  A sees a ban uh Sperrits Bright
  Dat tase de glo-ries dere—
    Mock groan from the audience.
  Dey are all robed in spotliss white
  an wavin palm dey bear.
  Ef Ah had wings—
    Another mock groan, a titter, a voice saying "a kovetkezo." Jack stops, the piano stops. A moment of uncertainty.
ELLIE: Oh, but look who has come to make us lively, Tom!

Tick enters as Topsy in a black wig and red checked dress, goes into a song number which the audience doesn't like any better than it did Jack's.

Ragosy pulls Tick from the stage and Jack and Ellie try to carry on, but the audience's derision breaks up the performance.

Scene 7: Belgrade, railway station

The sound of the audience's disapproval in the previous scene has changed
to the rumble of artillery. Jack, Ellie and Tick appear to be stranded, with
their luggage.

Smitty finds them in the railway station. He has a telegram—Jack's mother
is sinking fast. Perhaps Jack would like to reconsider the offer of a fixed fight,
in order to come home and see his mother one more time?

But Jack remains adamant: "Doan wan none today, man." Smitty starts to
leave but turns back, exasperated.

SMITTY:
> What the hell is it for though, all this.
> I mean, you're not a boyscout. What the hell is it, Jack?
> Keeping the belt a little bit longer? Staying champ
> a little while longer? I can't make you out.

JACK:
> Champ doan mean piss-all ta me, man.
> Ah bin it, all dat champ jive bin beat clear outa me.
> Dat belt a yours juss hardware, woulden even hole mah pants up.
> But Ahm stuck widdit, see, a hunk a junky hardware,
> but it doan let go, it turnin green on me,
> but it still ain lettin go, Ahm stuck as bad widdit
> as you all stuck wid needin it offa me—
> Shake it loose, man! Knock me fo ten and take it, unnerstan?
> Ah be much oblige!

SMITTY:
> Look, you know we'd rather
> have it straight—

JACK:
> Oh ya would, huh.

SMITTY:
> Sure,
> and Jack if you weren't so damned good—

JACK *(grabs him by his coat and swings him down to floor):*
> Hunnerd million people over dere, aintya?

SMITTY: Yes, but—

JACK: Picked out de bess Hope ya got dere, aintya—?

TICK: Jack—

JACK: Ah wants a match widdim.
> *Throws Smitty down.*

SMITTY: It's our way or nothing, feller.
> *Smitty picks himself up.*

JACK:
> Ah said a match widdim!

An if you doan wanna gimme one, Ah gonna makeya,
same's Ah done before, see—Ah gonna make em!
Gonna take mah funky suitcase an mah three-four hundred dollahs,
an get mahself ta Mexico, howya like dat, man,
right up nex ta ya, gonna sit on dat line dere
an wave you crummy belt at ya an sing out
Here Ah is—
SMITTY: It's not going to work, Jack.
JACK: Here Ah is! Here Ah is!
ELLIE *(goes to Jack):* Oh Jack—
JACK *(pushes her away):* Leave me alone!
　　　Lights fade as the guns grow louder. Curtain.

ACT III

Scene 1: Chicago, a street

Mourners, including Goldie and Clara, line up for the funeral of Jack's mother, Momma Tiny, with police to keep order. The Pastor sermonizes in praise of this patient, longsuffering woman who was born a slave and endured much tribulation.

Clara, the most frenzied of the mourners, turns on Goldie in Jack's absence and reproaches him bitterly for the trouble and neglect that led to Momma Tiny's death. The Pastor urges them all to be calm and endure, but Scipio enters with the sarcastic observation: "Dass right, chillun, suffer nice an easy—school em on it, boss!"

Scipio cries shame on "moanin low," on suffering in silence.

SCIPIO:
　　Yeah!
　　Shame on evvy Goodie-Book thumper like you!
　　White man keep pullin de teeth outa you head
　　an preacher here givin you de laughin-gas—
PASTOR: Ah warnin you, heathen—
SCIPIO:
　　Ah warnin evvybody!
　　(Warnin dat white gal an warnin dem po-lice
　　ain nothin lass foever!)
NEGRO: Tell em!
SCIPIO:
　　(Warnin dat dead woman
　　Jesus wuzn't swimmin! Warnin mah people
　　dat boy juss a shadow an dey livin black men
　　whut gotta live long—)
NEGRO: Amen!

SCIPIO:
> Doan Amen me!
> Makin believe you de Chillun of Isrel,
> fiery-furnacin an roll-on-Jordanin—
> you ain no Isrel! Dere—
>> *Points to Goldie.*
> *Dass* a Jew-man—
> see whut ya see! Look in de mirrah once
> an see whut ya see! Ah said de MIRRAH,
> not a lotta blue eyes you *usin* fo a mirrah,
> an hatin whut dey hates, de hair you got,
> de nose you got, de mouth you got, de—

PASTOR: Offissah, Ahm askin you—

POLICEMAN *(moves toward Scipio):* Right—

NEGRO: Whut dey doin—

SCIPIO:
> Hate dat woolly head you gotta hate de man whut got it, brudders,
> dat man YOU—

The police haul Scipio off, still protesting. Some of the black men move to help him, and the crowd becomes unruly. The police move in with clubs and force the crowd to move off with Momma Tiny's coffin, leaving Goldie alone onstage listening to the sounds of riot as the lights fade.

Scene 2: Pop Weaver's office

Jack's taunts from the other side of the Mexican border, as reported by newsmen ("Will Fight Kid for Carfare and a Watermelon"); the photos of him waving the belt in the white man's face, so to speak, have goaded Cap'n Dan into a fury. As each day passes, the Pop Weaver-Cap'n Dan contingent looks more and more foolish in refusing to accept Jack's challenge to a fair fight, waiting for him to accept their terms for a fixed fight with the Kid.

Cap'n Dan vows to "squeeze that dinge so goddam hard soon a fix is gonna look like a hayride to him." They'll cut off the money being sent him by friends, take away his sparring partners, isolate and starve him. The Kid's contingent is overextended (says Pop Weaver), but so is Jack's—"Let's see who goes under" (says Cap'n Dan). Blackout.

Monologue: Clara

CLARA *(enters as distant bell slowly chimes):*
> (Do it soon, soon, goin good now, drag him
> on down. Oh, wontya, for me and his momma
> an evvy black-ass woman he turn his back on
> for evvy gal wid a man longside dreamin him

a piece of what he got, for all his let-down
secon-bess sistahs, alla Mistah Number One's
lil ugly sistahs ssh—
we draggin on him with you
doan never stop now,
offa dat high horse an on down de whole
long mud-track in fronna him, years gawnta nothing,
limpin and slippin
an shrinkin and creepin and sinkin right in—
Call him to ya, Momma!
Soon, baby soon.)

Scene 3: Juarez, a barn

Jack is working out with crude equipment, with the help of Tick and a Mexican boy, Paco. Jack finishes and gets set for his rubdown. Tick comments that they'd better raise the punching bag a foot, the Kid is a very big man.

They are going to have to pawn the light boxing gloves. Tick wraps them in newspaper and hides them as Ellie comes in with a tray of food. Irritably, Jack forces Ellie to remind him that no cables have arrived, no help is near.

Paco and Tick (taking the gloves) depart, and Jack tries to push Ellie off with them, but Ellie is still trying to reach him across his frustration and tension. Clearly, Cap'n Dan's "squeeze" is hurting. Ellie begs him: "Cable them tonight, please—" Jack scorns Ellie for feeling the pressure. But Ellie persists: Jack's enemies have won this round with their isolation and starvation tactics. Jack must yield a little now in order to fight them another day.

ELLIE:

. . . . . they have you!
They do and you know it, you're theirs, at least
you can buy yourself back from them—

JACK:

Sold—
(one buck nigger fo de lady!)

ELLIE:

Let it sound the way it is!
Run when they push you and back when they pull you,
work yourself sick in this hell-hole for nothing,
and tell me you're not theirs—here,
look at the grease you swallow for them,
look at the bedbug bites on your arms,
and the change in your pockets and the blotches in your eyes—

JACK:

Doan leave de smell out—

ELLIE:

The two of us smell!

Whatever turns people into niggers—there—
> *Shows her neck.*
it's happening to both of us—

Maybe, Ellie insists, if Jack could get out of this trap, just maybe they could find a way to live. Jack mocks her; then, taking out his pain on her, he grabs Ellie and swings her against the edge of the table.

JACK:
Well Ah gonna tellya whut de livin like, baby,
far as Ah concern—
ELLIE:
Get away from me—
JACK:
Yeah,
Ah put you straight on it—(an alla you, too.
Ah wen inta a fair once and dere wuz dis old pug, see,
give anybody two bucks who stan up a roun widdim—
perfessional set-up, reggerlation ring an all,
cep dey had rope juss on three sides, dass right,
de back side wuz de tent. So Ah watches a couple
git laid out real quick in dere, but he doan look
dat red hot ta me, see, so Ah climbs in widdim.
An Ah doin awright fo a youngster, when all at once
he bulls me up gainss dat tent-side a de ring
an SLAM, WHAM, somebody behine dere conks me,
right through de canvas, musta use a two-by-four,
and evvy time Ah stans up he shove me back agin,
an SLAM, dere's anudder, down she come—
good story, huh?)
ELLIE: Jack—
> *Jack goes around the end of the table.*
JACK: Dass how it go like Ah knows it, baby—
ELLIE: Sometimes, sometimes—
JACK:
All de way now!
dass where Ah is and dass whut Ahm gittin,
gonna git it de same sayin Yassuh, Nossuh,
doan mattah whut Ah does—Ah in dere, unnderstan?
An Ah doan wan you watchin, or helpin, or waitin,
or askin, or hannin me you jive bout livin
or anythin fromya but OUT, Ah mean OUT—
ELLIE: What—
JACK: How goddam plain Ah gotta make it for ya!
ELLIE: Jack—if you want other girls—
JACK: Git you stuff ready, train out ten o'clock.

ELLIE: No, no I won't, no—

JACK: When Tick come Ah send him ovah—

ELLIE: Jack—

JACK: Bettah start movin—

ELLIE: Stop it—

JACK: Ah pologize actin so yellah up ta—

ELLIE: Wait, you have to stop it—

JACK: All Ah has to is be black an die, lady—

ELLIE *(goes toward him):* I want to stay, even if we—

JACK: Stay wid you own, lady.

Ellie begs Jack to let her stay, come what may. Jack pretends she is a dead weight hanging on him; he must get rid of her. As Jack told Ellie after his mother's death, "Leave me be a while!"

Still Ellie pleads to stay and try to make Jack happy. In the face of her resistance, Jack resorts to anger.

JACK: . . . . . you grey bitch—
> *Leaps onto table, grabs towel and jumps to floor, whipping Ellie with towel. Pushes her against table and steps back center.*

ELLIE: You can't make me go, stop doing this—

JACK:
> Why you think
> Ah aint put a han to ya for how long, why ya think
> it turn me off juss lookin atya

ELLIE: Stop it—

JACK:
> You stayin,
> stay fo it all—ya know why?
> Does ya, honeybunch? Cause evvy time you pushes
> dat pinch up face in fronna me, Ah sees
> where it done got me, dass whut Ah lookin at,
> the why, the wherefore and de Numbah One Who,
> right down de line, girl, an Ah mean YOU,
> an Ah doan wanna give you NOTHIN, unnerstan?
> Ah cut it off firss!

ELLIE: Oh I despise you—

JACK: Right, like alla resta ya—

ELLIE: Oh, I'd like to smash you—

JACK:
> Me an evvy udder dumb nigger who'd letya!
> Now go on home an hustle one up who doan know it yet,
> plenty for ya, score em up—(watch out, brudders!)
> Oughta hang a bell on so dey hear you comin.

ELLIE: You mean this.

JACK: Look in mah purple eyes.

ELLIE: You win, daddy.
She turns and goes off.

Jack takes a swig of water and shadow-boxes. The chief of this Mexican district enters. He, El Jefe, philosophizes to Jack that love of country is one of the few redeeming features of a hard life; but in reality El Jefe is merely marking time for Goldie, the government agent Dixon and another young agent who enter and greet Jack.

The government's offer to Jack has been sweetened—now he will receive only a suspended sentence for his original conviction as well as for the bail-jumping and passport-violating faults he has committed since. Still Jack refuses and defiantly prepares to walk out on them. But El Jefe, enforcing international law and agreements, pulls a revolver on Jack.

Jack continues toward the door in defiance of the gun, but he is stopped by the entrance of Tick and two Mexicans with Ellie's body—she has thrown herself down the well and died of a broken neck.

JACK *(kneels above table holding her limp arm):*
    Honey!
    Honey, baby, please, sugar, no—!
    Whut Ah—whut Ah—whut Ah—baby,
    whut Ah done to ya, whut you done, honey,
    honey whut dey done to us . . .
        Collapses behind table.
EL JEFE *(turns away):* No puedo mirarlo.
GOLDIE: Jack. Jack. Anything I can . . .
        Jack nods.
Anything. What, Jack.
JACK *(rising slowly):*
    Set dat fuckin fight up! Set it up, set it up!
    (Ah take it now!)
        Blackout.

Monologue: Cap'n Dan

The noise of printing presses is heard. Cap'n Dan is gratified at all the excitement and publicity the fight is rousing.

CAP'N DAN:
    (. . . . . I bet you can't guess who's refereein—Brady!
    Oh will they eat that up, when he's giving the count.
    and he's—what? no, he ain't in on it,
    neither is the Kid, who the hell wants that!
    But he's the one who lost it,
    and the whole world's gonna see him

take it in his hand again, and hold it up
and pass it on, like the Kid'll pass it—)
      Boat whistle interrupts him.
(OK!
This time we'll keep it in the family!)
      Lights fade.

Scene 4: *Chicago, a street*

Summoned by a beating bass drum, a group of Negroes is gathering to throw
nickels in a pail to send a telegram to Havana (where the fight is to take place)
in support of Jack Jefferson, "bess natchul fighter in de worl."

Scene 5: *Havana, Orienté Racetrack*

Outside the gate of Orienté Racetrack there is a crowd of white men without tickets, clustered under a banner advertising the fight. A Cuban Negro
boy is hawking cheap straw hats.

One man has climbed a ladder and can see into the arena. He is describing
the fight for the others, who can also follow it in the roars of the crowd within.
It is so hot that one of the men suffers a sunstroke and has to be helped away
by a Pinkerton man.

According to the man on the ladder, the Kid is getting much the worst of
it—he has lost all 10 rounds so far.

Smitty and Pop Weaver come in through a side door and are soon joined
by Fred, Brady's former manager. Two rounds ago, Smitty gave the signal and
Goldie caught it—he flipped his towel in acknowledgement. But Jack is fighting hard, in defiance of the fix. Pop is still certain that Jack will carry out his
part of the bargain.

Meanwhile, the crowd is shouting such remarks as "He's collapsin there but
so is the nigger," "Let's get mad, Kid," "Run, tar-baby, run back to your
barrel," "It's 102 degrees—Chalkasians ain't made for it," etc.

Rudy, the black baseball player who helped Jack escape from his mother's,
is sent for. He is persuaded to disguise himself as a handler, get to the ring and
remind his friend Jack of the agreement.

MAN 1 *(on ladder):*
   Kid—
   Cover, Kid, turn, turn—cover, he'll cave
   your ribs in—
         Roar.
MAN 2:
   Stop the goddam—
MAN 1:
   Wait, no, he's up—Oh
   the nigger's right on him, he's after it, he's—

MAN 6:
   Kid don't let him—
MAN 1:
   All he's got,
   he's workin like a butcher—
MAN 2:
   No—
MAN 7:
   He's gotta—
MAN 5:
   Kid—Kid!—
MAN 9:
   Kid—
MAN 1:
   Hookin him,
   sluggin—Oh that eye—
MAN 6:
   Ride him out—
MAN 7:
   Kid—
MAN 6:
   Bust your hand, you—
MAN 1:
   Murder, it's murder—
MAN 4:
   No more—
MAN 2:
   Clinch him—
MAN 1:
   Ref—
MAN 6:
   Clinch him, dummox—
MAN 2:
   No more—
MAN 1:
   REF!
MAN 5:
   Stop it—
MAN 2:
   Ref, ya—
NEGRO BOY:
   Eh! Eh! Eh! Eh!
MAN 1:
   He's
   on the ropes, he can't see, he's rollin,
   he's punchy—

MAN 2:
    How the hell does he—
        Roar.
MAN 6:
    Is he—
MAN 1:
    No, it's a bell, lemme down . . . lemme down . . .

Man 4 takes Man 1's place on the ladder and reports that the Kid has blood
and welts all over him, and the eye is damaged.

Pinkertons come in carrying Goldie from the arena in a chair. Goldie has
begged Jack to throw the fight as agreed, but Jack doesn't seem to hear him.

Excitedly the man on the ladder reports that the Kid is swinging wildly and
seems to be connecting. The steam has gone out of Jack's punches.

Now Jack has retreated to a corner where the Kid, blood in both eyes and
swinging blind, is battering the black fighter.

MAN 4 *(on ladder):*
    There—
    the nigger's grabbin for the rope—(he's bucklin)—
    he's swingin with his other—
MAN 6:
    You're through—
MAN 4:
    The Kid's
    poundin right down on him, he's grabbin,
    he's hanging, he's holdin, he can't, the Kid's
    drivin him down like a big black—
        Great roar. Man 1 follows the referee's count with his own arm;
        his voice barely audible.
MAN 1:
    Four—five—six—seven—eight—
        The crowd's roar pulsates with the last two counts and pandemo-
        nium breaks loose: hugging, dancing, etc.
    I love him, I love him—
MAN 2: Wahooo—
        Pop goes inside with Smitty.
MAN 6:
    (We got it—)

The Negro boy climbs the ladder to watch Jack, bloody, limp through the
gates with Tick and Goldie. In the background, the ring announcer can be
heard declaring the Kid the winner and new champion. The boy climbs down
from the ladder. Members of the press are badgering Jack to tell them how
and why it happened, and Jack stops.

JACK:

He beat me, dassall.

Ah juss din have it—

The boy spits on him and darts away.

Ain't dat right, boy?

TICK *(moving him on):* Take it slow, nice and slow . . .

PRESS 3: But why, Jack. Really.

JACK *(laughs, stops):*

Oh, man,

Ah ain't got dem realities frum de Year One . . .

(An if any a you got 'em, step right down and say 'em!)

Takes in audience. Drum-beating begins.

(No . . . You new here like Ah is—)

Music: a march triumphal.

Come on Chillun!

Let 'em pass by!

Spreading his arms, he sweeps Tick and Goldie to one side, moving slowly, as the cheering crowd surges out through the gates. The Kid rides on their shoulders: immobile in his white robe, with one gloved hand extended, the golden belt draped around his neck and a towel over his head—his smashed and reddened face is barely visible—he resembles the lifelike wooden saints in Catholic processions. Joyfully his bearers parade him before the audience and go off. Jack, Goldie and Tick go up center slowly as the lights fade. In the darkness they exit. Curtain.

IN THE MATTER OF
J. ROBERT OPPENHEIMER

A Play in Two Acts

BY HEINAR KIPPHARDT

Translated by Ruth Speirs

Cast and credits appear on page 390

HEINAR KIPPHARDT was born in Heidersdorf, Silesia in 1922. His father, a dentist, was imprisoned in concentration camps from 1933 to 1938 as an opponent of the Nazi regime. The son began medical studies in 1940 but was drafted into the German Army. As a member of a panzer division he took part in the retreat from Russia and then deserted in 1945. After the war, Kipphardt continued the medical phase of his career, taking a degree at Dusseldorf and specializing in psychiatry at various German hospitals.

In 1951, Kipphardt left his Berlin hospital and the medical profession to become a producer at the Deutsches Theater in East Berlin, where he remained nine years and became the chief producer-director. In 1959, because of political differences, he moved to Dusseldorf and in 1960 to Munich where he now lives and devotes his full time to playwriting.

Kipphardt's first produced play was Shakespeare Urgently Wanted *in 1953 at the Deutsches Theater, which also staged his satirical farce* The Chairs of Mr. Szmil *in 1956. The Munich Kammerspiele housed his* The General's Dog *in 1963 and* Joel Brand *in 1965. In the Matter of J. Robert Oppenheimer had its world premiere in October 1964 at the Free People's Theater in West Berlin and represented its author's New York playwriting debut in the Lincoln Center production. Kipphardt is also the author of many TV plays, a book of short stories and a new play* The Soldiers *(not to be confused with his compatriot Rolf Hochhuth's* Soldiers, *presented on Broadway in the 1967-68 season) which had its premiere in Dusseldorf in August 1968.*

234

INTRODUCTION BY THE DIRECTOR AND THE AUTHOR *

It might be rightly asked why an assemblage of documentary material should be fashioned into play form. As history it must inevitably be truncated and distorted, and as a play it violates traditional concepts of drama as action, plot and character. Why not make a film of the actual events or read out a verbatim transcript? Would it not be clearer, more precise, more factual—certainly! More enlightening—not at all! . . . . . Kipphardt focuses on fundamental issues within a society to prick the social conscience of us all. Life cannot do this, but our retelling of it can. . . .

In the Matter of J. Robert Oppenheimer is a celebration of the complex thought processes by which man comes to grips with his environment. The play is a distillation of 3,000 typewritten pages of transcript into 100 pages of drama. Film and slides are utilized in this production as documentation of real events and a continuing reminder of this as fact. The action on the stage is merely the abstraction of ideas embodied in human behavior; the film is the shadow of reality; the actor on stage is the three-dimensional existence of illusion. It asks the audience to reinterpret for itself what is being reinterpreted on the stage of the author's reinterpretation of something which really happened. The play answers no questions, rather it begs the question and poses problems with which the audience itself must wrestle.

GORDON DAVIDSON

The other authors who use documentary material (Peter Weiss and Rolf Hochhuth) have developed very different kinds of plays, both in terms of their approach to the word itself, and in terms of their dramatic techniques. Common to them, perhaps, is my attitude that in our time of slogans in which people tend to create ideologies of quick theses and premature judgments, one should be precise and base upon unassailable documentary evidence that which one presents in his works. . . . . Interestingly enough, writers of the so-called documentary drama have developed their techniques quite independently of one another as they were faced with the problem of bringing into the theater major political themes. But I would say that there are certain themes dependent upon documentations which can hardly be handled by any other than the documentary approach. These are themes in which artistic license has no place, in which one can focus on the essential core only by highlighting the contradictory mass of evidence to illuminate the heart of the matter. . . .

I don't know whether you can create a meaningful parable about Auschwitz, Hiroshima or Vietnam. This would seem somewhat obscene to me. As I began to work on *In the Matter of J. Robert Oppenheimer,* I experimented with var-

* These comments by Mr. Davidson, who directed the play in New York as well as in its American premiere last year in Los Angeles, and by Mr. Kipphardt appeared as notes in the program of the Lincoln Center Repertory production at the Vivian Beaumont Theater.

ious technical means. First, I considered an epic form akin to Shakespeare's plays, with the hearing merely the last act. It didn't satisfy me—it was too imprecise for me. I found that the problem of the contradictions between the grandiose development of the new sciences and the retarded development of our knowledge of society could not be portrayed as a parable or tale, but rather as a factual description, backed up by documentation. . . . . But of course, I did want to use the extreme case of Oppenheimer to portray the contradictions and conflicts of the scientist in our age. And these should be equally applicable to other fields of activity. The huge mass of facts is the basic source from which the dramatist tears the pertinent facets of his work, and he has to do a great deal more to come up with a viable end product.

HEINAR KIPPHARDT

Time: *April 12–May 6, 1954*

Place: *Room 2022, Building T3, Atomic Energy Commission, Washington, D.C.*

ACT I

SYNOPSIS: In a prologue, an amplified voice explains: "This is a theatrical event . . . . . and not an essay or assemblage of documentary material. Characters, such as the attorneys, appear on the stage who did not appear at the hearing, and additionally, there are some scientists and others who appear as witnesses who did not appear at the hearing." The aim here, the prologue explains, is not a plain documentary, but "a dramatization of fundamental issues."

An announcer continues to narrate while still photographs and documentary movie footage, projected on screens at the rear of the hearing room setting, recollect the explosion of the first atomic device at Los Alamos, N.M. and the dropping of the first atomic bomb on Hiroshima.

Scene 1

In Room 2022, on April 12, 1964, a hearing conducted by the Atomic Energy Commission is about to take place. At the center of the stage is a table with three armchairs for the members of the hearing board. At stage left is the witness chair, and stenographers are positioned at far left and right. Counsel for the Commission—Moffat and Spalding—are already in their places at right, going over stacks of documents. There is a place for Oppenheimer's counsel—Garrison, Hardiman and Stein—at left. On a lower level downstage is a small leather sofa facing up.

JOSEPH WISEMAN IN "IN THE MATTER
OF J. ROBERT OPPENHEIMER"

J. Robert Oppenheimer enters left; tall, ascetic, his suit appearing a size too large for his spare frame. He moves slowly, almost puppet-like. He is accompanied by two of his counsel, Hardiman and Stein, who take their places.

A clerk leads Oppenheimer across the room to the leather sofa. His counsel spread out their materials. He puts down his smoking paraphernalia and steps forward.

OPPENHEIMER: On the twelfth of April, 1954, a few minutes to ten, J. Robert Oppenheimer, a professor of physics at Princeton, formerly director of the Atomic Weapons Laboratories at Los Alamos, and, later, adviser to the government on atomic matters, entered Room 2022 in Building T3 of the Atomic Energy Commission in Washington—to answer questions put to him by a Personnel Security Board, concerning his views, his associations, his actions, suspected of disloyalty. The evening before this investigation, Senator McCarthy said in a television interview:

A huge picture of Senator McCarthy is projected on the white screens at the back. Oppenheimer goes to the leather sofa and fills his pipe. A voice shaking with agitation issues from the loudspeakers.

MCCARTHY'S VOICE: If there were no Communists in our government, why did we delay—for eighteen months—delay our research on the hydrogen bomb? Even though our intelligence agencies were reporting—day after day—that the Russians were feverishly pushing their development of the H-bomb? And may I say to America tonight that our nation may well die—our nation may well die because of that eighteen months' deliberate delay. And, I ask you, who caused it? Was it loyal Americans or was it traitors in our government?

The three members of the Commission's hearing board enter: the Messrs. Gray, Morgan and Evans. The others rise briefly as the board members take their seats at the table upstage.

Gray refers to Senator McCarthy's remarks of the previous evening, wondering whether they had any connection with this hearing, supposedly a secret one. Oppenheimer admits that some of his friends took the remarks as referring to him, including Einstein who phoned to say: "If I had the choice again I'd rather be a plumber or a peddler, if only to enjoy some small measure of independence."

The occupations of the hearing panel are stated for the record. Evans, a professor, is the only scientist. Morgan is a former Sperry Gyroscope Co. executive. Chairman Gray is a former newspaperman and Secretary of the Army, now chancellor of the University of North Carolina.

Oppenheimer agrees to testify under oath (he is not required to) and takes the witness stand. Under questioning by the Commission lawyer Moffat, he denies his publicity identification as "Father of the Atom Bomb," calls it "a pretty child—and it has about a hundred fathers."

Closely questioned by Moffat, Oppenheimer denies he took any major part in the decision to drop an A-bomb on Japan—that was "a political decision," not a scientific one. Once the decision was made, however, Oppenheimer helped advise on the choice of targets (photographs of various Japanese cities named by Oppenheimer are flashed on the screen at the back wall of the hearing room), as a member of an advisory council.

MOFFAT: And you had to select the targets?

OPPENHEIMER: No. We supplied the scientific data as to the suitability of the targets.

MOFFAT: What kind of target did you consider to be of the desired suitability?

OPPENHEIMER: According to our calculations, the area had to have a diameter of at least two miles, densely built-up, preferably with wooden buildings—because of the blast, and the subsequent wave of fire. Also, the selected targets had to be of a high military and strategic value, and unscathed by previous bombardments.

MOFFAT: Why, Doctor?

OPPENHEIMER: To enable us to measure exactly the effect of a single atomic bomb.

EVANS: These military considerations, I mean, after all, they were the business of the physicists, weren't they, at that time?

OPPENHEIMER: Yes. Because we were the only people who had the necessary experience.

EVANS: I see. I'm rather out of my depth here. How did you feel?

OPPENHEIMER: I asked myself that question, later. I don't know . . . I was very relieved when the Secretary of War followed our suggestions and crossed the famous temple city, Kyoto, off the list. It was the largest and most vulnerable target.

MOFFAT: But you did not oppose the dropping of the atom bomb on Hiroshima?

OPPENHEIMER: We set forth arguments against . . .

MOFFAT: I am asking you, Doctor, whether *you* opposed it.

OPPENHEIMER: I set forth arguments against dropping it. But I did not press the point. Not specifically.

MOFFAT: You mean to say that having worked day and night for three or four years to produce the atomic bomb, you then argued it should not be used?

OPPENHEIMER: No. When I was asked by the Secretary of War I set forth the arguments both for and against. I expressed my uneasiness.

Oppenheimer admits under questioning that he helped determine how to make the bomb's killing power most effective, yet after it was dropped he shared the terrible scruples felt by most people: "It is the kind of schizophrenia we physicists have been living with for several years now." Atomic energy could make the whole world a land of milk and honey, and instead it is being thought of as a weapon of war.

Oppenheimer tells the court that originally they developed the bomb as a preventative against it being used by Hitler, and then as it turned out it was America which used it: "We weren't asked *whether* it should be used, but only *how* it should be used in order to produce the maximum effect."

The scientific community set forth arguments for and against using the bomb, as opposed to demonstrating it to the Japanese in a test—Oppenheimer himself was undecided on this question: "We were physicists, not the military, not politicians. That was the time of heavy fighting on Okinawa. It was a horrible decision." The decision was made, the bomb was used, and the effect was "technically successful." Oppenheimer observes: "We scientists have been on the brink of presumptuousness in these years. We have known sin."

MOFFAT: . . . . . The reason I am digging up this old Hiroshima business is this: I want to find out why, at that time, you devoted yourself with such single-mindedness to your tasks, with a hundred per cent loyalty, I would say—and why, later, in the matter of the hydrogen bomb you adopted an entirely different attitude. Would you have supported the dropping of a hydrogen bomb on Hiroshima, Doctor?

OPPENHEIMER: It would have made no sense at all.

MOFFAT: Why not?

OPPENHEIMER: The target was too small . . . We were told that the atomic bomb was the only means of bringing the war to an end quickly and success-fully.

MOFFAT: You don't have to defend yourself, Doctor. Not on that count, anyway.

OPPENHEIMER: I know.

MOFFAT: Did the allegations contained in the letter of the Atomic Energy Commission surprise you?

OPPENHEIMER: They depressed me.

MOFFAT: What exactly depressed you, Doctor?

OPPENHEIMER: That twelve years' scientific work in the service of the United States should end in such allegations . . . Twenty-three points in that letter deal with my associations with Communists or Communist sympathizers. Points on which I have already been cleared in previous security investigations. The letter contains only *one* new point. A most surprising one.

MOFFAT: Which point, Doctor?

OPPENHEIMER: That I strongly opposed the development of the hydrogen bomb, on moral and other grounds; that I turned other scientists against the hydrogen bomb; that I thereby considerably slowed down the development of the hydrogen bomb.

MOFFAT: In your opinion, this allegation is not justified?

OPPENHEIMER: It is not true.

MOFFAT: Not true in any respect?

OPPENHEIMER: In no respect at all. Ever since our apprehensions concern-ing the monopoly of the hydrogen bomb have been proved right—ever since the two world powers have been facing each other like scorpions in a bottle—there have been people trying to persuade America that the blame lies with traitors.

The Atomic Energy Commission's letter to Oppenheimer, and the physi-cist's letter in reply, are placed in the record. Moffat wants to question Oppen-heimer on the old charges—he has what he claims is new evidence of a secret Communist meeting at Oppenheimer's residence in 1941. A witness named Paul Crouch—who has made anti-Communist testimony his profession in these troubled times—will be called. The board gives Moffat permission to open up the previous charges on which Oppenheimer has previously been cleared.

Moffat breaks from his place in the hearing and steps forward to address the audience directly, explaining that Oppenheimer was his idol until he stud-ied the physicist's dossier, the files which led the F.B.I. to believe that Oppen-heimer was "probably a camouflaged Soviet agent" and President Eisenhower to withhold all secrets from him. Moffat explains: "I have come to realize the inadequacy of being strictly confined to facts in our modern security investi-gations. Must we not examine the thoughts, the feelings, the motives—which underlie those facts—and make them the subject of our inquiries? It is the only method if we want to arrive at a conclusive judgment as to Oppenheimer's integrity. Do we dissect the smile of a Sphinx with butchers' knives? When the security of the free world depends on it, we must."

Scene 2

On the second day of the hearing, Moffat asks Oppenheimer, "Have you ever been a member of the Communist Party, Doctor?" and Oppenheimer answers "No."

Moffat probes the scientist's past. To Moffat's questions, Oppenheimer replies that his wife was a Communist up to about 1936, at the time of her first marriage to a husband who fell in the Spanish Civil War. Oppenheimer's brother, Frank, was a Communist until 1941.

Spalding takes up the questioning, and the scientist admits that he himself could be called a "fellow-traveller"—agreeing with certain parts of the Communist idea without joining or helping them. Even this degree of approval came to an end after the Nazi-Soviet pact of 1942, the year that Oppenheimer was placed in charge of Los Alamos and thus cut off from all his association with Communists except his onetime fiancee, Dr. Jean Tatlock, an admitted member of the party, who later killed herself.

MOFFAT: . . . . . You spent the night in a hotel with her, and . . .

OPPENHEIMER: What business is that of yours? What has it to do with my loyalty?

MOFFAT *(in a friendly tone):* Has it nothing to do with your loyalty, Doctor, when without informing the security authorities, when *you,* the man responsible for the atomic weapons project in Los Alamos, when *you* spend the night in a hotel with a Communist woman?

OPPENHEIMER: That Communist woman happened to be my former fiancee who was going through a severe emotional crisis and who wished to see me. A few days later, she was dead.

MOFFAT: What did you talk about, the two of you?

OPPENHEIMER: I do not propose to tell you.

MOFFAT: You won't tell me?

OPPENHEIMER: No.

The physicist leaves the witness stand, walks to the sofa and lights his pipe. His lawyer objects to this line of questioning, and Chairman Gray sustains the objection. Oppenheimer returns to the stand.

The board's only scientist, Professor Evans, comes forward to speak directly to the audience. He feels that such questioning is humiliating to a scientist. He wishes he hadn't agreed to join this board. He is disturbed by the State's increasing control over scientists, at the very time that scientists are giving man more and more control of his environment. "How can a thought be new, and at the same time conform?" Evans asks himself uneasily. "Is Oppenheimer only a beginning?"

Scene 3

The third day of the hearing, Oppenheimer is still being questioned by Moffat about his past Communist associations. The physicist gave $300 a month to the Spanish Loyalists because he saw Fascism as a greater threat to the world—and especially to the Jews—than Communism. But being a man of independent thought, he did not care to join the party.

Moffat refers to a report of the secret meeting at Oppenheimer's house in 1941. Oppenheimer admits being friends with such as Haakon Chevalier in those days, but flatly denies he ever took part in a secret Communist meeting. The aforementioned Paul Crouch and his wife are the only witnesses to this meeting, and Oppenheimer's lawyer, Stein, demands the right to call and question them, to demonstrate the falseness of their testimony. But the F.B.I. won't release the Crouches to attend this hearing.

Stein offers documentary evidence that Oppenheimer was in Mexico with his wife at the time that the alleged secret meeting was supposed to be taking place in Berkeley, Calif., thus disposing of Crouch's spurious charge.

Lawyer Stein leaves his place in the hearing and steps forward to address the audience, noting that "If Oppenheimer is condemned here, our present-day security system will have passed judgment on itself. The subjugation of science to the military will have been proclaimed, and in *their* ranks will be no room for independent spirits, for dissent. Are these proceedings fair? The Board has access to secret F.B.I. files, but we are not allowed to see them. Oppenheimer cannot look at his own correspondence, his own reports; they have been declared secret and confiscated. Are the atomic secrets supposed to vanish out of his head?"

Stein believes this hearing is a poor battlefield on which to fight—he'd rather air the whole matter publicly, even though his client's "faith in the power of arguments makes him a worse witness than Joan of Arc."

Scene 4

On the fifth day, Oppenheimer is being questioned by the industrialist on the panel, Morgan. Oppenheimer tells him that in the old days it was feasible to have an occasional Communist working on the atomic project, because Russia was an ally—but not today. At any rate, no known Communist was employed at Los Alamos. Even Oppenheimer feels that Party membership would raise problems of divided loyalty.

Moffat wonders what tests Oppenheimer applied to determine whether former party members were or were not spies—Oppenheimer's brother, for instance. Oppenheimer replies indignantly: "In the case of a brother you don't apply tests. At least I didn't. I knew my brother."

Moffat brings up Klaus Fuchs and other spies. Oppenheimer tells him that the Russians got a few details from them, but no essential information. Moffat returns to the subject of Oppenheimer's brother.

MOFFAT: When did your brother leave the Party?

OPPENHEIMER: In the autumn of 1941, I believe.

MOFFAT: But shortly after that, he was doing work on secret war projects?

OPPENHEIMER: About a year later.

MOFFAT: Did you, thereupon, inform the security authorities that your brother had been a member of the Communist Party?

OPPENHEIMER: Nobody asked me.

MOFFAT: Nobody asked you.

OPPENHEIMER: I don't think it is my duty to destroy my brother's career when I have complete confidence in him.

MOFFAT: Do you know that at that time, and also quite a while later, your brother publicly denied he had ever been a Party member?

OPPENHEIMER: I know he denied it in 1947.

MOFFAT: Why, in your opinion, did he deny it?

OPPENHEIMER: He probably wanted to go on working as a physicist—and not as a farmer, as he has been forced to do since then.

MOFFAT: Do you approve of his conduct, Doctor?

OPPENHEIMER: I don't approve of it. I understand it. I disapprove of a person being destroyed because of his past or present opinions. That is what I disapprove of.

MOFFAT: We are speaking about secret war projects and about the possibly disagreeable measures we have to take in order to protect our freedom, Doctor.

OPPENHEIMER: I know. There are people who are willing to protect freedom until there is nothing left of it.

Spalding, the other Commission lawyer, questions Oppenheimer about his recommendation of physicists with left-wing views for employment at Berkeley and Los Alamos. Oppenheimer explains that physicists tend to hold such views because of their interest in new ideas and thoughts. Oppenheimer admits that many of his friends and associates held such views, particularly before it became evident that the Soviet experiment was just another power play. But Oppenheimer holds to his opinion that these friends and associates were not security risks. Besides, he tells the lawyer, "You cannot produce an atomic bomb with irreproachable, that is conformist, ideas. Yes-men are convenient, but ineffectual."

When in 1947 Oppenheimer found that several of his associates—Weinberg, Bohm and others—were Party members, Spalding wants to know, did he break away from them?

OPPENHEIMER: No.

SPALDING: Why not?

OPPENHEIMER: Well, it isn't exactly my idea of good manners.

SPALDING: Is it your idea of security?

OPPENHEIMER: What?

SPALDING: Did you recommend your own lawyer to Weinberg, sir?

OPPENHEIMER: It was my brother's lawyer, I believe.

SPALDING: Did you give a party for Bohm?

OPPENHEIMER: I went to a farewell party given for him when he had been fired at Princeton and was going to Brazil.

SPALDING: And you found it quite easy to reconcile these sympathies for active Communists with the duties of your high office, as the adviser to the government on atomic matters?

OPPENHEIMER: What has that to do with atomic matters? I gave some advice to old friends, and I said goodbye to them.

SPALDING: Would you do the same again, today?

OPPENHEIMER: I should hope so.

SPALDING: Thank you, sir.

Professor Evans has a question: are there so many "red" physicists because, perhaps, they are all a little mad? It's because they're open-minded and curious, Oppenheimer informs him, they like to investigate why things don't work; why there are such things as hunger, joblessness, cruelty. Oppenheimer tried to read Marx but couldn't get past the first 50 pages.

Morgan the industrialist steps forward to speak to the audience. The question that must be decided here, he reasons, is not whether Oppenheimer's background and ideas are acceptable—that is no one's business—but whether he wrongfully allowed his subjective views to affect his objective work as a government atomic expert. "This is not small potatoes," Morgan decides. "It is bigger than Oppenheimer, and it is bigger than the Eisenhower administration. The question is whether you are going to have one security system for the scientist who built a bomb and another for a chauffeur who drives a Congressman around Washington."

Scene 5

The ninth day of the hearing is Oppenheimer's 50th birthday, and Moffat is still questioning him. Did Haakon Chevalier send him birthday greetings? Yes, he did. Oppenheimer still counts him as a friend, "One of the two or three friends one has in a lifetime."

Moffat wants Oppenheimer to recall a conversation he had with Chevalier, then a "pinkish-red" professor of French literature, at Oppenheimer's house the winter of 1942-43. Oppenheimer testifies that Chevalier and his wife came to the house for a social visit. They talked of Stalingrad, the Russian war effort.

GRAY: Did Chevalier introduce the subject of Stalingrad?

OPPENHEIMER: I don't know, it may be that we talked about it on some other day, but I think it was on that particular evening. One thing is certain, anyway: when I went into the kitchen to mix some drinks Chevalier followed me there and told me that he had recently met Eltonton.

GRAY: Would you tell us, for the record, who Eltonton is?

OPPENHEIMER: A chemical engineer, an Englishman, who had been working in Russia for several years.

GRAY: Party member?

OPPENHEIMER: Closely associated. Whether he actually was a party member? . . . I didn't know him all that well.

MOFFAT: What did Chevalier want from you?

OPPENHEIMER: I'm not sure he *wanted* anything. He told me that Eltonton was furious because we had left the Russians in the lurch, because we weren't opening up a second front, and didn't give them the technical information they needed, and that it was a bloody disgrace.

MOFFAT: Was this Chevalier's opinion?

OPPENHEIMER: He spoke about Eltonton. He said Eltonton had told him he knew certain ways and means of transmitting technical information to Soviet scientists.

MOFFAT: What ways and what means, Doctor?

OPPENHEIMER: Chevalier did not say what they were. I don't know whether Eltonton had said what they were. We did not discuss things, I mean, I just said: "But that is treason!". . . I'm not sure, but anyway, I said something to the effect that it was horrible and quite unspeakable. And Chevalier said he entirely agreed with me.

MOFFAT: Is that all that was said?

OPPENHEIMER: Then we talked about drinks, and about Malraux, I believe.

Oppenheimer didn't take this conversation seriously enough to report it. Besides, Chevalier didn't know that Oppenheimer was working on an atomic bomb. Then, six months later, a security man warned Oppenheimer that he was worried about the Berkeley situation. So Oppenheimer concocted a story, full of elaborate and false details about secret agents at the Soviet consulate. The purpose of this story was to warn the authorities about Eltonton without involving Chevalier. But the security people doubted his story. Finally Oppenheimer's commanding officer, General Groves, ordered him to tell the truth and name names. Oppenheimer then told the truth and named Chevalier and himself.

Why did Oppenheimer deliberately lie to the security people? "Because I was an idiot" is his only explanation.

Major Radzi, one of the counter-espionage officers to whom Oppenheimer told his cock-and-bull story, replaces the physicist on the witness stand. Radzi testifies that in May 1943 he was ordered to investigate suspected espionage at Berkeley. Each of four suspects—including the one finally revealed as the culprit—was connected in some way with Dr. Oppenheimer. So the F.B.I. was asked to investigate Oppenheimer, under Radzi's direction. They found that the physicist had "probably been a member of the Communist Party" and continued to have strong ties with known Party members. It was recommended that Oppenheimer be removed from U.S. Government employment, but the recommendation was rejected.

Radzi is still convinced that Oppenheimer's original story was true in all its fabricated sinister detail, and that only later did the physicist repudiate it and "admit" that it was a cock-and-bull story. "I wouldn't have cleared him then," Radzi concludes, "and I wouldn't clear him now."

Under cross-examination by Stein, Radzi claims to know Oppenheimer well, from his files. The physicist has been under investigation almost 14 years and yet—Radzi is forced to admit—there is no proof in these files that Oppenheimer ever committed an indiscretion. As for Chevalier, he was fired from his job at Berkeley (though he was never proved guilty of any act) and placed under surveillance.

STEIN: If Dr. Oppenheimer foresaw such consequences, would it not be understandable that he hesitated several weeks before naming him?

RADZI: No, not when the safety of the country is at stake. From a scientist of such stature, we must demand absolute loyalty.

STEIN: Do you know that, in 1946, the F.B.I. investigated the Chevalier incident a second time?

RADZI: Yes.

STEIN: And that Mr. Hoover, the F.B.I. chief, took an interest in it himself?

RADZI: Yes.

STEIN: And that Dr. Oppenheimer's clearance was granted, with no reservations?

RADZI: I'd have liked to see the man who'd have cast doubt on Dr. Oppenheimer's clearance in 1946, what with his prestige and influence! He was a god in those days.

STEIN: I have no more questions.

But Dr. Evans of the panel has something he wants to ask Major Radzi: is 100 per cent security possible? No, Radzi admits, but 95 per cent would be possible if scientists and technicians would cooperate. He tells Dr. Evans: "If we want to defend our freedom successfully we must be prepared to forego some of our personal liberty."

Radzi leaves the stand after testifying in answer to a question by Hardiman that Oppenheimer's alleged Communist sympathies influenced his attempt to protect his friend Haakon Chevalier. Oppenheimer tells the board he has seen Chevalier as recently as three months before, in Paris. Chevalier doesn't know yet that it was Oppenheimer who reported him to the authorities.

Lansdale, the expert in charge of security for the whole atomic weapons project during the war, takes the stand. He is questioned by Hardiman, one of Oppenheimer's lawyers. Lansdale testifies that he was disturbed by the F.B.I. reports and had the physicist closely watched. Also, he made the effort to study Oppenheimer personally, to get to know him.

HARDIMAN: What was your conclusion?

LANSDALE: That he was not a Communist, and that he should be granted his clearance no matter what the F.B.I. reports said.

HARDIMAN: Dr. Oppenheimer has been rebuked here for having refused to disclose the identity of his friend, Chevalier. What is your attitude in this matter?

LANSDALE: I think he was wrong. Also, it was rather naive of him to imagine that he would get away with it, when he had *us* to deal with. I always thought it was his brother, Frank, whom he wanted to protect, and General Groves thought the same.

HARDIMAN: Did his refusal endanger the security of the project?

LANSDALE: No. It just gave us a lot of extra work, that story he dished up to us. It was typical.

HARDIMAN: Typical of what?

LANSDALE: Scientists regard security officers either as extraordinarily stupid, or as extraordinarily cunning. And incompetent, in either case.

EVANS: Oh, how would you explain that?

LANSDALE: The scientific mind and the military security mind—well, it's like birds and rhinos sharing a ball game. Each thinks the other impossible, and both are quite right.

Lansdale doesn't agree with Radzi that Oppenheimer's made-up spy story about three mysterious agents at the Soviet consulate was actually true. Investigations in 1943, 1946 and 1950 revealed that it was just "a lot of hot air." By the criteria of those days—loyalty and discretion—Lansdale would still grant Oppenheimer his clearance.

Under cross-examination by Spalding, Lansdale refuses to discuss "presently existing security criteria." He insists that Oppenheimer was right in not abandoning Jean Tatlock just because she was a Communist: "If you should ever fall deeply in love with a woman who happens to have Communist views, and if she wants to see you because she is unhappy—then, I hope, you will go and comfort her, and leave your tape recorder behind."

Spalding tries to make Lansdale testify that Steve Nelson, a Communist functionary, might have learned of the existence of the atom bomb from Dr. Tatlock and/or Oppenheimer, but Lansdale insists that this too was investigated and no truth found in it. He cannot, however, deny the bare possibility that it might have happened.

Oppenheimer tells the hearing that Nelson was an acquaintance of his wife's, and Dr. Tatlock didn't know him well. If Dr. Tatlock knew anything about the bomb, she didn't learn it from Oppenheimer.

Spalding puts it to Lansdale that Oppenheimer deliberately lied to the security offers. Lansdale regards this simply as the eccentric attitude of scientists in general toward security in general. Angered by the lawyers' badgering, Lansdale declares: "I think that the current hysteria over Communism is a danger to our way of life and to our form of democracy." He objects particularly to judgments of 1940 actions in the light of 1950s hysteria. Oppenheimer's successes with the atomic device and bomb speak for themselves about his loyalty and motives.

Morgan, the industrialist on the panel, asks Lansdale to define a Communist. Lansdale replies: "A person more loyal to Russia than to his own country. You will note that this definition has nothing to do with philosophical or political ideas."

Morgan gives Lansdale a complicated analogy about a bank manager who neglects to report associations with known safe-crackers. Lansdale replies that he might have asked some questions in this situation, "but I wouldn't have done so twelve years later, when it turned out that none of those fellows had actually robbed a bank."

Evans asks Lansdale the same question about 100 per cent security he asked Radzi.

LANSDALE: In order to have one hundred per cent security, we would have to abandon all the freedoms we want to defend.

EVANS: It can't be done?

LANSDALE: It can't be done!

EVANS: What, in your opinion, can be done, then, to ensure a country the maximum amount of security?

LANSDALE: We must see to it that we have the best ideas and the best way of life.

EVANS: I'm no expert, but I feel I'd also have formulated it along these lines . . . It isn't easy.

LANSDALE: No.

EVANS: Not at all.

Lansdale rises to his feet.

When I look at the results of this strict secrecy, of these security ramifications on all sides, I mean, we are sitting rather uncomfortably on this powder keg of a world, everywhere, I think the question arises whether these secrets might not be safeguarded best of all by being made public?

LANSDALE: What do you mean?

EVANS: By re-establishing the age-old right of the scientists to publish the results of their researches, or maybe even demanding it of them?

LANSDALE: This is such a remote and Utopian dream, Dr. Evans, that even children are forbidden it . . . The world is divided into sheep and goats, and we are all in the slaughter house.

EVANS: As I said before, I'm no expert.

GRAY: Thank you very much, Mr. Lansdale.

Lansdale leaves the room.

Today's session is concluded, and we will now take a recess. We shall next deal with Dr. Oppenheimer's attitude in the matter of the hydrogen bomb. May I ask Mr. Hardiman and Mr. Moffat for the list of their witnesses.

End of Act I.

ACT II

The amplified voice of the announcer, in a prologue, comments on the first explosion of a hydrogen device, pictured on the screens behind the hearing room setting. The voice emphasizes that this staggeringly huge explosion was only a baby H-bomb.

Scene 1

In the hearing room, all the principals have returned. Oppenheimer is on the stand again. Gray, the chairman, steps forward to tell the audience that an exchange of correspondence between Oppenheimer and the Atomic Energy Commission has been released to the New York *Times* by the physicist's lawyers, "to counteract a subversive campaign against Oppenheimer." The hearing itself is now in the headlines all over the country.

Scene 2

Moffat is questioning Oppenheimer.

MOFFAT: I quote from a letter by the Atomic Energy Commission, page six, at the bottom: "It was further reported that in the autumn of 1949, and subsequently, you strongly opposed the development of the hydrogen bomb; One, on moral grounds, Two, by claiming it was not feasible, Three, by claiming that there were insufficient facilities and scientific personnel to carry on the development, and Four, that it was not politically desirable." Is this statement true?

OPPENHEIMER: Partly.

MOFFAT: Which parts of it are true, Doctor, and which are not?

OPPENHEIMER: I made that all clear in my answering letter.

MOFFAT: I would like to have it clearer still.

OPPENHEIMER: Let us try.

MOFFAT: I have a report here, from the General Advisory Committee, of which you were the chairman. It dates back to October 1949, and it is in answer to the question whether the United States should, or should not, initiate a crash program for the development of the hydrogen bomb. Do you remember that report?

He hands Oppenheimer a copy.

OPPENHEIMER: The majority report. I wrote it myself.

MOFFAT: It says there—Mr. Spalding will you read that excerpt . . .

SPALDING: It says here, in the majority report: "We all hope that the development of this weapon can be avoided. We are all agreed that it would be wrong at the present moment for the United States to initiate an all-out effort toward the development of this weapon."

MOFFAT: Does this not mean, Doctor, that you were against the development of the hydrogen bomb?

OPPENHEIMER: We were against *initiating* its development . . . The Russians had exploded their first atomic bomb, in 1949, and we reacted with nationwide shock. We had lost our monopoly of the atomic bomb, and our first reaction was: we must get a hydrogen bomb monopoly as quickly as possible.

MOFFAT: That was quite a natural reaction, was it not?

OPPENHEIMER: Maybe natural, but not sensible. The Russians also developed the hydrogen bomb.

MOFFAT: Were we not in a much better position, technically?

OPPENHEIMER: Perhaps, but in Russia there are only two targets suitable for a hydrogen bomb, Moscow and Leningrad, whereas we have more than fifty.

MOFFAT: One more reason to get ahead of the Russians, or is it not?

OPPENHEIMER: It seemed wiser to me to try for an international declaration of renunciation of that terrible weapon—the ability to extinguish all life upon earth is a new attribute.

Oppenheimer testifies to the devastating force of the hydrogen device. He began to feel "terrible scruples" after Hiroshima, when he understood that the forces he was harnessing would be actually used in war.

Regardless of anyone's scruples, the hydrogen bomb was quickly developed in 1951—not by Oppenheimer, but through the efforts of thermonuclear experts. Oppenheimer served only in an advisory capacity—not because of his scruples, he repeats under the lawyer's examination, but because he was not an expert in this field and therefore not the best man for the job.

Spalding introduces a patent application by Oppenheimer and Teller in 1944 for a device pertaining to the hydrogen bomb. Even so, Oppenheimer insists, he wasn't the man for the hydrogen-device job. He doubted the advisability of creating a hydrogen bomb, but after the President's decision to produce it he helped—but only as an adviser.

Moffat questions Oppenheimer's enthusiasm for this 1951 project.

OPPENHEIMER: I was enthusiastic about the fascinating scientific ideas.

MOFFAT: You thought the scientific ideas for the development of the hydrogen bomb were fascinating and wonderful—and you thought of the possible result, the hydrogen bomb itself, as horrible. Is that right?

OPPENHEIMER: I think that's right. It isn't the fault of the physicists that brilliant ideas always lead to bombs nowadays. As long as that is the case, it is possible to have a scientific enthusiasm for a thing and, at the same time, as a human being, one can feel a profound horror of it.

GRAY: Would you not say, Dr. Oppenheimer, that such an attitude might imply something like divided loyalty?

OPPENHEIMER: Divided between whom?

GRAY: Loyalty to a government—loyalty to mankind.

OPPENHEIMER: Let me think . . . I would like to put it this way: if governments show themselves unequal to, or not sufficiently equal to, the new scientific discoveries—then the scientist *is* faced with these conflicting loyalties.

GRAY: If you are facing such a conflict, Dr. Oppenheimer, and it obviously did happen in the case of the hydrogen bomb, to which loyalty would you give the preference?

OPPENHEIMER: I have always given undivided loyalty to my government, without losing my uneasiness or losing my scruples, and without wanting to say that this was right.

MOFFAT: You do not want to say that it is right to give one's undivided loyalty to the government in every case?

OPPENHEIMER: I don't know. I think about it. But I have always done it.

MOFFAT: Does this apply also to the hydrogen bomb program?

OPPENHEIMER: Yes.

After the President's decision, Oppenheimer supported the project, but "with grave doubts." Later, just after the Korean War and while the United States still had a hydrogen bomb monopoly, Oppenheimer was consulted on the advisability of waging a "preventive war." He advised against it on technical grounds. Would he have limited himself to a merely factual opinion, had the technical situation looked good? "I don't know," is Oppenheimer's reply, "I hope not."

Oppenheimer offered to resign from the General Advisory Committee at the time of the President's decision, because he had opposed the development of an H-bomb. Later, in 1952, Oppenheimer advocated postponing the testing of the hydrogen bomb, because of his belief that it would impair the chances of a disarmament agreement and test ban. The bomb was tested anyway. Moffat makes the point that not Oppenheimer, but Dr. Teller, earned the soubriquet "Father of the Hydrogen Bomb."

Morgan asks Oppenheimer whether he believes that American sovereignty should be limited in the sphere of atomic weaponry. Oppenheimer replies: "When things have gone so far that mathematicians have to calculate whether a certain test might not burn up the whole atmosphere—well, then national sovereignties begin to look slightly ridiculous."

MORGAN: Do you think the United States should make an effort towards reaching some understanding with Soviet Russia?

OPPENHEIMER: If the devil himself were on the other side, one would have to reach an understanding with the devil.

MORGAN: But you do draw a sharp distinction between the preservation of life as such and the preservation of a life that is worth living?

OPPENHEIMER: Oh yes. And I have great faith in the ultimate power of common sense.

MORGAN: It is my experience, Dr. Oppenheimer, that there is only as much common sense as we can enforce.

OPPENHEIMER: Quite right, yes. The question is, Mr. Morgan, who is "we?"

Oppenheimer is questioned by Evans about when he first began to fear the result while still working to achieve it. Right after the first explosion at Alamogordo, Oppenheimer tells him.

Oppenheimer is excused from the stand, and Dr. Edward Teller is called and sworn in as one of the witnesses called by Moffat. Teller testifies that he often discussed the possibilities of thermonuclear energy with Oppenheimer and other scientists at Berkeley and Los Alamos. After Hiroshima, in 1945, it was already possible to think of developing a hydrogen device. This was not done (Dr. Teller testifies) because Oppenheimer was against it, in harmony with the general mood of the community of physicists at that time. If Oppenheimer had chosen to lead, others would have followed and the hydrogen bomb might have been developed as early as 1948.

In contrast to many of his fellow-physicists and some elements of public opinion, Dr. Teller wanted in 1945 to develop the hydrogen bomb in order to remain comfortably ahead of the Russians. Even in 1949, when Teller, disturbed by the Russian explosion of an atomic device, phoned Oppenheimer to suggest they go all-out to create a hydrogen device, Oppenheimer's advice was "Keep your shirt on." If there was to be a U.S. hydrogen program, Dr. Teller realized, it would have to take place against Oppenheimer's inclination.

After the first tests were successful, Oppenheimer was interested in the technical achievement, but he never directly supported the program.

Stein, one of Oppenheimer's lawyers, wants to know how Teller feels about Oppenheimer's loyalty.

TELLER: Until I am given proof of the opposite, I shall believe that he wanted to act in the best interests of the United States.

STEIN: You consider him as perfectly loyal?

TELLER: Subjectively, yes.

STEIN: Objectively?

TELLER: Objectively, he has given wrong advice which was injurious to this country.

STEIN: Do you regard Dr. Oppenheimer as a security risk?

TELLER: His actions after the war appeared to me confused and complicated, and I personally would feel more secure if the vital interests of this country did not rest in his hands.

STEIN: Do you think that his former left-wing sympathies affected his attitude in the matter of the hydrogen bomb?

TELLER: I think a man's attitude is always affected by his philosophy.

Teller disagrees with Oppenheimer's political philosophy, and thinks he gave bad advice, but he wouldn't take away his clearance (although this has already been done, pending the hearing's results).

Questioned by Evans, Teller states that if his colleague Oppenheimer couldn't summon up any enthusiasm for the hydrogen project, he might at least have loaned it the support of his name and presence. Teller himself feels no scruples about the device. He doesn't think it his business to foresee all future uses and results, murderous or benign.

Evans wants to know what kind of people physicists are.

TELLER: . . . . . They need a little bit more imagination and a little bit better brains, for their job. Apart from that, they are just like other people.

EVANS: I have been asking myself this question ever since I've been sitting on this board . . . Thank you very much.

GRAY: Perhaps you would like to ask Dr. Teller some questions, Dr. Oppenheimer?

OPPENHEIMER *(haughtily):* No. *(Oppenheimer and Teller look at each other for a moment.)* No.

GRAY: Then I would like to thank you for your evidence, Dr. Teller, which has touched upon some essential points, I think.

TELLER: May I?

GRAY: Of course.

TELLER: I think it is necessary to say something about our problems. All great discoveries had, at first, a devastating effect on the state of the world and its image in our minds. They shattered it and introduced new conditions. They forced the world to move forward. But this was possible only because the discoverers were not afraid of the consequences of their discoveries. This was the case when the earth was discovered to be a planet among other planets; and this is the case now that we have been able to reduce matter, seemingly so complicated, to only a few elements which can be transformed, releasing immeasurable energies. If we shrink from the temporary aspect of discoveries, their powers of destruction—and I find this is the reaction of many a physicist —we'll get stuck halfway. We must use these new energies—no matter what the consequences—and put an end to that state of the world in which man is half free, half enslaved! Who knows? This might perhaps happen through a nuclear war which—limited or unlimited—would not necessarily mean more suffering than in former wars, and which would probably be shorter though more violent. I know! Because of my relentless logic, many people regard me as an incorrigible warmonger. I know that. I read that in the newspapers; but I hope the time will come when I shall be called a peace monger, when the unspeakable horror of our destructive weapons will have disqualified war once and for all.

EVANS: In case of survival, Dr. Teller, as they call it in the insurance business. But, supposing your prognosis turned out to be wrong, we perhaps ought to consider that mankind would have no chance of correcting the mistake. This is something new. Maybe even a physicist can't simply let it go at that.

TELLER: I don't think I do.

Having completed his testimony, Teller bows and leaves the room. Next on the stand is Hans Bethe, a German physicist who came to the United States in 1935 and worked at Los Alamos during the war as head of the Theoretical Physics Department. Questioned by Hardiman, one of Oppenheimer's lawyers, Bethe testifies that in those days Teller was so obsessed with the thermonuclear idea that he was less than useful on the atomic project. It was decided to replace him (and as it happened his replacement was Klaus Fuchs).

Teller and Oppenheimer never saw eye-to-eye (Bethe testifies). But the hydrogen bomb project was delayed, not by Oppenheimer's scruples, but rather by a lack of facilities and personnel. Scruples there were (Bethe admits) after Hiroshima, when the physicists came to realize that their discoveries would be used as weapons of war. Bethe shrank from going forward with the thermonuclear project and went to Cornell to teach. He came back to Los Alamos when, knowing the armaments race was on, he was convinced that America should get the H-bomb first.

Even then, Bethe had his scruples about the program. He doesn't think Oppenheimer's opposition delayed it; rather, "It was Teller's brilliant idea which made its production possible." Ideas like that cannot be delayed or advanced, they do not arrive on any schedule.

Bethe testifies that in a conflict of loyalties, Oppenheimer would be on the side of the United States. Under Spalding's cross-examination, he concedes that he worked with Fuchs for a year and a half without knowing or noticing that he was a security risk.

Bethe makes it clear that he was against the development of the H-bomb philosophically, even while helping to create it. Gray questions him on this point.

GRAY: Dr. Bethe, if I understand you correctly, you think it was wrong to develop the hydrogen bomb?

BETHE: I do.

GRAY: What should we have done instead?

BETHE: We ought to have come to an agreement by which nobody was allowed to produce this damned thing, and any breach of the agreement would mean war.

GRAY: Do you think there would have been the slightest chance of such an agreement in those days?

BETHE: Presumably it would have been easier to come by than to do the things we now have to do.

GRAY: What are you referring to?

BETHE: It seems the two power blocs haven't got much time left to decide whether to commit a double suicide with each other, or how to get that damn thing out of this world again.

Moffat shakes his head. Evans raises his hand.

EVANS: I would like to ask you something as an expert. Dr. Teller said here that a nuclear war, even if unlimited, would not necessarily mean more sufferings than in former wars. What is your opinion?

BETHE: That I can't bear to listen to such nonsense! . . . . .

After Bethe leaves the stand, Moffat requests the board to call Dr. Adams to comment on Bethe's testimony. While Dr. Adams takes the witness chair, Moffat and Stein lock horns in an argument.

MOFFAT: Dr. Bethe has strong moral reservations about the H-bomb, but he responds to a larger loyalty: the needs of his government. Dr. Oppenheimer, on the other hand, has a prior loyalty: he has never abandoned his Utopian ideals of an international classless society. Only by keeping faith with them can he reconcile his qualified loyalty to the United States.

STEIN: Is that an accusation of treason?

MOFFAT: It is "ideological treason." It has its origins in the deepest strata of the personality.

STEIN: Mr. Moffat, you are now confronting us with innovations in our code of law.

MOFFAT: I am not suggesting a *legal* base but an *ideological* base.

STEIN: Mr. Chairman, if we accept Mr. Moffat's odious concept of ideological treason, we would destroy the career of a great scientist and make a farce of these proceedings. Loyalty, discretion, honesty—these are the criteria. These, and the *whole* man—who he is, what he stands for, and what he means to our country.

MOFFAT: What he means to our country must now be examined in the light of *new* security criteria. Loyalty and discretion beyond a shadow of a doubt.

STEIN: These regulations must not be permitted to become self-destructive. We have in Dr. Oppenheimer an extraordinary individual such as nature can produce only once in a very great while. If we are to remain powerful, vital, America must not devour her own children.

Chairman Gray breaks up this argument to get on with Dr. Adams's testimony. Adams, a technical adviser to the Air Force, has seen all the reports and estimates submitted by Oppenheimer. "In the course of observation and analysis," says Adams, "I finally came to the conclusion that there was a silent conspiracy among some prominent scientists, a conspiracy directed against the hydrogen bomb. This group endeavored to prevent or delay the development of the hydrogen bomb, and it was led by Dr. Oppenheimer."

This conclusion was shared, says Adams, by Secretary of the Air Force Finletter and General Vandenberg. One day, in a discussion of whether or not to build and deploy an H-bomber fleet, an associate of Oppenheimer's wrote the code word "ZORC" on the blackboard (the initial letters of four physicists' names, with the "O" standing for "Oppenheimer") as a signal to those present to oppose the plan.

Once, when Adams accused Oppenheimer of spreading a false rumor about Finletter, and questioned his loyalty, Oppenheimer merely called Adams paranoid and walked away. Adams testifies that he believes Oppenheimer's decisions were influenced by his left-wing views, and that he is a "very serious" security risk.

At Oppenheimer's request, his lawyers refrain from cross-examining Adams. Evans questions Adams in order to point out the absurdity of serious conspiracy in a code word written out for all to see.

Adams leaves. The next witness is Jacob Lehmann, professor of physics at M.I.T. and adviser to the government in various capacities. Lehmann, examined by Stein, supports Oppenheimer in every way; he was right to oppose the hydrogen project, if only on the technical grounds that it might after all be against the laws of physics and therefore impossible.

Lehmann tries to ridicule Adams as a witness to anything, but is brought back to the subject: does he remember the "ZORC" meeting? He does—the incident was a big joke, the humor of which was appreciated by everyone at the conference except Adams. The word "ZORC," Lehmann testifies, was invented, not by conspirators, but by *Fortune* magazine in an article about the four scientists whose initials make up the word. Lehmann calls Oppenheimer "The most loyal person I know, myself included."

Under cross-examination by Moffat, Lehmann agrees that Oppenheimer acted foolishly in 1943 in trying to tell his cock-and-bull story to the security people. Lehmann hates the "backstairs" smell of the security reports when applied to a physicist without whose individual and team contributions there could have been no atomic device. "After that quite immaterial Chevalier incident," says Lehmann, "he produced the atom bomb," thus answering those who questioned his loyalty.

Lehmann ends his testimony by voicing his misgivings that any man should be judged by his views rather than by his actions. "We have a whole series of A-bombs," he tells the hearing, "This is just a tremendous achievement. What more do you want? Mermaids? If the end of the road is this kind of hearing . . ." which is not a trial and will end in no "verdict" but which is likely to carry even more weight with the public than a trial ". . . which can't help but be humiliating, then what in hell have we come to?"

As Lehmann leaves the stand and exits, Oppenheimer sums up for the audience: "Forty witnesses had testified in the matter of J. Robert Oppenheimer. The records of the hearings ran to three thousand typewritten pages. And on May 14th, 1954, a few minutes to ten, physicist J. Robert Oppenheimer entered, for the last time, Room 2022 of the Atomic Energy Commission in Washington, to hear the final decision of the board.

Scene 3

Gray reads the board's majority conclusion: He and Morgan, the industrialist, find that while there is "no indication of disloyalty," the incident of lying to the security officers was "incompatible with the interests of his country" and his attitude toward the development of the hydrogen bomb "disquieting." Therefore Dr. Oppenheimer "can no longer claim the unreserved confidence of the government."

Evans reads his minority report: He finds that Oppenheimer is "absolutely loyal," he is distressed because the interpretation of events can change according to the political climate, and he suggests that maybe Oppenheimer gave the best advice, after all, in the hydrogen bomb matter. Maybe it would have been better *not* to develop an H-bomb.

Gray sums up the conclusions of the board.

GRAY: It thus is evident that the majority of the Personnel Security Board of the Atomic Energy Commission recommends that Dr. Oppenheimer shall not be granted his security clearance. That concludes the present proceedings. I thank all for their participation, in particular—Dr. Oppenheimer.

The members of the board and counsel leave the room. Oppenheimer is left in the center of the stage; he steps forward to the footlights.

OPPENHEIMER: As I was thinking about myself, a physicist of our times, I began to ask myself whether there had not in fact been something like ideological treason, a category of treason Mr. Moffat proposed should be considered here. It has become a matter of course to us that even basic research in the field of nuclear physics is top secret nowadays, and that our laboratories are financed by the military and are being guarded like war projects. And when I think what might have become of the ideas of Copernicus, or the discoveries of Newton, under present-day conditions, I begin to wonder whether we were not perhaps traitors to the spirit of science when we handed over the results of our research to the military, without considering the consequences. Now we find ourselves living in a world in which people regard the discoveries of scientists with dread and horror, and go in mortal fear of new discoveries. And meanwhile there seems to be very little hope that people will soon learn how to live together on this ever smaller planet. We, the physicists, find that we have never before been of such consequence, and that we have never before been so completely helpless. I ask myself, therefore, whether we, the physicists, have not sometimes given too great, too indiscriminate loyalty to our governments, against our better judgment—in my case, not only in the matter of the hydrogen bomb. We have spent years of our lives in developing ever sweeter means of destruction, we have been doing the work of the military, and I feel it in my very bones that this was wrong. We have been doing the work of the devil, and now we return to our real tasks. We must devote ourselves entirely to research again. We cannot do better than keep the world open in the few places which can still be kept open.

Curtain.

FORTY CARATS

A Comedy in Two Acts

BY JAY ALLEN

Based on a play by Pierre Barillet and Jean-Pierre Gredy

Cast and credits appear on page 400

JAY ALLEN was born in Texas. After completing her education in the Lone Star State she ventured on a career as a writer, most notably for the Philco Playhouse in television. She gave up writing after a short while but came back to it years later when she became interested in the character of the teacher Jean Brodie in the Muriel Spark story. Robert Whitehead optioned the property for Miss Allen, who adapted it for the stage. The Prime of Miss Jean Brodie *was produced in London and New York (last season, with Zoe Caldwell winning the Tony Award for her performance as Miss Brodie) and in a motion picture for which Miss Allen wrote the screen play. She is also the author of the screen play for* The Borrowers. *For the second Broadway season in a row she has come up with a play of consequence—*Forty Carats—*which is also her second adaptation.*

PIERRE BARILLET and JEAN-PIERRE GREDY wrote a comedy called Le Don d'Adele *for the French theater 13 years ago. It ran for three years and was followed by their equally successful* Ami, Ami. *Over the years the French*

258

stage has enjoyed many other works by this leading comedy-writing team, including adaptations of the American plays Sunday in New York *and* Goodbye, Charlie. *Their* Fleur de Cactus *was a hit and a Best Play of the 1965-66 Broadway season as adapted to the American idiom by Abe Burrows in* Cactus Flower. *Their* Forty Carats *(same title in French,* Quarante Carats), *a hit in Paris during the 1967-68 season, was directed on Broadway by Mr. Burrows.*

Time: The present

Place: Somewhere in the Greek islands, and then the apartment and office of Ann Stanley in New York City

ACT I

Scene 1: The terrace of a little cafe in Greece

SYNOPSIS: A Greek folk melody is heard as the curtain rises on a cafe terrace with tables and stools shaded by reed matting. Behind is a mountainside dropping to the blue Mediterranean.

Standing behind one of the tables is Ann Stanley, an American tourist. She is dusty and hot and wiping her face and neck with Kleenex, which she carries with other necessities in a straw basket.

Half-visible upstage is a shiny American motorcycle, and its owner—a very young man in shorts and sandals—is talking into a wall phone near the cafe door. His name is Peter Latham. He is trying, without success, to find a mechanic for Ann, whose car has broken down.

Ann refuses the offer of a ride on Peter's motorcycle. She pleads that she is too old—36—for riding motorcycles. Peter goes into the cafe for drinks while Ann methodically packs the used Kleenexes into a Baggie and the Baggie into her basket. When Peter returns with a bottle and glass, Ann questions him. Peter is camped on the beach, painting—but he is neither artist nor student.

ANN: What are you then?
PETER: What do *you* think I am?
ANN: I think you're a nutty kid, bumming around on a motorcycle.
PETER *(amiably):* That's what I am. A nutty kid bumming around on a motorcycle.
ANN *(looks at drink):* What's this?
PETER: Ouzo. Try it.
    Ann reaches into her straw basket, takes out her own drinking glass, pours drink from glass on the table into her glass. Takes a sip, looks pleased.
ANN: How old are you?
PETER: Twenty-two.

ANN: You don't look twenty-two.
PETER: You don't look thirty-six.
ANN: I don't look thirty-six because I'm thirty-eight.
> *Sighs, empties glass.*

I took two years off for good behavior.
> *Pours another drink.*

So just don't expect me to go roaring off cross-country on *that* thing. That . . . thing.
> *With no warning, Ann's face puckers up and big tears begin to course down her cheeks.*

Ann is sorry for herself. It's hot, her car won't start and she's left her mother—who didn't want to come to Greece anyway—back at the hotel with an upset stomach. Ann can't get a mechanic until the next day at the earliest, and she has nowhere to sleep.

Peter tries to comfort her and plies her with more ouzo. She cannot stay at the local village hotel or in the uncomfortable car, but she can share his sleeping bag on the beach. Ann is hungry—well, Peter will spear her a fish and they can cook it on the beach after a swim. No matter that neither of them has a bathing suit on this island covered with myrtle, sacred to Aphrodite; this island where Paris first made love to Helen after carrying her off . . .

ANN: Of Troy Helen?
PETER *(turns, points another direction):* I think they're supposed to have spent a night over there too . . . It's the same legend all over Greece . . . Hey, before we go swimming . . . what's your name?
ANN *(a beat):* . . . Penelope.
PETER *(extending his hand):* I'm Peter Latham.
ANN: Peter Latham.
> *They shake hands.*

PETER: And what I'm offering here is a cool dip in the blue Aegean, a gourmet meal, civilized conversation . . . in *English* . . . *(Smiles charmingly.)* You'll forget your troubles.
ANN: Will I?
PETER: It's a promise. Come on.
ANN *(a beat):* Should I?
PETER: Sure.
ANN *(drinks):* Really?
PETER *(gently, seriously):* Yes, I really think you should.
ANN *(rises):* Should we bring the bottle?
PETER: Great. Come on.
> *He picks up the bottle. She starts for the motorcycle, then stops.*

ANN: Oh, dear . . .
PETER *(crosses to her):* What's the matter?
ANN: I was just wondering how Helen of Troy managed about her mother.
> *Blackout. Greek music.*

Scene 2: Ann's real estate office in the East Sixties

Furnishings of the office include a large map of Manhattan, a desk, files. At left is the entrance door. At right is the door to Ann's private office.

A customer (Mrs. Adams) is scanning a list of available apartments. Mrs. Margolin, the secretary, enters from Ann's office *("she is a motherly woman, sensible, good-natured, businesslike").* Mrs. Margolin calls to Ann that Mrs. Adams is still there. But for the moment, Ann is busy in her private office with another client.

Billy Boylan enters at left. He is *"not handsome but attractive and very sure of himself."* Mrs. Adams recognizes Billy as an actor she has seen in the movies and TV.

Ann comes in with some papers, embraces Billy, efficiently gets rid of Mrs. Adams. Ann must return to her client.

BILLY: Wait a minute. How was Greece?
ANN: It was covered with myrtle.
        She goes.
BILLY *(to Mrs. Margolin):* Myrtle . . . Hey, Margy, the trip seems to have done her good.
        He sits in chair in front of desk.
What's she up to? Is she happy?
MRS. MARGOLIN: In her opinion, she's happy. In my opinion, she should have a husband.
BILLY: She's had two husbands.
MRS. MARGOLIN: Are we counting you?
BILLY: Certainly, we're counting me. She got a customer in there?
MRS. MARGOLIN: A rich one. Owns a string of hotels.
BILLY: Great. *(Pause.)* How's business generally?
MRS. MARGOLIN: You can't be broke again.
BILLY: There's no such word as "can't!"
MRS. MARGOLIN: But you've had three shows in the last month. I read where you go from New York and L.A., L.A. and New York . . .
BILLY: I stop off in between.
MRS. MARGOLIN: Las Vegas.
BILLY: Where else? Newark? Margy, I'm a lonely, rootless man.

Ann comes back looking for some keys to an apartment she wants to show her client. Billy tells Ann he needs a thousand-dollar loan but will take five hundred. Ann promises to do something for him if she closes a deal with her client.

Ann goes back into her office. Billy leaves, just before Ann comes back in with the hotel man, Eddy Edwards, *"a big, well-set-up man in his 40s."* Eddy goes off to look at an apartment, and Mrs. Margolin hints to Ann that perhaps she ought to make an effort to attract a rich, eligible male like Eddy. Ann protests that she is "thirty-eight years old—going on thirty-nine. . . . . For the

JULIE HARRIS IN
"FORTY CARATS"

thousandth time, I am a middle-aged woman with a seventeen-year-old daughter." Ann leaves Mrs. Margolin talking to a client on the phone.

Scene 3: Ann's apartment

It is about 6 o'clock in the evening. Ann's living room is tastefully and comfortably furnished, and doors lead out of it to Ann's bedroom (down right), the hall (up right), the foyer (up a short flight of stairs to a landing at center) and the kitchen (left).

Maud, Ann's mother, is stretched out on the sofa wearing large pearl earrings and red stockings with a simple dress, listening to rock 'n' roll music.

Trina, Ann's 17-year-old daughter, comes in and turns off the music. She takes her earrings back from her grandmother. Obviously she's unable to repossess her red tights.

Maud wants to know what time Trina came in the night before.

TRINA: Five a.m.
MAUD: You haven't even the decency to lie. Who were you out with till five a.m.?
TRINA: Mark and Rudy and Bert.
MAUD: Mark *who?* Rudy *who?* Bert *who?*

TRINA: Who goes formal? They're just kids I go dancing with or shoot a little pool.

MAUD: Shoot a little pool! How feminine!

The doorbell rings.

TRINA *(starts for door):* It's Arthur for me.

MAUD *(assumes sitting position on sofa):* Arthur? You've never mentioned an Arthur. Arthur who?

TRINA: I'll ask him when he comes in.

> *Trina opens the door. We see the young man. He is the same one we met in Scene 1, Peter Latham. He is now wearing a white turtleneck sweater and is carrying a sports jacket.*

Peter has never met Trina—he is picking her up for Arthur, who is bringing Peter's date. Maud wants to know where they are going. While Peter explains that they're going to the Electric Circus, and Trina defies her grandmother's questioning, Ann enters from her bedroom, dressed in a bathrobe and carrying a towel.

ANN: My Vitabath's all gone! Who's been . . .

> *Crosses to Trina and Maud. Suddenly stops, turns, as she realizes Peter is standing there.*

TRINA: Granny did it.

MAUD *(facing Trina):* Ann, this young man, whom Trina has never met, not, I gather, even heard of, rings the doorbell as a proxy for Arthur . . .

TRINA: He had the decency to pick me up as a *favor* to Arthur!

> *Throughout the above exchange, Ann casts stunned glances at Peter. Peter looks amazed and then pleased.*

While Ann and Peter stare at each other, Maud and Trina continue their squabbling—until Maud discovers that Peter is the nephew of Isabella Latham. Maud went to school with her. Peter therefore must be a Hohenhauser. Maud beams and introduces Peter to Ann.

Peter and Ann pretend they've never met. Ann sends the young people off, then fixes herself a drink and questions her mother about the Hohenhausers. The Hohenhausers are rich, Maud tells Ann, and as for the Lathams, "this one brother married the Hohenhauser girl who must have inherited *everything* . . . and this boy . . . this *Peter* is the *son.*" Maud guesses he must be about twenty. Twenty-two, Ann informs her definitely, downing another drink.

Scene 4: Ann's office

In late afternoon two days later, Mrs. Margolin is typing away when Ann enters from her own office. Eddy, the hotel man, phones to make a dinner date with Ann. Eddy has taken the apartment, and Ann is helping him decorate.

Peter Latham enters, dressed in slacks and jacket, pretending to be a customer looking for a studio apartment. Mrs. Margolin is suspicious, but allows herself to be hustled out.

PETER *(crosses to desk):* Penelope. Penelope Schwartz.

Ann smiles, giving a small shrug.

That's a pretty strong defense. Give a guy the wrong name and number so that when he doesn't call, it's because he couldn't, not because he didn't want to.

ANN: Did you really try to find Miss Schwartz? It never occurred to me that you would.

PETER: Why did you cut out? The next morning you disappeared. You just cut out.

ANN: I'm sorry. But now you see why. I mean, among other things, I am the mother of a grown daughter.

PETER: Let's have dinner.

ANN: Peter, you're very sweet, but I can't have dinner with you. I can't see you again.

PETER: Look, there's no button on my lapel—"STANLEY REALTY SLEEPS AROUND."

ANN *(rises, crosses down right):* Now please listen to me. This entire situation is . . . is just horribly embarrassing.

PETER: Let's have dinner.

ANN *(turns to him):* Peter. I can't be seen running around with a . . . *(Smiles ruefully.)* You're just a kid. I could be arrested.

PETER *(grins):* Risk it.

ANN *(crosses back to desk):* You've got to understand my position.

PETER: I do. I understand your position.

ANN: Then you must realize why I can't see you again. I'm sorry, but that's the way it is.

PETER: I see.

ANN: I'm really sorry.

PETER: I'm sorry, too.

ANN: Thank you, Peter. You're very understanding.

Holds out her hand.

Goodbye, Peter.

Peter holds out his hand, but at this moment Maud enters, straight from the hairdresser's, taking refuge from a cloudburst. There are no taxis to be had. Peter explains that he has come to Ann's office looking for an apartment; he has his car and can take them home. Ann protests, but Maud jumps at the invitation and invites Peter to come for tea. Maud doesn't even notice Ann's hesitation—Maud has her eye on Peter for Trina (who, Peter tells Maud, beat him out of $17 at the poolroom on their last meeting).

Maud goes out to find Peter's Maserati while Ann and Peter linger behind for a moment. Yes, Ann tells Peter, she really *does* have another date that evening.

ANN *(turns to him):* Now, Peter, we're going out to the car. And you're going to drive Mother and me home. Then you're going to say you just remembered an appointment you forgot, and you're going to excuse yourself. You will then say goodbye and drive away into the sunset in your little red Maserati. You will definitely not come up. You are not to telephone me, you are not to come to this office again, and . . .

> *She goes through the door, but her voice goes on.*

. . . you will never again come to my apartment . . .

> PETER *(as he goes):* We'll talk about it up at your place.
>
> *Blackout.*

Scene 5: Ann's apartment

A little later, Maud has insisted that Peter come to the apartment. Peter, alone for a moment in the living room, notices that Ann keeps an ouzo bottle on the bar. Trina and Maud join him, then Maud leaves the two young people alone to talk. But after Trina demands and Peter hands over the $17 she won from him at pool, they find very little to talk about.

Maud returns and engages Peter in conversation about his family's life in Pittsburgh, at their house called "Belwood" (at the very mention of Pittsburgh, Trina exclaims "ecch!"). Peter looks at his watch, wonders how long it'll be before Ann emerges from the bedroom, where she's dressing.

Maud wonders who Ann's mysterious beau of the evening can be. Trina scoffs at the very idea of her mother having a romance.

> TRINA *(turns her attention directly to Peter):* I mean, you don't have to be diplomatic, but wouldn't you honestly say she was still pretty attractive? I mean for her age?
>
> PETER: Yes, I would.
>
> TRINA: I mean if you were an older man, *you'd* find her attractive.
>
> PETER *(judiciously):* I believe I would. Yes.
>
> TRINA: Well, she wouldn't find *you* attractive.
>
> MAUD: Trina! How can you be so rude!
>
> TRINA: Oh, Granny Maud, I'm just trying to say that Mummy doesn't find *anybody* attractive. She *refuses* to find anybody attractive. Two divorces and she's out of business.
>
> MAUD: Trina, I don't think Peter is interested in . . .
>
> > *Sits.*
>
> PETER: I see.
>
> TRINA: So she just *doesn't*. If you know what I mean.
>
> MAUD *(laughs as though it was a joke):* Trina!

Ann enters looking very glamorous in a short dinner dress. Even Maud and Trina are impressed; Peter is, obviously. Ann tells them she has a date with Eddy Edwards.

When Eddy arrives, he too is impressed with the way Ann looks. Ann introduces Eddy to the family. Eddy makes the natural mistake of assuming Peter is Ann's son, until Peter corrects him. Ann mixes Eddy a bourbon. Eddy, a rough diamond, uses a four-letter word by mistake. Ann quickly goes to get her purse and gloves, while her mother makes conversation.

MAUD *(social manner):* Has the rain let up, Mr. Edwards?
EDDY *(gratefully):* A bit.
MAUD: You stay, Peter. You can join us for a *petit diner.*
PETER *(smiles, looks at Trina, hesitates):* Well . . .
TRINA: It's okay, Pete. You can stay if you want.
    Puts legs up on coffee table.
PETER: Thanks, I'd like to.
TRINA: And later we can shoot some pool at McGirr's.
EDDY *(with interest):* A little girl like you shooting pool?
PETER *(to Eddy):* She just *looks* like a girl. She's really Paul Newman.

Ann returns and tries to whisk Eddy off, but Eddy is reluctant to leave "all these nice people." Ann says goodbye pointedly to Peter, but Peter puts his feet up on the coffee table and warns Ann he'll probably be there when she gets back.

Eddy says goodbye warmly to Trina. Ann opens the front door to depart, and there is Billy Boylan on the threshold, carrying cartons of Chinese food in a bag.

BILLY: I was just about to ring. I'm not too late?
ANN: About eight years.
BILLY: You invited me to dinner.
ANN: I said call me Wednesday and if it's convenient we can have dinner together.
BILLY: This is outrageous! I brought moo goo gai pan. You *love* moo goo gai pan.
    Shoves bag into her hand.
EDDY: Uh . . . Mrs. Stanley . . . if you really had a date with your beau . . .
ANN: He's not my beau, and I did *not* have a date with him. He's just a . . . part-time ex-husband.
EDDY *(puzzled):* Oh.
BILLY *(goes to Eddy, near bar, hand outstretched):* Billy Boylan.
EDDY: Eddy Edwards.
    Instantly recognizing the name, then the face, begins to beam. He
    takes the proffered hand, shakes it enthusiastically.
Billy Boylan. I've seen you on "Peyton Place." *(To Ann.)* Billy Boylan!
ANN *(wearily):* Billy Boylan. *(To Eddy.)* Eddy, let's go.

But Eddy will not be dragged away now; not from a party like this with a pretty 17-year-old *and* a celebrity. They can stay and make a Chinese meal of it, and Eddy will send his driver to the Caviarteria for extra delicacies, and wine.

Helplessly, Ann accepts the situation. Maud goes to fix the plates and Trina goes to her room to change. Billy introduces himself to Peter and shakes hands.

BILLY *(crossing toward kitchen):* Well, let's get this show on the road.
      Turns back.
Glad to have you aboard, Pete.
  PETER: Thanks.
      Billy exits, leaving Ann and Peter alone for a moment. She starts
      toward the kitchen.
How about you, Ann?
  ANN: What about me?
  PETER *(goes to her):* Are *you* glad to have me aboard?
  ANN *(stops):* What?
  PETER: Are *you* glad to have me aboard?
      He kisses her. She starts to respond. Suddenly pushes him away,
      looks at him thoughtfully.
Answer me!
  ANN: What was the question?
      Blackout. Fast Gypsy music.

Scene 6: Ann's apartment

It is Sunday afternoon, about 5 p.m. Billy is asleep on the sofa with the
TV set on. Trina comes in, turns it off, which wakes up Billy. Ann comes in,
having just finished the dishes from the night before. Trina goes off to the
movies with friends, leaving Billy and Ann alone to discuss the party. They
all wound up out on the town with Eddy. Billy noticed how "poised and attractive" Peter seemed, and he infuriates Ann with the suggestion that Peter
may be attractive to her—"Maybe as Mama gets older, she fancies 'em
younger." Ann denies this angrily—and of course Billy didn't really mean it.
    Ann calls herself a "creaky old lady" and finally admits to what is probably
her real age—40. She makes Billy confess that he is 42.
    Billy asks Ann to put in a good word for him with Eddy—no kidding, he
really needs a recommendation. It's not that he isn't getting all the acting jobs
he needs.

  BILLY: . . . . . I'm not pushing Richard Burton off the screen, but I think
I'll probably survive him.
  ANN: *Then what?*
  BILLY: Annie, the most extraordinary . . . the most unaccountable . . .
sensations have been zapping me for the last year . . .
  ANN *(deeply concerned):* What *is* it?
  BILLY: It comes over me at the damndest times . . . on the set, the cam-
eras grinding away, my nose down some stupid bird's bozoom . . . Suddenly
I hear this voice . . . "Is this any way for a grown man to make a living?" Or
I'm horsing around with the gang in Vegas. Everybody's having a million
laughs. And suddenly I find myself wondering if I wouldn't rather be home
with a book . . . I mean a home with an upstairs and a wife and a kid with

remedial reading. I tell you, at first I thought I was losing my effing mind! Annie, I've been putting on makeup and wearing elevator shoes for over twenty years. Now, suddenly, for *no reason,* it embarrasses me. I want to give up acting and go straight.

ANN: Billy, you? Give up acting? You're too good!

BILLY: True. But . . .

ANN *(bewildered):* What on earth could you do?

BILLY: Well, I thought maybe Eddy . . . Annie, I want to try to get a job. I mean, a real job.

ANN: Like what?

BILLY: Public relations.

ANN *(dubiously):* Public relations? Is that real?

BILLY *(crossly):* I've got to start somewhere. What do you want me to do, go cold turkey?

Ann feels tired, and Billy tells her to think of herself in terms of carats, not years. She isn't 40 years old, she's a 40-carat blue-white diamond. The phone rings. It's Eddy, breaking a date with Ann for this evening. He's going to the Coast on business for a week.

Ann, disappointed, asks Billy to stay on for dinner, but Billy can't. He really has a date—with a buxom 19-year-old blonde baby sitter named Elke who lives upstairs in this same building. Ann calls Billy an "old goat," and Billy admits: "Part of the growing-up process I was describing to you is this marvellous goatish thing for helpless young girls. I guess it's maturity."

Billy leaves Ann laughing over the absurdity of the situation. The bottle of ouzo and a Pan-Am ad on TV remind Ann of Greece. And just then the doorbell rings. This time it's Peter Latham. He watched until he saw Maud and Trina go out but figures "that bastard Boylan" was still here. When he finds that Boylan has gone upstairs, Peter prepares to spend the evening with Ann.

Ann decides to reason with Peter. He is an intelligent and sensitive boy, she tells him, he must know that their affair has got to stop. But Peter just reaches out for her. He kisses her to stop her talking, then takes his turn explaining.

PETER: . . . . . By the time I was ten I'd had four passports. My mother buzzed around a lot and I'll say this for her, she was always ready to yank me along with her. I wasn't left to the servants. My old man's kind of a standard son of a bitch and my mother . . .

ANN: Oh, Peter. I'm sure I remind you of your mother. You may not have been conscious of it, but . . .

PETER: I've never known a woman who reminded me less of my mother.

ANN: Huh?

PETER: You know who reminds me of my mother? *Trina* reminds me of my mother.

ANN *(laughs, then turns serious):* Oh, God.

PETER: All I'm trying to say is that I'm only twenty-two . . .

ANN *(softly):* I know.

PETER: . . . but I've been around. I've had my quota of girls . . . and their mothers . . .

Peter finds Ann "unsophisticated." He tells her she's right about him not coming there again; they'll take a small apartment together. And by the way, he tells her, "In all the hoo-ha around here, I think I forgot to tell you that I am in love with you."

Ann is "honored" and "flattered" but she is still concerned with preserving the order and tranquility of her life. Peter would like to muss it up a bit. Ann protests that she isn't attracted to youth; Peter argues that she is certainly attracted to *him*. Ann protests that she doesn't love him, but Peter insists that she is so hung up on their age difference she hasn't given herself a chance.

PETER: Who are all those people whose opinions count so much? Your mother? Your daughter? Mayor Lindsay? Your mother's charming but she wouldn't care if I were still in short pants as long as she hooks up with the Hohenhausers!

ANN: Why, you arrogant . . .

PETER *(going on):* As for Trina . . .

ANN: Please go.

PETER: You are a beautiful and desirable woman . . .
        Crosses to her.
I love you, Ann . . . Let me love you.
        *He takes her in his arms. They embrace. Ann pulls away when she
        hears key in the front door.*

ANN: Oh, God! It's my mother.

All including Maud are elaborately casual as Maud enters and takes off her hat and coat. Maud regrets that Trina isn't home to entertain Peter—but Peter is just going. Ann opens the door for him.

> *Peter kisses her hand. Maud is not watching; she's busy with her
> gloves, hat, etc. Peter keeps kissing both of Ann's hands. She tries
> to push him out the door, but he, with a twinkle in his eye, play-
> fully keeps kissing her hands. She finally gets him out the door. His
> hands still show and she's trying to avoid closing the door on his
> hands. She keeps pushing his hands the way one does with a cat's
> paws when trying to put the cat in a traveling box. She finally suc-
> ceeds in getting his hands outside and closes the door. She stands
> facing the door for a moment.*

MAUD: Has he been here long?

ANN: Huh?

MAUD: Has he been here long?

ANN: Who?

MAUD: Peter.

ANN: A few minutes.

MAUD: Of course he's courting you like mad!

ANN *(looks at her mother)*: Why would he be courting me?

MAUD: Because he's after Trina.

ANN: Oh.

MAUD: I think he's quite smitten with her.

ANN: You do?

MAUD: Why can't that silly Trina stay home occasionally?
Rises.

Oh, I'm so glad I'm not that age any more. Aren't you?
She goes. Ann looks in mirror, crosses down, sits on sofa, picks up apple from coffee table.

ANN *(in a small, childlike voice, sings softly)*: M-I-C-K-E-Y M-O-U-S-E . . .
Lights fade on "mouse." Rock 'n' roll music.

Scene 7: Ann's apartment

A month later, one evening, Trina is sitting on the sofa doing homework, wearing large sun glasses, listening to rock 'n' roll music. Maud comes in with a large basket of flowers. She turns off the radio and questions Trina about Peter. In Trina's opinion, Peter is not in love with her.

Maud tries to convince Trina of Peter's desirability as a catch, but Trina will have none of him. When the doorbell rings, Maud sends Trina to her room. It is Peter, and Maud wants to talk to him alone.

Peter enters, bringing a box of *marrons glaces*. He notices the flowers and is told that Eddy sent them to Ann.

Maud clears the card table and sits down to a game of gin rummy with Peter, who is dressed more carefully even than usual because his father is in town, and Peter had lunch with him.

Over the cards, Maud startles Peter by telling him: "I know what's going on, Peter . . . why you come here so often. And I know it isn't to play gin rummy with an old lady. Do you think I'm so old I no longer recognize love when it's right under my nose?"

Of course, Maud thinks it's Trina whom Peter loves, and Maud argues that the difference in their ages—22 and 17—really doesn't matter. Trina's mother must be made to understand this, Maud insists: "Ann doesn't see things head-on. What will be hard for her to grasp is that age is not the question here. The question is simply what is best for the two individuals involved. You will have to convince her that marriage is possible. Possible and desirable."

Peter is fascinated by Maud's words simply because he applies them in his own mind, not to himself and Trina, but himself and Ann. He has lost track of the game and has drawn a handful of useless cards. He has been made to consider, for the first time, that marriage with *Ann* might be possible in spite of their age difference. His parents' consent isn't necessary; he is not dependent on them.

Maud goes on convincing him (she thinks) to speak to Ann about marrying

Trina. But all Maud's arguments are just as applicable to a match between Peter and Ann herself.

Ann comes home, and Maud leaves the two alone after trouncing Peter at this round of gin rummy. Ann is tired from "a million rotten things at the office." Peter suggests that she needn't work any more if only she will marry him. Ann decides to treat his proposal as a joke, but Peter is serious.

PETER *(hands her a drink):* I'm not kidding, Ann. I'm asking you. Will you marry me?

ANN: I'm not kidding, Peter. I'm telling you. No.

PETER *(quietly):* Why?

ANN: Because I know what would happen.

PETER: What would happen?

ANN: You know how old I am.

PETER *(turns away impatiently):* Oh God! Look. Suppose you were thirty-five. Would you marry me if you were thirty-five?

ANN: No.

PETER: Thirty?

ANN: No.

PETER: Twenty-nine?

ANN *(starts to say no, stops):* I don't think so . . . no, of course I wouldn't.

PETER: Twenty-five?

ANN *(hesitates, then smiles):* I'd be tempted.

PETER: You know you would.

ANN: I might.

PETER: So let's suppose you're twenty-five and we get married. Then what happens?

ANN *(sharply):* How do I know?

PETER *(leans toward her): Exactly.*

ANN *(puzzled, then annoyed):* How does anyone know what will happen in a marriage . . . or in life?

PETER: *Exactly.*
Ann slowly begins to understand what he's trying to say.
All anybody ever really has is *now.*
There is a moment of silence, then Ann takes a deep breath.

ANN *(starts for bedroom, turns, heads for kitchen):* Peter, please go. This is my night to . . . *(Reaching.)* I've really got to polish the silver.

PETER *(follows her):* All right. But while you're polishing the silver, will you think about it? And try to think about yourself. Nobody else.

ANN *(still bewildered):* I'll try.
He kisses her, goes to door and turns back.

PETER: Okay, go on, polish the silver.
He goes. Ann stands there lost in thought for a moment. Maud, followed by Trina, enters from hallway, crosses to sofa.

MAUD: Did I hear Peter leave? What did he say?

TRINA: What did Peter say to you?

ANN *(puzzled):* About what?

TRINA: I guess you know that Granny practically put a shotgun in his back!

ANN *(stares at Maud):* Mother! What on earth did you say to him?

MAUD *(very pleased with herself):* I simply brought it to his attention that his feelings were perfectly obvious to me and that I thoroughly approved. And I said I wanted to know his intentions.

ANN: Oh, you did.

MAUD: He was surprised.

ANN: He was surprised.

MAUD: But when I said I thought he should speak to you, he very quickly agreed. *(Silence.)* Well? What happened? Did he declare himself?

ANN: *He certainly did.*

TRINA *(starts left):* Look, Mummy . . .

MAUD *(stopping her, impatiently):* Please be quiet, Trina. I'm trying to talk to your mother about Peter.

TRINA: It's not *you* he wants to marry, Granny. It's *me.*

ANN *(gazes from Maud to Trina):* Actually . . . actually, what he's got in mind is something in between—a kind of compromise.

    Sits on sofa.

Well, let's put it this way . . .

    Fast curtain.

ACT II

Scene 1: Ann's apartment

A few days later, in the evening, Ann and Eddy are alone, picking colors for Eddy's apartment.

Gradually the conversation gets more personal—what Eddy *really* needs is a home in Connecticut, something that Ann might approve of. Eddy has been lonely since his wife died (he tells Ann), and he feels he might be happy settling down with the right woman. Eddy goes on: "I'd give her everything. She'd be a regular little queen. What I want above everything else is a family. My wife . . . my late wife . . . couldn't have children. I don't think a man's lived his life unless he leaves children. I'd like to have . . . Hell! I'll take as many as I can get! . . . . . I'm only forty-five and at forty-five a man is at his peak! And I just *know* I'll make a good husband for Trina."

Yes, it's Trina whom Eddy loves—they love each other, Eddy informs astonished Ann—and they intend to get married right away. They have been in love since that first night they met, but Trina has been afraid that Ann might be jealous.

Ann's immediate reaction is that Trina is too young at seventeen to be married. Eddy had thought she was eighteen—Trina had told him so, and he chuckles at her deception. In any case, Eddy and Trina have made up their minds what they intend to do.

ANN: Eddy . . . how would you like ten to twenty in the state pen?

EDDY *(takes her shoulders):* You've got a lot to think about, Ann. I'm going to run along.

> *Starts for door.*

ANN: Now wait a minute, Eddy.

EDDY *(blandly going on. At door):* And honey, you just bear in mind what good care I'll take of Trina. And of you too.

ANN: Of me?

EDDY: Naturally. I'm going to be your son-in-law.

> *Eddy goes.*

ANN *(calls out):* Trina!

> *Trina appears immediately, goes to Ann.*

TRINA: I might as well tell you right now, Mummy, that if you pull something square like trying to keep me from seeing Eddy, I'll just talk him into taking me to Tahiti or some place out of your reach until I'm eighteen and then we'll be married anyway.

ANN *(cutting in):* You are playing Juliet to a fairly sedate Romeo.

TRINA *(coolly):* Mummy, I shouldn't think you'd want me to answer that in kind.

ANN *(trying to stay calm):* Trina, my big mistake was not sending you to a good, tough military school.

TRINA: I'm going to marry Eddy.

ANN: Do you love him?

TRINA: I think so.

ANN: You think so.

TRINA: He's crazy about me. He makes all the decisions. It's so easy to be with him. You thought Eddy was nice enough for *you,* didn't you?

ANN: I wasn't contemplating marrying Eddy.

TRINA: You don't contemplate marrying *anybody.* You'd have let Eddy hang around just the way you let a kid like Peter. Just hang around. Only Eddy would never have asked you to marry him because you'd have brushed him off long before he got to the point. Because *he's* too *possible.* He's a darling man, and I decided I'd be damned if I'd let you waste *him.* So I swiped him.

> *Sits in chair.*

Trina goes on to tell Ann that even if she had wanted Peter she couldn't have taken him away from Ann—but she doesn't want him. Eddy is the man she wants. Eddy takes care of her.

Ann has "done okay" as a mother, Trina reassures her. It's all going to be all right. Ann is gradually beginning to reconcile herself to the inevitable. Mother and daughter embrace. Maud comes in, looking around for Eddy, sensing that she has walked into the middle of something.

ANN: What you walked in in the middle of was a proposal.

MAUD: *Eddy?* Oh, Ann!

Crosses to Ann, embraces her warmly.
Oh, my precious girl! I'm so happy for you!

ANN *(gently disentangling herself):* Mother . . . it's not me Eddy wants to marry, Mother . . . it's Trina.

MAUD *(disengages herself after a moment):* What? What in the world is *wrong* with everybody? Everyone's gone mad! Or is it me?

Doing a complete about-face, crosses to Trina.
Trina! My darling girl! I'm so happy for you!

It is Trina now who suffers Maud's embrace. Blackout. Rock 'n' roll music.

Scene 2: Ann's office

A few days later, around noon, Billy comes to see Ann, at her invitation. Discreetly, Mrs. Margolin departs early for lunch, leaving them to discuss the astonishing news of Trina's engagement to Eddy.

Billy thinks the marriage is the best thing that could have happened to Trina, even though (as Ann points out) Eddy is 28 years her senior. Billy tells Ann that the 40s seem to be a very sexy age—he has noticed that young girls are attracted to *him.*

Ann tells Billy of Peter Latham's proposal. Billy is astonished, even shocked.

ANN: He has money of his own, a mind of his own and he wants to marry *me.* Raddled old broken-down, liver-spotty *me.* He's even met you and Maud and he *still* wants to marry me.

Billy stares open-mouthed for a long moment.

BILLY: He must have a thing about his mother. Has he talked much about his mother?

ANN: He says she's very like Trina.

BILLY: Annie! You don't mean you're taking this seriously! He's a baby! A little, bitty baby!

Holding his hand about a foot from the floor.

ANN: He's twenty-two. Were you a baby at twenty-two?

BILLY: You're damn right I was. A little, bitty baby!

Repeating the hand gesture and kicking the imaginary baby.

ANN: Well, he isn't.

BILLY *(peers at her):* Are you *serious?* I can't believe it.

ANN *(grimly):* Believe it.

BILLY: But . . . Jesus, honey! Have you thought . . .

ANN: What people would say?

BILLY: Yes.

If Billy saw them together (he tells Ann) he would assume she was paying his way. But Ann doesn't think they look so incongruous together. She tells Billy: "I don't know if you are aware of it, but the latest statistics prove that a woman comes into her full sexual flowering at forty, while a man attains his at twenty."

Billy tells her generously to go have a fling if she feels that way about it. Ann tries to make Billy understand that there's more to it: "It's not his *youth* that's to my taste. It bothers me terribly. But he's really a marvelous person. He's quite extraordinary. Very strong-*minded*. And he has a good deal of money. Once I stopped to think about it . . . the overall picture, you understand . . . it suddenly seemed . . . rather marvelous. I'd given up thinking about . . . well, actually, I guess I kind of put myself out to pasture. And suddenly, here is this handsome, intelligent, *rich, young* man who thinks that *I* . . . am the *greatest*. Billy, he loves me. He could have anybody he wants, and he wants *me*."

Billy is touched by this confession. What's more, he knows something Ann doesn't—Ann is in love with Peter. Billy realizes he himself no longer has a chance with Ann and departs, half in anger.

Ann calls Peter on the phone: "Hello, is that you Peter? . . . Well this is me. And I called to say that, after thinking it over carefully, weighing everything, pro and con, I've decided that . . . Peter, don't interrupt me! . . . Well, *okay!* The answer's *okay!*"

Scene 3: Ann's apartment

Three weeks later, Ann is in a panic because Peter has invited his mother and father to meet her, without giving her any advance notice. Peter tells Ann she needn't be scared. His parents will probably like Ann—but whether they do or not, he and Ann are getting married next week.

PETER: If this meeting goes down moderately well, everything will be a hell of a lot easier, that's all. And if they don't like it . . . *(He grins.)* Screw 'em.

ANN: Screw 'em.

PETER: I'll be interested to see how you react to the old man. He's something on wheels. Self-made, you know.

ANN: I thought he married . . . I mean, your mother is a Hohenhauser.

PETER: Oh, that's not the way my father went about it. He grabbed the company away from my grandfather, kicked the old boy into astonished retirement, *then* took over the daughter. Along with everything else in sight.

ANN: My goodness! Your poor grandfather.

PETER: Don't waste your sympathy *there*. My grandfather Hohenhauser was tough and mean and greedy. Bashed his way through a picket line once with a seven iron. He used to show it to me. Six notches on it. *Still* . . . my father took the old boy on and whipped him and set himself up there as king of the hill before he was thirty-five. *(Grins.)* Want to know something? He's next.

Peter's father will probably approve their marriage because he knows Peter is breathing down his neck. Maybe Ann will be a distraction.

The doorbell rings—it's Mr. and Mrs. Latham *("Mrs. Latham is very trim with a youthful bearing. She is extremely elegant; she wears the best jewels . . . the best everything. Very lacquered, in quiet, deadly professional good taste").*

Peter introduces them to Ann. Peter mixes a drink while Mrs. Latham notices an old photograph of Ann, remarks tactlessly that she used to wear her hair the same way as in the photo, when she was carrying Peter.

Latham is in a hurry, and he goes to the point at once: he likes Ann's looks, but why is she marrying Peter? He is only twenty-two . . . Ann won't like Pittsburgh, etc. Peter warns his father that he is just making a fool of himself. But Latham persists.

LATHAM: Of course you're not interested in the subject of money.
          Turns his back to Ann.
ANN: Oh, yes, I am.
LATHAM *(turns to her, laughs):* Ah—well, in that case . . .
PETER: Dad . . .
LATHAM: I can easily top anything you might expect from Peter—
PETER: Dad . . .
LATHAM: And we can all shake hands.
PETER: How about me, Dad? Who do *I* shake hands with?
LATHAM: With yourself, son. You shake hands with yourself.
ANN *(firmly):* Mr. Latham.
LATHAM *(turning back to her):* Yes, Mrs. Stanley?
ANN: I know the value of money. I wouldn't marry Peter if he didn't have some. But I'm not marrying him *for* his money. And I'm not throwing him over for *yours*.
          They lock stares.
LATHAM *(gives her a small bow):* Mrs. Stanley.
ANN *(small bow):* Mr. Latham.
LATHAM *(starting to door):* Christine.
MRS. LATHAM *(small bow):* Edgar.

So it's all settled. Latham leaves, and Peter goes with his father, arm around him, to buy him a drink. Mrs. Latham stays behind, and after an embarrassing moment or two she admits that probably Ann will make Peter happy. Mrs. Latham agrees with Ann that "Youth in a woman is frightfully overrated" and that "One's responses to life at forty are infinitely more tender." Mrs. Latham finally confesses that Ann and Peter are lucky. Here she is, stuck with her husband Edgar: "One must simply organize one's life *around* the Edgars."

The doorbell rings. Ann admits Patrick Graham, *"a handsome young man very fashionably turned out."* Patrick has become impatient waiting for Mrs. Latham, particularly after he saw her husband leave. Mrs. Latham introduces Ann to *her* young man.

ANN: How do you do?
MRS. LATHAM: Patrick is one of our most promising young golfers. He was second at Pinehurst last year. I can't tell you how thrilling it was!
PATRICK *(pouting):* But she's sending me off alone to the big Phoenix Open. All by myself.

Smiles shyly, sexily at Ann.
Tell her she shouldn't do that.
    MRS. LATHAM *(to Patrick):* Don't bother, pet.
    Touches his arm.
You can't win 'em all. She's already booked. Booked, booked, booked.
    Pushes him toward the door. Turns tranquilly to Ann, smiles, holds
    out her hand.
Goodbye, Ann.
    They brush cheeks. She goes to the door.
    ANN: Goodbye.
    MRS. LATHAM: I'm so glad we've met.
    PATRICK: Goodbye.
    MRS. LATHAM *(looks at Patrick, turns back to Ann):* Welcome to the family.
    Blackout. Fast gypsy music.

Scene 4: Ann's apartment

A week later, Maud enters from the kitchen, dressed in tweeds and carrying a pot of poinsettias. Billy Boylan is mixing a drink. Peter and Ann plan to fly to Mexico to be married on Christmas Eve. Maud disapproves. For that matter, Trina disapproves too. Trina and Eddy are taking Maud to the country for a proper Christmas, and Maud goes to finish packing as Peter comes in.

Pointedly, Billy asks Peter for a drink instead of mixing another for himself, as a sign that there's a new man in charge here now. They approach each other warily; Billy can't resist a few conversational digs, and Peter is frankly hostile.

Ann comes in with a new, youthful hairdo and dress. To Billy's dismay, Ann seems to love the young excitement of evenings on the town and getting arrested while speeding on Peter's motorcycle.

Trina and Eddy come in, and Maud joins them. Trina wants to have a word with her mother, and the two of them disappear into Ann's bedroom. Meanwhile, Maud and Eddy discuss with anticipatory glee the tree, the turkey and all the conventional Christmas delights they expect to enjoy. As for Billy, he plans to spend Christmas right here in the building—with his buxom blonde, Elke.

Eddy and Trina are to be married soon—before she finishes high school. Maud is concerned only that they wait until Trina's trousseau is ready.

Ann and Trina return from the bedroom, and there is a round of Merry Christmases and half-tearful partings. Trina, Eddy and Maud go off for the country, Billy starts to go, but Ann stops him to tell him that Trina is pregnant. She is going to be a grandmother. Peter feels that Trina might have kept this to herself until after Ann's wedding.

Finally Billy leaves, admitting that he is now, at last (and to his own amazement), jealous of Peter. And Peter, alone with Ann, now admits that he is jealous of Billy.

    PETER: . . . . . I feel very threatened by Billy.
    ANN: Well, you needn't. You're terribly possessive, you know.

PETER: I know. Every time I see you even shake hands with another guy, I get a big blast of the old territorial imperative.

ANN: I can never believe it will last . . .

PETER: It will last as long as you want it. I'll be here as long as you'll have me.

ANN: *Why?*

PETER: Because you're very neat with Kleenex.

ANN *(steps right to him):* Peter. I do wish I'd known you sooner.
    They embrace.

PETER: I like now.

ANN: Oh, I like now, too. Do you know that for the first time in my life I can really *count* on someone else? And a little child shall lead her . . .

PETER *(steps back):* Ann, I swear to God, if you make one more joke about my age . . .

ANN: Shut up. I'm older than you.
    She kisses him.

PETER: Let's skip the Electric Circus.
    Embraces her.

ANN: Not on your life! I'm already plugged in.
    She does a dance step. Blackout. Rock 'n' roll music.

Scene 5: Ann's apartment

The same evening, around midnight, Ann and Peter return—Ann is exhausted and shattered by the night club noise, and astonished by the beautiful 18-year-old Botticelli-type who seemed to know Peter so well. Ann confesses that it was all a little too much for her. She sends Peter home and heads toward the bedroom. But Billy appears in the bedroom doorway, in his shirt sleeves. Maud gave him a key to take care of the plants. He is waiting here for Elke to finish work.

Billy makes drinks for them while he tells Ann his news: he has a publicity job with an important Italian producer in Rome. Ann feels that Billy is going off and abandoning her, just when she needs her friends around her. The whole Electric Circus experience has shaken her. She's not yet ready to admit that she is in love with Peter.

The doorbell rings. Billy guesses it's probably Elke and doesn't want her to find him here with Ann. He hides in the bedroom. Ann, playing a joke on him, places his cigar in full view and opens the door. It's Peter, bringing Ann some sleeping pills.

> *Peter suddenly is conscious of the cigar smoke. He looks curiously around, spots it, crosses down to coffee table, picks up cigar, looks at bedroom door, stubs out cigar and heads for front door.*

PETER: I . . . guess I made a mistake . . . coming back unexpectedly.

ANN: No, no . . .

PETER: Sorry I barged in. I should have known better. Good night, Ann.
    Peter closes the door.

ANN: Peter! Wait a minute . . . oh, Peter, let me exp . . .

> *He is gone. She stands frozen staring at the door. After a moment, Billy sticks his head out.*

BILLY: All cleared away?

ANN *(quietly):* You might say that.

> *Suddenly whirls on him.*

Get out of here! Go pollute somebody else's air for a change! You bastard! You swine! *You goddam actor!*

BILLY *(who has been trying to stop this assault):* What did I do?

ANN: He saw your cigar and went storming out of here. *(Starts to cry.)* Billy, I've begged you for years to give up smoking.

> *Slumps over on sofa. Blackout. Fast Gypsy music.*

Scene 6: Ann's apartment

The next day, late on a sunny morning, Ann is telling all to Mrs. Margolin, who advises Ann to phone Peter. But Ann has already written Peter a letter calling everything off. Billy is delivering it by hand.

Billy comes in. Mrs. Margolin leaves, advising Ann to marry "anybody but him." Ann asks for Billy's reassurance: now that it's all over with Peter, hasn't she done the right thing? Billy reassures her, and she goes to get her coat. But while Ann is out of the room, Peter enters by the front door. When Ann comes back and sees Peter standing there, she is stunned.

ANN: What are you doing here?

PETER: Our plane leaves in an hour.

ANN: Oh.

PETER: Look, Ann, I've spent the whole night kicking myself . . . and then I went over to Billy's place and let him kick me . . . and well, here I am. So, say goodbye while I get your bags.

> *He puts her coat and bag on the chair right, pushes her left toward Billy. He starts for the bedroom.*

ANN: But . . .

BILLY *(grabs her shoulders):* Behave.

> *Peter has disappeared into the bedroom.*

ANN: You knew he was coming here.

BILLY: We rode over together.

ANN: Didn't you give him my letter?

BILLY: Letter? Oh, the letter. What the hell did I do with that . . .

> *Starts searching his pockets.*

ANN: But, Billy . . .

Peter comes back into the room with two more suitcases. Ann tries to argue with him, but Billy stops her: let well enough alone. Peter disappears again.

ANN: Why, Billy? You were so against it.

BILLY *(shrugs):* Do you know how many "B" pictures I've made?
> *They embrace.*

ANN: It's a gigantic mistake.

BILLY *(solemnly):* It has been obvious to me for some time that that is what God put us here for. To make gigantic mistakes. It is His Supreme Design.
> *Peter re-enters with two more bags.*

PETER: Is this all?

ANN: I think so.

PETER *(shakes Billy's hand):* Thanks, Billy.

BILLY: Beat it.

PETER *(starting off):* I'll ring for the elevator . . .
> *Pointing to bags on floor.*

. . . and come back for those two.

BILLY: I'll get them.
> *Peter goes. Billy gets Ann's coat, puts it on her. He takes out letter from his pocket, slowly tears it into small pieces and puts them into Ann's hand.*

ANN: Thanks, Billy.

BILLY: I've finally decided that you're grown up enough to marry the kid.

ANN: Goodbye, Billy.
> *He embraces her, suddenly lets her go, picks up bags.*

Billy . . .
> *Steps towards Billy. Peter reappears in the doorway.*

PETER: The elevator's here. Come on, love.
> *Greek music softly under.*

BILLY: Go on, hold it. I got these.
> *Peter disappears. Billy goes for the bags, starts for the door.*

Come on, Ann.
> *Ann is just standing there. Billy, at door, stops and looks at her.*

ANN: Oh, dear . . .

BILLY: What's the matter?

ANN: I was just wondering how Helen of Troy managed about her ex-husband.

BILLY: He was an older guy, you know. They let him take care of the luggage.
> *He goes. Ann, left alone, looks around the room, crosses up to the door, and then looks down at the torn letter in her hand and flips the pieces into the air as though they were rice or confetti. She flips them so they come down around her head.*

ANN: Here comes the bride. Oh, God!
> *She goes. Music swells. Curtain.*

HADRIAN VII

A Play in Two Acts

BY PETER LUKE

Based on Hadrian the Seventh *and other works by Fr. Rolfe (Baron Corvo)*

Cast and credits appear on page 401

PETER LUKE was born in England of Anglo-Irish and Hungarian parentage and grew up between the two wars in the British Isles and Austria, Pakistan and Malta. He was educated, he says, "in the holidays from Eton." He studied painting in London and Paris and worked in a wine-shipping firm for nine years before entering show business as a play producer for the BBC.

Luke's three-year record with the BBC included productions of A Passage to India *and* Silent Song *(winner of the 1967 Italia Prize). In Spain, he wrote and directed on location a movie about Garcia Lorca entitled* Black Sound— Deep Song. *At the same time, two of Luke's own scripts—*A Man on Her Back *and* The Devil a Monk Wou'd Be—*appeared on the BBC.* Hadrian VII *is its author's professional playwriting debut. It is based on the life and works of Frederick William Rolfe, and it is interesting to note that Luke's father, Sir Harry Luke, was acquainted with Rolfe at Oxford in 1906.*

INTRODUCTION BY THE PLAYWRIGHT

The play of *Hadrian VII* is an attempt to biography Frederick Rolfe in dramatic terms and in terms of his own fantasy. The play is primarily based on Rolfe's book of the same title, but I refuse to accept the term "adaptation" because it is also based on other works by Rolfe and on my own imagination. In fact, there is a good deal more original Luke in it than I have been given credit for. Even some of the widely quoted *bons mots,* ascribed to Rolfe, have been mine. I should also like to make it known that the play owes nothing to the excellent work by A.J. Symons, *The Quest for Corvo,* except insofar as this was referred to once or twice for biographical purposes. The "other works" referred to (in the "based on" credit) were many and various, both published and unpublished. For these last I am indebted to Mr. Cecil Woolf and I have acknowledged his help, and that of other Corvines, elsewhere.

That the play is a *dramatic* success is manifest. That the play does not depend on a star actor is proved by the fact that, at this time of writing, *Hadrian* is running successfully both in London and New York with two different stars giving very different performances. The criticism that "it is not as good as the book" is irrelevant. But the criticism that the subplot characters, Jeremiah Sant and Mrs. Crowe, are out of tone with the rest of the play is more or less valid. The justification for their existence is that they are the two-dimensional figments of a paranoid's imagination.

The point of the play, beyond trying to present a good piece of theater, is to make some sort of plea for Rolfe's belief in his Vocation. The Roman Catholic hierarchy now, as then, may or may not believe that he had one. In any case they could argue that a man sick in mind is not fit to be a priest. But we know today, as was less well known at the turn of the century, that sickness of mind can be cured. It is my belief that an enlightened bishop might have cured Rolfe, body, mind and soul, by offering the priesthood he so earnestly desired.

—PETER LUKE

Time: Around 1903

Place: London and Rome

ACT I

Scene 1: A corner of Frederick Rolfe's bed-sitting room in London

SYNOPSIS: Frederick Rolfe is seated in an armchair in his room, smoking, writing a manuscript, wrapped in a blanket but shivering with cold. His room *"is the abode of a poor scholar of fastidious habits and austere tastes"* with books, a small gas heater, wooden furniture (one chair is propped against the door to hold it shut). It is conspicuously decorated with a large crucifix and other religious objects.

Frederick William Rolfe is a smallish, spare man of about 40. He wears his greying hair very short, is myopic and can hardly see without his plain, steel-rimmed spectacles, but he is slim, agile and erect. . . . . He smokes a lot, always rolling his own and tucking the ends in with a pencil. Cat-like, his movements are swift, lithe and silent. Likewise, there are moments when he remains utterly still. . . . . He wears a threadbare clerical grey suit.

After a moment, there is a knocking and a rattling of the door handle. Rolfe's landlady, Mrs. Crowe, is trying to get in.

MRS. CROWE *(off):* . . . . . Mr. Rolfe, I know you're there.

ROLFE: Tickle your ass with a feather, Mrs. Crowe.

MRS. CROWE *(off):* What did you say?

ROLFE: Particularly nasty weather, Mrs. Crowe.

MRS. CROWE *(off):* Mr. Rolfe, I haven't climbed all these stairs just to be insulted. There are two gentlemen below who wish to see you.

ROLFE *(starting up; noticeably startled):* To see *me?*

MRS. CROWE *(off):* Yes, to see you.

Rolfe removes the barricade and lets Mrs. Crowe into the room. The visitors below won't state their business, but Rolfe asks his landlady to send them up. While she does so, Rolfe quickly puts on a collar and tie and straightens up the room.

The visitors enter; they are bailiffs. The First Bailiff is *"a venerable-looking old man with white hair";* the Second Bailiff is *"a tall, amiable, healthy-looking fellow in his early 40s."* The bailiffs address Rolfe by various aliases (which Rolfe denies): Baron Corvo, Frank W. Hochheimer, F. Austin. Finally they address him as Frederick William Rolfe (pronounced as in "golf"). Rolfe corrects them; his name is pronounced to rhyme with "oaf."

The Second Bailiff comments that the way Rolfe signs his name—Fr. Rolfe —might almost be mistaken for Father Rolfe, designating a priest. Rolfe tells him: "My name is Frederick Rolfe. I have never taken Holy Orders. Had I done so, no doubt I should have been a bishop by now—not a mere priest."

The bailiffs inform Rolfe that there is a court judgment standing against him, and that he must sign a paper promising not to remove any of his belongings from these premises. Rolfe refuses to sign, and the bailiffs depart, threatening him with a Warrant of Execution.

Mrs. Crowe returns, and Rolfe admits to her that these were bailiffs with a judgment against him. Mrs. Crowe hints to Rolfe that she could help him with his money problems "if you wanted me to." Loathing her touch and her advances, Rolfe jumps away. Mrs. Crowe, now a woman scorned, demands her quarter's rent by the end of the week, or out Rolfe goes. It happens that Mrs. Crowe wants the room for an old "friend" of Rolfe's—one Jeremiah Sant, the very mention of whose name sends Rolfe into a rage. Mrs. Crowe leaves the room with Rolfe shouting.

ROLFE *(closes the door and puts the blanket round his shoulders):* Someone will have to suffer for this.

He rolls and lights a cigarette, holding it cupped in his two hands for warmth.

All those curves and protuberances—breeding, that's all they're good for.

He sits.

Jeremiah Sant is a gerrymandering gouger!

After a moment he hears footsteps on the stairs again. He listens, wondering if it is Mrs. Crowe coming back to apologize. Instead, a letter is thrust under the door. He rises, looks at it suspiciously, then picks it up and turns it over, looking at the seal.

What—what's that? Archbishop House?

He tears the letter open and reads it with trembling hands.

(Savagely.) Hell and damnation! Imbeciles! Owl-like Hierarchs! Degenerates! *(After a pause.)* God, if You ever loved me, hear me. They have denied me the priesthood again. Not a chance do You give me, God—ever. Listen! How can I serve You—*(To the crucifix.)*—while You keep me so sequestered? I'm intelligent. So, O God, You made me. But intelligence must be active, potent, and perforce I am impotent and inactive always; futile in my loneliness. Why, O God have You made me strange, uncommon, such a mystery to my fellow-creatures? Am I such a ruffian as to merit total exile from them? You have made me denuded of the power of love—to love anybody or be loved. I shall always be detached and apart from the others. I suppose I must go on like that to the end *(Grimly.)* because they are frightened of me—frightened of the labels I put on them.

He puts out his cigarette savagely.

O God, forgive me smoking. I quite forgot. I am not doing well at present. They force me into it: a pose of haughty genius, subtle, learned, inaccessible. Oh, it's wrong, wrong altogether, but what can I do? God, tell me clearly, unmistakably and distinctly, tell me, tell me what I must do—and make me do it.

He sits.

Oh Lord, I am sick—and very tired.

Kindly Agnes, an elderly charlady, knocks and enters carrying a bowl of bread and milk for Rolfe, and a newspaper. Feeling how cold Rolfe's room is, Agnes puts a coin in the gas meter, over Rolfe's protests.

Rolfe eats the bread and milk hungrily, until he glances at the paper and sees that the Pope is dead. There will be an immediate Conclave of the Sacred College to choose a successor. Agnes, dusting Rolfe's room, comments, "It's about time they had an English Pope for a change."

Agnes leaves, but she has set Rolfe to thinking—he takes down a reference book, sits with paper and pencil and begins to write feverishly. He finds that from 1154 to 1159 one Nicholas Brakespeare reigned as Hadrian IV, the first and only British Pope (there have been two Hadrians since, one from Genoa and one from Utrecht).

Rolfe's imagination goes to work. He writes, and the lighting changes to a warmer hue. Once again Mrs. Crowe knocks on his door. There are two clergymen calling to see Rolfe—His Grace the Archbishop of Pimlico and the Bishop of Caerleon (Drs. Courtleigh and Talacryn). They are ushered in. Except for their canonical garb, they exactly resemble the First and Second Bailiffs of the preceding visit.

Talacryn—whom Rolfe claims as his personal friend—introduces Rolfe to Courtleigh. Courtleigh opens the subject of the church's rejection of Rolfe for holy orders and finds that Rolfe is angry and intransigently aggrieved: "I have lost faith in man, and I have lost the power of loving."

As the head of the Roman Communion in England, Courtleigh is the target of some of Rolfe's resentment. But Courtleigh asks Rolfe to speak his mind, even if his words must be disagreeable.

ROLFE: The Catholic and Apostolic Church, with its championing of learning and beauty, was always to me a real and living thing. It was with the highest hopes, therefore, that I entered Oscott College to begin my career as a clerk in Holy Orders. I was soon obliged to leave, however, after a dispute with the principal, who seemed to see no offense in grubs grazing on the lettuces and caterpillars cantering across the refectory table. The Archbishop of Agneda then invited me, on recommendation, to attend St. Andrew's College at Rome. I gladly went, on the assurance that my expenses would be borne by the Archbishop. They never were and, in consequence, I was several hundred pounds out of pocket.

COURTLEIGH: Dear me!

He looks at Talacryn for confirmation. Talacryn nods agreement. Yes?

ROLFE: Then after four months in college, I was expelled suddenly and brutally.

COURTLEIGH: And what reason was given?

ROLFE: No reason was ever given. The gossip of my fellow-students—immature cubs prone to acne and versed in dog Latin—was that I had no Vocation.

COURTLEIGH: I see. Go on.

ROLFE: Then there was the occasion in Wales when the machinations of a certain cleric, whose cloven hoof defiled the shrine of the Blessed Saint Winefred of Holywell, defrauded me of my rightful deserts for two years of arduous work undertaken at his request. Having been robbed by the said priest not only of my means of livelihood, but also of health, comfort, friends and reputation, and brought physically to my knees, he then gave me the *coup de grace* by debarring me from the Sacraments. I then had no option but to leave Wales and start life from scratch. I walked to London. Two hundred and fourteen miles. It took me eighteen days.

COURTLEIGH: Good gracious! But did no one come forward to assist you at this time?

ROLFE: The Bishop of Caerleon, who somewhat belatedly received me back into Communion; one other Catholic, a man of my own trade, who later betrayed me, so I'll say no more of him; women, of course, I neglect. Eventually, others, moved no doubt by the last twitchings of their dying consciences, made tentative overtures. To these I quoted St. Matthew twenty-five, verses forty-one to forty-three.

COURTLEIGH: Now, how does that go?

He feels in the air with his hand for the quotation.

ROLFE: From "I was hungered and ye gave me no meat" down to "Depart from me ye cursed, into aeonial fire."

COURTLEIGH: You are hard, Mr. Rolfe, very hard.

ROLFE: I am what you and your fellow Catholics have made me.

Destitute and abandoned, Rolfe set out to occupy himself with writing and painting until such time as God would permit him to resume following his true Vocation, which he recognized in himself at the age of 15 and in which he still persists: "I am not a bog-trotting Fenian or one of your Sauchiehall Street hybrids—but English and sure; born under Cancer. Naturally I persist."

Rolfe informs the bishops he means to continue his writing career until he gets out of debt and has enough money to go to Rome to confront the priest who dismissed him from college. "Until I'm the posessor of a checkbook, I do not propose to start commerce with the clergy again."

Courtleigh insists that the money question need no longer trouble Rolfe. He has come to offer Rolfe his heart's desire: Holy Orders without delay, in recognition of the persistence of Rolfe's Vocation through 20 years of hardship.

But Rolfe is not ready—he must have money first. He has already learned how little an archbishop's promise of support can be worth. Courtleigh reassures him that the money will be offered to him as a token of restitution for the lost years. But Rolfe will not accept charity.

TALACRYN: Well, then, Freddy, in what form will you accept this act of justice from us? Do make an effort to believe we are sincerely in earnest and that in this matter we are in your hands.

Turning to Courtleigh.

I may say that, Your Eminence?

COURTLEIGH: Unreservedly.

There is a pause while Rolfe considers.

ROLFE *(quietly but with determination):* I will accept a written expression of regret for the wrongs which have been done to me by both Your Eminence and by others who have followed your advice, command or example.

COURTLEIGH *(taking a folded piece of paper from his breviary):* It is here.

ROLFE *(at first surprised, then reading it with care):* I thank Your Eminence.

He tears the paper into pieces.

COURTLEIGH: Man alive!

ROLFE: I do not care to preserve a record of my superiors' humiliation.

COURTLEIGH *(with an effort):* I see that Mr. Rolfe knows how to behave nobly, Frank.

ROLFE: Only now and again. But I had long ago arranged to do just that. *The prelates make a gesture of incomprehension to each other. Courtleigh stands. Rolfe kneels and receives benedictions.*

Rolfe agrees to meet them the next day for confession and investiture. Meanwhile, just before they leave, he borrows five pounds for new clothing from his friend Talacryn.

The priests have left and Rolfe is giving his mirror image an episcopal blessing, when behind him he sees the figure of his old enemy Jeremiah Sant standing in the doorway. Sant has come to gloat over Rolfe's misfortune and to look over the room that is to be his after Rolfe is dispossessed.

Rolfe wants to know why Sant keeps hounding him, and Sant reminds Rolfe of a childhood incident in Belfast, whose slums they both remember. Sant lived on a militantly Protestant street, next to a street of Catholics. One day, Sant's little brother, age 11, wandered onto the Catholic street by mistake and was badly beaten.

SANT: . . . . . They went on kicking him till he stopped moving.
ROLFE: I heard.
SANT: Aye, they left him for dead. But he wasn't—not quite. Whenever I'm back in Belfast I go and see him at the asylum. He was thirty-two last birthday, but he's still only eleven in his mind. Just lately he's taken to wetting his bed again.
ROLFE: Tragic. But one act of hooliganism begets another.
SANT: That may be what you call it. But the Lord saith, an eye for an eye and a tooth for a tooth—and I'm still biding my time.
He moves to the door.
When you go, leave the window wide, will ye. It's the smell of a Papish I can't abide.
> *Sant exits, leaving the door open, and singing as he goes "The Sash My Father Wore:"*
Our Father knew the Rome of old
And evil is thy fame.
Thy kind embrace the galling chain,
Thy kiss the blazing flame.
> *Rolfe rises and stands quite still for a moment. His triumphant mood has vanished and, once more, he looks trapped and hunted. After a moment's thought he springs into action. Pulling a holdall out from the corner, he puts it on the chair, takes a few effects from the chest of drawers and throws them in, then goes to the door and listens to make sure the coast is clear. Having satisfied himself on this count, he picks up the holdall and tiptoes out, as the lights fade to a blackout.*

Scene 2: A room in Archbishop House

At 7:30 the following morning, Rolfe makes his confession to his friend the Bishop of Caerleon. Rolfe's conscience is burdened only with trifling technical offenses—except in a general confession of his whole life's shortcomings. Group worship is distasteful to him—he prefers to worship God in private. "My mind has a twist toward frivolity, toward perversity," Rolfe declares, admitting to the telling of off-color stories. "Sometimes I catch myself extracting elements of esthetic pleasure from unesthetic situations," as for example, noticing the beautiful texture of the human skin while assisting at an amputation.

Does Rolfe love God? Talacryn asks. "I don't know. I really don't know," is Rolfe's reply. "He is the Maker of the World to me. He is Truth and Righteousness and Beauty. He is first, He is last. He is Lord of all to me. I absolutely believe in Him. I unconditionally trust Him. So far I clearly see. Then in my mind, there comes a great gap—filled with fog."

Rolfe is certain that he does not love his neighbor—in fact he detests "him —and her. Most people are repulsive to me, because they are ugly in person, or in manner, or in mind." Does Rolfe love himself? No, he despises himself, and though he cultivates himself he takes little pleasure in either his own body or mind.

Talacryn advises Rolfe that he should make an effort to increase his capacity to love in order to get nearer to God. Talacryn recites the ritual of penance with Rolfe, then gives him a piece of news: Rolfe is to accompany Talacryn and Courtleigh to Rome, where Rolfe is to serve as private chaplain to Courtleigh during the Conclave at which the new Pope is to be chosen.

Scene 3: A chapel in the Vatican

The Liturgy is heard in the remote background. Acolytes enter to light the altar candelabra and then depart. Rolfe (now a priest, in black soutane and biretta) and Talacryn enter, discussing the election. The Conclave is deadlocked. Cardinal Ragna, the Papal Secretary of State, is described by Rolfe as "the short-odds favorite" but doesn't have enough votes to overcome the bloc against him, of which Courtleigh is a prominent member. Courtleigh (Rolfe observes) would nominate anyone, even a parish priest, just to keep Ragna out.

A bell begins to clang, and there is a stir. Apparently the cardinals have found a Pope.

> *The nine Cardinal Compromissaries, in full purple, led by the Cardinal Archdeacon, and in company with thurifers and cross-bearers, appear from the rear of the auditorium and move in procession down the aisles to the stage, chanting the Christus Vincit as they move. Arriving on the stage, they form an arc. Lastly comes an acolyte bearing the Papal crown—the triple tiara—on a cushion.*

*All bow in the direction of the altar, then turn inwards. As soon as
everyone is in position the bell ceases.*

ROLFE *(in a whisper to Talacryn):* What is it? What is happening?

TALACRYN: I think God has given us a Pope.

ROLFE: Whom?

*The litany ceases, and all turn to face Rolfe and Talacryn. All ex-
cept Rolfe kneel.*

CARDINAL ARCHDEACON: Reverend Lord, the Sacred College has elected
thee to be the successor to St. Peter. Wilt thou accept pontificality?

*Since all present are now facing toward Rolfe and Talacryn, Rolfe
assumes it is the latter who is being addressed. He turns toward
Talacryn with a happy smile. Talacryn, however, is kneeling. Confused, Rolfe turns back to look at the Cardinal Archdeacon.*

(With greater emphasis.) Reverend Lord, the Sacred College has elected thee
to be the successor to St. Peter. Wilt thou accept pontificality?

*There is another pause. Rolfe, looking round to where all are on
their knees facing inwards towards him, at last realizes that the aw-
ful question is addressed to him.*

ROLFE: *Reverend Lord? Will I?*

TALACRYN *(in a whisper):* The response is *Volo*—or *Nolo*.

*Rolfe takes a deep breath, crossing his right hand over his left on
his breast.*

ROLFE: *Volo*—I will.

An organ peals out, as the curtain falls.

ACT II

Scene 1: Mrs. Crowe's parlor in London

Mrs. Crowe is seated on the chaise longue with Jeremiah Sant. They are
drinking while discussing the front-page news: the coronation of the first English Pope since 1154. Sant raves, "Begod, doesn't it make you want to puke
to think of an Englishman sinking so low." But Sant's cloud has one silver
lining: perhaps the fact of an Englishman as Pope will cause distress and revolution among Irish Catholics.

Sant is a member of an organization of fanatics called the Fellowship of
Religious Segregation dedicated to anti-Catholic action. Sant has been dele-
gated by the FRS to make a trip to Rome to demand safeguards for Protestants
from the new Pope. Plying Mrs. Crowe with drink, Sant asks her to come to
Rome on the trip with him—"and I wouldn't insult your intelligence by trying
to pretend that it was just for business reasons only."

Mrs. Crowe is pleased at Sant's attentions and hints that things were not
easy between herself and Rolfe, who left without paying the rent or making
any attempt to write her after he reached Rome. Sant presses Mrs. Crowe to
tell him all about her relations with Rolfe. She resists, but finally gives in and
"confesses," lying to Sant about Rolfe, who in fact had repulsed her.

MRS. CROWE: Oh, Jerry, it's been going on for years. He—he wouldn't leave me alone, never. He was always—always trying to—to do things to me, even when Mr. Crowe was alive. I've had no peace whenever he was around, Jerry, and I—I just couldn't keep him away.

She turns and buries her head in Sant's shoulder, sobbing.

SANT *(surprised):* Well I'll be damned!

MRS. CROWE: Well, don't sound so surprised. Aren't I attractive any more?

SANT: No, no. Of course you are, sweetheart. It's just that I always thought . . . Anyway, no Papish traitor shall defile with his dirty touch a respectable Protestant lady and get away with it. He shall pay right dearly for this or my name's not Jeremiah Sant.

MRS. CROWE *(quietly and viciously):* Make him squirm, Jerry. Make him squirm.

Sant kisses her violently on the mouth as the lights fade to a blackout.

Scene 2: An audience chamber in the Vatican

The Pontifical Throne is set on a dais at center. Cardinal Ragna the Secretary of State *("an elderly, bull-like Italian"),* Cardinal Berstein *("a cold, arrogant German")* and Father St. Albans the Propositor-General of the Jesuits *("the truculent 'Black Pope,' an Englishman")* are discussing the election of the nonentity Rolfe to the Papacy. They are disgusted at this turn of events, set in motion by Cardinal Courtleigh when he suggested in the deadlocked Conclave that "We must search outside the Vatican for a man of Faith and Constancy, a man of Simplicity and Humility." Now they have acquired a Pope who calls himself Hadrian VII instead of Pius or Leo or Gregory and who demands an amethyst ring instead of an emerald one.

"He who was a frog, is now a king," Ragna comments. And the new Pope insisted they all walk to the Lateran, exposing themselves to the perils of a city "full of Jews and Freemasons." When Ragna complained of the danger, the new Pope's only comment was, "Good, the Church needs a new martyr."

Courtleigh (in a wheelchair with gout), Talacryn and other members of the Sacred College enter. They have been summoned, and St. Albans has made it his business to find out why. The Pope is issuing a bull renouncing all claim to temporal sovereignty, in direct contradiction of the policy of his predecessors.

Ragna is furious—if the Pope renounces temporal power, of what State can he be Secretary? Talacryn tries feebly to justify the Pope's decision: "His Holiness believes the world is sick for want of the Church. He believes, I think, that we should turn all our efforts and attention to the pursuit of non-secular matters."

But Ragna and the others are adamant. They do not mean to give up temporal power without a struggle. They call Rolfe anti-Pope and suggest convening the Ecumenical Council, adjourned since 1870, to reverse his decision. The Sacred College must act—must *demand* if necessary.

Hadrian VII (Rolfe) enters dressed in white and carrying a briefcase, at first unnoticed by the others.

HADRIAN *(very quietly):* Pray, what must the Sacred College demand, Lord Cardinal?
> *All react to the sudden appearance of the Pope. Ragna, taken off guard, can only work his jaw defiantly. Hadrian persists in his most ominously gentle voice.*

Your Eminence is free to address Us.

RAGNA *(recovering his truculence slightly):* I wish rather to address the Sacred College.

HADRIAN *(sweetly):* You have Our permission to do so.
> *He looks round the room, noting the reactions of those present.*

RAGNA: I wish to . . . *(He clears his throat to gain time.)* I wish to . . .

HADRIAN: You wish to denounce Us as Heretic and Pseudo-pontiff. And to do so, you wish to convene an Ecumenical Council. Is that not correct?
> *Ragna, his own words taken from his mouth, remains silent, his face working.*

That generally is done by oblique-eyed cardinals who cannot accustom themselves to new pontiffs.
> *Mounting the dais.*

But Lord Cardinals, if such an idea should be presented to you, be ye mindful that none but the Supreme Pontiff can convoke an Ecumenical Council, and that the decrees of such are ineffective without the express sanction of the Supreme Pontiff. We are conscious of your love and of your loathing for Our Person and Our Acts. We value the one and regret the other. But ye voluntarily have sworn obedience to Us, and We claim it. Nothing must and nothing shall obstruct Us. Let that be known.
> *He sits on the throne.*

Wherefore Most Eminent Lords and Venerable Fathers, let not the sheep of Christ's flock be neglected while the shepherds exchange anathemas. Try, Venerable Fathers, to believe that the time has come for taking stock. Ask yourselves whether we really are as successful as we think we are—whether in fact we are not abject and lamentable failures in the eyes of God. We have added and added to the riches, pomp and power of the Church, yet everywhere there is great wealth alongside dire poverty; there are strong nations brutally holding small ones to slavery; above all there are millions of people of good will looking to us for moral and spiritual leadership who get from us only dogmatic interpretations of Canon Law in return. If, then, we have so far failed in spreading Christ's Gospel, let us try anew. Let us try the road of Apostolic simplicity—the simplicity of Peter the Fisherman. At least let us try.
> *There is total silence.*

Your Eminences have permission to retire.
> *For a moment there is silence. Then Talacryn goes quickly to reaffirm his allegiance by kissing the Pontifical ring. Hesitantly at first, the others follow. Ragna, still recalcitrant, makes the briefest*

> *possible acknowledgement. Courtleigh alone is left, in his chair. Having made obeisance, the prelates move off, murmuring.*

Hadrian asks Courtleigh to remain behind. The Pope is worried about the conduct of English Catholics who have petitioned Parliament to set up some control over Roman Catholic finances, because the Church gives no account to the public of bequests received and expenditures made. Hadrian finds other fault with the English Church—the custom of pew rentals to discourage "improper" people from attending services, and the conduct of some clergy in setting up schemes to bring in money. Hadrian wants such practices stopped, so that the English Church will become a shining instead of a tarnished example.

Courtleigh protests, but Hadrian is firm: "The Barque of Peter is way off course. Lord Cardinal, can the new captain count on the loyal support of His Lieutenant in trying to bring her head round?" Courtleigh struggles with himself and finally, with an effort, agrees to carry out the Pope's wishes.

At once Hadrian adopts the role of the solicitous companion, instead of the master, and wheels the embarrassed Courtleigh out to the garden for an airing.

Scene 3: Outside a cafe in Rome

Mrs. Crowe sits at a cafe table under her parasol, while Sant fans himself with his Panama hat. The Pope has not favored them with an audience as emissaries of the Fellowship of Religious Segregation. Sant is composing a note to Hadrian which will put his case more firmly and meaningfully.

Scene 4: The audience chamber

Hadrian sits on the throne, smoking, while Talacryn reads him the last part of Sant's note. It smacks of blackmail: ". . . I therefore trust that in view of the not altogether pleasant facts that are in the possession of myself and another party well known to yourself, you will see fit to accord me a private interview at your earliest convenience. . . . ."

Hadrian, furious, decides to ignore this message and its sender, although Talacryn warns him that his opponents in the Sacred College would welcome a scandal, should Sant decide to take his case to the newspapers. Hadrian insists on changing the subject, and Talacryn remarks that he has just paid a visit to Rolfe's old college, St. Andrew's, where the same Rector who expelled him years ago for having "no Vocation" is now an old man.

The thought of this incident still hurts, Hadrian admits. He determines to cauterize the wound once and for all by visiting the college immediately, accompanied by Talacryn.

Scene 5: St. Andrew's College

In the background is a suggestion of cloisters, as Hadrian and Talacryn enter with the Rector, who is expressing his appreciation of the Pope's visit.

Hadrian has noticed an older boy, unhappier-looking than most, who took only bread and water at lunch. He is George Arthur Rose (the Rector tells the Pope), a problem student who in the Rector's opinion has no real Vocation. The Pope reminds the embarrassed Rector of a past error in just such a judgment. He sends the Rector to fetch the young seminarist Rose.

Hadrian decides to appoint Talacryn Protector of the College and instructs him to befriend the students "and see what you can do to take that horrible secretive suppressed look out of their young eyes."

The Rector comes back with young Rose, and the Pope sends him off with Talacryn to inspect the kitchens. Questioning Rose, Hadrian finds that the young man is 29, uncomfortable at the college but uncomplaining. The Pope asks him why the others make fun of him.

ROSE: Because for my ablutions I carry two cans of water up two hundred and two steps every day.

HADRIAN: No doubt they say you must be a very unclean person to need so much washing.

ROSE: Sanctity, you are quoting the Rector. How does Your Holiness know so exactly?

HADRIAN (laughing): Have they even put a snake in your water cans?

ROSE: No, they have not done that.

HADRIAN: They did in Ours. Isn't it absurd?

ROSE: It is—and very disconcerting.

HADRIAN: But you try not to let it disconcert you?

ROSE: I try but I fail. My heart is always on my sleeve and the daws peck it. So I try to protect myself in isolation.

HADRIAN: That they call "sulkiness!"

ROSE: Yes, Your Holiness knows so exactly . . .

HADRIAN (almost to himself): We also were never able to arrange to be loved.
          He circles slowly above Rose.
Do you always live on bread and water?

ROSE: Yes, except for eggs.

HADRIAN: Why?

ROSE: I have been into the kitchen and seen—things. They cannot deposit sputum inside the shells of boiled eggs.

HADRIAN: Do you like bread and water?

ROSE: No, but in order not to be singular I eat and drink what I can of what is set before me. But because of that, I am deemed more singular than ever.

HADRIAN (moving around above Rose as before): Yet you choose to persevere, my son!

ROSE: Sanctity, I must, I am called.

HADRIAN: You are sure of that?

ROSE: It is the only thing in all the world of which I am sure.

Unhappy as he is at the college, Rose will stick it out because his diocesan sent him here, and he will wait 20 years if necessary (just the time Rolfe waited, in fact) to obtain his priesthood. Hadrian suggests to Rose that maybe there is a favor the Pope could grant him, but Rose refuses to ask. Then Hadrian gives what was not asked for. He tells Rose to come to the Vatican next day, for the fulfillment of his desires. Rose kneels for Hadrian's blessing and then departs, as Talacryn returns.

HADRIAN: What a delicious day it has been, Frank. You persuaded Us and We are grateful.

TALACRYN: I think the walk did Your Holiness good.

HADRIAN: It was not just the walk, but something quite other—as though a curtain had been lifted, or, more exactly, as if We had been given a brief glimpse into a human heart.

TALACRYN: That is a rare and wonderful experience, Holiness.

HADRIAN: Rare? You are Our confessor. You must know that for Us the experience is unique. Frank, We have just had the first feeling of undiluted enjoyment of human society which We can ever remember.

TALACRYN: Do you remember what I said to you in London, Holiness? I said that if You could find it in Yourself to love your neighbor it would lead You to love God.

HADRIAN: Love—yes—We have recognized for the first time in Ourselves a new and unborn power, a perfectly strange capability. Today, We have made experience of a feeling which—well, which We suppose—at any rate will pass for—Love.

Blackout.

Scene 6: The audience chamber

Agnes, the charlady who was kind to Rolfe in London, is seated in a small chair facing the throne. It is some days later, and young Rose is now a priest and private chaplain to His Holiness; he is keeping Agnes company pending the arrival of the Pope.

Hadrian enters and greets Agnes warmly. Agnes is glad to see him but somewhat uncomfortable in the Vatican surroundings—she can't help thinking of Hadrian as plain Mr. Rolfe "I used to do for."

Agnes offers Hadrian an envelope containing money left over from a sum the Pope sent her to buy a lodging-house; but of course Hadrian presses her to keep the money. Agnes's establishment is already doing well, overflowing with lodgers. She has brought "Mr. Rolfe" a jar of her special pickles he likes so well.

After receiving the Pope's blessing and promising to pray for him "every day for as long as I'm spared," Agnes departs. Hadrian arranges for a specially conducted tour of the Vatican before she leaves (though it seems Agnes will cherish Hadrian's signature on a card more than the tour for which it is the passport).

Talacryn enters with the alarming news that calumnies about the Pope's previous life have been published in an Ulster paper and even in a church publication. Ragna enters on Talacryn's heels, waving a sheaf of papers, smelling blood. Hadrian scans the newspaper columns and protests that the stories are untrue distortions.

RAGNA: The English reporters are careful to begin at the beginning—His Holiness was expelled from ecclesiastical college in Roma because he is owing everybody money. He makes friends with old Italian lady, the Duchess of Sforza-Cesarini, who is very rich.

HADRIAN (to himself): Unanswerable, because it is half-truth.

RAGNA: Back in England, His Holiness becomes "Baron Corvo," a fine gentleman who inherited title from his noble Italian friend. He used title to gain influence and obtain more money.

HADRIAN (still to himself): Half-truth again. Who could have attacked with such malign ingenuity?

RAGNA: The Baron tries to buy some property, but people find he is not "Baron." He has no money to buy property. He is a fraud, an adventurer.

HADRIAN (searching the column): Anonymous! Anonymous half-truths. I should be able to recognize the filthy paw of this muckraker.

RAGNA: So "Baron Corvo" runs away—to another town where he makes more trouble and owes more money; this time in Wales.

HADRIAN: We were not in Wales this time—but in Belfast. Yes, of course—Sant! Jeremiah Sant!

RAGNA: But in Ireland it is also the same story; he is again the great gentleman—the writer, photographer, inventor of many things, a friend of many famous people. But it is all lies. He has no money. He has no friends. He is nothing, he owes money to the people where he is living. They take him from bed and put him in the street. They throw his clothes after him so he must dress in the street.

Talacryn reacts sharply to this humiliating revelation.

Hadrian tells Ragna that there are fifteen deliberate lies in this report, but Ragna will not be satisfied. As Secretary of State, he demands action. Hadrian strips off his Papal ring, places it on the throne and offers himself to the cardinals for interrogation as Frederick William Rolfe.

Courtleigh asks Hadrian gently to refute the lies. Hadrian agrees to do so, after which he will never return to the subject again.

First, Hadrian explains the pseudonyms: after being expelled from the college he needed to earn his living but did not want to associate his real name with secular pursuits. He was driven from one occupation to another by "Church malfeasance" and changed his name to suit: "as Baron Corvo I wrote and painted and photographed; as F. Austin I designed decorations; as Frank Hockheimer I did journalism." The name Frederick William Rolfe he hoped to save for the resumption of his Divine Vocation.

Ragna presses Hadrian to explain his debts, and Hadrian does so: he worked for the Church and expected to be paid, so he accepted credit. When the Church did not pay, Hadrian found himself in difficulty.

Berstein presses Hadrian on the charge of luxurious living. Courtleigh and Talacryn try to end the interrogation, but Hadrian insists on answering everything.

HADRIAN (*mounting the dais*): But you shall hear more. They say that I gorged myself with sumptuous banquets at grand hotels. Once, after several days of starvation, I got a hard-earned begrudging and overdue fee from a magazine. I went and had an omelette at a small-town commercial doss-house which called itself "The Grand Hotel." They also say that, in my lodgings, I demanded elaborate dishes to be made from my own cookery book. Since I was beholden to my landlords I did indeed ask for special dishes—dishes of lentils and carrots—I do not touch meat—anything that was cheapest, cleanest, easiest and most filling. Each dish cost a few pence and I sometimes had one each day. And occasionally when I earned a little bit I spent a few shillings on apparatus conducive to personal cleanliness, soap, baths and so on. That is the story of my luxurious living, My Lords.
There is a pause, and all keep silent.
I have been provoked, abused, calumniated, traduced with insinuation, innuendo, misrepresentation, lies; my life has been held up to ridicule and most inferior contempt. I tell you this because, officially, I must correct an error. You may take it as an example of how your Catholics, laymen and clergy alike, can tire out and drive almost to death a man's body—perhaps even his soul. But understand this, My Lords: by no words will I ever defend myself outside these walls. Nor do I speak in my own defense, Venerable Fathers, even to you. I personally and of predilection, am indifferent to opinions, but it is your right to hear that which you have heard.
There is another silence, then Ragna speaks out.
RAGNA (*waving the newspapers*): An enemy hath done this!
HADRIAN (*with candid delight*): Those are the first genuine words I have heard from Your Eminence's heart.
RAGNA (*in a voice of thunder*): Who is it has done this evil thing?
TALACRYN: A reactionary blackmailer and a disappointed woman—two worms that have turned.
RAGNA (*roaring*): Anathema sint: let them be smothered in the dunghill.
Slowly, Hadrian picks up the Pontifical ring, places it on his finger and sits.

Hadrian indicates his wish to be alone with Ragna, and the others leave. Hadrian has now won Ragna, who offers his apologies for past antagonisms.
Gently, Hadrian tells Ragna he is thinking of giving away the Vatican treasure, because "the Church exists for the service of God in His creatures. She does not serve . . . . . by keeping costly and beautiful things shut up in cupboards." What is Ragna's opinion on this subject? Ragna is shaken, but he holds fast to his new loyalty to Hadrian: "Holy Father, I am with You with all my heart. Under Your inspired guidance let the Church once more meet the

ALEC MCCOWEN IN "HADRIAN VII"

world in the pure missionary spirit of Her greatest days. I shall follow wherever Your Holiness may lead."

And there is one more blow in store for Ragna: the Pope insists that they walk together to St. John Lateran.

RAGNA: But, Holy Father, the political situation is very, very dangerous.
   Father Rose enters with the white, Pontifical sunshade with its green lining. Hadrian takes it from him.

HADRIAN *(smiling):* Quite. But as We mentioned to Your Eminence once before . . .

RAGNA *(raising his hands to heaven):* But, Holiness, I am too fat to become a martyr.

HADRIAN (*opening the sunshade*): My Lord Cardinal, in every fat priest, there is always a bony martyr crying out for Beatitude.
> *Hadrian leads off, followed by the now faithful Ragna crossing himself and tut-tutting, as the lights fade to a blackout.*

Scene 7: *The audience chamber*

Mrs. Crowe and Jeremiah Sant are escorted by chamberlains and Swiss Guards to two chairs set up facing the Papal throne. The guards stand in an arc facing the visitors, who sit awkwardly awaiting the arrival of the Pope.

MRS. CROWE (*in a stage whisper*): Oh dear, why don't they hurry up? Oh, I do wish I'd never come.
SANT (*also in a stage whisper*): Shut up, Nancy. Do you want them to hear you?
MRS. CROWE: I just wish it was all over, that's all.
SANT: Can't you see that's just what he wants? He wants to get us rattled. But I'll rattle him first. (*He clinks the loose change in his pocket.*) Ay.
MRS. CROWE: Oh, I do hope you're right, Jerry.
SANT: Of course I am. You don't imagine I gave the papers all I know, do you? Not by a long chalk I didn't. Not by a very long chalk. He'll listen to me this time, or my name's not Jeremiah . . .

Hadrian enters with his entourage of Cardinals and Father Rose and sits on the throne. He dismisses the guards, then confronts Sant and Mrs. Crowe coolly. He has summoned them to hear what they have to say. The conversation is to be recorded—but Sant objects to this, and the Pope concedes. He also concedes that Sant may speak for Mrs. Crowe as well as himself.

Sant tells Hadrian he wants reparation and damages for the time and trouble of waiting eight months in Rome for a Papal audience—20,000 pounds for himself and the same sum for Mrs. Crowe, "and we'll cry quits."

Mrs. Crowe suggests that perhaps it would be best if she had "a private word with His Holiness." Hadrian refuses, with the comment: "Daughter, your notorious conduct bars you from a private conversation with any clergyman except in the open confessional."

Mrs. Crowe, scorned again and furious, urges Sant to tell everything. Sant objects to the presence of so many onlookers. Hadrian, over all protests, dismisses everyone except Father Rose and faces his two visitors determinedly.

Hadrian points out to Sant that he didn't ask Sant to waste his time in Rome and therefore owes him nothing. Sant becomes angrier and angrier as Hadrian terms his errand "a foolish and dirty business." Sant accuses Hadrian of skipping out on his London rent, and Father Rose merely produces a receipt for this rent which Hadrian paid as soon as he could. And Hadrian repeats that he owes Sant nothing and will pay him nothing.

Sant hints at "a bit more about yer scabby little self in the papers," but Hadrian is not perturbed—he sees Sant as a person suffering deeply by his own fault. He pities Sant; he goes so far as to tell Sant he will help him, which only makes Sant angrier.

SANT *(shouting):* I want what I came here to get—my money.

HADRIAN: If you wish honestly to earn a better living, We shall give you that opportunity.

SANT: The hell with that. What about damages for the past?

HADRIAN *(rising):* We promise you a chance for the future.

SANT *(with menace):* You won't pay, then?

HADRIAN: On your terms—not one farthing. But We will help you to save your soul.

SANT *(almost out of his mind):* You'll *save* my soul? You?

MRS. CROWE *(urgently):* Jerry, sit down—please.

SANT *(to Hadrian):* You make me sick, you dirty Taigh.

MRS. CROWE *(rising; desperately):* Jerry, I want to go. Please. It's no good.

SANT *(taking a step towards Hadrian):* He's just a little insect. Aren't ye?

MRS. CROWE: Jerry, please . . .

ROSE *(in alarm):* Guard! Presto! Presto!

SANT *(quite out of his mind, drawing a revolver):* And ye know what to do with insects, don't ye? Tread them underfoot.

MRS. CROWE *(shrieking):* Jerry!

> *Swiss Guards, not knowing what is required of them, rush in shouting "Pronto! Pronto!"*

SANT: Vengeance is mine, Saith the Lord! Halleluya!

> *Before anyone can move, Sant fires once. Hadrian stands quite still. Father Rose rushes forward. The guards' reactions are slower, but they follow. Sant fires for the second time, and Mrs. Crowe screams. Hadrian remains still, though he seems to sway. As Sant fires for the third time, Father Rose tries to interpose himself between Sant and Hadrian. He fails, but manages to catch Hadrian who now slowly subsides as a patch of crimson defiles the apostolic whiteness of his robe. Ragna, Talacryn and other cardinals rush in. The guards overpower Sant, half killing him and holding him on the floor. The cardinals surround the throne. All eyes are turned to Hadrian who is supported by Talacryn on one side and Ragna on the other. The guards fling Sant on his knees before the dying Pope.*

HADRIAN *(weakly):* Father, forgive them for they know not—*(He struggles for breath.)*—what they . . . Venerable Fathers, Our will and pleasure is . . .

TALACRYN: Speak it, Most Holy Father.

HADRIAN: Venerable Fathers, We name you all the ministers of Our will.

> *He turns toward Sant.*

Son, you are forgiven. You are free.

The Swiss Guards drag Sant away, and Mrs. Crowe follows. Hadrian gives Father Rose his pectoral cross, and the room begins to fill with members of the Sacred College, as Talacryn prepares to administer the last rites.

Hadrian asks to be lifted to his feet; he gives the cardinals his blessing, and dies. The dead Pope is carried offstage by the guards, as a bell tolls; the company departs and the throne is removed, leaving Father Rose alone on a bare stage intoning a prayer in Latin. Then a procession escorts Hadrian's bier slowly across the stage.

ROSE: It had to happen. It was inevitable. By his own will he rejected the beautiful solitude of peace in intellectual silence. Instead of watching from the illimitable distance of his psychic altitude, by his own wish he chose the inevitable certainty of ceaseless and ferocious conflict among the ugly and obscene mob. It was the old bitter feeling of disgust with himself that inspired him to do this, so fearful was he that he might have seemed to be pleading for sympathy. But he really had gone far, far beyond the realm of human sympathy. There was not a man on earth who would have dared to risk rebuff, to persist against rebuff, to soar to him with that blessed salve of human sympathy for which—underneath his armor—and behind his warlike mien—he yearned. Pity perhaps, horror perhaps, dislike perhaps might have met him. But he only emphasized his fastidious aloofness by disclosing the cold of marble, not the warmth of human flesh. And so it happened. So died Hadrian the Seventh, Bishop, Servant of the Servants of God—and maybe Martyr.

> As the end of the procession crosses, Rolfe, as he appeared at the beginning of Act I, walks on and watches with approval the funeral cortege. He is smoking a cigarette and carries in his arms a huge bundle of manuscript. The remaining lights start to fade.

ROLFE: (In unison.)   ROSE:
Let us pray for the repose of his soul.   He was so tired.
> The lights fade to a blackout.

Scene 8: Rolfe's room in London

Rolfe is clutching his bundle of manuscript as Mrs. Crowe knocks and enters to tell him that two men have called to see him again. For a moment Rolfe imagines that they might be Their Lordships—he puts the manuscript on a chair and tries to straighten himself up. But no—his callers are the bailiffs, come back with a Warrant of Execution to take possession of Rolfe's property.

Rolfe stands trembling while the bailiffs prepare to remove the room's meager furnishings.

FIRST BAILIFF (looking suspiciously at the pile of manuscript): Hadrian the Seventh. What's this then?

ROLFE (picking up the manuscript and holding it to him): A book.

SECOND BAILIFF (piling books and all small items onto the chest of drawers): Write books, do you?
> He takes down the crucifix, the mirror and puts them on the chest of drawers. Rolfe does not deign to answer.

FIRST BAILIFF (helping the other): What's it about, then?

ROLFE: About? It's about a man who made the fatuous and frantic mistake of living before his time.

FIRST BAILIFF: Any value?

The Second Bailiff takes out the small chair and returns.

ROLFE: It's a masterpiece and, therefore, probably not worth tuppence.

The two bailiffs exchange glances of incomprehension.

At the same time, it is possibly beyond price.

He passes his hands gently over the manuscript. The bailiffs look more than ever confused.

FIRST BAILIFF *(to his colleague):* All right, then, let's get these out.

The Second Bailiff takes out the chair while the First moves the chest of drawers around. The Second Bailiff re-enters and between them they take out the chest of drawers. Rolfe stands quite still, holding his manuscript. After a moment the First Bailiff returns, moves to Rolfe, takes the manuscript and goes to the door.

FIRST BAILIFF: Best not to take any chances, Mr. Rolfe. After all, you could be right.

The First Bailiff exits. Rolfe is left all alone in the bare room, standing rigidly as he has done from the moment the bailiffs came in. As he stands there, one knee begins to tremble violently. Curtain.

○ ○ ○
○ ○ ○
○ ○ ○
○ ○ ○
○ ○ ○
○ ○ ○ # CELEBRATION

A Musical in Two Acts

BOOK AND LYRICS BY TOM JONES

MUSIC BY HARVEY SCHMIDT

Cast and credits appear on page 402

TOM JONES (book, lyrics) was born in Texas in 1928, the son of a turkey hatcheryman—the only appearance of this show-biz-significant bird in Jones's life so far. He and his collaborator Harvey Schmidt are co-authors of the long-est-running show of record in the professional American theater: The Fantasticks, *the off-Broadway musical based on a Rostand play, which opened May 1, 1960, was exactly 3,800 performances old and still running as of May 31, 1969 and has played in more than 50 countries and 800 American cities.*

The Jones-Schmidt collaboration began in 1951 at the University of Texas, where Jones was a drama major, and continued in the Army when the two wrote songs together by mail. Their New York career began with Julius Monk's Upstairs-at-the-Downstairs shows and blossomed into The Fantasticks, *their*

first full-length post-college work. The team's first Broadway musical was 110
in the Shade *in triple collaboration with N. Richard Nash, who wrote the book
from his own play* The Rainmaker. *It opened Oct. 24, 1963 and ran for 330
performances. The next was* I Do! I Do! *with Jones doing both lyrics and
book from Jan de Hartog's play* The Fourposter, *starring Mary Martin and
Robert Preston for 560 Broadway performances beginning Dec. 5, 1966.
Their fourth and shortest-running work,* Celebration *(109 performances)—is
the team's first original musical, the first directed by Jones himself and their
first appearance on the Best Plays list.*

*HARVEY SCHMIDT (music) like his collaborator Tom Jones was born in
Texas, in 1929, the son of a Methodist minister. At the University of Texas
Schmidt majored in art, not drama, but he joined the Curtain Club, an organization for those who wanted to participate in theater activities. In this way
he became acquainted with his co-author of future college and professional
musicals. Their illustrious career with* The Fantasticks, 110 in the Shade *and*
I Do! I Do! *is detailed above, with Schmidt composing the music and Jones
supplying the "words," as their formal* Celebration *billing terms it. Schmidt
and Jones are also co-authors of a short film* A Texas Romance—1909 *which
won a first prize at the San Francisco Film Festival.*

Our method of synopsizing Celebration *in these pages differs from that used
for the other nine of the Best Plays.* Celebration *is represented partly in pictures, in order to record the total "look" of a Broadway show in the season
of 1968-69—and also because its design is exceptionally effective.*

*The photographs depict the succession of scenes as produced by Cheryl
Crawford and Richard Chandler and directed by Tom Jones, as of the musical's opening Jan. 22, 1969 at the Ambassador Theater, with scenery and costumes by Ed Wittstein. Our special thanks are enthusiastically tendered to the
authors, producers and their press representatives—Lee Solters, Harvey B.
Sabinson and David Powers—for their help in obtaining this material including the excellent photographs by Robert Alan Gold and Friedman-Abeles.*

INTRODUCTION BY THE LIBRETTIST-LYRICIST

Everybody loves the movies. And why not? A huge screen. With huge stars
on it. Zoom lenses. Helicopter shots. Technological achievements. Color.
Julie Andrews in *The Sound of Music.* Your local butcher in cinema verite.
There's no doubt about it. It's "what's happening." It's "now." Everybody
loves the movies. Except me.

I love the theater. And I love it not because it's "now" but because it's
"then." It's ancient. Primitive. I love it because it touches something basic
within myself. It is a ceremony. A ritual. And something in me craves that
ritual, *needs* it. People gather in a circle. An invocation is offered. A parable
is enacted. And somehow, through these ancient "mysteries" of movement

and music and poetry, I am revealed unto myself. I am confirmed. Here, gathered with my fellow creatures, I am part of a group knowledge that goes beyond any simple reasoning of the mind. Winter and summer. Regeneration and decay. There they are up in the spotlight, same as always: battling, struggling, making us laugh and cry. It is delicious. And somehow it is also ennobling.

It's like a fire. Like sitting by a fire. That is a primitive thing too. It is inefficient and ridiculously archaic for our day and time. But in some strange and ancient way it heals and soothes us more than turning up the central heating. It "roots" us. It connects us with the past. And it releases us to dream about the future.

Celebration is an attempt to write for this kind of primitive theater. It is not (repeat: NOT) a musical comedy. It is an attempt at a ritual experience. With laughs. And a few naked girls.

TOM JONES

Time: New Year's Eve
Place: A Platform

ACT I

The Invocation and Procession

It is dark and wintry. The sun is in eclipse. A narrator, Potemkin (Keith Charles), explains that men once gathered by fires in the long winter dark, singing, acting plays, hoping for a sign that the light would return. Masked revelers join him, as for a ritual.

POTEMKIN & REVELERS *(sing):*
    Some people say
    That tonight is the night
    When the bird will fly
    And eat away the light;
    And it may be so.
    I just don't know

    All I know is up until we have
       to go,
    I want to celebrate! . . . . .
POTEMKIN *(speaks):*
    We're like those ancient people, in
      a way.

(continued on next page)

Photos by Robert Alan Gold except when otherwise credited

POTEMKIN (continued):
   We've gathered by the fire to do
      a play.
   Our night is dark like theirs.
   Our world is cold.
   Our hopes seem frozen
   Underneath the snow—
   And yet, if you will just assist us
   With your imagination,
   We'll try to make this humble stage
   A place for celebration!
POTEMKIN & REVELERS (sing):
   Some people say
   That today is the day
   When the cold will come

And never go away.
When the bird will fly—
The wind will blow—
But something deep inside me says
   it can't be so.
I want to celebrate!
Make a celebration!
I want to celebrate!
Savor each sensation.
Something deep inside. . . . .
Says—"Beneath the snow. . . . .
There's a tiny seed. . . . .
And it's gonna grow!". . . . .
I want to celebrate. . . . .
Celebration!

The Parable

It is New Year's Eve (says Potemkin) when a boy named Orphan sets out on a quest. He is cold and hungry and sings to "Mr. Somebody in the sky" to guide his footsteps. In the city, Revelers mock Orphan (Michael Glenn-Smith, *left*).

Orphan meets Potemkin, who has changed into the garb of a hobo and the personality of a con man. Potemkin wonders what treasure Orphan may be carrying. Orphan tells him, "the sun." He worked in the garden at his orphanage and liked it—until everyone he knew began to disappear, teachers and priests as well as children.

ORPHAN: Finally there wasn't anybody left at all except me.—And then some men came with machines, and they began to eat all the buildings. They had a ball on a great long chain and they swung it—way, way out—above the trees and the garden. It was beautiful. But then, when it came back, it smashed into the Face of God.

POTEMKIN: The Face of God?

ORPHAN: Yes.—in the stained glass window of the Chapel. Well, I ran over and I took the Eye of God—that was all that was left.—Look, I'll show you. *(Gets "Eye of God" from bag and holds it up.)*

Orphan is on his way to see Edgar Allen Rich, who owns the orphanage, to ask for his garden back. Rich gives a big party every New Year's Eve. Potemkin offers to guide Orphan through the world of the social climbers.

POTEMKIN *(sings):*
> Everywhere you go, it is all the same.
> People, high or low, play the same old game.
> Learn to push and shove,
> Carve yourself a niche,

(continued on next page)

POTEMKIN *(continued):*
    And we'll wind up right on top
    With Mr. Rich.
POTEMKIN & RICH PEOPLE:
    So come with us
    And we will show
    You all the crooked
    Tricks we know.
    We'll steal and cheat
    And we'll connive
    But it's worth it all if we
       survive.

Major-domo welcomes beautiful people to Rich's party *(right)*. Potemkin steals invitations for himself and Orphan.

Exploring Rich's eerie house, Potemkin and Orphan come upon Angel (Susan Watson). Taking her for an apparition, they are awed *(left)*. But Angel is only a costumed entertainer, hired for the party. A flick of the zipper, and her costume disappears. Orphan lifts her down from the platform, admires her beauty *(below)*. But Angel is much too ambitious to waste time with a poor nobody like Orphan.

ANGEL *(joined by troupe; sings):*
    At twenty, you've had it!
    If you know what I mean—
    And you start aging very fast
    The day you reach thirteen!
    And so, before these golden days,
    These Lolita days, are through—
    I'm gonna get myself some Pucci
        pants,
    And here's what I'm gonna do:

    I'm gonna be—Somebody!
    Before they lay me in my grave!
    I'm gonna be—Somebody!
    So everyone'll be my slave! . . . . .
    I need—Somebody!
    Who'll buy me all the things I need
    And help me be—Somebody!
    Just like the people that I see—
    Makin' money on tee vee—
    Posin' in the magazines—
    Dancin' on the movie screen!

Rich (Ted Thurston) is brought forward by attendants. He expresses his restless mood in the form of a song *(below).*

RICH *(sings):*
    When I'm in a state of depression—
    Craving some fresh titillation—
    I just dial the world's finest intercom:
    Instantly they send exhibitionists
    Who perform the latest atrocities
    Meant to whet the deadliest of appetites.
    As they show each sexy spectacular,
    And erect each pulsating pyramid,
    Rising to a climax!
    I'm bored! Bored! Bored! *Bored!*
    I'm the richest man in the western world:
    There is nothing I can't afford!
    I'm the president of the stock exchange:
    I'm the chairman of every board!
    I've got everything that they say it takes:
    But no matter how much I hoard—
    I'm bored, bored, bored, bored!

All around him is wintertime and ice, Rich laments. Just then he hears a voice singing "The sun! The sun! The sun!" It is Orphan, with the Eye of God. Rich warns Orphan: "I haven't laughed in twenty-five years. I haven't cried in twenty-five years. I haven't felt anything—*not anything at all*— in almost a quarter of a century. So, do you know what I say? I say you can just take that Eye of God and shove it!" Potemkin intervenes.

Potemkin reminds Rich that he was *not* bored while he was talking to Orphan. Orphan asks Rich to give his orphanage back, and Rich challenges him: "Okay, make me feel." Potemkin advises Orphan to tell Rich all about his garden, try to arouse his interest. Orphan obliges.

ORPHAN *(sings):*
  My garden.
  My garden.
  Each seed conceals a mystery.
  My garden.
  My garden.

Each season has its history.
Reaching for the sun!
Dying when the time
Has come—
My Garden.

(continued on next page)

ORPHAN *(continued; sings):*
    My garden.
    How patiently it teaches me!
    Summertime—
    Wintertime—
    Are one—!

Rich exclaims: "Son of a bitch.
That's beautiful!" He demands several
encores, then admits: "I think—I'm
—about—to—feel—something!" The
crowd gasps as Rich sheds a tear,
and then another. Suddenly Rich
knows that Orphan has caused him to
feel by reminding him of himself as
he used to be, 30 years ago.

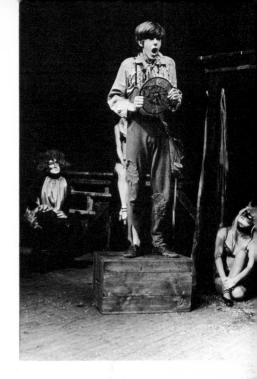

Rich tells of his past life, with violins *(below).* Once he was
young and carefree like Orphan, but then he became a millionaire
peddling imitations of all kinds, including artificial flowers. But
then time began to move ever faster, and youth disappeared.
Rich sings: "Ten minutes ago I was only a kid/I was kiddin'
around with the gals/Ten minutes ago I was John Barrymore/But
now look at me: covered with jowls!"

Four revelers join Rich *(right)* in his lament for his vanished youth. He becomes sadder and sadder, becomes suicidally depressed.

Orphan fights Rich's dark mood with "The sun! The sun!" Potemkin advises Orphan to attempt a love song with Angel—perhaps that will put Rich in the mood to grant Orphan's request.

Angel and Orphan prepare to stage a love song for Rich's benefit.

ANGEL *(sings):*
  This is a love song—
  Made up of moments.
  Made up of moments that
  We've never known together

  This is a love song
  Composed of longings—
  And secret daydreams where
  We swear to love forever. . . . .

  Since I first saw you,
  The song's been growing—
  And now that you are close
  It's almost overflowing!

  Come sing beside me.
  Come share my love song!
  Come join the chorus!

As the love song continues, Revelers bring in placards with green images of summer. Rich begins to feel spring stirring in his blood. He joins the love song. So does Orphan. Angel moves toward Orphan at first, but as the love song ends she rushes to Rich, who exclaims happily: "A beautiful young girl reaching out her arms to *me!*" Instantly Angel finds herself elegantly gowned and covered with jewels *(below)*.

Photo by Friedman-Abeles

Rich makes Potemkin master of revels to take place in Orphan's garden. All depart, leaving Orphan alone.

ORPHAN *(sings):*
A song of laughter
And sweet desire

A secret melody in me
That you inspire.

Potemkin comes back to deliver a special message: Angel wants to meet Orphan in the garden, early, before the others arrive. Orphan exits, singing joyously.

Potemkin tells the audience that in his career as a magician his big effect was sawing a woman in half: "I learned one little bit of wisdom, and this seems to be an appropriate time to pass it on to you—You can saw all you want to. But you never know how the trick's turned out till you see the second half."
    Curtain.

The Parable (continued)

The scene has changed from Rich's house to Orphan's garden, and other changes are taking place (Potemkin notes). The boy is losing some of his innocence. The girl is now covered in diamonds. Orphan and Angel meet as planned and agree politely that now they have their hearts' desire—she is Somebody and he will have his garden back (Angel will see to it). They sing "goodbye" to each other, as Rich comes in with "exterior decorators" who will turn this place into a Garden of Eden with artificial blooms. Rich and Angel are to play Adam and Eve, wearing fig leaves, and at midnight at the climax of the pageant they will eat the forbidden fruit.

RICH (sings to Angel):
It's you who makes me young
When I start feelin' old.
It's you who makes me sunny
When the autumn turns to gold.
And when the seasons change,
And the winter's on its way,
Then it's you who makes me dance,

Makes me celebrate each da—aa—ay
It's you—it's you—
Who makes me young!

Rich dances for joy (above) until he reaches the point of collapse. Meanwhile Orphan has noticed that Angel shivered when Rich touched her.

"Exterior Decorators" *(left)* have done their work—the garden is overdressed in false flowers. Orphan complains that they don't belong in "his" garden.

ORPHAN: My garden is here. Underneath the earth.

RICH: Prove it.

ORPHAN: I don't have to prove it. When the snows melt, the seeds I planted will come up—thousands of them.

RICH: What makes you think so?

ORPHAN: Because it's natural.

RICH: Natural?—It'll happen because it's "Natural?" *(And Rich laughs. He laughs so hard, in fact, that tears come streaming down his face.)* My! My! *(Wipes his eyes.)* Thank you, my boy. Thank you. I haven't had a laugh like that since I divorced my wife.—Oh, me! *(Blows his nose.)* Why you homeless, half-wit, orphan idiot. All I have to do is raise my finger and all those thousands of seeds can be ripped up by machines! This garden is mine.

ORPHAN *(aghast):* But you promised.

RICH: I've changed my mind. Besides, I've got a better present for you: knowledge. Experience. The world! You don't like my values? All right. Make your own values. You don't like my falsies? Okay. Make your own. Get rid of the machines if you think you can do it. Live off flowers and love. Wonderful! But in the meantime . . . this stage is mine!

ORPHAN: No!

RICH: Yes it is. I've worked for it. I've sweated my ass off. This is my set. My scene. My night!

Rich, being prepared for the pageant *(right),* directs Potemkin to tear up the garden with machines and as for "Mr. 'Natural'—kick him out on his ass!"

Orphan appeals to Potemkin, reminds him of his promise to help. Potemkin tells Orphan he was once a holy man. "And then one day I found out that God is dead. So you know what I did? I looked at the world around me and I said O.K."

POTEMKIN (sings):
    The earth is being eaten by machines.
    Not my problem. . . . .
    Taking "speed" can rearrange your
        genes.
    Not my problem. . . . .

    I've become a humble bum—
    A drop-out from humanity.
    You may think my morals stink,

But at least I keep my sanity. . . . .
(Slower and more menacing.)
Somebody screams in terror on the
    street.
Not my problem. . . . .
People die of hunger; I repeat:
Not my problem. . . . .

God is dead
That's what they said.
Done in by Darwin, Marx and Freud.
Free are we from deity.
Of course it sort of leaves a little void.

I used to care about my fellow man.
But now—hurrah—I'm free.
And it's simply not my problem!

Orphan fights back with the "Eye of God." The machines retreat. Orphan resolves to fight Rich for the girl too.

ORPHAN (sings):
    Fifty million years ago
    Something in the sea—
    Reached above the water
        eagerly!
        (continued on next page)

ORPHAN *(continued; sings):*
  Fifty thousand years ago—
  Something on the land
  Suddenly decided it could stand!

  Does this lonely road just go to
    nowhere?
  Can it be that there's no reason why?
  When in spite of all the strife
  And the endless dying—
  Life keeps reaching higher
  For the sky!

  Fifty seconds from right now—
  Anything can be!

I'm the future.
Please—believe in me!

Having been carefully prepared for the pageant by body-builders and beauticians, Rich believes he looks young again. Helping to deceive him, Orphan poses as though he were a mirror image of Rich's new youthfulness *(below)*.

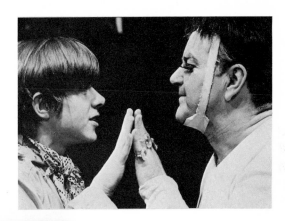

The pageant takes place. In the Saturnalia *(left)* a Mock-King presides over a debauch. Within the pageant's action, Orphan, disguised, makes love to Angel, and she responds while pretending it is Rich who has her attention. Finally it is time for Rich and Angel to play their scene as Adam and Eve.

Angel, costumed as Eve, takes her place in the garden.

ANGEL *(sings):*
    Under the tree,
    Under the tree,
    Down where the leaves billow
        —billow—
    Under the tree,
    Under the tree,
    There is a green pillow—
        pillow—

    I know the way!
    Follow me, follow me.
    Don't be afraid;
    Follow me, follow me.
    Give me your hand.
    Undo my hair,
    Open my heart,
    Take me! Take me!

In a dance of animals, Orphan, masked, seduces Angel before Rich's eyes. When Orphan takes off his animal mask, Rich realizes he's been tricked.

Before Rich can act, Potemkin gives the signal for a ritual battle between winter and summer. While this takes place, Rich drags Angel away from Orphan. But as summer overcomes winter in the ritual, Revelers in white masks bring in mirrors in which Rich sees himself for what he is, an old man whose time of youth is over. Father Time's clock strikes twelve. Rich is destroyed.

The Revelers line up behind Angel and Orphan, who peer at the audience.

ORPHAN: What's out there? Do you know? Out there in the streets? Outside the theater?

ANGEL: The world. The *real* world.

ORPHAN *(squinting his eyes):* It's dark, isn't it?

ANGEL: It's grey.

ORPHAN: The air is being poisoned.

ANGEL: Half of the people are starving.

ORPHAN: We're destroying the other animals.

ANGEL: People don't know what to believe in any more. *(Pause. She looks at him.)* I'll never be Somebody, will I? *(He shakes his head. She smiles sadly. . . . .)*

ORPHAN: The garden is gone, isn't it? *(She nods. He looks around.)* I'm going to miss it, in a way. You could always count on it. You know? *(Drumbeat. It grows darker.)*

ANGEL: Are you afraid?

ORPHAN: Yes.

ANGEL: So am I.

Gravely, the boy and girl join hands and kneel in front of Potemkin, who blesses them: "In this time of cold and darkness/In this terrifying night/In this seemingly endless winter/Let us pray that they'll be all right." Orphan and Angel exit up the aisle of the theater, as the Revelers line up behind Potemkin *(below)*, now appearing without the masks they've worn in previous scenes, carrying images of the full sun.

The Celebration

POTEMKIN & REVELERS *(sing):*
Some people say
That today is the day
When the cold will come
And never go away—
When the bird will fly—
The wind will blow—
But something deep inside me says it can't be so.
I want to celebrate! Celebrate!
Make a celebration!

I want to celebrate! Celebrate!
Savor each sensation. . . . .
Every day! Every day!
Make a celebration—
Every day!
Celebration!

And as they all hold up their images on the poles, the large sun which has reappeared in eclipse above the platform moves out of the eclipse and becomes the full sun. And the play is done.

O
O
O

1776

A Musical in One Act

BASED ON A CONCEPTION OF SHERMAN EDWARDS

BOOK BY PETER STONE

MUSIC AND LYRICS BY SHERMAN EDWARDS

Cast and credits appear on page 410

O
O
O

PETER STONE was born in 1930 in Los Angeles, the son of the late John Stone, movie producer and writer. He took his B.A. degree at Bard and his M.F.A. at Yale Drama School. The first 12 years of his writing career were spent in France, where he contributed to all media including TV. His first Hollywood screen play was Charade, *followed by* Mirage, Arabesque, *and* Father Goose, *for which he won an Oscar. He is also the recipient of an Emmy Award for his work on the TV series* The Defenders.

Stone, who is married, continues to divide his time between stage and screen. He wrote the librettos for two previous Broadway musicals, Kean *and* Skyscraper, *and the movie version of* Sweet Charity. *His new project following* 1776 *was the movie* Skin Game.

SHERMAN EDWARDS (composer and lyricist) is a New Yorker, born in 1919 and educated at New York University and Cornell, where he majored in and developed his keen interest in history. After serving in the Air Force in

World War II, Edwards taught history at James Monroe High School and also pursued a distinguished career in music as a song writer ("Wonderful, Wonderful," "See You in September," "Johnny Get Angry," "Broken Hearted Melody"), as a pianist (with Benny Goodman, Tommy Dorsey, Louis Armstrong and other jazz greats) and as an actor (in Pins and Needles and My Sister Eileen). His love for both history and music led him to the conception for 1776 as early as 10 years ago, and now it has materialized on Broadway as his highly successful musical theater writing debut. Edwards is married to a ballet dancer, Ingrid Secretan, and they have two children.

INTRODUCTION BY THE LIBRETTIST AND COMPOSER-LYRICIST

The concept of *1776* was brought to me by its composer-lyricist, Sherman Edwards, who had been working toward its realization for almost a decade.

Upon hearing that he was seriously proposing a Broadway musical dealing with the signing of the Declaration of Independence, I was not terribly anxious to hear more. But producer Stuart Ostrow persuaded me to listen, not only to the songs Sherman had written, but to a detailed account of this historical occasion and the events leading to it as Sherman had researched it.

I was enthralled. The suspense, the intrigue, the courage and compromise, the richness of the men, their vagaries, vanities and fears, the issues and convictions motivating the thirteen colonies, the factions within them, the differences between them, their individual pride and their collective heritage—all of it held me spellbound for over three hours.

And then I was appalled. Why hadn't I known any of this? I had gone through grade and high school, through college and graduate degrees—I had enjoyed history and had absorbed all that was offered—and still I knew nearly nothing; it was all a revelation!

And then it occurred to me that *nobody* knew anything about our national legend. Why? Could it somehow be subversive? Might it corrupt children? Is it possible it would undermine the Republic? I am still waiting for the answers to those questions.

1776 was conceived as entertainment. But if it is indeed entertaining, it is, I believe, more than the songs and the jokes and the theatricality that make it so—it is the surprise of discovering that our founding fathers were men of flesh and blood and not cardboard, that our history is fascinating—and that the events of July 4, 1776 mean more to us during these troubled times than most of us could ever imagine.

PETER STONE

Regarding a successful work in retrospect is always a happy luxury. The quarrying, the polishing, the setting of ideas, words and music is done. The total effort is made.

In the case of *1776* re-observed, the moment of emergence provides an even lovelier indulgence: to come out of the "cave of creation"—not a lonely place, certainly, not with those characters of history who became alarmingly alive as they demanded attention, drained one of energy, invaded sleep, sought sympathy, understanding, interpretation—no, not lonely, but still a place of being alone; and then to emerge into the arms of agent Flora Roberts, producer Stuart Ostrow, librettist Peter Stone, director Peter Hunt—people of talent and integrity who dedicated themselves completely to the original conception.

It's a pleasant indulgence to remember working with them and with the eternally young Jo Mielziner, one of the giants of theater; with Patricia Zipprodt, so sensitive to the psychology of the characters through fabric, color and cut; with Onna White who created great dash with dignity—and with the ladies and gentlemen of *1776* who understood the uniqueness of the project and gave it a splendid united quality.

SHERMAN EDWARDS

Time: May, June and July 1776

Place: The Chamber and an anteroom of the Continental Congress, a mall, high street and Thomas Jefferson's room, in Philadelphia; and certain reaches of John Adams' mind.

Scene 1

SYNOPSIS: Part of the setting juts forward in front of the closed curtain. Out onto this steps John Adams—peppery, irate, declaring himself chagrined at the situation this 8th day of May, 1776. Adams' own Massachusetts constituents have stood up to British soldiers on more than one occasion. But this Congress, now in session in Philadelphia, won't even debate the subject of Independence openly: "Good God, what in hell are they waiting for!"

The curtain rises suddenly to reveal, behind the cursing Adams, the representatives of the thirteen colonies seated in their places in the Chamber of the Second Continental Congress. (A group of 20 delegates, including Adams, symbolizes the much larger number who actually took part in these events.)

It's very hot in Philadelphia. The delegates are sweating, and they let John Adams know how much they resent his gadfly insistence on pleading his cause at such a time, making them feel even more uncomfortable.

CONGRESS *(sings):*
Sit down, John!
Sit down, John!
For God's sake John, sit down! . . . . .
VOICE:

Someone ought to open up a window!
CONGRESS:
   It's ninety degrees!
   Have mercy, John, please!
   It's hot as hell in
   Philadel-phia!
TWO VOICES:
   Someone ought to open up a window!
JOHN:
   I say vote "Yes!"
   Vote "Yes!"
   Vote for Independency!
CONGRESS VOICES:
   Someone ought to open up a window!
JOHN:
   I say vote "Yes!"
CONGRESS:
   Sit down, John! . . . . .
   Oh, for God's sake, John,
   Sit down!
        They freeze.
JOHN *(spoken; roaring): Good God!!* Consider yourselves fortunate that
you have John Adams to abuse, for no sane man would tolerate it!
   CONGRESS *(action resumes; sings):*
   John, you're a bore!
   We've heard this before!
   Now, for God's sake, John,
   Sit down!!

Congress continues to urge John Adams to desist, but Adams declares he
will never stop pleading for Independence. Congress has been in session a
year and has done nothing. John strides downstage and lifts his voice to God
in an appeal to get Congress moving, expressed in a song.
   The song is interrupted by a discussion between John Hancock, who is pre-
siding over this session as President of the Congress, and Judge James Wilson
of Pennsylvania over a $20 claim for a dead mule.

   JOHN: *Good God!! (Sings.)*
   They may sit here for years and years in
   Philadelphia . . . !
   These indecisive grenadiers of
   Philadelphia!
   They can't agree on what is right or wrong
   Or what is good or bad.
   I'm convinced the only purpose
   This Congress ever had . . . was to

Gather here, specifically,
To drive John Adams mad!

You see . . . we
Piddle, twiddle and resolve.
Not one damned thing do we solve.
Piddle, twiddle and resolve
Nothing's ever solved in
Foul, fetid, fuming, foggy, filthy . . .
Philadelphi—

John's song is interrupted as his wife Abigail *("a handsome woman of 32")* appears on the stage as an embodiment of his imagination.

Abigail orders John to get on with Independency and come home where he is sorely needed. John wonders why Abigail has not sent him the saltpetre he requested for making gunpowder. They will make and send the saltpetre, Abigail tells her husband, if John will arrange to send pins to the ladies of Massachusetts, where there is a shortage. John's fond dream of his wife Abigail dissolves. Congress once again orders him: "Sit down, John!"

Scene 2

Outdoors on a mall, John joins Benjamin Franklin, who is sitting on a bench having his portrait painted. John continues to fret about Congress's do-nothing attitude.

JOHN: . . . . . With one hand they can raise an army, dispatch one of their own to lead it and cheer the news from Bunker's Hill—while with the other they wave an olive branch begging the King for a happy and permanent reconciliation. Why damn it, Fat George has declared us in rebellion—why in bloody hell can't *they?!*

FRANKLIN: John, really! You talk as if Independence were the rule! *It's never been done before!!* No colony has ever broken from the parent stem in the history of the world!

JOHN: Damnit, Franklin, you make us sound treasonous!

FRANKLIN: Do I? *(Thinking.)* Treason—"Treason is a charge invented by winners as an excuse for hanging the losers."

JOHN: I have more to do than stand here listening to you quote yourself.

FRANKLIN: No, that was a new one!

JOHN: Damnit, Franklin, we're at war!

FRANKLIN: To defend ourselves, nothing more. *We* expressed our displeasure, the English moved against us and *we,* in turn, have resisted. Now our fellow Congressmen want to effect a reconciliation *before* it becomes a war.

JOHN: Reconciliation, my ass! The *people* want Independence!

FRANKLIN: The people have read Mr. Paine's *Common Sense.* I doubt the Congress has.

He studies John.

John—why don't you give it up? Nobody listens to you—you're obnoxious and disliked.

JOHN: I'm not promoting John Adams—I'm promoting Independence.

FRANKLIN: Evidently they cannot help connecting the two.

Franklin is suggesting that they find someone less controversial to make the proposal in Congress. At this moment Richard Henry Lee *("a tall, loose-jointed Virginia aristocrat of 45")* comes onto the scene. Franklin outlines the situation: at present only Massachusetts, New Hampshire and Delaware have declared for Independence. Virginia favors it, but the formal resolution hasn't yet passed the House of Burgesses in Williamsburg. Would there be a Virginian of sufficient stature and influence to get the resolution passed and make the proposal in Congress? . . .

Lee jumps at the suggestion, adopting it for his own. Virginia, the state that produced the military commander-in-chief, George Washington (a drum-roll accompanies the mention of this name), will make the proposal for Independence.

Richard Henry Lee puffs up into song about the power and influence of the Lee family of Virginia.

LEE *(sings):*

. . . . . And may my horses turn to glue
If I can't deliver up to you
A resolution—on Independency!

For I am F.F.V.
That is, the first family
In the sovereign colony of Virginia.
The F.F.V.
The oldest family
In the oldest colony in America!
And, may the British burn my land
If I can't deliver to your hand
A resolution—on Independency!

Y'see it's—Here a Lee
          There a Lee
          Everywhere a Lee, a Lee!

FRANKLIN and LEE *(alternating):*

Social—Lee!
Political—Lee!
Financial—Lee!
Natural—Lee!
*In*ternal—Lee!
*Ex*ternal-Lee!
*Fra*ternal—Lee!

E-ternal—Lee!
> *Together.*

The F.F.V.
The first family
In the sovereign colony of Virginia!

Lee departs on his mission, in a strut that is a continuation of his song-and-dance. John is dubious about this strategy, but Franklin is encouraged.

Scene 3

In the Chamber, the calendar now reads June 7. Andrew McNair, the custodian, is readying the room for the day's session with the help of a "Leather Apron," an assistant. Each of the thirteen colonial delegations has its appointed place in this room, with President John Hancock's desk upstage and elevated above the level of the others. Behind it on the wall is a voting tally board listing the name of each colony opposite three headings: YEA, NAY and ABSTAIN.

Dr. Lyman Hall of Georgia enters—he is 55 years old and new to the Congress. The custodian directs him to his place at stage left near the representatives of the two Carolinas.

Stephen Hopkins of Rhode Island enters—he is *"a thin, round-shouldered man of 70, wearing a black suit, black Quaker hat and his gray hair at shoulder length."* He shouts for his rum. McNair goes off grudgingly to fetch it.

Edward Rutledge of South Carolina—*"a young, handsome, dandified aristocrat of 26"*—enters. Meeting Dr. Hall, he remarks airily that Georgia will vote with South Carolina, but Dr. Hall tells Rutledge gently that he is uninstructed, he may vote his own conscience on Independence. More earnestly, Rutledge tells him: "Dr. Hall—the deep South speaks with one voice. It is traditional—even more, it is historical."

Enter the Delaware delegation: Caesar Rodney, *"48, thin and pale, wears a green scarf around his face, covering some infirmity;"* George Read, *"43, small and round, speaks with a high voice,"* and Col. Thomas McKean, *"42, tall and florid, has a booming voice decorated with a Scottish brogue."* Rodney and McKean detest their fellow-delegate Read and take no pains to hide their feelings.

Other Congressmen enter: Lewis Morris and Robert Livingston of New York, Roger Sherman of Connecticut, Joseph Hewes of North Carolina, Samuel Chase of Maryland, Josiah Bartlett of New Hampshire and others including, almost unnoticed, Thomas Jefferson of Virginia, *"33, six feet three, with copper-colored hair."*

Rodney takes Dr. Hall aside, not to talk to him of Independence, of which he is one of the most ardent advocates, but to ask to consult him later on his physical condition. They are joined by two of the Pennsylvania delegates: John Dickinson, *"44, a thin, hawkish man, not without elegance,"* and James Wilson, *"33, a bespectacled, cautious little sycophant."*

The third Pennsylvania delegate enters—Benjamin Franklin, now suffering from an attack of gout. He is soon joined by John Adams, and: *"It is now evident that the colors and styles of the various costumes change gradually from colony to colony—from the fancy greens and golds of the Deep South to the somber blacks of New England."*

John Adams is impatient for Lee's return; meanwhile he is making an effort to keep silent, even though Dickinson baits him.

> *Dickinson turns to Wilson and addresses him in a loud voice, for all to hear.*

DICKINSON: Tell me, James—how do you explain the strange, monumental quietude that Congress has been treated to these past thirty days?

Everyone, including John, has turned to listen.

Has the ill-wind of Independence finally blown itself out?

WILSON: If you ask me—

DICKINSON: For myself, I must confess that a month free from New England noise is more therapeutic than a month in the country! Don't you agree, James?

WILSON: Well, I—

DICKINSON *(turning):* Mr. Adams—pray look for your voice, sir—it cannot be far and God knows we need the entertainment in this Congress!

> *Laughter from his fellow-conservatives. Everyone turns to Adams, who is trembling with rage.*

FRANKLIN: Congratulations, John—you've just made your greatest contribution to Independence—you kept your flap shut!

JOHN: One more day . . . !

President John Hancock sits at his desk and calls the session to order. His first action is to cut Hopkins off from the rum supply for three days—the Rhode Island delegate has been abusing this Congressional privilege.

The Congress's pedantic secretary, Charles Thomson, notes that the whole New Jersey delegation is absent. (Franklin's son is Royal Governor of New Jersey; the two are no longer in touch.) Young Jefferson reports on the weather (hot) and tells President Hancock of his intention to go home to his wife in Virginia this very night on "family business."

> *A uniformed courier, dusty from his long ride, enters and approaches Thomson, removing a communique from his pouch. He tosses it onto the secretary's desk and leaves, wearily.*

THOMSON *(ringing his bell):* From the Commander, Army of the United Colonies; in New York, dispatch number one thousand one hundred and thirty-seven—

MCNAIR: Sweet Jesus!

THOMSON *(reading):* —"To the Honorable Congress, John Hancock, President. Dear Sir: It is with grave apprehension that I have learned this day of the sailing, from Halifax, Nova Scotia, of a considerable force of British troops

in the company of foreign mercenaries and under the command of General Sir William Howe. There can be no doubt that their destination is New York, for to take and hold this city and the Hudson Valley beyond would serve to separate New England from the other colonies permitting both sections to be crushed in turn. Sadly, I see no way of stopping them at the present time as my army is absolutely falling apart, my military chest is totally exhausted, my Commissary General has strained his credit to the last, my Quartermaster has no food, no arms, no ammunition, and my troops are in a state of near mutiny! I pray God some relief arrives before the armada but fear it will not. Y'r ob'd't—
> *Drum roll.*
—G. Washington."
> *During the brief silence that follows, Thomson shrugs and files the dispatch.*
MCKEAN: Mr. President—!
HANCOCK: Colonel McKean—
MCKEAN: Surely we've managed to promote the gloomiest man on this continent to the head of our troops. Those dispatches are the most depressing accumulation of disaster, doom and despair in the entire annals of military history!
HANCOCK *(pounding his gavel):* Please, Colonel McKean—it's too hot. . . . .

Just as Bartlett is introducing an austerity resolution, Lee arrives on the scene. After conveying to Thomas Jefferson his wife's wishes that he would come home, Lee reads the proposal which Virginia has prepared and ratified: "Resolved: that these united colonies are (and of a right ought to be) free and independent states, that they are absolved from all allegiance to the British Crown, and that all political connection between them and the state of Great Britain is (and ought to be) totally dissolved!"

Adams seconds the proposal. Dickinson moves that this question of Independence "be postponed—indefinitely," and his fellow Pennsylvanian, Wilson, automatically seconds his motion. But a colony cannot second its own motion, so the "weasel" from Delaware, Read, seconds it.

Hancock orders those who are for debating Independence to vote "Yea," and those for postponement to vote "Nay." McNair takes his place at the tally board and records each vote as it is announced by Secretary Thomson, as follows:

New Hampshire	YEA		
Massachusetts	YEA		
Rhode Island	YEA		
Connecticut	YEA		
New York			ABSTAIN
New Jersey			(Absent)
Pennsylvania		NAY	
Delaware	YEA		

Maryland	NAY
Virginia	YEA
North Carolina	NAY
South Carolina	NAY
Georgia	NAY

Thus, by one vote the motion to debate Independence is approved. During the voting, some of the delegates had explained their colonies' positions as they cast their ballots. Adams had tried to make a speech and was shouted down. Connecticut had been witholding its "Yea" vote until some state outside of New England moved Independence. In casting New York's vote, Lewis Morris had noted that his state "abstains—courteously" but with no further explanation. North Carolina had yielded to South Carolina, and Rutledge had explained the South's position: the South has considered Independence but, unlike New England, is not impatient for it and will wait and see. If all the other states want it, South Carolina will not stand in their way. Rutledge voted "Nay" and North Carolina followed suit. Hall of Georgia had declared himself for Independence but voted against the motion because he felt the people he represents would be against it.

Hopkins of Rhode Island had been out of the room when the roll was called and returned just in time to cast the deciding "Yea" vote, whereupon Hancock restored his rum privilege.

Adams has won his point at last—Independence is to be debated in the Congress. Dickinson is the first to speak. He declares himself proud to be part of the British Empire, part of its glorious history. Adams reminds him of England's "cruel repressions and abolished rights," and Dickinson responds angrily.

DICKINSON: . . . . . Some men are patriots—like General Washington—and some are anarchists—like Mr. Paine—some, even, are internationalists—like Dr. Franklin. But you, sir—you are merely an—a-gi-ta-tor—disturbing the peace, creating disorder, endangering the public welfare—and for what? Your petty little personal complaints—your taxes are too high. Well, sir—so are mine. Come, come, Mr. Adams—if you have grievances—and I'm sure you have—our present system must provide a gentler means of redressing them short of—
> Suddenly his manner changes as he brings his fist down on the desk with a crash.
—revolution! (Wheeling to the Congress.) That's what he wants—nothing short of it will satisfy him! Violence! Rebellion! Treason!! Now, Mr. Adams— are these the acts of Englishmen?

JOHN: Not Englishmen, Dickinson—Americans!

DICKINSON (again pounding the desk): No, sir! Englishmen!!

FRANKLIN (he's been asleep, his chin on his chest; now an eye opens): Please, Mr. Dickinson—but must you start banging? How is a man to sleep?
> Laughter.

DICKINSON: Forgive me, Dr. Franklin, but must you start speaking? How is a man to stay awake?

Laughter.

We'll promise to be quiet, sir—I'm sure everyone prefers that you remain asleep.

FRANKLIN: If I'm to hear myself called an Englishman, sir, then I assure you I'd prefer I'd remained asleep.

DICKINSON: What's so terrible about being called an Englishman? The English don't seem to mind.

FRANKLIN: Nor would I, were I given the full rights of an Englishman. But to call me one *without* those rights is like calling an ox a bull—he's thankful for the honor but he'd much rather have restored what's rightfully his.

Laughter, Franklin laughing the longest.

DICKINSON *(finally):* When did you first notice they were missing, sir?

Laughter.

Under England's mishandling of her colonies (Franklin continues), America has developed a new breed of men, a new nationality which requires a new nation.

Adams accuses Dickinson of being strongly concerned with protecting his own property. Dickinson is not ashamed to admit it, and he accuses Massachusetts of trying to drag them all into its private quarrel with the King.

Rutledge reminds the gathering that it is South Carolina's wish to be truly free, governed neither by England nor New England. He proposes "a nation of sovereign states—united for our mutual protection but separate for our individual pursuits."

Chase of Maryland advises that they wait and see how General Washington makes out—if he wins, this Congress can declare anything it wishes. Adams argues that the army needs a cause, a new flag under which to conquer, *now*.

Dickinson labels John Adams "madman" and Adams retaliates with "Pennsylvania proprietors—cool, considerate men. You keep to the rear of every issue . . . . . coward!" Dickinson and Adams come to blows. They are separated by Rodney, who collapses from the effort. Dr. Hall goes to Rodney's side, looks under the bandage and sees that he is suffering grievously from cancer.

Rodney decides it is time to go home to die. McKean will escort him and return as soon as possible. Rodney departs, begging Adams' pardon for leaving behind a divided Delaware.

Now Rutledge calls for a vote on Independence, stepping to the tally board and changing Delaware's vote from "Yea" to "Nay" (with Rodney and McKean absent, only Read is left behind to cast Delaware's vote). This change would defeat Independence, perhaps once and for all. Trying to gain time, Franklin asks that the Virginia resolution be read aloud once more.

As the secretary re-reads the resolution, the Rev. Jonathan Witherspoon, *"a lean, ascetic clergyman of 54,"* comes into the Chamber. Here, at last, is the representative of New Jersey (he has news for Franklin that his Royalist son has been deposed, arrested and transported to a Connecticut prison for his own safety). New Jersey has undergone a change of policy and is now prepared to vote in *favor* of Independence.

With the addition of New Jersey's vote, Independence is now assured of at least a tie, which Adams expects to be broken in his favor by President Hancock. But Dickinson moves that "any vote in favor of Independence must be unanimous." He argues that it would be wrong for any colony to be "torn from its mother country without its consent."

On the question of unanimity, their vote is divided six to six, with New York once against abstaining "courteously."

HANCOCK: Mr. Morris—why does New York constantly abstain? Why doesn't New York simply stay in New York? Very well—the vote is tied.
He covers his eyes for a moment.
The principles of Independence have no greater advocate in Congress than its President—and that's the reason I must join those who vote *for unanimity.*
As the Congress reacts, stunned, John jumps up, horrified.
JOHN: Good God! What're y'doing, John? You've sunk us!
HANCOCK: Hear me out. Don't you see that any colony who opposes Independence will be forced to fight on the side of England—that we'll be setting brother against brother—that our new nation will carry as its emblem the mark of Cain? I can see no other way—either we walk together or together we must stay where we are.

Before Secretary Thomson can proceed to record an obviously non-unanimous vote on the Virginia resolution (and thus defeat it, perhaps forever), John leaps up and declares a need for a postponement. How can they vote on Independence until their motives, goals, etc., are spelled out in writing? They need a Declaration of some sort. Adams is supported by Franklin and Jefferson, who declares that Congress ought to "place before mankind the common sense of the subject—in terms so plain and firm as to command their assent."

The motion to postpone is again tied six to six, with New York again abstaining (Morris explains this time that their legislature has never instructed them). Hancock rules in favor of a postponement until a Declaration can be drafted. Adams, Franklin, Livingston of New York and Sherman of Connecticut are appointed a committee to draft the Declaration, along with Thomas Jefferson who protests mightily that he wants to go home to his wife. He is placed on the committee nevertheless.

Congress adjourns this session, and Adams holds an immediate meeting of the committee as soon as the others have left. They argue—in song—about who is to write the Declaration.

FRANKLIN *(sings):*
Mr. Adams, I say you should write it
To your legal mind and brilliance we defer . . .

JOHN:
>   Is that so!
>   Well, if I'm the one to do it
>   They'll run their quill pens through it
>   I'm obnoxious and disliked, you know that, sir!

FRANKLIN *(spoken):* Yes, I know.

JOHN:
>   Then, I say you should write it, Franklin, yes, you!

FRANKLIN *(sings):*
>   . . . . . Mr. Adams!—
>   But—Mr. Adams!
>   The things I write
>   Are only light extemporanea . . .
>   I won't put politics on paper
>   It's a mania . . .
>   So, I refuse to use the pen . . . in Pennsylvania!

Sherman and Livingston sing their objections in similar style: Sherman cannot write, and Livingston is going home to New York to celebrate the birth of a new son.

All eyes turn to Jefferson. He protests that he is eager to go home to his wife. Adams quotes from a Jefferson pamphlet on the "Necessity of Taking Up Arms" to demonstrate the young Virginian's talent with words. "Will you be a patriot," Adams challenges Jefferson, "or a lover?!"

JEFFERSON: A lover!

JOHN: No!

JEFFERSON *(sings):*
>   But I burn, Mister "A"!

JOHN *(sings):*
>   So do I, Mister "J"!
>   *Everything stops.*

JEFFERSON *(spoken): You—?!*

SHERMAN: You do?

FRANKLIN: John!

LIVINGSTON: Who'd'a thought it?

JOHN *(sings):*
>   Mr. Jefferson
>   Dear Mr. Jefferson
>   I'm only forty-one,
>   I still have my virility!
>   And I can romp through Cupid's grove
>   With great agility!
>   But life is more than
>   Sexual combustability!

OTHERS:
  Bust-a-bility!
  Bust-a-bility!
  Com-bust-a-bil-i—
JOHN *(spoken):* Quiet! *(Sings.)*
  Now, you'll write it, Mister "J"!
JEFFERSON *(six feet three):*
  Who will make me, Mister "A"?
JOHN *(five feet eight):* I . . . !
JEFFERSON: You . . . ?!
JOHN: Yes . . . !
JEFFERSON: How . . . ?!
JOHN *(spoken):* By physical force if necessary! It's your duty—*your duty, damnit!!*
JEFFERSON *(sings):*
  Mr. Adams!
  Damn you, Mr. Adams!
  You're obnoxious and disliked,
  That cannot be denied
      This is agreed to by all.
  Once again you stand between me
  And my lovely bride!

Adams, furious, thrusts a pen into Jefferson's hand and tells him to do as he likes with it. The others leave Jefferson alone studying the pen.

Scene 4

In his room, Jefferson is making false starts on the Declaration, writing, crumpling the page, throwing it away, toying with his violin. Adams and Franklin join him to see how he is doing. Adams picks up one of the crumpled pages and reads: " 'There comes a time in the lives of men when it becomes necessary to advance from that subordination in which they have hitherto remained—' —this is terrible." The Declaration is not even begun.

Outside on the street a cloaked woman appears; she enters Jefferson's house. It is his wife, Martha Jefferson, *"a lovely girl of 27"* who even makes Franklin sit up and take notice.

Jefferson and his wife fall into each other's arms at once, ignoring the others. John explains to Franklin that he sent for Martha Jefferson to join her husband and encourage him in his vital task.

Franklin and Adams exit, leaving the lovers in the privacy of their embrace, and soon Franklin departs for a rendezvous of his own, leaving John by himself. As it grows dark, John conjures up his vision of his wife Abigail.

JOHN: I'm very lonely, Abigail.
ABIGAIL: Are you, John? Then as long as you were sending for wives, why didn't you send for your own?

JOHN: Don't be unreasonable, Abigail.

ABIGAIL: Now I'm unreasonable—you must add that to your list.

JOHN: List?

ABIGAIL: The catalogue of my faults you included in your last letter.

JOHN: They were fondly intended, madame!

ABIGAIL: That I play at cards badly?

JOHN: A compliment!

ABIGAIL: That my posture is crooked?

JOHN: An endearment!

ABIGAIL: That I read, write and think too much?

JOHN: An irony!

ABIGAIL: That I am pigeon-toed?

JOHN: Ah, well, there you have me, Abby—I'm afraid you *are* pigeon-toed. *(Smiling.)* Come to Philadelphia, Abigail—please come.

But she can't. The children have the measles and the Braintree farm is in trouble. They sing to each other of their mutual loneliness: she is living like a nun, he like a monk.

ABIGAIL *(sings):*
>Write to me with sentimental effusion
>Let me revel in romantic illusion.

JOHN:
>Do y' still smell of vanilla and spring air?
>And is my fav'rite lover's pillo' still firm and fair?

ABIGAIL:
>What was there, John!
>Still is there, John!
>Come soon as you can to my cloister
>I've forgotten the feel of your hand.

JOHN:
>Soon, madame, we shall walk in Cupid's grove together . . .

JOHN & ABIGAIL:
>And we'll fondly survey that promised land!

Their song ends with Abigail's promise to remember about the saltpetre for gunpowder.

The daylight returns, and with it comes Franklin, joining Adams outside Jefferson's house. The shutters are still closed. Adams remarks that "It's positively indecent!"

FRANKLIN: Oh, John—they're young and they're in love.

JOHN: Not them, Franklin—us! Standing out here— *(Gesturing vaguely at the shuttered room.)* —waiting for them to—I mean, what will people think?

FRANKLIN: Don't worry, John—the history books will clean it up.

JOHN: It doesn't matter—I won't appear in the history books, anyway—

only you. *(Thinks about it.)* Franklin did this, Franklin did that, Franklin did some other damned thing—Franklin smote the ground and out sprang George Washington, fully grown and on his horse—Franklin then electrified him with his miraculous lightning rod and the three of them—Franklin, Washington *and* the horse—conducted the entire revolution all by themselves.

FRANKLIN *(a pause):* I like it!

Martha Jefferson opens the shutters, and the two men introduce themselves. Martha joins them in the street. They talk of her husband. All agree, Jefferson is not a talker. How does he express himself to his wife?

MARTHA *(sings):*
>He plays the violin
>He tucks it right under his chin . . .
>And he bows . . .
>Oh, he bows . . .
>For he knows . . .
>Yes, he knows . . . That it's . . .
>
>Heigh, heigh, heigh diddle-diddle . . .
>'Twixt my heart, Tom, and his fiddle . . .
>My strings are unstrung . . .
>Heigh-heigh-heigh-heigh-igh-igh . . .
>Heigh . . . I am undone!

Sometimes Martha and Tom dance, too (she explains in song), persuading first Franklin and then Adams to waltz a step or two with her.

Jefferson comes out of the house carrying his fiddle. He escorts Martha back toward the house, as Adams snatches a piece of paper stuck in the bow. Tom and Martha disappear. Adams reads the paper: "Dear Mr. Adams: I am taking my wife back to bed. Kindly go away. Y'r ob'd't, T. Jefferson."

Adams and Franklin are left in the street to sing another chorus of the violin song.

Scene 5

In the Chamber, Congress is in session. The calendar reads "June 22." The secretary, Thomson, is reading a dull list of committees. Many of the delegates are paying no attention, chatting among themselves.

John Adams strides in and glances at the tally board. There are, he reminds Franklin, six "Nays" to be won over, and without delay. It seems impossible, but they must get to work—"one foot in front of the other."

They start with Delaware. McKean is back from escorting Rodney home. They urge him to work on the "weasel" Read to change his vote. McKean feels this is a futile effort, with so many other "Nays" registered, but on Adams's urging he agrees to see what he can do about Read's vote.

Adams takes on the assignment of persuading Chase of Maryland, while

Franklin, whose Pennsylvania delegation consists of himself, Dickinson and Wilson, goes to work on Dickinson's yes-man.

FRANKLIN (*drawing Wilson aside*): Mr. Wilson, it's time to assert yourself. When you were a judge, how in hell did you ever make a decision?

WILSON: The decisions I made were all based on legality and precedence. But there is no legality here—and certainly no precedent.

FRANKLIN: Because it's a new idea, you clot! We'll be setting our own precedent!

Adams is faring no better with Chase, who complains that George Washington's army is falling apart; were it otherwise, Maryland would favor Independence. Adams tries to reassure him that the army is in good shape, but his argument is belied by the reappearance of Washington's dusty courier dragging his heels and his spurs into the Chamber with message Number 1,157. Washington reports "despair," "confusion" and lack of discipline and asks Congress for a War Committee to come to New Jersey to help him deal with the situation.

Adams challenges Chase: if he thinks Washington can win, will he vote for Independence? Chase says he will. Adams challenges him to come to New Jersey with Franklin and himself, as a War Committee, to reassure himself on the state of Washington's forces (despite the General's gloomy letter, Adams is convinced that the troops are in good condition). Chase agrees, and the Committee departs.

All the Liberals follow the trio out of the Chamber, leaving the Conservatives—the "cool, cool conservative men" like Dickinson, Rutledge, Wilson, Read, Morris, Hall, Livingston, Hewes.

DICKINSON (*sings*):
 Oh say do you see what I see?
 Congress sitting here in sweet serenity
 I could cheer,
 The reason's clear
 For the first time in a year
 Adams isn't here . . . !
 And, look!
 The sun is in the sky
 The breeze is blowing by
 And there's not a single fly!

 Oh sing "hosanna," "hosanna"
CONSERVATIVES:
 "Hosanna," "hosanna"
DICKINSON:
 . . . And it's cool!

 Oh ye cool cool conservative men
 Our like may never ever be . . . seen again

We have land
Cash in hand
Self-command
Future planned . . .
Fortune thrives
Society survives
In neatly order'd lives
With well-endower'd wives . . .
CONSERVATIVES:
Come sing "hosanna," "hosanna"
DICKINSON:
In our breeding and our manner
CONSERVATIVES:
. . . We are cool!

They dance a minuet and sing additional "hosannas" to their own coolness, as Washington's messenger enters again. This time the dispatch reports that British General Howe is in control of New York and preparing to march on Philadelphia. The Conservatives congratulate each other on not entering the game until they are sure of winning.

Hancock is present but will not join them in their song and dance—he prefers John Adams's tune, he tells them. Hancock reminds the Conservatives that there aren't enough men of property in America to control the government. Dickinson agrees, but argues: "Most men with nothing would rather protect the possibility of becoming rich than face the reality of being poor."

The Conservatives sing another self-satisfied chorus of coolness, with cash in hand. Then all the Congressmen depart from the Chamber, leaving only McNair, the Leather Apron and the Courier. McNair pours drinks all around. The Courier is a Massachusetts man, so McNair directs him to have a seat in the Massachusetts area of the Chamber.

> *The Courier goes to John's chair and touches it reverently before he sits.*

LEATHER APRON: You see'd any fightin'?

COURIER *(proudly)*: Sure did—I see'd my two best friends git shot dead on the very same day! Right on the village green it was, too! *(The recollection takes hold.)* An' when they didn't come home f'r supper—their mommas went down the hill lookin' for 'em. Miz Lowell—she foun' Tim'thy right off—but Miz Pickett—she looked near half the night f'r Will'm 'cuz he'd gone 'n' crawl'd off the green 'fore he died—

> *He is silent for a moment—then he sings:*

Momma, hey Momma
Come lookin' for me.
I'm here in the meado'
By th' red maple tree.
Momma, hey Momma,

Look sharp—here I be . . .
Hey, hey,
Momma, look sharp! . . . . .

My eyes are wide open
My face to th' sky
Is that you I'm hearin'
In th' tall grass nearby?
Momma, come find me
Before I do die . . .
Hey, hey,
Momma, look sharp!

I'll close y'r eyes, my Billy
Them eyes that cannot see
An' I'll bury ya, my Billy
Beneath th' maple tree
An'—never ag'in
Will y' whisper t' me . . .
"Hey, hey—
Oh Momma—look sharp! . . ."
      The lights fade.

Scene 6

In an anteroom to the Chamber, Thomas Jefferson listens through the door as Secretary Thomson begins to read the now-finished Declaration: "When in the Course of Human Events it becomes necessary for one People to dissolve the Political Bands which have connected them with another. . . . ."

Franklin and Jefferson enter, dressed in capes and hats, back from New Jersey, reporting good news. Chase, impressed by the rabble army's skill with the rifle, is going to place Mary-land (as John Adams pronounces it) in the "Yea" column.

As the Declaration is being read, the three discuss what kind of a bird is ready to hatch from this egg of Independence. What should new America's national symbol be? John says "Eagle," Jefferson says "Dove," Franklin says "Turkey."

> *John and Jefferson look at Franklin in surprise, then at each other.*
> JOHN: The eagle.
> JEFFERSON: The dove.
> JOHN: The *eagle.*
> JEFFERSON *(shrugging):* The eagle.
> FRANKLIN *(a pause):* The turkey.
> JOHN: The eagle is a majestic bird.
> FRANKLIN: The eagle is a scavenger, a thief, a coward and the symbol of more than ten centuries of European mischief.

JOHN: And the turkey—?

FRANKLIN: A truly noble bird, a native of America, a source of sustenance to our settlers and an incredibly brave fellow who would not flinch from attacking an entire regiment of Englishmen single-handedly! Therefore the national bird of America is going to be—

JOHN: The eagle.

FRANKLIN AND JEFFERSON *(shrugging):* The eagle.

They sing of the eaglet waiting to be hatched on this very hot day. Then John voices his confidence.

JOHN: The Declaration will be a triumph, I tell you—a triumph! If I was ever sure of anything I'm sure of that—a triumph!
    A pause.
And if it isn't, we've still got four days left to think of something else. *(Sings:)*
    The eagle's going to
    Crack the shell
    Of the egg that England laid!
ALL:
    Yessir! We can
    Tell! Tell! Tell!
    On this humid Monday morning
    In this—Congressional incubator!
FRANKLIN:
    And just as Tom, here has written . . .
    Tho' the shell may belong to Great Britain . . .
    The eagle inside . . .
    Belongs to us!

The three repeat this chorus and then move into the Chamber.

Scene 7

In the Chamber, all are present as Thomson ends his reading of the Declaration: ". . . . . And for the support of this Declaration we mutually pledge to each other our Lives, our Fortunes and our sacred honor."

After a prolonged silence, Hancock asks if there are any amendments or other changes. Every hand is raised but those of Adams, Jefferson and Franklin. For example, McKean wants the word "Scottish" expunged from the phrase "Scottish and foreign mercenaries." Jefferson strikes it out.

Rev. Witherspoon of New Jersey urges a reference to the Supreme Being, not mentioned in the document; Jefferson complies. He makes other changes suggested by Read of Delaware, Bartlett of New Hampshire, Sherman of Connecticut—though clearly, as the suggestions get closer and closer to the heart of the document, it pains Jefferson to alter his carefully constructed sentences.

McNair, who is changing leaves on the calendar to signify that this process of revision is taking several days, removes the leaves for June 29 and 30. He offers the opinion that "I'm not very fond of the United States of America as a name for a new country" but is ignored because he is not a member of the Congress.

Dickinson suggests that it is wrong to call the King a "tyrant" when all human rights came from him in the first place. But here Jefferson takes a stand. He will not consent to the removal of the word "tyrant." Hancock rules in his favor. It is July 1.

Hewes of North Carolina suggests they should mention fishing rights, and at this Adams loses his patience. Hancock tries to cut off further suggestions, but before he can do so Rutledge of South Carolina rises and asks that a portion of the Declaration be read again.

THOMSON (*clears his throat and reads*): "He has waged cruel war against human nature itself, in the persons of a distant people who never offended him, captivating and carrying them into slavery in another hemisphere. Determined to keep open a market where *men* should be bought and sold, he has prostituted—"

RUTLEDGE: That will suffice, Mr. Thomson, I thank you. Mr. Jefferson, I can't quite make out what it is you're talkin' about.

JEFFERSON: Slavery, Mr. Rutledge.

RUTLEDGE: Ah, yes. You're referring to us as slaves of the King.

JEFFERSON: No, sir—I'm referring to *our* slaves. Black slaves.

RUTLEDGE: Ah! Black slaves. Why didn't you say so, sir? Were you tryin' to hide your meanin'?

JEFFERSON: No, sir.

RUTLEDGE: Just another literary license, then.

JEFFERSON: If you like.

RUTLEDGE: I don't like at all, Mr. Jefferson—to us in South Carolina, black slavery is our peculiar institution and a cherished way of life.

JEFFERSON: Nevertheless, we must abolish it. Nothing is more certainly written in the Book of Fate than that this people shall be free.

RUTLEDGE: I am not concerned with the Book of Fate right now, sir—I'm more concerned with what's written in your little paper there.

JOHN: That "little" paper there deals with freedom for Americans!

RUTLEDGE: Oh, really! Mr. Adams is now callin' our black slaves Americans—are-they-now?

JOHN: They are! They're people and they're here—if there is any other requirement I've never heard of it.

RUTLEDGE: They are here, yes, but they are not people, sir—they are *property*.

JEFFERSON: No, sir! They are people who are being treated as property. I tell you the rights of human nature are deeply wounded by this infamous practise!

RUTLEDGE: Then see to your own wounds, Mr. Jefferson, for you are a—*practitioner*—are you not?

JEFFERSON: I have already resolved to release my slaves.

RUTLEDGE: Then I'm sorry, for you have also resolved the ruination of your personal economy.

JOHN: Economy. Always economy. There's more to this than a filthy purse-string, Rutledge—it's an offense against man and God.

HOPKINS: It's a stinking business, Mr. Rutledge—a stinking business!

Rutledge, infuriated, comments on the hypocrisy of the North which, though unwilling to own slaves, is willing to accept the profits earned by transporting and selling them.

Rutledge's anger is expressed in song: "Molasses . . . to rum . . . to slaves." New England ships, blackbirders, sail with a cargo of Bibles and rum (sings Rutledge), and ply the triangular trade to the African coast, the South and home with a pocketful of gold. Bitterly, Rutledge reminds the group that the faces at the African slave auctions are "New England faces—sea-faring faces."

RUTLEDGE (sings):
Molasses . . . to
Rum . . . to
Slaves . . . !

Who sail the ships back to Boston . . .
Laden with gold . . . see it gleam?!
Whose fortunes are made
In the triangle trade . . . ?
Hail, slavery! The New England
Dream!

Mr. Adams—I give you a toast!
Hail, Boston!
Hail, Charleston!
—Who stinketh—the most??!!
    He turns and walks straight out of the chamber. Hewes of North
    Carolina follows and Hall of Georgia is right behind them.

The cause of Independence seems lost indeed, even though Chase enters with the good news that Maryland is changing its vote to "Yea." With a unanimous vote required to adopt the Declaration, the tally board now looks as follows:

New Hampshire	YEA	
Massachusetts	YEA	
Rhode Island	YEA	
Connecticut	YEA	
New York		ABSTAIN
New Jersey	YEA	
Pennsylvania		NAY

HOWARD DA SILVA AS BENJAMIN FRANKLIN (LOWER LEFT) SURROUNDED BY
PAUL HECHT, CLIFFORD DAVID, WILLIAM DANIELS (SEATED), RONALD HOLGATE
AND KEN HOWARD IN "1776"

Delaware		NAY
Maryland	YEA	
Virginia	YEA	
North Carolina		NAY
South Carolina		NAY
Georgia		NAY

John Adams refuses to give up. Feverishly, he asks McKean to go to Delaware and bring back Caesar Rodney, a dying man, so that Rodney and McKean can outvote Read on the Delaware delegation. McKean departs on this mission.

Other Adams supporters, filing out, voice their hopelessness—after all, the vote is to take place tomorrow. They have less than a day to change the votes of all the "Nay" colonies. Finally only Adams, Hancock, Jefferson and Franklin remain. Franklin tells them the anti-slavery clause must go, it is "a luxury we can't afford."

JOHN: A *luxury?!* A half million souls in chains and Dr. Franklin calls it a luxury! Maybe you should've walked out with the South!

FRANKLIN: You forget yourself, sir! I founded the first anti-slavery society on this continent!

JOHN: Don't wave your credentials at me! Perhaps it's time you renewed them!

FRANKLIN: The issue here is Independence—maybe you've lost sight of that fact but I have not! How *dare* you jeopardize our cause when we've come so far?! These men, no matter how much we disagree with them, are not ribbon clerks to be ordered about—they're proud, accomplished men, the cream of their colonies—and whether you like it or not they and the people they represent will be a part of the new country you'd hope to create! Either start learning how to live with them or pack up and go home—but in any case, stop acting like a Boston fishwife!

Franklin turns from him, and Adams comes downstage alone, reflecting on his own errors, summoning up his vision of Abigail to ask her what he must do. Abby agrees with John, smiling, that he is "pig-headed". But she encourages him to keep trying—she reminds him of his own respect for the concept of commitment.

As the vision of his wife Abby leaves him, John sees that McNair is bringing in the two kegs of saltpetre she had promised. John orders McNair to "go out and buy every damned pin in Philadelphia!"

Once again, John leaps into action and maps strategy for his friends: "Talk and talk and talk." In his agitation, John turns the details of the plan into song. Jefferson must talk to Rutledge, all night if necessary.

JOHN (sings):
    Franklin!
    Time's running out!
FRANKLIN:
    I know . . . get out of my chair!
    Do I have to talk to Wilson?
JOHN:
    Yes, you do!
    If it takes all night,
    Keep talking . . .
JOHN, FRANKLIN, JEFFERSON:
    Talk and talk and talk!

Franklin and Jefferson depart. Hancock offers to support John, but John advises him to remain aloof from political maneuvering, as the President of the Congress should.

John is left alone in the Chamber. He looks at Washington's latest dispatch which asks "Is anybody there? Does anybody care?" His reverie becomes a song in which he declares that he is now committed and will not retreat.

JOHN (sings):
    Is anybody there . . . ?
    Does anybody care . . . ?

Does anybody see . . .
What I see . . . ?

I see . . .
Fireworks!
I see the pageant and pomp and parade!
I hear the bells ringing out!
I hear the cannons' roar!
I see Americans . . . all Americans . . .
Free! . . . For evermore!
>   *He "comes to" and looks around, realizing that it's dark and that
>   he's alone.*
How quiet . . .
How quiet the Chamber is.
How silent . . .
How silent the Chamber is . . .

Is anybody there . . . ?
>   *He waits for an answer; there is none.*
Does anybody care . . . ?
>   *Again, nothing.*
Does anybody see . . . what I see . . . ?

A voice answers Adams: "Yes, Mr. Adams—I do." It is Dr. Hall of Georgia, who has decided to follow Edmund Burke's advice that a representative owes his constituents his best judgment, even if it does not coincide with their opinion of the moment. Hall goes to the tally board and changes Georgia's vote to "Yea."

The members of Congress file in. It is time to call the roll for Independence —and a single "Nay" vote defeats the motion. While the role is called, Franklin, Wilson and Dickinson are seen to be engaged in argument. All votes are "Yea" to New York. New York abstains "courteously." Pennsylvania, its delegation still arguing, passes for the time being. It is then Delaware's turn, and dying Rodney, now back in the hall, rises to vote "Yea" with McKean, putting Delaware back in the "Yea" column.

Maryland and Virginia are both "Yeas," and then North Carolina yields to South Carolina. Rutledge takes his stand: strike out the anti-slavery clause, or South Carolina will vote "Nay." Adams senses that posterity will never forgive them if they now yield on the slavery question, but Franklin argues: "What will posterity think we were—demigods? We're men—no more, no less—trying to get a nation started against greater odds than a more generous God would have allowed. John—first things first! Independence! America! For if we don't secure that, what difference will the rest make?"

Adams waits for Jefferson to dispute Franklin, but he cannot. Jefferson goes to the secretary's table and strikes the anti-slavery clause from the Declaration. South Carolina, North Carolina and Georgia all vote "Yea." Now the tally board reads as follows:

New Hampshire	YEA	
Massachusetts	YEA	
Rhode Island	YEA	
Connecticut	YEA	
New York		ABSTAIN
New Jersey	YEA	
Pennsylvania		NAY
Delaware	YEA	
Maryland	YEA	
Virginia	YEA	
North Carolina	YEA	
South Carolina	YEA	
Georgia	YEA	

Dickinson rises to tell the Congress that they have wasted their effort, Pennsylvania's vote is *still* "Nay." But before he can cast this vote, Franklin requests that the delegation be polled. The secretary complies. Franklin votes "Yea." Dickinson votes "Nay." Now the whole matter is up to Judge James Wilson, who will cast the deciding vote on Independence. Wilson is silent. Dickinson orders him to speak up, warns him that Franklin is merely trying to create "one of his confusions." John Adams needles Wilson.

JOHN *(quietly; turning the screw):* It would be a pity for a man who handed down hundreds of wise decisions from the bench to be remembered only for the one unwise decision he made in Congress.

DICKINSON: James—you're keeping everybody waiting. The secretary has called for your vote.

WILSON *(to Dickinson):* Please don't push me, John, I know what you want me to do. But Mr. Adams is correct about one thing—I'm the one who'll be remembered for it.

DICKINSON: What do you mean?

WILSON: I'm different from you, John—I'm different from most of the men here. I don't want to be remembered! I just don't want the responsibility!

DICKINSON: Yes, well, whether you want it or not, James, there's no way of avoiding it.

WILSON: Not necessarily—if I go with them I'll only be one among dozens —no one will ever remember the name of James Wilson. But if I vote with you I'll be the man who prevented American Independence. I'm sorry, John— I just didn't bargain for that.

DICKINSON: And is that how new nations are formed—by a nonentity trying to preserve the anonymity he so richly deserves?

FRANKLIN: Revolutions come into this world like bastard children, Mr. Dickinson—half improvised and half compromised. Our side has provided the compromise—now Judge Wilson is supplying the rest.

WILSON *(to Dickinson):* I'm sorry, John—my vote is "Yea."

FRANKLIN: Mr. Secretary—Pennsylvania says "Yea."

THOMSON: Pennsylvania says "Yea"—
> *There is a stunned silence as all eyes go to the tally board and Pennsylvania's marker is moved into the "Yea" column. Finally:*
The count being twelve to none with one abstention—the resolution on Independence—*(Surprised.)*—is adopted.

It is done. Hancock suggests they sign their Declaration at once. Dickinson states that in all conscience he cannot sign the document—he still hopes for an adjustment of the differences with England. But he will join the army to fight for America, even though he believes the cause to be hopeless. As he departs, he carries with him the respect of the members of Congress, even of John Adams.

Adams quibbles with Jefferson over the word "inalienable"—it should be "*un*alienable," he believes, but he yields the point. The signing begins with Hancock writing his name large for King George to read easily.

A dispatch arrives from Washington: the General is preparing to make a stand at Brooklyn Heights with 5,000 men against 25,000 of the enemy. He has evacuated Manhattan and in doing so he has rescued Mrs. Lewis Morris and eight Morris children after their estate was destroyed.

As McNair changes the date on the calendar to July 4, Morris declares: "The hell with New York—I'll sign it anyway." Now the delegates of all thirteen colonies step up to Hancock's desk to sign the document—all except Rodney, who signs it where he sits.

> *As the last man signs, the sound of the tolling Liberty Bell in the belfry above becomes deafening. Then the scene freezes for a brief instant—and the pose of the familiar Trumbull painting of this occasion has been captured. A scrim curtain falls, the scene visible through it. Then as the back-light dims and the curtain is lit from the front it becomes opaque and reveals the lower half of the Declaration, featuring the signatures. Curtain.*

NO PLACE TO BE SOMEBODY

A Play in Three Acts

BY CHARLES GORDONE

Cast and credits appear on page 434

CHARLES GORDONE was born Oct. 12, 1925 and grew up in Elkhart, Indiana, where he attended Elkhart High School. His mother is Camille Morgan, former carnival and circus performer and acrobat who now teaches elocution. Gordone entered UCLA but left to join the Army. Upon his return he entered Los Angeles City College as a music major. He came to New York in 1952 and immediately found work as an actor in Moss Hart's The Climate of Eden *on Broadway. In 1959 he directed The Judson Poets Theater's first production* (Faust) *and has directed many other shows. In 1961 he appeared in the original off-Broadway production of Jean Genet's* The Blacks, *and last season he appeared in the title role of the Negro Ensemble Company's production of Wole Soyinka's* The Trials of Brother Jero.*

Gordone was founder and co-chairman, with Godfrey Cambridge, of the Committee for Employment of Negro Performers, and he was the associate producer of the movie Nothing But a Man. No Place To Be Somebody *is his first produced play. Speaking of his background, Gordone describes himself as a black who is also part French, part Italian, part Irish and part American Indian. He is married, with one child, a daughter.*

Time: The past 15 years

Place: Johnny's Bar in the West Village

ACT I

Scene 1

SYNOPSIS: Upstage is a bar with stools and a juke box at right and the door to the kitchen at left. Tables and chairs take up about half the space on the cigarette-butt-strewn floor. The front entrance is down right. The back entrance is half-covered by a dart board down left.

Gabe Gabriel—a young Negro, light-skinned, neatly dressed—is sitting at one of the tables, typing. He rips the page angrily from the typewriter. He lights a marijuana cigarette and tells the audience: "Right now I'm working on a play. They say if you wanna be a writer you gotta go out an' live. I don't believe that shit no more. Take my play for instance. Might not believe it but I'm gonna make it all up in my head as I go along. Before I prove it to you, wanna warn you not to be thinkin' I'm tellin' you a buncha barefaced lies. An' no matter how far out I git. Don't want you goin' out'a here with the idea— what you see happenin' is all a figment a my grassy imagination. 'Cause it ain't. *(He picks up Bible from table, raises it above his head. Without looking, he turns pages.)* 'And I heard a voice between the banks of the U'lai. And it called, Gabriel! Gabriel! Make this man understand the vision! So he came near where I stood; and when he came, I was frightened and fell upon my face!' "

Gabe exits as the lights dim. When the lights come up, Shanty Mulligan is at the juke box putting on a jazz number. Shanty is a skinny, long-haired, seedy-looking white youth in bell-bottomed trousers. He carries drumsticks thrust into his belt. Now he draws them and begins tapping on the bar and furniture.

Johnny Williams enters and hangs up raincoat and umbrella. He is compact, confident, dark with a black mustache, a take-charge type. He directs Shanty to stop fooling around with the sticks and start sweeping up—it's time to open the bar, which Johnny owns and operates.

Dee (white) and Evie (black) enter the barroom and hang up their coats.

JOHNNY: You broads let them two ripe apples git away from you, huh?
DEE: Don't look at me!
EVIE: . . . . . you an' your rich Texas trade!
DEE: Just gettin' too damn sensitive!
EVIE: Sensitive my black behin'! Excuse me, I mean black ass!
    Evie goes to juke box. Punches up number.
DEE: Last night we bring those two johns up to her pad! An' like, Jack?

One with the cowboy hat? Stoned? Like out of his skull. And like out of nowhere he starts cryin'!

EVIE: All weekend it was, "nigger this an' nigger that!"

DEE: Never bothered you before! I didn't like it when he started sayin'
things like, "black son'sa bitches are gettin' to be untouchables! Takin' over
the country!"

EVIE: Bet he'll think twice before he says sump'n like that ag'in!

DEE: That lamp I gave her? One the senator brought me back from Russia? Evie goes an' breaks it over his head!

JOHNNY: What the hell'd you do that for?

EVIE: Sure hated to lose that lamp!

JOHNNY: Wouldn't care if they b'longed to the Ku Klux Klan long's they
gimme the bread!

He goes into Dee's purse.

SHANTY: Sure had plenty of it too! When they was in here, they kept buyin'
me drinks! Thought I was the boss!

JOHNNY: Crackers cain't 'magine niggers runnin' nothin' but elevators an'
toilets!

DEE: Leave me somethin', please!

EVIE: Ain't goin' do nothin' with it nohow!

Johnny finds a pair of baby shoes in Dee's purse.

JOHNNY: Thought I tole you to git rid'a these?

Johnny strongly advises Dee to throw the shoes away—"Worrin' over
sump'n pass, over an' done with!"—but Dee is determined to keep them.

Cora Beasely enters dressed in a white uniform, a newspaper over her head
to shield her from the rain. Her manner is ladylike and proud; she is attractive looking, a practical nurse, no one's servant; when she is seen wheeling a
baby it'll be her own. Hostility between Cora and the two hustlers flares in
angry sarcasms, and they come to the verge of a physical fight, with Evie
drawing a switchblade. Johnny orders them to stop, and they obey him.

After the hustlers depart, Cora orders a martini and reminisces with Johnny
about the past. Cora had promised Johnny's mother she would watch out for
him, but "that bad nigger, Sweets Crane got holt you an' ruint ya!"

But Johnny insists that Sweets was a father to him.

JOHNNY: Fixed it so's I didn't have to go to that orphan-house, didn't he?
Took me in, treated me like I was his own son, didn't he? Damned sight more'n
you or that drunken bitch of a mama'a mine did!

CORA: Jay Cee? Might God strike you dead! Maybe I ain't yo' flesh an'
blood! But yo' mama? She couldn't he'p none'a the things she did!

JOHNNY: Do me one favor, bitch! Leave my mama on the outside! 'Nother
thing, if you cain't say nothin' boss 'bout Sweets Crane, you don't have to come
in here yo' dam-self!

He slaps her on the behind. Exits to kitchen.

CORA: Well, fan me with a brick! That's one Nigro you jus' cain't be civil
with!

She sips drink as Shanty finishes sweeping floor.
Eb'm as a chile, give him a piece'a candy! Wudn't the kin' he wanted, he'd rare back an' th'ow it at you! 'Nen he'd stan' there lookin' all slant-eyed— darin' you to touch him!

Cora watches Shanty beat on the bar as she tells him that Johnny never had a father; his mother would never tell who his father was. She had known Johnny's mother down South.

Melvin enters; he is black, well-muscled, shaven-headed and mild-mannered, a ballet dancer who also works as the short-order cook at Johnny's Bar. Johnny re-enters, ribs Melvin about shaking his "tukus" for free, but Melvin is devoted to pure art and calls the TV dancers "prostitutes."

Johnny goes to juke box. Punches up number. Classical music comes on.
JOHNNY: Go with a little sample what you jokers is puttin' down!
MELVIN: Nothing doing! To appreciate true art, one must first be familiar with it!
CORA: Talk that talk, Mel! What do Jay Cee know 'bout bein' artistic?
Johnny rejects the music.
JOHNNY: This Wineberg you study with? He's a Jew, ain't he?
MELVIN: So what?
JOHNNY: Gotta give it to him! Connin' spades into thinkin' they gotta be taught how to dance!
MELVIN: You're just prejudice, Johnny! That's why you got no appreciation!
JOHNNY: When you start teachin' him maybe I'll git me some pre-she-a-shun!

Gabe saunters into the bar in grand manner, with umbrella and briefcase, goes through an elaborate ritual of friendly greeting with Johnny. Johnny pours Gabe a tumblerful of whisky, which Gabe drinks down.
Gabe has been to an audition for black actors. His skin is so light that the director told him casting for white actors would take place the next day. The show is a musical about slavery, it seems. Gabe wants no part of it.
Cora and Shanty urge Gabe to recite "one of his crazy poems." Gabe recites a description of the day "They met on the banks of the Potomac,/The rich, the great and the small!" for a civil rights rally. A famous black speaker whose name Gabe can't remember (the poem continues) harangued them, urging them "Don't rock no boat!/Don't cut ne'r th'oat!" Instead, they should accept bourgeois values and work hard, in order to rise in the world.

GABE *(quoting the "speaker"):*
. . . . . "Now, here are the bare facks,
Grab yo'selves by the bootblacks!
Leave heroin Nanderson on the side!

An' all you take notice,
You'll all git yo' lettuce!
You'll own the Post Office yet!
Offsprings off mixed couples
Who're more than a han'full,
You'll make the cover of Jet!
We'll have invented a machine that delivers
A cream to make crackers pay the debt!
Now junkies don't dilly
You husslers don't dally!
Don't waste yo' time smokin' pot
In some park or some alley,
'Cause Charley is watchin' you!"
  Everyone claps.
. . . . . A cracker preacher there, then said a prayer!
Said civil rights you could not fo'ce!
By this time I was so confused my head was in
A spin!
Somebody else got up with a grinnin' face!
Said to leave that place like we found it!
Tha's when I reached in my pocket an' pulled
Out my packet an' before everybody took a
Sip'a my wine!
Then we lef' that place without ne'r trace!
An' we didn't leave ne'r chit'lin behin'!
  Everyone laughs and claps again.

JOHNNY: If you ask me, it's all a big-ass waste'a time an' energy! Jus' how long you gon' keep this up? Ought'a be in some office makin' a white man's pay!

Cora hastens to depart before Johnny and Gabe get into another of their arguments. As she leaves, she drops Shanty an invitation for supper (Shanty and Cora have an understanding, acknowledged by the others).

Johnny gives Gabe some money to get on with till he finds a job. Gabe has a standing invitation to come in with Johnny, but Gabe is reluctant to get involved in illegal activity. Johnny scoffs: "Ain't no law! Kill you an' me in the name'a the law! You an' me wouldn't be where we at, if it wasn't for that law! Even that law they write for us makes us that worse off!"

Johnny and his friend Sweets Crane are planning to grab themselves "a piece'a this town" when Sweets gets out of jail. Johnny is making plans. Gabe warns him that he may wind up on the bottom of the East River. Johnny replies: "Okay, Hollywood! Keep knockin' on doors with yo' jeans at half-mast! Sellin' yo'-self like some cheap-ass whore! If I know one thing about you, you ain't even that good'a actor! Whitey knows right away you can't even stan' to look at him!" Gabe picks up the money and departs, grinning as the scene goes to blackout.

Scene 2

A week later, Gabe stands at stage center and warns the audience: "Because I call myself a black playwright, don't git the impression I'm hung up on crap like persecution and hatred! 'Cause I ain't!" In reality, Gabe fears violence and has been hiding in his house because he imagines violence waiting for him in the street.

Nor is his play about Negro self-pity, nor social protest (he explains, as the lights dim out).

The lights come up on Johnny lying on the floor of his bar next to an empty bottle and glass. Johnny rouses himself, sees a telegram has been pushed under the door. He studies it as Dee enters and goes behind the bar to fix a bromide.

Johnny hands Dee the telegram, orders her to read it to him. She does so—it's from Sweets, telling Johnny he'll be released in three weeks' time.

Johnny is overjoyed, but Dee has "a bad feelin'" and wants Johnny to go away with her somewhere for a couple of weeks. It's Dee's birthday and Johnny tries to give her some money for a present, but she refuses it—all she wants is his company. Johnny promises her a birthday celebration—just the two of them, in Johnny's apartment. Dee goes out.

Cora and Shanty enter and report that Dee is outside, sitting in the car, crying. Johnny leaves the bar in Shanty's charge and runs out to join Dee.

Alone with Shanty, Cora asks him about his divorce. Shanty's wife Gloria will never give him one (he says), but Cora is perfectly willing for Shanty to live with her anyway. What's more, she'll help "Shangy" (as she pronounces his name) get that set of drums he's been wanting.

Shanty dreams of setting the drums up here in the bar and playing them to impress Johnny.

CORA: Lawd, Shangy! I wouldn't miss that for nothin' in this worl'!
> *Shanty takes out marijuana cigarette, wets it, lights it, smokes.*
Lawd, Shangy! I done tole you 'bout smokin' them ol' nasty things!
> *He passes cigarette to her. She grins.*
Guess it won't hurt none once in awhile!
> *She inhales, coughs.*
SHANTY: I was just thinkin' about ol' Gloria. How much she hated jazz! Nigger music, she called it! Man, every time I'd set up my skins to practise! She'd take the kids an' go over to her mother's!
> *They pass the cigarette back and forth.*
Dig. One night after a gig! Brought some cats over for a little game! Some spade cat grabs her between the legs when I wasn't lookin'.
CORA: Spent the bes' part'a my life on Nigroes that wasn't no good! Had to baby an' take care all of 'em!
SHANTY: Never heard the last of it! You'd think he raped her or somethin'!
CORA: Can't hol' no job! Take yo' money an' spen' it all on likker!

SHANTY: Got this job playin' the Borsh-belt! My skins was shot. Had to borrow a set from Champ Jones!

CORA: Can't make up their min's! Jus' be a man, I says!

SHANTY: Gone about a week! Come home! Shades all down! Key won't fit in the door!

CORA: Git evil! Nex' thing you know they goin' up 'side yo' head!

SHANTY: She's over at her mother's! Says she gonna sue me for desershun!

CORA: I thought you was a dif-rent kind'a nigger! I'm gon' git me a white man! One that'll take care me! Or he'p me take care myse'f!

They continue like this, each with a private fantasy, he of beating up his wife, she of the cruelty of a lover. They re-establish contact with each other just as the scene ends in a blackout.

Scene 3

Three weeks later, Shanty is busy behind the bar and Melvin is doing his dance exercises as Johnny enters. Johnny and Melvin discuss the shopping list. Melvin goes off to buy food.

Mary Lou Bolton, a pretty young white girl, well and simply dressed, enters carrying a civil rights placard, on the way to some sort of demonstration. She orders a daiquiri. Johnny learns that she has just graduated from Elmira College and is the daughter of a judge who was once a criminal lawyer. She's picketing construction work up the street because they won't hire qualified Negroes. Johnny's sarcastic reaction is "Why don't them qualified Nigroes do they own pickitin'?"

Much to Johnny's amusement, Mary Lou feels a deep sense of responsibility. Irritated by Johnny's attitude, she puts down money for the unfinished daiquiri and moves to leave the bar, but Johnny catches her arm, determined to shock her.

JOHNNY: Know what's in that daiquiri, baby?

MARY LOU: Let me go, please!

JOHNNY: Jizzum juice. A triple dose of jizzum jismistic juice! Any minute now you gonna turn into a depraved sex maniac! A teenage Jeckle an' Hide! Yo' head is gon' sprout fuzzy like somebody from the Fee-jee Eye-lan's! Yo' tongue'll roll out'a your mouth like'a fat snake! You'll pant like'a go-rilla in heat! Yo' buzzooms will blow up like gas galloons an' the nipples will swell an' hang like ripe purple plums! Yo' behin' will begin to work like the ol' gray mare an' you'll strut aroun' flappin' yo' wings like'a raped duck! Then you'll suck me up with one mighty slurp an' fly out'a here a-screamin' vampire. They will finally subdue an' slay you on top'a the Empire State buildin' with ray guns where you'll be attemptin' to empale yo'self astride that giant antennae! An' nobody will ever know that you, li'l Mary Lou Bolton! Who jus' graduated from Elmira College, was lookin' to lay down in front of a big, black bulldozer, to keep America safe for democracy!

MARY LOU: I think I get your point!

Another girl from the picket line enters and summons Mary Lou back to business. Cora comes in with the news that Shanty is moving in with her today.

Johnny warns Cora: he hired Shanty when none of the white proprietors in the district would, and now he doesn't want Cora turning Shanty's head. Cora believes she and Shanty have some happiness coming and should grab it. Shanty believes that Cora is going to help him get his drums. But Johnny warns Shanty: Cora will try to turn him into a white man. "She'll make you so damn white you won't be able to bang two spoons together!"

When Johnny suggests that Shanty will never be able to play the drums, Cora rushes him and Johnny throws her to the floor. Shanty tries to counter-attack but can't—he isn't strong enough. He winds up in tears, with Cora comforting him. Cora warns Johnny that he has a hurt coming to him. She and Shanty leave the bar.

Gabe enters and sees Johnny getting champagne out to celebrate Sweets Crane's arrival. A black man comes in the door, so ragged that Johnny commands him: "On yo' way, wine!" But it is Sweets, fresh out of jail. Johnny and Sweets fall into each other's arms. One of Sweets' prison souvenirs is an ominous cough.

Johnny introduces Gabe and brings out glasses and the bottle—"Some'a Pete Zerroni's bes'". Zerroni has been running things everywhere but, as Johnny remarks, "We gon' change all that, ain't we Sweets?" as he prepares to pull the cork from the champagne.

SWEETS: Sonny boy, we wasn't much on sendin' kites! Wha's been happenin' since I been in the joint?

JOHNNY: Jews, Irish an' the Ginees still runnin' things as usual!

SWEETS: No, I mean with you, sonny boy!

JOHNNY: Like you know I had a tough gaff gittin' my divorce. Whole thing started when I wanted her to do a little merchandizin' for me! Real Magdaleen, she was! One thing led to 'nother! Boom! Back to Mama, she went! Had a helluva time gittin' her to sign this joint over to me! Went into my ack! Fell down on my deuce'a benders! Gave her the ol' rutine! Like how the worl' been treatin' us black folk an' everything—

> *He pops cork, pours. Johnny holds his glass up. The two men clink their glasses.*

Well, look here Sweets, here's to our li'l piece'a this town!

> *Sweets looks into his glass as Johnny sips.*

SWEETS: Speakin' a'husslers, Sonny boy!

> *He coughs. Gabe goes to bar. Gets large glass and fills it with champagne.*

You runnin' any kind'a stable?

JOHNNY: You kiddin', Sweets?

SWEETS: Pushin' or bookin'?

JOHNNY: Hay, that ain't my stick!

SWEETS: Sonny boy, when I was yo' age, I was into some'a ev'thing.

JOHNNY: Wish you wouldn't call me that, Sweets! I ain't that little boy runnin' up an' down Saint Nicklas Avenue for you nomore.

SWEETS: Jus' habit, Johnny! But I sort'a was hopin' you was into sump'm on yo' own, like!

JOHNNY: Hell! I was tryin' to stay clean! Waitin' on you, man! Like we planned!

Sweets informs Johnny he is through with the rackets, he has made up his mind. Johnny, upset at this news, at first touches Sweets and then grabs him violently, as though he could shake the thought out of him. Gabe sees that Sweets is a sick man and tries to intervene, but Johnny takes Gabe out with a punch to the stomach.

Sweets uses this opportunity to lift Gabe's wallet, then turns on Johnny and accuses him of catching "Charlie fever," while admitting that he himself probably exposed Johnny to the disease: "Couldn't copy Charlie's good points an' live like men! So we copied his bad points! That was the way it was with my daddy an' his daddy before him! We just pissed away our lives tryin' to be like bad Charlie! With all our fine clothes an' big cars! All it did was make us hate him all the more an' ourselves too! Then I tried to go horse-to-horse with 'em up there in the Bronx! An' ended up with a ten! All because'a the Charlie fever! I gave you the Charlie fever, Johnny! An' I'm sorry! Seems to me, the worse sickness'a man kin have, is the Charlie fever!"

Sweets leaves—he must be faking, Johnny is convinced, he has changed so much. Gabe looks for his watch, finds that it's gone, along with his wallet and the money Johnny gave him. Now Johnny laughs: "It's Sweets! The bastard *is* fakin'. He snatched it!" *(Blackout.)*

ACT II

Scene 1

Two days later, Gabe is alone at the bar, sitting at a table with a whisky bottle, obviously drunk. He sings a few lines of the hymn "Whiter Than Snow," then launches into a chant about moving away from a "dirty-black slum" full of "dirty-black people" into a nice "clean-white" suburban neighborhood. . . . .

GABE:
>Now those clean-white people thought we were
>Dirty-black people!
>And they treated us like we were
>Dirty-black people!
>But we stuck it out!
>We weathered the storm!
>We cleansed and bathed

And tried to be and probably were
Cleaner than most of those clean-white people!

The dirty-black people on the other side of the tracks envied them (Gabe's chant continues) and would catch them and beat them up whenever they could. The clean-white people were ready to make a place for them, but they realized that the world was not really clean, so they returned to the black slum, where the "dirty-black people," still angry, disowned and reviled them.

GABE:
　　And we still were exceedingly glad!
　　For at last they knew
　　We were not like our clean-white neighbors!
　　Most of all! We were safe!
　　Assured at last!
　　We could never more be
　　Like those dirty-black niggers!
　　Those filthy, dirty-black niggers!
　　Who live far away!
　　Far away, in hovels across the tracks!
　　　He bursts into song:
　　"Whiter than snow! Yes! Whiter than snow!
　　Oh, wash me and I shall be whiter than snow!"

The lights dim out on Gabe and then come up to reveal Shanty behind the bar. Mike Maffucci, a white man in suit and necktie who looks like he might be any kind of a white-collar straw boss but happens to be a gangster, is throwing darts into the board at right.

Sweets enters. Shanty, who doesn't know who he is, takes him for a wino and tries to eject him, but Sweets brushes Shanty aside and goes into the back in search of a broom to clean the place up with. Shanty is astonished at Sweets' behavior.

At this moment Johnny enters and recognizes Maffucci as an old acquaintance. Maffucci calls him "Johnny cake," and Johnny calls Maffucci "little snotty-nosed wop kid." Playfully, Maffucci throws a dart at Johnny who ducks, laughs and pours his old "friend" a drink. Warily, they discuss the old days. Maffucci's father died shortly after Johnny went to jail (Maffucci was in on the crime, too, but his father, who had "connections," got him off). The nicknames "Jay Cee" and "Johnny cake" come from Johnny's onetime hero worship of a gangster named Joe Carneri.

Sweets comes in with a broom and proceeds to sweep the floor. This act irritates Johnny, but he says nothing.

Maffucci touches Johnny in a half-hearted gesture of apology for what happened years ago, and this triggers a sharp physical revulsion in the black man. The two nearly come to blows, but Maffucci backs away.

Controlling his temper, Maffucci tells Johnny he is "one of Pete Zerroni's local boys" working in the field of "community relations." Zerroni is a little concerned because of one Sweets Crane, who dropped some threats in jail and might be tempted to carry them out now that he's out. Johnny reassures Maffucci (who of course fails to recognize the sweeper) that Sweets Crane plans to go straight. "Wanna believe you," Maffucci tells Johnny, "But just in case you an' this Sweets are thinkin' 'bout makin' a little noise! Pete wants me to give you the six-to-five!"

Sweets, sweeping close to Maffucci, deliberately bumps into him and causes him to spill wine on his shirt. The gangster brushes off Sweets' apologies and ministrations and tells Johnny that his boss Zerroni "don't like jigs! Says, the minute they git a little somethin' they start actin' cute!" Commenting that Johnny might have gone far in the rackets if he had been white, Maffucci departs.

Johnny grabs the broom from Sweets and thrusts it at Shanty, who takes it into the back, now realizing who Sweets is. "What's this game you playin'?" Johnny asks Sweets, who is looking over the watch he just stole from Maffucci. The pilfering is just for the hell of it: "Cain't see no point in watchin' George Raff on tee vee ev'a night! All my life I been into things! Always active!"

For the rest of it, Sweets has brought Johnny his will. He hands it over and Johnny summons Shanty from the kitchen to read it. Both Shanty and Johnny are surprised to learn that Johnny will inherit "interest in barber shops, meat markets, stores an' a whole lotta Harlem real estate!" Sweets never dared tell anyone about his holdings, not even Johnny, for fear of a tax rap.

Johnny suspects that Sweets may be contemplating "some kind'a back gate commute—suicide?" but this is far from the case. The truth is, with his cough and all, Sweets has only six months to live, according to the doctors.

JOHNNY: Goddamit, Sweets! What the hell kin I say? I sho' been a real bastard! Guess it don't help none for me to say I'm sorry!

SWEETS: Might he'p some if you was to turn all this into sump'n worth while an' good! Maybe the Lawd will f'give me f'the way I got it!

Sweets bursts into laughter and coughs.

JOHNNY: Git off it, Sweets! Jus' 'cause you s'pose to chalk out on us, don't mean you gotto go an' 'brace relijun!

SWEETS: Figger it won't hurt none if I do!

JOHNNY: Shit. That good Lawd you talkin' 'bout is jus' as white as that judge who sent yo' black ass to Fedsville!

SWEETS: How you know? You ever seen him? When I was down there in that prison, I reads a lot! Mos'ly the Bible! Bible tells me, the Lawd was hard to look upon! Fack is, he was so hard to look upon that nobody eva looked at him an' lived! Well, I got to figgerin' on that! An' reasons that was so, 'cause he was so black!

Sweets goes into loud laughter and coughs again.
Lawd knows! White's easy nuff to look at!

Johnny throws the will upon the floor. Sweets goes to his knees and clutches the will.

What you doin', Sonny boy? My life is in them papers!

Sweets hits Johnny with hat. Johnny reaches under the bar and comes up with a revolver, levels it at Sweets.

JOHNNY: See this, Sweets? My firs' and only pistol! You gave it to me when I was a lookout for you when you was pullin' owl jobs in Queens! I worshipped the groun' you walked on! I thought the sun rose an' set in yo' ass! You showed me how to make thirteen straight passes without givin' up the dice. Stood behin' me an' nudged me when to play my age! Hipped me how to make a gappers cut! How to handle myself in a pill joint! Taught me to trust no woman over six or under sixty! Turned me on to the bes' horse players an' number runners! Showed me how to keep my ass-pocket full'a coins without goin' to jail! Said the wors' crime I ever committed was comin' out'a my mama screamin' black! Tole me all about white folks an' what to expect from the best of them. You said as long as there was white man on the face of this earth, the black man only had one free choice! That was the way he died! When you went to jail for shootin' that cracker, you said, "Sonny boy, git us a plan!" Well, I got us a plan! Now, you come back here nutty an' half dead, dancin' all over me about me goin' through a change'a life! An' how you want me to help you git ready to meet yo' Lawd. Well, git ready, mother fucker! Tha's exactly what I'm gon' do! Help you to meet him!

Johnny pulls back the hammer of the gun. Sweets coughs and looks at the barrel of the gun.

SWEETS: You ain't gon' shoot me, Johnny! You cain't shoot me! They's a whole lotta you, I ain't even touched!

Sweets exits. Blackout.

Scene 2

Two weeks later, Gabe and Melvin are in the bar, both disconsolate—Gabe because the role he wants calls for a guitar player and he can't seem to get the hang of the instrument, and Mel because he lost his balance and fell at his solo dance recital, much to his teacher's dismay.

Shanty is in place behind the bar. When Dee enters, he pours her a drink. She takes the glass and the whole bottle and sits down with Gabe.

Gabe questions Dee about her past. Dee met Johnny through her friend Evie. Evie came home with Johnny one night while a boy friend was beating Dee up, and Johnny intervened and saved her. Dee got into the profession after she worked as a salesgirl and kept getting propositions all the time from rich men—finally she accepted one. Dee remembers her childhood sweetheart who "Got me pregnant! Nice decent boy! Only, he was black! Went to my folks! Said, 'I'll marry her.' The crazy bastard! They made his life miserable!"

They disposed of the baby for her, Dee tells Gabe, and that was that. She launches into a wild tale, told in a Southern dialect, of how her father raped her and how after that she came to New York.

In the middle of this extravagant narrative, Gabe is reminded of his own childhood sweetheart, Maxine—Maxine was Jewish (Gabe tells Dee, going into his own first-person story) and taught him a lot: "Said I was a good lover! Said white boys got their virility in how much money they made an' the kind'a car they drove! Said I related better 'cause I was black an' had nothin' to offer but myself! So I quit my job! Used to hide in the closet when her folks came in from Connecticut! Listened to 'em degradin' her for livin' with an' supportin' a nigger! . . . . . Didn't really want to marry me! Jus' wanted my baby so she could go on Welfare! She out there somewhere! Maxine is! She's out there, waitin' on me to come back to her! Maxine is!"

Johnny comes in. Soon Gabe is gone and Johnny is admitting to Dee that maybe they'd better get away for a while, after all. But Dee—who by now has had a great many drinks—has something else on her mind. She wants to get out of "the life." She wants a more lasting arrangement—marriage, maybe. Johnny pleads that business is so bad "Wasn't for the coins you bring in, I'd go under 'fore the week was out!" She offers to help him improve the business, but he tells her "Ain't no woman'a mine gon' be workin'. She b'long at home!"

Johnny orders Dee to make reservations for them this weekend at Bimini. Dee goes, but she is no longer to be satisfied with such partial favors.

Scene 3

The next day, Melvin is straightening the place up as Gabe enters. Gabe didn't get the part he wanted. Instead, they picked what Johnny calls a "Nigra type."

JOHNNY: . . . . . When whitey pick one'a y'all you gotta either be a clown, a freak or a Nigra type!

GABE: They do the same thing among themselves, too!

JOHNNY: 'Mongst themselves, they ain't so damn choosey!

GABE: Should'a seen the cat they did pick! Hell! I'm as black as he is!

JOHNNY: Gabe, ain't they no mirrors in yo' house?

GABE: I mean black in here!

MELVIN: You people are more preoccupied with color than white people are!

JOHNNY: They won't let us be porcupined with nothin' else!

GABE: Don't make no difference what color I am. I'm still black!

JOHNNY: Yeah! But you ain't gon' git no chance to prove it! Not on no stage, you ain't! You remin' whitey'a too many things he don't wanna take'a look at! Figgers he's got nuff problems dealin' with niggers who jus' look black, like me.

Johnny hands Gabe some more money. Gabe balks at the handout, but Johnny offers him a chance to earn it by minding the bar while he goes to Bimini.

Cora and Shanty make a dramatic entrance carrying the set of drums which Shanty has at long last acquired. Johnny tries to prevent Shanty from setting the drums up and making a spectacle of himself, but Cora insists: They swore they were going to show Johnny, and now they will do it.

Shanty has already grabbed his familiar broom, but Cora announces to Johnny that Shanty is quitting his job as of today, and she insists that he play his drums.

> *Shanty hands Johnny the broom, approaches the drums reluctantly.*

JOHNNY: Some reason, Shangy! You don't look so happy! Now I want you to jump up there an' give ol' Jay Cee a little wham-bam-thank-ya-mam! Piece'a the funky nitty-gritty! Like the time they said you played like'a spade! Guess I kin risk gittin' a summons on that!

CORA: Ne'min', Jay Cee! Go 'head, honey! Git yo'se'f together! Take all the time you need!

GABE: Whale, baby!

> *Shanty sits upon the stool. Fumbles. Accidentally puts foot on pedal. Strikes pose. Taps cymbals. Moves to snares. Mixes. Pumps. Works. Gets loud. Cora fidgets, anxious. Shanty fakes. Can't cover up. Becomes frustrated. Louder. Stands. Begins to beat wildly. Moves around the drums banging for all he's worth. Cora is ashamed. Gabe frowns. Cora grabs Shanty's arm. He pushes her away, becomes a windmill.*

CORA: Stop it, Shangy! Stop it, I said!

> *Shanty beats as if possessed. Cora is helpless. Johnny calmly reaches behind the bar. Gets a pitcher of water. Pours it over Shanty's head.*

SHANTY: Ya-hoooo!

> *Leaps into the air.*

I had it! I was on it! I was into it, babee!

> *He moves around doing the pimp walk.*

Ol' Red Taylor said I had the thing! Said, "Shanty man! You got the thing."

> *Goes to Melvin.*

Gimme some skin, motherfucker.

> *Melvin gives him some skin. Goes to Gabe.*

Gimme some skin.

> *Gabe doesn't put his hand out.*

Ah, fuck you, man. Didn't I hip you to my happenin's, Johnny? Didn't I show you where it's at?

JOHNNY: You burned, baby, you burned!

> *Shanty gives Johnny some skin.*

CORA: Shangy? I—think you better start packin' up now!

SHANTY: Git away from me! You funky, black bitch!

CORA: Shangy!

SHANTY: Just stay away from me—you evil piece'a chunky!

Cora is just like Gloria (Shanty tells her). She thought she could make a fool of him by bringing the drums in here and making him play in public, but he showed them all. Cora can take the drums away with her, Shanty will get his own drums—and he and Cora are "Splitsville!"

Shanty goes into the kitchen for a change of clothes. Cora departs. Melvin follows Shanty into the kitchen. Johnny and Gabe begin dismantling the drums, but Gabe, still feeling strong sympathy for Shanty, can't go through with it, and leaves. While Johnny's attention is held by the drums, Mary Lou Bolton enters and orders a daiquiri. Johnny knows it isn't for the drink that Mary Lou came back.

Maffucci enters with a truck driver delivering a case of whisky—it is part of Maffucci's job to keep an eye on things, make sure the customers are happy. Maffucci spots Mary Lou, identifies her as Judge Bolton's daughter, rudely grabs her by the arms, sends "Hello" to Judge Bolton, then releases her and leaves the bar.

Maffucci knows the Judge (Mary Lou tells Johnny) because her father defended Zerroni and others in a case involving bribery and murder. He got them acquitted.

MARY LOU: What's your interest? You know this Pete Zerroni?
JOHNNY: Not personal!
MARY LOU: He's not a very good person to know!
JOHNNY: With Pete, sometimes you ain't got no choice!
          She prepares to leave.
Here! Lemme freshen up yo' drink!
MARY LOU: No thanks! I'm getting—I'm getting a headache!
          She moves to the street door.
Goodbye, Mister—
JOHNNY: Johnny! Johnny Williams!
MARY LOU: Goodbye, Johnny—
          She exits, leaving her purse. He picks it up. Thinks for a moment.
          Goes to phone. Dials.
JOHNNY: Hey, Dee? Cancel them reservations! Sump'm important jus' came up! Won't be able to after all! Now don't hand me no crap! Just cancel.
          Blackout.

ACT III

Scene 1

Two weeks later, a newspaper announcing "Negroes Riot" is folded to make a display arrangement with a small American flag, a Molotov cocktail and an automatic pistol lying on a plate, in the center of one of the tables.

Gabe enters and announces to the audience "There's more to being black than meets the eye!" Like a preacher reciting the Beatitudes, Gabe tells the audience how it is.

GABE: . . . . . Bein' black, is eatin' chit'lin's an' wah-tah-melon, an' to hell with anybody, if they don't like it! Bein' black has a way'a makin' ya wear bright colors an' knowin' what a fine hat or a good pair'a shoes look like! An' then—an' then—it has a way'a makin' ya finger pop! Invent a new dance! Sing the blues! Drink good scotch! Smoke a big seegar while pushin' a black Cadillac with white sidewall tires! It's conkin' yo' head! Wearin' a black rag to keep the wave! Carryin' a razor! Smokin' boo an' listenin' to gut-bucket jazz . . . . Bein' black is gittin' down loud and wrong! Uh-huh! It's makin' love without no hang-ups! . . . . . Bein' black has a way'a makin' ya mad mos' of the time, hurt all the time an' havin' so many hang-ups, the problem'a soo-side don't even enter yo' mind! It's buyin' what you don't want, beggin' what you don't need! An stealin' what is yo's by rights! . . . . . It's the body that keeps us standin'! The soul that keeps us goin'! An' the spirit that'll take us thooo! . . . . .

His liturgy completed, Gabe sits at the table with the display and pulls the plate with the gun toward him. He bites into the gun, chews and swallows, takes a drink from the Molotov cocktail canister, as the lights black out.

When the lights come up, Dee is sitting at a table with a bottle of whisky. Shanty is sitting on a stool reading *Downbeat*. Dee wishes she could find out where Johnny has disappeared to, suspects he's with a woman. Shanty is mum.

Evie comes in. It seems that she has quit the life, has a job tending an IBM machine. Evie warns Dee about her drinking and her behavior. Evie has heard that Dee paid a visit to a place named Jack's way uptown the night before and warns Dee that she will get hurt if she strays often into that territory. Dee explains that she went there to buy, not to sell, and found herself a lover —"the biggest, blackest cat you ever saw." Evie warns Dee again that Johnny will have to kill her if he ever finds out.

Drunkenly, Dee smears black shoe polish on her face just as Johnny enters. Johnny is surprisingly tender toward Dee; helps her to wipe her face. Evie makes Dee angry by suggesting that she leave Johnny and the life. Johnny also twits Evie: "I know what's eatin' yo' ass! You don't like it 'cause I went for her and not you! Tha's it—ain't it?"

To show her utter contempt for Johnny, Evie grabs Dee, kisses her roughly on the mouth and pushes her into Johnny's arms. Johnny pushes Dee aside, and she slumps to the floor. Johnny goes after Evie, but Evie gets in the first blow, low and accurate. Johnny is doubled over. Evie leaves just as Mary Lou comes in.

Mary Lou surveys the obviously messy situation, and Dee in turn surveys Mary Lou.

MARY LOU: Johnny—I—
JOHNNY: Stay where you at, Mary.
MARY LOU: Johnny, maybe I'd better—
DEE: Well, well, well. And just who might you be, Miss Baby Cakes?
MARY LOU: Johnny!

JOHNNY: I said stay where you at!
Dee struggles to her feet. Gathers her belongings.
DEE: Baby Cakes, let me give you the best advice you ever had in your whole little life! Run away from here fast! Run for your life!
She goes into her purse. Comes up with the baby shoes. Drops them on the floor. Exits.
MARY LOU: Who is she, Johnny—?
JOHNNY: Some chick with a problem—
MARY LOU: She—she looked—
JOHNNY: She was wiped out.
MARY LOU *(picks up the baby shoes):* Who do these belong to—
He snatches them out of her hands and throws them into the waste basket.
JOHNNY: Don't ask me! Never had no kid'a mine if tha's what you're thinkin'!

Mary Lou tells Johnny someone has phoned her father and threatened to stop Mary Lou and Johnny from seeing each other. Johnny sends Shanty out and locks the street door. Johnny then confides in Mary Lou: Pete Zerroni "don't like it if a nigger's got a place'a business in his ter'tory," and "this ain't no ord'nary type 'scrimunashun! They give you the signals you ignore it! Place burns down."

Perhaps—Johnny suggests—there might be something in Mary's father's possession that could be used, if not as direct evidence, at least as a deterrent against the Zerroni people. But Mary Lou couldn't steal from her father—besides, he keeps such things locked in the office safe.

Johnny caresses Mary Lou, kisses her, points up the irony of their position—Mary Lou's father is a judge, yet they can't go to him for help. Johnny intimates that Judge Bolton may even be an accomplice of Zerroni's, which angers Mary Lou. A developing quarrel is interrupted by a pounding on the door. It is Gabe with the news that Dee has slit her wrists and is dead—up in Harlem, at the Hotel Theresa.

Scene 2

Three days later, Shanty is drumming on the bar to the juke box accompaniment, when Johnny enters with Gabe. They have just come back from Dee's funeral, at which "every damned whore in town showed up!"

Shanty's drumming irritates Johnny, who orders Shanty rather sharply to stop. Shanty reminds Johnny of the bad publicity he has received over Dee's death, as the result of some things Dee wrote on the wall with lipstick just before she died. Shanty liked Dee—she was a good tipper.

Cora comes in to tell them all that she is married at last, to a heart specialist she met at the hospital. She's on her way to Quebec for a honeymoon and to meet her husband's family.

Cora tries to create a moment of tender goodbye with Johnny, telling him she'll always think of him fondly as the little boy who was left alone in the world—but Johnny's surface remains rock-hard. Cora tries to say goodbye to Shanty, but he just keeps staring out the window. Happy at last in spite of everything, Cora exits.

JOHNNY: Married a doctor! Ain't that a bitch! Say one thing for her! That number don't give up! She—
SHANTY: Shut up, man.
JOHNNY: What you say?
SHANTY: I said, shut up, nigger.
JOHNNY: Now, look! I know you upset 'bout Cora but—
SHANTY: Will you cool it! Big man! Mister Hot Daddy! Think you know everything in the whole goddam world don't you!? Well, lemme tell you somethin', man. You don't know a mu-thah-fuc-kun thing!
He rips off his apron and flings it into Johnny's face.
Here! Do your own dirty, nigger work! I've done all I'm gonna do! Took all I'm gonna take!
He pulls out his drumsticks. Boldly beats upon the bar.
Stood behind this bar! Let you put me down for the last time! 'Cause my skin is white!
He beats harder upon the bar.
Yeah, baby. I'm white! An' I'm proud of it! Pretty an' white! Dynamite! Eh, mothahfuckah. Know what else I got that you ain't got? I got soul. You ain't got no soul. Mothahfuckah's black an' ain't got no soul. If you're an example of what the white race is ag'inst, then baby, I'm gittin' with 'em! They are gonna need a cat like me. Somebody that really knows where you black sons-a-bitches are at!
He picks up the butcher knife. Plunges it into the top of the bar.
That's what I think of this ol' piece of kind'lin! Take it an' stick it up you black, rusty, dusty!
He moves quickly to the street door. Turns. Gives Johnny the finger and exits quickly.
JOHNNY: Well, looks like ol' Corabelle Beasely done turn Shanty into a real white man, after all! . . . . .

Johnny turns to Melvin and invites him to walk out, too, but Melvin has no wish to go. They're not doing enough business to keep the kitchen open, Johnny informs Melvin, but Melvin is willing to stay on doing the chores in Shanty's place. He has dropped his dancing for the time being. He tells Johnny and Gabe of a dreadful experience at a marijuana party at his dance teacher's penthouse, where he was forced to take part in an orgy against his will.

Mary Lou comes in carrying material she has stolen from her father's safe in a paper bag. It's all there, she tells Johnny—tapes and documents indicating that Maffucci committed a murder on orders from Zerroni. Mary Lou decided, after a great deal of thought, that there wasn't any other way out for Johnny, so she worked in her father's office for an afternoon, surreptitiously watching him turn the safe dial until she had memorized the combination.

Johnny suggests that Mary Lou stay out of sight for a while, at a girl friend's. Mary Lou had of course believed that she could move in with Johnny.

Gabe, who along with Melvin has been witnessing all this with Johnny's permission, suddenly takes an interest in the situation.

GABE: And you stole that material from your father?

MARY LOU: Yes, I stole that material from my father! There was nothing else we could do!

GABE: Why you stupid naive little bitch! Don't you know what he wants that stuff for?

MARY LOU: To keep Zerroni from forcing him out of business!

GABE: That's a lie! He wants it so he kin blackmail his way into his own dirty racket!

MARY LOU: That's not true! Tell him, Johnny!

GABE: A black Mafia! That's what he wants! (Laughs.)

MARY LOU: You're crazy! Johnny, are you going to stand there and—

JOHNNY: I gotta right to my own game! Just like they do!

Mary Lou sees that Gabe is telling the truth about Johnny's ambitions. Gabe informs Mary Lou that Johnny hates everything she stands for: "Lemme tell you something! Before he kin lay one hot hand on you! You gonna have to git out there on that street an' hussle your ass off!"

Gabe moves on Johnny and demands that he hand over the paper bag. Johnny aims his revolver at Gabe, but Gabe reads him correctly: Johnny will not fire, and if he did he'd no longer be in a position to make use of the evidence against Zerroni. Johnny is forced to hand Gabe the paper bag. Gabe puts it into his briefcase, but before he can get it out of the bar Judge Bolton and Maffucci push their way in through the door.

Mary Lou is ordered out, and Bolton demands that Johnny hand over the papers. Johnny in his turn demands to see Zerroni—"horse to horse." Maffucci draws a gun, but Bolton orders him to put it away.

BOLTON: Williams, you'd better listen to me and listen good! You're in dangerous trouble! If you don't hand over that material, I'm not going to be responsible for what happens to you!

JOHNNY: And I sho' ain't gon' be responsible for what happens to you neither, Judge!

Both Johnny and the Judge laugh. Bolton starts to exit.
Judge?

Bolton turns. Johnny tosses him Mary Lou's purse. Bolton exits.

MAFFUCCI: Johnny cake?

JOHNNY: What?

MAFFUCCI: Right now, your life ain't worth a plug nickel!

JOHNNY: Footch?
> *Johnny puts his thumbnail under his upper teeth and flicks it at Maffucci. Maffucci exits.*

Johnny wants to know how come Gabe didn't hand the file over to the Judge? Gabe just couldn't bring himself to betray his friend Johnny to those two "bastards."

Johnny sends Melvin out with the file to make copies. He knows that they will probably get him, but "Gabe, we was got the day we was born! . . . . . Jus' bein' black ain't never been no real reason for livin'!" Gabe can't agree: "If I thought that! I'd probably go crazy or commit suicide!"

Scene 3

The next day, Gabe exits to the kitchen as Johnny sits at the bar checking his revolver. Machine Dog appears—he is indeed an apparition, something perhaps out of Johnny's subconscious. He is tall, black, wearing a shabby paramilitary uniform and black beret and carring a huge spanner.

Machine Dog orders Johnny to attention, delivers to him the "edick" of the "brothers": "Brother Williams! The brothers have jus' senunced an' condemned you to death! Now, repeat after me! I have been chosen to be the nex' brother to live on in the hearts an' min's'a the enemy host!"

It will be Johnny's solemn duty, Machine Dog tells him, to haunt and agonize the enemy's innermost soul, aided by all the brothers who have gone before and all those who will come after. Johnny accepts this duty. The odd ritual ends in a handshake and an exchange of "Se la! An' ay-man!" Machine Dog exits, just as Judge Bolton and two plainclothesmen enter.

This is a vice squad raid—Mary Lou has been arrested for soliciting. They bring in Mary Lou, who with great effort testifies that, yes, she was working for Johnny, and runs out.

Threatened with arrest by the vice squad, Johnny gives the paper bag back to Judge Bolton, who checks its contents and exits with the plainclothesmen— the charge is dropped. Johnny puts his revolver in his back pocket and awaits developments, meanwhile warning Gabe he'd better go while the going's good. Gabe prefers to stay.

Sweets Crane comes in carrying a large assortment of soul food, sits down to eat, invites Gabe to join him. First Gabe wants to know how come Sweets stole his watch and wallet? Sweets tells him, "Son, all my life I been one kind'a thief or 'nother! It's jus' in me! 'Course I don't have to steal! But I steals for the pure enjoyment of it! Jus' the other day I stole a rat-la from a baby!"

Sweets returns Gabe's watch and wallet—the money is all there. Maffucci comes into the bar with another white gunman, Louie. Sweets ignores the gunmen, just keeps on eating; invites Maffucci to join him and have a little maccaroni salad; gives Maffucci back his watch.

Johnny pretends that his attempt to blackmail Pete Zerroni has now failed, that the whole affair can be forgotten. But Maffucci tells him otherwise.

MAFFUCCI: . . . . . Matters a helluva lot to me! Pete now, he's willin' to forget the whole thing! Says the trick is not to take you jigs too serious! I can't do nothin' like that, Johnny! Don't look good on my record!

JOHNNY: What you gonna do about it, Footch?

Maffucci quickly pulls his gun. Levels it at Johnny. Backs to the street door. Locks it. Pulls shades. He takes a large sign from his pocket. It reads "CLOSED." He puts it on the bar in front of Johnny.

MAFFUCCI: The sign in both hands, Johnny cake!

Johnny slowly picks up the sign.

Pops, you an' that other joker stay put!

Maffucci nods to Louie who moves behind Sweets and Gabe. Johnny starts to tear sign.

Ah-ah! I want you to lick that sign an' paste it right up there on the door. Start lickin', Johnny cake!

Johnny begins to wet sign with his tongue.

That's it! Wet it a little more! That's enough! Now start walkin' real careful like.

Johnny moves to door with sign.

Now, paste it up there!

Johnny does so.

Now, back up! Real slow!

Johnny backs up. Maffucci seats Johnny on bar stool.

SWEETS: You don't have to do that, Sonny boy!

Sweets goes to the door with the knife he has been eating with.

You don't have to do nothin' like that!

He pulls the sign from the window and tears it up.

MAFFUCCI: What are you doin', Pops? Look, if you don't want hi-call-it to get hit—

JOHNNY: Keep out'a this, Sweets! This is my game!

SWEETS: Not any more, it ain't! You don't have to do nothin' like that.

Sweets advances to Maffucci.

MAFFUCCI: What'a ya, crazy, Pops? Put that ax away!

JOHNNY: Lay out of it, Sweets! Lay out of it, I said!

MAFFUCCI: I'm warnin' you, Pops! Take another step an—

Sweets lunges at Maffucci as Maffucci fires. Knife penetrates Maffucci's heart. Johnny kills Louie. Whirls and fires three shots into Maffucci. Rushes to Sweets.

JOHNNY: Goddamit, Sweets, I tole you I could handle it!

It's too late for a doctor to do Sweets any good. He barely has the strength to make Johnny promise he'll go straight from now on, and to call attention to the will in his pocket. Then, after warning Johnny "git rid'a the—the Ch-Charlie fever—" Sweets goes limp and dies.

But Johnny has no intention of keeping any promise to Sweets. He has always kept a copy of Sweets' will—and of the file on Zerroni. Johnny will go ahead with his plans, with Sweets' money to help him.

To Gabe, this is all wrong. Gabe feels they should go to the police with the truth. He feels Johnny should keep his vow to Sweets. Gabe has "no stomach for this personal war you got ag'inst the white man!"

They are already at war and committed to war, white against black, Johnny insists. Johnny presses the revolver into Gabe's hand.

JOHNNY: Take this gun in yo' han'! Feel that col' hard steel! Bet you ain't never held a heater in yo' han' like that in yo' life! Well, you gon' have to, Gabe! They gon' make you do it! 'Cause we at war, Gabe! Black ag'inst white!

GABE: I—I don't wanna—kill-you—

JOHNNY: You ain't got the guts! You wanna believe you kin sell papers an' become President! You're a coward, Gabe! A lousy, yellow, screamin' faggot coward!

> Enraged, Gabe fires at Johnny. Johnny tumbles backward and then forward into Gabe's arms. Gabe eases Johnny to the floor. Johnny goes limp. Gabe weeps softly.

Machine Dog enters, startling Gabe, who protests "He made me kill him!" Gabe presses the gun into Johnny's hand after wiping it clean of fingerprints, covers Johnny with a tablecloth and exits as Machine Dog delivers an accusation which turns into a kind of eulogy for all black sufferers: "You has crushed the very life fum black an' profane souls! Hordes'a un-re-gen-rants an' smashed the spirit an' holy ghost fum rollers an' dancers who founded they faith on black, human sufferin' burnt an' tortured souls who knew th'ough the power of love that they trials an' trib'lashuns could not be leg'slated away by no co'ot, no congruss, not eb'n God hisse'f! You has scorched an' scalded them black Mo-heekans an' stuffed them in the very stoves they cooked on! Se la! An' ay-man!" (Blackout)

Epilogue

> Gabe enters, dressed as a woman in mourning. A black shawl is draped over his head.

GABE: Like my costume? You like it? You don't like it! I know what I am by what I see in your faces! You are my mirror! But unlike a metallic reflection, you will not hold my image for very long! Your capacity for attention is very short! Therefore, I must try to provoke you! Provoke your attention! Change my part over and over again! I am rehearsing at the moment! For tomorrow, I will go out amongst you, "The Black Lady in Mourning!" I will weep, I will wail, and I will mourn! But my cries will not be heard! No one will wipe away my bitter tears! My black anguish will fall upon deaf ears! I will mourn a passing! Yes! The passing and the ending of a people dying! Of a people dying into that new life! A people whose identity could only be measured by the struggle, the dehumanization, the degradation they suffered! Or allowed themselves to suffer! Perhaps! I will mourn the ending of those years! I will mourn the death of a people dying! Of a people dying into that new life!

> *Blackout. Curtain.*

○○○
○○○
○○○
○○○
○○○
○○○ # ADAPTATION/NEXT
A Program of Two One-Act Plays
ADAPTATION
BY ELAINE MAY
NEXT
BY TERRENCE McNALLY
Cast and credits appear on page 446

*ELAINE MAY (Adaptation) was born Elaine Berlin in 1932, the daughter
of an actor in the Yiddish theater. In 1949 her name was changed by marriage
to May, which she has retained in her career. She studied acting with Maria
Ouspenskaya. Later, Miss May was a member of the Compass, a Chicago
group of revue performers specializing in improvisations. Another Compass
performer—Mike Nichols—later teamed up with Miss May in one of the outstanding acts of modern times, much of it created during performances. In
New York City they appeared at the Blue Angel, the Village Vanguard and on
the concert stage at Town Hall. Finally they reached Broadway in* An Evening
with Mike Nichols and Elaine May *October 8, 1960 at the Royale Theater for
306 performances.*

Miss May's play A Matter of Position *was produced on tour in October
1962. Off Broadway, her* Not Enough Rope *was produced at the Maidman*

Theater February 27, 1962 and she directed The Third Ear *in a production at the Premise May 21, 1964. She directed both her own* Adaptation *and Terrence McNally's* Next *on this 1969 off-Broadway program. The two one-act plays are linked not only physically on this bill but also in theme and mood, making up the first program by different authors ever to be named a collective Best Play. In private life Miss May is married and has one child, a daughter, by her first husband. She was also married to Sheldon Harnick, the renowned Broadway musical author.*

TERRENCE McNALLY (Next) *was born and raised in Corpus Christi, Texas. He received his B.A. in English at Columbia, where in his senior year he wrote the varsity show. After graduation he was awarded the Harry Evans Travelling Fellowship in creative writing (and more recently he was the recipient of a Guggenheim). He made his Broadway debut with* And Things That Go Bump in the Night *on April 26, 1965 at the Royale Theater, after a production of the play at the Tyrone Guthrie Theater in Minneapolis. Last season his play* Tour *was produced off Broadway as part of the program* Collision Course, *and three of his short plays were produced on National Educational Television under the title* Apple Pie.

McNally's work was much produced in New York this season. Besides Next, *off Broadway saw two of his one-acters under the title* Sweet Eros. *On Broadway, his* Noon *segment of* Morning, Noon and Night, *another program of one-acters, was produced by Circle in the Square at Henry Miller's Theater. McNally has also written* Bringing It All Back Home *for the new La Mama Theater. A collection of his work is in preparation by Random House.*

ADAPTATION

SYNOPSIS: The stage is a game board marked off for a contest called "Adaptation" and furnished with a few cubes on which the actors can sit. Upstage is a panel where scores, words, etc. may be projected.

The atmosphere is that of a TV studio before a game show. A games master (Narrator) and his two assistants (Players, male and female) enter and begin checking equipment and props. They will play all the roles in the game except that of contestant.

The contestant—Phil Benson—is brought in and stands nervously while the recorded voice of an announcer explains that the point of the game is to find, somewhere on the board, a hidden Security Square. If he succeeds in doing so, the contestant receives a Super Bonus Card entitling him to any prize he wishes.

Phil Benson is led into position behind the starting panel. The voice of the announcer confides to the audience: "Ladies and gentlemen, what Mr. Benson does *not* know is that *he, himself,* may label *any* space on the Board the Security Square and declare himself the winner at any time it *occurs* to him to do so."

A buzzer signals the beginning of the game. The starting panel opens and the Narrator tells Phil: "You are born. Move three spaces forward and enter the world as the son of urban, liberal, middle-income, Protestant, white, American parents."

MOTHER: Harry, it's a boy.

FATHER: I heard.

MOTHER: I'm going to name him Phil. There's no reason for it. I just like the sound of the name.

FATHER: It's a good name, Phyllis.

MOTHER: Have the painters finished yet?

FATHER: Not yet. As a matter of fact they haven't shown up yet. Neither has the girl from the State Employment Agency, and I didn't have time to clean the apartment myself because the freezer defrosted during the power failure on Thursday and I had to spend all day Saturday shopping for specials. I'm going to take them up to the apartment as soon as the elevators are fixed, which I hope will be soon because the garbage is piling up in the service hall and the Sanitation Department says there's nothing they can do about garbage unless it's piling up in the street. But there isn't any immediate crisis, because the boiler broke down during the cold wave on Wednesday and there's no heat in the building . . . which means that the entire building is like a refrigerator, so, of course, the garbage won't spoil . . . and the food specials in the lobby will stay fresh—which is fortunate because after I paid the hospital bill I had to get the bank to extend our loan for another thirty days so I could pay the rent, and the first premium on a new all-inclusive life insurance policy which guarantees that should I have a coronary before Phil is twelve you and he will be able to maintain the same standard of living you enjoy now.

MOTHER: Oh Harry. I can't wait to get home and get back to normal.

The Narrator directs the contestant, Phil, to "Leave the hospital and start life." He gets one Maturity Point for getting home even though the only available taxi refuses to go in his direction, but loses the point by confusing the identities of his mother and father.

Phil reaches the square on which he asks his mother where babies come from, and what sex is all about. Mother explains casually, in the most careful clinical detail. But when Phil asks her "Mom, what's a Negro?" mother sits him down and gravely explains to him about dark flowers and white flowers growing side-by-side in the same garden.

Phil is sent to school, where the rules are many and confusing, but he reaches the Third Grade Square safely. After a heart-to-heart talk with his father in which neither of them says anything, Phil is ordered to take a giant step into prepubescence and then into puberty, along with other members of his school grade, among them a boy and a girl whom Phil watches closely.

They go through various phases of development leading to puberty. The boy rolls down his pants, the girl takes off her bow, the boy becomes aware of his muscles, feels his face for hair, covertly studies the girl. The girl becomes aware of her looks, feels her breasts tentatively, covertly looks at the boy. Phil studies both of them, alternately flexing his muscles and feeling his breast.

NARRATOR *(blowing whistle):* You are having an identity crisis . . . Your mother is called to school for a conference with the school principal. Go to your nearest Isolation Square.

MOTHER: What did he do, Mr. Ashley?

ASHLEY: He wrote something scurrilous on the walls about one of the students—who happens to be colored.

MOTHER: What did he write?

ASHLEY *(reading from a slip of paper):* "Jim is a dark flower." Naturally Jim is outraged. We're trying to appease his mother now, but she's threatened to release the story to the New York Post . . . which would destroy the image we have tried to build up for this school as sub-standard but equal. Frankly, Mrs. Benson, it's a dilemma.

NARRATOR: Your parents are in Conflict. Remain on your Isolation Square until a decision has been made.

Phil's parents decide to send him to a progressive private school where marching on Washington is part of the regular curriculum. Before long, Phil is writing *really* shocking phrases on the wall, like "Phyllis can't make a commitment." But his mother is relieved that at least he isn't writing about dark flowers.

The Narrator sends Phil on to high school, where he has trouble deciding which extracurricular activity to pursue. He tries to adapt to one of the female intellectuals in his class.

NORMA: I don't care what people think, Phil. I have to be the way I am. I won't conform. Last year I read *The Prophet* aloud at my parents' Seder. My mother cried. She didn't understand. I wanted them to hear *The Prophet* so they could understand love—but too many people spell it f-i-t.

PHIL: F-i-t?

NORMA: Yes, ironic isn't it? That's how they spell everything.

PHIL: F-i-t spells fit.

NORMA: I know. That's why *The Prophet* is meaningless to them.

PHIL: Oh. They spell *prophet* f-i-t.

NORMA: That's right. That's the absurdity.

PHIL: Yeah . . . well, nobody knows how to spell any more. I mean bright guys . . . and they can't even spell their own names. I blame it on the schools and a lack of interest on the part of the establishment.

NORMA: I'm not talking about that. I'm talking about an attitude on the part of a society.

PHIL: Yeah, well, that, I think, is because they're taught to read by sounding out words instead of memorizing them. They think of words as sounds rather than symbols. But that's changing now in a lot of schools.

NORMA: Phil, I'm talking about values, not spelling. I'm saying that people don't care.

PHIL: Wow. You know that's really true. They really don't. Never mind looking it up. If it sounds like "f" spell it with an "f". Why bother to check up and see if it's "p-h". No one bothers to use a dictionary any more.

There is a pause.

NORMA: Give me back the book.

NARRATOR: You have failed in your Emotional Interest. Advance to your nearest Narcissistic Consolation square and try to Recover Status.

MARK: How'd you make out last night, Phil?

PHIL: Boy, I tell you Thomas Wolfe was right about Jewish girls. They don't just discuss it . . . if you know what I mean.

MARK: I know what you mean.

Phil and Mark nudge each other and laugh dirtily for several seconds.

NARRATOR: You have just successfully Enhanced Your Image without actually having accomplished anything. Move two squares sideways toward Security.

PHIL: I hope I haven't ruined her reputation or anything.

NARRATOR: You are feeling Guilt which entitles you to another Maturity Point but forfeits your last move. Go back two squares to a Moral Position.

PHIL: But on the other hand, who knows what she's saying about me.

NARRATOR: You are having an Adolescent Crisis. Enter a New Phase in which you Lie Around at Home. Do not shave. Do not collect any Maturity Cards. Do not change clothes until your parents notice you.

Phil's father engages him in a heart-to-heart talk, which is to say an assortment of cliches about making the most of youth while it lasts—the rat race begins all too soon, as Father can testify. He wants to be close to his son—but somehow they don't seem to have the friendly father-and-son arguments you see on TV. They should have more talks like this one. And in the meantime, Phil's father instructs him: "Could you step a little to one side. You're standing in front of the set."

Phil starts to think about college and long-term goals. He applies for Yale, Berkeley and Chicago and is admitted to the University of Miami. He is urged by his friend Mark to go ahead and follow his Impossible Dream (the Players hum a chorus of the *Man of La Mancha* song while Phil tells his parents of his decision).

PHIL: Mom, I've decided to major in Hotel Management.

MOTHER: That's nice. Then you can manage a hotel.

PHIL: Dad, I've decided to major in Hotel Management. Dad? Dad? Am I standing in front of the set?

FATHER: Yes . . . but I can talk to you and watch, Phil. You see, I'm thinking about another kid, Phil. A young, crazy kid very much like you, Phil. Me. A kid with a dream . . . who wanted more than anything in the world to own a liquor store. I was a wild kid like you, Phil. And even though everyone told me I was crazy I went ahead. I learned everything there was to know about liquor. But I always knew I had to have something to fall back on, Phil. That's why I joined the Civil Service. You understand what I'm trying to tell you?

PHIL: Yes, sir. You're trying to tell me to have something to fall back on.

FATHER: That's right, Phil.

PHIL: I've already done that, Dad. I'm minoring in Cinema.

FATHER: Good boy.

At college, the Hotel Management professor lectures Phil on O.A.M.— organization, administration and management—which he calls the secret of success. Phil has brought a copy of *Fortune* to class and is penalized by the Narrator when a quote from it about the high cost of public relations in the hotel business antagonizes the professor.

Phil tries to decide which political front and which fraternity to join. He is ordered to take an Opportunity Card, which reads: "You make friends with a Negro."

Phil puts his arm around the other man's shoulder and leaves it there for the rest of the scene.

PHIL: This is a real time of crisis for you, isn't it Harve?

HARVE: It sure is. I don't know whether to join the Urban League and attempt to seek equality by peaceful methods or join SNICC and attempt to stir the conscience of the white man by gutting my own neighborhood.

PHIL: I want to tell you something, Harvey. I believe—and this may sound crazy to you—but I believe the future of civil rights may lie to a great extent in the hands of hotel managers. That's one of the things I'm trying to do, Harve. That's one of the reasons I want to make it in O.A.M.

NARRATOR: You join SNICC and are thrown out of the organization after your first meeting. Remain where you are.

HARVE: What happened, Phil?

PHIL: I don't know, Harve. It all seemed very pleasant at first. One of the speakers was saying that the end of the white man had come and all we could contribute was money because our services weren't worth anything and I was applauding along with the rest of the audience and suddenly he leaned forward and called, "Can you understand that, Whitey?" And I called back "I sure can, Blacky" and I was removed from the hall and deprived of my civil rights button.

Phil is accepted by a very exclusive fraternity and so he decides to join the establishment and effect change from within. "You have made a social adjustment," the Narrator informs him, "take a Success Card and rise to the top ten per cent of your class."

After scoring high in O.A.M. during the visit of a Hilton relative to the classroom, Phil starts a search for the Right Girl. He is engaged almost before he knows it, to a girl named Doris. In rapid succession Phil accepts an assignment to spy on his class for the C.I.A., graduates, gets a job with the Hilton Hotel chain and marries Doris, his college sweetheart.

Phil goes into debt for a house. Upwardly mobile, he accosts Mr. Hilton drunkenly, at a party, and tells him what he really thinks of him.

PHIL: ..... you're not good, Mr. Hilton. You wanna know what you are? You're great! That's what you are. Just goddamned, unbelievably great. Now go ahead and fire me if you want to.

NARRATOR: You are transferred to a larger city and have your first child. Advance to Fatherhood.

DORIS: It's a boy, Phil.

PHIL: I heard. What are you going to name him, Doris?

DORIS: I thought I'd name him Dore. After . . . one of the great liberals of our time. Dore Schary. In fact I'd like his middle name to be Schary.

BOTH (smiling at the baby): Dore Schary Benson.

NARRATOR: You receive a raise and buy your second house. Advance one space toward Prosperity.

PHIL: Doris, I'd like to have a den. Do you think we could afford one?

DORIS: Could you move a little to one side, Phil. You're standing in front of the set.

The C.I.A. drops Phil from its payroll, which sets him back. But he recovers. Soon he is a chain manager, and Dore is in school. Then his dream comes true—he is to manage the Chicago Hilton during the National Democratic Convention.

PHIL: I've spent all my life preparing for this moment, Doris. This is what it's all about. *This* is O.A.M. Oh, wait till my father hears about this.

FATHER: You're standing in front of the set.

PHIL: Dad, take a close look at the screen. Do you notice who's being interviewed on camera?

FATHER: Yes. It's you. You should have moved a little to one side. You're standing in front of Gabe Pressman.

NARRATOR: You have reached a Long Term Goal. Advance to Emotional Fulfillment and take another step toward Success.

DORIS: Well, how was it? Did you meet anyone important? Were you photographed with Mayor Daley? Phil? Phil, what is it?

PHIL (slowly): One hundred and two top sheets and forty-one towels—gone.

DORIS: Well, that's not unusual.

PHIL: Not to mention twenty-seven washcloths and four pillow cases.

DORIS: Tell me about the convention.

PHIL: And two ash trays.

DORIS: Phil, stop itemizing and answer me.

PHIL: I can't believe it. Those men were my heroes.

Phil's father dies watching TV but leaves Phil's mother well provided for. Phil tries to communicate with his own long-haired son the way he remembers his father talking to him.

PHIL: Hang on to your youth.

DORE: For what? I didn't ask to be born. Who wants it? Who needs it? What do I have that's so great?

PHIL: I'm sorry I'm so busy.

DORE: You've sold out. That's why you're so busy. You've all sold out.

PHIL: I wanted you and your mom to have a little security when I was gone.

DORE: In this rotten world? With the bomb ten minutes away? There's no way you can make it up to me. Just give me my allowance and let me go.

PHIL: I don't have any cash on me right now.

DORE: Then could you move a little to one side? You're standing in front of the set.

NARRATOR: You have failed to Reach Your Son. Advance three squares to Domestic Upheaval and try to Do Better.

Phil quarrels with Doris. He also quarrels with his mistress, and so returns to Doris. At last the Hilton Hotel Chain retires him. The Narrator instructs him: "You have retired with moderate wealth. Take two steps sideways toward Security and have a Coronary Occlusion."

Phil, staggering, is supported by Doris. She tries to get him home, but of course the taxi will not go in their direction.

DORIS: Sit down and rest. I'll call an ambulance.

PHIL: No, no. It will never get crosstown in time. Doris . . . did you pay the premium on the life insurance?

DORIS: Yes, Phil.

PHIL: I wish I didn't have to quit so soon. If I could have played a little while longer I know I could have found the Security Square.

DORIS: We're secure, Phil. The house is almost paid for. We own the lien on the car. The AT & T stock brings in a small but steady income.

PHIL: But I wanted so much more. I had so many dreams . . .

The Players begin humming "The Impossible Dream."

. . . I wanted to earn a Super Bonus Card and have a house in the country with a small heated pool and maybe one or two little hotels and a high yield stock with minimum risk. I wanted to send Dore to a really good college where he could make contacts and wear the best clothes and drive the best car that money could buy and be a real college boy. I wanted to eat out without fear and tip lavishly so that headwaiters would know me and I'd get a good table. I wanted to be on intimate terms with a congressman or a movie star so that my father would be proud of me before he died, and my mother would think I was somebody. And I never had any of those things. Where did I go wrong, Doris?

DORIS: You aimed too high, Phil.

The actors' singing gradually swells during the following speech.

PHIL: Maybe. But it was worth it, Doris. I had a dream, a simple American dream . . . and I would rather have had that dream and never realize it than have nothing but the reality of what I have. See to it . . . that Dore . . . carries the torch.

NARRATOR: You have spoken your last words. Remain where you are and die.

Curtain.

NEXT

Time: The present

Place: An examination room

SYNOPSIS: The stage is set with an examination table, a cabinet full of medical equipment, a scale. At right is a desk and two chairs, at center is an American flag.

The voice of Sergeant Thech is heard offstage calling "Next!" Marion Cheever enters—*"He is a fat man in his late 40s and he is nattily dressed. He carries a briefcase."* He lights a cigarette and finally Sergeant Thech enters. She is in uniform, hefty, businesslike. She tells Marion there is no smoking and demands his "card and bottle."

Marion hands her his card. She begins to type.

MARION: I thought to myself there must be someone else in my building with the same name because why else would I get a card to come down here?

SGT. THECH: Is your name Marion Cheever?

MARION: Yes, it is. But you know I just had a fortieth birthday and I thought to myself nobody sends a card like this to a man like me.

SGT. THECH: They're taking older men.

MARION: How old exactly?

SGT. THECH: It's inching up all the time. May I have your bottle, please?

MARION *(looking in briefcase):* Inching up all the time, is it? The bottle, yes, here it is!

He hands her his urine specimen.

SGT. THECH: Strip.

MARION: I didn't know it . . . the inching up all the time.

SGT. THECH: Remove all articles of clothing including your shoes and socks.

MARION: Who are you?

SGT. THECH: Sergeant Thech, your examining officer. And by the authority vested in me by this government, I order you to strip.

MARION: A lady examining officer! Oh that's funny! They must be pretty hard up these days.

SGT. THECH: And if you have not begun to strip in the next ten seconds I will complete these forms without further examination and report you to the board of examiners as fit for duty.

She begins to count off the ten seconds: "One one-thousand, two one-thousand . . . . ." Marion realizes she means business. He begins to strip while she asks him routine questions. He admits he is 48, not 40. He tries to joke with her, but she takes everything so literally that he is forced to play it absolutely straight.

Marion tells Sgt. Thech he has been the assistant manager of the Fine Arts Theater, a New York art movie house, for 15 years. He has now stripped down to a torn and dirty undershirt and is looking desperately for some place to hide. He wraps himself in the flag as he continues to strip. He is standing behind Sgt. Thech, who cannot see what he is doing and continues to ask him questions so routine that they almost seem to be statements requiring no question mark. Marital status—divorced twice, with three children, all girls. Education—high school but not college. Religion—Roman Catholic.

SGT. THECH: Do you live alone.

MARION: At the present time I do. I get a lot of company, of course, but unh, officially, for the record, I live alone.

SGT. THECH: Do you own your own home.

MARION: No. It's a . . . you know . . . residential hotel for . . . unh . . . men. Single men.

Marion has undressed now and is sitting on a low stool. The flag is draped across him.

SGT. THECH *(turning to a new page):* Measles.

MARION: What?

SGT. THECH: Have you ever had the measles.

MARION: Oh measles! No, no I haven't!

Sgt. Thech questions Marion about his general health and allergies. He tries to persuade her that he is a nervous wreck, a chain smoker, a compulsive drinker, but she is unimpressed.

Turning to order him onto the scales, she sees that he is draped in the flag. She gives him a sheet to drape himself in, pulls the flag away from him, salutes it. Then she prepares herself for the examination, ominously washing her hands and putting on a white coat.

Marion is angry (he is going to complain to somebody about this) and then alarmed at the way she callously weighs and measures him, spinning the measuring pole close to his head. As she orders him to sit at the edge of the examining table, he at first complains of the humiliation in this whole process, but then decides to change his tune: "I'm sorry. I'm not cooperating. You have your job to do and I'll try to help in every way I can."

But Marion cannot elicit any humanitarian reaction or response from Sgt. Thech by means of cooperation, any more than he could by joking or complaining. She is imperturbable, as unreachable as a machine. She tests his heart, his hearing, his eyes. She calls him "Private," and he objects—he hasn't passed the physical yet. She warns him that this is his one chance to *fail* the physical, he'd better cooperate. Sgt. Thech orders Marion "Keep your head down."

MARION: What do they want with me anyway? I'm on the verge of my big break. Do you know what that means to a civilian? I've stood in the back of that lousy theater for eleven years and they are going to promote me next winter. Unh-hunh, sergeant, I'm not going into any army, war or peace!

SGT. THECH *(while she makes ready to take a blood sample):* I want you to close your eyes and count to ten slowly and then touch the tip of your nose with your left index finger.

MARION: Oh, all right, that sounds easy. I don't mind this part at all. One, two, three, four . . . this is very restful . . . five, six—*(Suddenly sitting up.)* Wait! Wait, wait, wait, wait, wait! I saw it.

Sgt. Thech is holding a syringe.

I hate needles. I'm not afraid of them, I just don't like them.

SGT. THECH: Shall I complete the forms, Mr. Cheever, or will you let me continue with the examination?

MARION: I know you must do your job, but please be very careful. I have very small veins. Don't be nervous.

She proceeds to take the blood sample, then orders him to stand up and drop his shorts. It turns out that he is wearing a girdle, and he is forced to drop it. She reaches under his sheet to test him for hernia. While Marion is haranguing her, comparing her to his first wife whom he divorced for mental cruelty in Juarez, Mexico, she completes some forms. Then she tells him that the physical is over and he has passed it. He objects violently. She hasn't examined his feet, his sinuses, his teeth, his hair . . . he snatches off his toupee.

MARION: . . . . . And what about my mind? You haven't asked me one single question about my mind. For all you know I could be a raving lunatic. I could be a—

SGT. THECH *(she's into the psychological and intelligence tests):* I have twelve apples.

MARION *(thrown):* You have what?

SGT. THECH: You have twelve apples. Together we have . . .

MARION *(involuntarily):* Twenty-four apples. *(He realizes what he's done and groans.)*

SGT. THECH: I have a pie which I wish to divide as follows: one-fourth of the pie to Fred, one-fourth of the pie to Phyllis, one-fourth of the pie to you. How much of the pie will I have left for myself.

MARION *(thinks a moment):* Who are Fred and Phyllis. I mean maybe Phyllis didn't finish all her piece and there'd be more for you. A quarter and a half!

Sgt. Thech continues to ask routine test questions, to which Marion supplies answers which are as absurd as he can make them. She asks him what he would do if he were seated in a theater and noticed a fire before the rest of the audience. "This one's right up my alley," he replies. "As a theater manager I know about this. The main thing is I wouldn't want to start a panic. So I'd very quietly leave and go home."

Sgt. Thech puts him through the various kinds of aptitude questions and his ridiculous answers fail to ruffle a feather of her military composure. She probes every avenue of his psyche with word-associations and questions, until Marion abandons all reality in his answers.

SGT. THECH: Compulsive eating.

MARION: No, I've never been bothered by that. About my anxiety states—

SGT. THECH: Have you ever indulged in homosexual activities.

MARION: They have been very good to me.

SGT. THECH: When did you stop.

MARION: Who said anything about stopping? They're a small but vital minority. The Fine Arts Theater welcomes them.

SGT. THECH: Did you have a normal relationship with your mother?

MARION: I'm sure she thought so!

SGT. THECH: Did you have a normal relationship with your father.

MARION: After we stopped dating the same girl, everything was fine.

SGT. THECH: Do you have any history of bedwetting.

MARION: Even my top sheet is rubber.

SGT. THECH: Have you ever attempted suicide.

MARION: No, but I've thought of murder.

SGT. THECH: Are you now or have you ever been a member of the Communist Party.

MARION: I wouldn't be surprised. I mean you join anything nowadays and next thing you know it's pinko.

SGT. THECH: What is your responsibility to your community.

MARION: Unh . . . to shovel the snow.

SGT. THECH: What is your responsibility to your family.

MARION: To be there.

SGT. THECH: What is your responsibility to your country.

MARION: To be there.

SGT. THECH (abruptly): All right, Mr. Cheever, you may go now. The examination is over.

Sgt. Thech reassures Marion that on the basis of his answers to the psychological exam the Army probably won't accept him. He can go, she tells him, she is through with him. But she has turned Marion inside out, and he cannot return to normal so easily. He begins to talk compulsively as he puts his clothes back on. Sgt. Thech types out a form, ignoring Marion, but Marion persists. The more he talks, the more indignant he becomes at the humiliation he has suffered. He demands his blood and urine samples back.

Sgt. Thech concentrates on her typing while Marion pours it all out. He is a citizen, he performs his duty to his family and country, and he demands his rights. He even feels he is entitled to some kind of reward: "You owe me something. My country owes me something. Somebody owes me something. Because I have nothing! My children don't give a damn. What do I get on Father's Day? A lot of crap from Woolworth's their mothers picked out. My father doesn't recognize my voice on the telephone. My mother is dead. I've been married twice. You think it's fun, a man my age going home alone at night? Who looks at men like me after a while? I know what I look like! I'm no fool! *(Sgt. Thech continues typing.)* You know what the ushers at the theater call me behind my back? Fatso. Yeah! that hurts. But when I become *the* manager I am going to fire those ushers and hire new ushers and *they* will call me Fatso behind my back. Because that is exactly what I am. A Fatso. I am nothing but what I eat. But I feed myself. Nobody feeds me. And I eat everything I want. When I want candy, I eat candy. When I want a pizza at two a.m., I call up and order pizza. I'm going to get older and fatter and some day I'm going to die from overweight and smoking. But when I go, I'm paying for my own funeral and I'm going to give myself the best funeral that money can buy. Because dead or alive I pay my own way! Those niggers on relief, can they say that? They cannot! And they get to do everything. They get to riot, they get to loot, they get to yell, they get to hate, they get to kill! They get in the papers, they get on television and everybody pays attention. Everybody cares. And what do I get? There's nothing on television about me. My name's not in the Sunday papers. And I'm the one who does everything he should. I'm the one who never makes trouble. I'm the good citizen. But everybody else gets to do everything! You see those teen-age girls with their skirts up to here strutting around with their hair all piled up and driving a man crazy. And those men all like fags with that hair and those pants. They do anything they want. They have anything they want. And I get shit!"

Instead of being happy to fail the examination, he is indignant that Sgt. Thech should dismiss him so cavalierly as "unacceptable." He wants consideration and attention. He orders Sgt. Thech to stop typing and listen to him. When she doesn't, he stops her by placing his hands over the keys.

As Sgt. Thech folds the paper, checks her equipment and leaves the room, Marion orders her to make each movement and gesture as though she were performing precisely at his command. Then he begins to give himself orders. He, Marion, orders Marion through successive stages of the physical exam. He orders himself onto the scale, onto the examination table. Finally he puts himself through the questions about his family life and his past.

MARION: Tell me about it. I was thirteen years old. Yes, go on. I came home and she wasn't there. Yes. It was so sudden. None of us knew. We all thought she would always be there and then when she wasn't . . . *(His voice trails off in tears.)* You must have been very sad. I was, I was. I felt so cold. Didn't you tell anyone how you felt? Nobody asked me. I'm asking you. I never got to say goodbye. I understand. *(Short pause.)* On your feet now. I don't think I can. Yes, Cheever, you can do it. You're very strong now and very brave and very acceptable.

> *Marion gets up off the table.*

Up now, shoulders back, walk tall. That's it. You're doing fine.

> *Marion goes to Sgt. Thech's desk, puts on her white examination coat which she has left over her chair, sits, types a moment, then looks up.*

You have ten seconds to strip. By the power vested in me by the United States government I order you to remove all articles of clothing. One one-thousand, two one-thousand, three one-thousand, four one-thousand. Sorry. You are not acceptable.

> *His head spins around as he looks straight ahead into the audience.*

NEXT!

> *Lights snap off. Curtain.*

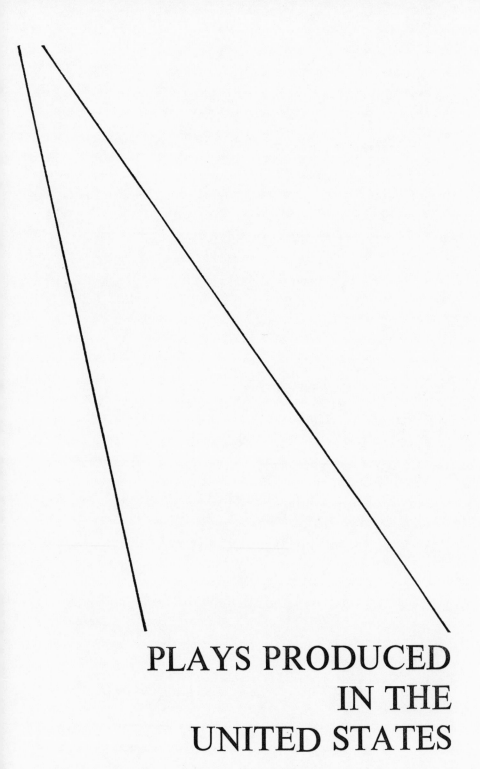

PLAYS PRODUCED
IN THE
UNITED STATES

PLAYS PRODUCED ON BROADWAY

Figures in parentheses following a play's title indicate number of performances. Plays marked with an asterisk (*) were still running on June 1, 1969, and their number of performances is figured from opening night through May 31, 1969, not including extra non-profit performances. In a listing of a show's numbers—dances, sketches, musical scenes, etc.—the titles of songs are identified by their appearance in quotation marks (").

HOLDOVERS FROM PREVIOUS SEASONS

Plays which were running on June 1, 1968 are listed below. More detailed information about them is to be found in previous *Best Plays* volumes of appropriate years. Important cast changes are recorded in a section of this volume.

* **Hello, Dolly!** (2,210). Musical suggested by Thornton Wilder's *The Matchmaker;* book by Michael Stewart; music and lyrics by Jerry Herman. Opened January 16, 1964.

* **Fiddler on the Roof** (1,956). Musical based on Sholom Aleichem's stories; book by Joseph Stein; music by Jerry Bock; lyrics by Sheldon Harnick. Opened September 22, 1964.

* **Man of La Mancha** (1,467). Musical suggested by the life and works of Miguel de Servantes y Saavedra; book by Dale Wasserman; music by Mitch Leigh; lyrics by Joe Darion. Opened November 22, 1965.

Cactus Flower (1,234). By Abe Burrows; based on a play by Pierre Barillet and Jean-Pierre Gredy. Opened December 8, 1965. (Closed November 23, 1968)

* **Mame** (1,260). Musical based on the novel *Auntie Mame* by Patrick Dennis and the play by Jerome Lawrence and Robert E. Lee; book by Jerome Lawrence and Robert E. Lee; music and lyrics by Jerry Herman. Opened May 24, 1966.

* **Cabaret** (1,153). Musical based on John van Druten's play *I Am a Camera* and stories by Christopher Isherwood; book by Joe Masteroff; music by John Kander; lyrics by Fred Ebb. Opened November 20, 1966.

I Do! I Do! (560). Musical based on Jan de Hartog's play *The Fourposter;* book and lyrics by Tom Jones; music by Harvey Schmidt. Opened December 5, 1966. (Closed June 15, 1968)

You Know I Can't Hear You When the Water's Running (755). Program of four one-act plays by Robert Anderson. Opened March 13, 1967. (Closed January 4, 1969)

Rosencrantz and Guildenstern Are Dead (420). By Tom Stoppard. Opened October 16, 1967. (Closed October 19, 1968)

There's a Girl in My Soup (321). By Terence Frisby. Opened October 18, 1967. (Closed July 27, 1968)

The Repertory Theater of Lincoln Center. 1967-68 schedule of four revivals ended with **Cyrano de Bergerac** (52). By Edmond Rostand; new English version by James Forsyth. Opened April 25, 1968. (Closed June 8, 1968)

Association of Producing Artists (APA-Phoenix) Repertory Company. 1967-68 repertory of plays. **Pantagleize** (59). By Michel de Ghelderode; translated by George Hauger. Opened November 30, 1967. **The Show-Off** (81). Revival of the play by George Kelly. Opened December 5, 1967. **Exit the King** (47). By Eugene Ionesco; translated by Donald Watson. (Repertory closed June 22, 1968 after 225 performances including 38 of *The Cherry Orchard*)

How Now, Dow Jones (220). Musical based on an original idea by Carolyn Leigh; book by Max Shulman; music by Elmer Bernstein; lyrics by Carolyn Leigh. Opened December 7, 1967. (Closed June 15, 1968)

Spofford (202). By Herman Shumlin; based on Peter DeVries' novel *Reuben, Reuben*. Opened December 14, 1967. (Closed June 8, 1968)

The Prime of Miss Jean Brodie (378). By Jay Allen; adapted from the novel by Muriel Spark. Opened January 16, 1968. (Closed December 14, 1968)

The Happy Time (285). Musical based on the play by Samuel Taylor and the book by Robert L. Fontaine; book by N. Richard Nash; music by John Kander; lyrics by Fred Ebb. Opened January 18, 1968. (Closed September 28, 1968)

A Day in the Death of Joe Egg (154). By Peter Nichols. Opened February 1, 1968. (Closed June 15, 1968)

Golden Rainbow (383). Musical based on a play by Arnold Schulman; book by Ernest Kinoy; music and lyrics by Walter Marks. Opened February 4, 1968. (Closed January 12, 1969)

The Price (429). By Arthur Miller. Opened February 7, 1968. (Closed February 15, 1969)

* **Plaza Suite** (537). Program of three one-act plays by Neil Simon. Opened February 14, 1968.

George M! (427). Musical with book by Michael Stewart and John and Fran Pascal; music and lyrics by George M. Cohan; lyric and musical revisions by Mary Cohan; musical supervision by Laurence Rosenthal. Opened April 10, 1968. (Closed April 26, 1969)

* **Hair** (455). Musical with book and lyrics by Gerome Ragni and James Rado; music by Galt MacDermot. Opened April 29, 1968.

Leonard Sillman's New Faces of 1968 (52). Musical revue conceived by Leonard Sillman. Opened May 2, 1968. (Closed June 15, 1968)

The Only Game in Town (16). By Frank D. Gilroy. Opened May 20, 1968. (Closed June 1, 1968)

The King and I (22). Musical revival based on the novel *Anna and the King of Siam* by Margaret Landon; book and lyrics by Oscar Hammerstein II; music by Richard Rodgers. Opened May 23, 1968. (Closed June 9, 1968)

The Venetian Twins (I Due Gemelli Veneziani) (32). Revival of the play in the Italian language by Carlo Goldoni. Opened May 28, 1968. (Closed June 23, 1968)

PLAYS PRODUCED JUNE 1, 1968—MAY 31, 1969

My Fair Lady (22). Musical revival adapted from George Bernard Shaw's play *Pygmalion* and Gabriel Pascal's movie; book and lyrics by Alan Jay Lerner; music by Frederick Loewe. Produced by The City Center Light Opera Company, Jean Dalrymple director, at New York City Center. Opened June 13, 1968. (Closed June 30, 1968)

Mrs. Eynsford-Hill ....Claire Waring	Alfred P. Doolittle ....George Rose
Eliza Doolittle ....Inga Swenson	Mrs. Pearce ....Leta Bonynge
Freddy Eynsford-Hill ....Evan Thomas	Mrs. Hopkins;
Colonel Pickering ....Byron Webster	Lady Boxington ....Blanche Collins
Bystander; Jamie;	Mrs. Higgins ....Margery Maude
Lord Boxington ....James Beard	Chauffeur ....Todd Butler
Henry Higgins ....Fritz Weaver	Footman; Flunkey;
Selsey Man; Harry;	Bartender ....Darrell Sandeen
Ambassador ....Charles Goff	Footman ....Peter Costanza
Hoxton Man; 3d Cockney ....Jack Fletcher	Constable ....Richard Maxon
1st Cockney ....Laried Montgomery	Flower Girl ....Kiki Minor
2d Cockney ....Stokely Gray	Zoltan Karpathy ....Erik Rhodes
4th Cockney; Butler ....William James	Queen of Transylvania ....Maggie Worth
Bartender ....Larry Devon	Mrs. Higgins' Maid ....Jeanne Shea

Buskers: George Bunt, John Johann, Kiki Minor. Servants: Jeanne Shea, Hanna Owen, Maggie Worth, Joyce Olson, William James, Stokely Gray.

Singing ensemble: Marcia Brushingham, Spring Fairbank, Maryann Kerrick, Joyce Olson, Hanna Owen, Jeanne Shea, Barbara Sorenson, Maggie Worth, Jim Connor, Peter Costanza, Larry Devon, Jack Fletcher, Stokely Gray, William James, Laried Montgomery, Darrell Sandeen.

Dancing ensemble: Lisa Ackerman, Judith Austin, Cindi Bulak, Joyce Maret, Mari McMinn, Kiki Minor, Skiles Ricketts, Britt Swanson, Margot Travers, Oscar Anthony, George Bunt, Todd Butler, Richard Dodd, Joe Helm, John Johann, Donald Mark, Richard Maxon, Duane Taylor, Jimmy White.

Understudies: Mr. Weaver—Jack Fletcher; Miss Swenson—Jeanne Shea; Mr. Rose—Charles Goff; Mr. Webster—James Beard; Mr. Thomas—Jim Connor; Misses Bonynge, Collins—Maggie Worth.

Directed by Samuel Liff (originally staged by Moss Hart); musical director, Anton Coppola; choreography and musical numbers, Hanya Holm (restaged by Harry Woolever); scenery, Oliver Smith; costumes, Cecil Beaton; lighting, Feder; costume supervision, Stanley Simmons; musical arrangements, Robert Russell Bennett, Phil Lang; dance music arrangements, Trude Rittman; production stage manager, Herman Shapiro; stage managers, James Stevenson, Hamilton Gregg; press, John Clugstone.

Time: 1912. Place: London.

My Fair Lady was first produced March 15, 1956 by Herman Levin at the Mark Hellinger Theater for 2,717 performances, Broadway's longest run for a musical. It was previously revived May 20, 1964 by the New York City Center Light Opera Company for 47 performances.

The list of scenes and musical numbers in *My Fair Lady* appears on pages 378 and 379 of the 1955-56 *Best Plays* volume.

West Side Story (89). Musical revival based on a conception of Jerome Robbins; book by Arthur Laurents; music by Leonard Bernstein; lyrics by Stephen Sondheim. Produced by Music Theater of Lincoln Center, Richard Rodgers president and producing director, at the New York State Theater. Opened June 24, 1968. (Closed September 7, 1968)

The Jets:
Riff, the Leader ....Avind Harum
Tony, His Friend ....Kurt Peterson
Action ....Ian Tucker
A-Rab ....Robert LuPone
Baby John ....Stephen Reinhardt
Snowboy ....George Ramos
Big Deal ....Roger Briant
Diesel ....Victor Mohica
Gee-Tar ....Chuck Beard
Mouth Piece ....Joseph Pichette
Tiger ....Kenneth Carr
Their Girls:
Graziella ....Garet de Troia
Velma ....Nancy Dalton
Minnie ....Rachel Lampert
Clarice ....Sherry Lynn Diamant
Pauline ....Carol Hanzel
Pucky ....Jeanne Frey
Anybody's ....Lee Lund
The Sharks:
Bernardo, the Leader ....Alan Castner
Maria, His Sister ....Victoria Mallory

Anita, His Girl ....Barbara Luna
Chino, His Friend ....Bobby Capo Jr.
Pepe ....Edgar Coronado
Indio ....Peter De Nicola
Luis ....Pat Matera
Anxious ....Steven Gelfer
Nibbles ....Ramon Caballero
Juano ....Pernett Robinson
Toro ....Byron Wheeler
Moose ....George Comtois
Their Girls:
Rosalia ....Kay Oslin
Consuelo ....Lee Hooper
Teresita ....Connie Burnett
Francisca ....Eileen Barbaris
Estella ....Judith Lerner
Marguerita ....Carol Lynn Vazquez
Felicia ....Diane McAfee
The Adults:
Doc ....Martin Wolfson
Schrank ....Joseph Mascolo
Krupke ....Josip Elic
Gladhand ....Bill McCutcheon

Understudies: Miss Mallory—Diane McAfee; Mr. Peterson—Kenneth Carr; Miss Luna—
Carol Hanzel; Mr. Castner—Edgar Coronado; Mr. Wolfson—Bill McCutcheon; Mr. Harum—
Roger Briant; Mr. LuPone—Al De Sio; Swing dancer—Susan Platt.

Original production directed and choreographed by Jerome Robbins; direction and choreography reproduced by Lee Theodore; musical director, Maurice Peress; scenery, Oliver Smith;
costumes, Winn Morton; lighting, Peter Hunt; orchestrations, Leonard Bernstein, Sid Ramin,
Irwin Kostal; production stage manager, George Quick; stage managers, Philip Mandelker,
William Hammond; press, Frank Goodman, Martin Shwartz, Alan Eichler.

Time: The last days of summer. Place: The West Side of New York City.

West Side Story was first produced September 26, 1957 by Robert E. Griffith and Harold S.
Prince by arrangement with Roger L. Stevens at the Winter Garden for 732 performances. It
was revived by the same management April 27, 1960 at the Winter Garden for 249 performances and by The City Center Light Opera Company April 8, 1964 for 31 performances.

The list of scenes and musical numbers in *West Side Story* appears on page 287 of the 1957-
58 *Best Plays* volume.

Compagnie du Théâtre de la Cité de Villeurbanne. Repertory of three plays in the
French language. **The Three Musketeers** (9). Adapted by Roger Planchon from
the novel by Alexandre Dumas. Opened June 25, 1968. **George Dandin** (4). Revival of the play by Molière. Opened June 27, 1968. **Tartuffe** (6). Revival of the
play by Molière. Opened July 2, 1968. Produced by Lincoln Center Festival '68
at the Vivian Beaumont Theater. (Repertory closed July 14, 1968)

THE THREE MUSKETEERS

The Royal Personages:
Louis XIII ....Claude Lochy
Anne of Austria ....Isabelle Sadoyan
Cardinal Richelieu ....Gérard Guillaumat
Duke of Buckingham ..Jean-Pierre Bernard
Milady de Winter ....Julia Dancourt
Lord de Winter ....Jean Bouise
The Musketeers:
Tréville ....Pierre Meyrand
Athos ....Michel Herbault
Porthos ....Armand Meffre
Aramis ....François Gabriel
D'Artagnan ....Claude Brasseur
Boistracy ....Pierre Bianco

The Supporters of Cardinal Richelieu:
Rochefort ....Pierre Le Rumeur
Jussac ....Gilbert Vilhon
Baron Guillaume ....Gérard Pichon
Boisrenard ....Pierre Bianco
Cahusac ....Martin-Barbaz
Chancellor Séguier ....Jean Bouise
The People:
Madame Bonacieux ...Colette Dompiétrini
Monsieur Bonacieux; d'Artagnan's Father;
Baron de Clarick;
Passerby ....Michel Robin
D'Artagnan's Sister;
Estafena ....Mireille Calvo

D'Artagnan's Brother; Planchet; Patrick; 2d Chandelier Cleaner; Ferryman; Passerby ....Julien Mallier Major-domo; Innkeeper; Passerby ....René Morard Felton; Meung Innkeeper ....Gilles Chavassieux

Lady's Maid ....Elisabeth Rosner 1st Chandelier Cleaner; Commentator ....Jean Bouise Georges ....Gilbert Vilhon Executioner ....Pierre Le Rumeur

PERFORMER	"GEORGE DANDIN"	"TARTUFFE"
Michel Auclair		Tartuffe
Nelly Borgeaud		Elmire
Jean Bouise	George Dandin	M. Loyal
Claude Brasseur		Damis
Ferna Claude	Servant	
Julia Dancourt	Claudine	
Jacques Debary		Orgon
Colette Dompiétrini		Mariane
Gérard Guillaumat	Clitandre	Cléante
Danièle Lebrun	Angélique	
Lucienne Le Marchand		Mme. Pernell
Claude Lochy	de Sottenville	Adjutant
Julien Mallier	Valet	
Pierre Meyrand	Lubin	
René Morard	Valet	Laurent
Michel Robin	Colin	
Michel Rulh		Valère
Isabelle Sadoyan	Mme. de Sottenville	Flipote
Françoise Seigner		Dorine

Théâtre de la Cité company under the direction of Robert Gilbert and Roger Planchon; all plays directed by Roger Planchon; scenery and Molière costumes, René Allio; associate director, Jacques Rosner; music, Claude Lochy; press, Sol Jacobson, Lewis Harmon.

THE THREE MUSKETEERS furnishings and accessories, Françoise Darne; costumes, Isabelle Sadoyan.

Time: The 17th Century. Place: France. Prologue: The burial of a Marshal of France. Scene 1: In the chateau of the elderly d'Artagnan. Scene 2: The Inn at Meung. Scene 3: The Palais du Louvre. Scene 4: At Monsieur de Tréville's. Scene 5: The barefooted Carmelites. Scene 6: At the home of His Eminence the Cardinal the Duke de Richelieu. Scene 7: At the home of d'Artagnan. Scene 8: At the home of Richelieu. Scene 9: The trap. Scene 10: The streets of Paris. Scene 11: The apartments of the Queen. Scene 12: The battle of La Rochelle. Intermission. Scene 13: A summary of the preceding events. Scene 14: The royal apartments. Scene 15: Pursuit of Monsieur Bonacieux. Scene 16: The Musketeers and the supporters of the Cardinal. Scene 17: The Colombier Rouge Inn. Scene 18: The game of goose. Scene 19: Portsmouth. Scene 20: The sea. Scene 21: The ball at City Hall in Paris. Scene 22: The forest. Scene 23: Finale.

The Three Musketeers treats the events of Dumas' novel from d'Artagnan's departure from home to the execution of Milady as an often comic adventure with strong elements of fantasy. A foreign play previously produced in France.

GEORGE DANDIN—Time: 1668. Place: The house of George Dandin, a married countryman. The play is divided into three acts.

George(s) Dandin is Molière's play about a cuckolded husband. Its last New York revival of record was by the Provincetown Players at the Provincetown Playhouse April 6, 1924.

TARTUFFE—Time: Mid-winter, 1665. Place: Orgon's estate in France.

Tartuffe was presented in French last season off Broadway at the Barbizon-Plaza Theater April 16, 1968 for 29 performances in Le Tréteau de Paris Repertory. Its last New York production in English was by the Repertory Theater of Lincoln Center in Richard Wilbur's English verse translation at the ANTA-Washington Square Theater January 14, 1965, for 74 performances.

Lovers (148). Program of two one-act plays by Brian Friel: *Winners* and *Losers*. Produced by Helen Bonfils and Morton Gottlieb by arrangement with Oscar Lewenstein at the Vivian Beaumont Theater. Opened July 25, 1968. (Closed November 30, 1968)

Andy Tracey (Commentator) ....Art Carney

Mag ....Fionnuala Flanagan
Joe ....Eamon Morrissey

Hanna ....Anna Manahan
Cissy ....Beulah Garrick
Mrs. Wilson ....Grania O'Malley

Standbys: Mr. Carney—Vincent Dowling; Miss Manahan—Beulah Garrick; Mr. Morrissey—Roger McIlree; Miss Flanagan—Susan Anspach, Blythe Danner; Misses Garrick, O'Malley—Peg Mayo.

The Edwards-MacLiammoir Dublin Gate Theater Production directed by Hilton Edwards; scenery, William Ritman; costumes, Noel Taylor; lighting, Tharon Musser; production stage manager, Warren Crane; stage manager, Roger McIlree; press, Dorothy Ross.

Time: The present. Place: The town of Ballymore, County Tyrone, Northern Ireland.

In *Winners* a young couple eagerly look forward to their wedding day, while the Commentator explains that they are soon to be the victims of a fatal accident. In *Losers* the Commentator both describes and takes part in the action; he is a middle-aged husband locked in a battle of wills with his demanding invalid mother-in-law. A foreign play previously produced in Dublin.

Lovers moved from the Vivian Beaumont at Lincoln Center after 60 performances to the Music Box on 9/17/68, where it played 88 additional performances.

Peter Lind Hayes replaced Art Carney 11/4/68.

A Best Play; see page 171

Association of Producing Artists (APA-Phoenix) Repertory Company. Schedule of two return engagements. **Pantagleize** (9). By Michel de Ghelderode; translated by George Hauger. Opened September 3, 1968. (Closed September 12, 1968). **The Show-Off** (19). Revival of the play by George Kelly. Opened September 13, 1968. (Closed September 28, 1968). Produced by APA-Phoenix (a project of Theater Incorporated), T. Edward Hambleton managing director, at the Lyceum Theater. (The 1968-69 repertory schedule of APA-Phoenix appears in a separate entry in this listing of "Plays Produced on Broadway.")

PANTAGLEIZE

Pantagleize ....Ellis Rabb
Bamboola ....Nat Simmons
Innocenti ....James Greene
A Poet ....Nicholas Martin
A Policeman ....Richard Easton
An Anarchist ....Keene Curtis
Rachel Silbershatz ....Patricia Conolly
General MacBoom ....Joseph Bird

Bank Managers ....Alan Brasington,
                              Harley Hackett
1st Soldier ....George Pentecost
2d Soldier ....James Whittle
Distinguished Counsel ......Richard Woods
The Generalissimo ....Gordon Gould
An Officer ....Alan Fudge

Soldiers, Waiters, Jurymen: Alan Brasington, Michael Durrell, Alan Fudge, Harley Hackett, Chet Leaming, Drew Snyder.

Directed by John Houseman and Ellis Rabb; scenery and lighting, James Tilton; costumes, Nancy Potts; assistant director, Jack O'Brien; music, Bob James; incidental lyrics, Jack O'Brien; stage managers, George Darveris, Nikos Kafkalis; press, Ben Kornzweig, Reginald Denenholz.

Time: The eve of one war and the morrow of another. Place: The City.

This production of *Pantagleize* was presented by APA-Phoenix in its 1967-68 Broadway repertory November 30, 1967 for 50 performances.

THE SHOW-OFF

Clara ....Suzanne Grossmann
Mrs. Fisher ....Helen Hayes
Amy ....Jennifer Harmon
Frank Hyland ....Alan Fudge
Mr. Fisher ....Alexander Clark

Joe ....George Pentecost
Aubrey Piper ....Clayton Corzatte
Mr. Gill ....James Greene
Mr. Rogers ....Gordon Gould

Directed by Stephen Porter; scenery and lighting, James Tilton; costumes, Nancy Potts; stage managers, R. Derek Swire, Harley Hackett, C. Leaming.

Time: 1924. Place: The home of the Fisher family in North Philadelphia.

This production of *The Show-Off* was presented by APA-Phoenix in its 1967-68 Broadway repertory December 5, 1967 for 69 performances.

Lovers and Other Strangers (69). Program of four untitled one-act comedies by Renee Taylor and Joseph Bologna. Produced by Stephanie Sills in association with Gordon Crowe at the Brooks Atkinson Theater. Opened September 18, 1968. (Closed November 16, 1968)

I.

Jerry ....Ron Carey
Brenda ....Zohra Lampert

II.

Johnny ....Gerald S. O'Loughlin
Wilma ....Renee Taylor

III.

Susan ....Mariclare Costello
Mike ....Marvin Lichterman

IV.

Frank ....Richard Castellano
Bea ....Helen Verbit
Richy ....Bobby Alto
Joan ....Candy Azzara

Understudies: Johnny Armen, William Lazarus, Stella Longo, Barbara Young.

Directed by Charles Grodin; scenery, Robin Wagner; costumes, Domingo A. Rodriguez; lighting, John Gleason; associate producer, Maury Kanbar; production associate, Lee Beltzer; production stage manager, Joe Calvan; stage manager, Hal Halvorsen; press, Merle Debuskey, Violet Welles, Faith Geer.

Time: A Saturday night in spring. Place: Apartments in New York City.

The first comedy deals with the preliminaries to a seduction; the second with a married couple's bedroom quarrel; the third with a groom's panicky second thoughts on the eve of his wedding; the fourth with a father and mother fumbling their attempts to help their son make a go of his marriage.

The Cuban Thing (1). By Jack Gelber. Produced by Ivor David Balding & Associates Ltd. at Henry Miller's Theater. Opened and closed at the evening performance, September 24, 1968.

The Family:

Roberto ....Rip Torn	
Barbara ....Jane White	
Alicia ....Maria Tucci	
Juan ....Harold Scott	
Mamma ....Jenny Egan	
Their Servant Chan ....Raul Julia	

Their Friends:

Carlos ....Michael Wager
Paco ....Robert Fields

Their Visitors:

Appleby ....Conrad Bain
O'Hara ....Harry Packwood
Ray ....Richard Steele-Reed

The Prostitutes:

Daisi ....Rose Gregorio
Billi ....Carla Pinza
Cuqui ....Jeanne Kaplan

The Guard Angel ....Henry Proach

Directed by Jack Gelber; scenery, Robin Wagner; costumes, Patricia Quinn Stuart; lighting, Jules Fisher; sound, Val Peters; documentary film, Lee Lockwood; production supervisor, Richard Scanga; associate producer, Samuel Bronstein; film sequences, P.G.L. Productions; production stage manager, Roger Johnson Jr.; stage manager, Joel Walker; press, Michael Alpert.

Time: 1958 to 1964. Place: Havana, Cuba. Act I, Scene 1: 1958, evening. Scene 2: 1959, late afternoon. Act II, Scene 1: 1961, midnight. Scene 2: 1962, early afternoon. Scene 3: 1964, early evening.

The Castro revolution in Cuba seen through the eyes of a family which lived comfortably under Batista but comes gradually to accept Castro and his principles. Previously produced at the Berkshire Theater Festival, Stockbridge, Mass.

Woman Is My Idea (5). By Don C. Liljenquist. Produced by the Magniquest Corporation at the Belasco Theater. Opened September 25, 1968. (Closed September 28, 1968)

Ruel	Sean Simpson	Bessie Wendridge	Diane Moore
Lehi Hardiman	Jon Richards	Victoria Wendridge	Tracy Brooks Swope
Bascombe	David Huddleston	Emily Wendridge	Lara Parker
Brigham Young	Hugh Marlowe	Sarah Hardiman	Martha Greenhouse
John Rocky Park	John Heffernan		

Standbys: Messrs. Heffernan, Marlowe—David Vaughan; Messrs. Huddleston, Richards—James Harwood; Misses Parker, Swope, Moore—Marie Puma; Mr. Simpson—William Dolive; Miss Greenhouse—Jane Rose.

Directed by Don C. Liljenquist; design, Lloyd Burlingame; production stage manager, Gigi Cascio; press, Max Eisen, Carl Samrock.

Time: The 1870s. Place: The home of John Rocky Park in Salt Lake City, Utah. Act I, Scene 1: An evening in early December 1872. Scene 2: Early morning of the second day after. Act II: A beautiful afternoon in May 1873. Act III: A dark evening, six days later.

Comedy, romance among the Mormons in the Brigham Young days.

The Man in the Glass Booth (268). By Robert Shaw. Produced in association with Glasshouse Productions and Peter Bridge by Ivor David Balding & Associates Ltd. and Edward M. Meyers with Leslie Ogden at the Royale Theater. Opened September 26, 1968. (Closed May 17, 1969)

Arthur Goldman	Donald Pleasence	Steiger	Paul Manfred
Sam	Graham Brown	Durer	Michael Ebert
Jack; Marowski	Madison Arnold	Presiding Judge	Boris Tumarin
Charlie Cohn	Lawrence Pressman	Judges	Martin Rudy, Ben Kapen
Flower Man	John Coe	Mrs. Levi	Florence Tarlow
Dr. Kessel; Prosecutor	Jack Hollander	Landau	Abe Vigoda
Rudin;		Mrs. Lehmann	Tresa Hughes
Tzelniker	F. Murray Abraham	Sergeant	Clinton Atkinson
Mrs. Rosen	Ronni L. Gilbert	Guards	Walter Allen, Robert Anthony

Understudies: Mr. Pleasence—John Coe; Messrs. Pressman, Arnold, Abraham—Ben Kapen; Messrs. Tumarin, Hollander—Martin Rudy; Misses Gilbert, Hughes—Florence Tarlow.

Directed by Harold Pinter; scenery, Ed Wittstein; costumes, Joseph G. Aulisi; lighting, Jules Fisher; original London design, Voytek; production supervisor, Richard Scanga; production stage manager, John Drew Devereaux; press, Michael Alpert.

Time: 1964-65. Place: New York and Israel. The play is divided into two acts.

Multimillionaire Jew, a victim of Nazi cruelty, poses as a Nazi war criminal in order to present the enemy as he really was—evil and unrepentent—while acting as the defendant in a trial in Israel. A foreign play previously produced in London.

Jack Warden replaced Donald Pleasence 3/31/69.

A Best Play; see page 187

Noel Coward's Sweet Potato (44). Musical revue with words and music by Noel Coward; assembled and adapted by Roderick Cook and Lee Theodore from a conception by Roderick Cook. Produced by Robert L. Steele at the Ethel Barrymore Theater. Opened September 29, 1968. (Closed November 23, 1968; see note)

George Grizzard	Stephen Reinhardt
Tom Kneebone	Bonnie Schon
Dorothy Loudon	Carole Shelley
Robert LuPone	Ian Tucker
Arthur Mitchell	

Standby: Mr. Mitchell—Judd Jones.

Directed and choreographed by Lee Theodore; musical direction and vocal arrangements, Charles Schneider; scenery, Helen Pond, Herbert Senn; costumes, David Toser; lighting, Peter Hunt; co-choreographer, Robert Tucker; musical supervision and arrangements, Fred Werner;

production supervisor, Robert Linden; produced in association with the Erani Corporation; production stage manager, Charles Gray; press, John Springer Associates, Louise Weiner.

NOTE: *Noel Coward's Sweet Potato* suspended on 10/12/68 after 17 performances, then resumed 11/1/68 at the Booth Theater for 27 more performances.

Mary Louise Wilson replaced Dorothy Loudon 11/1/68.

ACT I: A Beginning—The Company; Useful Phrases—George, Dorothy, Arthur, Bonnie; "Dance, Little Lady" (music arranged by Roland Hanna)—Bonnie, Boys; "Mad Dogs and Englishmen"—George, Dorothy, Carole, Tom; "World Weary"—Arthur, Bonnie, Boys; "A Bar on the Piccola Marina"—George; Literature—Dorothy and Tom; "Why Does Love Get in the Way?"—Carole; "Men About Town"—George, Dorothy, Tom; "Matelot"—Arthur, Carole, Bonnie; Eve—Tom; "Consecutive Fifths" (music by Fred Werner and Roderick Cook) —George; "Mad About the Boy"—Dorothy, Carole, Bonnie, Boys; I Wonder What Happened to Him?—George, Tom; Karate—Bonnie; "A Room With a View"—Dorothy; Waltzes—George, Boys; "I Like America"—The Company.

ACT II: "Let's Do It" (music by Cole Porter)—The Company; "Three White Feathers"— Dorothy, Tom; "Don't Put Your Daughter on the Stage, Mrs. Worthington"—George, Boys; Headless Dance (music: "Never Again")—Arthur, Ron Carter; "Alice"—Tom. Social Grace— Arthur, Bonnie, Ian, Dorothy, Tom; Sweet Potato—Carole, Boys; Party Chat/Amanda, Elyot and Friends—Carole, George, The Company; "If Love Were All"—Dorothy; Sex Talk— Tom; "Sunset in Samolo" (music by Fred Werner and Roderick Cook)—Carole; "Teach Me To Dance Like Grandma"—Dorothy, Arthur; Boy Actor—George; "World Weary" (Reprise) —The Company; An Ending—The Company.

Theater 1969 Playwrights Repertory. Repertory of four programs. **Box and Quotations from Chairman Mao Tse-Tung** (12). Program of interrelated plays by Edward Albee. Opened September 30, 1968. **The Death of Bessie Smith** and **The American Dream** (12). Program of two one-act revivals by Edward Albee. Opened October 2, 1968 matinee. **Krapp's Last Tape** by Samuel Beckett and **The Zoo Story** by Edward Albee (5). Program of two one-act revivals. Opened October 9, 1968 matinee. **Happy Days** (3). Revival of the play by Samuel Beckett. Opened October 12, 1968 matinee. Produced by Theater 1969 (Richard Barr and Edward Albee) at the Billy Rose Theater. (Repertory closed October 26, 1968)

BOX

The voice of Ruth White

QUOTATIONS FROM CHAIRMAN MAO TSE-TUNG

Chairman Mao	Wyman Pendleton	Old Woman	Sudie Bond
Long Winded Lady	Nancy Kelly	Minister	George Bartenieff

THE DEATH OF BESSIE SMITH

The Father	George Bartenieff	The Orderly	Lisle Wilson
The Nurse	Rosemary Murphy	2d Nurse	Carolyn Coates
Jack	J.A. Preston	The Intern	Ben Piazza

THE AMERICAN DREAM

Mommy	Sada Thompson	Mrs. Barker	Carolyn Coates
Daddy	Donald Davis	The Young Man	Stephen McHattie
Grandma	Sudie Bond		

KRAPP'S LAST TAPE

Krapp ....Donald Davis

THE ZOO STORY

Jerry	Ben Piazza	Peter	Donald Davis

HAPPY DAYS

Winnie	Sada Thompson	Willie	Wyman Pendleton

All plays: designed and lighted by William Ritman; executive producer, Mark Wright; associate producer, Michael Kasdan; production stage manager, Bruce A. Hoover; stage managers, Charles Kindl, Curt Dempster; press, David Rothenberg, Mary Bryant.

BOX and QUOTATIONS FROM CHAIRMAN MAO TSE-TUNG directed by Alan Schneider.

A recorded philosophical comment on life *(Box)* while the stage remains empty is later interpolated in re-play through a scene *(Quotations from Chairman Mao Tse-Tung)* in which one character recites Will Carlton's poem *Over the Hill to the Poorhouse*, another tells her troubles to a minister while the fourth, Chairman Mao, recites some of his sayings. The plays (commonly abbreviated as *Box-Mao-Box*) are performed together without intermission. They were previously produced by Studio Arena Theater, Buffalo.

THE DEATH OF BESSIE SMITH directed by Michael Kahn; music by William Flanagan.

Time: Afternoon and early evening, September 26, 1937. Place: In and around the city of Memphis.

The Death of Bessie Smith was first produced by Theater 1961 off Broadway, joining *The American Dream* on a double bill March 1, 1961 and playing for 328 performances.

THE AMERICAN DREAM directed by Edward Albee.

The American Dream was first produced by Theater 1961 off Broadway January 24, 1961 for 370 performances. It was revived off Broadway by Theater 1962 in repertory February 11, 1962; by Theater 1963 on September 4, 1962 for 30 performances; by Theater 1964 on May 28, 1963 for 143 performances and on April 21, 1964 for 232 performances.

KRAPP'S LAST TAPE directed by Alan Schneider.

Time: A late evening in the future. Place: Krapp's den.

Krapp's Last Tape was first produced on a double bill with *The Zoo Story* off Broadway by Theater 1960 and Harry Joe Brown Jr. on January 14, 1960 for 582 performances. It was revived off Broadway on the same double bill September 12, 1961 for 32 performances; and by Theater 1965 on June 8, 1965 for 168 performances.

THE ZOO STORY directed by Richard Barr.

Time: A Sunday afternoon in Central Park. Place: New York City.

In addition to its original production and revivals on a double bill with *Krapp's Last Tape* (see above), *The Zoo Story* was revived off Broadway in repertory by Theater 1962 on February 11, 1962; by Theater 1963 on September 4, 1962 for 30 performances; by Theater 1964 on May 28, 1963 for 143 performances; and by Theater 1965 on November 8, 1964 as a replacement on a double bill.

HAPPY DAYS directed by Alan Schneider.

Happy Days was first produced off Broadway by Theater 1962 on September 17, 1961 for 28 performances. It was revived off Broadway in its French version September 14, 1965 for 14 performances, and in its English version September 28, 1965 for 16 performances, both produced by Theater 1966.

* The Great White Hope (276). By Howard Sackler. Produced by Herman Levin at the Alvin Theater. Opened October 3, 1968.

ACT I

Scene 1: Parchment, Ohio, Brady's farm

Brady .... Gil Rogers
Fred .... George Ebeling
Cap'n Dan .... George Mathews
Smitty .... Peter Masterson
Goldie .... Lou Gilbert

And Reporters, Trainers, Photographers

Scene 2: San Francisco, a small gym

Tick .... Jimmy Pelham
Jack Jefferson .... James Earl Jones
Eleanor Bachman .... Jane Alexander
Clara .... Marlene Warfield

And Goldie, Smitty, Reporters

Scene 3: Reno, Nevada, the fight

Roller .... Edward McNally
Bettor .... Joseph Hamer
Tout .... George Harris II
Blackface .... Hector Elizondo
Colonel Cox .... Dan Priest

Weigher-in ....George Curley
Deacon ....Garwood Perkins
Young Negro ....Woodie King
Boy ....Terrance Phillips
And Brady, Fred, Cap'n Dan, Jack, Goldie, Tick, Smitty, Crap Players, Rangers, Men at
Fight, Handlers, Reporters
Monologue: Cap'n Dan
Scene 4: Chicago, Cafe de Champion
Barker ....David Connell
Mr. Donnelly ....Michael Prince
Mrs. Bachman ....Ruth Gregory
Mr. Dixon ....Brooks Rogers
And Jack, Tick, Ellie, Goldie, Smitty, Jack's Friends, Policeman, Civic Marchers
Scene 5: Chicago, District Attorney's Office
Mr. Cameron (D.A.) ....John Cypher
Detective ....Edward McNally
A Distinguished Negro ....Clark Morgan
And Ellie, Mr. Dixon, Smitty, Mr. Donnelly, Civic Leaders
Scene 6: Beau Rivage, Wisconsin, a cabin
Jack, Ellie, Mr. Dixon, Deputies
Monologue: Scipio ....Antonio Fargas
Scene 7: Chicago, Mrs. Jefferson's house
Pastor ....L. Errol Jaye
Mrs. Jefferson ....Hilda Haynes
Rudy ....Mel Winkler
And Jack, Goldie, Tick, Clara, Members of the Congregation, Rudy's Teammates

ACT II

Scene 1: London, the Home Office
Mr. Eubanks ....Larry Swanson
Mr. Treacher ....David Thomas
Sir William Griswold ....Thomas Barbour
Mr. Coates ....Max Wright
Mrs. Kimball ....Sheila Coonan
Inspector Wainwright ....Gil Rogers
Mr. M. Bratby ....Joseph Hamer
Mr. Farlow ....George Curley
And Jack, Ellie, Goldie, Tick
Scene 2: Le Havre, a customs shed
Official ....Bob Horen
Klossowski ....Jon Cypher
Porter ....Lance Cunard
And Reporters
Scene 3: Paris, Vel d'Hiver
Promoter ....Bob Horen
French Handler ....Hector Elizondo
And Jack, Ellie, Tick, Goldie, Smitty
Scene 4: New York, Pop Weaver's office
Pop Weaver ....Eugene R. Wood
And Cap'n Dan, Fred, Mr. Dixon
Scene 5: Berlin, an outdoor cafe
Waiter ....George Harris II
Ragosy ....Marshall Efron
An African Student ....Don Blakely
And Jack, Ellie, Tick, Goldie, German Officers
Scene 6: Budapest, a cabaret
Juggler ....Lou Meyer
And Jack, Ellie, Tick, Ragosy, Stage Hands
Scene 7: Belgrade, railway station
Jack, Ellie, Tick, Smitty

ACT III

Scene 1: Chicago, a street
Pastor, Goldie, Rudy, Clara, Scipio, Mourners, Photographers, Policemen

Scene 2: New York, Pop Weaver's office
  Cap'n Dan, Smitty, Fred, Pop Weaver
Monologue: Clara
Scene 3: Juarez, a barn
  Paco ....Donald Girard
  El Jefe ....Hector Elizondo
  Government Agent ....Edd K. Gasper
  And Jack, Ellie, Tick, Mr. Dixon, Goldie, Mexicans
Monologue: Cap'n Dan
Scene 4: Chicago, a street
  Pailman ....David Connell
  Signature Recorder ....Yvonne Southerland
  Drummer ....Woodie King
  And Contributors
Scene 5: Havana, Orienté Racetrack
  1st Man on Ladder ....Burke Byrnes
  2d Man on Ladder ....Dan Priest
  The Kid ....Sean J. Walsh
  Cuban Boy ....Luis Espinosa
  And Smitty, Pop Weaver, Fred, Government Agent, Goldie, Tick, Jack, Cap'n Dan, Rudy,
  Fight Fans, Pinkerton Men

Reporters, Trainers, Photographers, Crap Players, Rangers, Men at Fight, Handlers, Jack's Friends, Policemen, Civic Marchers, Civic Leaders, Deputies, Members of the Congregation, Rudy's Teammates, German Officers, Stage Hands, Mourners, Mexicans, Contributors, Fight Fans, Pinkerton Men: Thomas Anderson, Thomas Barbour, Verona Barnes, Don Blakely, Dave Brown, Burke Byrnes, David Connell, Lawrence Cook, Sheila Coonan, Lance Cunard, George Curley, John Cypher, Marshall Efron, Hector Elizondo, Luis Espinosa, Joanna Featherstone, Edd K. Gasper, Joseph Hamer, George Harris II, Bob Horen, Woodie King, Ed Lauter, Jerry Laws, Philip Lindsay, Edward McNally, Lou Meyer, Clark Morgan, Terrence O'Connor, Garwood Perkins, Terrance Phillips, Richard Pittman, Dan Priest, Michael Prince, Gil Rogers, Dolores St. Amand, Danette Small, Yvonne Southerland, Larry Swanson, Judy Thames, Christine Thomas, David Thomas, Glory Van Scott, Sean J. Walsh, Mel Winkler, Eugene R. Wood, Max Wright.

Directed by Edwin Sherin; scenery, Robin Wagner; costumes, David Toser; lighting, John Gleason; music arrangements, Charles Gross; choral supervision and arrangements, Howard A. Roberts; production stage manager, William Dodds; stage manager, Tom Ellis; press, Martin Shwartz.

Time: The years before and during World War I. Place: See list of scenes above.

The rise and fall of a Negro heavyweight boxing champion, spread over many scenes in two continents, suggested by the career of Jack Johnson. The play was previously produced by Arena Stage in Washington, D.C.

A Best Play; see page 204

Marlene Dietrich (67). Return engagement of the one-woman program of songs performed by Marlene Dietrich. Produced by Alexander H. Cohen in a Nine O'Clock Theater production at the Mark Hellinger Theater. Opened October 3, 1968. (Closed November 30, 1968)

Arrangements by Burt Bacharach; orchestra conducted by Stan Freeman; lighting, Joe Davis; production stage manager, Bennett Thomson; press, John Springer Associates, Louise Weiner.

Miss Dietrich's program was presented without intermission. Song numbers, mostly in English, were "Look Me Over Closely," "You're the Cream in My Coffee," "Boomerang Baby," "Lola," "Where Have All the Flowers Gone," "The Laziest Gal in Town," "Shir Hatan-Biem," "La Vie en Rose," "Jonny," "Go 'Way from My Window," "Lili Marlene," "Das Lied Ist Aus," "I Wish You Love," "Marie Marie," "Honeysuckle Rose," "When the World Was Young," "White Grass," "Everyone's Gone to the Moon" and "Falling in Love Again."

Marlene Dietrich's one-woman program of songs was previously produced by Alexander H. Cohen on October 9, 1967 at the Lunt-Fontanne Theater for 48 performances.

Gilbert Becaud Sings Love (24). One-man program of songs performed by Gilbert Becaud; music by Gilbert Becaud; lyrics, most of them in the French language, by

Pierre Delanoe, Louis Amade, Maurice Vidalin, Charles Aznavour, Jean Broussolle, Mack David, Carl Sigman and Gilbert Becaud. Produced by Norman Twain and Marcel Akselrod by arrangement with Feliz Marouani at the Cort Theater. Opened October 6, 1968. (Closed October 26, 1968)

Musical director, Raymond Bernard; scenery and lighting, Ralph Alswang; orchestra—pianist, Gilbert Segrist, drummer, Pierre Lemarchand, bass, Herbert Tissier, Spanish guitar, Harry Katz, electric guitar, Pierre DorRagon; production stage manager, Michael Thoma; press, Frank Goodman.

PART I: "Le Jour ou la Pluie Viendra," "Les Jours Meilleurs," "C'Etait Mon Copain," "Le Bateau Blanc," "Rosy and John," "L'Etoile," "La Grande Roue," "Je t'Attends," "Je Partirai," "T'es Venu de Loin," "Le Pianiste de Varsovie," "Cornelius."

PART II: "L'Oiseau de Toutes les Couleurs," "The Other Three," "Les Cerisiers Sont Blancs," "La Grosse Noce," "La Riviere," "Les Cloches," "Je Reviens Te Chercher," "Nathalie," "Et Maintenant," "L'Importance C'est la Rose."

A foreign show previously performed in Paris and elsewhere.

Gilbert Becaud previously appeared in a one-man show on Broadway at the Longacre Theater October 31, 1966 for 19 performances.

Association of Producing Artists (APA-Phoenix) Repertory Company. Repertory of four revivals. **The Cocktail Party** (44). By T.S. Eliot. Opened October 7, 1968. **The Misanthrope** (86). By Molière; English version by Richard Wilbur. Opened October 9, 1968. **Cock-A-Doodle Dandy** (40). By Sean O'Casey. Opened January 20, 1969. **Hamlet** (45). By William Shakespeare. Opened March 3, 1969. Produced by APA-Phoenix (a project of Theater Incorporated), T. Edward Hambleton managing director, at the Lyceum Theater. (The 1968-69 APA-Phoenix schedule of two return engagements appears in a separate entry in this listing of "Plays Produced on Broadway.") (Repertory closed April 26, 1969)

PERFORMER	"THE COCKTAIL PARTY"	"THE MISANTHROPE"	"COCK-A-DOODLE DANDY"	"HAMLET"
Brian Bedford	Edward	Acaste		
Joseph Bird		Clitandre	Porter	
Barry Bostwick			The Cock	Ghost; Osric; Player
Alan Brasington			Julia's Father	Francisco; Priest; Player
Peter Coffield			1st Rough	Rosencrantz
Patricia Conolly	Celia	Eliante	Marion	
Keene Curtis	Gibbs	Oronte	Sergeant	Player
Jake Dengel			Bellman	2d Gravedigger
Michael Durrell		Guard	2d Rough	Laertes
Richard Easton		Alceste	Messenger	Claudius
Alan Fudge				Marcellus
Amy Levitt				Ophelia
Betty Miller		Arsinoe	Julia	Gertrude
Philip Minor				1st Gravedigger
Donald Moffat			Sailor Mahan	Horatio
Etain O'Malley	Nurse-Secretary			
Christine Pickles		Celimene	Lorna	Player
Ellis Rabb			Shanaar	Hamlet
Drew Snyder			Jack	Guildenstern
Frances Sternhagen	Lavinia		Loreleen	
James Tripp				Bernardo
Nancy Walker	Julia			
Sydney Walker	Sir Henry	Philinte	Michael	
James Whittle	Caterer's Man	Servant		
Ralph Williams	Peter	Valet	One-Eyed Larry	
Richard Woods			Domineer	Polonius

ELLIS RABB IN "HAMLET"

All plays: artistic director, Ellis Rabb; scenery and lighting, James Tilton; costumes, Nancy Potts; press, Ben Kornzweig, Reginald Denenholz.

THE COCKTAIL PARTY directed by Philip Minor; assistant director, Jack O'Brien; stage managers, George Darveris, Harley Hackett, Nikos Kafkalis.

Time: The present. Place: London.

The Cocktail Party was first produced on Broadway by Gilbert Miller January 21, 1950 at the Mansfield Theater for 409 performances. This is its first New York revival.

THE MISANTHROPE directed by Stephen Porter; music, Conrad Susa; stage managers, Nikos Kafkalis, R. Derek Swire.

Time: 1666. Place: Celimene's house in Paris.

The Misanthrope was last performed on Broadway (in the French language) by the Madeleine Renaud-Jean-Louis Barrault Repertory Company, in a repertory of eight plays at the Winter Garden beginning January 30, 1957.

COCK-A-DOODLE DANDY directed by Jack O'Brien and Donald Moffat; music, Bob James; production stage manager, George Darveris; stage managers, Harley Hackett, Chet Leaming.

Time: The present. Place: The front garden outside Michael Marthraun's house in Nyadnanave. Act I: Morning. Act II: The same; midday. Act III: The same; dusk.

Cock-A-Doodle Dandy was previously produced in New York in 1958 off Broadway for 31 performances. This is its Broadway debut.

HAMLET directed by Ellis Rabb; assisted by Jack O'Brien; music, Conrad Susa; duel staged by Rod Colbin; production stage manager, George Darveris; stage managers, Harley Hackett, Nikos Kafkalis, Chet Leaming.

This production of *Hamlet*, with text based partially on the 1603 Quarto, appeared previously in Ann Arbor, Mich. Joseph Papp produced his version of the play last season, December 26, 1967, at the New York Shakespeare Festival Public Theater for 56 performances, and events of *Hamlet* were the subject of Tom Stoppard's *Rosencrantz and Guildenstern Are Dead,* a Best Play of the same season produced at the Alvin Theater October 16, 1967 for 420 performances. Recent New York revivals of *Hamlet* were the Bristol Old Vic production at the City Center February 16, 1967 for 9 performances and the Richard Burton *Hamlet* produced by Alexander H. Cohen at the Lunt-Fontanne Theater April 9, 1964 for 137 performances.

The Megilla of Itzik Manger (78). Musical partly in the Yiddish language; original Israeli version by Shmuel Bunim, Hayim Hefer, Itzik Manger and Dov Seltzer; adapted by Shmuel Bunim; music by Dov Seltzer; English commentaries by Joe Darion. Produced by Zvi Kolitz, Solomon Sagall and Alice Peerce at the John Golden Theater. Opened October 9, 1968. (Closed December 15, 1968)

Interlocutor, Fastrigosso, Fanfosso, others ....Mike Burstein
Ahasueras, Mordechai, others ....Pesach Burstein
Vashti, Zeresh, Innkeeper, Mothers ....Lillian Lux
Haman, Tailor, Fanfosso's Daughter, others ....Zisha Gold
Esther, Apprentice, 1st and 2d Girls, others ....Susan Walters
2d Interlocutor, Vayzatha, others ....Ariel Furman

Standbys: Messrs. Burstein, Gold—Menasha Oppenheim; Misses Lux, Walters—Evelyn Kingsley.
Directed by Shmuel Bunim; musical conductor, Max Meth; original Israeli production designed by Shlomo Vitkin; lighting, Eldon Elder; assistant director, Amnon Kabatchnik; production stage manager, Bernard Sauer; press, David Lipsky, Lisa Lipsky.
Time: The present. Place: A small town in Eastern Europe. The play is divided into two acts of thirteen scenes each.
The libretto is an adaptation of the Old Testament's Book of Esther, in which Esther marries a Persian king and with her uncle's help contrives to end the king's persecution of the Jews. The characters of the story have become Jewish shtetel characters. A foreign play previously produced in Jaffa and Tel Aviv.
ACT I—"The Tailors' Megilla," "Theme of the Megilla," "Oom Pa Pa Pa," "Vashti's Farewell," "Song of the Walnut Tree," "Theme of the Megilla" (Reprise), "Fastrigossa's Lament," "Fastrigossa's Lament" (Reprise), "Song of the Golden Peacock," "Fly Little Bird."
ACT II—"Gevald Aria," "The Tailors' Drinking Song," "S'a Mechaye," "Song of the Walnut Tree" (Reprise), "From Stopchet to Kolomay," "Revolutionary Song," "A Mother's Tears," "'Cause Uncle Mordechai is So Smart," "Chiribim," "Lechaim."
The Megilla of Itzik Manger played a return engagement of 12 performances 4/19/69-4/26/69 at the Longacre Theater, with Evelyn Kingsley replacing Susan Walters.

The Flip Side (4). By Hugh and Margaret Williams. Produced by Frederick Brisson and Charles Forsythe by arrangement with Michael Codron at the Booth Theater. Opened October 10, 1968. (Closed October 12, 1968)

Candida (The Publisher's Wife) ....Monica Evans
Sharon (The Author's Wife) ....Gwyda Donhowe
Julian (Successful Young Publisher) ....David McCallum
Theo (Famous Author) ....Don Francks

Understudies: Messrs. McCallum, Francks—Chet London; Misses Evans, Donhowe—Samantha Dean.
Directed by Fred Hebert; production designed by Hutchinson Scott; lighting, Lloyd Burlingame; production stage manager, Ben Janney; press, Harvey B. Sabinson, Lee Solters, Harry Nigro.
Time: The present. Place: A country home in Sussex. Act I, Scene 1: Late Saturday afternoon in mid-June. Scene 2: The same evening, after dinner. Act II, Scene 1: The next morning. Scene 2: Some considerable time later—just before Christmas.
Comedy about wife-swapping. A foreign play previously produced in London.

We Bombed in New Haven (85). By Joseph Heller. Produced by Helen Bonfils, Morton Gottlieb, Harold Leventhal and Joseph Stein at the Ambassador Theater. Opened October 16, 1968. (Closed December 29, 1968)

Captain Starkey	Jason Robards	Pfc. Joe Carson	Maxwell Glanville
Ruth	Diana Sands	Private Fisher	Tom Brannum
The Major	William Roerick	Frank	Frank Andre
Sergeant Henderson	Ron Leibman	Vic	Victor Arnold
Corporal Bailey	Anthony Holland	Bob	Robert Christian
Corporal Sinclair	Don Billett	Garry	Garry Mitchell

David ....David Piel   Young Fisher ....Dale Williams
Hunter ....Hansford Rowe   Starkey's Son ....Gene Scandur
Golfer ....Elek Hartman

Standbys: Mr. Robards—John Harkins; Miss Sands—Alexandra Berlin. Understudies: Mr. Roerick—Elek Hartman; Mr. Liebman—Victor Arnold; Young Fisher—Lewis Rosen.

Directed by John Hirsch; scenery, William Ritman; costumes, Noel Taylor; lighting, John Gleason; production stage manager, Warren Crane; stage manager, Lewis Rosen; press, Dorothy Ross, Ruth D. Smuckler.

Time: The present. Place: The Ambassador Theater, New York City. The play is divided into two parts.

Satire on entrapment into violence and war, as actors take on the roles of Air Force personnel in a "play" about bombing missions to incredible targets being "rehearsed." Previously produced in New Haven, Conn.

Her First Roman (17). Musical based on George Bernard Shaw's *Caesar and Cleopatra;* book, music and lyrics by Ervin Drake. Produced by Joseph Cates and Henry Fownes in association with Warner Brothers-7 Arts at the Lunt-Fontanne Theater. Opened October 20, 1968. (Closed November 2, 1968)

Ftatateeta ....Claudia McNeil   Achillas ....Larry Douglas
Rufio ....Bruce MacKay   Pothinus ....Earl Montgomery
Roman Centurion ....Jack Dabdoub   Ptolemy ....Phillip Graves
Caesar ....Richard Kiley   Britannus ....Brooks Morton
Cleopatra ....Leslie Uggams   Roman Sentry ....George Blackwell
Iris ....Barbara Sharma   Apollodorus ....Cal Bellini
Charmian ....Diana Corto   Palace Official ....Marc Jordan

Roman Soldiers: John Baylis, Paul Berné, George Blackwell, Gerry Burkhardt, Robert Carle, Gordon Cook, Bill Gibbens, Scott Hunter, Sean Nolan, Doug Spingler, Don StomsVik, Ronald Stratton.

Egyptians: Pamela Barlow, Diana Corto, Priscilla Lopez, Sally Neal, Trina Parks, Suzanne Rogers, Renee Rose, Fran Stevens, Geri Seignious, Henry Baker, Marc Jordan, George Nestor, Alexander Orfaly, Kenneth Scott.

Standbys: Mr. Kiley—Larry Douglas; Miss McNeil—Fran Stevens. Understudies: Miss Uggams—Diana Corto; Ptolemy—Jason Howard; Swing Girl—Myrna White; Swing Boy—Ron Schwinn.

Directed by Derek Goldby; dances and musical scenes staged by Dania Krupska; musical direction, dance and incidental music, Peter Howard; scenery and costumes, Michael Annals; lighting, Martin Aronstein; orchestrations and vocal arrangements, Don Walker; production supervised by Robert Weiner, George Thorn; production associate, Irwin T. Denberg; production manager, Tom Porter; stage managers, Ellen Wittman, George Rondo; press, Max Eisen, Carl Samrock.

Time: October 48 through March 47 B.C. Place: Egypt.

The romance between Caesar as an elderly philosopher-warrior and Cleopatra as a barbaric sex kitten, as imagined by G.B.S. The play *Caesar and Cleopatra* was last presented on Broadway December 13, 1951 at the Alvin Theater for 67 performances with Laurence Olivier and Vivien Leigh in the leading roles.

ACT I

Prologue
"What Are We Doing in Egypt?" ....Roman Soldiers
Scene 1: The Sphinx
"Hail Sphinx" ....Caesar
"Save Me from Caesar" ....Cleopatra, Caesar
Scene 2: The Throne Room at Memphis
"Many Young Men from Now" ....Cleopatra
Scene 3: The Council Chamber at Alexandria
Scene 4: The Queen's Chamber
"Ptolemy" ....Cleopatra, Egyptian Women
Scene 5: Caesar's Chamber
"Kind Old Gentleman" ....Caesar

JASON ROBARDS AND DIANA SANDS IN
"WE BOMBED IN NEW HAVEN"

Scene 6: A Roman Guard Room
  "Her First Roman" ....Rufio, Britannus, Roman Soldiers
Scene 7: Caesar's Chamber
  "Magic Carpet" ....Cleopatra, Iris, Charmian, Egyptians
Scene 8: The Lighthouse
  "Rome" ....Caesar
  "The Things We Think We Are" ....Caesar, Cleopatra, Britannus, Apollodorus

ACT II

Scene 1: A Palace Garden
  "I Cannot Make Him Jealous" ....Cleopatra
Scene 2: The Roof of the Palace
  "The Dangerous Age" ....Rufio, Britannus
  "In Vino Veritas" ....Caesar, Rufio, Britannus, Apollodorus
  "Caesar Is Wrong" ....Caesar
  "Just for Today" ....Cleopatra
Scene 3: The Wharf at Alexandria

Maggie Flynn (81). Musical with book, music and lyrics by Hugo Peretti, Luigi
Creatore and George David Weiss; book in collaboration with Morton Da Costa;
based on an idea by John Flaxman. Produced by John Bowab at the ANTA Theater. Opened October 23, 1968 (Closed January 5, 1969)

Mulligan Sergeant ....David Vosburg
Sprague Sergeant;
  Lieutenant ....Larry Pool

Garibaldi Sergeant; Lena,
  the Gorilla ....James Senn
Donnelly ....Austin Colyer

O'Malley ....George Tregre	Officer O'Reilly ....Nick Malekos
1st Soldier ....Roger Bigelow	Effram ....Peter Norman
Carter; Fireman;	Molly; Mrs. Van Stock;
Capt. Piedmont ....Charles Rule	Tessie ....Hazel Steck
O'Brian ....Stanley Simmonds	Mick ....John Stanzel
Clancy ....Mario Maroze	Bellini; Gen. Parkinton .....Robert Mandan
Timmy ....William James	Atlas ....Robert Roman
Walter ....Douglas Grant	Phineas ....Jack Cassidy
Maggie Flynn ....Shirley Jones	Young Girl ....Kathleen Robey
William ....Clarence Espinosa	Goliath ....Roy Barry
Andrew ....Gian Carlo Esposito	Acrobats ....George Bunt, Don Bonnell
Erasmus ....Vincent Esposito	Col. John Farraday ....Robert Kaye
Violet ....Sharon Brown	Mrs. Vanderhoff ....Sybil Bowan
Hyacinth ....Jewel Hoston	Mrs. Opdyke ....Jeannette Seibert
Iris ....Irene Cara	2d Lady ....June Eve Story
Pansy ....Stephanie Mills	Mrs. Savage;
Chrysanthemum ....Cheri Welles	Lady of the Evening ....Sandie Fields
Mary O'Cleary ....Jennifer Darling	Deaf Lady ....Betty Hyatt Linton
Bob Jefferson ....Bill Barrian	Soldier Ed Walters ....Dallas Johann
Will Jefferson ....Mitch Taylor	Lady of the Evening ....Reby Howells

Standbys: Miss Jones—Marilyn Child; Mr. Cassidy—Robert Roman. Understudies: Mick—George Tregre; Effram—Derick Jones.

Directed by Morton Da Costa; choreography, Brian Macdonald; musical direction and vocal arrangements, John Lesko; scenery, William and Jean Eckart; costumes, W. Robert LaVine; lighting, Tharon Musser; orchestrations, Philip J. Lang; dance music arrangements, Trude Rittmann; production stage manager, Terence Little; stage manager, Lee Murray; press, Harvey B. Sabinson, Lee Solters, Jay Russell.

Time: 1863. Place: New York City.

Resourceful Maggie Flynn guides her Negro orphans and orphanage through the days of unrest leading up to the Civil War draft riots.

ACT I

Prologue: Streets of New York City, 1863
"Never Gonna Make Me Fight" ....Soldiers, Saloon Boys, Timmy
Scene 1: Dormitory and facade of Meagan Orphan Home
"It's a Nice Cold Morning" ....Maggie, Children
Scene 2: Barlow's Saloon
"I Wouldn't Have You Any Other Way" ....Maggie, Saloon Boys
Scene 3: Christopher Street
"Learn How To Laugh" ....Phineas, Townspeople
Scene 4: Dressing Tent
"Maggie Flynn" ....Phineas
Scene 5: Parlor and facade of orphanage
"The Thank You Song" ....Maggie, Mary, Children
"Look Around Your Little World" ....Col. Farraday, Phineas
Scene 6: Kitchen of orphanage and street
"Maggie Flynn" (Reprise) ....Phineas, Maggie, Children, Saloon Boys
Scene 7: Kitchen of orphanage
"I Won't Let It Happen Again" ....Maggie
Scene 8: Solarium of Vanderhoff Mansion
"How About a Ball?" ....Phineas, Maggie, Mrs. Vanderhoff, Ladies
Scene 9: Union Army Headquarters and the kitchen
"Pitter Patter" ....Phineas
"I Won't Let It Happen Again" (Reprise) ....Maggie

ACT II

Scene 1: Barlow's Saloon and a street
"Never Gonna Make Me Fight" (Reprise) ....Donnelly, O'Brian, Timmy, Men
Scene 2: Veranda of the Vanderhoff mansion
"Why Can't I Walk Away?" ....Phineas
Scene 3: The Basement of the orphanage
"The Game of War" ....Children

RICHARD KILEY AS CAESAR AND LESLIE
UGGAMS AS CLEOPATRA IN "HER FIRST
ROMAN"

Scene 4: The parlor
Scene 5: A jail
"Mr. Clown" ....Phineas, Maggie, Children, Bums, Ladies of the Evening
"Pitter Patter" (Reprise) ....Maggie
Scene 6: The jail office
Scene 7: Various New York Streets
The Riot ....Full Company
Scene 8: The kitchen and facade of the orphanage
"Don't You Think It's Very Nice?" ....Maggie, Phineas, Children
"Mr. Clown"—"Maggie Flynn" (Reprise) ....Maggie, Phineas

Rockefeller and the Red Indians (4). By Ray Galton and Alan Simpson; adapted
from a play by Rene de Obaldia. Produced by David Merrick with Arthur Lewis
at the Ethel Barrymore Theater. Opened October 24, 1968. (Closed October 26,
1968)

Caroline Rockefeller ....Joyce Grant	Partridge Eye;
Pamela Rockefeller ....Jennie Woodford	Lynx Eye ....John Golightly
Tom Rockefeller ....Norman Allen	Virginia ....Ann Hamilton
William Butler ....Peter Bayliss	Wayne Nelson ....Simon Oates
John Emery Rockefeller ....Frankie Howerd	

Understudies: Misses Grant, Hamilton—Rosalind Ross; Messrs. Oates, Golightly—Lucas
White; Mr. Allen—Bruce Heighley; Miss Woodford—Katherine Glass.
Directed by Burt Shevelove; scenery and costumes, Hayden Griffin; lighting, Lloyd Burlin-
game; associate producer, Samuel Liff; stage manager, James Stevenson; press, Harvey B.
Sabinson, Lee Solters, Leo Stern.
Time: 1879 . . . or thereabouts. Place: John Emery Rockefeller's ranch near that den of
iniquity, Pancho City. The play is divided into three parts.

Comedy, a spoof of movie and TV Westerns. A foreign play previously produced in London under the title *The Wind in the Sassafras Trees.*

D'Oyly Carte Opera Company. Repertory of five operetta revivals with librettos by W.S. Gilbert; music by Arthur Sullivan. **H.M.S. Pinafore** (4). Opened October 29, 1968. **Patience** (4). Opened October 31, 1968. **The Mikado** (8). Opened November 1, 1968. **The Pirates of Penzance** (3). Opened November 6, 1968. **Iolanthe** (4). Opened November 8, 1968. Produced by S. Hurok at New York City Center. (Repertory closed November 17, 1968; see note)

PERFORMER	"H.M.S. PINAFORE"	"PATIENCE"	"THE MIKADO"	"THE PIRATES OF PENZANCE"
Donald Adams	Dick Deadeye	Col. Calverly	Mikado	Pirate King
George Cook	Bill Bobstay		Go-To	Sergeant
Julia Goss				Isabel
Susan Jackson	(Josephine)	Patience		
Peggy Ann Jones		Angela	Pitti-Sing	Edith
Thomas Lawlor	Capt. Corcoran		Pish-Tush	
Betti Lloyd-Jones			(Katisha)	
James Marsland		Solicitor		
Ralph Mason	Ralph Rackstraw	Dunstable		
Valerie Masterson	Josephine		Yum-Yum	Mabel
Christene Palmer	Buttercup	Jane	Katisha	Ruth
Clifford Parkes	Bob Becket			
Philip Potter			Nanki-Poo	Frederic
John Reed	Sir Joseph	Bunthorne	Ko-Ko	Maj.-Gen. Stanley
Kenneth Sandford		Archibald	Pooh-Bah	
Anne Sessions		Ella		
Pauline Wales	Hebe	Saphir	Peep-Bo	Kate
John Webley				Samuel
Howard Williamson		Murgatroyd		(Maj.-Gen. Stanley)

(Parentheses indicate roles in which the actors alternated)

IOLANTHE

Lord Chancellor ....John Reed
Earl of Mountararat ....Donald Adams
Earl Tolloller ....Ralph Mason
Private Willis ....Kenneth Sandford
Strephon ....Thomas Lawlor
Queen of the Fairies ......Christene Palmer

Iolanthe ....Peggy Ann Jones
Celia ....Anne Sessions
Leila ....Pauline Wales
Fleta ....Alison Parker
Phyllis ....Susan Jackson

Small Parts, Understudies, Chorus: Glyn Adams, John Ayldon, Derek Booth, Jeffrey Cresswell, Jon Ellison, Arthur Jackson, Gordon Mackenzie, Brian Peach, David Rayson, Brian Sharpe, Michael Tuckey, David Young, Brenda Atherton, Susan Minshull-Browne, Christine Bull, Anne Eggleston, Frances Gregory, Glenys Groves, Anne Guthrie, Abby Hadfield, Elizabeth Lowry, Marian Martin, Beverly Milno, Elizabeth Mynett.

All plays produced under the personal supervision of Bridget D'Oyly Carte; musical director, James Walker; chorus master and assistant conductor, William Cowley; director of productions, Herbert Newby; scenery, Peter Goffin; stage manager, Peter Riley; press, Martin Feinstein, Michael Sweeley, James Murtha.

H.M.S. PINAFORE costumes, Peter Goffin; backcloth, Joseph and Phil Harker. THE MIKADO directed by Anthony Besch; artistic director, Peter Goffin; costumes, Charles Ricketts; Nanki-Poo Act I costume, Disley Jones. PATIENCE costumes, Peter Goffin.

The last Broadway visit of the D'Oyly Carte Opera Company from the Savoy Theater, London, was November 15, 1966 under S. Hurok's management at New York City Center for 32 performances. Note: In addition to the 23 repertory performances during this 1968 visit, the D'Oyly Carte staged a Mystery Program of Gilbert & Sullivan numbers, solo acts and commentary for its 24th and final performance.

* The Repertory Theater of Lincoln Center. Repertory of two plays. **King Lear** (72). Revival of the play by William Shakespeare. Opened November 7, 1968.

(Closed February 12, 1969) **A Cry of Players** (72). By William Gibson. Opened November 14, 1968. (Closed February 15, 1969). And schedule of two plays. **In the Matter of J. Robert Oppenheimer** (64). By Heinar Kipphardt; translated by Ruth Spiers. Opened March 6, 1969. (Closed April 20, 1969) * **The Miser** (27). Revival of the play by Molière; based on a translation by H. Baker and J. Miller. Opened May 8, 1969. Produced by The Repertory Theater of Lincoln Center, under the direction of Jules Irving, at the Vivian Beaumont Theater.

KING LEAR

Earl of Gloucester ....Stephen Elliott	Oswald ....Tom Sawyer
Edmund ....Stacy Keach	Edgar ....Robert Stattel
Earl of Kent ....Philip Bosco	Gentleman ....Ronald Weyand
Lear, King of Britain ....Lee J. Cobb	Curan ....Ray Stewart
Goneril ....Marilyn Lightstone	Cornwall's Servant ....Brendan Fay
Regan ....Patricia Elliott	Old Man ....Don McHenry
Cordelia ....Barbette Tweed	Messenger to Albany ....Jean-Pierre Stewart
Duke of Cornwall ....John Devlin	Messenger to Cordelia .....Mervyn Haines
Duke of Albany ....Charles Cioffi	Doctor ....William Myers
King of France ....Robert Phalen	Captain ....Joseph Schroer
Duke of Burgundy ....Bill Moor	Herald ....Paul Rudd
Fool ....Rene Auberjonois	Soldier with Knife ....Robert Phalen

Soldiers, Servants, Knights, Priests: Ruth Attaway, Joseph Attles, Gerry Black, Samual Blue Jr., Virgilia Chew, James Cook, Stan Dworkin, Barnett Epstein, Mervyn Haines, Douglas Hayle, Martin Herzer, Robert Levine, Judith Mihalyi, Robert Molock, Paul Rudd, Joseph Schroer, Jean-Pierre Stewart, Susan Tyrell.

Understudies: Mr. Cobb—Charles Cioffi; Miss Tweed—Judith Mihalyi; Mr. Keach—John Devlin; Mr. Stattel—Robert Phalen; Mr. Auberjonois—James Cook; Misses Lightstone, Elliott —Joan Jeffri.

Directed by Gerald Freedman; scenery, Ming Cho Lee; costumes, Theoni V. Aldredge; lighting, John Gleason; music, John Morris; production stage manager, Tim Ward; stage manager, Barbara-Mae Phillips; press, Susan Bloch.

King Lear's most recent major New York revival was in the Royal Shakespeare Company production May 18, 1964 at the New York State Theater of Lincoln Center for 12 performances.

A CRY OF PLAYERS

Will ....Frank Langella	Arthur ....Kristoffer Tabori
Fulk ....Michael Egan	Sir Thomas ....Stephen Elliott
Meg ....Rosetta LeNoire	Berry ....Brendan Fay
Richards ....Ray Fry	Sandells ....Bill Moor
Susanna ....Jackie Paris	Roche ....Ray Stewart
Anne ....Anne Bancroft	Jenny ....Susan Tyrrell
Kemp ....Robert Symonds	Hodges ....Jerome Dempsey
Ned ....Rene Auberjonois	Old John ....Don McHenry
Heming ....Tom Sawyer	Gilbert ....Ronald Weyand
Pope ....Gerry Black	

Townspeople: Ruth Attaway, Joseph Attles, Samual Blue Jr., Virgilia Chew, James Cook, Patricia Elliott, Leslie Graves, Mervyn Haines, Douglas Hayle, Robert Levine, Judith Mihalyi, Robert Molock, William Myers, Robert Phalen, Paul Rudd, Joseph Schroer, Jean-Pierre Stewart, Barbette Tweed.

Understudies: Mr. Langella—Robert Phalen; Miss Bancroft—Marilyn Lightstone.

Directed by Gene Frankel; scenery, David Hays; costumes, Patricia Quinn Stuart; lighting, John Gleason; music, Richard Peaslee; production stage manager, Ronald Schaeffer; stage manager, Frank Bayer.

Time: One autumn in the 1580s. Place: A backwater town in England. Act I, Scene 1: A hill, at night. Scene 2: The town square, next morning. Scene 3: The hill, that evening. Scene 4: The tavern, later. Act II, Scene 1: The home, later that night. Scene 2: The hill, midnight. Scene 3: The town square, next afternoon. Act III, Scene 1: The Guild Hall, later. Scene 2: The town square, immediately following.

LEE J. COBB IN "KING LEAR"

Play about a young Englishman named "Will," depicting him as a rebellious youth at odds with his squire, his wife Anne and his society, until finally he runs away to join a band of players. The name Shakespeare is not mentioned, but the implication is clear. Previously produced in Stockbridge, Mass.

IN THE MATTER OF
J. ROBERT OPPENHEIMER

J. Robert Oppenheimer	Joseph Wiseman	Franklin S. Hardiman	Cec Linder
Personnel Security Board:		Witnesses:	
Gordon Gray	Harry Townes	Major Nicholas Radzi	Charles Cioffi
Ward V. Evans	Eduard Franz	John Lansdale	Stephen Elliott
Thomas A. Morgan	Whitfield Connor	Edward Teller	Herbert Berghof
Counsel:		Hans Bethe	Stefan Schnabel
Curtis Moffat Jr.	Philip Bosco	Walker Leroy Adams	Ronald Weyand
H. Thomas Spalding	Robert Phalen	Jacob Lehmann	Tony van Bridge
Aaron Stein	Ralph Bell		

Stenographers: Robert Molock, Douglas Hayle. Security Guards: Jean-Pierre Stewart, Joseph Schroer, Paul Rudd. Custodians: Barnett Epstein, Patrick Horrigan, Robert Molock, Douglas Hayle.

Standby: Mr. Wiseman—Paul Sparer. Understudies: Messrs. Bosco, van Bridge—Ray Fry; Messrs. Berghof, Elliott, Connor—Ben Hammer; Messrs. Schnabel, Franz—William Myers; Messrs. Linder, Townes, Weyand—Ray Stewart.

Directed by Gordon Davidson; scenery, Peter Wexler; costumes, Constance Ross; lighting, John Gleason; still projections, Elinor Bunin, Peter Wexler; production stage manager, Barbara-Mae Phillips; stage manager, Patrick Horrigan.

Time: April 12-May 6, 1954. Place: Room 2022, Building T3, Atomic Energy Commission, Washington, D.C. The play is divided into two acts.

Dramatization of the A.E.C. hearing on the security clearance of Dr. Oppenheimer, "father of the atom bomb." The facts have been freely adapted so that characters represent points of view on the issues rather than actual lawyers and witnesses at the hearing, which took place at the end of the witch-hunt era of McCarthyism. Previously produced at the Mark Taper Forum, Los Angeles, Calif.

A Best Play; see page 234

THE MISER

Harpagon	Robert Symonds	La Merluche	James Cook
Valere	Lloyd Battista	Master Jacques	Ray Fry
Elise	Blythe Danner	Mariane	Maeve McGuire
Cleante	David Birney	The Magistrate	Stephen Elliott
La Fleche	Roger Robinson	The Clerk	Robert Levine
Master Simon	Ronald Weyand	Anselme	Philip Bosco
Frosine	Lili Darvas	Criquet	William Myers
Dame Claude	Leta Bonynge	Attendants	Robert Molock, Joseph Schroer,
Brindavoine	Douglas Hayle		Jean-Pierre Stewart

Understudies: Mr. Symonds—Jerome Dempsey; Mr. Battista—Jean-Pierre Stewart; Miss Mc-Guire—Jane Altman; Mr. Birney—Joseph Schroer; Miss Danner—Joan Jeffri; Miss Darvas—Leta Bonynge.

Directed by Carl Weber; scenery, David Hays; lighting, John Gleason; costumes, James Hart Stearns; music, William Bolcom; production stage manager, Frank Bayer; stage manager, Barnett Epstein.

Time: 17th century. Place: Paris. The play was presented in two acts.

The Miser's last New York professional production of record was by the Federal Theater Project May 13, 1936 for 3 performances.

* **Zorbá** (224). Musical with book by Joseph Stein; music by John Kander; lyrics by Fred Ebb; adapted from *Zorba the Greek* by Nikos Kazantzakis. Produced by Harold Prince in association with Ruth Mitchell at the Imperial Theater. Opened November 17, 1968.

Constable	David Wilder	Aristos	Charles Kalan
Nikos	John Cunningham	Georgi	Johnny La Motta
Alexis	Alex Petrides	Antonis	Anthony Marciona
Hortense	Maria Karnilova	Tasso	Susan Marciona
Manolako	James Luisi	Thanos	Lewis Gundunas
Panayotis	Nat Horne	Pavli	Richard Dmitri
Widow	Carmen Alvarez	Father Zacharia	Gerard Russak
Mimiko	Al De Sio	Aliki	Miriam Welch
Konstandi	Joseph Alfasa	Mavrodani	Paul Michael
Sofia	Marsha Tamaroff	Chyristo	Louis Garcia
Kyriakos	Jerry Sappir	Zacharias	Edward Nolfi
Leader	Lorraine Serabian	Belly Dancer	Jemela Omar
Kanakis	Al Hafid	Old Man	Robert Bernard
Kostantinos	Angelo Saridis	Katapolis	Richard Nieves
Marina	Alicia Helen Markarian	Despo	Nina Dova
Fivos	Gerrit De Beer	Irini	Connie Burnett
Efterpi	Lee Hooper	Athena	Peggy Cooper
Zorba	Herschel Bernardi	Grigoris	Wayne Boyd
Loukas	Loukas Skipitaris	Vasilis	Martin Meyers
Meropi	Juliette Durand		

Instrumental Interlude Soloists: Jerry Sappir, Ali Hafid, Angelo Saridis.

Understudies: Mr. Bernardi—James Luisi; Miss Karnilova—Nina Dova; Mr. Cunningham—Loukas Skipitaris; Miss Alvarez—Lee Hooper; Miss Serabian—Peggy Cooper; Female Dancers—Anna Maria Fanizzi; Male Dancers—Terry Violino.

Directed by Harold Prince; choreography, Ronald Field; musical director, Harold Hastings; scenery, Boris Aronson; costumes, Patricia Zipprodt; lighting, Richard Pilbrow; orchestrations, Don Walker; dance music arrangements, Dorothea Freitag; production consultant, Vassili Lambrinos; production stage manager, Ruth Mitchell; stage manager, James Bronson; press, Mary Bryant, David Rothenberg, Ellen Levene.

Time: The present (and 1924). Place: A Bouzouki circle (and Piraeus, Greece, and Crete).

As in the movie version of *Zorba the Greek,* a young man learns from his life-loving companion on a visit to Crete how to realize and enjoy the full possibilities of each moment of time.

ACT I

"Life Is" .... Leader, Company

"The First Time" .... Zorba

"The Top of the Hill" ....Leader, Chorus
"No Boom Boom" ....Hortense, Zorba, Nikos, Admirals
"Vive La Difference" ....Admirals, Dancers
"The Butterfly" ....Nikos, Leader, Widow, Chorus
"Goodbye, Canavaro" ....Hortense, Zorba
Belly Dance ....Jemela
"Grandpapa" ....Zorba, Leader, Chorus
"Only Love" ....Hortense
"The Bend of the Road" ....Leader, Chorus
"Only Love" (Reprise) ....Leader

ACT II

Bells ....Dancers
"Y'assou" ....Nikos, Zorba, Hortense, Leader, Chorus
"Why Can't I Speak?" ....Widow, Girl
Mine Celebration ....Zorba, Company
"The Crow" ....Leader, Women
"Happy Birthday" ....Hortense
"I Am Free" ....Zorba
"Life Is" (Reprise) ....Leader, Company

Morning, Noon and Night (52). Program of three one-act plays: *Morning* by Israel Horovitz, *Noon* by Terrence McNally and *Night* by Leonard Melfi. Produced by Circle in the Square on Broadway, Theodore Mann artistic director, Paul Libin managing director, Gillian Walker associate director, at Henry Miller's Theater. Opened November 28, 1968. (Closed January 11, 1969)

MORNING

Tillich ....John Heffernan
Gertrude ....Charlotte Rae
Updike ....Sorrell Booke
Sissy ....Jane Marla Robbins
Junior ....Robert Klein

NOON

Kerry ....John Heffernan
Asher ....Robert Klein
Allegra ....Jane Marla Robbins
Beryl ....Charlotte Rae
Cecil ....Sorrell Booke

NIGHT

Miss Indigo Blue ....Jane Marla Robbins
Robin Breast Western ....John Heffernan
Filigree Bones ....Charlotte Rae
Fibber Kidding ....Sorrell Booke
Cock Certain ....Robert Klein

General Male Understudy: Walter Rosen Scholz.

All plays: directed by Theodore Mann; scenery and costumes, Michael Annals; lighting, Martin Aronstein; music, John Hall; lyrics, Israel Horovitz; production stage manager, Randall Brooks; stage manager, Walter Rosen Scholz; press, Merle Debuskey, Violet Welles, Faith Geer.

MORNING—Time: Now. Place: Harlem. A Negro family of misfits has taken medicine which turned them white.

NOON—Time: Now. Place: A large loft. A practical joker summons a group of sex perverts with different hang-ups to an intimate rendezvous.

NIGHT—Time: Now. Place: Somewhere outdoors in any American cemetery and perhaps other places, too. Four mourners meet to honor the memory of a departed friend, and a fifth to bury a dog.

MARIAN MERCER, JERRY ORBACH, JILL O'HARA (IN FOREGROUND), NORMAN
SHELLY, VINCE O'BRIEN, DICK O'NEILL, PAUL REED, A. LARRY HAINES AND
DONNA MCKECHNIE IN "PROMISES, PROMISES"

* **Promises, Promises** (208). Musical with book by Neil Simon; music by Burt
Bacharach; lyrics by Hal David; based on the screenplay *The Apartment* by Billy
Wilder and I.A.L. Diamond. Produced by David Merrick at the Sam S. Shubert
Theater. Opened December 1, 1968.

Chuck Baxter	Jerry Orbach	Company Nurse	Carole Bishop
J.D. Sheldrake	Edward Winter	Company Doctor	Gerry O'Hara
Fran Kubelik	Jill O'Hara	Peggy Olson	Millie Slavin
Bartender Eddie;		Lum Ding Hostess;	
Karl Kubelik	Ken Howard	Miss Wong	Baayork Lee
Mr. Dobitch	Paul Reed	Waiter	Scott Pearson
Sylvia Gilhooley	Adrienne Angel	Madison Square Garden Attendant;	
Mr. Kirkeby	Norman Shelly	Bartender Eugene	Michael Vita
Mr. Eichelberger	Vince O'Brien	Dining Room Hostess	Betsy Haug
Vivien Della Hoya	Donna McKechnie	Miss Polansky	Margo Sappington
Dr. Dreyfuss	A. Larry Haines	Marge MacDougall	Marian Mercer
Jesse Vanderhof	Dick O'Neill	Helen Sheldrake	Kay Oslin
Dentist's Nurse	Rita O'Connor	New Young Executive	Rod Barry

Clancy's Lounge Patrons: Carole Bishop, Rita O'Connor, Julane Stites, Rod Barry, Gene
Cooper, Bob Fitch, Neil Jones, Scott Pearson, Michael Shawn. Clancy's Employees: Graciela
Daniele, Betsy Haug, Margo Sappington. Interns and Their Dates: Barbara Alston, Graciela
Daniele, Gerry O'Hara, Michael Shawn. Orchestra Voices: Kelly Britt, Margot Hanson, Bettye
McCormick, Ilona Simon.
Standby: Messrs. Orbach, Winter—Peter Lombard. Understudies: Miss O'Hara—Margo Sap-
pington; Mr. Haines—Norman Shelly; Mr. Reed—Dick O'Neill; Messrs. O'Neill, O'Brien—
Henry Sutton; Miss Mercer—Kelly Britt.
Directed by Robert Moore; musical numbers staged by Michael Bennett; musical direction
and dance arrangements, Harold Wheeler; scenery, Robin Wagner; costumes, Donald Brooks;
lighting, Martin Aronstein; orchestrations, Jonathan Tunick; associate producer, Samuel Liff;

production stage manager, Charles Blackwell; stage manager, Henry Velez; press, Harvey B. Sabinson, Lee Solters, David Powers.

Time: The present. Place: New York City.

As in the movie comedy *The Apartment,* a young executive gets ahead in a large corporation by lending the key to his bachelor apartment to his bosses for their romantic escapades.

ACT I

Scene 1: The offices of Consolidated Life; Second Ave. bar
"Half as Big as Life" ....Chuck
Scene 2: Chuck's apartment house
"Upstairs" ....Chuck
Scene 3: Medical office
"You'll Think of Someone" ....Fran, Chuck
Scene 4: Mr. Sheldrake's office
"Our Little Secret" ....Chuck, Sheldrake
Scene 5: Lobby
"She Likes Basketball" ....Chuck
Scene 6: Lum Ding's Restaurant and Madison Square Garden
"Knowing When to Leave" ....Fran
Scene 7: Lobby; Executive Dining Room; Executive Sun Deck
"Where Can You Take a Girl?" ....Dobitch, Kirkeby, Eichelberger, Vanderhof
"Wanting Things" ....Sheldrake
Scene 8: At the elevator
Scene 9: 19th Floor Christmas party
"Turkey Lurkey Time" ....Vivien, Miss Polansky, Miss Wong

ACT II

Scene 1: Clancy's Lounge
"A Fact Can Be a Beautiful Thing" ....Chuck, Marge, Bar Patrons
Scene 2: Chuck's apartment
"Whoever You Are" ....Fran
"A Young Pretty Girl Like You" ....Chuck, Dr. Dreyfuss
"I'll Never Fall in Love Again" ....Fran, Chuck
Scene 3: The offices of Consolidated Life
Scene 4: Lum Ding's Restaurant and Street
"Promises, Promises" ....Chuck
Scene 5: Chuck's apartment

The Goodbye People (7). By Herb Gardner. Produced by Feuer and Martin at the Ethel Barrymore Theater. Opened December 3, 1968. (Closed December 7, 1968)

Arthur Korman ....Bob Dishy
Max Silverman ....Milton Berle
Nancy Scott ....Brenda Vaccaro

Eddie Bergson ....Jess Osuna
Michael Silverman ....Tony Lo Bianco
Marcus Soloway ....Sammy Smith

Standbys: Miss Vaccaro—Hildy Brooks; Mr. Dishy—Tony Lo Bianco; Mr. Berle—Monroe Arnold.

Directed by Herb Gardner; scenery and lighting, David Hays; costumes, Alvin Colt; production supervisor, Porter Van Zandt; stage manager, Ellen Wittman; press, Merle Debuskey, Violet Welles, Faith Geer.

Time: The present. Place: The beach at Coney Island. Act I: Just before dawn. Act II, Scene 1: Before dawn of the next morning. Scene 2: Three days later, early evening. Scene 3: 8:30 the following morning.

An aged Coney Island concessionaire comes out of retirement to risk everything, including his life, on a glorious, hopeless, gala midwinter reopening of his hot dog stand.

Jimmy Shine (153). By Murray Schisgal. Produced by Claire Nichtern and Zev Bufman at the Brooks Atkinson Theater. Opened December 5, 1968. (Closed April 26, 1969)

MARTYN GREEN, GEORGE ROSE, HERMIONE BADDELEY, ED EVANKO AND SANDY
DUNCAN (IN BED) IN "CANTERBURY TALES"

Jimmy Shine ....Dustin Hoffman	Arnold ....Arnold Wilkerson
Rosie Pitkin ....Rose Gregorio	Boy ....John Pleshette
Miss Green ....Barbara Cason	2d Boy ....Joel Warfield
Elizabeth Evans ....Susan Sullivan	Millie ....Gale Dixon
Constance Fry ....Pamela Payton-Wright	Rita ....Dorothy Emmerson
Michael Leon ....Charles Siebert	Boy Dancer ....Johnny Evans
Sally Weber ....Rue McClanahan	Girl ....Kim Lang
Man in Closet ....David Sabin	Girl Dancer ....Susan Segal
Lee Haines ....Cleavon Little	Mr. Lepke ....Eli Mintz

Musicians: David Nichtern, Kenneth Altman, Michael Sachs.

Understudies: Mr. Hoffman—John Pleshette; Misses Gregorio, Emmerson—Kim Lang; Misses
Sullivan, Cason—Dorothy Emmerson; Mr. Mintz—Joseph Leon.

Directed by Donald Driver; music and lyrics, John Sebastian; scenery, Edward Burbridge;
costumes, Lewis Brown; lighting, Thomas Skelton; musical director, Irving Joseph; production
stage manager, William Krot; stage manager, Carol Raymont; press, Ben Kornzweig, Reginald
Denenholz.

Time: The present. Place: A loft. The play is divided into two acts.

Jimmy Shine, a not-yet-successful abstract painter, reenacts romantic and other events,
mostly failures, of his growing up—and occasionally he expresses himself in song.

Carnival! (30). Musical revival with book by Michael Stewart; music and lyrics
by Bob Merrill; based on material by Helen Deutsch. Produced by The City Center Light Opera Company, Jean Dalrymple director, at New York City Center.
Opened December 12, 1968. (Closed January 5, 1969)

Jacquot ....Pierre Olaf	Strongman ....David Berk
Mr. Schlegel ....Carmine Caridi	Gladys Zuwicki ....Mary Ann Niles
Grobert ....George Nestor	Gloria Zuwicki ....Christina Bartel
Dog Trainer ....Leonard Brook	Gypsy ....Roberta Vatske
Wardrobe Mistress ....Maria Hero	Marco the Magnificent ......Richard France
Bear Girl ....Maureen Hopkins	The Incomparable Rosalie ....Karen Morrow
Princess Olga ....Dorothy D'Honau	Greta Schlegel ....Jennifer Rose
Band ....Art Ostrin, Nate Barnett	Lili ....Victoria Mallory
Stilt Walker; Clown;	Paul ....Leon Bibb (Richard Barclay)
Aerialist ....Dean Crane	Dr. Glass ....Robert L. Hultman
Jugglers ....Martin Brothers	Puppets performed by ......Richard Barclay
Clown ....John Drew	

Roustabouts: Chuck Beard, Marcello Gamboa, Fred Randall, Steven Ross, Paul Solen.
Harem Girls and Blue Birds: Nina Janik, Dottie Lester, Maralyn Miles, Linda Rankin.

Standby: Mr. France—Ted Forlow. Understudies: Miss Mallory—Roberta Vatske; Miss Morrow—Maria Hero; Mr. Olaf—Art Ostrin; Miss D'Honau—Maureen Hopkins; Mr. Caridi—George Nestor.

Directed by Gus Schirmer; restaging of original choreography, John Nola; musical director, Peter Howard; production and lighting, Feder; associate designer, Richard Fuhrman; costumes, Harry Curtis; based on the original designs by Freddy Wittop; musical and vocal arrangements, Saul Schechtman; orchestrations, Philip J. Lang; dance arrangements, Peter Howard; original production directed and choreographed by Gower Champion and produced by David Merrick; designer and supervisor of magic and illusion, Jack Adams; assistants to choreographer, Mary Ann Niles, Jerry Fries; production stage manager, Herman Shapiro; stage managers, Forrest Carter, Larry Ziegler; press, John Clugstone.

Place: The outskirts of a town in Southern Europe.

Carnival's story is based on the same material as was the motion picture *Lili*. *Carnival* was first produced April 13, 1961 at the Imperial Theater for 719 performances. This is its first New York revival.

The list of musical numbers in *Carnival* appears on page 337 of the 1960-61 *Best Plays* volume.

The Minnesota Theater Company. Repertory of two revivals. **The House of Atreus** (17). Adapted by John Lewin from the *Oresteia* of Aeschylus. Opened December 17, 1968. **The Resistible Rise of Arturo Ui** (14). By Bertolt Brecht; translated by George Tabori. Opened December 22, 1968. Produced by The Minnesota Theater Company, Peter Zeisler managing director, at the Billy Rose Theater. (Repertory closed January 11, 1969)

	"THE HOUSE OF ATREUS"			"THE RESISTIBLE RISE OF ARTURO UI"
PERFORMER	*Agamemnon*	*Choephori*	*The Furies*	
James Alexander	Chorus		Hermes	Bowl; etc.
Paul Ballantyne	Chorus Leader			Hindborough
Don Barshay	Soldier	Chorus	Priest	Smith; etc.
Emery Battis	Soldier		Chorus	Gardener; Actor
Fran Bennett		Chorus Leader	Chorus	
Douglas Campbell	Clytemnestra	Clytemnestra	Clytemnestra's Ghost; Athena	
Helen Carey	Handmaiden	Chorus	Chorus	
Len Cariou		Orestes	Orestes	
Richard Cottrell	Soldier	Chorus	Priest	Inna; etc.
Jon Cranney	Soldier		Priestess; Juryman	Mulberry, etc.
Nicholas DeJoria	Soldier	Chorus	Priest	Shorty
David Feldshuh				Etc.
Larry Ferguson	Soldier	Chorus	Juryman	Greenwool
Katherine Ferrand	Chorus		Priest	Lady; etc.
Robin Gammell	Cassandra	Electra		Arturo Ui
Katherine Garnett	Handmaiden		Chorus	
Ron Glass	Chorus		Chorus	Jim Crocket
Carol Gustafson	Chorus		Singer	Woman

| PERFORMER | "THE HOUSE OF ATREUS" | | | "THE RESISTIBLE RISE OF ARTURO UI" |
	Agamemnon	Choephori	The Furies	
Allen Hamilton	Chorus	Servant; Chorus	Juryman	Butcher; Doctor
Helen Harrelson	Chorus	Chorus	Singer	
Charles Keating	Chorus	Pylades	Juryman	Giri
James J. Lawless	Chorus		Chorus Leader	Sheet; Judge; Minister
Roberta Maxwell	Handmaiden	Chorus	Chorus	Mrs. Dullfeet
Michael Moriarty	Chorus		Chorus	Ragg; Fish; Dullfeet
Robert Pastene	Aegisthus	Aegisthus	Juryman	Clark
Lauri Peters	Handmaiden	Chorus	Singer	
Michael Pierce				Etc.
Alek Primrose	Chorus		Chorus	Barker; O'Casey; etc.
Richard Ramos	Soldier	Cilissa; Chorus	Chorus	Givola
John Ramsey		Chorus	Juryman	
Nancy Reardon			Singer	Dockdaisy
Lee Richardson	Watchman; Agamemnon		Apollo	Roma
Michael Sevareid	Chorus		Juryman	Prosecutor; Narrator
Tony Swartz	Soldier	Chorus	Juryman	Young Hindborough
Granville Van Dusen	Soldier	Chorus	Singer	Flake; Defense Attorney

Both plays: design associate, John Jensen; press, Arthur Cantor, Stanley Gaither, Susan L. Sculman.

THE HOUSE OF ATREUS directed by Tyrone Guthrie; designed by Tanya Moiseiwitsch; music, Dominick Argento; masks, Carolyn Parker; stage manager, Milt Commons; assistant to the director, Fran Bennett.

Act I *(Agamemnon)*: Argos, the palace of Agamemnon. Act II *(The Bringers of Offerings)*: Argos, the tomb of Agamemnon and the palace, some years later. Act III *(The Furies)*: Delphi, the shrine of Apollo; later, Athens, the shrine of Pallas Athene.

Aeschylus' *Oresteia*, from which *The House of Atreus* was adapted, is a trilogy of plays: *Agamemnon, Choephori (The Bringers of Offerings)* and *Eumenides (The Furies)*. This is *Agamemnon's* first Broadway production of record. *Choephori* and *Eumenides* were produced September 19, 1961 by the City Center of Music and Drama, Inc. in association with the Greek Theater Association at the New York City Center for 16 performances. *The House of Atreus* was originally produced in 1967 in Minnesota Theater Company repertory at the Tyrone Guthrie Theater, Minneapolis, Minn.

THE RESISTIBLE RISE OF ARTURO UI directed by Edward Payson Call; scenery and costumes, Richard L. Hay; music, Herbert Pilhofer; film sequences, S. Leonard Auerbach; assistant to the director, Jonathan Gillman; stage manager, Gordon Smith.

Time: The early 1930s. Place: Chicago.

Brecht's parable of Hitler's rise to power, told as a Chicago gangland drama, was first produced on Broadway November 11, 1963 by David Merrick at the Lunt-Fontanne Theater for 8 performances.

The Sudden and Accidental Re-education of Horse Johnson (5). By Douglas Taylor. Produced by Gene Persson, Orin Lehman, Jay Harnick and Cora Gay Carr at the Belasco Theater. Opened December 18, 1968. (Closed December 21, 1968)

Horse Johnson	Jack Klugman	Dolly	Jill Clayburgh
Herman Slovaski	Fred Kareman	Bud	William Bogert
Connie	Kathleen Maguire	Clint Barlowe	Mitchell Ryan

Understudies: Messrs. Kareman, Bogert, Ryan—Gene Williams. Misses Maguire, Clayburgh—Elisabeth Farley.

Directed by George Morrison; scenery, Robert D. Mitchell; costumes, Domingo A. Rodriguez; lighting, Roger Morgan; production stage manager, Jack Leigh; stage manager, Gene Williams; press, Harvey B. Sabinson, Lee Solters, Harry Nigro.

Time: The present. Place: San Francisco. Act I, Scene 1: Late afternoon. Scene 2: Several minutes later. Act II, Scene 1: Later that evening. Scene 2: Early the next morning.

Comedy about a warehouse worker who takes some time off to study in order to figure out a way to change the world. Previously produced in Milwaukee.

* Forty Carats (180). By Jay Allen; adapted from a play by Pierre Barillet and Jean-Pierre Gredy. Produced by David Merrick at the Morosco Theater. Opened December 26, 1968.

Ann Stanley	Julie Harris	Maud Hayes	Glenda Farrell
Peter Latham	Marco St. John	Trina Stanley	Gretchen Corbett
Mrs. Adams	Iva Withers	Mrs. Latham	Nancy Marchand
Mrs. Margolin	Polly Rowles	Mr. Latham	John Cecil Holm
Billy Boylan	Murray Hamilton	Pat	Michael Nouri
Eddy Edwards	Franklin Cover		

Standby: Miss Harris—Iva Withers. Understudies: Messrs. Hamilton, Cover—David Baker; Mr. St. John—Michael Nouri; Misses Farrell, Withers, Rowles—Cele McLaughlin; Miss Corbett—Susan King; Mr. Nouri—Jeff Chambers.

Directed by Abe Burrows; scenery, Will Steven Armstrong; costumes, William McHone; lighting, Martin Aronstein; associate producer, Samuel Liff; production stage manager, James Burrows; stage manager, Jeff Chambers; press, Harvey B. Sabinson, Lee Solters, Leo Stern.

Time: The present. Place: The play begins somewhere in the Greek islands and then moves on to the apartment and the office of Ann Stanley in New York City. The play is divided into two acts.

Comedy about the May-August romance between an attractive divorcee of 40, in the prime of her life, and a discerning youth in his early 20s.

Violet Dunn replaced Glenda Farrell 2/24/69. Sudie Bond replaced Polly Rowles 3/17/69.

A Best Play; see page 258

The Fig Leaves Are Falling (4). Musical with book and lyrics by Allan Sherman; music by Albert Hague. Produced by Joseph Harris, Lawrence Carr and John Bowab at the Broadhurst Theater. Opened January 2, 1969. (Closed January 4, 1969)

Harry Stone	Barry Nelson	Mother-in-Law	Helon Blount
Lillian Stone	Dorothy Loudon	Billy	David Cassidy
Pookie Chapman	Jenny O'Hara	Cecelia	Louise Quick
Mr. Mittleman	Jay Barney	Le Roy	Alan Weeks
Hodgekins	Joe McGrath	Mary Queen of Scots	Anna Pagan
Rev. Walters	Darrell Sandeen	Elizabeth Marsden	Pat Trott
Gelb; Queen Victoria	Frank DeSal	Mao-Tse	John Joy
Mildred; Marlene	Jean Even	Grace	Mara Landi
Mimsy	Marilyne Mason	Cynthia	Jocelyn McKay
Charley Montgomery	Kenneth Kimmins	Tough Guy	Lathan Sanford
Marty	Patrick Spohn		

Dancers: Jean Even, Mary Jane Houdina, Renata Powers, Sally Ransone, Charlene Ryan, Pat Trott, Frank DeSal, John Medeiros, Michael Misita, Lathan Sanford, Tony Stevens, Patrick Spohn, Pi Douglas.

Singers: Sherry Lambert, Mara Landi, Rosemary McNamara, Anna Pagan, Jocelyn McKay, Edmund Gaynes, John Joy, Joe McGrath, Darrell Sandeen, Alan Weeks.

Standbys: Miss Loudon—Ellen Hanley; Messrs. Nelson, Kimmins—Jack Drummond. Understudies: Miss Quick—Sherry Lambert; Mr. Cassidy—Edmund Gaynes; Miss O'Hara—Marilyne Mason.

Directed by George Abbott; dances and musical numbers staged by Eddie Gasper; musical direction, Abba Bogin; scenery, William and Jean Eckart; costumes, Robert Mackintosh; lighting, Tharon Musser; orchestrations, Manny Albam; dance music arrangements and orchestra conducted by Jack Lee; production stage manager, Terence Little; stage manager, Wally Engelhardt; press, David Lipsky, Lisa Lipsky.

Time: The present. Place: Larchmont and New York.
A Larchmont husband is torn between the wife at home and the attractive secretary in town.

ACT I

Prologue
"All Is Well in Larchmont" ....Choir
Scene 1: The Stones' living room in Larchmont
"Lillian" ....Company
Scene 2: Limbo
"Like Yours" ....Pookie, Wallstreeters
Scene 3: Harry's office
"All of My Laughter" ....Pookie, Harry
Scene 4: The park
"Give Me a Cause" ....Protestors
Scene 5: Harry's office
"Today I Saw a Rose" ....Harry
Scene 6: The Stones' living room (off to Europe)
"We" ....Lillian
Scene 7: The Stones' living room
"For Our Sake" ....Billy, Cecelia
Scene 8: Limbo
Scene 9: The park
"Light One Candle" ....Le Roy, Queen Victoria, Mary Queen of Scots, Hippies, Yippies, etc.
Scene 10: Limbo
"Oh, Boy" ....Choir
Scene 11: The Stones' bedroom (nightmare)

ACT II

Scene 1: The Fig Leaves Are Falling
"The Fig Leaves Are Falling" ....The Boys Club
Scene 2: Limbo
Scene 3: The Stones' living room
"For the Rest of My Life" ....Lillian
Scene 4: The theater
"I Like It" ....Harry, Pookie
Scene 5: Limbo
Broken Heart ....Lillian
Scene 6: Charley's apartment
Scene 7: Pookie's pad
"Old Fashioned Song" ....Charley, Ensemble
"Lillian, Lillian, Lillian" ....Lillian, Cecelia, Billy
Scene 8: Limbo
Scene 9: The Stones' living room
Scene 10: Limbo
"Did I Ever Really Live" ....Harry
Scene 11: The Stones' living room
"All of My Laughter" (Reprise) ....Harry

* **Hadrian VII** (166). By Peter Luke; based on *Hadrian the Seventh* and other works by Fr. Rolfe (Baron Corvo). Produced by Lester Osterman Productions (Lester Osterman, Richard Horner, Lawrence Kasha), Bill Freedman and Charles Kasher at the Helen Hayes Theater. Opened January 8, 1969.

Fr. William Rolfe ....Alec McCowen
Mrs. Crowe ....Sydney Sturgess
Bailiff; Bishop of
  Caerleon ....William Needles
Bailiff; Cardinal-Archbishop
  of Pimlico ....Gillie Fenwick
Agnes ....Marie Paxton
Jeremiah Sant, F.R.S. ....Gerard Parkes
The Cardinal-Archdeacon ..Richard Nicholls

Prepositor-Gen. of
  Jesuits ....Christopher Hewett
Cardinal Ragna ....Louis Zorich
Cardinal Berstein ....Truman Gaige
Rector of St. Andrew's
  College ....Neil Fitzgerald
George Arthur Rose ....Peter Jobin
Papal Chamberlain ....John Hallow

Cardinals: William A. Bush, Tom Gorman, Robert Hewitt, Theodore Tenley. Papal Guards: William Engel, Michael Stein. Acolytes, Seminarists, Swiss Guards: B.J. DeSimone, Carl Jessop, John Kramer, Joseph Neal, Alan Rachins, Robert Shattuck.

Standbys: Mr. McCowen—Roderick Cook; Misses Sturgess, Paxton—Sylvia O'Brien.

Directed by Peter Dews; scenery and costumes, Robert Fletcher; lighting, Lloyd Burlingame; production stage manager, Ben Janney; stage manager, Wayne Carson; press, Harvey B. Sabinson, Lee Solters.

Time: Around 1903. Place: London and Rome. Act I, Scene 1: A corner of Frederick Rolfe's bed-sitting room in London. Scene 2: A room in Archbishop House. Scene 3: A chapel in the Vatican. Act II, Scene 1: Mrs. Crowe's parlor in London. Scene 2: An audience chamber in the Vatican. Scene 3: Outside a cafe in Rome. Scene 4: The audience chamber. Scene 5: St. Andrew's College. Scene 6: The audience chamber. Scene 7: The audience chamber. Scene 8: Rolfe's room in London.

Frederick William Rolfe (who called himself Fr. Rolfe or Baron Corvo) has been rejected for the priesthood and is living impoverished and alone, and he escapes his misery into a dream that he is elected Pope. A foreign play previously produced in Birmingham and London.

A Best Play; see page 281

Celebration (109). Musical with book and lyrics by Tom Jones; music by Harvey Schmidt. Produced by Cheryl Crawford and Richard Chandler at the Ambassador Theater. Opened January 22, 1969. (Closed April 26, 1969)

Potemkin	Keith Charles	Angel	Susan Watson
Orphan	Michael Glenn-Smith	Rich	Ted Thurston

The Revelers: Glenn Bastian, Cindi Bulak, Stephan de Ghelder, Leah Horen, Patricia Lens, Norman Mathews, Frank Newell, Pamela Peadon, Felix Rice, Sally Riggs, Gary Wales, Hal Watters. Percussion Ensemble: Keyboards—Rod Derefinko, Clay Fullum, Paulette Haupt; Percussion—Dennis Glick, Leon Oxman, Cholli Simons; Harp—Kathryn Easter; Guitar—Jack Hotop; Bass—Sam Bruno.

Standbys: Mr. Thurston—David Sabin; Mr. Charles—John Boni. Understudies: Miss Watson—Pamela Peadon; Mr. Glenn-Smith—Hal Watters; Revelers—Tip Kelley, Nina Trasoff.

Directed by Tom Jones; musical numbers staged and choreographed by Vernon Lusby; musical director, Rod Derefinko; scenery, costumes, lighting, Ed Wittstein; orchestrations, Jim Tyler; production coordination, Robert Alan Gold; production stage manager, May Muth; stage manager, Robert Schear; press, Harvey B. Sabinson, Lee Solters, David Powers.

Time: New Year's Eve. Place: A platform.

Fable about the time and life cycle passing through the cold winter season of disillusionment and satiation to the inevitable spring of rebirth, renewal and love.

A Best Play; see page 302

ACT I

"Celebration"	Potemkin, Revelers
"Orphan in the Storm"	Orphan, Revelers
"Survive"	Potemkin, Revelers
"Somebody"	Angel, Hittites
"Bored"	Rich
"My Garden"	Orphan, Revelers
"Where Did It Go"	Rich, Sycophants
"Love Song"	Angel, Potemkin, Rich, Orphan, Revelers
"To the Garden"	Everyone

ACT II

"I'm Glad To See You've Got What You Want"	Angel, Orphan
"It's You Who Makes Me Young"	Rich, Revelers
"Not My Problem"	Potemkin, Machines
"Fifty Million Years Ago"	Orphan
"The Beautician Ballet"	Rich, Revelers
"Saturnalia"	Potemkin, Revelers
"Under the Tree"	Angel, Animals
"Winter and Summer"	Everyone
"Celebration" Finale	Everyone

Red, White and Maddox (41). Musical with book by Don Tucker and Jay Broad; music and lyrics by Don Tucker. The Theater Atlanta Production produced by Edward Padula at the Cort Theater. Opened January 26, 1969. (Closed March 2, 1969)

Lester Maddox ....Jay Garner	Buttercup Boy ....Ted Harris
Alberta ....Georgia Allen	Bombardier ....Christopher Lloyd
Student Leader ....Fran Brill	Rock Singer ....Bettye Malone
Cynical Campaigner ....Lois Broad	Boy from New Left ....Ted Martin
The Senator ....Ronald Bush	The Redneck ....Sandy McCallum
Air Force General ....Fred Chappell	Virginia Maddox ....Muriel Moore
Governor of Indiana ......Mitchell Edmonds	Girl from New Left ....Arlene Nadel
Standard Bearer ....Karl Emery	Political Commentator ....Steve Renfroe
The Interlocutor ....Clarence Felder	Little Mary Sue ....Judy Schoen
General of the Armies ....Gary Gage	Protester ....Susan Shaloub
Radio Commentator ......William Gammon	C.I.A. Chief ....William Trotman
Student Delegate ....Elaine Harris	Rock Singer ....James Weston

Directed by Jay Broad and Don Tucker; scenery and costumes, David Chapman; design supervision and lighting, Richard Casler; visual materials, Bill Diehle Jr.; associate producers, William Domnitz, Arthur Miller; production stage manager, Peter J. Perry; press, Sol Jacobson, Lewis Harmon.

Act I ("One hundred years later") satirizes Lester Maddox as owner of the Pickrick Restaurant in Atlanta, Ga., and later as governor of his state. Act II ("One hundred years too late") imagines a future in which Maddox becomes an all-destroying president of the United States.

ACT I—"What America Means to Me," "Givers and Getters," "Jubilee Joe," "Ballad of a Redneck," "First Campaign Song," "Hoe Down," "Phooey," "Second Campaign Song," "God Is an American."

ACT II—"Hip-Hooray for Washington," "City Life," "Song of the Malcontents," "The General's Song," "Little Mary Sue," "Billy Joe Ju," "The Impeachment Waltz," "Red, White and Maddox Kazoo March."

Fire! (6). By John Roc. Produced by David Black in association with Jonathan Burrows at the Longacre Theater. Opened January 28, 1969. (Closed February 1, 1969)

Lorna ....Carolyn Coates	Walter ....John Wardwell
Jason ....Peter MacLean	Delia ....Jennifer Darling
Ronald ....Roy K. Stevens	Sarah ....Audra Lindley
Stanley ....Louis Edmonds	Marco ....Rene Auberjonois

Understudies: Misses Coates, Lindley—Ann D'Andrea; Miss Darling—Dorrie Kavanaugh; Messrs. Auberjonois, Edmonds—William Grannell; Messrs. MacLean, Wardwell—Albert Stratton; Mr. Stevens—Tommy Breslin.

Directed by Charles Werner Moore; scenery and lighting, Howard Bay; costumes, Lewis Brown; electronic effects, Alvin Lucier; production supervisor, Jose Vega; production stage manager, Charles Gray; press, Frank Goodman, Alan Eichler.

The play is divided into two acts. It is a timeless, placeless assemblage of people for a meeting of some kind, at which a bully repeatedly forces other characters into confessing their weaknesses and in saying aloud the word "Fire" as though it were a cleansing punishment. Previously produced at Brandeis University, Waltham, Mass.

The Mother Lover (1). By Jerome Weidman. Produced by Leland Hayward in association with Joseph E. Levine and Avco Embassy Pictures Corp. Opened and closed at the evening performance, February 1, 1969.

Mrs. Haber ....Eileen Heckart	Griselda ....Valerie French
Seymour ....Larry Blyden	

Directed by Larry Blyden; scenery and lighting, Ben Edwards; costumes, Jane Greenwood; stage manager, Hal Halvorsen; press, Frank Goodman, Alan Eichler.

Time: The present, during one of Seymour Haber's weekly visits to his mother. Place: Mrs. Haber's apartment in the Borough of Queens. Act I: Morning. Act II, Scene 1: Immediately thereafter. Scene 2: A half-hour later.

Mother and son, mutually detesting but going through the motions of a family relationship, are joined during one of their get-togethers by a call-girl friend.

Canterbury Tales (121). Musical with book by Martin Starkie and Nevill Coghill; music by Richard Hill and John Hawkins; lyrics by Nevill Coghill; based on a translation from Geoffrey Chaucer by Nevill Coghill. Produced by Management Three Productions Ltd. and Frank Productions Inc. by arrangement with Classic Presentations Ltd. at the Eugene O'Neill Theater. Opened February 3, 1969. (Closed May 18, 1969 matinee)

The Pilgrims:
Chaucer .... Martyn Green
Host .... Edwin Steffe
Miller .... Roy Cooper
Wife of Bath .... Hermione Baddeley
Cook .... David Thomas
Merchant .... Leon Shaw
Knight .... Reid Shelton
Steward .... George Rose
Prioress .... Ann Gardner
Nun .... Evelyn Page
Priest .... Garnett Smith
Clerk of Oxford .... Bruce Hyde
Squire .... Ed Evanko
Friar .... Richard Ensslen
Pardoner .... Garnett Smith
Summoner .... Bert Michaels
The Sweetheart .... Sandy Duncan
The Miller's Tale
Nicholas .... Ed Evanko
Alison .... Sandy Duncan
The Carpenter .... George Rose

Absalon .... Bruce Hyde
Gervase .... Roy Cooper
Robin .... Terry Eno
Parishioners .... Mary Jo Catlett,
                                Suzan Sidney
The Steward's Tale
Miller .... Roy Cooper
Miller's Wife .... Evelyn Page
Molly .... Sandy Duncan
Alan .... Ed Evanko
John .... Bruce Hyde
The Merchant's Tale
January .... George Rose
Justinus .... Martyn Green
Placebo .... Garnett Smith
May .... Sandy Duncan
Damian .... Ed Evanko
Pluto .... Roy Cooper
Proserpina .... Ann Gardner
Duenna .... Evelyn Page
Page .... Tod Miller

Bridesmaids: Patricia Michaels, Marianne Selbert, Karen Kristin, Joyce Maret. Attendants: Terry Eno, Tod Miller, Gene Myers, Ron Schwinn, Jack Fletcher.

The Wife of Bath's Tale
King .... Reid Shelton
Queen .... Ann Gardner
Old Woman .... Hermione Baddeley

Young Knight .... Bruce Hyde
Executioner .... Roger Franklin
Housewife .... Mary Jo Catlett
Sweetheart .... Sandy Duncan

Courtiers: Terry Eno, Ron Schwinn, Tod Miller, Gene Myers. Court Ladies: Karen Kristin, Marianne Selbert, Joyce Maret, Patricia Michaels.

Other Pilgrims; Workmen: Terry Eno, Jack Fletcher, Tod Miller, Gene Myers, Ron Schwinn, David Thomas. Village Girls: Mary Jo Catlett, Betsy Dickerson, Karen Kristin, Joyce Maret, Patricia Michaels, Marianne Selbert, Suzan Sidney.

Understudies: Mr. Rose—Garnett Smith; Miss Baddeley—Evelyn Page; Mr. Green—David Thomas; Mr. Cooper—Dick Ensslen; Miss Gardner—Patricia Michaels; Miss Page—Mary Jo Catlett; Mr. Evanko—Jack Fletcher; Mr. Hyde—Terry Eno; Miss Duncan—Karen Kristin.

Directed by Martin Starkie; musical numbers and dances staged by Sammy Bayes; musical direction, vocal and dance arrangements, Oscar Kosarin; orchestrations, Richard Hill and John Hawkins; scenery, Derek Cousins; costumes, Loudon Sainthill; lighting, Jules Fisher; scenery supervision, Richard Seger; assistant choreographer, Bert Michaels; production stage manager, Elizabeth Caldwell; stage manager, Wade Miller; press, Harvey B. Sabinson, Lee Solters, Jay Russell.

Time: In the spring during the latter part of the 14th century. Place: Between the Tabard Inn and Canterbury Cathedral.

Incidents on the road to Canterbury, plus four stories of love and marriage as told by four of the pilgrims, adapted from Geoffrey Chaucer's *The Canterbury Tales*. A foreign play previously produced in London.

ACT I

"Song of Welcome" ....Host, Company
"Good Night Hymn" ....Company
"Canterbury Day" ....Company
Pilgrim Riding Music ....Company
The Miller's Tale
  "I Have a Noble Cock" ....Nicholas
  "Darling, Let Me Teach You How To Kiss" ....Absalon
  "There's the Moon" ....Nicholas, Alison
"It Depends on What You're At" ....Wife of Bath, Nun, Company
"Love Will Conquer All" ....Prioress, Village Girl (Suzan Sidney), Company
The Steward's Tale
  "Beer Is Best" ....Miller, Miller's Wife, Alan, John, Molly
"Canterbury Day" (Reprise) ....Company

ACT II

"Come on and Marry Me Honey" ....Wife of Bath, Company
Mug Dance ....Company
"Where Are the Girls of Yesterday" ....Host, Company
The Merchant's Tale
  "Hymen, Hymen" ....Company
  "If She Has Never Loved Before" ....January
  "I'll Give My Love a Ring" ....Damian, May
  "Pear Tree Quintet" ....Damian, January, Pluto, Proserpina, May
"I Am All A-Blaze" ....Squire
"Love Pas de Deux" ....Pilgrim (Ron Schwinn), Village Girl (Marianne Selbert)
The Wife of Bath's Tale
  "What Do Women Want" ....Young Knight, Court Ladies
"April Song" ....Company
"Love Will Conquer All" (Reprise) ....Prioress, Village Girl (Suzan Sidney), Company

Dear World (132). Musical with book by Jerome Lawrence and Robert E. Lee; music and lyrics by Jerry Herman; based on *The Madwoman of Chaillot* by Jean Giraudoux, as adapted by Maurice Valency. Produced by Alexander H. Cohen at the Mark Hellinger Theater. Opened February 6, 1969. (Closed May 31, 1969)

The Chairman of the Board . . William Larsen	The Peddler ....John Taliaferro
The Prospector ....Joe Masiell	Countess Aurelia, The Madwoman of
Julian ....Kurt Peterson	Chaillot ....Angela Lansbury
Nina ....Pamela Hall	The Sewerman ....Milo O'Shea
The Waiter ....Gene Varrone	Gabrielle, The Madwoman of
The Doorman ....Michael Davis	Montmartre ....Jane Connell
The Busboy ....Ty McConnell	Constance, The Madwoman of
The Juggler ....Ted Agress	the Flea Market ....Carmen Mathews
The Deaf-Mute ....Miguel Godreau	

Board Members: Clifford Fearl, Charles Karel, Zale Kessler, Charles Welch. People of Paris: Nicole Barth, Bruce Becker, Toney Brealond, Jane Coleman, Jack Davison, Jacque Dean, Richard Dodd, John Grigas, Marian Haraldson, Tony Juliano, Gene Kelton, Carolyn Kirsch, Urylee Leonardos, Larry Merritt, Ruth Ramsey, Orrin Reiley, Patsy Sabline, Connie Simmons, Margot Travers, Mary Zahn.

Standbys: Miss Lansbury—M'el Dowd; Misses Connell, Mathews—Camila Ashland. Understudies: Mr. O'Shea—Zale Kessler; Mr. Larsen—Clifford Fearl; Mr. Peterson—Ty McConnell; Miss Hall—Merrill Leighton; Ensemble—Barbara Blair, Merrill Leighton, Joe Nelson.

Directed by Joe Layton; musical direction and vocal arrangements, Donald Pippin; scenery, Oliver Smith; costumes, Freddy Wittop; lighting, Jean Rosenthal; orchestrations, Philip J. Lang; dance and incidental arrangements, Dorothea Freitag; associate producer, Hildy Parks; production supervisor, Jerry Adler; production associate, Roy A. Somlyo; stage manager, Robert L. Borod; press, James D. Proctor, Ted Goldsmith.

Time: An early spring. Place: Paris.

Musical is based on Giraudoux *The Madwoman of Chaillot,* which made its New York debut December 27, 1948 at the Belasco Theater for 369 performances and was named a Best Play

of its season and received the Critics Award for Best Foreign Play. It played a return engagement of 17 performances at the New York City Center beginning June 13, 1950.
Zale Kessler replaced Milo O'Shea 4/16/69.

ACT I

"The Spring of Next Year" ....Chairman, Prospector, Corporation
"Each Tomorrow Morning" ....Countess, Company
"I Don't Want To Know" ....Countess
"I've Never Said I Love You" ....Nina
"Garbage" ....Sewerman, Countess, Gabrielle, Constance, Company
Ballet: I Don't Want To Know ....Entire Company
"Dear World" ....Countess, Company

ACT II

"Kiss Her Now" ....Countess
The Tea Party
  "Memory" ....Constance
  "Pearls" ....Countess, Gabrielle
  "Dickie" ....Gabrielle
  "Voices" ....Constance
  "Thoughts" ....Countess
"And I Was Beautiful" ....Countess
"Each Tomorrow Morning" (Reprise) ....Julian
"One Person" ....Countess, Company
Finale ....Entire Company

* **Play It Again, Sam** (128). By Woody Allen. Produced by David Merrick in association with Jack Rollins and Charles Joffe at the Broadhurst Theater. Opened February 12, 1969.

Allan Felix	Woody Allen	Sharon Lake	Diana Walker
Nancy	Sheila Sullivan	Gina	Jean Fowler
Bogey	Jerry Lacy	Vanessa	Cynthia Dalbey
Dick Christie	Anthony Roberts	Go-Go Girl	Lee Anne Fahey
Linda Christie	Diane Keaton	Intellectual Girl	Barbara Press
Sharon; Barbara	Barbara Brownell		

Understudies: Messrs. Roberts. Lacey—Ted Tinling; Miss Sullivan—Diana Walker.
Directed by Joseph Hardy; scenery, William Ritman; costumes, Ann Roth; lighting, Martin Aronstein; associate producer, Samuel Liff; production stage manager, Mitchell Erickson; stage manager, Ted Tinling; press, Harvey B. Sabinson, Lee Solters, Leo Stern.
Time: The present. Place: The apartment of Allan Felix on West 10th Street, New York. Act I, Scene 1: A late summer afternoon. Scene 2: Later that night. Act II: Several weeks later. Act III: The following morning.
Comedy, a mousy film critic tries to console himself, after his wife leaves him, with a glamorous fantasy life in which he is coached by his image of Humphrey Bogart.

The National Theater of the Deaf (16; see note). Programs of pantomime and sign language based on dramatic and poetic material. Produced by the Eugene O'Neill Memorial Theater Foundation at the Longacre Theater. Opened February 24, 1969. (Closed March 8, 1969)

THE TALE OF KASANE

Narrator	Andrew Vasnick	Yoemon	Joe Velez
Readers	William Rhys, Jacqueline Awad	Policeman	Edmund Waterstreet
Kasane	Audree Norton		

By Tsurya Namboku; adapted by Sahomi Tachibana and Robert F. Panara; directed by Yoshio Aoyama; scenery, David Hays; costumes, Patricia Zipprodt; lighting, John Gleason.
Time: The 17th century. Place: By the River Kine in Japan.
The Tale of Kasane (Iromyo Chotto Karimane) is a Kabuki drama of love, murder and doom.

ON THE HARMFULNESS OF TOBACCO

Nyukhin ....Lou Fant   Master of Ceremonies ....William Rhys

By Anton Chekhov; adapted by Bernard Bragg; directed by Alvin Epstein; costumes, Fred Voelpel.

GIANNI SCHICCHI

Schicchi ....Bernard Bragg	Zita ....June Russi
Rinuccio ....Richard Kendall	Marco ....Joe Velez
Betto ....Edmund Waterstreet	Ciesca ....Mary Beth Miller
Gherardo ....Andrew Vasnick	Lauretta ....Linda Bove
Nella ....Audree Norton	Spinelloccio; Notary ....Lou Fant
Gherardino ....Morton Steinberg	Witness ....Dorothy Miles
Simone ....Charles Corey	Readers .....William Rhys, Jacqueline Awad

Adapted by Robert F. Panara and Eric Malzkuhn from a commedia dell'arte farce; directed by Joe Layton; associate director, Rhoda Levine; scenery and cosumes, Fred Voelpel; lighting, John Gleason.

Time: 1299. Place: Florence, the bedchamber of Buoso Donati.

THE CRITIC

Dangle ....Bernard Bragg	Singer; Niece; Bank ....Linda Bove
Mrs. Dangle ....June Russi	Singer; Underprompter ....Lou Fant
Maid; Sentinel; Seamstress;	Singer; Master of Horse; Beefeater;
Dog; Bank ....Jacqueline Awad	Spanish Ship ....Richard Kendall
Hairdresser; Sentinel; Musician;	Musician ....John Basinger
English Ship ....William Rhys	French Interpreter; Don Ferolo Whiskerandos;
Servant; Leicester; Burleigh;	English Ship ....Morton Steinberg
Thames ....Edmund Waterstreet	Hatton; Governor;
Puff ....Joe Velez	Spanish Ship ....Andrew Vasnick
Ritornello; Raleigh;	Confidante; Niece ....Audree Norton
Spanish Ship ....Charles Corey	Tilburina ....Mary Beth Miller

By Richard Brinsley Sheridan; adapted by Lou Fant and Eric Malzkuhn; directed by Joe Layton; assistant to the director, Rhoda Levine; scenery and costumes, Fred Voelpel; lighting, John Gleason.

TYGER! TYGER! AND OTHER BURNINGS—Adaptations by Eric Malzkuhn from *The Tyger* by William Blake, *On His Deafness* by Robert F. Panara, *Jabberwocky* by Lewis Carroll, *How Do I Love Thee* from *Sonnets from the Portuguese* by Elizabeth Barrett Browning, *Flowers & Moonlight of the Spring River* by Yang Ti, *Poems by Children* from *Miracles: Poems by Children of the English-Speaking World*, collected by Richard Lewis; directed by John Hirsch. With Bernard Bragg, Charles Corey, Richard Kendall, Audree Norton, June Russi, Joe Velez, Edmund Waterstreet, William Rhys, Jacqueline Awad.

BLUEPRINTS: PROJECTIONS AND PERSPECTIVES—Adapted by Bernard Bragg and Lou Fant from works by Rainer Maria Rilke, e.e. cummings, Randall Jarrell, Muriel Rukeyser, Leonard Cohen, Anne Halley, Theodore Roethe and Edward Field; directed by Gene Lasko; scenery, David Hays, lighting, John Gleason. With the Company.

All productions—managing director, David Hays; production stage manager, Rilla Bergman; stage managers, Ken Swiger, Bernard Tansey; press, Ben Kornzweig, Reginald Denenholz, Fred Weterick.

Plays and poetry dramatizations presented in sign language and pantomime for deaf audiences, with readers speaking the words for others. Note: The opening program consisted of *The Tale of Kasane, Blueprints: Projections and Perspectives* and *Gianni Schicchi* and was presented 10 times through 3/4/69. The second bill, *On the Harmfulness of Tobacco, The Critic* and *Tyger! Tyger! and Other Burnings,* played the final 6 performances beginning with the matinee 3/5/69.

Does a Tiger Wear a Necktie? (39). By Don Petersen. Produced by Philip Rose and Huntington Hartford in association with Jay Weston at the Belasco Theater. Opened February 25, 1969. (Closed March 29, 1969)

Ringo	M. Emmet Walsh	Rita	Catita Lord
Hugo	Kenneth Rosaly	Fullendorf	Bruce Scott
Raul	Hector Troy	Prince	Michael Brandon
Conrad	Roger Robinson	Tonto	Lazaro Perez
Deek	Bob Christian	Bickham	Al Pacino
Marietta	Laura Figueroa	Mr. O'Malley	Jon Richards
Linda	Lauren Jones	Dr. Werner	David Opatoshu
Ponti	Jose Perez	Lee	Sam Watson
Mr. Winters	Hal Holbrook		

Standbys: Mr. Holbrook—Joe Ponazecki; Miss Jones—Hattie Winston; Messrs. Opatoshu, Richards, Walsh—Mitchell Jason. Understudies: Mr. Robinson—Bob Christian; Messrs. Scott, Pacino—Michael Brandon; Messrs. Perez, Brandon—Hector Troy; Miss Lord—Laura Figueroa; Messrs. Rosaly, Troy, Christian—Nate Barnett.

Directed by Michael A. Schultz; scenery, Edward Burbridge; costumes, David Toser; lighting, Thomas Skelton; special sound, James Reichert; associate producer, Irving Cooper; production stage manager, Leonard Auerbach; stage manager, Nate Barnett; press, Merle Debuskey, Violet Welles, Faith Geer.

Time: The present. Place: A rehabilitation center for juvenile narcotics addicts located on an island in a river bordering on a large industrial city. Act I, Scene 1: The English classroom and hallway, 2 p.m., a wintry Friday in December. Scene 2: A storage room, the following Sunday night, around midnight. Act II, Scene 1: The English classroom, 8 p.m. the following Wednesday. Scene 2: A psychiatrist's office in the hospital, 3 p.m. Thursday. Act III: The school auditorium and stage, 8 p.m. one week later and a few days before Christmas.

Juvenile addicts in detention, whose temperaments range from placid to dangerous, react to clinical and intellectual influences, most notably an English teacher trying to stimulate their imaginations. Previously produced at Brandeis University and Stockbridge, Mass.

But, Seriously . . . (4). By Julius J. Epstein. Produced by Gerard Oestreicher, Joseph Kipness and Harold Leventhal at Henry Miller's Theater. Opened February 27, 1969. (Closed March 1, 1969)

Walter London	Tom Poston	Robert Arnold	Steven Gravers
Carol London	Bethel Leslie	The Hon. Newton Prince	Dick Van Patten
Helga	Lee Billington	Barbara Prince	Jen Jones
A Young Man	Harry Packwood	Helen Arnold	Sally Gracie
Vincent	Louis Guss	Louella Ann Pringle	Beverly Penberthy
Stanley	Richard Dreyfuss	David Harley	Robert Mandan
Clinton Evans Keith	Nicolas Coster		

Understudies: Messrs. Poston, Mandan, Gravers—Michael Kane; Misses Leslie, Gracie, Penberthy, Jones—Jodean Russo; Messrs. Dreyfuss, Packwood—Schorling Schneider; Miss Billington—Elizabeth Forman.

Directed by John Allen; scenery, Oliver Smith; costumes, Pearl Somner; lighting, Jules Fisher; assistant to the producers, Madeline Lee Gilford; production supervised by Gerard Oestreicher; production stage manager, Burry Fredrik; stage manager, Schorling Schneider; press, Merle Debuskey, Violet Welles, Faith Geer.

Time: The present. Place: Beverly Hills, Calif. Act I: A Saturday mid-morning. Act II: Early the same evening.

Marital and other problems of a Hollywood scenarist.

The Wrong Way Light Bulb (7). By Leonard Spigelgass. Produced by Elliot Martin at the John Golden Theater. Opened March 4, 1969. (Closed March 8, 1969)

Harold Axman	James Patterson	Mrs. Devereaux	Claudia McNeil
Arnie Erickson	Daniel Keyes	Carlton Devereaux	Lawrence Cook
Judge Belknap	Barnard Hughes	Miss Sullivan	Mildred Clinton
Gus Haber	Sammy Smith	Joshua Chibuchnick	Donnie Melvin
Mrs. Rosen	Nancy R. Pollock	Sergeant Colvin	John McCurry
Dolores Gonzales	Miriam Colon	Police Officer	George Guidall

Understudies: Mr. Patterson—George Guidall; Messrs. Keyes, Hughes, Smith—Ralph Stantley; Miss Pollock—Mildred Clinton; Miss Colon—Irene De Bari; Miss O'Neil—Alyce Webb; Mr. Cook—John McCurry; Mr. McCurry—Lloyd Hollar; Mr. Melvin—Lee Franklin.

Directed by Stephen Porter; scenery and lighting, Donald Oenslager; costumes, Jane Greenwood; production stage manager, Ben D. Kranz; stage manager, Alfred Hinckley; press, Nat Dorfman.

Time: The present, a recent summer. Place: The living room of an apartment house in Brooklyn. Act I: An afternoon. Act II, Scene 1: Some weeks later. Scene 2: An hour later. Scene 3: Early the next morning.

Liberal writer inherits an apartment house in a changing neighborhood, finds old cliches and bromides inadequate in the face of modern racial, religious and social antagonisms.

Zelda (5). By Sylvia Regan. Produced by Arthur Hoffe and Charles Isenberg in association with Gerald B. Seiff at the Ethel Barrymore Theater. Opened March 5, 1969. (Closed March 8, 1969)

David Hartman	Robby Benson	Rose Hartman	Lilia Skala
Alexander Hartman	Ed Begley	Elliott Hartman	Alfred Sandor
Suzy Corey	Julie Anne	Geraldine Hartman	Renee Roy
Steffi Hartman	Nita Talbot	Jim Corey	Maxwell Glanville
Norman Hartman	Tom Keena	Christine Corey	Zaida Coles

Standbys: Mr. Begley—Robert H. Harris; Miss Skala—Viola Harris. Misses Talbot, Roy—Dale Berg; Messrs. Sandor, Keena—Laurence Feinstein; Mr. Benson—Bob Hennessey; Mr. Glanville—Stanley Greene; Miss Coles—Javotte Green; Miss Anne—Karen Anderson.

Directed by Delbert Mann; scenery and lighting, Will Steven Armstrong; costumes, Theoni V. Aldredge; production supervisor, Howard Whitfield; stage manager, William Weaver; press, Frank Goodman, Alan Eichler.

Time: The present, a Labor Day weekend. Place: A beach cottage located on a spit of land off the southern shore of Long Island. Act I: Friday afternoon. Act II, Scene 1: The following morning. Scene 2: Late the same afternoon. Act III: Early the following morning.

Comedy about a modern Noah and his family preparing to survive the end of the world, coming in the form of a September hurricane named Zelda.

The Watering Place (1). By Lyle Kessler. Produced by Gene Persson and James Walsh at the Music Box. Opened and closed at the evening performance March 12, 1969.

The Mother	Vivian Nathan	The Father	Ralph Waite
Janet	Shirley Knight	Sonny	William Devane

Directed by Alan Schneider; scenery, Robin Wagner; costumes, Jeanne Button; lighting, Jules Fisher; associate producer, Rick Hobard; production stage manager, Frederic deWilde; stage manager, John Actman; press, Harvey B. Sabinson, Lee Solters, Harry Nigro.

Time: The present. Place: A house on the edge of an American city. Act I, Scene 1: A summer day. Scene 2: One hour later. Scene 3: Tuesday evening, two days later. Act II, Scene 1: One hour later. Scene 2: Sunday, noon. Scene 3: One hour later, afternoon.

Vietnam War veteran moves in with a dead friend's family and disrupts their already neurotic existence.

The Dozens (4). By Laird Koenig. Produced by Hale Matthews at the Booth Theater. Opened March 13, 1969. (Closed March 15, 1969)

Via Hillman	Paula Kelly	Kgaravu	Morgan Freeman
Stanley Pollack	Al Freeman Jr.		

Understudy: Miss Kelly—Susan Taylor

Directed by Edward Parone; production designed by Rouben Ter-Arutunian; lighting, Martin Aronstein; associate producer, Terry Fay; production stage managers, Joe Calvan, Charles Gray; press, Frank Goodman.

Time: The present. Place: The revolution-torn African Republic of Chaka. Act I: Late afternoon. Act II, Scene 1: Later that night. Scene 2: Early the next morning.

Night club singer and her ineffectual husband meet a fugitive leader of an African country, spend a night in hiding with him.

* 1776 (89). Musical with book by Peter Stone; music and lyrics by Sherman Edwards; based on a conception of Sherman Edwards. Produced by Stuart Ostrow at the Forty-Sixth Street Theater. Opened March 16, 1969.

Members of the Continental Congress

President
   John Hancock ....David Ford
New Hampshire
   Dr. Josiah Bartlett ....Dal Richards
Massachusetts
   John Adams ....William Daniels
Rhode Island
   Stephen Hopkins ....Roy Poole
Connecticut
   Roger Sherman ....David Vosburgh
New York
   Lewis Morris ....Ronald Kross
   Robert Livingston ....Henry Le Clair
New Jersey
   Rev. Jonathan
     Witherspoon ....Edmund Lyndeck
Pennsylvania
   Benjamin Franklin ......Howard Da Silva
   John Dickinson ....Paul Hecht
   James Wilson ....Emory Bass
Delaware
   Caesar Rodney ....Robert Gaus

   Col. Thomas McKean .....Bruce MacKay
   George Read ....Duane Bodin
Maryland
   Samuel Chase ....Philip Polito
Virginia
   Richard Henry Lee ....Ronald Holgate
   Thomas Jefferson ....Ken Howard
North Carolina
   Joseph Hewes ....Charles Rule
South Carolina
   Edward Rutledge ....Clifford David
Georgia
   Dr. Lyman Hall ....Jonathan Moore
          and
Congressional Sec.
   Charles Thomson ....Ralston Hill
Congressional Custodian
   Andrew McNair ....William Duell
   A Leather Apron ....B.J Slater
   Courier ....Scott Jarvis
   Abigail Adams ....Virginia Vestoff
   Martha Jefferson ....Betty Buckley

Standby: Mr. Da Silva—Rex Everhart. Understudies: Mr. Daniels—Jonathan Moore; Mr. Hecht—Bruce McKay; Mr. David—Dal Richards; Mr. MacKay—Charles Rule; Messrs. Howard, Jarvis—B.J. Slater; Misses Vestoff, Buckley—Gretchen Cryer; general understudy—Hal Norman.

Directed by Peter Hunt; musical numbers staged by Onna White; musical direction and dance music arrangements, Peter Howard; scenery and lighting, Jo Mielziner; costumes, Patricia Zipprodt; orchestrations, Eddie Sauter; vocal arrangements, Elise Bretton; associate to Miss White, Martin Allen; production stage manager, Peter Stern; stage manager, Lee Murray; press, Harvey B. Sabinson, Lee Solters, Harry Nigro.

Time: May, June and July 1776. Place: A single setting representing the Chamber and an anteroom of the Continental Congress, a mall, High Street and Thomas Jefferson's room, in Philadelphia; and certain reaches of John Adams' mind. The action takes place continuously, without intermission.

Drama with music about events leading to the signing of the American Declaration of Independence.

David Cryer replaced Clifford David and John Fink replaced Ken Howard 5/30/69.

A Best Play; see page 305

Scene 1: The Chamber of the Continental Congress
   "Sit Down, John" ....Adams, Congress
   "Piddle, Twiddle and Resolve" ....Adams
   "Till Then" ....Adams, Abigail
Scene 2: The Mall
   "The Lees of Old Virginia" ....Lee, Franklin, Adams
Scene 3: The Chamber
   "But, Mr. Adams" ....Adams, Franklin, Jefferson, Sherman, Livingston
Scene 4: Jefferson's room above High Street
   "Yours, Yours, Yours" ....Adams, Abigail
   "He Plays the Violin" ....Martha, Franklin, Adams
Scene 5: The Chamber
   "Cool, Cool, Considerate Men" ....Dickinson, Conservatives
   "Momma Look Sharp" ....Courier, Custodian, Leather Apron
Scene 6: The Congressional anteroom
   "The Egg" ....Franklin, Adams, Jefferson

Scene 7: The Chamber
"Molasses to Rum" ....Rutledge
"Yours, Yours, Yours" (Reprise) ....Abigail
"Is Anybody There?" ....Adams

Come Summer (7). Musical with book and lyrics by Will Holt; music by David Baker; based on *Rainbow on the Road* by Esther Forbes. Produced by Albert W. Selden and Hal James at the Lunt-Fontanne Theater. Opened March 18, 1969. (Closed March 22, 1969)

Phineas Sharp ....Ray Bolger
Nathaniel Burnap ....William Cottrell
Jude Scribner ....David Cryer
Dorinda Pratt ....Margaret Hamilton
Labe Pratt ....John Gerstad
Submit Pratt (Mitty) ....Cathryn Damon

Mrs. Meserve ....Dorothy Sands
Emma Faucett ....Barbara Sharma
Francis Faucett ....William LeMassena
Dancing characters:
Lovers ....Evelyn Taylor, David Evans
Head Logger ....William Glassman

The Populace: Marcia Brushingham, Ellen Everett, Sunny Hannum, Lucia Lambert, Mary Ann Rydzeski, Lana Sloniger, Sarah Jane Smith, Britt Swanson, Jeanette Williamson, Toodie Wittmer, Jenny Workman, James Albright, Paul Berné, Bjarne Buchtrup, Dennis Cole, Leonard John Crofoot, Harry Endicott, David Evans, William Glassman, Walter Hook, Doug Hunt, Del Horstmann, John Johann.

Standbys: Mr. Bolger—Ben Kapen; Misses Damon, Sharma—Tanny McDonald; Miss Hamilton—Dorothy Sands. Understudies: Mr. Cryer—David Evans; Miss Sands—Mary Ann Rydzeski; Mr. LeMassena—Del Horstmann; Mr. Gerstad—Doug Hunt; Mr. Cottrell—Walter Hook.

Directed by Agnes de Mille; musical direction, Milton Rosenstock; scenery, Oliver Smith; costumes, Stanley Simmons; lighting, Thomas Skelton; orchestrations, Carlyle Hall; vocal arrangements and musical continuity, Trude Rittman; dance music, David Baker and John Berkman; directorial assistant, James Mitchell; choreographic assistant, Vernon Lusby; production stage manager, Phil Friedman; stage manager, Frank Hamilton; press, Merle Debuskey, Violet Welles, Faith Geer.

Time: The peddlers' season, early spring to late fall in the year 1840, just before the factories took over. Place: The towns and surrounding countryside along the Connecticut River in New England.

Veteran peddler and young friend find romantic adventures as they work their way along the Connecticut River Valley.

ACT I

"Good Time Charlie" ....Phineas, Peddlers
"Think Spring" ....Phineas, Jude, Populace
"Wild Birds Calling" ....Jude, Mitty
"Goodbye, My Bachelor" ....Phineas
"Fine, Thank You, Fine" ....Emma
"Road to Hampton" ....Jude
"Come Summer" ....Phineas, Jude, Emma, Mitty, Visions of Lovers
"Let Me Be" ....Mitty, Jude
"Feather in My Shoe" ....Phineas
"The Loggers' Song" ....Phineas, Jude, Loggers, Populace

ACT II

"Jude's Holler" ....Jude, Populace
"Faucett Falls Fancy" ....Phineas, Populace
"Rockin' " ....Emma, Jude
"Skin and Bones" ....Phineas
"Moonglade" ....Phineas, Jude, Mitty, Emma, Dorinda, Labe, Faucett, Populace
"Women" ....Mitty
"No" ....Phineas, Populace
"So Much World" ....Jude

Billy (1). Musical with book by Stephen Glassman; music and lyrics by Ron Dante and Gene Allan; suggested by Herman Melville's *Billy Budd*. Produced by

Bruce W. Stark in association with Joseph Shoctor at the Billy Rose Theater. Opened and closed at the evening performance, March 22, 1969.

Capt. Edward Vere ......Laurence Naismith
Lt. William Radcliffe ...William Countryman
Lt. Roger Mordant ....Michael Tartel
John Claggart,
    Master-at-Arms ....John Devlin
Cpl. John Bernard ....Simm Landres
Marine Cpl.; Stoker .....Laried Montgomery
Marine Cpl. ....Danny Villa
Billy Budd ....Robert Salvio
Dansker ....John Beal
Whiskers ....Dolph Sweet
Campbell ....George Marcy
Boscombe ....Alan Weeks
Boyer ....Igors Gavon
Gilbert ....Al Cohen

Donald Taff ....Peter De Maio
Rawley ....Danny Carroll
John Thorp ....Joseph Dellasorte
Stafford ....Bill Schustik
Fallon ....Pascual Vaquer
Smithy ....Howard Girven
Rush ....Steven Broockvor
Potter ....Christopher Chadman
Roper ....Michael Peters
Marsten ....Tim Ramirez
Harker ....Ron Tassone
Seeger ....Frank De Sal
Grimer ....De Wayne Oliver
Molly ....Barbara Monte

Directed by Arthur A. Seidelman; musical sequences staged by Grover Dale; musical director, Jack Lee; scenery, Ming Cho Lee; costumes, Theoni V. Aldredge; lighting, Martin Aronstein; orchestrations, Ronald Frangipane; dance music arrangements, Coleridge Perkinson; incidental music and special arrangements, Wally Harper; production stage manager, Frank Rembach; stage manager, Tom Porter; press, Harvey B. Sabinson, Lee Solters, David Powers.

Time: 1796. Place: Aboard a man-of-war. The action takes place continuously, without intermission.

Herman Melville's *Billy Budd* story was previously produced on Broadway as a straight play by Chandler Cowles and Anthony B. Farrell February 10, 1951 for 105 performances.

MUSICAL NUMBERS

"Molly" ....Billy
"Chanty" ....Stafford, Fallon, Smithy, Stoker
"Watch Out for Claggart/Work" ....Boscombe, Claggart, Crew
"Shaking Hand with the Wind" ....Billy
"Whiskers' Dance" ....Whiskers, Crew
"Billy" ....Molly, Billy
"It Ain't Us Who Make the Wars" ....Campbell, Crew
"The Bridge to Nowhere" ....Vere
"The Night and the Sea" ....Billy, Claggart
"Whiskers' Dance" (Reprise) ....Whiskers, Billy, Fallon, Taff, Thorp
"In the Arms of a Stranger" ....Dansker
"The Fiddlers' Green" ....Whiskers, Campbell, Boyer, Stoker, Rawley, Gilbert
"My Captain" ....Vere, Billy
"Requiem" ....Billy

Cop-Out (8). Program of two one-act plays by John Guare. Produced by Norman Twain in association with Albert I. Fill at the Cort Theater. Opened April 7, 1969. (Closed April 13, 1969)

HOME FIRES

Mr. Catchpole ....George Bartenieff
Peter Smith ....MacIntyre Dixon
Nell Schmidt ....April Shawhan

Rudy Smythe ....Charles Kimbrough
Margaret Ross-Hughes ....Carrie Nye

COP-OUT

Ron Leibman   Linda Lavin

Standby: Miss Lavin—Barbara Gilbert. Understudies: Mr. Leibman—Charles Kimbrough; Messrs. Bartenieff, Dixon—Eugene Stuckmann.

Directed by Melvin Bernhardt; scenery and costumes, Fred Voelpel; lighting, John Gleason; environmental sound, James Reichert; songs, John Guare; production stage manager, Nelle Nugent; stage manager, Eugene Stuckmann; press, Frank Goodman, Ruth Cage.

HOME FIRES—Time: November 12, 1918, the day after the Armistice ending World War I was signed. Place: Catchpole's Funeral Parlor, a very elegant establishment on the Boulevard in Swampscott, Mass.
Comedy of snobbism within a family of German immigrants in various degrees of Americanization.
COP-OUT—Time: 50 years later.
Comedy of relationships between various policemen (all played by the same actor) and the women in their lives (all played by the same actress). *Cop-Out* and *Home Fires* were previously produced at the Eugene O'Neill Memorial Theater Foundation, Waterford, Conn.

The Gingham Dog (5). By Lanford Wilson. Produced by Haila Stoddard, Mark Wright, Duane Wilder, Harold Scott at the John Golden Theater. Opened April 23, 1969. (Closed April 26, 1969)

Gloria	Diana Sands	Robert	Roy London
Vincent	George Grizzard	Barbara	Karen Grassle

Standbys: Miss Sands—Micki Grant; Mr. Grizzard—Jordan Charney; Miss Grassle—Kristina Callahan; Mr. London—Joseph Cali.
Directed by Alan Schneider; scenery, William Ritman; costumes, Theoni V. Aldredge; lighting, Tharon Musser; associate producer, David G. Meyers; production stage manager, Bruce Hoover; stage manager, Joseph Cali; press, Robert Ganshaw & John Prescott.
Time: The present. Place: A New York apartment living room. Act I: A Saturday in March, about noon. Act II: The following morning, 5:30 a.m.
The breakup of a marriage between a white Southern liberal and a black girl from Harlem. Previously produced at the Washington, D.C. Theater Club.

Trumpets of the Lord (7). Musical adapted by Vinette Carroll from James Weldon Johnson's *God's Trombone;* music and lyrics based on gospel hymns. Produced by Circle in the Square, Theodore Mann artistic director, Paul Libin managing director, Gillian Walker associate director, at the Brooks Atkinson Theater. Opened April 29, 1969. (Closed May 3, 1969)

Sister Henrietta Pinkston	Theresa Merritt	Rev. Ridgley Washington	Bernard Ward
Rev. Bradford Parham	Lex Monson	Rev. Marion Alexander	Cicely Tyson

Female Voices: Berniece Hall, Ella Eure, Camille Yarborough. Male Voices: Earl Baker, Bill Glover, Milton Grayson, William Stewart.
Understudies: Miss Tyson—Camille Yarborough; Messrs. Monson, Ward—Milton Grayson.
Directed by Theodore Mann; musical adaptations, arrangements and direction, Howard Roberts; scenery, Marsha Eck; lighting, Jules Fisher; costumes, Domingo A. Rodriguez; production stage manager, Randall Brooks; press, Merle Debuskey, Faith Geer.
The show, in the form of a revival meeting with sermons and hymns, was presented without intermission. Previously produced off Broadway 12/29/63 at the Astor Place Playhouse for 160 performances.

MUSICAL NUMBERS

"So Glad I'm Here"	Company
"Call to Prayer"	Company
"Listen Lord—A Prayer"	Rev. Parham
"Amen Response"	Company
"In His Care"	Glover, Miss Hall, Company
"The Creation"	Rev. Parham
"God Lead Us Along"	Sister Pinkston
Noah Medley	
"Noah Built the Ark"	Rev. Alexander
"Run Sinner Run"	Miss Yarborough, Company
"Didn't It Rain"	Miss Hall, Company
"The Judgment Day"	Rev. Washington
"In That Great Gettin Up Morning"	Rev. Washington, Company
Funeral Suite	
"Soon One Morning"	Miss Hall, Company

"There's a Man" ....Sister Pinkston, Baker, Company
"Go Down Death" ....Rev. Parham
"He'll Understand" ....Sister Pinkston
"Were You There" ....Rev. Alexander
"Calvary" ....Male Voices
"Crucifixion" ....Female Voices
Freedom Suite
  "Reap What You Sow" ....Rev. Alexander, Company
  "I Shall Not Be Moved" ....Company
  "We Are Soldiers" ....Company
  "Woke Up This Morning" ....Company
  "Let My People Go" ....Rev. Washington
  "We Shall Overcome" ....Sister Pinkston, Company
  "Jacob's Ladder" ....Company
Postlude: "God Be With You"

* **Hamlet** (34). Revival of the play by William Shakespeare. Produced by Albert I. Fill, Joseph H. Shoctor, Marcel Akselrod and Norman Twain by special arrangement with Woodfall, Ltd. at the Lunt-Fontanne Theater. Opened May 1, 1969.

Francisco; 1st Sailor ....Michael Elphick	Reynaldo ....Mark Griffith
Barnardo ....John Trenaman	Rosencrantz ....Ben Aris
Horatio ....Gordon Jackson	Guildenstern ....Clive Graham
Marcellus ....John J. Carney	First Player; Gravedigger .....Roger Livesey
Claudius ....Patrick Wymark	Player Queen ....Richard Everett
Gertrude ....Constance Cummings	Player King ....John J. Carney
Polonius ....Mark Dignam	Captain ....Malcolm Terris
Laertes ....Michael Pennington	Priest ....Ian Collier
Hamlet ....Nicol Williamson	Osric ....Peter Gale
Ophelia ....Francesca Annis	

Courtiers, Soldiers, Players: Ian Collier, Michael Elphick, Richard Everett, Mark Griffith, Anjelica Huston, Bill Jarvis, Michael Martin, Malcolm Terris, John Trenaman, Jennifer Tudor, Jason Twelvetrees, Christopher Walsh.

Understudies: Mr. Williamson—Clive Graham; Mr. Wymark—John Trenaman; Miss Cummings—Jennifer Tudor; Mr. Dignam—Ben Aris; Miss Annis—Anjelica Huston.

Directed by Tony Richardson; scenery and costumes, Jocelyn Herbert; scenery supervision, Michael Annals; lighting, John Gleason; production stage manager, Kevin Palmer; stage manager, Howard Panter; press, Frank Goodman, Ruth Cage.

The play was presented in two acts. *Hamlet* was most recently revived on Broadway earlier this season by APA-Phoenix (see its entry in this listing).

* **The Front Page** (25). Revival of the play by Ben Hecht and Charles MacArthur. Produced by Theater 1969 (Richard Barr, Edward Albee and Charles Woodward) at the Ethel Barrymore Theater. Opened May 10, 1969.

Wilson, *American* ....Tom Atkins	Mollie Malloy ....Peggy Cass
Endicott, *Post* ....Robert Milli	Sheriff Hartman ....Charles White
Murphy, *Journal* ....James Flavin	Peggy Grant ....Katharine Houghton
McCue, *City Press* ....Don Porter	Mrs. Grant ....Julia Meade
Schwartz, *News* ....Morison Gampel	The Mayor ....John McGiver
Kruger, *Journal of Commerce* Conrad Janis	Mr. Pincus ....Arnold Stang
Bensinger, *Tribune* ......Harold J. Kennedy	Earl Williams ....Geoff Garland
Woodenshoes Eichorn ......Walter Flanagan	Walter Burns ....Robert Ryan
Diamond Louis ....Val Avery	Carl ....Bruce Blaine
Hildy Johnson,	Tony ....Patrick Desmond
Herald Examiner ....Bert Convy	Policemen ....Will Gregory, Ed Riley
Jenny ....Doro Merande	Boy Scouts ....Rick & Scott Hagan

Understudies: Mr. Ryan—Will Gregory; Mr. Convy—Ed Riley; Mr. Janis—Patrick Desmond.

Directed by Harold J. Kennedy; designed by Will Steven Armstrong; costumes, Sara Brook; production stage manager, Elissa Lane; press. John Springer Associates, Louise Weiner.

Time: 1928. Place: The Press Room of the Criminal Courts Building in Chicago.

The Front Page was first produced August 14, 1928 at the Times Square Theater by Jed Harris, for 276 performances, and was named a Best Play of its season. It was last revived on Broadway September 4, 1946 at the Royale Theater for 79 performances.

Jesse White replaced John McGiver and Ed Riley replaced Don Porter 5/19/69.

The World's a Stage (6). One-man program of hypnotism performed by Sam Vine. Produced by Richard Kagan at the Lyceum Theater. Opened May 12, 1969. (Closed May 17, 1969)

Scenery, David F. Segal; press, Ben Kornzweig, Reginald Denenholz.

Hypnotism designed for theatrical presentation, with audience participation.

* **My Daughter, Your Son** (23). By Phoebe and Henry Ephron. Produced by David Hocker and Chandler Warren at the Booth Theater. Opened May 13, 1969.

Joe Ellis	Gene Lindsey	Jimmy Gordon	Don Scardino
Anne Gordon	Lee Lawson	Sally Ellis	Dody Goodman
Arthur Gordon	Robert Alda	Daddy Ellis	Bill McCutcheon
Maggie Gordon	Vivian Vance		

Standbys: Misses Vance, Goodman—Merle Albertson; Mr. Alda—Donald Buka. Understudy: Mr. Lindsey—William C. Poore.

Directed by Larry Arrick; scenery, Robin Wagner; costumes, Ann Roth; lighting, John Harvey; production associate, Alan J. Zuch; production stage manager, D.W. Koehler; stage manager, William C. Poore; press, Nat Dorfman.

Time: The present. Place: New York, Los Angeles and Columbus. The play was presented in two acts.

Comedy about the families' preparations for a white wedding between a screen writer's daughter and a dentist's son, who have been living together for some time.

* **Fiesta in Madrid** (5). Musical in the Spanish language by Tito Capobianco; adapted from the *La Verbena de La Paloma* by Tomas Breton. Produced by City Center of Music and Drama Inc., Norman Singer general administrator, at New York City Center. Opened May 28, 1969.

Photographer	Chavo Ximinez	Casta	Kay Creed
Don Hilarión	Nico Castel	Tia Antonia	Antonia Rey
Don Sebastian	Alfonso Manosalvas	1st Maid;	
Don Pepe	Nino Garcia	1st Little Sailor	Muriel Greenspon
Seña Rita	Claramae Turner	Grenadiers	Roberto Lorca, Luis Olivares,
Julián	Franco Iglesias		Manolo Rivera
Susana	Isabel Penagos	Policeman	Dan Kingman
Teresa	Teresa	Juggler	Harry De Dio

Singers: Arlene Adler, Marilyn Armstrong, Renee Herman, Suzy Hunter, Diana Kehrig, Donna Owen, Hanna Owen, Frances Pavlides, Sandra Jean Schaeffer, Henrietta Valor, Maria West, Marie Young, Ron Bentley, George Bohachevsky, Don Carlo, Tony Darius, Harris Davis, Joseph Galiano, Nino Garcia, Don Henderson, Douglas Hunnikin, Karl Krause, Raymond Papay, Dick Park. Dancers: Martha Calzado, Deardra Correa, Andrea Del Conte, Liliana Morales, Juana Ortega, Dini Roman.

Conceived and directed by Tito Capobianco; conductor, Odon Alonso; choreography, Teresa; scenery and costumes, Jose Varona; lighting, Hans Sondheimer; associate director, Elena Denda; production associate, Clifford Stevens; associate set designer, David Mitchell; choral director, Martinez Palomo; lyric arrangement, G. Roepke and J. Varona; production stage manager, Dan Butt; press, Seymour Krawitz, Ellen Levene.

Based on a popular Zarzuela about a wealthy apothecary infatuated with two beautiful girls.

ACT I

Overture

"Fiesta in Madrid" ....Chorus, Dancers

"Times Have Changed" ....Hilarión, Sebastian, Pepe

"I Also Have a Heart" ....Julián, Seña Rita

"The Tarantula" ....Susanna, Friends
"Blondes and Brunettes, I Like Them All" ....Hilarión
"On a Girl's Hard Life" ....Maids
   (Music, Chueca and Valverde; lyrics, J. Perez)
Patio Espanol ....Dancers
   (Music, R. Chapi)
"Flamenco Song" ....Casta, Antonia, Susana, Chorus, Dancers
"The Grenadiers" ....Three Grenadiers
"O, What a Lovely Evening" ....Hilarión, Casta, Susana, Antonia
"Forget That Girl, Once and For All" ....Seña Rita, Julián
"Where Are You Going Wearing That Shawl From Manila?" ....Susana, Julián
"The Fight" ....Susana, Casta, Antonia, Julián, Seña Rita, Hilarión, Policemen,
                                                                       Chorus, Dancers

ACT II

Prelude
"The Streets of Madrid" ....Chorus
   (Music, Chueca and Valverde; lyrics, J. Perez)
"Who Cares for Love?" ....Susana
   (Music, J. Serrano; lyrics, V. Sevilla and Carreño)
"The Barquilleros" ....Chorus, Dancers
   (Music, Chueca and Valverde; lyrics, J. Perez)
Danza Española ....Dancers
   (Music, Giminez)
"Three Little Sailors" ....Soloists, Chorus
   (Music, Chueca and Valverde; lyrics, J. Perez)
"Mazurka" ....Chorus, Dancers
"The Best Woman in the World" ....Seña Rita
   (Music, J. Ileo; lyrics, Perrin and Palacios)
"The Milord's Waltz" ....Hilarión
   (Music, Chueca and Valverde; lyrics, J. Perez)
"The Second Fight" ....Seña Rita, Hilarión, Julián, Casta, Susana, Antonia, Policemen,
                                                                       Chorus, Dancers
"You Are the Only One for Me" ....Susana, Julián
   (Music, R. Chapi; lyrics, Shaw and Silva)
"Fiesta in Madrid" (Reprise) ....Soloists, Chorus, Dancers

PLAYS WHICH CLOSED
PRIOR TO BROADWAY OPENING

Plays which were organized in New York for Broadway presentation, but
which closed during their tryout performances or in New York previews, are
listed below.

A Mother's Kisses. Musical with book by Bruce Jay Friedman; music and lyrics by
Richard Adler. Produced by Lester Osterman Productions (Lester Osterman, Richard Horner, Lawrence Kasha) in association with Frederic S. and Barbara Mates
in a pre-Broadway tryout at the Shubert Theater in New Haven. Opened September 23, 1968. (Closed at the Morris A. Mechanic Theater in Baltimore October 19,
1968)

Meg	Beatrice Arthur	Maid	Anna Franklin
Joseph	Bill Callaway	Father	Carl Ballantine
Kathleen	Renee Roy	Ditcher; Bess	Maggie Task

Dr. Hurwitz; Rabbi .... Ned Wertimer
The Cop; Commander .... Alan North
The Druggist; Chris;
Professor .... Del Horstman
The Butcher .... Taylor Reed
Salamandro .... Rudy Bond
Harley; Camp Doctor; Schulz;
Dr. Peretz .... Arthur Anderson
Ruffio .... Steven Ross
Kenzie .... John Johann
Hortz; Buffkins .... Daniel Goldman
Campers ...... Teddy Williams, Joseph Neal

Frenchie .... Caryl Hinchee
Mrs. Rhinelander;
Chambermaid .... Kate Wilkinson
Lifeguard .... Joseph Corby
Hester .... Ruth Jaroslow
Bellhop; Camper .... Patrick Cook
Barbara .... Cyndi Howard
Co-eds ...... Carol Estey, Jacquie Ullendorf,
Lori Cesar
Philly .... Don Wonder
Woman Attendant .... Maggie Worth

Singers: Patrick Cook, Joseph Corby, Larry Devon, Del Horstman, Joseph Neal, Taylor Reed, Don Wonder, Lori Cesar, Sheila Hogue, Luba Mauro, Mary Ann Rydjeski, Maggie Task, Maggie Worth.

Dancers: Ray Chabeau, Gene Gavin, John Johann, Steven Ross, Terry Violino, Teddy Williams, Linda Campagna, Carol Estey, Lois Etelman, Caryl Hinchee, Cyndi Howard, Jacquie Ullendorf.

Directed by Gene Saks; dances and musical numbers staged by Onna White; musical direction and arrangements, Colin Romoff; scenery, William and Jean Eckart; costumes, Alvin Colt; lighting, Tharon Musser; associate producer, Orin Lehman; orchestrations, Jack Andrews; dance music, Roger Adams; assistant choreographer, Pat Cummings; production stage manager, Phil Friedman; stage manager, Wayne Carson; press, Frank Goodman, Alan Eichler, Abby Hirsch.

Time: About 20 years ago. Place: The city, the camp, across the lake, back to the city, a plain's state.

Satire on momism adapted by Bruce Jay Friedman from his own novel.

ACT I

"There Goes My Life" .... Meg
"Look at Those Faces" .... Parents, Neighbors, Young People
"With a Little Help from Your Mother" .... Meg
"Left by the Wayside" .... Joseph, Campers
"When You Gonna Learn" .... Meg
"We've Got Meg" .... Meg, Shopkeepers, Neighbors
"Where Did the Summer Go" .... Joseph
"People of Passionate Nature" .... Commander, Mrs. Rhinelander
"They Won't Regret It" .... Joseph, Neighborhood People

ACT II

"I Told Them We Were Lovers" .... Meg
"I Have a Terrible Secret" .... Joseph, Barbara, Co-eds
"A Course in Your Mother" .... Meg
"We've Got Meg" (Reprise) .... Meg, Hotel Friends

Love Match. Musical with book by Christian Hamilton; music by David Shire; lyrics by Richard Maltby Jr. Produced by Center Theater Group by arrangement with Elliot Martin and Ivor David Balding Associates in a pre-Broadway tryout at the Palace West Theater in Phoenix. Opened November 3, 1968. (Closed at the Ahmanson Theater in Los Angeles January 4, 1969)

Dance Valentine
Victoria .... Anne Marie Longtin
Dance Valentine Albert .... Brynar Mehl
Dance Attendant; 2d Lady;
2d Nursemaid .... Marilyn D'Honau
Dance Attendant;
3d Nursemaid .... Betty Lynn

Victoria .... Patricia Routledge
Lord Melbourne .... Michael Allinson
Victoria (as a child) .... Lee Wilson
Duchess of Kent .... Patricia Ripley
Ernest .... Hal Linden
Albert .... Laurence Guittard
1st Footman; Major Domo ..... Keith Perry

2d Footman; Doctor ....Michael Amber	Boy Jones ....Bill Hinnant
Lord Conyngham ....Martin Ambrose	Sailor ....Don Percassi
Archbishop of	Spanish Count;
Canterbury ....Ronald Drake	3d Footman ....Phillip Filiato
Servant Girl ....Anne Wallace	1st Lady; 1st Nursemaid ......Helen Wood
Messenger; Drummer .........J.J. Jepson	4th Footman ....Rodney Griffin
Inspector Plank ....Rex Robbins	Thomas Moore ....Carl Nicholas

Ladies in Waiting: Barbara Gregory, Jacqueline Britt. Rosenau Footmen: Fred Albee, Rodney Griffin, Don Percassi, Phillip Filiato.

Singers: Jacqueline Britt, Karen Ford, Barbara Gregory, Miriam Lawrence, Joyce O'Neil, Julie Sargant, Michael Amber, Martin Ambrose, Peter Costanza, Carl Nicholas, Keith Perry, Ken Richards.

Dancers: Marilyn D'Honau, Janet Fraser, Ann Marie Longtin, Betty Lynn, Kuniko Narai, Anne Wallace, Lee Wilson, Helen Wood, Fred Albee, Kim Bray, Phillip Filiato, Rodney Griffin, J.J. Jepson, George Lee, Brynar Mehl, Don Percassi.

Directed and choreographed by Danny Daniels; entire production supervised by Noel Willman; musical conductor, Theodore Seidenberg; scenery, Robin Wagner; costumes, Ray Diffen; lighting, Jules Fisher; orchestrations, Hershy Kay; dance music and vocal arrangements, David Shire; production stage manager, William Ross; stage manager, Michael Sinclair; press, Nat Dorfman.

Time: Sometime after the death of Prince Albert, Queen Victoria's consort. Place: England. The courtship, marriage and public and private lives of Queen Victoria and her husband Prince Albert.

ACT I

"These Two Hands" ....Victoria, Melbourne
"Coronation Parade" ....1st Nursemaid, Ensemble
"Play It Again ....Victoria, Melbourne, Duchess, Archbishop, Ensemble
"The Packing Song" ....Albert, Footmen
"As Plain as Daylight" ....Victoria
"I Hear Bells" ....Jones, Plank
"I May Want To Remember Today" ....Victoria
"A Meaningful Life" ....Albert
"The Grand Diversion" ....Victoria, Albert, Melbourne, Duchess, Ernest, Ensemble
"I Won't Sleep a Wink Tonight" ....Duchess, Ernest, Plank, Two Ladies
"Waiting for Morning Alone" ....Victoria
"Beautiful" ....Victoria, Albert, Ensemble

ACT II

"I Don't Believe It" ....Ernest, Melbourne, Archbishop, Jones, Plank
"A World of Love" ....Thomas Moore
"Mine" ....Victoria
"A Woman Looking for Love" ....Ernest
"The Little Part of Me That's Mine" ....Albert
"Never Again" ....Victoria, Entire Company
"The World and You" ....Albert, Ensemble
"Play It Again" (Reprise) ....Victoria, Entire Company

A Way of Life. By Murray Schisgal. Produced by Edgar Lansbury and Marc Merson in preview performances at the ANTA Theater. Opened January 18, 1969. (Closed February 1, 1969)

Lilly Seltzer ....Melinda Dillon	Janice Krieger ....Estelle Parsons
Alex Krieger ....Bob Dishy	Max Krieger ....Lou Jacobi
Mr. Tarkis ....John McGiver	

Directed by Harold Stone; scenery, William and Jean Eckart; lighting, Tharon Musser; costumes, Theoni V. Aldredge; produced in association with Josephine Forrestal Productions, Inc.; production stage manager, Gigi Cascio; stage manager, William Callan; press, Max Eisen, Cheryl Sue Dolby.

Act I, Scene 1: Reception and sportswear manager's offices at Dunfee's Department Store, late afternoon. Scene 2: The Krieger apartment, immediately following. Scene 3: Lilly Seltzer's apartment, that night. Act II, Scene 1: The Krieger apartment, next morning. Scene 2: The Dunfee offices, one year later. Scene 3: A park, some time later.

About two brothers, one of whom is dominated by a nagging wife and an overbearing boss.

Jeremy Troy. By Jack Sharkey. Produced by Daniel Hollywood and Wally Peterson in association with Harvey Granat in a pre-Broadway tryout at the Forrest Theater in Philadelphia. Opened February 24, 1969. (Closed at the National Theater in Washington, D.C. March 22, 1969)

Jeremy Troy .... Will Hutchins	Tina Winslow .... Ann Willis
Kathryn Troy .... Beverly Ballard	Mr. Ivorsen .... Murvyn Vye
Charlie Bickle .... Charles Braswell	

Directed by Ronny Graham; scenery, costumes and lighting by Robert T. Williams; production stage manager, Wally Peterson; stage manager, Wallace Englehardt; press, Mary Bryant, David Rothenberg, Ellen Levene.

Time: The present, mid-winter. Place: The Troy home in West Rutherford, N.J. Act I: A weekday morning. Act II, Scene 1: The same evening. Scene 2: The following morning.

Comedy about a young lawyer who never really went to law school and is faking it with a New York firm.

PLAYS PRODUCED OFF BROADWAY

Figures in parentheses following a play's title indicate number of performances. Plays marked with an asterisk (*) were still running on June 1, 1969, and their number of performances is figured from opening night through May 31, 1969, not including extra non-profit performances. In a listing of a show's numbers—dances, sketches, musical scenes, etc.—the titles of songs are identified by their appearance in quotation marks ("). Entries of off-Broadway productions which ran less than 16 performances are somewhat abbreviated.

HOLDOVERS FROM PREVIOUS SEASONS

Plays which were running on June 1, 1968 are listed below. More detailed information about them appears in previous *Best Plays* volumes of appropriate years. Important cast changes are recorded in a section of this volume.

* **The Fantasticks** (3,800; longest continuous run of record in the American theater). Musical suggested by the play *Les Romantiques* by Edmond Rostand; book and lyrics by Tom Jones; music by Harvey Schmidt. Opened May 3, 1960.

* **You're a Good Man Charlie Brown** (895). Musical based on the comic strip "Peanuts" by Charles M. Schulz; book, music and lyrics by Clark Gesner. Opened March 7, 1967.

* **Scuba Duba** (674). By Bruce Jay Friedman. Opened October 10, 1967.

* **Curley McDimple** (647). Musical with book by Mary Boylan and Robert Dahdah; music and lyrics by Robert Dahdah. Opened November 22, 1967.

* **Your Own Thing** (580). Musical with book by Donald Driver; suggested by William Shakespeare's *Twelfth Night;* music and lyrics by Hal Hester and Danny Apolinar. Opened January 13, 1968.

The Indian Wants the Bronx and **It's Called the Sugar Plum** (204). Program of two one-act plays by Israel Horovitz. Opened January 17, 1968. (Closed July 14, 1968 following a recess 6/23-7/11 for performances at the Spoleto Festival in Italy)

* **Jacques Brel Is Alive and Well and Living in Paris** (562). Cabaret revue with music by Jacques Brel; production conception, English lyrics, additional material by Eric Blau and Mort Shuman; based on lyrics and commentary by Jacques Brel. Opened January 22, 1968.

The Repertory Theater of Lincoln Center. Schedule of two programs in the Forum Theater (see entry in 1967-68 *Best Plays* volume) concluded with **Summertree** (127). By Ron Cowen. Opened March 3, 1968. (Closed June 22, 1968)

The American Place Theater. Schedule of four programs (see entry in 1967-68 *Best Plays* volume) included **The Electronic Nigger and Others** (90). Program of three one-act plays by Ed Bullins. Opened March 6, 1968. Moved to the Martinique Theater 3/28/68 and continued its run under the title *Three Plays by Ed Bullins.* (Closed June 2, 1968)

Tom Paine (295). By Paul Foster. Opened March 25, 1968. (Closed December 8, 1968)

* **The Boys in the Band** (471). By Mart Crowley. Opened April 15, 1968.

Muzeeka by John Guare and **Red Cross** by Sam Shepard (65). Program of two one-act plays. Opened April 28, 1968. (Closed June 23, 1968)

New York Shakespeare Festival Public Theater. Indoor schedule of four plays (see entry in 1967-68 *Best Plays* volume) concluded with **The Memorandum** (49). By Vaclav Havel; translated by Vera Blackwell. Opened May 5, 1968. (Closed June 16, 1968)

Collision Course (80). Program of eleven one-act plays by Lanford Wilson, Leonard Melfi, Jack Larson, Rosalyn Drexler, Harvey Perr, Jean-Claude van Itallie and Sharon Thie, Terrence McNally, Robert Patrick, Martin Duberman, Jules Feiffer and Israel Horovitz. Opened May 8, 1968. (Closed July 14, 1968)

The Believers (310). Musical with book by Josephine Jackson and Joseph A. Walker; music by Benjamin Carter, Dorothy Dinroe, Josephine Jackson, Anje Ray and Ron Steward; lyrics by Benjamin Carter, Dorothy Dinroe, Josephine Jackson, Anje Ray, Ron Steward and Joseph A. Walker. Opened May 9, 1968. (Closed February 2, 1969)

PLAYS PRODUCED JUNE 1, 1968—MAY 31, 1969

The Negro Ensemble Company. 1967-68 schedule of four plays (see entry in 1967-68 *Best Plays* volume; also, for 1968-69 Negro Ensemble Company schedule, see entry elsewhere in this listing of "Plays Produced Off Broadway") concluded with **Daddy Goodness** (64). By Richard Wright; translated and adapted from a play by Louis Sapin. Opened June 4, 1968; see note. **Song of the Lusitanian Bogey** (24). By Peter Weiss; translated from the German by Lee Baxandall. Return engagement of the 1967-68 Negro Ensemble Company production in repertory with *Daddy Goodness*. Opened July 23, 1968. Produced by The Negro Ensemble Company, Douglas Turner Ward artistic director, Robert Hooks executive director, Gerald S. Krone administration director, at the St. Marks Playhouse. (Repertory closed September 1, 1968)

DADDY GOODNESS

Sam	Bill Jay	Daddy Goodness	Moses Gunn
Lena	Denise Nicholas	Postman	Richard Mason
Thomas	Douglas Turner	Milkman	Buddy Butler
Jeremiah	Arthur French	Luke	Norman Bush
A Preacher	Allie Woods	Chauffeur	Richard Mason
Annie	Clarice Taylor	A young man	Theodore Wilson
Fanny	Rosalind Cash	An old woman	Clarice Taylor
Sarah	Judyann Jonsson	The mayor	Arthur French
David	David Downing		

Directed by Douglas Turner Ward; scenery, Edward Burbridge; costumes, Gertha Brock; lighting, Michael A. Schultz; press, Howard Atlee.

Time: A hot sultry August in the recent past. Place: An unidentified American city. Act I, Scene 1: A graveyard. Scene 2: Meeting hall of the New Faith a week and a half later. Act II: Three weeks later. Act III, Scene 1: Five days later. Scene 2: Graveyard—that night.

A satire on religious fakery and its exploitation.

Note: *Daddy Goodness* suspended performances 7/7/68 and reopened 7/23/68 in repertory with the return engagement of *Song of the Lusitanian Bogey*.

Now (22). Musical revue conceived by Marvin Gordon; lyrics and sketches by George Haimsohn; music by John Aman; additional material by Steve Holden, John Kuntz, Sue Lawless and Mart Panzer. Produced by the PF Company and John H. Beaumont at the Cherry Lane Theater. Opened June 5, 1968. (Closed June 23, 1968)

John Aman	Rosalind Harris
Frank André	Sue Lawless
Lauree Berger	Ted Pugh

Directed by Marvin Gordon; musical direction and arrangements, Barry Manilow; scenery, Jack Robinson; women's costumes, Betsey Johnson and Michael Mott for Paraphernalia; special men's costumes, The Different Drummer; lighting, Skip Palmer; visuals designed by Staging Techniques; production stage manager, Larry Whiteley; press, Samuel J. Friedman, Jane Friedman.

Time: Now. Place: Here. The show was presented without intermission.

Topical revue which opened after the shooting and before the death of Sen. Robert F. Kennedy. A song number "Bobby Baby" was eliminated from the production; a skit satirizing Andy Warhol, who had been recently injured in an assassination attempt, was not.

"Come Along with Us"—Entire Company; You Get Me High—Aman, André, Misses Lawless, Berger, Harris; "Space Idiocy"—André, Pugh; "Come Along with Us" (Reprise)—Entire Company; Room Service (by Gerald Smith)—Aman, Miss Lawless; "Save a Sinner Tonight"—Pugh, Congregation; Randy Girls—Pugh (Randy, Pope, Dorian), André (Izzy), Miss Berger (Mary, Teenie Bopper, Zena), Aman (Daniel), Miss Harris (Mom), Miss Lawless (Cruella, Ida); Lonely Are They—André; Sex Can Be Funny—Miss Lawless (TV Announcer), Miss Berger (Judy), Miss Harris (Bozo), Pugh (Peter), André (Hermie), Aman (Pianist); "Come Along with Us" (Reprise)—Entire Company; Drill Team—Pugh, Miss Lawless; "Acre of Grass"—Farmers, Farmerettes; "Sidney"—Miss Harris; "Peonies"—Pugh, Miss Lawless; "Flower Children" (lyric by John Aman)—Miss Lawless, Friends; Cinderella (by John Kuntz)—Entire Company; "The Third Lady" (music by Barry Manilow, lyric by Marty Panzer)—Pugh; Hello Hubert—Aman, Miss Berger; U.S. Patent Office (by Sue Lawless)—André, Pugh; "Leather Love" (lyric by John Aman)—Miss Lawless; "Minimal"—Entire Company; Acrobats—Pugh, Miss Lawless; Speed Kills—André; "Climb Up Here With Daddy on the Boom Boom" (lyric by Steve Holden)—Aman, André, Miss Harris; "Beautiful People"—Entire Company; "California Style" (lyric by John Aman)—Miss Berger; Dark Horse—Entire Company; "Now" (lyric by John Aman)—Entire Company.

Frere Jacques (13). Musical by Gerard Singer. Produced by Singer Productions, Inc. at Theater 802. Opened June 6, 1968. (Closed June 16, 1968)

Directed by Richard Balin; orchestrations and musical direction, Harry Goodman; stage manager, Richard Gibson; press, Howard Atlee, Bill Cherry. With Sy Cohen, Carolyn Dahl, Joe Disraeli, Nina Dova, Douglas Fisher, Pamela Hall, Michael Makman, David Tabor.

Young man returns to his relatives in Brooklyn after being raised by Tibetan monks.

New York Shakespeare Festival. Summer season of three revivals of plays by William Shakespeare. **Henry IV, Part 1** (23½; see note). Opened June 11, 1968. (Closed August 3, 1968) **Henry IV, Part 2** (18½; see note). Opened June 18, 1968. (Closed August 3, 1968) **Romeo and Juliet** (21). Opened August 7, 1968. (Closed August 31, 1968). Produced by New York Shakespeare Festival, Joseph Papp producer, Gerald Freedman artistic director, Bernard Gersten associate producer, in cooperation with the City of New York, Hon. John V. Lindsay Mayor, Hon. August Heckscher Commissioner of Parks, at the Delacorte Theater in Central Park.

PERFORMER	"HENRY IV, PART 1"	"HENRY IV, PART 2"
Rae Allen		Doll Tearsheet
Reathel Bean		Surrey
Peter Burnell	Prince John	Prince John
Mitchell Carrey	Traveller; Carrier	Mouldy
Herb Davis	Peto	Scroop; Peto
John Davis		Servant
Stephen Elliott	Glendower	Chief Justice
Victor Eschbach		Porter
Penny Fuller	Lady Percy	Lady Percy
Peter Galman	Chamberlain; Traveller; Servant	Travers; Bullcalf
Douglas Hayle	Traveller; Carrier	Beadle; Feeble
George Hearn	Poins	Poins
Stacy Keach	Falstaff	Falstaff
Robert Keesler	Traveller; Vintner	Coleville
Sharon Laughlin	Lady Mortimer	Lady Northumberland
Christopher Lee		Falstaff's Page
Stephen McHattie	Mortimer	Lord Bardoll
Joseph Mydell	Ostler	Groom
David O'Brien	Westmoreland; Northumberland	Westmoreland; Northumberland
Gary A. Poe		Snare; Wart; Groom
J.A. Preston	Blunt	Mowbray
Barry Primus	Hotspur	Pistol
Charlotte Rae	Hostess Quickly	Hostess Quickly
James Ray	Henry IV	Henry IV
Robert Ronan		Shallow
Paul Rudd		Messenger; Groom
Edward Rudney	Gadshill; Douglas	Hastings
Joseph Schroer	Sheriff	Warwick
Joseph R. Sicari	Francis	Rumor; Francis; Davy; Fang
Robert Stattel	Worcester	Silence
Joseph Stern	Bardolph	Bardolph
Jean Pierre Stewart		Gower; Blunt
Stephen Temperley		Clarence
Donald Warfield	Servant; Messenger	Shadow; Gloucester
Sam Waterston	Prince Hal	Prince Hal
Russell Garland Wiggins		Harcourt

Ensemble: Daniel Greenblat, Michael Hassett, Stephen Tice, Jenny Maybruck, Angela Pietropinto. Bagpiper: James Maxwell.

Both plays directed by Gerald Freedman; scenery, Ming Cho Lee; lighting, Martin Aronstein; costumes, Theoni V. Aldredge; songs and music, John Morris; *Henry IV, Part I* battle staged by Joyce Trisler; production stage manager, D.W. Koehler; stage managers, Michael Chambers, Edmond Faccini; press, Merle Debuskey.

ROMEO AND JULIET

Prologue; Old Man; Apothecary	Fred Warriner	Romeo	Martin Sheen
Sampson; Balthasar	Antonio Fargas	Paris	Robert Stattel
Gregory; Chief Watchman	William Devane	Peter	William Duell
Abram; Officer; Friar John	Robert Keesler	Nurse	Charlotte Rae
Benviolio	Michael Heit	Juliet	Susan McArthur
Tybalt	Tom Aldredge	Mercutio	Joseph Bova
Capulet	Moses Gunn	Anthony; Watchman	Russell Garland Wiggins
Lady Capulet	Eleanor Stewart	Potpan; Watchman; Rebeck	Douglas Hayle
Montague	Albert Quinton	Friar Laurence	John Call
Lady Montague	Helen Dalby	Catling; Page	Gary A. Poe
Prince Escalus	William Kiehl	Soundpost	Edward Harris

Dance Ensemble: Mary Barnett, Matthew Cameron, Sidney C. Collier, Maria Di Dia, Richard Gordon, Phillip Jonson, Sharron Miller, Monica Moseley, Ernest Royster, Daniel A. Sloan, Clay Taliaferro. Musicians: Fred Hand, Arthur Krilov, Theodore Wilson.

Directed by Joseph Papp; scenery, Ming Cho Lee; lighting, Martin Aronstein; costumes, Theoni V. Aldredge; music, John Morris; choreography, Joyce Trisler; duels, James J. Sloyan; production stage manager, D.W. Koehler; stage manager, Edmond Faccini.

Note: The two parts of *Henry IV* were played in repertory, except that on the evening and morning of 7/13-7/14 both plays were performed between 7 p.m. and 3 a.m., divided by an intermission of about one hour. The odd ½ performances represent evenings on which the shows were rained out during the performance (including the opening 6/11 performance).

A Moon for the Misbegotten (199). Revival of the play by Eugene O'Neill. Produced by Circle in the Square, Inc., Theodore Mann artistic director, Paul Libin managing director, Gillian Walker associate director, at Circle in the Square. Opened June 12, 1968. (Closed December 1, 1968.)

Josie Hogan	Salome Jens	James Tyrone, Jr.	Mitchell Ryan
Mike Hogan	Jack Kehoe	T. Stedman Harder	Garry Mitchell
Phil Hogan	W.B. Brydon		

Directed by Theodore Mann; scenery, Marsha Eck; lighting, Jules Fisher; costumes, Domingo A. Rodriguez; stage manager, George Blanchard; press, Merle Debuskey, Violet Welles, Faith Geer.

Time: Early September 1923. Place: A farmhouse.

A Moon for the Misbegotten was first produced in New York at the Bijou Theater May 2, 1957 for 68 performances and was named a Best Play of its season.

Jack Davidson replaced Gary Mitchell 8/26/68.

Walk Down Mah Street! (135). Musical revue with script and lyrics by Patricia Taylor Curtis; music by Norman Curtis; special material by James Taylor, Gabriel Levenson and the members of The Next Stage Theater Company. Produced by Audience Associates Inc. at the Players Theater. Opened June 12, 1968. (Closed October 6, 1968)

The Next Stage Theater Company:

Denise Delapenha	Kenneth Frett
Freddy Diaz	Vaughn Martinez
Lorraine Feather	Gene Rounds

Directed by Patricia Taylor Curtis; scenery, Jack Logan; costumes, Bob Rogers; lighting, Bruce D. Bassman; musical arrangements, Norman Curtis; musicians, Norman Curtis, James Taylor, Johnny Castro; stage manager, Rick Rotante; press, Howard Atlee, Margie Clay, Bill Cherry.

Topical revue with most skits and songs directed to racial subjects.

ACT I: "We're Today"—Entire Company; Taxi!—Rounds; "Walk Down My Street"—Frett; Is She or Ain't She—Misses Delapenha, Feather; Zap!—Martinez, Miss Delapenha; "If You Want to Get Ahead"—Diaz, Frett, Rounds, Misses Delapenha, Feather; Don't Be a Litterbug—Martinez; "Just One More Time"—Miss Delapenha, Diaz; Walk Down Mah Street Courageous Award of the Year—Rounds; Where and with What?—Diaz, Martinez, Miss Delapenha, Company; "I'm Just a Statistic"—Miss Delapenha, Diaz, Rounds; Minus One—Frett, Miss Feather; Unknown Factor—Misses Feather, Delapenha; "Someday, if We Grow Up"—Martinez; Candid Camera—Rounds, Frett; "Basic Black"—Entire Company.

ACT II: "What Shadows We Are"—Diaz; "Want To Get Retarded?"—Misses Delapenha, Feather; What's for Dinner?—Martinez, Miss Delapenha; "Teeny Bopper"—Martinez, Rounds; Plus One—Miss Feather, Frett; "Flower Child"—Frett, Miss Feather; "For Four Hundred Years"—Rounds; Walk Down Mah Street Courageous Award of the Year—Frett; "Don't Have To Take It Any More"—Diaz, Rounds, Miss Delapenha, Company; Plus Two—Miss Feather, Frett; "Lonely Girl"—Martinez; The American Way—Miss Delapenha; "Clean Up Your Own Backyard"—Diaz, Rounds, Martinez; Walk Down Mah Street Courageous Award of the Year—Rounds. "Walk, Lordy, Walk"—Frett, Company; "Walk Down My Street" (Reprise)—Entire Company.

Futz! (233). By Rochelle Owens. Produced by Harlan P. Kleiman in association with David Cryer, Albert Poland and Theodore Hoffman at the Theater de Lys. Opened June 13, 1968. (Closed December 31, 1968.)

Narrator	Sally Kirkland	Sheriff Tom Sluck	Peter Craig
Cyrus Futz	John Bakos	Father Satz	Jerry Cunliffe
Majorie Satz	Beth Porter	Mother Satz	Victor Lipari
Oscar Loop	Seth Allen	Mrs. Loop	Marilyn Roberts
Bill Marjoram	Fred Forrest	Sugford	Fred Forrest
Ann Fox	Mari-Claire Charba	Buford	Peter Craig

Music and direction by Tom O'Horgan; scenery, Nicholas Russiyan; costumes, Sandra Jones; lighting, John Patrick Dodd; sculpture, Saito; presented by special arrangement with Lucille Lortel Productions, Inc.; production stage manager, Nicholas Russiyan; press, Robert Ganshaw, John Prescott, Michael F. Goldstein, Inc.

Time: The present. Place: Somewhere in rural America. The play is performed without intermission.

A farmer's unnatural love for his pig shocks and disrupts his community. Previously produced at Cafe La Mama, at the Edinburgh Festival and in London.

In Circles by Gertrude Stein; music by Al Carmines. **Songs by Carmines** (56). Return engagement of the Judson Poets Theater Production, plus a one-man performance by Al Carmines. Produced by Dina and Alexander E. Racolin and Samuel J. Friedman at the Gramercy Arts Theater. Opened June 25, 1968. (Closed August 11, 1968)

IN CIRCLES

Cousin	Theo Barnes	Sylvia	Arlene Rothlein
Mildred	Jacque Lynn Colton	Dole	Al Carmines
Mable	Lee Crespi	Ollie	Andrew Roman
Jessie	Lee Guilliatt	The Citizen	Arthur Williams
George	George McGrath	Lucy Armitage	Julie Kurnitz

Directed by Lawrence Kornfeld; scenery, Roland Turner and Johnnie Jones; lighting, Barry Arnold; stage manager, Steven Jarrett; press, Jane Friedman.

In Circles was originally produced off Broadway at the Cherry Lane Theater November 5, 1967 for 222 performances. *Songs by Carmines* was a one-man program of some of his own songs sung and played by Al Carmines.

Atelje 212. Repertory of four plays in the Serbo-Croatian language. **The Progress of Bora, the Tailor** (6). By Alexander Popovic. Opened June 26, 1968. **Ubu Roi** (6). By Alfred Jarry; adapted by Ljubomir Draskic; translated by Ivanka Markovic and Svetlana Termacic. Opened June 28, 1968. **Who's Afraid of Virginia Woolf?** (7). By Edward Albee; translated by Ileana Cosic. Opened July 3, 1968. **Victor, or The Children Take Over** (5). By Roger Vitrac. Opened July 7, 1968. Produced by Lincoln Center Festival '68 in the Atelje 212 production at the Forum Theater. (Repertory closed July 14, 1968)

PERFORMER	"THE PROGRESS OF BORA"	"UBU ROI"	"VICTOR"	"WHO'S AFRAID OF VIRGINIA WOOLF?"
Milutin Butkovic	Piklja	Bordure; Bonaparte	Charles	
Dejan Cavic		Leczinski; Judge; Capt.; Financier		
Vera Cukic				(Esther)
Maja Cuckovic		Mama Ubu		
Dragutin Dobricanin	Spira			
Alexander Gruden	Milosavljevic			

PERFORMER	"THE PROGRESS OF BORA"	"UBU ROI"	"VICTOR"	"WHO'S AFRAID OF VIRGINIA WOOLF?"
Olga Ivanovic	Lina			
Liljana Krstic				Martha
Nikola Milic		Wenceslas; Alexis		
Danica Mokranjac			Therese	
Tasco Nacic		Cotice; Lascy	Doctor	
Bozidar Pavicevic	Milisav	Ladislas; Grand Duke; Sobiesky; Financier; Judge		
Slobodan Perovic				George
Branko Plesa	Bora			
Vladimir Popovic			Victor	Nick
Zoran Radmilovic		Papa Ubu		
Zoran Ratkovic	Miloje	Giron; Bear		
Jelisaveta Sablic	Goca	Bourgelas	(Esther)	
Ruzica Sokic	Rozika		Emilie	Honey
Neda Spasojevic		Rosemonde	Lili	
Danilo Stojkovic	Selimir	Pile; Rensky	Gen. Lonsegur	
Bora Todorovic	Vitomir	Boleslas; Vitebsk; Judge; Financier	Antoine	
Mira Vacic			Ida	

(Parentheses indicate role in which the actors alternated)

THE PROGRESS OF BORA, THE TAILOR directed by Branko Plesa; scenery, Radenko Misevic; costumes, Biljana Dragovic; music, Vojislav Kostic; choreography, Irena Kis; assistant, Alexander Gruden; assistant designer, Slobodan Pajic; press, Sol Jacobson, Lewis Harmon.

Satire about the decline of a candle-making co-operative under the direction of an unscrupulous boss. The play is divided into four scenes.

UBU ROI directed by Ljubomir Draskic; songs adapted by Ivan Lalic; scenery and costumes, Vladislav Lalicki; music, Vojislav Kostic.

Ubu Roi was first performed in Paris in 1896, and the text has been freely adapted in this version, divided into two acts and 22 scenes.

WHO'S AFRAID OF VIRGINIA WOOLF? directed by Mira Trailovic; scenery, Petar Pasic; costumes, Mara Finci.

Who's Afraid of Virginia Woolf? was first presented 10/13/62 at the Billy Rose Theater for 664 performances. It was named a Best Play of its season.

VICTOR, OR THE CHILDREN TAKE OVER directed by Mica Popovic; artistic adviser, Srboljub Stankovic; scenery, Mica Popovic; costumes, Vera Bozickovic-Popovic; scenic movement, Tamara Polonska.

Victor, or The Children Take Over is the drama of a 9-year-old boy's last day of life. The play is divided into two acts.

The Firebugs (8). Revival of the play by Max Frisch; translated by Mordecai Gorelik. Produced by Artemis Productions at the Martinique Theater. Opened July 1, 1968. (Closed July 7, 1968)

Directed by Jacques Cartier; scenery, John Conklin; lighting, Peter Hunt; costumes Kate Vachon; stage manager, Stephen Coleman; press, Howard Atlee, Margie Clay and Bill Cherry. With Barbara Cason, Glenn Kezer, Swoosie Kurtz, Madison P. Mason, James F. Murtaugh, David Rohan Sage, Frank Savino, Noel Schwartz, Richard Ward and Billy Dee Williams.

The Firebugs was first produced off Broadway 2/11/63 at the Maidman Theater for 8 performances.

The Fourth Wall (141). Program of improvisation. Produced by Jay H. Fuchs in association with Barry Diamond at Theater East. Opened September 4, 1968. (Closed January 4, 1969)

Kent Broadhurst
James Manis
Bette-Jane Raphael

Jeremy Stevens
Marcia Wallace

Directed by Jeremy Stevens; production designed by Kent Broadhurst; press, Seymour Krawitz. Program of sketches, some set and some improvised at each performance, presented without intermission.

The Happy Hypocrite (17). Musical with book and lyrics by Edward Eager; music by James Bredt; additional material by Tony Tanner; based on the short story by Max Beerbohm. Produced by Arete Spero at the Bouwerie Lane Theater. Opened September 5, 1968. (Closed September 19, 1968)

The People of London:
Cheapside ....Howard Girven
Shoreditch ....Keith Cota
Mistress Bow ....Rose Roffman
Lord George Hell ....John Aman

Sir Follard Follard ....Kevin O'Leary
La Gambogi ....Rosemarie Heyer
The Merry Archer ....George Feeney
Jenny Mere ....Joan Kroschell
Aeneas Aeneas ....Edward J. McPhillips

Directed by Tony Tanner; musical direction and orchestrations, Richard J. Leonard; scenery, Michael Horen; costumes, Deidre Cartier; lighting, Jules Fisher; assistant to the director, Vernon Wendorf; production stage manager, Wil Richter; press, Jane Friedman.

Time: The Regency. Place: England. Scene 1: A London street. Scene 2: Boodle's gambling den. Scene 3: Garble's Theater. Scene 4: A sylvan dell. Scene 5: The shop of Aeneas Aeneas. Scene 6: Boodle's gambling den. Scene 7: The dell. Scene 8: A London street. Scene 9: A stagecoach. Scene 10: The dell. The action is presented without intermission.

Tale of a rake reformed by true love, presented as a satire on operetta plots.

MUSICAL NUMBERS

"Street Song and Opening" ....Cheapside, Shoreditch, Mistress Bow
"Deep in Me" ....La Gambogi, Lord George
"The Amorous Arrow" ....Mistress Bow
"Echo Song" ....Jenny
"Miss Mere" ....Lord George
"Mornings at Seven" ....Lord George
"The Song of the Mask" ....Aeneas and Lord George
"Deep in Me" (Reprise) ....La Gambogi
"Almost Too Good to Be True" ....Lord George, Jenny
"Wedding Pantomime" ....Company
"Don't Take Sides" ....Cheapside, Shoreditch, Mistress Bow
"Almost Too Good to Be True" (Reprise) ....Lord George, Jenny, Cheapside, Shoreditch, Mistress Bow
"Hell Hath No Fury" ....La Gambogi, Cheapside, Shoreditch, Mistress Bow
"I Must Smile" ....Lord George
"Once, Only Once" ....La Gambogi, Ensemble
"The Face of Love" ....Jenny, Lord George, Ensemble

An Ordinary Man (24). By Mel Arrighi. Produced by Margaret Hayes at the Cherry Lane Theater. Opened September 9, 1968. (Closed September 29, 1968.)

The Judge ....Robert Ackerman
Andy Neff ....Michael Baseleon
Monica Lambert ......Caroline McWilliams
Harris Fisher ....John Carpenter
Rod Korman ....Jerome Dempsey
Helen Neff ....Kathleen Murray

Dick Preble ....Frank Bara
Mr. Swanson ....Tom Keena
Austin Coker ....Lloyd Hollar
Connie Frager ....Beatrice Ballance
Steve Frager ....Robert Ackerman
Shirley Korman ....Sunja Svensen

Directed by Harold Stone; scenery and lighting, C. Murawksi; associate producer, Robert D. Feldstein; special sound effects, Reichert & Ross; stage manager, Stephen Jarrett; press, David Lipsky.

Parallel between American treatment of the Negroes and Nazi treatment of the Jews, as a white man stands trial for mass murder of blacks. The play is divided into two acts.

Month of Sundays (8). Musical with book by Romeo Muller; music by Maury Laws; lyrics by Jules Bass; based on the play *The Great Git-Away* by Romeo Muller. Produced by Arthur Rankin Jr. and Jules Bass at the Theater de Lys. Opened September 16, 1968. (Closed September 22, 1968)

Directed by Stone Widney; scenery, Robert T. Williams; costumes, Sara Brook; lighting, Joan Larkey; musical direction and orchestrations, Irv Dweir; press, Seymour Krawitz. With Pamela Hall, Patti Karr, Joe Morton, John Bennett Perry, Dan Resin, Gil Robbins, Martha Schlamme, Allen Swift, Amanda Trees.

Survivors of a Flood-to-be are towed to Paradise on a floating house by a whale. Previously produced at the Tyrone Guthrie Theater in Minneapolis.

The Empire Builders (6). By Boris Vian; translated from the French by Simon Watson Taylor. Produced by Michael Twain and Vera Cochran in association with Ruth Kalkstein at the Astor Place Theater. Opened October 1, 1968. (Closed October 5, 1968)

Directed by Larry Arrick; scenery, costumes and lighting, Lester Polakov; production stage manager, Rosemarie Ticholas; press, Ben Kornzweig, Reginald Denenholz. With Meg Foster, Connie Keyse, Matthew Tobin, Michael Twain and Erica Yohn.

A dramatic examination of the relation between life and death, in the story of a family moving into smaller and smaller rooms. A foreign play previously produced in Paris and London.

Another City, Another Land (7). By Guy Hoffman. Produced by Mildred Torffield at the Gramercy Arts Theater. Opened October 8, 1968. (Closed October 13, 1968)

Directed by Guy Hoffman; scenery and lighting, Jack Blackman; costumes, John E. Hirsch; production stage manager, Bryan Sheedy; press, Howard Atlee, David Roggensack, Martin Cohen. With Frederick Ainsworth, Frank A. Ammirati, Suzanne Beckman, Joan Bellomo, Bob Berger, Michael Crosby, Julie Elkins, Marietta Federici, Charles Hull, Robert Lehman and Patrick Suraci.

About a hairdresser and New York City's hair industry.

How To Steal an Election (89). Musical with book by William F. Brown; music and lyrics by Oscar Brand. Produced by Stephen Mellow, Seymour Vall and IPC at the Pocket Theater. Opened October 13, 1968. (Closed December 22, 1968)

D.R. Allen	Carole Demas
Barbara Anson	Del Hinkley
Beverly Ballard	Thom Koutsoukos
Ed Crowley	Bill McCutcheon
Clifton Davis	

Directed by Robert H. Livingston; musical director, Bhen Lanzaroni; scenery and lighting, Clarke Dunham; musical staging, Frank Wagner; musical arrangements and orchestrations, Bhen Lanzaroni and Jay Dryer; costumes, Mopsy; film sequences, George Pickow; production stage manager, Clifford Ammon; visual research, Bonnie Buchanan; press, Howard Atlee, David Roggensack, Martin Cohen, Bill Cherry.

Time: Yesterday, today and tomorrow. Place: The United States of America.

Satire of American political chicanery from George Washington's administration to the present.

ACT I

"The Plumed Knight" ....Ed Crowley
"Clay and Frelinghuysen" ....Barbara Anson, Beverly Ballard, Crowley
"Get on the Raft With Taft" ....Bill McCutcheon
"Silent Cal" ....Crowley, McCutcheon, Del Hinkley, Thom Koutsoukos, Misses Anson, Ballard
"Nobody's Listening" ....Clifton Davis
"The Right Man" ....Carole Demas
"How To Steal an Election" ........D.R. Allen, Hinkley, Crowley, Koutsoukos, McCutcheon
"Van Buren" ....Koutsoukos
"Tippecanoe and Tyler Too" ....McCutcheon, Ensemble

"Charisma" ....Allen
"Nobody's Listening" (Reprise) ....Davis
"Lincoln and Soda" ....Miss Ballard
"Lincoln and Liberty" ....Crowley, Hinkley, Koutsoukos, McCutcheon
"The Right Man" (Reprise) ....Allen, Ensemble

ACT II

"Grant" ....Crowley, Hinkley, Koutsoukos, McCutcheon
"Law and Order" ....Crowley
"Lucky Lindy" ....Misses Anson, Ballard
"Down Among the Grass Roots" ....Allen, Ensemble
"Get Out the Vote" ....Ensemble
"Mr. Might've Been" ....Davis, Miss Demas
"We're Gonna Win" ....Davis, Miss Demas, Ensemble
"More of the Same" ....Davis, Miss Demas

Before I Wake (16). By Trevor Reese. Produced by Charles Harrow and Frank S. Stuart (Jordan Productions) at the Greenwich Mews Theater. Opened October 13, 1968. (Closed October 27, 1968)

F. Scott Fitzgerald ....Martin Donegan   Ernest Hemingway ....Vincent McNally

Directed by Sandy Lesberg; production designed by Robert Troie; incidental music, Frank S. Stuart; stage manager, John Martin Giles; press, David Lipsky, Marian Graham.

Act I, Scene 1: Mid-1920s, Ernest's small room over Sawmill, Paris. Scene 2: Same day, Scott and Zelda's room, Paris. Scene 3: Months later, on the banks of the Seine, Paris. Scene 4: Same day, Scott and Zelda's room, Paris. Scene 5: A few months later, a sidewalk cafe, Paris. Act II, Scene 1: Mid-1930s, a bar in New York. Scene 2: Months later, a New York hotel room and a Baltimore home. Scene 3: Late 1930s, library of a home in Hollywood. Scene 4: Shortly afterward, Ernest's hotel room in Hollywood and Scott's apartment in Hollywood. Scene 5: December 1940, an apartment in New York. Scene 6: July 1962, Ketchum, Idaho.

About the 17-year friendship of F. Scott Fitzgerald and Ernest Hemingway.

Tea Party and **The Basement** (147). Program of two one-act plays by Harold Pinter. Produced by Richard Lee Marks and Henry Jaffe at the Eastside Playhouse. Opened October 15, 1968. (Closed March 16, 1969)

TEA PARTY

Sisson ....Richard Neilsen   Disley ....David Sage
Wendy ....Hildy Brooks   Lois ....Rose Roffman
Diana ....June Emery   Mother ....Hazel Jones
Willy ....John Tillinger   Father ....Bert Bertram
John ....Jeffrey Edmond   Waiters .....David Cromer, Manfred Taron
Tom ....Riley Mills

THE BASEMENT

Law ....Ted van Griethuysen   Jane ....Margo Ann Berdeshevksy
Stott ....James Ray

Directed by James Hammerstein; scenery, Ed Wittstein; lighting, Neil Peter Jampolis; costumes, Deidre Cartier; production stage manager, Ian Cadenhead; press, Frank Goodman, Alan Eichler.

Tea Party presents the gradual destruction of a successful business man by his wife, secretary and children. *The Basement* is a triangular story of two men and a girl in a basement apartment on a rainy night. Foreign plays previously produced in London, on TV; this was their world stage premiere.

Valerie French replaced Hildy Brooks 1/7/69.

Just for Love (6). Musical by Jill Showell and Henry Comor; score by Michael Valenti. Produced by Seymour Vall in association with Investors Production Company and Maurice Rind at the Provincetown Playhouse. Opened October 17, 1968. (Closed October 20, 1968)

Directed by Henry Comor; musical direction and arrangements, George Taros; scenery and lighting, Jack Blackman; costumes, Sara Brook; production stage manager, Martha Knight; press, Howard Atlee, David Roggensack, Martin Cohen. With Henry Comor, Jacqueline Mayro, Steve Perry, Jill Showell.

An anthology of love, some of it based on familiar literary works.

The American Place Theater. Schedule of four programs. **The Cannibals** (40). By George Tabori. Opened October 17, 1968; see note. (Closed November 23, 1968). **Trainer, Dean, Liepolt and Company** (44). Program of three one-act plays: *The Acquisition* by David Trainer, *This Bird of Dawning Singeth All Night Long* by Phillip Dean and *The Young Master Dante* by Werner Liepolt. Opened December 12, 1968; see note. (Closed January 18, 1969). **Boy on the Straight-Back Chair** (38). By Ronald Tavel. Opened February 14, 1969; see note. (Closed March 22, 1969) **Papp** (39). By Kenneth Cameron. Opened April 17, 1969; see note. (Closed May 24, 1969). Produced by The American Place Theater, Wynn Handman director, at The American Place Theater, St. Clement's Church of the Episcopal Diocese of New York.

THE CANNIBALS

Heltai	Gene Gross	Somlo	Michael McGuire
Hirschler	Jack Somack	Mad Mr. Reich	William Macy
Puffi	George Terry	Weiss	James S. Tolkan
Klaub	Andy Robinson	Professor Glatz	Vincent Milana
Uncle	Harris Yulin	Little Lang	Ed Clein
Ramaseder Kid	George Linjeris	Ghoulos	Dimo Condos
Silent Haas	Constantine Katsanos	S.S. Schreckinger	Sam Schacht
Gypsy	Gregory Rozakis	Kapo	Richard Vos

Directed by Martin Fried; production design and lighting, Wolfgang Roth; costumes, Ruth Morley; sound, Vladimir Ussachevsky; stage manager, Kate M. Pollack; press, Gifford/Wallace.

Drama set in Auschwitz, probing into reasons for individual survival under extreme conditions.

William Macy replaced Harris Yulin and M.M. Streicher replaced William Macy 11/19/68.

THE ACQUISITION

Sam	Philip Bruns	Edna	Betty Henritze
Agnes	Dixie Marquis	Leo	John Dorman

THE BIRD OF DAWNING SINGETH
ALL NIGHT LONG

Anne Jillett	Leora Dana	Nancy Ferrett	Billie Allen

THE YOUNG MASTER DANTE

Mrs. W.	Meggin Myles	Anticrustus	Gary Maxwell
Warlock	Philip Bruns	Cannilingus	Terri Teague
Dante	Andy Robinson	Grosslipper	Herve Villechaize
Monsters:		Omnivicious	Richard Vos
Sodomantis	John Bottoms	Buckentaur	Jane Whitehill
Innocensuous	Ted Leplat		

ALL PLAYS—Scenery, Douglas W. Schmidt; costumes, Carrie Fishbein; lighting, Dennis Parichy; press, Howard Atlee, David Roggensack.

THE ACQUISITION directed by Tom Bissinger; stage manager, Kate M. Pollack. About an intrusion of the older generation into a younger-generation household.

THIS BIRD OF DAWNING directed by Martin Fried; stage manager, Mitchell Kessler. Nightmarish encounter between a white woman and a black woman who claims to be her sister.
THE YOUNG MASTER DANTE directed by Tom Bissinger; music and organized sound, James Reichert. Special movement, Joel Zwick; stage manager, Kate M. Pollack. About a young poet searching for manhood.

BOY ON THE STRAIGHT-BACK CHAIR

Toby	Kevin O'Connor	May	Nancy McCormick
Stella	Katherine Squire	Ray	Ernestine Mercer
Della	Alice Beardsley	Maude	Jacque Lynn Colton
Singer	Orville Stoeber	Lynn	Lori Shelle
Stripper	Gloria LeRoy	Bad Butch	Norman Thomas Marshall
Mary	Martha Whitehead	Musician	Richard Vos
Romeo	Clark Burckhalter	The Sound Man	John Lefkowitz

Directed by Lee Von Rhau; music, Orville Stoeber; lighting, Dennis Parichy; stage manager, Kate M. Pollack.
Study of a youngster who commits multiple murders. The play is divided into two acts.

PAPP

Papp	Albert Paulsen	Whore of Babylon	Barbara Hayes
Curio	Arnold Soboloff	Mak	Rudy Bond

Directed by Martin Fried; scenery, Kert Lundell; costumes, Willa Kim; lighting, Roger Morgan; special sound, James Reichert; stage manager, Bruce Paul Eisensmith.
Time: A future. The play was presented without intermission. Allegorical treatment of formal religion in the world to come, following a global disaster.
NOTE: In this volume, the off-Broadway subscription companies like The American Place Theater are exceptions to our rule of counting the number of performances from the date of press coverage, because usually the press opening night takes place late in the play's run of public performances (after previews) for its subscription audience. In these cases, therefore, we count the first subscription performance, not the press review date, as opening night.

Don't Shoot Mable It's Your Husband (1). By Jerome Kilty. Produced by The Wilding Ones at the Bouwerie Lane Theater. Opened and closed at the evening performance October 22, 1968.

Directed by Mr. Kilty; scenery, Stuart Wurtzel; lighting, Joan Larkey; costumes, Patrizia von Brandenstein; production under the supervision of Frank Gero; production stage manager, Bruce Lovelady; press, Max Eisen, Carl Samrock, Reuben Rabinovitch. With Sue Lawless, Barry MacGregor, Zora Margolis, Ted Pugh, Michael Shepard and Peter Stuart.
Comedy, satire of social ills from World War II to the present. Previously produced by the American Conservatory Theater in San Francisco.

The People vs. Ranchman (41). By Megan Terry. Produced by Linda Otto, Geoffrey Johnson and Rick Hobard at the Fortune Theater. Opened October 27, 1968. (Closed December 1, 1968)

The Burning Crowd:
    Baseball Player .... Angelo Nazzo
    Housewife .... Jane Whitehill
    Student .... Wai Ching Ho
    Soldier .... Gary Poe
The Crusading Crowd:
    Pregnant Woman .... Leslie Karakas
    Photographer .... Jeff Chandler
    Young Man .... Dewayne Oliver
    Young Woman .... Sonya Hollmann
Policeman; Asst. Executioner .... Sherman Hemsley
Policeman; Nancy's Father; Executioner .... John M. Miranda

Policeman; Judge ....Alfred Hinckley
Ranchman ....William Devane
Nancy ....Joy Stark
Prosecutor ....Pierre Epstein
Woman Who Looks Up ....Greta Markson
Woman Who Looks Down ....Ceci Perrin
William ....Don Warfield
John Jay ....Vernon Joyce

Directed by Robert Greenwald; settings, Kurt Lundell; costumes, Morgan; lighting, Neil Peter Jampolis; music, Tom Sankey; production stage manager, Michael Frank; press, Max Eisen, Carl Samrock, Reuben Rabinovitch.

Irate citizens are more vicious than the criminal, Ranchman, they seek to execute for rape. The play is performed without intermission.

The David Show (1). By A.R. Gurney Jr. Produced by Donald H. Goldman at the Players Theater. Opened and closed at the evening performance October 31, 1968.

Directed by Ben Tarver; production designed by Barry Arnold; original music, Sergio Mihanovich; production stage manager, Gail Bell; press, Saul Richman, Eleanor McCann. With Jay Barney, Milton Earl Forrest, Tom Keena, Glenn Kezer, Ira Lewis, Holland Taylor.

Satire on the Biblical king, set in a TV studio.

Triple Play (17). Program of three one-act plays by Randolph Carter. Produced by Joel Reed and Robert Gibson in association with Milo Wood at the Cherry Lane Theater. Opened November 3, 1968. (Closed November 17, 1968)

I SAW A MONKEY

Larry Evans ....Matthew Cowles

THE LATE LATE SHOW

Laura Langston ....Hortense Alden   Gertrude ....Elaine Eldridge
Ted ....Lloyd Carter

SAVE IT FOR YOUR DEATH BED

George Moore ....Lloyd Carter   Mrs. Moore ....Elaine Eldridge
Josephene ....Brandy Alexander   Nick ....Victor Argo

Directed by Mr. Carter; scenery and lighting, Barry Arnold; production stage manager, Tex Wood; press, Max Eisen, Carl Samrock, Reuben Rabinovitch.

I SAW A MONKEY—Time: The present. Place: A corner of a drawing room in an apartment in the East Sixties, New York City. Monologue by a pathetic male homosexual prostitute.

THE LATE LATE SHOW—Time: 3 a.m. Place: Drawing room of a town house in the East Seventies, New York City. About a fading female movie star resorting to exaggerated camp.

SAVE IT FOR YOUR DEATH BED—Time: The present. Place: The basement of an old house in Queens. Scene 1: 2 a.m. Scene 2: Night, two weeks later. Scene 3: Afternoon, several days later. About a murderer wanted by the Mafia and a homosexual "marriage."

The Grab Bag (32). Program of three one-act plays by Robert J. Thompson. Produced by Thespis at the Astor Place Theater. Opened November 4, 1968. (Closed December 1, 1968)

THE SUBSCRIBER

Millicent ....Jean Francis   Wife ....Fern Sloan
Subscription Salesman ....Michael Saposnick   Husband ....Oreste Matachena
Alberto ....Hector Elias   Whore ....Jen Jones
Waitress ....Josephine Lemmo

SUSIE IS A *GOOD* GIRL

Susie	Josephine Lemmo	Sister Apollonia	
Mother Superior		Liguori	Hector Elias
Zachery Michael	Fern Sloan	Sister Felicity	
Sister Anne Immaculata	Jen Jones	Scholastica	Jean Francis
Sister Wilhamena		Xavier	Oreste Matachena
Lydwina	Michael Saposnick		

THE GRAB BAG

Pig Lady	Jen Jones	Second Girl	Josephine Lemmo
Patrick	Hector Elias	Matron's Son	Michael Saposnick
Matron	Jean Francis	Policeman	Oreste Matachena
First Girl	Fern Sloan		

Directed by Miguel Ponce; scenery, E.A. Smith; lighting, Jennifer Tipton; costumes, Michele Van Saun; production stage manager, Rand Michels; press, Howard Atlee, David Roggensack.
The Subscriber is about a deviate who is sublimated while making obscene phone calls. *Susie is a Good Girl* concerns a bevy of fake nuns commanded by a pimp. *The Grab Bag* is about an exhibitionist with a mother complex.

Walk Together Children (24). One-woman program of readings performed by Vinie Burrows. Produced by Robert Hooks and Michael Tolan in association with Ananse Productions at the Greenwich Mews Theater. Opened November 11, 1968. (Closed December 1, 1968)

Lighting, Fritz deBoer; costumes, Arthur McGee; press, Dorothy Ross, Ruth D. Smuckler.
Miss Burrows presents the black scene in prose, poetry and occasional interpolations of portions of songs.
PART I—John Brown's Body—Prelude, The Slaver, (by Stephen Vincent Benet), Speech (by Sojourner Truth), Runagate Runagate (by Robert Hayden), The Party (by Paul Laurence Dunbar), Life Cycle in the Delta (by George Houston Bass), Scarlet Woman (by Fenton Johnson), W.E.B. to Booker T. (by Dudley Randall), Between the World and Me (by Richard Wright).
PART II—Alberta K. Johnson (by Langston Hughes), Jazz Poem (by Carl Wendell Hines), I Know Jesus Heard Me (by Charles Anderson), Benediction (by Bob Kaufman), "Revolutionary Cradle Song" (by Edward Reicher), Conversation (anonymous), Jitterbugging in the Streets (by Calvin Hernton), Poem for Certain Cats (by Roland Snellings), Three Movements and a Coda (by LeRoi Jones), Status Symbol (by Mari Evans), Let America Be America Again (by Langston Hughes).

Die Brücke (The Bridge). German theater ensemble for overseas in a schedule of two plays in the German language. **Minna von Barnhelm** (8). By Gotthold Ephraim Lessing. Opened November 12, 1968. (Closed November 17, 1968). **Das Schloss** (The Castle) (6). By Max Brod; based on Franz Kafka's novel. Opened November 19, 1968. (Closed November 24, 1968). Produced by The Goethe-Institut München and Gert von Gontard at the Barbizon Plaza Theater.

PERFORMER	"MINNA VON BARNHELM"	"THE CASTLE"
Dieter Brammer	The Innkeeper	Parish Warden
Klaus Dierig	Chasseur	Arthur
Ursula Dirichs	Lady in Mourning	Frieda
Ingeborg Lapsien		Innkeeper's Wife
Peter Lieck	Riccaut	K.
Peter Lühr		The Speaker
Fred Maire	Servant	Jeremias
Helmut Oeser	Paul Werner	Innkeeper "Gentleman's Inn"
Inge Rassaerts	Franziska	Olga
Christian Rode	Maj. von Tellheim	Schwarzer; Teacher
Joost Siedhoff	Just	Barnabas

PERFORMER	"MINNA VON BARNHELM"	"THE CASTLE"
Sigfrit Steiner	von Bruchsall	Innkeeper "Bridge Inn"; Bürgel
Antje Weisgerber	Minna von Barnhelm	Amalia

MINNA VON BARNHELM directed by Axel von Ambesser; scenery and costumes, Jörg Zimmermann; press, Nat Dorfman.
Time: 1763. Place: Prussia. Comedy of the romantic and legal difficulties faced by a returning veteran of the Seven Years War.
DAS SCHLOSS directed by Jochen Heyse; scenery and costumes, Hansheinrich Palitzsch; music, Dieter Schönbach.
Symbolic Kafka work in which all K.'s efforts to establish himself are thwarted by strange obstacles.

Piraikon Theatron (Piraikon Theater). Schedule of two plays by Euripides; translated by Dimitrios Sarros and presented in the modern Greek language. **Iphigenia in Aulis** (8). Opened November 12, 1968. (Closed November 17, 1968). **Hippolytus** (8). Opened November 19, 1968. (Closed November 24, 1968). Produced by Piraikon Theatron, Dimitrios Rondiris founder-director, at The Felt Forum.

PERFORMER	"IPHIGENIA IN AULIS"	"HIPPOLYTUS"
Frini Arvanitou	Chorus Leader	Chorus Leader
Christos Christopoulos	Messenger	Servant
Akti Drini	Chorus Leader	Chorus Leader
Christos Frangos	Achilleus	Servant
Kostis Galanakis		Hippolytus
Thanos Kanellis	Old Man	Servant
Nikos Lykomitros	Menelaus	Messenger; Servant
Krinio Pappa		Nurse
Karmen Rougeri	Chorus Leader	Aphrodite; Chorus Leader
Elsa Vergi	Clytaemnestra	Phaedra
Antonis Xenakis	Agamemnon	Theseus
Miranda Zafiropoulou	Iphigenia	Artemis
Kiki Zakka	Chorus Leader	Chorus Leader
Dmitra Zeza	Chorus Leader	

Chorus: Kiki Rota, Yanna Lykomitrou, Anna Landou, Mimika Balaska, Olga Tsakrali, Mina Tounta, Maria Assimakopoulou, Ritsa Kimouli, Ketty Passa, Mika Romanou, Ketty Romanoy, Konstantina Rondiri.
Directed by Dimitrios Rondiris; choreography, Loukia; *Iphigenia* music, Konstantinos Kydoniatis; *Hippolytus* music, Dimitrios Mitropoulos; press, Bill McGuire.
Iphigenia in Aulis was last revived here last season, in English translation, 11/21/67 for 232 off-Broadway performances. This is the first New York professional production of record for *Hippolytus*.

* **New York Shakespeare Festival Public Theater.** Indoor schedule of four plays. **Huui, Huui** (51). By Anne Burr. Opened November 16, 1968; see note. (Closed December 29, 1968). **Cities in Bezique** (67). Program of two one-act plays by Adrienne Kennedy: *The Owl Answers* and *A Beast's Story*. Opened January 4, 1969; see note. (Closed March 2, 1969) **Invitation to a Beheading** (67). By Russell McGrath; adapted from the novel by Vladimir Nabokov. Opened March 8, 1969; see note. (Closed May 4, 1969). * **No Place To Be Somebody** (30). By Charles Gordone. Opened May 4, 1969; see note. Produced by Joseph Papp for the New York Shakespeare Festival, Gerald Freedman artistic director, Bernard Gersten associate producer, at the Public Theater.

HUUI, HUUI

Minnie	Eda Reiss Merin	Elly	Margaret Linn
Feisel	Barry Primus	Ramona	Sharon Laughlin

Jerry ....David Congdon
Kay-Kay ....Jacque Lynn Colton
Al ....William Alderson
Girl #1 ....Betty Harmon

Hickman ....George Riddle
Girl #2 ....Karen Ludwig
Daddy ....Charles Durning
Gentleman ....Robert Frink

Directed by Joseph Papp; scenery, Douglas W. Schmidt: poem *When I'm Old* by Roy Harvey.

A young man, estranged from his family, strives to maintain his identity but is finally driven to suicide.

THE OWL ANSWERS

She who is Clara Passmore who is the
  Virgin Mary who is the Bastard who
  is the Owl ....Joan Harris
Bastard's Black Mother—Reverend's
  Wife—Anne Boleyn .....Cynthia Belgrave
Goddam Father—Richest White Man—
  Dead White Father—
  Reverend Passmore ....Moses Gunn

White Bird—Reverend's Canary—
  God's Dove ....Henry Baker
The Negro Man ....Paul Benjamin
Shakespeare ....Tony Thomas
Chaucer ....Joseph Walker
William the Conqueror ....Clee Burtonya

A BEAST'S STORY

Woman ....Amanda Ambrose
Man Beast ....Moses Gunn

Woman Beast ....Cynthia Belgrave
Human ....Tony Thomas

Girl Beasts: Robbie McCauley, Theta Tucker, Camille Yarborough. Other Beasts: Pawnee Sills, Deloris Gaskins, Henry Baker, Paul Benjamin, Clee Burtonya, Joseph Walker.

Directed by Gerald Freedman; scenery, Ming Cho Lee; music and sound score supervised by John Morris; assistant director, Amy Saltz.

The *Cities in Bezique* program note for *The Owl Answers* states: "The characters change slowly back and forth out of themselves leaving some garment from their previous selves upon them. . . . . The scene is a New York Subway is the Tower of London is a Harlem Hotel Room is St. Peter's," in a series of reveries of a mulatto girl who can find no place for herself in either white or black society. *A Beast's Story's* scene is Beast's House in the Forest, and it is a symbolic, introspective piece about sexual fear.

INVITATION TO A BEHEADING

Rodion ....Charles Durning
Cincinnatus ....John Heffernan
Rodrig ....Robert Ronan
Emmie ....Eloise Harris
Roman ....John Svar
The Librarian ....Steven Shaw
Marthe ....Susan Tyrell
M'sieur Pierre ....Joseph Bova
Father-in-Law;
  Minister of Opacity ....Fred Warriner

Young Man; Sec'y of
  Impenetrability ....Stephen Temperley
Old Lady;
  Minister of Propriety ....Susan McArthur
Brother-in-Law; Minister of
  Deconstruction ....John Glennon
Brother-in-Law; Sec'y of
  Re-education ....Irwin Pearl
Cecilia C. ....Janet Dowd

Directed by Gerald Freedman; scenery, Ming Cho Lee; music, John Morris; assistant director, Amy Saltz.

Time: Sometime now in the future. Place: The artist's mind. The play is presented in two acts. Dramatization of Nabokov's novel about a Kafka-esque victim in jail and awaiting execution.

ALL PLAYS: Costumes, Theoni V. Aldredge; lighting, Martin Aronstein; associate to Miss Aldredge, Milo Morrow; stage manager, Michael Chambers; press, Merle Debuskey.

NO PLACE TO BE SOMEBODY

Gabe Gabriel ....Ron O'Neal
Shanty Mulligan ....Ronnie Thompson
Johnny Williams ....Nathan George
Dee Jacobson ....Susan Pearson
Evie Ames ....Lynda Westcott

Cora Beasely ....Marge Eliot
Melvin Smeltz ....Henry Baker
Machine Dog ....Paul Benjamin
Mary Lou Bolton ....Laurie Crews
Ellen ....Iris Gemma

Sweets Crane ....Walter Jones	Sergeant Cappaletti ....Charles Seals
Mike Maffucci ....Nick Lewis	Harry ....Malcolm Hurd
Judge Bolton ....Ed VanNuys	Louie ....Martin Shakar

Directed by Ted Cornell; scenery and lighting, Michael Davidson; stage manager, Adam Perl. Time: The past 15 years. Place: Johnny's Bar in the West Village. The play was presented in three acts.

An aggressive, ambitious Negro tavern owner and his patrons are symbols of the contemporary distressed black urban condition.

A Best Play; see page 332

NOTE: In this volume, the off-Broadway subscription companies like New York Shakespeare Festival Public Theater are exceptions to our rule of counting the number of performances from the date of press coverage, because usually the press opening night takes place late in the play's run of public performances (after previews) for subscription audiences. In these cases, therefore, we count the first subscription performance, not the press review date, as opening night.

Sweet Eros and **Witness** (78). Program of two one-act plays by Terrence McNally. Produced by Michael Ellis at the Gramercy Arts Theater. Opened November 21, 1968. (Closed January 26, 1969)

SWEET EROS

Young Man ....Robert Drivas	The Girl ....Sally Kirkland

WITNESS

Young Man ....Joe Ponazecki	Window Washer ....James Coco
Man ....Richard Marr	Miss Presson ....Sally Kirkland

Directed by Larry Arrick; scenery and costumes, Peter Harvey; lighting, Roger Morgan; associate producer, Samuel Bronstein; production stage manager, Otis Bigelow; press, Howard Atlee, David Roggensack.

In *Sweet Eros,* a young man has tied a girl to a chair and is both haranguing and stripping her as he prepares to rape her. *Witness* is a black comedy about violence in America.

Chad Mitchell's Counterpoint (12). One-man program of songs performed by Chad Mitchell. Produced by Bert Wainer at The Bitter End. Opened November 25, 1968. (Closed December 7, 1968)

Directed by Moni Yakim; production designed by Chuck Eisler; production stage manager, Chuck Eisler; press, Dorothy Ross, Ruth D. Smuckler.

21 songs of "the new Renaissance" of 1960s American song writing.

Up Eden (7). Musical with book and lyrics by Robert Rosenblum and Howard Schuman; music by Robert Rosenblum. Produced by Jack Farren in association with Evan William Mandel at the Jan Hus Theater. Opened November 27, 1968. (Closed December 1, 1968)

Directed by John Bishop; musical direction, Wally Harper; musical staging, Patricia Birch; scenery and costumes, Gordon Micunis; lighting, Louise Guthman; vocal arrangements, Jack Lee; orchestrations, Wally Harper, Richard Hurwitz; production stage manager, Dale Whitman; press, Harvey B. Sabinson, Lee Solters, Harry Nigro. With Bob Balaban, David Burrow, George Connolly, Blythe Danner, Deborah Deeble, Diana Goble, Richard Hall, Laurie Hutchinson, Stacy McAdams, Barbara Porter, Denny Shearer, Sally Soldo.

A free adaptation of Mozart's *Cosi fan Tutte.*

Bil and Cora Baird's Marionettes. Schedule of two marionette programs. **The Wizard of Oz** (118). Conceived by Bil Baird; music by Harold Arlen; lyrics by E.Y. Harburg; adapted by Bil Baird and Arthur Cantor from the book by L. Frank Baum. Opened November 27, 1968. (Closed March 2, 1969 after 114 performances but gave four additional performances on April 7 and 8, 1969) **Winnie the Pooh** (58). Return engagement of the marionette show conceived by Bil Baird; adapted by A.J. Russell from the book by A.A. Milne; music by Jack Brooks; lyrics by A.A. Milne and Jack Brooks. Opened March 7, 1969. (Closed April 27, 1969) Produced by The American Puppet Arts Council, Arthur Cantor executive producer, at the Bil Baird Theater.

PERFORMER	"THE WIZARD OF OZ"	"WINNIE THE POOH"
Bil Baird	Tanglefoot; Cowardly Lion	Eeyore
Franz Fazakas	Tin Woodman	Winnie-the-Pooh
Jerry Nelson	Toto; Wizard	Piglet
Phyllis Nierendorf	Dorothy	Christopher Robin
The Simon Sisters		Mice
Fania Sullivan	Aunt Em; Glinda	Kanga
Frank Sullivan	Uncle Henry; Scarecrow	Rabbit; Owl
Byron Whiting	Kalidah; Guardian; Witch	Roo; Tigger
	of the West	

THE WIZARD OF OZ directed by Bil Baird and Arthur Cantor; musical director and arranger, Alvy West; assistant to the director, Gordon Hunt; production manager, Carl Harms; general understudy, Billy Mitros; press, Stanley Gaither.

Place: In and around Kansas, U.S.A. and the Land of Oz. The play is divided into two acts. The story is based on the Baum Oz fantasy, in which a Kansas farm girl, Dorothy, dreams that she is deposited by a cyclone into a strange land full of wonderful creatures and events.

WINNIE THE POOH directed by Fania Sullivan; musical director and arranger, Alvy West. *Winnie the Pooh* was originally presented at the Bil Baird Theater 11/23/57 for 185 performances.

NOTE: A PAGEANT OF PUPPET VARIETY, a demonstration of the art of the marionette theater, was presented on both programs.

Papers (2). By Hans Ruesch. Produced by Robert D. Feldstein at the Provincetown Playhouse. Opened December 3, 1968. (Closed December 4, 1968)

Directed by Anthony J. Stimac; scenery and lighting, C. Murawski; costumes, Charles D. Tomlinson; production stage manager, Charles E. Hale; press, David Lipsky, Marian Graham, M.J. Boyer. With Irene Bunde, John Canemaker, Herbert Foster, Russell Horton, Charlotte Jones, William Metzo, Thomas Ruisinger, Virginia Sandifur and Raymond Thorne.

Losing struggle of an individual against the establishment.

Possibilities (1). By Arthur Pittman. Produced by Stanley Gordon, Burry Fredrik, Selma Tamber and Edward A. Wolpin Enterprises, Inc. at the Players Theater. Opened and closed at the evening performance December 4, 1968.

Directed by Jerome Kilty; scenery and lighting, Jo Mielziner; costumes, Noel Taylor; press, Betty Lee Hunt. With Elizabeth Hubbard, Richard Jordan, Toni Darnay, Eileen Dolphin, Hugh Franklin, Schorling Schneider, Nancy Jane-Stephens, Donald Symington, Millee Taggert, Neil Vipond.

Four possible outcomes in the life of a young woman having an affair in the 1940s.

* The Repertory Theater of Lincoln Center. Repertory of two programs. **Bananas** (42). By John White. Opened December 5, 1968. **An Evening for Merlin Finch** (35). Program of two one-act plays by Charles Dizenzo: *A Great Career* and the title play. Opened December 29, 1968. (Repertory closed February 22, 1969). And schedule of two plays. **The Inner Journey** (36). By James Hanley. Opened March 20, 1969. (Closed April 20, 1969). *** The Year Boston Won the Pennant** (12). By John Ford Noonan. Opened May 22, 1969. Produced by The Repertory Theater of Lincoln Center, Jules Irving director, Robert Symonds associate director, at the Forum Theater.

BANANAS

Talking Woman ....Patricia Roe	Green Banana ....Larry Robinson
Ripe Banana ....Arnold Soboloff	Pianist ....James Hodges
Sour Banana ....Ralph Bell	Drummer ....Richard Fitz
The Critic ....Ray Fry	

Directed by Robert Symonds; original concept by Anna Sokolow; scenery, Karl Eigsti; lighting, John Gleason; costumes, Holly Haas; music and songs, James Hodges; sound, Pril Smiley; production stage manager, Christopher Kelly; press, Susan Bloch.

Time: The present. Place: The stage of a dilapidated burlesque theater. Act I: Entire Company. Act II: Patricia Roe, Larry Robinson. Act III: Entire Company. Act IV: Patricia Roe, Ray Fry. Finale: Entire Company.

Farcical parody of old time burlesque shows, used to satirize various other elements of society, with incidental musical numbers.

A GREAT CAREER

George & Phoebe .............R.G. Brown	Linda ....Mary Louise Wilson
Zelda & Mr. Gray ....Philip Bosco	

AN EVENING FOR MERLIN FINCH

Mrs. Darlene Finch ....Sada Thompson	Mrs. Fanny Lawson ....Priscilla Pointer
Mr. Frank Finch ....Jerome Dempsey	Mr. Jack Lawson ....Ed Crowley
Merlin Finch;	Bill Lawson ....Paul Rudd
Darlene's Mother ....James Cahill	

Directed by George Sherman; scenery, Tom Munn; lighting, John Gleason; costumes, Holly Haas; production stage manager, Barbara-Mae Phillips.

A GREAT CAREER—Time: The present. Place: An office in Manhattan. Satire on the personalities and events of a day in the office of a large corporation.

AN EVENING FOR MERLIN FINCH—Time: The present. Place: A suburban living room. The play was presented in two parts. Black comic cartoon of suburban family life.

THE INNER JOURNEY

Dominic Christian ....Robert Symonds	Antaeus Christian ....Michael Dunn
Mrs. Leekens ....Eda Reiss Merin	Mrs. Peeles ....Aline MacMahon
A Worker ....Robert Levine	Mrs. Garsides ....Leta Bonynge
His Wife ....Joan Jeffri	Father Duriere ....Ray Stewart
Lizzie Christian ....Priscilla Pointer	Doctor Reznin ....William Myers

Directed by Jules Irving; scenery, Douglas W. Schmidt; lighting, John Gleason; costumes, Carrie Fishbein Robbins; sound, Pril Smiley; production stage manager, Christopher Kelly; assistant director, Tim Ward; stage manager, Ronald Schaeffer.

Scene 1: A room in Mrs. Leekens' boarding house, late morning. Scene 2: A room in Mrs. Peeles' boarding house, late at night, two years later; Scene 3: Radford Music Hall, late evening. Scene 4: Lizzie's room, late afternoon, some months later. Scene 5: A room in Mrs. Garsides' boarding house, near midnight, 18 months later. Scene 6: A Catholic hospital for the dying, 1 a.m. the next morning. Scene 7: A dressing room at the Music Hall, the same evening. Scene 8: On stage, moments later. The play was presented in two parts.

Mutually distressing relationship between an old vaudevillian and his crippled, dwarflike son. A foreign play previously produced in Europe.

THE YEAR BOSTON WON THE PENNANT

Dillinger, Peabody ....Lenny Baker	Marcus Sykowski ....Roy R. Scheider
Shattuck, Star ....Jerome Dempsey	Man in Raincoat ....William Myers
Kolkowski, Technician,	La Monde, Oscar ....Richard Woods
Delivery Man ....Ronald Schaeffer	Candy Cane Sykowski ....Marcia Jean Kurtz
O'Connor, Delivery Man,	Martha, Anne, LaVerne ......Marilyn Sokol
Frisch ....Joseph Schroer	Pepper, Cakes ....Jane Altman
Kuckta, Jones, George ....Paul Benjamin	P.J. ....Joan Jeffri
Delorenzo, Lurtsema,	
Groundskeeper ....Ralph Drischell	

Directed by Tim Ward; scenery, Holly Haas; costumes, Carrie Fishbein Robbins; lighting, John Gleason; production stage manager, Patrick Horrigan; stage manager, Ronald Schaeffer.
Scene 1: The caddies at the country club. Scene 2: Marcus collects his money. Scene 3: Candy Cane gets a surprise. Scene 4: Marcus visits an old friend. Scene 5: Marcus is asked a favor. Scene 6: Candy and Marcus make love. Scene 7: Marcus visits his hero. Scene 8: Marcus gets a surprise. Scene 9: Marcus attends the funeral. Scene 10: Candy asks some questions. Scene 11: General strike at the country club. Scene 12: Candy asks a favor. Scene 13: Marcus crashes the party. Scene 14: Reunion in Fenway Park. The play was presented in two parts, with the intermission following Scene 9.
A star right-hander has lost his left arm in some mysterious, unexplained manner and is struggling to make a comeback, in a symbolic drama of the human condition.

Big Time Buck White (124). By Joseph Dolan Tuotti. Produced by Zev Bufman in association with Ron Rich and Leonard Grant at the Village South Theater. Opened December 8, 1968. (Closed March 30, 1969)

Hunter	Kirk Kirksey	Rubber Band	Arnold Williams
Honey Man	David Moody	Jive	Ron Rich
Weasel	Van Kirksey	Big Time Buck White	Dick Williams

Directed by Dick Williams; scenery, Edward Burbridge; costumes, Sara Brook; lighting, Thomas Skelton; produced in association with Seymour Vall & I.P.C.; production stage manager, Vahan Gregory; press, Robert Ganshaw & John Prescott, Tom Trenkle, Stan Brody.
Time: The present. Place: The meeting hall of the Beautiful Alleluiah Days organization. Comedy about goings-on at an anti-poverty agency turns serious with the arrival of a black power leader who expounds his views and answers questions from the audience. Previously produced at the Watts Writers' Workshop and the Coronet Theater, Los Angeles.

Americana Pastoral (8). By Yabo Yablonsky. Produced by The Art Theater Guild in association with Chuck Brent and Louis K. Sher at the Greenwich Mews Theater. Opened December 10, 1968. (Closed December 15, 1968)

Directed by Mr. Yablonsky; lighting, Paul Holland; theme music by Howard Fenton and Gene Bone; production stage manager, Alan Charlet; press, Dorothy Ross. With Stanley Brock, Cashmere Ellis, Gladys Fry, Eliot Karpack, Marcella Lowery, Linda Manley, Norman Matlock, Ron O'Neal, Suzanne Pred, Martin Shakar, Louise Stubbs, Lance Taylor, Dan Tyra and Lisle Wilson.
Wealthy Negro buys a cotton mill for poor North Carolinians.

Lemonade and **The Autograph Hound** (28). Program of two one-act plays by James Prideaux. Produced by M.P.C. Ltd. at the Jan Hus Playhouse. Opened December 13, 1968. (Closed January 5, 1969)

Directed by William E. Hunt; scenery and lighting, David Segal; costumes, Deborah Foster; press, Saul Richman. With Nancy Coleman, Kendall March, Jan Miner, Michael Vale.
In *Lemonade* two upper-class matrons discuss life while peddling the beverage. In *The Autograph Hound* a rabid celebrity-chaser sacrifices her family for her hobby.

Ballad for a Firing Squad (7). Musical with book by Jerome Coopersmith; music by Edward Thomas; lyrics by Martin Charnin. Produced by Edward Thomas at the Theater de Lys. Opened December 13, 1968. (Closed December 15, 1968)

Directed by Martin Charnin; choreography, Alan Johnson; musical direction, Joyce Brown; scenery and lighting, James Tilton; costumes, Theoni V. Aldredge; orchestrations, Larry Wilcox; dance arranger, Joe Rago; production stage manager, Jon Froscher; press, Saul Richman. With Dominic Chianese, Stanley Church, Joseph Corby, James Hurst, George Marcy, Adelle Rasey, Irma Rogers, Elliott Savage, Bruce Scott, Peter Shawn, Liz Sheridan, Neva Small, Renata Vaselle, Vi Velasco.
About the ill-fated love between Mata Hari and the French intelligence officer who hunted her down. Previously produced in the 1967-68 season in a pre-Broadway tryout.

Beclch (48). By Rochelle Owens. Produced by Norma Productions in association with Theodore A. Pennington Jr. and Marlene Brockmeier at the Gate Theater. Opened December 16, 1968. (Closed January 26, 1969)

Najdina; Old Woman ....Abigail Rosen	Thin Man; Waiter ....Gene Romeo
African Men ....Gene Romeo, Theodore	Boy; Hermes ....George Coleman
Toussant, Clay Taliaferro	Missionary Woman ....Evelyn Ave
Nuala ....Gwynne Tomlan	Jose ....Monty Montgomery
Mank ....Thomas Martell Brimm II	Cockfighters ....Clay Taliaferro,
Beclch ....Jean David	Theodore Toussant
Yago ....Donald L. Brooks	

Directed by Don Signore; scenery, Paulita Sedgwick; lighting, Leo; costumes, Susan Gingrich; production stage manager, Cliff Tobey; press, Robert Ganshaw & John Prescott, Tom Trenkle, Stan Brody.

Time: Any time. Place: Someplace in Africa. The play is divided into two acts.

Sadistic white woman establishes herself as a jungle queen and revels in cruelty until she betrays a sign of weakness by falling in love herself, and is executed by the natives. Previously produced at Theater of the Living Arts, Philadelphia.

The Negro Ensemble Company. Schedule of four programs. **"God Is a (Guess What?)"** (32). Morality play by Ray McIver with music by Coleridge-Taylor Perkinson. Opened December 17, 1968; see note. (Closed January 12, 1969). **Ceremonies in Dark Old Men** (40; see note). By Lonne Elder III. Opened February 4, 1969; see note. (Closed March 9, 1969). **An Evening of One Acts** (32). Program of three one-act plays: *String* by Alice Childress, *Contribution* by Ted Shine and *Malcochon* by Derek Walcott. Opened March 25, 1969; see note. (Closed April 20, 1969). 1969 schedule will also include *Man Better Man,* musical play by Earl Hill opening 7/2/69. Produced by The Negro Ensemble Company, Douglas Turner Ward artistic director, Robert Hooks executive director, Gerald S. Krone administrative director, at St. Marks Playhouse.

"GOD IS A (GUESS WHAT?)"

The Chorus ....The Company	First Extraordinary
First End Man ....Arthur French	Spook ....Judyann Jonsson
Second End Man ....David Downing	Second Extraordinary
Jim ....Julius W. Harris	Spook ....Hattie Winston
Officer ....Theodore Wilson	Third Extraordinary
Reba ....Clarice Taylor	Spook ....Rosalind Cash
Boy ....William Jay	Cannibal ....Esther Rolle
Lady ....Frances Foster	Priest ....Norman Bush
Voice ....Graham Brown	Accolyte ....Mari Toussaint
A Man ....Allie Woods	Bla-Bla ....Graham Brown

Directed by Michael A. Schultz; choreography, Louis Johnson; scenery, Edward Burbridge; costumes, Bernard Johnson; lighting, Marshall Williams; stage managers, Edmund Cambridge, James S. Lucas Jr.; press, Howard Atlee, David Roggensack, William Cherry, Irene Gandy.

Time: Now. Place: Here. The play was presented without intermission. Ironic juxtaposition of minstrel show form with drama of a lynching prevented by the invention of God.

MUSICAL NUMBERS

"A Mighty Fortress"	Chorus
"The Lynch-Him Song"	French, Downing
"The Sonny-Boy Slave Song"	Bush, Jay, Toussaint, Wilson
"The Black-Black Song"	Chorus, Downing, French
"The Golden Rule Song"	French, Downing
"God Will Take Care"	Bush, Jay, Toussaint, Wilson
"The Darkies Song"	Downing, French
"The Sit Down Song"	Cash, Jonsson, Winston, Woods
"The Lynchers' Prayer	The Company

CEREMONIES IN DARK OLD MEN

Mr. Russell B. Parker . . . . Douglas Turner	Adele Eloise Parker . . . . Rosalind Cash
Mr. William Jenkins . . . . Arthur French	Blue Haven . . . . Samual Blue Jr.
Theopolis Parker . . . . William Jay	Young Girl . . . . Judyann Jonsson
Bobby Parker . . . . David Downing	

Directed by Edmund Cambridge; scenery, Whitney Le Blanc; costumes, Gertha Brook; lighting, Shirley Prendergast; stage manager, James S. Lucas Jr.

Time: The present, late spring. Place: A barber shop, Harlem, U.S.A. Act I, Scene 1: 4:30 p.m. Scene 2: Six days later, late afternoon. Act II, Scene 1: Two months later, 9 p.m. Scene 2: Same night, two hours later.

Onetime hoofer, now a barber, cannot prevent disaster from overtaking his children as they reach maturity and turn to pleasure-seeking and crime.

NOTE: *Ceremonies in Dark Old Men* was produced a second time in the 1968-69 off-Broadway season, beginning 4/28/69 at the Pocket Theater (see its separate entry in this listing).

STRING

Mrs. Beverly . . . . Esther Rolle	Maydelle . . . . Frances Foster
Mrs. Rogers . . . . Clarice Taylor	L.V. Craig . . . . Julius W. Harris
Joe . . . . Arthur French	(Sadie) . . . . Stephanie Mills, Bambi Jones

(Parentheses indicate role in which the actresses alternated)

CONTRIBUTION

Mrs. Gracie Love . . . . Clarice Taylor	Eugene Love . . . . Allie Woods
Katy Jones . . . . Esther Rolle	

MALCOCHON

Conteur . . . . Rosalind Cash	Chantal . . . . Arthur French
Charlemagne . . . . Graham Brown	The Moumou . . . . Allie Woods
Sonson . . . . Samual Blue Jr.	Chorus Leader . . . . Sonny Morgan
Popo . . . . Norman Bush	Chorus . . . . Mari Toussaint, Theodore Wilson
Madeleine . . . . Frances Foster	

String and *Malcochon* directed by Edmund Cambridge; *Contribution* directed by Douglas Turner Ward; scenery, Edward Burbridge; costumes, Gertha Brock; lighting, Buddy Butler; music, Coleridge-Taylor Perkinson; stage manager, James S. Lucas Jr.

STRING—Time: The present, a summer Sunday morning. Place: A picnic ground, near New York City; a picnic given by the Neighborhood Association. Based on a De Maupassant story, a ne'er-do-well is unjustly accused of stealing at a civic outing.

CONTRIBUTION—Time: Sometime during the era of the sit-ins. Place: A Southern town. Satire on white attitudes of paternalism toward the Negro.

MALCOCHON—Time: The rainy season. Place: An abandoned copra shed on a coconut estate on a West Indian island. West Indian folk legend about a John Henry of the sugar cane fields.

NOTE: In this volume, the off-Broadway subscription companies like the Negro Ensemble Company are exceptions to our rule of counting the number of performances from the date of press coverage, because usually the press opening night takes place late in the play's run of public performances (after previews) for its subscription audience. In these cases, therefore, we count the first subscription performance, not the press review date, as opening night.

* **Dames at Sea** (182). Musical with book and lyrics by George Haimsohn and Robin Miller; music by Jim Wise. Produced by Jordan Hott and Jack Millstein at the Bouwerie Lane Theater. Opened December 20, 1968.

Mona Kent . . . . Tamara Long	Dick . . . . David Christmas
Joan . . . . Sally Stark	Lucky . . . . Joseph R. Sicari
Hennessey . . . . Steve Elmore	The Captain . . . . Steve Elmore
Ruby . . . . Bernadette Peters	

Directed and choreographed by Neal Kenyon; scenery and costumes, Peter Harvey; lighting, Martin Aronstein; musical director, Richard J. Leonard; assistant choreographer, Bonnie Ano;

associate producer, Robert S. Mankin; production stage manager, T.L. Boston; press, Howard Atlee, David Roggensack.

Time: The early 1930s. Place: Any 42nd Street theater and on the battleship. A lampoon of the movie musicals of the 1930s. Previously produced at Caffe Cino in 1960.

ACT I

"Wall Street"	Mona
"It's You"	Dick and Ruby
"Broadway Baby"	Dick
"That Mister Man of Mine"	Mona and Chorus
"Choo-Choo Honeymoon"	Joan and Lucky
"The Sailor of My Dreams"	Ruby
"Singapore Sue"	Lucky and Company
"Good Times are Here to Stay"	Joan and Company

ACT II

"Dames at Sea"	Company
"The Beguine"	Mona and Company
"Raining in My Heart"	Ruby and Chorus
"There's Something About You"	Company
"Raining in My Heart" (Reprise)	Ruby
"The Echo Waltz"	Mona, Joan, Ruby, Company
"Star Tar"	Ruby and Chorus
"Let's Have a Simple Wedding"	Company

Yes Yes, No No (1). By Ronnie Paris. Produced by Beverly Landau at the Astor Place Theater. Opened and closed at the evening performance December 31, 1968.

Directed by Leonardo Shapiro; scenery, costumes and lighting, John Braden; incidental music, Alonzo Levister; production stage manager, Robert Buzzell; press, Howard Atlee, David Roggensack, Henry Luhrman. With Suzan Devon, Patricia Hamilton, Marcia Jean Kurtz, Lucille Patton, Susann Randall, Wendy Wynters.

Fantasy about a cold, matriarchal world of women without men.

* To Be Young, Gifted and Black (172). Excerpts from the work of Lorraine Hansberry; adapted by Robert Nemiroff. Produced by Harry Belafonte/Chiz Schultz and Edgar Lansbury in association with Robert Nemiroff at the Cherry Lane Theater. Opened January 2, 1969.

Barbara Baxley	Janet League
John Beal	Stephen Strimpell
Rita Gardner	Cicely Tyson
Gertrude Jeannette	Andre Womble

Directed by Gene Frankel; designed by Merrill Sindler; lighting, Barry Arnold; photographic effects, Stuart Bigger; musical coordinator, William Eaton; production state manager, Gigi Cascio; press, The Mike Merrick Co., Max Eisen.

Part I: 1930-1959. Part II: 1960-1965. Subtitled "The World of Lorraine Hansberry in Her Own Words," the play draws on material, much of it autobiographical, from her plays *A Raisin in the Sun, The Sign in Sidney Brustein's Window, Les Blancs, The Drinking Gourd,* and *What Use Are Flowers;* her novel *All the Dark and Beautiful Women* and other writings.

Dolores Sutton replaced Barbara Baxley 1/19/69. Bruce Hall replaced John Beal 1/19/69. Tina Sattin replaced Cicely Tyson 4/1/69. Alice Borden replaced Rita Gardner 4/4/69. William Suplee replaced Bruce Hall 4/25/69.

* Little Murders (168). Revival of the play by Jules Feiffer. Produced by Circle in the Square, Inc., Theodore Mann artistic director, Paul Libin managing director, Gillian Walker associate director, Orin Lehman co-producer, at the Circle in the Square. Opened January 5, 1969.

Kenny Newquist ....Jon Korkes   Alfred Chamberlain ....Fred Willard
Marjorie Newquist ....Elizabeth Wilson   Judge Stern ....Shimen Ruskin
Carol Nequist ....Vincent Gardenia   Rev. Dupas ....Paul Benedict
Patsy Newquist ....Linda Lavin   Lt. Practice ....Andrew Duncan

Directed by Alan Arkin; scenery, Ed Wittstein; costumes, Albert Wolsky; lighting, Neil Peter Jampolis; sound, Terry Ross; production stage manager, James E. Dwyer; press, Merle Debuskey, Violet Welles, Faith Geer.

Time: The present. Place: The Newquist apartment. *Little Murders* was previously produced on Broadway 4/25/67 at the Broadhurst Theater for 7 performances.

Carole Shelley replaced Linda Lavin 3/25/69. Jay Devlin replaced Fred Willard 4/29/69.

* **Geese** (159). Program of two one-act plays by Gus Weill: *Parents and Children* and *Geese*. Produced by Jim Mendenhall at the Players Theater. Opened January 12, 1969.

PARENTS AND CHILDREN

Bill ....John Scanlan   Little Bill ....Kenneth Carr
Helen ....Adele Mailer   Hank ....Dan Halleck

GEESE

Miss Lucy ....Dorothy Vann   Deborah Mobley ....Jennifer Williams
Mrs. Mobley ....Martha Sherrill   Sandy ....Paula Shaw
Paul Mobley ....John Scanlan

Directed by Philip Oesterman; scenery, Douglas W. Schmidt; costumes, Terry Leong; music, Richard Kimball; lighting, Dean Mendenhall, Bob Engstrom; production stage manager, Chuck Vincent; press, Marc Olden, Bob Perilla Associates.

Parents and Children compares a homosexual relationship with a heterosexual one and *Geese* compares a lesbian relationship with loneliness, both favorably, and both with nudity and explicit love making.

Gwen Van Dam replaced Adele Mailer 2/2/69. Jim Sink replaced Kenneth Carr and Joan Maxham replaced Jennifer Williams 2/23/69. Gwen Saska replaced Dorothy Vann 4/20/69. Schorling Schneider replaced Jim Sink 5/4/69. J. Frank Lucas replaced John Scanlan 5/27/69. *Geese* was revised to make adjustments to audience response, and the new version began playing 5/21/69.

Horseman, Pass By (37). Musical by Rocco Bufano and John Duffy; based on writings of W.B. Yeats; music by Mr. Duffy. Produced by John A. McQuiggan at the Fortune Theater. Opened January 15, 1969. (Closed February 16, 1969)

Intellect ....Barbara Barrie   Spirit ....Terry Kiser
Imagination ....George Hearn   Vanity ....Novella Nelson
Sensuality ....Laurence Luckinbill   Timidity ....Maria Tucci
Political Man ....Clifton Davis   The Voice ....Will Geer

Directed by Mr. Bufano; scenery, Dennis Dougherty; costumes, Nancy Potts; lighting, Jennifer Tipton; music director, Stanley Walden; orchestrations, Robert Dennis, John Duffy, Stanley Walden; choreographer, Rhoda Levine; production stage manager, Joseph Cali; press, Fred Weterick.

Yeats's poetry with a rock score.

MUSICAL NUMBERS

"What Then?" ("Dead Man's Tango") ....Company
"This Great Purple Butterfly" ....Spirit
"Brown Penny" ....Sensuality
"Girl's Song" ....Intellect
"A Soldier Takes Pride in Saluting His Captain" ....Political Man
"Before the World Was Made" ....Vanity
"Last Confession" ....Timidity

"Mad as the Mist and Snow" ....Imagination
"Crazy Jane on the Day of Judgment" ....Vanity, Sensuality, Spirit
"Her Anxiety" ....Vanity
"Salley Gardens" ....Spirit
"Soulless a Faery Dies" ....Timidity
"A Drunken Man's Praise of Sobriety" ....Company
"To an Isle in the Water" ....Imagination
"Consolation" ....Company
"For Anne Gregory" ....Intellect and Sensuality
"Three Songs to the One Burden" ("Henry Middleton") ....Political Man
Final Choral Blessing ....Company

Tango (67). By Slawomir Mrozek; translated by Teresa Dzeduszycka and Ralph Manheim. Produced by Arthur Cantor, Ninon T. Karlweis, Martin Rubin in association with Zvi Kolitz at the Pocket Theater. Opened January 18, 1969. (Closed March 16, 1969)

Eugenia	Muriel Kirkland	Eleanor	Lilyan Wilder
Eddie	Clifford A. Pellow	Stomil	Stefan Schnabel
Eugene	Arthur Ed Forman	Ala	Elizabeth Swain
Arthur	David Margulies		

Directed by Heinz Engels; based on original direction by Erwin Axer; American adaptation of scenery, Jason Phillips; American adaptation of costumes, John E. Hirsch; lighting, Paul Holland; original production designed by Eva Starowieska; costume stylist, Zoe Brown; dance arranged by Jon Devlin; production stage manager, Aida Alvarez; press, Arthur Cantor, Stanley Gaither, Susan L. Schulman.

Place: A large, high room. The troubles of our times (generation gap, rise of totalitarianism), reflected in the story of a family of nonconformists. A foreign play previously produced in Poland.

Get Thee to Canterbury (20). Musical with book by Jan Steen and David Secter; music by Paul Hoffert; lyrics by David Secter; adapted from Chaucer's *The Canterbury Tales*. Produced by David Secter at Sheridan Square Playhouse. Opened at the matinee performance January 25, 1969. (Closed February 9, 1969)

Carpenter	Will B. Able	Miller	Marc Jordan
Priest	Norman Allen	Pardoner	John Mintun
Summoner	Al Cohen	Allan	Paul Renault
Geoffrey Chaucer	Walker Daniels	Host	Shev Rodgers
John	Michael Harrison	Prudence	Shoshanna Rogers
Wife of Bath	Travis Hudson	Friar	Tom Sinclair

Directed by Jan Steen; musical numbers staged by Darwin Knight; musical director, Jerald B. Stone; orchestrations, Paul Hoffert; scenery, James F. Gohl; lighting, Michael Davidson; costumes, Jeanne Button; production stage manager, Martha Knight; press, Howard Atlee, David Roggensack, Henry Luhrman.

Free adaptation of several of Chaucer's tales. A foreign play previously produced, in part, as a straight play in Canada.

ACT I

"Get Thee to Canterbury" ....Company
"The Journey" ....Host
"Take a Pick" ....Company
"Death Beware" ....Friar, Summoner, Priest
"Buy My Pardons" ....Pardoner
"Dreams" ....Host, Wife
"Canter Banter" ....Summoner
"Day of Judgment I" ....Company
"Ballad of Sir Topaz" ....Chaucer

ACT II

"Bottom's Up" ....Male Company
"A Simple Wife" ....Wife
"Shadows" ....Allan, Prudence
"Day of Judgement II" ....Company
"Alison Dear" ....Chaucer
"Where are the Blossoms?" ....Carpenter
"On the Relative Merits of Education & Experience" ....Miller, John, Allan
"Everybody Gets It In the End" ....Company
"The Prologue" ....Chaucer

* **Peace** (142). Musical with book and lyrics by Tim Reynolds; music by Al Carmines; based on the play by Aristophanes. Produced by Albert Poland and Franklin DeBoer at the Astor Place Theater. Opened January 27, 1969.

Lisa	Julie Kurnitz	War	David Pursley
Rastus	George McGrath	Gen. Disorder	David Tice
Trygaeus	Reathel Bean	Peace	Arlene Rothlein
His Daughters	Essie Borden, Ann Dunbar	Prosperity	Margaret Wright
Hermes	David Vaughan	Abundance	Lee Crespi

Six Mortals: Jeffrey Apter, Essie Borden, Ann Dunbar, Craig Kuehl, Margot Lewitin, Dallett Norris.

Directed by Lawrence Kornfeld; costumes, Nancy Christofferson; lighting, Roger Morgan; Al Carmines, piano; John Kaye, percussion; choreography for Goddess Peace, Arlene Rothlein; production stage manager, Charles Atlas; press, Robert Ganshaw & John Prescott, Tom Trenkle, Warren Pincus.

Act I: Earth, then Heaven. Act II: Earth. Minstrel musical version of Aristophanes' *Peace*, in which a nobleman rescues Peace from Paradise and brings her back to earth.

Carol Fox replaced Julie Kurnitz 5/6/69. Violet Santangelo replaced Lee Crespi 5/20/69.

Shoot Anything With Hair That Moves (17). By Donald Ross. Produced by Seymour Vall in association with IPC and Peter Aiello at the Provincetown Playhouse. Opened February 2, 1969. (Closed February 16, 1969)

Peter	Bert Convy	Steve	Laurence Feinstein
Roz	Judi West	Frank	Danny DeVito
Vic	Susan Batson		

Directed by David Goldman; scenery and lighting, C. Murawski; costumes, David Toser; production stage manager, Charles Briggs; press, Seymour Krawitz, Anne Woll.

Time: The present. Place: Apartment in Manhattan. Act I, Scene 1: Late at night. Scene 2: A few minutes later. Scene 3: One week later. Act II, Scene 1: One week later. Scene 2: A few minutes later. Scene 3: Twenty-four hours later.

Two hippie girls move into the apartment of a 30-year-old film publicist who is estranged from his wife.

* **Adaptation** by Elaine May and **Next** by Terrence McNally (126). Produced by Lyn Austin and Oliver Smith, Seymour Vall in association with Robert J. Gibson (IPC) at the Greenwich Mews Theater. Opened February 10, 1969.

ADAPTATION

Games Master	Graham Jarvis	Players (female)	Carol Morley
Players (male)	Paul Dooley	Contestant	Gabriel Dell

NEXT

Marion Cheever	James Coco	Sgt. Thech	Elaine Shore

Directed by Elaine May; scenery, William Pitkin; lighting, Michael Davidson; production associate, Tessie Hill; production stage manager, Paul Holland; press, Howard Atlee, David Roggensack.

Adaptation represents life as a TV game with the player struggling to understand the rules and advance along the board to death. *Next* finds a middle-aged theater manager facing, for some unaccountable reason, an army physical exam. Previously produced at Stockbridge, Mass.
A Best Play; see page 354

Open 24 Hours (22). Program of two one-act plays by Roger Cornish: *Satisfaction Guaranteed* and the title play. Produced by John Grissmer and Patricia Vollmar at the Actors Playhouse. Opened February 11, 1969. (Closed March 2, 1969)

SATISFACTION GUARANTEED

Black Woman ....Louise Stubbs	Girl ....Joy Rinaldi
White Woman ....Pamela Duncan	Boy ....Russell Horton
Man ....Bill Steele	Attendant ....Joseph C. Davies

OPEN 24 HOURS

Black Woman ....Louise Stubbs	George ....Juan DeCarlos
White Woman ....Pamela Duncan	Attendant ....Joseph C. Davies
Harold ....Arlen Dean Snyder	Policeman ....Bill Steele
Number One ....Thurman Scott	

Directed by William DeSeta; scenery, Joseph McArdle; lighting, Marshall Williams; production stage manager, Robert Burgos; press, Jane Friedman, Rod Jacobson, The Goldstein Organization.
Time: The present. Place: A laundromat in New York's Upper West Side.
Satisfaction Guaranteed is about an unmarried father's fear of diaper rash. *Open 24 Hours* studies what might have been if black and white roles had been reversed. Previously produced at the University of Minnesota.

* An Evening with Max Morath at the Turn of the Century (123). One-man musical revue arranged, compiled and performed by Max Morath. Produced by Norman Kean at the Jan Hus Playhouse. Opened February 17, 1969.

Scenery and lighting, Dennis Dougherty; stage manager, Deborah Foster; press, Ben Kornzweig, Reginald Denenholz.
Monologues and ragtime piano reminiscences of such as Irving Berlin, Bert Williams, Jelly Roll Morton, Scott Joplin, Noble Sissle, etc. The show was presented in two parts.

A Corner of the Bed (6). By Allen Jack Lewis. Produced by Cora Gay Carr in association with Richard-Allan Productions, Inc. at the Gramercy Arts Theater. Opened February 26, 1969. (Closed March 2, 1969)

Directed by Demetrius Ambandos; scenery and costumes, Mischa Petrow; lighting, Michael Davidson; stage manager, Clifford Ammon; press, Sol Jacobson, Lewis Harmon. With Jon Barron, John Carpenter, Vera Lockwood, Salem Ludwig and Myrna Strom.
Portrays how American women figuratively castrate their man.

Spitting Image (49). By Colin Spencer. Produced by Zev Bufman in association with Columbia Pictures by arrangement with Oscar Lewenstein and Donald Flamm at the Theater de Lys. Opened March 2, 1969. (Closed April 13, 1969)

Tom Dart ....Walter McGinn	
Gary Rogers ....Sam Waterston	
Doctor, Psychiatrist, Perkins, Dr. Grapielkoff ....Phil Bruns	
Nun, Supervisor, Grey Lady, Mrs. Dart, Landlady, Miss Saunders ....Barbara Cason	
Sally ....Madeleine Fisher	
Intern ....Wil Albert	

Directed by Michael Gil; scenery, Edward Burbridge; costumes, Fred Voelpel; lighting, Jack Blackman; music composed by Arthur Rubinstein; American adaptation, Godfrey Danvers; presented by special arrangement with Lucille Lortel Productions, Inc.; production stage manager, Bud Coffey; press, Robert Ganshaw & John Prescott.

The play was presented without intermission. Comedy-fantasy in which a male homosexual couple has a baby. A foreign play previously produced in London.

The Millionairess (16). Revival of the play by George Bernard Shaw. Produced by Edgar Lansbury and Alexander E. Racolin at the Sheridan Square Playhouse. Opened March 2, 1969. (Closed March 16, 1969)

Julius Sagamore	Robert Moberly	Doctor	Nicholas Kepros
Epipfania	Barbara Caruso	Man	Kermit Brown
Alistair Fitzfassenden	Peter Coffeen	Woman	Liz Engleson
Patricia Smith	Marla Lennard	Manager	Nicholas Martin
Adrian Blenderbland	Tom Lacy		

Directed by Philip Minor; scenery, John Wright Stevens; costumes, Carrie Fishbein Robbins; lighting, Barry Arnold; stage manager, Frank Schmitt; press, Max Eisen.

The Millionairess was last revived on Broadway 10/17/52 at the Shubert Theater for 83 performances with Katharine Hepburn in the leading role.

Of Thee I Sing (21). Musical revival with book by George S. Kaufman and Morrie Ryskind; music by George Gershwin; lyrics by Ira Gershwin. Produced by Musical Heritage Productions at the New Anderson Theater. Opened March 7, 1969. (Closed March 23, 1969)

Sen. Robert E. Lyons	Edward Penn	Emily Benson	Joyce Orlando
Frances X. Gilhooley	Sandy Sprung	Mary Turner	Joy Franz
Chambermaid; Tourist	Jeannie Johnsen	Chief Justice	Bob Freschi
Matthew Arnold Fulton	William Martel	Guide; Doctor	Richard Stack
Sen. Carver Jones	John Aman	Tourist	Gale Swymer
Alexander Throttlebottom	Lloyd Hubbard	French Ambassador	Larry Whiteley
John P. Wintergreen	Hal Holden	Scrubwoman	Dorothy Lister
Diana Devereaux	Katie Anders	Senate Clerk	Ronald Dennis
Sam Jenkins	Danny Franklin		

Singing and dancing ensemble: Joan Ashlyn, Ronald Dennis, Bob Freschi, Jeannie Johnsen, Linda Larson, Dorothy Lister, Richard Stack, Gayle Swymer, Robert Yarri.

Directed by Marvin Gordon; choreography, Michael C. Penta; musical director, dance & special arrangements, Leslie Harnley; design, Bob Olson; costumes, James Bidgood; lighting, William Marshall; assistant director, Larry Whiteley; press, Sol Jacobson, Lewis Harmon.

Act I, Scene 1: The Parade (Main Street). Scene 2: The Committee (Hotel Room). Scene 3: The Contest (Atlantic City). Scene 4: The Rally (Madison Square Garden). Scene 5: The Returns (Election Night). Scene 6: The Inauguration (Washington). Act II, Scene 1: The New Administration (The White House). Scene 2: The Impeachment (The Capitol; The Senate). Scene 3: The Happy Ending (White House; Yellow Room). Scene designations in parentheses are those of a previous production of this musical.

Of Thee I Sing was first produced on Broadway 12/26/31 at the Music Box for 441 performances. It became the first musical to be designated a Best Play and to win the Pulitzer Prize. It reappeared on Broadway 5/15/33 at the Imperial theater for a return engagement of 32 performances, and was revived 5/5/52 at the Ziegfeld Theater for 72 performances.

ACT I

"Wintergreen for President" ....Company
"Because" ....Diana, Jenkins, Ensemble
Finaletto for Scene 3 ....Wintergreen, Diana, Committee, Ensemble
"Love Is Sweeping the Country" ....Jenkins, Benson, Ensemble
"Of Thee I Sing" ....Wintergreen, Mary, Ensemble
Finale for Act I ....Company

ACT II

"Hello, Good Morning" ....Jenkins, Benson, Ensemble
"Who Cares?" ....Wintergreen, Mary, Committee, Male Ensemble
"The Illegitimate Daughter"; Finaletto for Scene 1 ....French Entourage, Ambassador,
Wintergreen, Mary, Diana, Ensemble

"Love Is Sweeping the Country" (Reprise) ....Mary, Throttlebottom, Wintergreen
"The Illegitimate Daughter" (Reprise); "Jilted" ....French Ambassador, Diana, Ensemble
Mary's Announcement ....Mary, Ensemble
"Posterity" ....Wintergreen, Mary, Company
"Trumpeter, Blow Your Golden Horn" ....Benson, Jenkins, Female Ensemble
Finale ....Company

Frank Gagliano's City Scene (16). Program of two one-act plays by Frank Gagliano: *Paradise Gardens East* and a revival of *Conerico Was Here To Stay*. Produced by Doris Kuller and Simon L. Saltzman at the Fortune Theater. Opened March 10, 1969. (Closed March 23, 1969)

CITY SCENE I:
PARADISE GARDENS EAST

Workmen ....Dominic Chianese, Terry Kiser, Raul Julia
Sis ....Lynn Milgrim
Mrs. Super ....Fran Stevens
Brother ....Lenny Baker
William Saroyan O'Neill ....M.K. Douglas
Narrator ....Phillip Giambri

Musical numbers (lyrics by Frank Gagliano; music by Mildred Kayden): "Harmony" and "The Beat of the City"—Workmen; "I'll Bet You're a Cat Girl" and "Gussy and the Beautiful People"—Mrs. Super; "Look at My Sister," "Black and Blue Pumps" and "That's Right Mr. Syph"—Brother; "The Incinerator Hour"—William Saroyan O'Neill.

CITY SCENE II:
CONERICO WAS HERE TO STAY

Yam ....Terry Kiser
Blind Man ....Dominic Chianese
Woman ....Fran Stevens
Girl with Cello ....Lynn Milgrim
Boy with Eye Patch ....M.K. Douglas
Young Man ....Lenny Baker
Jesus ....Raul Julia

Directed by Neil Israel; scenery and lighting, David F. Segal; costumes, John David Ridge; musical arrangements, Wolfgang Knittel; associate producer, Wendy Levine; production supervisor, Frank C. Prince; production associate, Kerry Haymen; production stage manager, Stephen Jarrett; press, Robert Ganshaw & John Prescott.

PARADISE GARDENS EAST—Place: A newly-painted efficiency on New York's Upper East Side. Like *Conerico*, this one-acter is about urban violence.

CONERICO WAS HERE TO STAY—Place: A subway platform. Originally produced off Broadway in the Theater 1965 New Playwrights Series 3/3/65 at the Cherry Lane Theater for 21 performances.

Stop, You're Killing Me (39). Program of three one-act plays by James Leo Herlihy: *Laughs, Etc., Terrible Jim Fitch* and *Bad Bad Jo-Jo*. Produced by Dick Duane in the Theater Company of Boston production at Stage 73. Opened March 19, 1969. (Closed April 20, 1969)

LAUGHS, ETC.

Gloria ....Sasha von Scherler

TERRIBLE JIM FITCH

Lonesome Sally ....Rochelle Oliver   Terrible Jim Fitch ....Larry Bryggman

BAD BAD JO-JO

Kayo Hathaway ....William Young   Dennis ....Phillip Piro
Frank ....Matthew Cowles

Directed by David Wheeler; production designed by Robert Allen; music, Boynton-Devinney; lighting, Ray Long; production supervisor, Frank Cassidy; production stage manager, Robert Stevenson; press, Ben Kornzweig, Reginald Denenholz, Fred Weterick.

LAUGHS, ETC.—Place: An apartment in the East Village. Monologue by an insensitive matron describing unhappy developments at a party in her apartment.

TERRIBLE JIM FITCH—Place: A motel room on Route 66 near Albuquerque, N.M. A thief who has scarred his mistress's face tries to persuade her to forgive him.

BAD BAD JO-JO—Place: Kayo's penthouse apartment in Sutton Place. Black comedy about a popular novelist, supposedly being interviewed by an inept questioner.

The Perfect Party (21). By Charles H. Fuller Jr. Produced by Jeff G. Britton at Tambellini's Gate Theater. Opened March 20, 1969. (Closed April 6, 1969)

Ed	Woodie King	Bella	Tracee Lyles
Laura	Susan Willerman	Mark	Victor Eschbach
Cornish	Art Wallace	Jill	Beverly Hayes
Kate	Ceci Perrin	Leon	Harold Miller
Helen	Virginia Kiser	Nick	Moses Gunn

Directed by Perry Bruskin; scenery and lighting, Kert Lundell; costumes, Bernard Johnson; associate producer, Ruth Kalkstein; production stage manager, Michael Frank; press, David Lipsky, M.J. Boyer.

Concerns five interracial couples. Previously produced at Princeton, N.J.

World War 2½ (1). By Roger O. Hirson. Produced by Gerald Freeman, Julien J. Studley, Joseph S. Siegel, Seymour Vall in association with IPC at the Martinique Theater. Opened and closed at the evening performance March 24, 1969.

Directed by Arthur Sherman; scenery, Eugene Lee; costumes, Jeanne Button; lighting, Roger Morgan; original music composed and performed by The Open Window; production stage manager, Janet Beroza; press, Freeman-Halpern-Maisel, Inc. With Robert Loggia, Kathleen Widdoes.

Eternal war between sexes.

Lime Green Khaki Blue (14). Program of two one-act plays by Ben Piazza. Produced by Lawrence P. Fraiberg at the Provincetown Playhouse. Opened March 26, 1969. (Closed April 6, 1969)

Directed by Peter Masterson; scenery and lighting, C. Murawski; production stage manager, Martha Knight; press, Chester Fox, Harold Rand & Company, Inc. With Clinton Allmon, Dolores Dorn-Heft, Louise Lasser, Robert Walden.

Lime Green is the meeting, wooing and bedding of a pair of virgins. In *Khaki Blue*, a Southern belle has turned promiscuous after her lover was killed.

God Bless You, Harold Fineberg (9). By Maxine Fleischman. Produced by Paul Scott at the Actors Playhouse. Opened March 30, 1969. (Closed April 6, 1969)

Directed by Sherwood Arthur; scenery and costumes, Richard Fuhrman; lighting, Barbara Nollman; stage manager, Gage Andretta; press, Vasiliki Sarant. With Hy Anzell, Sylvia Gassell, Marty Greene, Natalie Priest.

An unhappy housewife rents an off-Broadway theater in order to psychoanalyze her husband, father and best friend.

Someone's Comin' Hungry (16). By McCrea Imbrie and Neil Selden. Produced by Preston Fischer and Bruce W. Paltrow at the Pocket Theater. Opened March 31, 1969. (Closed April 13, 1969)

Paul Odum	Cleavon Little	Connie Odum	Blythe Danner
Tamara Bissy	Jonelle Allen	Mrs. Gershon	Jane Hoffman
James C. Odum	W. Benson Terry		

Directed by Burt Brinckerhoff; scenery, Robert D. Mitchell; costumes, Joseph G. Aulisi; lighting, Jules Fisher; associate producer, Mitchell Fink; production stage manager, David Semonin; press, Ben Kornzweig, Reginald Denenholz, Anne Woll.

Place: The Odum apartment in the East Village, Manhattan. Act I: An April day, late afternoon. Act II: Four days later.

About an interracial couple, living with the husband's father and expecting a baby.

Le Tréteau de Paris. Schedule of two programs in the French language. **Quoat-Quoat** (10). By Jacques Audiberti. Opened April 13, 1969. (Closed April 27, 1969). **Pique-Nique en Campagne** and **Guernica** (15). Program of two one-act plays by Fernando Arrabal. Opened April 30, 1969. (Closed May 14, 1969). Produced by Le Tréteau de Paris, Jean de Rigault executive director, in cooperation with Jacques Courtines and Seff Associates at the Barbizon-Plaza Theater.

QUOAT-QUOAT

Le Capitaine	Jacques Dumesnil	Le Gendarme	Michel Fortin
Amédée	Jean-Pierre Leroux	La Mexicaine	Antoinette Moya
Le Mousse	Jacques Audoux	Madame Batrilant	Jacqueline Duc
Clarisse	Jacqueline Coué		

Directed by Georges Vitaly; scenery and costumes, Jacques Marillier; produced by special arrangement with the Théâtre La Bruyère.

Comedy, an allegory in the form of a voyage in search of Maximilian's treasure in Mexico. Previously produced in Paris.

PIQUE-NIQUE EN CAMPAGNE

Zapo	Michel Degand	Zépo	Yves-Marie Maurin
Monsieur Tepan	Pierre Leroux	1er Brancardier	Pierre Peyrou
Madame Tepan	Arlette Thomas	2ième Brancardier	Marc Jolivet

GUERNICA

Fanchou	Pierre Leroux	L'ecrivain	Pierre Peyrou
Lira	Arlette Thomas	Journaliste	Marc Jolivet

Directed by Pierre Peyrou; *Pique-Nique en Campagne* scenery and costumes, Jean-Paul Vieuille; *Guernica* decor, Rafael Esteve.

Pique-Nique en Campagne is theater of the absurd applied to war, as a soldier's parents visit him for a picnic at the front. *Guernica* is an allegory of loneliness and death among the falling bombs.

ALL PLAYS produced by Jean de Rigault under the sponsorship of L'Association Française D'Action Artistique of the Government of the French Republic and with the patronage of Edouard Morot-Sir, Cultural Counselor to the French Embassy in the United States; stage manager, Harry Abbott; press, Arthur Cantor.

War Games (22). By Neal Weaver. Produced by Rick Mandell in association with Jim Stevenson at the Fortune Theater. Opened April 17, 1969. (Closed May 4, 1969)

John Flagstad	Don Warfield	General Patrick Flagstad	Shev Rodgers
Mrs. Moylan	Dorothy Greener	Anastasia Flagstad	June Graham
Ted Montefiore	Jean-Claude Vasseux	Sandra Cates	Jane Whitehill

Directed by James E. Dwyer; scenery, Neil Jampolis; lighting, Dennis Parichy; costumes, Victor Joris; stage manager, Hank Schob; press, Robert Ganshaw & John Prescott, Warren Pincus, Ted Goldsmith.

Time: Spring. Place: Small one-room apartment in a private house near University of Toronto. Act I, Scene 1: Early evening, Saturday. Scene 2: The following morning, Sunday. Act II, Scene 1: Early the following morning, Monday. Scene 2: Late in the day, just before nightfall.

About two draft dodgers in Canada and their homosexual relationship.

The Honest-to-God Schnozzola (8). Program of two one-act plays by Israel Horovitz: *Leader* and the title play. Produced by Jay H. Fuchs, Barry Diamond, David G. Meyers in association with Victor Resnick at the Gramercy Arts Theater. Opened April 21, 1969. (Closed April 26, 1969)

Directed by Rip Torn; associate producer, E.H. Davis; music, John Hall; lyrics, Israel Horovitz; scenery, Charles Brandon; lighting, Roger Morgan; associate director, Timmy Everett; press, Howard Atlee, David Roggensack. With David Edgell, Julie Garfield, Salem Ludwig, Lane Smith, Hervé Villechaize, Ann Wedgeworth.

The Honest-to-God Schnozzola is the symbolic adventure of two Americans in a West German cabaret. *Leader* is an American political allegory told in terms of a bad vaudeville act.

* **The Man with the Flower in His Mouth** (46). Program of three one-act plays by Luigi Pirandello; American translation by William Murray. Produced by Morel Productions at the Sheridan Square Playhouse. Opened April 22, 1969.

THE MAN WITH THE FLOWER IN HIS MOUTH

A Commuter ....Tony Capodilupo	The Man ....Jay Novello

THE LICENSE

Judge D'Andrea ....Mitchell Jason	2d Judge ....Steve Parris
Marranca ....Danny De Vito	Rosinella ....Claire Malis
1st Judge ....Tony Capodilupo	Rosario Chiarchiaro ....Jay Novello

THE JAR

Carminella ....Claire Malis	Mule Driver ....Leonhard Britton
Trisuzza ....Gloria Tofano	Scime' ....Mitchell Jason
Tana ....Alberta Cuozzo	Tarara' ....Joseph Della Sorte
The Repeater ....Pat Maniccia	Fillico' ....Steve Parris
Friend Pe' ....Danny De Vito	Uncle Dima Lirasi ....Jay Novello
Don Lolo' Zirafa ....Tony Capodilupo	

Directed by Michael Simone; scenery and lighting, C. Murawski; costumes, Robert J. Pusilo; production stage manager, Gigi Cascio; press, Jane Friedman, Rod Jacobson.

The Man with the Flower in His Mouth—Time: After midnight. Place: The sidewalk in front of an all-night cafe in some large city. Details of life become more meaningful to a man who has been told he has a fatal disease.

The License—Place: The chambers of Judge D'Andrea in a small provincial town of Southern Italy. American premiere, a phony warlock tries to have his supernatural powers authenticated.

The Jar—Time: Late October, late in the afternoon. Place: A Sicilian countryside. American premiere, handyman accidentally glues himself into a huge earthen jug.

* **Ceremonies in Dark Old Men** (38). Second 1968-69 production of the play by Lonne Elder III. Produced by Michael Ellis at the Pocket Theater. Opened April 28, 1969.

Mr. Russell B. Parker ....Richard Ward	Adele Eloise Parker ....Bette Howard
Mr. William Jenkins ....Arnold Johnson	Blue Haven ....Carl Lee
Theopolis Parker ....Billy Dee Williams	Young Girl ....Denise Nicholas
Bobby Parker ....Richard Mason	

Directed by Edmund Cambridge; scenery, Whitney Le Blanc; costumes, Gertha Brock; lighting, Shirley Prendergast; stage manager, Nate Barnett; press, Howard Atlee, David Roggensack.

Ceremonies in Dark Old Men was first produced this season by the Negro Ensemble Company at St. Marks Playhouse 2/4/69 for 40 performances (see its separate entry in this listing).

A Home Away From (8). By Glenn Allen Smith. Produced by Jane Reid Petty at the Village South Theater. Opened April 28, 1969. (Closed May 4, 1969)

Directed by Ivan Rider; scenery, Frank Hains; lighting, David F. Segal; costumes, Sara Brook; production stage manager, Dale Whitman; press, Ben Kornzweig, Reginald Denenholz, Anne Woll. With Bruce Davison, Sue Jones, Christopher Wines.

Triangle composed of a high school teacher, his wife and a former pupil renting a room in their house.

The Triumph of Robert Emmet (15). By Bache McEvers Whitlock. Produced by the Frances Adler Theater, Ltd. in association with Sarah B. Dona at the Frances Adler Theater. Opened May 7, 1969. (Closed May 18, 1969)

Directed by Neil Flanagan; music and lyrics, Lou Rodgers, costumes and lighting, David Adams; scenery, Elwin Charles Terrell II; stage manager, Judith Kayser; press, Howard Atlee, David Roggensack. With Jeremy Brooks, Julia Curry, Stephen Harrison, Pat McNamara and Jean Robbins.

Drama about the Irish patriot, by a direct descendant of his brother.

* In the Bar of a Tokyo Hotel (23). By Tennessee Williams. Produced by Richard Lee Marks and Henry Jaffe at the Eastside Playhouse. Opened May 11, 1969.

Barman	Jon Lee	Hawaiian Lady	Elsa Raven
Miriam	Anne Meacham	Leonard	Lester Rawlins
Mark	Donald Madden		

Directed by Herbert Machiz; scenery and lighting, Neil Peter Jampolis; costumes, Stanley Simmons; musical effects, Hayward Morris; production stage manager, George Rondo; press, Frank Goodman, Ruth Cage.

Time: The present. Place: The bar of a Toyko hotel. Part I: Mid-day. Part II: Noon, a few days later.

An artist on his last legs of talent and endurance gets no help from his selfish wife.

* De Sade Illustrated (22). By Josef Bush, from an original idea by Bill Haislip; translated and adapted from *Philosophy in the Boudoir* by the Marquis de Sade. Produced by Lester Persky at the Bouwerie Lane Theater. Opened May 12, 1969.

The Stage Manager	Bill Haislip	The Cavalier	Dale Reynolds
Madame Angela	Ann Sweeny	Dolmance	David Gallagher
Eugenie	Zita Litvinas		

Directed by Walter Burns; scenery, Josef Bush, Bill Haislip; costumes, Andrew Greenhut; lighting, Leo B. Meyer; produced in association with Divine Marquis Co. and Cinemex, Intl.; production stage manager, Lindsay Law; press, Robert Ganshaw & John Prescott, Ted Goldsmith, Warren Pincus.

Time: Now. Place: Wherever the play is performed. The play was presented in two acts.

Six de Sade episodes of the boudoir are narrated and mimed and illustrated with slide projections—the first of two 1968-69 adaptations of this de Sade work (see separate entry on *Philosophy in the Boudoir* in this listing).

Make Me Disappear (7). By Marjorie L. Stuart and J. Marberger Stuart. Produced by J. Marberger Stuart at the Mercury Theater. Opened May 13, 1969. (Closed May 18, 1969)

Directed by Michael Holmes; lighting. V.C. Fuqua; costumes, A. Christina Giannini; stage manager, Robert Buzzell; press, Bernard Simon. With Terri Baker, Judy Guyll, Vinnie Holman, Jana Klenburg, Richard Marr, Charles Regan, Rosemary Shevlin, Del Shorter, Maureen Tionco, Ron Vaad, Fred Vinroot, Valerie von Volz.

Magic show with a plot about a menaced man seeking a magician's help.

Pets (15). Program of three one-act plays by Richard Reich: *Baby with a Knife, Silver Grey Toy Poodle* and the title play. Produced by Jack Beekman and Jules Itts in association with Roy Baxter at the Provincetown Playhouse. Opened May 14, 1969. (Closed May 25, 1969)

Directed by Tony Calabrese; scenery, Hui Mei Lin; costumes, Gene Galvin; lighting, Ed Devany; stage manager, Raymond Thorne; press, Max Eisen. With Marlene Clark, William Grannell, Frances Helm, Carol E. Marnay, Laura Wallace, Alan Weeks.

Trio of sadistic concepts, about people who dominate, brutalize and even encage others.

Exhibition (6). By Frank Spiering. Produced by William J. Addy at the Actors Playhouse. Opened May 15, 1969. (Closed May 18, 1969)

Directed by Paul Bengston; scenery and lighting, David F. Segal; costumes, Deidre Cartier; sound collage, Mildred Kayden; stage manager, Kirk Morris; press, Robert Ganshaw & John Prescott, Ted Goldsmith, Warren Pincus. With Morgan Freeman, Jeanne Rostaing and Vera Lockwood.

About witchcraft.

* Spiro Who? (15). By William Meyers; music composed and recorded by Phil Ochs. Produced by Robert L. Steele at Tambellini's Gate Theater. Opened May 18, 1969.

Christopher Endal	Oliver Clark	Mrs. Ferngrow	Anne Shropshire
Stuart Ferngrow	Ryan Listman	1st Dopester	Mike Mearian
Neil Lapides	James J. Sloyan	2d Dopester	Peter Collins
Elsie Sondheim	Mary Hamill	Mr. Endal	Henry Calvert

Directed by Bernard Barrow; scenery, Eldon Elder; costumes, Winn Morton; lighting, Howard Becknell; production stage manager, Ron Abbott; press, Sol Jacobson, Lewis Harmon.

Time: Midnight. Place: A college apartment. The play was presented without intermission.

Three about-to-be-graduates express their ideals and discontentments in three episodes.

The Transgressor Rides Again (1). By Aldo Giunta. Produced by Jerome Rudolph and Fred Entman at the Martinique Theater. Opened and closed at the evening performance May 20, 1969.

Directed by Hal Raywin; scenery, Robert Guerra; costumes, Joseph G. Aulisi; lighting, Dennis Parichy; sound, Walter Gustafson; stage manager, Joel Foster; press, John Springer Associates, Louise Weiner, Howard Haines. With David Carradine, Aurelia De Felice, James Hall, Patrick McVey, John Newton, Tom Spratley.

A hippie Christ-symbol in a small Southern town.

* Philosophy in the Boudoir (13). By Eric Kahane; adapted from the play by the Marquis de Sade; English translation by Alex Szogyi. Produced by Noel Weiss and Leonard Soloway at the Gramercy Arts Theater. Opened May 21, 1969.

Chevalier de Mirvel	DeVeren Bookwalter	Lapierre; Sans Culotte	Vincent Baggetta
Mme. de Saint-Ange	Gwyda Donhowe	Dolmance	Dean Santoro
Maid; Knitting Girl	Joan Shepard	Augustin	Gordon Fearing
Eugenie de Mistival	Anna Shaler	Mme. de Mistival	Sylvia Gassell

Directed by Tom Gruenewald; scenery and lighting, Clarke Dunham; costumes, Joseph F. Bella; production stage manager, Bruce Coffey; stage manager, Philip Larson; press, Merle Debuskey, M.J. Boyer, Faith Geer.

Time: The spring of 1790. Place: The boudoir and bedroom of Mme. de Saint-Ange's country house not far from Paris. The play was presented without intermission.

Second of this season's two versions of the de Sade work about the sex education of a young girl by a group of libertines (see separate entry on *De Sade Illustrated* in this listing). This version is a foreign play previously produced in Paris 10/9/64 and shut down after 7 performances.

Arf and **The Great Airplane Snatch** (5). Program of two one-act plays by Dan Greenburg. Produced by David Dretzin at Stage 73. Opened May 27, 1969. (Closed May 31, 1969)

Directed by Richard Benjamin; scenery and costumes, Marsha Eck; lighting, Neil Peter Jampolis; stage manager, George Blanchard; press, Dorothy Ross, Fred Weterick. With Nancy Douglas, Lawrence Pressman, Lily Tomlin, Fred Willard, Joe Young.

In *Arf* a female dog is transformed into a woman. In *The Great Airplane Snatch* a young man is held aboard an airliner by the pilot and stewardess.

Some Additional Productions

This selected listing of off-off-Broadway and other experimental productions was compiled by R.J. Schroeder (see his article on the 1968-69 off-off-Broadway scene in "The Season in New York" section of this volume). Leading producing groups are identified in alphabetical order in **bold face type** and examples of their outstanding 1968-69 work are noted. Performances, opening dates and other details are given when available, but in most cases there was no premiere or engagement of record.

Afro-American Studio. This Harlem-based performing group led by Ernie McClintock features works from the Afro-American literature. Typical of the works presented was:

BLACK NATIVITY by Langston Hughes. Directed by Ernie McClintock.

The American Theater Club. Richard Kuss and Alice Scudder co-promote this group's series of revivals of American near-classics. Notable among this season's presentations in the auditorium of the Church of the Holy Communion were:

THE DOUBLE AXE by Robinson Jeffers, as adapted and directed by Richard Kuss.

PYRAMUS AND THISBE and THE SALON, two plays by Henry James. Directed by Ellis Santone.

ANTA Matinee Theater Series. The Series, sponsored by the American National Theater and Academy, presented 4 productions in its 13th season under the direction of Lucille Lortel at the Theater de Lys.

HELLO AND GOODBYE by Athol Fugard (2). November 11 and 12, 1968. Directed by Barney Simon.

CUBA SI by Terrence McNally, and GUNS OF CARRAR by Bertolt Brecht (2). December 9 and 10, 1968. Directed by Harris Yulin.

NEIGHBORS by James Saunders, directed by John Chace, and THE PROJECTION ROOM by Robert Somerfeld, directed by Kenneth Harvey (2). January 13 and 14, 1969.

AGEE, a selection from the writings and films of James Agee, arranged by David McDowell, directed by Paul Leaf (2). February 10 and 11, 1969. Music by Robert Dennis.

Cafe 4. The only off-off-Broadway house specializing in Latin-American playwrights presented in English. Typical of this season's presentations was:

THE ELEVATOR by Nelly Vivas. Directed by George Dal Lago.

Chelsea Theater Center. This experimental play production unit originated in Manhattan's Chelsea district, and has now moved to the newly-remodelled "Third Stage" of the Brooklyn Academy of Music, where it presents a series of new works. Among this year's presentations were:

THE INNOCENT PARTY and THE WAX
MUSEUM by John Hawkes. Directed by Robert Kalfin.

A BLACK QUARTET, four plays by Ed
Bullins, Ben Caldwell, Ronald Milner, and
LeRoi Jones. Directed by Woodie King.

The Cooper Square Arts Theater. This house, under new management this season,
books packages prepared outside its jurisdiction. Outstanding among the presentations this season was:

GEORGIE-PORGIE by George Birimisa, directed by the author.

CSC Repertory. Christopher Martin's troupe has recently reopened downtown at
273 Bleecker St. after several years in the Rutgers Church uptown. Classic and
reputable "establishment" plays are presented in repertory. Among this season's
works were:

THE CAVERN by Jean Anouilh. Directed
by Christopher Martin.

THE REVENGER'S TRAGEDY by Cyril
Tourneur. Directed by Christopher Martin.

Equity Library Theater. The following plays were produced by Equity Library Theater at the Master Theater:

OF THEE I SING (15). Musical with book
by George S. Kaufman and Morrie Ryskind,
lyrics by Ira Gershwin, music by George
Gershwin. October 18, 1968. Directed by
Marvin Gordon, choreography by Michael C.
Penta.

ALL MY SONS (9). By Arthur Miller. November 15, 1968. Directed by Albert Lipton.

AS YOU LIKE IT (9). By William Shakespeare. December 6, 1968. Directed by Robert Moss.

FIVE FINGER EXERCISE (9). By Peter
Shaffer. January 10, 1969. Directed by Gail
Bell.

SACCO-VANZETTI! (15). Musical with
book and lyrics by Armand Aulicino, and

music and orchestration by Frank Gaskin
Fields. February 7, 1969. Directed by Allan
Lokos, choreography by Diane Adler.

PURLIE VICTORIOUS (9). By Ossie Davis.
March 7, 1969. Directed by Gordon Hunt.

NIGHT MUST FALL (9). By Emlyn Williams. March 28, 1969. Directed by Clifford
V. Ammon.

SHE LOVES ME (15). Musical with book
by Joe Masteroff, lyrics by Sheldon Harnick,
music by Jerry Bock. April 18, 1969. Directed
by Leland Ball.

ACCENT ON YOUTH (9). By Samson Ra-
phaelson. May 16, 1969. Directed by Charlie
Briggs.

Equity Theater Informals. The following shows were among those presented by
Equity Library Theater in early-evening or matinee performances at the Library
and Museum of the Performing Arts at Lincoln Center:

OX-ROAST (3). By Dolores Walker and
Andrew Piotrowski. October 21, 1968. Directed by Chuck Vincent.

JOHN BROWN'S BODY (3). By Stephen

Vincent Benet. March 3, 1969. Directed by
Neil Flanagan.

THE DRINKING PARTY (3). An adaptation of the dialogues of Plato by Paul Shyre.
March 17, 1969. Directed by Paul Shyre.

The Extension. Walter Leyden Brown's theater club presents both new and established works in a beautiful church chapel at 277 Park Ave. South—one of the most
esthetically pleasing off-off-Broadway arenas. Recent productions included:

THE WHITE WHORE AND THE BIT
PLAYER by Tom Eyen. Directed by Ron
Link.

LEONCE AND LENA by Georg Büchner.
Directed by Peter Wilson Strader.

LE GRAND PANIC CIRCUS, an intentionally anonymous concoction by cohorts of the Spanish-French playwright Arrabal, played by a traveling company of its perpetrators.

Free Store Theater. Paradoxically, off-off-Broadway's most expensive ticket. Ed Wode's enterprise features advanced nudity and sexual maneuvering. The season's most publicized "attractions":

GIZMO DOES THE AUDITION by Dan Daniels. Directed by Ed Wode.

CHE! by Lennox Raphael. Directed by Ed Wode.

James Weldon Johnson Theater Arts Center. Under Mical Whitaker's direction, this group presents plays of particular interest to a Harlem and Spanish Harlem audience. Among the presentations were:

MESSAGE FROM THE GRASSROOTS by Robert Riche. Directed by Mical Whitaker.

A RAISIN IN THE SUN by Lorraine Hansberry. Directed by Mical Whitaker.

The Judson Poets Theater. Under the supervision of Al Carmines, and "house director" Lawrence Kornfeld, new plays or adaptations of established plays are presented in the large Sanford White-designed auditorium, or in an intimate loft. Noteworthy among this season's productions were:

PEACE, a free adaptation of the Aristophanes play by Timothy Reynolds, with music by Al Carmines. Directed by Lawrence Kornfeld. (A revised version of this production was subsequently presented off Broadway.)

ARENAS OF LUTETIA, by Ronald Tavel. Directed by the author.

La Mama Experimental Theater Club. Ellen Stewart's pioneer off-off-Broadway unit, after having been dark for most of the season while its new quarters were being readied, opened temporarily in a storeroom on St. Marks Place, and then, in the spring of 1969, began operations on two stages in its new home in a four-story building on 4th Street in the East Village. The work of the Plexus group, strongly influenced by Grotowski's Polish Laboratory Theater, is house-controlled. But most of the productions continue to be packages originating and rehearsed off the premises. Recent productions included:

FOUR NO PLAYS by Tom Eyen, directed by the author.

NEVER TELL ISOBEL by John Gruen. Directed by Gaby Rodgers.

The Living Theater. Julian Beck's and Judith Malina's itinerant troupe played a three-week season, and a short repeat engagement, at the Brooklyn Academy of Music. 4 productions were presented in repertory:

FRANKENSTEIN, created by the Living Theater Company. October 2, 1968. Directed by Julian Beck and Judith Malina.

MYSTERIES AND SMALLER PIECES, created by the Living Theater Company. October 9, 1968. Directed by Julian Beck and Judith Malina.

THE ANTIGONE OF SOPHOKLES, as adapted by Judith Malina from the Bertolt Brecht adaptation. Matinee, October 10, 1968. Directed by Julian Beck and Judith Malina.

PARADISE NOW, created by the Living Theater Company. October 14, 1968. Directed by Julian Beck and Judith Malina.

The Mannhardt Theater Foundation, Inc. The production unit of the Mannhardt theater school mounts 6 to 7 productions a year, usually under "house" direction. Among this year's presentations were:

CLAUDINE, by Don Kvares, as adapted by Robert Schroeder, directed by John Chace.

VIMAZOLULEKA, by Levy Rossell, directed by the author.

The New Lafayette Theater. Under the supervision of Robert Macbeth, plays by black authors are presented by and for blacks. Whites are not excluded, nor are they invited. Noteworthy among this year's works was:

WHO'S GOT HIS OWN by Ronald Milner, a revival of the play originally presented at the American Place Theater, in a radically revised staging by Robert Macbeth.

OM Theater Workshop. Based in Boston, this troupe presented a New York run of a Boston success in the Broadway United Church of Christ auditorium.

RIOT, created by the OM Theater Workshop, under the direction of Julie A. Portman.

The Open Theater. Offshoot of The Living Theater, this troupe, led by Joseph Chaikin, features group-improvised "improvements" of new or old scripts. Major productions this season were:

THE SERPENT: A CEREMONY, created by the Open Theater ensemble, words and structure by Jean-Claude van Itallie. Directed by Joseph Chaikin.

UBU COCU by Alfred Jarry, as translated by Albert Bermel. Music by Walter Caldon. Directed by Peter Feldman.

The Other Stage. Joseph Papp's workshop for new plays and playwrights operates in the Public Theater. Representative of this year's work were:

ROMAINIA THAT'S THE OLD COUNTRY by Allen Joseph. Directed by Amy Saltz.

NO PLACE TO BE SOMEBODY by Charles

Gordone. Directed by Ted Cornell. (Named a Best Play of 1968-69 in a subsequent off-Broadway production by Joseph Papp.)

The Performance Group. Richard Schechner's outgrowth of the acting class Jerzy Grotowski of the Polish Laboratory Theater taught at NYU. Grapplings, writhings, moanings in the neo-modern manner. Current production is:

DIONYSUS IN '69, an "environmental theater" production of an uncredited adaptation of Euripides's *The Bacchae*. Directed by Richard Schechner.

Playbox Studio. Robert Weinstein's facility is devoted almost equally to packages prepared outside, and to revivals he himself directs. This year's work included:

A DAY IN THE LIFE OF by Michael Shurtleff, directed by Michael Holmes.

FALLEN ANGELS by Noel Coward. Directed by Robert Weinstein.

Roundabout Theater. Off-off-Broadway's most successful, both artistically and financially, repertory theater, supervised by Gene Feist, and usually presenting plays he directs. Included this season were:

JOURNEY'S END by R. C. Sherriff. Directed by Gene Feist.

CANDIDA by George Bernard Shaw. Directed by Gene Feist.

KING LEAR by William Shakespeare. Directed by Gene Feist.

Theater Genesis. The East Village's established outpost of the "far-out", as explored under the aegis of Ralph Cook. The season's most gone:

THE HUNTER by Murray Mednick. Directed by Ralph Cook.

Thresholds. Led by Donna Carlson and John Parkinson, this experimental theater group is among New York's most artistically responsible. The season's work included:

THE SUNDAY PROMENADE by Lars Forssell. Directed by Donna Carlson.

FINNEGANS WAKE by James Joyce, as adapted for the stage and directed by David Kerry Heefner.

Universalist Theater. An uptown troupe led by James Monos, specializing in the classics and near-classics. Recent productions included:

THE UNDERPANTS by Carl Sternheim. Directed by James Monos.

Workshop of the Players' Art. David Gale has moved and re-named his former Der Grüne Kakadu operation. He either directs himself, or supervises closely, the productions at the WPA. Outstanding among this season's presentations was:

THE GAMBLER by Ugo Betti. Directed by David Gale.

CAST REPLACEMENTS AND TOURING COMPANIES

The following is a listing of the more important cast replacements in productions which opened in previous years, but which were still playing in New York during a substantial part of the 1968-69 season; or were still on a first-class tour; or opened in 1968-69 and cast a first-class touring company in that same season. The name of the character is listed in italics beneath the title of the play in the first column, and in the second column appears the name of the actor who created the role. Immediately beneath the actor's name are subsequent replacements. The third column gives information about first-class touring companies of these shows (produced under the auspices of their original Broadway managements). Where there is more than one roadshow company, #1, #2, #3, etc. appear before the name of the performer who created the role in each company. Their subsequent replacements, if any, are listed beneath. A note on bus-truck touring companies appears at the end of this section.

	NEW YORK COMPANY	TOURING COMPANIES
THE BOYS IN THE BAND		
Michael	Kenneth Nelson 4/15/68	#1 Kenneth Nelson 2/11/69
	Eric James 1/25/69	#2 Dennis Cooney 3/10/69
	David Daniels 3/4/69	#3 George Pentecost 5/3/69
Donald	Frederick Combs 4/15/68	#1 Frederick Combs 2/11/69
	Leon Russom 1/25/69	#2 Brian Taggert 3/10/69
		#3 Christopher Carroll 5/3/69
Emory	Cliff Gorman 4/15/68	#1 Tom Aldredge 2/11/69
	Tom Aldredge 10/22/68	#2 Cliff Gorman 3/10/69
	Matthew Tobin 1/25/69	#3 Jere Admire 5/3/69
Larry	Keith Prentice 4/15/68	#1 Keith Prentice 2/11/69
	Christopher Bernau 1/25/69	#2 Peter Ratray 3/10/69
		#3 Alan Castner 5/3/69
Hank	Laurence Luckinbill 4/15/68	#1 Laurence Luckinbill 2/11/69
	Konrad Matthaei 1/25/69	#2 Konrad Matthaei 3/10/69
	Wayne Tippit 3/11/69	#3 Rex Robbins 5/3/69
Bernard	Reuben Greene 4/15/68	#1 Reuben Greene 2/11/69
	Harold Scott 1/25/69	#2 Guy Edwards 3/10/69
		#3 Robert Christian 5/3/69

NEW YORK COMPANY		TOURING COMPANIES

Cowboy Robert La Tourneaux 4/15/68 #1 Robert La Tourneux 2/11/69
Ted Le Plat 1/25/69 #2 Roger Herren 3/10/69
#3 Paul Rudd 5/3/69
Alan Peter White 4/15/68 #1 Peter White 2/11/69
David O'Brien 1/25/69 #2 Richard Roat 3/10/69
#3 Nicholas Pryor 5/3/69
Harold Leonard Frey 4/15/68 #1 Leonard Frey 4/15/69
Michael Lipton 1/25/69 #2 Michael Lipton 3/10/69
Edward Zang 3/11/69 #3 Bill Moor 5/3/69

CABARET

Emcee Joel Grey 11/20/66 #1 Robert Salvio 12/26/67
Martin Ross 1/1/68 Charles Abbott 10/30/68
#2 Barry Dennen 2/28/68
Clifford Bradshaw Bert Convy 11/20/66 #1 Gene Rupert 12/26/67
John Cunningham 7/31/68 #2 Kevin Colson 2/28/68
Ken Kercheval 8/26/68
Larry Kert 12/9/68
Sally Bowles Jill Haworth 11/20/66 #1 Melissa Hart 12/26/67
Anita Gillette 11/4/68 #2 Judi Dench 2/28/68

CACTUS FLOWER

Stephanie Lauren Bacall 12/8/65 Elizabeth Allen 7/31/67
Betsy Palmer 10/17/66 Betty Garrett
Lauren Bacall 10/24/66 Alexis Smith 10/27/68
Betsy Palmer 11/20/67
Julian Barry Nelson 12/8/65 Hugh O'Brian 7/31/67
Kevin McCarthy 5/8/67 Larry Parks
Barry Nelson 5/29/67 Craig Stevens 10/27/68
Lloyd Bridges 10/16/67

CURLEY McDIMPLE

Jimmy Paul Cahill 11/22/67
Ray Becker 5/7/68
Don Emmons 5/24/68
Sarah Helon Blount 11/22/67
Nell Evans 9/24/68
Mary Boylan 10/29/68
Alice Joyce Nolen 11/22/67
Ronni Richards 1/7/69
Curley McDimple Bayn Johnson 11/22/67
Robbi Morgan 1/7/69
Miss Hamilton Norma Bigtree 11/22/67
Jane Stuart 8/20/68

THE FANTASTICKS

The Narrator Jerry Orbach 5/3/60
Gene Rupert
Bert Convy
John Cunningham
Don Stewart
David Cryer
Keith Charles
John Boni 1/13/65
Jack Mette 9/14/65
George Ogee
Keith Charles
Tom Urich
John Boni
Jack Crowder 6/13/67

NEW YORK COMPANY		TOURING COMPANIES

	Nils Hedrick	
	Keith Charles 9/18/67	
	Robert Goss 11/7/67	
	Joe Bellomo 3/11/68	
The Girl	Rita Gardner 5/3/60	
	(Sybil Lamb	
	Understudy from	
	5/3/60-5/31/69)	
	Carla Huston	
	Liza Stuart	
	Eileen Fulton	
	Alice Cannon	
	Royce Lennelle	
	B.J. Ward 12/1/64	
	Leta Anderson 7/13/65	
	Carol Demas 11/22/66	
	Leta Anderson 8/7/67	
	Carol Demas 9/4/67	
	Anne Kaye 1/23/68	
	Carol Demas 2/13/68	
	Anne Kaye 5/28/68	
The Boy	Kenneth Nelson 5/3/60	
	Gino Conforti	
	Jack Blackton	
	Paul Giovanni	
	Ty McConnell	
	Richard Rothbard	
	Gary Krawford	
	Bob Spencer 9/5/64	
	Erik Howell 6/28/66	
	Gary Krawford 12/12/67	
	Steve Skiles 2/6/68	
	Craig Carnelia	

FIDDLER ON THE ROOF

Tevye	Zero Mostel 9/22/64	Luther Adler 4/11/66
	Luther Adler 8/15/65	Paul Lipson
	Herschel Bernardi 11/8/65	(matinees only) 9/20/67
	Harry Goz 8/14/67	(all perfs.) 10/9/67
	Herschel Bernardi 9/18/67	Theodore Bikel 12/28/67
	Harry Goz 11/6/67	Paul Lipson 7/2/68
	Jerry Jarrett 5/12/69	
Golde	Maria Karnilova 9/22/64	Dolores Wilson 4/11/68
	Martha Schlamme 4/9/68	Mimi Randolph 4/2/68
	Dolores Wilson 7/1/68	
	Rae Allen 7/15/68	

GEORGE M!

George M. Cohan	Joel Grey 4/10/68	Joel Grey 5/8/69
	Jerry Dodge 12/16/68	
	Joel Grey 12/23/68	

HAIR

(Owing to the multiplicity of short-term cast changes and regional productions, we list only the actors who have played the major roles for a length of time in the New York companies)

Berger	Gerome Ragni 10/29/67	
	(off Broadway)	
	Steve Curry 12/22/67	

NEW YORK COMPANY	TOURING COMPANIES

Claude	Gerome Ragni 4/29/68 (on Broadway) Steve Curry Barry McGuire Peter Link Otis Stevens Walker Daniels 10/29/67 (off Broadway) James Rado 4/29/68 (on Broadway) Barry McGuire Joseph Campbell Butler Kim Milford Eric Robinson	
Sheila	Jill O'Hara 10/29/67 (off Broadway) Lynn Kellogg 4/29/68 (on Broadway) Diane Keaton Heather MacRae	

HELLO, DOLLY!

Mrs. Dolly Gallagher Levi	Carol Channing 1/16/64	#1 Mary Martin 4/17/65
	Ginger Rogers 8/9/65	Dora Bryan 5/14/65
	Martha Raye 2/27/67	#2 Carol Channing 9/6/65
	Betty Grable 6/12/67	Eve Arden 5/66
	Bibi Osterwald 11/6/67	Carol Channing 10/66
	Pearl Bailey 11/12/67	#3 Betty Grable 11/3/65
	Thelma Carpenter 1/29/69	#4 Ginger Rogers 4/19/67
	(Wed. matinees)	Dorothy Lamour (alternate) 8/23/67
		Ginger Rogers 10/20/67
		#5 Pearl Bailey 10/11/67
Horace Vandergelder	David Burns 1/16/64	#1 Loring Smith 4/17/65
	Max Showalter 3/13/67	Bernard Spear 5/14/66
	Cab Calloway 11/12/67	#2 Horace McMahon 9/6/65
		Milo Boulton 11/65
		#3 Max Showalter 11/3/65
		#4 David Burns 4/19/67
		Max Showalter 8/23/67
		#5 Cab Calloway 10/11/67

JACQUES BREL IS ALIVE AND WELL AND LIVING IN PARIS

(Alternates cast at nearly every performance; has had many regional productions but no road companies until summer 1969. Listed below are those who have performed in New York)

Original cast	Shawn Elliott 1/22/68
	Mort Shuman
	Elly Stone
	Alice Whitfield
Others	June Gable 5/7/68
	Robert Guillaume 5/31/68
	Chevi Colton 7/1/68
	Joe Masiell 7/1/68
	Betty Rhodes 7/1/68
	Fleury D'Antonakis 9/9/68
	Stan Porter 9/17/68
	George Ball 3/30/69

NEW YORK COMPANY	TOURING COMPANIES

LOVERS

Andy Tracey   Art Carney 7/25/68   Art Carney 2/10/69
Peter Lind Hayes 11/4/68

MAME

Mame   Angela Lansbury 5/24/66   #1 Celeste Holm 9/28/67
Sheila Smith 2/13/67   #2 Angela Lansbury 5/30/68
Angela Lansbury 2/27/67   #3 Susan Hayward 12/30/68
Janis Paige 4/1/68   Celeste Holm 3/10/69
Jane Morgan 12/2/68   #4 Janet Blair 1/24/69
Ann Miller 5/26/69

Vera Charles   Beatrice Arthur 5/24/66   #1 Vicki Cummings 9/28/67
Sheila Smith 3/27/67   #2 Anne Francine 5/30/68
Beatrice Arthur 4/10/67   #3 Delphi Lawrence 12/30/68
Anne Francine 7/10/67   #4 Elaine Stritch 1/24/69
Audrey Christie 4/1/68
Anne Francine 9/23/68

THE MAN IN THE GLASS BOOTH

Arthur Goldman   Donald Pleasence 9/26/68   Jack Warden 5/19/69
Jack Warden 3/31/69

MAN OF LA MANCHA

Quixote (Cervantes)   Richard Kiley 11/22/65   #1 José Ferrer 9/24/66
José Ferrer 5/28/66   Richard Kiley 4/11/67
John Cullum 2/24/67   José Ferrer 7/17/67
José Ferrer 4/11/67   Richard Kiley 8/7/67
David Atkinson 7/14/67   Keith Andes 9/19/67
Hal Holbrook 7/1/68   José Ferrer 9/23/68
Bob Wright 9/23/68   #2 Keith Michell

Aldonza   Joan Diener 11/22/65   #1 Maura K. Wedge 9/24/66
Marion Marlowe 1/17/67   Joan Diener 4/11/67
Maura K. Wedge 4/11/67   Marion Marlowe 7/31/67
Bernice Massi 7/25/67   Carolyn Maye 11/7/68
Carolyn Maye   Natalie Costa 3/18/68
   (matinees only 3/20/68)   Maura K. Wedge 10/15/68
Barbara William   #2 Joan Diener 4/24/68
   (matinees only 11/11/68)
Gaylea Byrne 5/5/69
Marilyn Child
   (matinees only 5/28/69)

A MOON FOR THE MISBEGOTTEN

Josie Hogan   Salome Jens 6/12/68   Salome Jens 5/12/69
Phil Hogan   W.B. Brydon 6/12/68   Stefan Gierasch 5/12/69
James Tyrone Jr.   Mitchell Ryan 6/12/68   Mitchell Ryan 5/12/69

PLAZA SUITE

Sam, Jesse, Roy   George C. Scott 2/14/68   #1 Dan Dailey 9/16/68
Nicol Williamson 5/27/68   #2 Forrest Tucker 10/14/68
George C. Scott 6/17/68
E.G. Marshall 9/9/68
Dan Dailey 3/3/69
Lawrence Weber 5/19/69
Don Porter 5/26/69

Karen, Muriel, Norma   Maureen Stapleton 2/14/68   #1 Lee Grant 9/16/68
Barbara Baxley 2/13/69   #2 Betty Garrett 10/14/68

NEW YORK COMPANY		TOURING COMPANIES

THE PRICE

Victor Franz	Pat Hingle 2/7/68	Albert Salmi 3/4/69
	Albert Salmi 10/14/68	
Esther Franz	Kate Reid 2/7/68	Kate Reid 3/4/69
Gregory Solomon	Harold Gary 2/7/68	Harold Gary 3/4/69
	David Burns 6/10/68	
	Harold Gary 2/10/69	
Walter Franz	Arthur Kennedy 2/7/68	Shepperd Strudwick 3/4/69
	Shepperd Strudwick 10/14/68	

ROSENCRANTZ AND GUILDENSTERN ARE DEAD

Rosencrantz	Brian Murray 10/16/67	Brian Murray 1/6/69
Guildenstern	John Wood 10/16/67	George Bachman 1/6/69
The Player	Paul Hecht 10/16/67	W.B. Brydon 1/6/69

SCUBA DUBA

Harold Wonder	Jerry Orbach 10/10/67	
	Judd Hirsch 8/5/68	
	Jim Friedman 5/13/69	
	(alternate)	

THE SHOW-OFF

Mrs. Fisher	Helen Hayes 12/5/67	Helen Hayes 9/30/68
	Nancy Walker 6/20/68	
	Helen Hayes 9/13/68	
Aubrey	Clayton Corzatte 12/5/67	Clayton Corzatte 9/30/68

YOU KNOW I CAN'T HEAR YOU WHEN THE WATER'S RUNNING

Pawling, George, Chuck	Martin Balsam 3/13/67	Eddie Bracken 10/16/67
	Larry Blyden 2/27/68	
	Eddie Bracken 12/2/68	
Harriet, Edith, Muriel	Eileen Heckart 3/13/67	Ruth Manning 10/16/67
	Irene Dailey 2/27/68	
	Michaele Myers 12/2/68	
Jack, Salesman, Herbert	George Grizzard 3/13/67	Robert Elston 10/16/67
	William Redfield 2/27/68	
	Robert Elston 12/2/68	

YOU'RE A GOOD MAN CHARLIE BROWN

Charlie Brown	Gary Burghoff 3/7/67	Ken Kube 12/21/68
	Sean Simpson 3/4/68	Bob Lydiard
	Bob Lydiard	
	Alfred Mazza	
Lucy	Reva Rose 3/7/67	Ann Gibbs 12/21/68
	Boni Enten 6/11/68	Ann Hodapp
	Ann Gibbs	
Snoopy	Bill Hinnant 3/7/67	T.D. Johnston 12/21/68
	Don Potter	Alfred Roberge

YOUR OWN THING

(Owing to the multiplicity of short-term cast changes and regional productions, we list only the actors who have played the major roles in New York and in the touring company)

Sebastian	Rusty Thacker 1/13/68	Gerry Glasier 4/21/69
	Bruce Scott	
	Frank Andre	
	Kim Milford	

NEW YORK COMPANY		TOURING COMPANIES
Viola	Leland Palmer 1/13/68	Priscilla Lopez 4/21/69
	Sandy Duncan	
	Priscilla Lopez	
	Jill Choder	
Orson	Tom Ligon 1/13/68	Bruce Jacobs 4/21/69
	Les Carlson	
Olivia	* Marian Mercer 1/13/68	Paula Kelly 4/21/69
	Marcia Rodd	
	June Compton	
	Sally Stark	
	Donna Christie	
	Lee Chamberlin	

* Miss Mercer was replaced shortly after the opening by Miss Rodd, who was incorrectly listed in the 1967-68 volume of *Best Plays* as having created this role.

BUS-TRUCK TOURS

These are touring productions designed for maximum mobility and ease of handling in one-night and split-week stands (with occasional engagements of a week or more). Among Broadway shows on tour in the season of 1968-69 were the following bus-truck troupes:

Cactus Flower with Jeannie Carson and Biff McGuire, 95 cities, 9/20/68-3/7/69
The Apple Tree with Tom Ewell and Rosemary Prinz, 63 cities, 10/24/68-3/20/69
Black Comedy with Jan Sterling, 41 cities, 2/3/69-4/20/69
Fiddler on the Roof with Joe Cusanelli/Harry Goz, 94 cities, 8/27/68-5/31/69 (continuing)
The Star-Spangled Girl with Sandy Baron, Joan McCall and Lyman Ward, 78 cities, 10/21/68-3/2/69
You Know I Can't Hear You When the Water's Running with Imogene Coca and King Donovan, 10/18/68-3/1/69
Man of La Mancha with David Atkinson and Patricia Marand, 110 cities, 9/27/68-4/26/69
Mame with Janet Blair and Elaine Stritch, 16 cities, 1/24/69-5/18/69
Funny Girl with Carmen Natiku/Evalyn Baron, 90 cities, 10/20/68-3/31/69
Hello, Dolly! with Yvonne de Carlo and Don De Leo, 32 cities, 12/26/68-4/21/69.

Some other shows on bus-truck tours in 1968-69 were the following:

Lamp at Midnight by Barrie Stavis, with Morris Carnovsky, 48 cities, 1/14/69-5/10/69
Mrs. Warren's Profession, Hay Fever, An Ideal Husband, The Beaux' Stratagem in The Theater Royal Windsor repertory, 61 cities, 8/27/68-12/14/68
In Search of Dylan, 30 cities, 3/31/69-5/3/69
Les Ballets Africains, 70 cities, 9/27/68-12/14/68
Big Country, Ballet America variety, 25 cities, 1/17/69-2/23/69
Othello, The Taming of the Shrew, Murder in the Cathedral in National Shakespeare repertory, 120 cities, 10/6/68-5/9/69
Much Ado About Nothing, Macbeth in National Theater repertory, 40 cities, 2/10/69-4/26/69.

FACTS AND
FIGURES

LONG RUNS ON BROADWAY

The following shows have run 500 or more continuous performances in a single production, usually the first, not including previews or extra non-profit performances, allowing for vacation layoffs and special one-booking engagements, but not including return engagements after a show has gone on tour. Where there are title similarities, the production is identified as follows: (p) straight play version, (m) musical version, (r) revival.

THROUGH MAY 31, 1969

(PLAYS MARKED WITH ASTERISK WERE STILL PLAYING JUNE 1, 1969)

Plays	Number Performances	Plays	Number Performances
Life With Father	3,224	Lightnin'	1,291
Tobacco Road	3,182	*Mame (m)	1,260
My Fair Lady	2,717	The King and I	1,246
Abie's Irish Rose	2,327	Cactus Flower	1,234
Oklahoma!	2,212	Guys and Dolls	1,200
*Hello, Dolly! †	2,210	Mister Roberts	1,157
*Fiddler on the Roof	1,956	*Cabaret	1,153
South Pacific †	1,925	Annie Get Your Gun	1,147
Harvey	1,694	The Seven Year Itch	1,141
Born Yesterday	1,642	Pins and Needles	1,108
Mary, Mary	1,572	Kiss Me, Kate	1,070
The Voice of the Turtle	1,557	The Pajama Game	1,063
Barefoot in the Park	1,530	The Teahouse of the August	
*Man of La Mancha	1,467	Moon	1,027
Arsenic and Old Lace	1,444	Damn Yankees	1,019
The Sound of Music	1,443	Never Too Late	1,007
How To Succeed in Business		Any Wednesday	982
Without Really Trying	1,417	A Funny Thing Happened on	
Hellzapoppin	1,404	the Way to the Forum	964
The Music Man	1,375	The Odd Couple	964
Funny Girl	1,348	Anna Lucasta	957
Angel Street	1,295	Kiss and Tell	956

† Both *South Pacific* and *Hello, Dolly!*—and probably many other shows over the years— interrupted their runs for special one-booking engagements outside New York City. *South Pacific's* run was originally recorded as 1,925 performances but was cut back starting with the 1960-61 *Best Plays* volume to the 1,694 performances it played prior to just such a special booking. In the opinion of the present editor *South Pacific's* record should show the full 1,925 performances, which are restored in this volume's long-run list.

Plays	Number Performances	*Plays*	Number Performances
The Moon Is Blue	924	Li'l Abner	693
Bells Are Ringing	924	Peg o' My Heart	692
Luv	901	The Children's Hour	691
Can-Can	892	Dead End	687
Carousel	890	The Lion and the Mouse	686
Hats Off to Ice	889	White Cargo	686
Fanny	888	Dear Ruth	683
Follow the Girls	882	East Is West	680
Camelot	873	Come Blow Your Horn	677
The Bat	867	The Most Happy Fella	676
My Sister Eileen	864	The Doughgirls	671
Song of Norway	860	The Impossible Years	670
A Streetcar Named Desire	855	Irene	670
Comedy in Music	849	Boy Meets Girl	669
You Can't Take It With You	837	Beyond the Fringe	667
La Plume de Ma Tante	835	Who's Afraid of Virginia Woolf?	664
Three Men on a Horse	835	Blithe Spirit	657
The Subject Was Roses	832	A Trip to Chinatown	657
Inherit the Wind	806	The Women	657
No Time for Sergeants	796	Bloomer Girl	654
Fiorello!	795	The Fifth Season	654
Where's Charley?	792	Rain	648
The Ladder	789	Witness for the Prosecution	645
Oliver	774	Call Me Madam	644
State of the Union	765	Janie	642
The First Year	760	The Green Pastures	640
You Know I Can't Hear You		Auntie Mame (p)	639
When the Water's Running	755	A Man for All Seasons	637
Two for the Seesaw	750	The Fourposter	632
Death of a Salesman	742	The Tenth Man	623
Sons o' Fun	742	Is Zat So?	618
Gentlemen Prefer Blondes	740	Anniversary Waltz	615
The Man Who Came to Dinner	739	The Happy Time (p)	614
Call Me Mister	734	Separate Rooms	613
West Side Story	732	Affairs of State	610
High Button Shoes	727	Star and Garter	609
Finian's Rainbow	725	The Student Prince	608
Claudia	722	Sweet Charity	608
The Gold Diggers	720	Bye Bye Birdie	607
Carnival	719	Broadway	603
The Diary of Anne Frank	717	Adonis	603
I Remember Mama	714	Street Scene (p)	601
Tea and Sympathy	712	Kiki	600
Junior Miss	710	Flower Drum Song	600
Seventh Heaven	704	Don't Drink the Water	598
Gypsy (m)	702	Wish You Were Here	598
The Miracle Worker	700	A Society Circus	596
Cat on a Hot Tin Roof	694	Blossom Time	592

Plays	Number Performances	Plays	Number Performances
The Two Mrs. Carrolls	585	The Music Master	540
Kismet	583	Pal Joey (r)	540
Detective Story	581	What Makes Sammy Run?	540
Brigadoon	581	What a Life	538
No Strings	580	*Plaza Suite	537
Brother Rat	577	The Unsinkable Molly Brown	532
Show Boat	572	The Red Mill (r)	531
The Show-Off	571	A Raisin in the Sun	530
Sally	570	The Solid Gold Cadillac	526
Golden Boy (m)	568	Irma La Douce	524
One Touch of Venus	567	The Boomerang	522
Happy Birthday	564	Rosalinda	521
Look Homeward, Angel	564	The Best Man	520
The Glass Menagerie	561	Chauve-Souris	520
I Do! I Do!	560	Blackbirds of 1928	518
Wonderful Town	559	Sunny	517
Rose Marie	557	Victoria Regina	517
Strictly Dishonorable	557	Half a Sixpence	511
A Majority of One	556	The Vagabond King	511
Toys in the Attic	556	The New Moon	509
Sunrise at Campobello	556	The World of Suzie Wong	508
Jamaica	555	Shuffle Along	504
Stop the World—I Want to Get Off	555	Up in Central Park	504
		Carmen Jones	503
Floradora	553	The Member of the Wedding	501
Ziegfeld Follies (1943 r)	553	Panama Hattie	501
Dial "M" for Murder	552	Personal Appearance	501
Good News	551	Bird in Hand	500
Let's Face It	547	Room Service	500
Milk and Honey	543	Sailor, Beware!	500
Within the Law	541	Tomorrow the World	500

LONG RUNS OFF BROADWAY

Plays	Number Performances	Plays	Number Performances
*The Fantasticks	3,800	The Boy Friend (r)	763
The Threepenny Opera	2,611	The Pocket Watch	725
The Blacks	1,408	The Connection	722
Little Mary Sunshine	1,143	The Knack	685
Leave It to Jane (r)	928	*Scuba Duba	674
*You're a Good Man Charlie Brown	895	The Balcony	672
		*Curley McDimple	647
The Mad Show	871	America Hurrah	634
A View From the Bridge (r)	780	Hogan's Goat	607

Plays	*Number Performances*	Plays	*Number Performances*
The Trojan Women (r)	600	*Jacques Brel Is Alive and Well and Living in Paris	562
Krapp's Last Tape and The Zoo Story	582	The Hostage (r)	545
*Your Own Thing	580	Six Characters in Search of an Author (r)	529
The Dumbwaiter and The Collection	578	Happy Ending and Day of Absence	504
The Crucible (r)	571	The Boys From Syracuse (r) ..	500
The Iceman Cometh (r)	565		

DRAMA CRITICS CIRCLE VOTING 1968-69

The New York Drama Critics Circle voted *The Great White Hope* the best play of the season regardless of origin on the second ballot, by a plurality of 25 points in weighted voting to 19 points for *Hadrian VII* and 14 for *Ceremonies in Dark Old Men*. Other plays which received points on this ballot, on which each critic awarded 3 points for his first choice, 2 for his second and 1 for his third, were: *The Man in the Glass Booth* 4, *Little Murders* 4, *In the Matter of J. Robert Oppenheimer* 4, *Frankenstein* 3, *Paradise Now* 3, *Hamlet* 3, *Adaptation/Next* 2, *The Misanthrope* 2, *No Place To Be Somebody* 2, *Boy in the Straight-Back Chair* 2, *The Front Page* 1, *Futz* 1, *We Bombed in New Haven* 1. The winner, *The Great White Hope*, received a plurality of 6 first-place votes out of 18 cast on the first ballot, short of the majority necessary to win the Critics Award on the first ballot. 19 critics were represented in the voting, 4 by proxy, with one abstaining across the board.

The critics voted *1776* the season's best musical on the first ballot in that category, with a majority of 9 first-place votes against 3 for *Hair*, 2 for *Zorbá*, 2 for *Promises, Promises*, 1 for *The Great White Hope* and 2 abstentions.

Since an American play won the best-regardless-of-origin citation, the question of whether to give an award for the best foreign play was put to a vote and the "nays" had it.

In some instances, votes were cast facetiously, possibly as a comment upon the procedural methods of the critics' organization. Here's the way the individual members of the New York Drama Critics Circle voted on the first and second ballots for best play and the first ballot for best musical:

FIRST BALLOTS FOR BEST PLAY AND BEST MUSICAL

Critic	Best Play	Best Musical
Clive Barnes *Times*	Hamlet	Hair
Whitney Bolton *Morning Telegraph*	The Great White Hope	Zorbá
John Chapman *Daily News*	White Hope	1776
Harold Clurman *The Nation*	Ceremonies in Dark Old Men	Zorbá

Ethel Colby *Journal of Commerce*	White Hope	1776
Richard Cooke *Wall St. Journal*	Hadrian VII	Promises, Promises
Jack Gaver UPI	White Hope	1776
William H. Glover AP	Ceremonies	1776
Martin Gottfried *Women's Wear Daily*	Paradise Now	White Hope
Henry Hewes *Saturday Review*	Little Murders	Hair
Edward S. Hipp *Newark News*	Hadrian VII	1776
Ted Kalem *Time*	(Abstain)	(Abstain)
Walter Kerr *Times*	White Hope	1776
Jack Kroll *Newsweek*	Frankenstein	(Abstain)
Emory Lewis *Bergen Record*	Ceremonies	Hair
Hobe Morrison *Variety*	White Hope	1776
George Oppenheimer *Newsday*	We Bombed in New Haven	1776
William Raidy Newhouse Papers	Hadrian VII	1776
Richard Watts Jr. *Post*	Hadrian VII	Promises, Promises

SECOND BALLOT FOR BEST PLAY

Critic	*1st Choice (3 pts.)*	*2d Choice (2 pts.)*	*3d Choice (1 pt.)*
Clive Barnes	Hamlet	The Misanthrope	The Front Page
Whitney Bolton	(Abstain)		
John Chapman	(Abstain)		
Harold Clurman	Ceremonies in Dark Old Men	The Great White Hope	In the Matter of J. Robert Oppenheimer
Ethel Colby	White Hope	Hadrian VII	The Man in the Glass Booth
Richard Cooke	Hadrian VII	White Hope	Oppenheimer
Jack Gaver	White Hope	Hadrian VII	Glass Booth
William H. Glover	Ceremonies	White Hope	Hadrian VII
Martin Gottfried	Paradise Now	White Hope	Oppenheimer
Henry Hewes	Little Murders	Ceremonies	Futz
Edward S. Hipp	(Abstain)		
Ted Kalem	(Abstain)		
Walter Kerr	White Hope	No Place To Be Somebody	Glass Booth
Jack Kroll	Frankenstein	Boy in the Straight-Back Chair	White Hope
Emory Lewis	Ceremonies	White Hope	Oppenheimer
Hobe Morrison	White Hope	Hadrian VII	We Bombed in New Haven
George Oppenheimer	Hadrian VII	Adaptation/Next	Ceremonies
William Raidy	Hadrian VII	White Hope	Little Murders
Richard Watts Jr.	Hadrian VII	Ceremonies	Glass Booth

Choices of some other critics:

Critic	Best Play	Best Musical
Judith Crist "Today"	Hadrian VII	1776
Edwin Newman WNBC-TV	Glass Booth	(Abstain)
Theodore Hoffman Westinghouse Broadcasting	Glass Booth	Zorbá
Stanley Kauffmann Channel 13	The Serpent	(Abstain)
Norman Nadel Scripps-Howard	White Hope	1776
Tom Prideaux Life	Glass Booth	Promises, Promises
Leonard Harris WCBS-TV	White Hope	(Abstain)

NEW YORK DRAMA CRITICS CIRCLE AWARDS

Listed below are the New York Drama Critics Circle Awards, classified as follows: (1) Best American Play, (2) Best Foreign Play, (3) Best Musical, (4) Best, regardless of category.

1935-36—(1) Winterset
1936-37—(1) High Tor
1937-38—(1) Of Mice and Men, (2) Shadow and Substance
1938-39—(1) No award, (2) The White Steed
1939-40—(1) The Time of Your Life
1940-41—(1) Watch on the Rhine, (2) The Corn Is Green
1941-42—(1) No award, (2) Blithe Spirit
1942-43—(1) The Patriots
1943-44—(2) Jacobowsky and the Colonel
1944-45—(1) The Glass Menagerie
1945-46—(3) Carousel
1946-47—(1) All My Sons, (2) No Exit, (3) Brigadoon
1947-48—(1) A Streetcar Named Desire, (2) The Winslow Boy
1948-49—(1) Death of a Salesman, (2) The Madwoman of Chaillot, (3) South Pacific
1949-50—(1) The Member of the Wedding, (2) The Cocktail Party, (3) The Consul
1950-51—(1) Darkness at Noon, (2) The Lady's Not for Burning, (3) Guys and Dolls
1951-52—(1) I Am a Camera, (2) Venus Observed, (3) Pal Joey (Special citation to Don Juan in Hell)
1952-53—(1) Picnic, (2) The Love of Four Colonels, (3) Wonderful Town
1953-54—(1) Teahouse of the August Moon, (2) Ondine, (3) The Golden Apple
1954-55—(1) Cat on a Hot Tin Roof, (2) Witness for the Prosecution, (3) The Saint of Bleecker Street

1955-56—(1) The Diary of Anne Frank, (2) Tiger at the Gates, (3) My Fair Lady
1956-57—(1) Long Day's Journey Into Night, (2) The Waltz of the Toreadors, (3) The Most Happy Fella
1957-58—(1) Look Homeward, Angel, (2) Look Back in Anger, (3) The Music Man
1958-59—(1) A Raisin in the Sun, (2) The Visit, (3) La Plume de Ma Tante
1959-60—(1) Toys in the Attic, (2) Five Finger Exercise, (3) Fiorello!
1960-61—(1) All the Way Home, (2) A Taste of Honey, (3) Carnival
1961-62—(1) The Night of the Iguana, (2) A Man for All Seasons, (3) How To Succeed in Business Without Really Trying
1962-63—(4) Who's Afraid of Virginia Woolf? (Special citation to Beyond the Fringe)
1963-64—(4) Luther, (3) Hello, Dolly! (Special citation to The Trojan Women)
1964-65—(4) The Subject Was Roses, (3) Fiddler on the Roof
1965-66—(4) The Persecution and Assassination of Marat as Performed by the Inmates of the Asylum of Charenton Under the Direction of the Marquis de Sade, (3) Man of La Mancha
1966-67—(4) The Homecoming, (3) Cabaret
1967-68—(4) Rosencrantz and Guildenstern Are Dead, (3) Your Own Thing
1968-69—(4) The Great White Hope, (3) 1776

PULITZER PRIZE WINNERS

1917-18—Why Marry?, by Jesse Lynch Williams

1918-19—No award

1919-20—Beyond the Horizon, by Eugene O'Neill

1920-21—Miss Lulu Bett, by Zona Gale

1921-22—Anna Christie, by Eugene O'Neill

1922-23—Icebound, by Owen Davis

1923-24—Hell-bent fer Heaven, by Hatcher Hughes

1924-25—They Knew What They Wanted, by Sidney Howard

1925-26—Craig's Wife, by George Kelly

1926-27—In Abraham's Bosom, by Paul Green

1927-28—Strange Interlude, by Eugene O'Neill

1928-29—Street Scene, by Elmer Rice

1929-30—The Green Pastures, by Marc Connelly

1930-31—Alison's House, by Susan Glaspell

1931-32—Of Thee I Sing, by George S. Kaufman, Morrie Ryskind, Ira and George Gershwin

1932-33—Both Your Houses, by Maxwell Anderson

1933-34—Men in White, by Sidney Kingsley

1934-35—The Old Maid, by Zoë Akins

1935-36—Idiot's Delight, by Robert E. Sherwood

1936-37—You Can't Take It with You, by Moss Hart and George S. Kaufman

1937-38—Our Town, by Thornton Wilder

1938-39—Abe Lincoln in Illinois, by Robert E. Sherwood

1939-40—The Time of Your Life, by William Saroyan

1940-41—There Shall Be No Night, by Robert E. Sherwood

1941-42—No award

1942-43—The Skin of Our Teeth, by Thornton Wilder

1943-44—No award

1944-45—Harvey, by Mary Chase

1945-46—State of the Union, by Howard Lindsay and Russel Crouse

1946-47—No award.

1947-48—A Streetcar Named Desire, by Tennessee Williams

1948-49—Death of a Salesman, by Arthur Miller

1949-50—South Pacific, by Richard Rodgers, Oscar Hammerstein II and Joshua Logan

1950-51—No award

1951-52—The Shrike, by Joseph Kramm

1952-53—Picnic, by William Inge

1953-54—The Teahouse of the August Moon, by John Patrick

1954-55—Cat on a Hot Tin Roof, by Tennessee Williams

1955-56—The Diary of Anne Frank, by Frances Goodrich and Albert Hackett

1956-57—Long Day's Journey into Night, by Eugene O'Neill

1957-58—Look Homeward, Angel, by Ketti Frings

1958-59—J. B., by Archibald MacLeish

1959-60—Fiorello!, by Jerome Weidman, George Abbott, Sheldon Harnick and Jerry Bock

1960-61—All the Way Home, by Tad Mosel

1961-62—How to Succeed in Business Without Really Trying, by Abe Burrows, Willie Gilbert, Jack Weinstock and Frank Loesser

1962-63—No award

1963-64—No award

1964-65—The Subject Was Roses, by Frank D. Gilroy

1965-66—No award

1966-67—A Delicate Balance, by Edward Albee

1967-68—No award

1968-69—The Great White Hope, by Howard Sackler

ADDITIONAL PRIZES AND AWARDS, 1968-69

The following is a list of major prizes and awards for theatrical achievement. In all cases the names of winners—persons, productions or organizations—appear in **bold face type.**

MARGO JONES AWARDS (for encouraging production of new playwrights). **Washington Theater Club** of Washington, D.C. and its director **Davey Marlin-Jones. Ellen Stewart** and her **La Mama Experimental Theater Club.**

BRANDEIS UNIVERSITY CREATIVE ARTS AWARD (for excellence). **Boris Aronson,** scene designer. **The Negro Ensemble Company.**

GEORGE FREEDLEY MEMORIAL AWARD. **Louis Sheaffer** for the biography *O'Neill, Son and Playwright.*

GEORGE JEAN NATHAN AWARD (for criticism). **Martin Gottfried.**

NATIONAL INSTITUTE OF ARTS AND LETTERS GOLD MEDAL FOR DRAMA. **Tennessee Williams.**

OUTER CIRCLE AWARDS (voted by critics of out-of-town periodicals, for distinctive achievement in the New York theater this season). **Sherman Edwards,** composer-lyricist of *1776.* **Edwin Sherin,** director of *The Great White Hope.* **Elaine May,** director of *Adaptation/Next* and author of its first part. **Lonne Elder III,** author of *Ceremonies in Dark Old Men.* **Lorraine Serabian,** for her performance in *Zorbá.* The off-Broadway musical *Dames at Sea.* **Linda Lavin,** for performances in *Little Murders* and *Cop-Out.* **Jules Feiffer,** author of *Little Murders.* The late **Jean Rosenthal,** for her contributions to stage lighting. **David Hays,** for his work with the National Theater of the Deaf.

JOSEPH MAHARAM FOUNDATION AWARDS (for design by an American). Musical scene design, **Jo Mielziner** for *1776.* Straight play design, **The Living Theater Company** under the direction of **Julian Beck** for *Frankenstein.* Costume design, **Patricia Zipprodt** for *1776.*

LOLA D'ANNUNZIO AWARD. **Ted Mann** for his service to the plays of Eugene O'Neill. Citation to **Moses Gunn** for his fine performances with the Negro Ensemble Company and the New York Shakespeare Festival.

VERNON RICE AWARD (for outstanding contribution to the off-Broadway theater). **The Open Stage** and its director **Joseph Chaikin.**

VILLAGE VOICE OFF-BROADWAY (OBIE) AWARDS (for off-Broadway excellence; categories unspecified). **The Living Theater** for *Frankenstein,* **Jeff Weiss** for *International Wrestling Match,* **Julie Bovasso** for *Gloria & Esperanza,* **Judith Malina** and **Julian Beck** for *Antigone,* **Arlene Rothlein** for *The Poor Little Match Girl,* **Nathan George** and **Ron O'Neal** for *No Place To Be Somebody,* **Theater Genesis** for sustained excellence, **Jules Feiffer** for *Little Murders,* **Ronald Tavel** for *Boy on the Straight-Back Chair,* **Israel Horovitz** for *The Honest-to-God Schnozzola,* **Open Theater** for *The Serpent,* **Performance Group** for *Dionysius in '69* and **Boston Om Theater** for *Riot.*

CLARENCE DERWENT AWARDS (for best non-featured performances). **Marlene Warfield** in *The Great White Hope.* **Ron O'Neal** in *No Place To Be Somebody.* Derwent Awards in London: **Gordon Jackson** as Horatio in *Hamlet.* **Elizabeth Spriggs** as Claire in *A Delicate Balance.*

SAM S. SHUBERT AWARD (for outstanding service to the American theater). **Harold Prince.**

KELCEY ALLEN AWARD. **Ellen Stewart.**

DRAMA DESK AWARDS. Those with the greatest proportion of citations in the voting of Drama Desk members in each category were: Best Performance, **James Earl Jones** in *The Great White Hope;* Best Direction, **Edwin Sherin** for *White Hope;* Best Scene Design, **Ming Cho Lee** for *Invitation to a Beheading;* Best Costume Design, **Tania Moiseiwitsch** for *The House of Atreus;* Best Composer, **Al Carmines** for *Peace;* Best Lyricists, **George Haimsohn** and **Robert**

Miller for *Dames at Sea;* Best Musical Book Writer, **Peter Stone** for *1776;* Best Choreographer, **Grover Dale** for *Billy;* Most Promising Playwrights (also winners of Kahn Performing Arts Foundation grants), **Charles Gordone** for *No Place To Be Somebody,* **Lonne Elder III** for *Ceremonies in Dark Old Men,* **Elaine May** for *Adaptation.*

THE TONY AWARDS

The Antoinette Perry (Tony) Awards are voted by members of The League of New York Theaters, by the governing bodies of the Dramatists Guild, Actors Equity, the Society of Stage Choreographers and the United Scenic Artists, and by members of the first and second night press lists, from a list of four nominees in each category. Nominations are made by a committee serving by invitation of The League of New York Theaters, which is in charge of the Tony Awards procedure. The 1968-69 nominating committee was composed of Sidney Kingsley, Richard Watts Jr., Judith Crist, Tom Prideaux, Rose Franzblau and Charles Freeman. 434 ballots were sent out for voting on the following list of nominees (winners are listed in **bold face type**):

BEST PLAY (award goes to both producer and author). ***The Great White Hope*** by **Howard Sackler**, produced by **Herman Levin**. *Hadrian VII* by Peter Luke, produced by Lester Osterman Productions (Lester Osterman, Richard Horner, Lawrence Kasha), Bill Freedman and Charles Kasher. *Lovers* by Brian Friel, produced by Helen Bonfils and Morton Gottlieb by arrangement with Oscar Lewenstein. *The Man in the Glass Booth* by Robert Shaw, produced by Ivor David Balding & Associates Ltd. and Edward M. Meyers with Leslie Ogden, in association with Glasshouse Productions and Peter Bridge.

BEST MUSICAL (award goes to producer, author, composer, lyricist; separate composer-lyricist category now eliminated). *Hair,* book and lyrics by Gerome Ragni and James Rado, music by Galt MacDermit, produced by Michael Butler in the Natoma Production. *Promises, Promises,* book by Neil Simon, music by Burt Bacharach, lyrics by Hal David, produced by David Merrick. *1776,* book by **Peter Stone**, music and lyrics by **Sherman Edwards**, produced by **Stuart Ostrow**. *Zorbá,* book by Joseph Stein, music by John Kander, lyrics by Fred Ebb, produced by Harold Prince in association with Ruth Mitchell.

ACTOR—Dramatic star. Art Carney in *Lovers,* **James Earl Jones** in *The Great White Hope,* Alec McCowen in *Hadrian VII,* Donald Pleasence in *The Man in the Glass Booth.*

ACTRESS—Dramatic star. **Julie Harris** in *Forty Carats,* Estelle Parsons in *The Seven Descents of Myrtle,* Charlotte Rae in *Morning, Noon and Night,* Brenda Vaccaro in *The Goodbye People.*

ACTOR—Musical star. Herschel Bernardi in *Zorbá.* Jack Cassidy in *Maggie Flynn.* Joel Grey in *George M!* **Jerry Orbach** in *Promises, Promises.*

ACTRESS—Musical star. Maria Karnilova in *Zorbá.* **Angela Lansbury** in *Dear World.* Dorothy Loudon in *The Fig Leaves Are Falling.* Jill O'Hara in *Promises, Promises.*

ACTOR—Dramatic featured or supporting. **Al Pacino** in *Does a Tiger Wear a Necktie?* Richard Castellano in *Lovers and Other Strangers.* Anthony Roberts in *Play It Again, Sam.* Louis Zorich in *Hadrian VII.*

ACTRESS—Dramatic featured or supporting. **Jane Alexander** in *The Great White Hope.* Diane Keaton in *Play It Again, Sam.* Lauren Jones in *Does a Tiger Wear a Necktie?* Anna Manahan in *Lovers.*

ACTOR—Musical featured or supporting. A. Larry Haines and Edward Winter in *Promises, Promises.* **Ronald Holgate** in *1776.* (William Daniels in *1776* nominated but withdrew.)

ACTRESS—Musical featured or supporting. Sandy Duncan in *Canterbury Tales.* **Marian Mercer** in *Promises, Promises.* Lorraine Serabian in *Zorbá.* Virginia Vestoff in *1776.*

DIRECTOR—Play. **Peter Dews** for *Hadrian VII.* Joseph Hardy for *Play It Again, Sam.*

Harold Pinter for *The Man in the Glass Booth*. Michael A. Schultz for *Does a Tiger Wear a Necktie?*

DIRECTOR—Musical. **Peter Hunt** for *1776*. Robert Moore for *Promises, Promises*. Tom O'Horgan for *Hair*. Harold Prince for *Zorbá*.

SCENE DESIGNER. **Boris Aronson** for *Zorbá*. Derek Cousins for *Canterbury Tales*. Jo Mielziner for *1776*. Oliver Smith for *Dear World*.

COSTUME DESIGNER. **Michael Annals** for *Morning, Noon and Night*. Robert Fletcher for *Hadrian VII*. **Loudon Sainthill** for *Canterbury Tales*. Patricia Zipprodt for *Zorbá*.

CHOREOGRAPHER. **Sammy Bayes** for *Canterbury Tales*. Ronald Field for *Zorbá*. **Joe Layton** for *George M!* Michael Bennett for *Promises, Promises*.

SPECIAL AWARDS. **Laurence Olivier, Carol Burnett, Leonard Bernstein, Rex Harrison, Negro Ensemble Company.**

ORIGINAL CAST ALBUMS
OF NEW YORK SHOWS

The following albums were issued during the 1968-69 season. The first number appearing after each title is the number of the monaural version, the second the number of the stereo version. If there was only one version it is indicated in parentheses by (M) monaural, (S) stereo or (C) compatible (playable either way).

The Believers. RCA Victor. LOC-1151; LSO 1151.
Canterbury Tales. Capitol. (S) SW-229.
Celebration. Capitol. (S) SW-198.
Dear World. Columbia. (S) BOS 3260.
Fiddler on the Roof (orig. German cast). London. (S) 99470.
Hair (orig. London cast). Atco. (S) S-7002.
House of Flowers (orig. 1968 cast). United Artists. (S) 5180.
How To Steal an Election. RCA Victor. (S) LSO-1153.
Maggie Flynn. RCA Victor. (S) LSOD-2009.
The Megilla of Itzik Manger. Columbia. (S) OS-3270.
Originals: Musical Comedy, 1909-35. RCA Victor. (S) LPV-560.
Promises, Promises. United Artists. (S) 9902.
1776. Columbia. (C) VOS-3310.
Zorbá. Capitol. (S) SO-118.

1968-69 PUBLICATION
OF RECENTLY-PRODUCED PLAYS

Box and *Quotations from Chairman Mao Tse-Tung* (Box-Mao-Box). Edward Albee. Atheneum.
The Boys in the Band. Mart Crowley. Farrar, Straus and Giroux.
A Cry of Players. William Gibson. Atheneum.
The Cuban Thing. Jack Gelber. Grove Press.
Ergo. Jakov Lind. Hill and Wang.
Fire. John Roc. Atheneum.
The Great White Hope. Howard Sackler. Dial Press.
Hadrian VII. Peter Luke. Alfred E. Knopf.
I Never Sang for My Father. Robert Anderson. Random House.
Jimmy Shine. Murray Schisgal. Atheneum.
Kingdom of Earth (originally *The Seven Descents of Myrtle*). Tennessee Williams. New Directions.
The Man in the Glass Booth. Robert Shaw. Grove Press.
The Only Game in Town. Frank D. Gilroy. Random House.
Plaza Suite. Neil Simon. Random House.
The Serpent. Jean-Claude van Itallie. Atheneum.
Spofford. Herman Shumlin. Random House.
Summertree. Ron Cowen. Random House.
Tango. Slawomir Mrozek; translated by Teresa Dzeduzycka and Ralph Manheim. Grove Press.
We Bombed in New Haven. Joseph Heller. Alfred A. Knopf.

A SELECTED LIST OF OTHER PLAYS PUBLISHED IN 1968-69

The Amen Corner. James Baldwin. Dial.
Best Short Plays of the World Theater, 1958-1967. Stanley Richards, editor. Crown.
Best Short Plays of 1968. Stanley Richards, editor. Chilton.
The Bonds of Interest. Jacinto Benavente. Frederick Ungar.
Cascando and Other Dramatic Pieces: Cascando; Words and Music; Eh Joe; Play; Come and Go; Film. Samuel Beckett. Grove Press.
Coat of Many Colors. Barrie Stavis. A.S. Barnes.
Collision Course. Edward Parone, editor. Random House.
The Duke of Palermo and Other Plays: The Duke of Palermo; Dr. McGrath; Osbert's Career, or The Poet's Progress; An Open Letter to Mike Nichols (an essay). Edmund Wilson. Farrar, Straus and Giroux.
Enter a Free Man. Tom Stoppard. Faber and Faber.
Father Uxbridge Wants To Marry. Frank Gagliano. Grove Press.
The Fighting Cock. Jean Anouilh. Methuen.
First Season: Line; The Indian Wants the Bronx; It's Called the Sugar Plum; Rats. Israel Horovitz. Random House.
The Hawk. Murray Mednick and Tony Barsha. Bobbs-Merrill.
House of Blue Leaves and *Muzeeka*. John Guare. Grove Press.
House of Flowers (musical). Book by Truman Capote, music by Harold Arlen, lyrics by the Messrs. Capote and Arlen. Random House.
Little Boxes. John Bowen. Methuen & Co.
New Black Playwrights: Happy Ending by Douglas Turner Ward; *Day of Absence* by Douglas Turner Ward; *Ceremonies in Dark Old Men* by Lonne Elder III; *A Rat's Mass* by Adrienne Kennedy; *Goin' a Buffalo* by Ed Bullins; *Family Meeting* by William Wellington Mackey. Louisiana State University Press.
A Night Out, Night School, Revue Sketches. Harold Pinter. Grove Press.
Plays from Black Africa: The Rhythm of Violence by Lewis Nkosi; *The Rain Killers* by Alfred Hutchinson; *The Jewels of the Shrine* by James Ene Henshaw; *Song of a Goat* by John Pepper Clark; *Edufa* by Efua T. Sutherland; *The Literary Society* by Henry Ofori. Hill and Wang.
Plays of Three Decades: Thunder Rock (1939), *Jeb* (1946), *Shadow of Heroes* (1958) by Robert Ardrey. Atheneum.
The Sean O'Casey Reader. Brooks Atkinson, editor. *Juno and the Paycock; The Plough and the Stars; Red Roses for Me; Cock-A-Doodle Dandy; The Drums of Father Ned; The Silver Tassie; Within the Gates; Bedtime Story; Purple Dust*. Also extracts from 6 volumes of autobiography and essays. St. Martins.
Time Present and *The Hotel in Amsterdam*. John Osborne. Faber and Faber.
The Undertaking, Thief, The Pig. David Trainer. Random House.

NECROLOGY

JUNE 1, 1968—MAY 31, 1969

PERFORMERS

Ahearne, Tom (63)—January 7, 1969
Ayres, Robert (54)—November 5, 1968
Bagley, Sam (65)—July 3, 1968
Bainbridge, Julian (91)—March 7, 1969
Balin, Mireille (59)—November 8, 1968
Ballantine, E. J. (80)—October 20, 1968
Bankhead, Tallulah (65)—December 12, 1968
Barrett, Roger (47)—November 17, 1968
Barzell, Wolfe (72)—February 14, 1969
Bates, Barbara (43)—March 18, 1969
Beal, Royal (69)—May 21, 1969
Bellarina, Bella (72)—February 1, 1969
Benaderet, Bea (62)—October 13, 1968
Bennett, Raymond (68)—February, 1969
Berry, James J. (54)—January 28, 1969
Bishop, Jane—January 30, 1969
Blake, Madge—February 19, 1969
Boles, John (73)—February 27, 1969
Bonanova, Fortunio (73)—April 2, 1969
Bowes, Alice (79)—January 3, 1969
Brady, Mary—May 24, 1968
Brindley, Madge—August 28, 1968
Carol, John (58)—November, 1968
Casson, Sir Lewis (93)—May 16, 1969
Castle, Irene (75)—January 25, 1969
Chan, Peter (68)—March 15, 1969
Cherry, V. Ewing (76)—March 30, 1969
Cianelli, Alma (76)—June 23, 1968
Clark, Fred (54)—December 6, 1968
Close, Ivy (78)—December 4, 1968
Collins, Marty (72)—November 24, 1968
Copley, Joan (69)—May, 1969
Corey, Wendell (54)—November 8, 1968
Cullis, Brian (41)—March, 1969
Dawson, Gladys (71)—March 7, 1969
Deutsch, Ernst (78)—March 22, 1969
Douglas, Valerie (31)—March 2, 1969
Duryea, Dan (61)—June 7, 1968
Eliscu, Fernanda (88)—September 27, 1968
Endersby, Paul (69)—June, 1968
Evans, Rex (66)—April 3, 1969
Fife, Evelyn Henderson (81)—April 12, 1969
Fischer, Charlotte Andrews (58)—November 24, 1968
Flanagan, Bud (72)—October 20, 1968
Fleming, Ian (80)—January 1, 1969
Foley, Red (58)—September 20, 1968
Forbes, Edward—May 15, 1969
Forster, Rudolf (84)—October 25, 1968

Francis, Kay (63)—August 26, 1968
Galloway, Hunter (59)—February 14, 1969
Gardner, Helen Louise—November 20, 1968
Gish, Dorothy (70)—June 4, 1968
Glenn, Cynda (59)—September 1, 1968
Glenville, Shaun (84)—December 28, 1968
Gough, John (74)—June 30, 1968
Graff, Wilton (64)—January 13, 1969
Green, Mitzi (48)—May 24, 1969
Granville, Louise (73)—December 22, 1968
Hale, Malcolm (27)—October 30, 1968
Hancock, Tony (44)—June 22, 1968
Harvey, Lilian (61)—July 27, 1968
Hawley, Esther (62)—November 4, 1968
Hazzard, Alice Dovey (84)—January 11, 1969
Hemsley, Estelle (81)—November 4, 1968
Henry, Sam H.—June 21, 1968
Herbert, Lew (65)—July 30, 1968
Hibbert, Geoffrey (48)—February 3, 1969
Hilary, Ruth (61)—June 20, 1968
Hilton, Violet and Daisy (60)—January 4, 1969
Hitchcock, Flora Zabelle (88)—October 7, 1968
Hobbs, Jack (74)—June 4, 1968
Hornblow, Mrs. Juliette Crosby (73)—May 1, 1969
Hylan, Donald (69)—June 20, 1968
Ingram, Jack (66)—February 20, 1969
Jessel, Patricia (47)—June 8, 1968
Karloff, Boris (81)—February 2, 1969
Kelly, Kitty (66)—June 29, 1968
Kelton, Pert (61)—October 30, 1968
Kent, Willard (85)—September 5, 1968
Kirby, Mae Elaine (87)—October, 1968
Lahtinen, Warner H. (Duke) (58)—December 12, 1968
Lanphier, James F. (48)—February 11, 1969
Laurier, Jay (89)—April, 1969
Leduc, Claudine—February 15, 1969
Lewis, Cathy (50)—November 20, 1968
Locher, Felix (87)—March 13, 1969
Lockerbie, Beth (53)—September 21, 1968
Logan, Ella (56)—May 1, 1969
Lord, Lucy (70)—January 23, 1969
Lord, Philip (89)—November 25, 1968
MacLane, Barton (66)—January 1, 1969
Malleson, Miles (80)—March 15, 1969
Margulies, Virginia M. (53)—February 16, 1969
Martin, Lewis H. (74)—February 21, 1969

479

Mason, Marjorie—November 21, 1968
Maunsell, Charles—August 1, 1968
McDonald, Francis (77)—September 18, 1968
McKee, Donald M. (69)—June 27, 1968
McNear, Howard (64)—January 3, 1969
Merton, Collette (61)—July 24, 1968
Metz, Lucius Wells (71)—January 7, 1969
Mohr, Gerald (54)—November 10, 1968
Montt, Cristinia (72)—April 22, 1969
Moran, Patsy (63)—December 10, 1968
Mowbray, Alan (72)—March 25, 1969
Navarro, Carlos (47)—February 24, 1969
Nelson, Virginia Tallent (57)—September 26, 1968
Nordstrom, Clarence (75)—December 13, 1968
Novarro, Ramon (69)—October 31, 1968
O'Keefe, Dennis (60)—August 31, 1968
O'Neill, Sally (55)—June 18, 1968
Piesen, Margery Korman (62)—November 14, 1968
Plimmer, Rev, Walter J. (67)—September 18, 1968
Powell, Maud Morton—March, 1969
Puccio, Mae Crane (44)—April 15, 1969
Ridgewell, Audrey (64)—October 27, 1968
Riga, Nadine (59)—December 11, 1968
Ritter, Thelma (63)—February 5, 1969
Roberts, Sara Jane (44)—August 19, 1968
Rorke, Margaret Hayden (85)—March 2, 1969
Ruben, Jose (80)—April 28, 1969
Russell, Marie (86)—March 29, 1969
Ryan, Ben—July 5, 1968
Ryken, Mabel (77)—May 27, 1968
Schwartz, Wendie Lee (45)—August 23, 1968
Seaton, Scott (97)—June 3, 1968
Servoss, Mary (80)—November 20, 1968
Sheehan, Margaret T. (Flavin) (88)—March 18, 1969
Sherman, Frederick (64)—May 20, 1969
Shoshano, Rose (73)—November 2, 1968
Simonov, Ruben (69)—December 5, 1968
Skelly, James (33)—April 19, 1969
Spear, Harry (56)—February 10, 1969
Stafford, Hanley (69)—September 9, 1968
Strassberg, Max (55)—July 17, 1968
Sutherland, Victor (79)—August 29, 1968
Tabor, Joan (35)—December 18, 1968
Talman, William (53)—August 30, 1968
Talva, Galina (41)—December 27, 1968
Terranova, Dino (65)—April 27, 1969
Tone, Franchot (63)—September 18, 1968
Tracy, Lee (70)—October 18, 1968
Tripp, Frederick (76)—December, 1968
Tully, Ethel (70)—October 1, 1968
Turner, Aidan (60)—August 6, 1968
Turner, Dorothy (79)—April 5, 1969
Turner, George—July 27, 1968
Twinem, Leo L. (78)—October 16, 1968
Valli, Virginia (70)—September 24, 1968
van Saber, Mrs. Lilla Alexander (56)—July 15, 1968

Washington, Lamont (24)—August 25, 1968
White, Frances (71)—February 14, 1969
Williams, Rhys (71)—May 28, 1969
Winninger, Charles (84)—January 19, 1969
Woods, Harry L. (79)—December 28, 1968
York, Elizabeth (46)—March 24, 1969
Young, Margaret (69)—May 3, 1969

PLAYWRIGHTS

Atkins, Thomas C. (80)—June 18, 1968
Bardoli, Louis (75)—May 22, 1969
Burns, Anne K. (82)—September 20, 1968
Bynner, Witters (86)—June 1, 1968
Byrne, John J.—July 4, 1968
Carroll, Paul Vincent (68)—October 20, 1968
Claman, Julian (51)—April 24, 1969
Corrie, Joe (74)—December 11, 1968
Dratler, Jay (57)—September 25, 1968
Dunning, Philip (76)—July 20, 1968
Hiken, Nat (54)—December 7, 1968
Jackson, Charles (65)—September 21, 1968
Kennaway, James (40)—December 21, 1968
Kirkland, Jack (66)—February 22, 1969
Manger, Itzik (67)—about February 18, 1969
O'Brien, Justin (62)—December 7, 1968
Percy, Edward (born Edward Percy Smith)—May 28, 1968
Steinbeck, John (66)—December 20, 1968
Sullivan, Mrs. Pamela W. (30)—February 8, 1969
Weinstock, Jack (62)—May 23, 1969
Weisenborn, Guenther (66)—March 26, 1969
Woolrich, Cornell (64)—September 25, 1968

COMPOSERS AND LYRICISTS

Anderson, Cecil (62)—November 17, 1968
Arce, Juan F. Acosts (78)—May 21, 1968
Boyd, Jeanne (78)—August 8, 1968
Brooks, Harvey O. (69)—June 17, 1968
Bunch, Boyd—February 18, 1969
Butler, Ralph (82)—April 8, 1969
Clifford, Gordon (65)—June 11, 1968
Cooper, Evelyne Love—September 7, 1968
Davies, Lew (57)—December 12, 1968
Duke, Vernon (65)—January 17, 1969
English, Granville (73)—September 1, 1968
Fields, Frank Gaskin (59)—March 5, 1969
Gerber, Alex (74)—April 21, 1969
Kahn, Marvin (54)—April 2, 1969
Kendrick, Merle T. (71)—May 23, 1968
Komeda, Christopher (36)—April 23, 1969
Kramer, A. Walter (79)—April 7, 1969
Labate, Bruno (85)—November 23, 1968
La Prade, Ernest (79)—April 20, 1969
Lewis, Morgan (Buddy) (63)—December 8, 1968
McHugh, Jimmy (74)—May 23, 1969
McLaughlin, John (71)—June 15, 1968
Nelson, Ed (84)—March 30, 1969
Phillips, Montague (83)—January 4, 1969
Richards, Johnny (56)—October 7, 1968

Rosemont, Walter (91)—February 22, 1969
Ross, Roy Irving (56)—July 23, 1968
Schoenfeld, William C. (75)—January 8, 1969
Skinner, Frank (69)—October 11, 1968
Smalley, Eugene B. (Bud) (46)—June 15, 1968
Sowerby, Leo (73)—July 7, 1968
Stegmeyer, William J. (51)—August 19, 1968
Weber, Edwin J. (75)—August 26, 1968
Young, Victor (79)—September 2, 1968

PRODUCERS, DIRECTORS, CHOREOGRAPHERS

Akimov, Nikolai (67)—September 6, 1968
Arnold, Tom (72)—February 2, 1969
Carr, Lawrence (51)—January 17, 1969
Cassel, Rita Allen (56)—July 2, 1968
Castle, Nick (56)—August 29, 1968
Cobb, John S. (37)—March 5, 1969
Colina, Fernando (37)—January 30, 1969
Darnel, Hale (44)—April 24, 1969
Davies, William Arthur (84)—May 6, 1969
Fleischmann, Julius (68)—October 22, 1968
Johnson, Virginia (59)—February 7, 1969
Kretlow, Arthur (73)—October 18, 1968
McKenna, Edwin (Boots) (68)—March 16, 1969
Miller, Gilbert (84)—January 2, 1969
Vinaver, Steven (31)—July 28, 1968
Wanger, Walter (74)—November 18, 1968
White, George (78)—October 11, 1968
Willis-Croft, Stanley—March 8, 1969

CONDUCTORS

Ansermet, Ernest (86)—February 20, 1969
Dantzig, Eli (70)—July 9, 1968
Hirst, George S. (77)—June 19, 1968
Munch, Charles (77)—November 6, 1968

DESIGNERS

Graham, Shad E. (72)—January 28, 1969
Rosenthal, Jean (57)—May 1, 1969
Shelving, Paul—June 5, 1968
Stevenson, Edward (62)—December 2, 1968

CRITICS

Barstow, James S. Jr. (49)—June 23, 1968
Brackett, Charles (76)—March 9, 1969
Brown, John Mason (68)—March 16, 1969
Cail, Harold J. (66)—August 30, 1968
Chujoy, Anatole (74)—February 24, 1969
Fitzgerald, William C. (53)—April 7, 1969
Hoffman, Irving (59)—December 9, 1968
Millar, Robins (79)—August 12, 1968
Pihodna, Gottlieb (Joe) (61)—January 4, 1969
Sabin, Robert (57)—May 17, 1969
Sherman, John K. (70)—April 18, 1969

MUSICIANS

Barbarin, Adolph Paul (69)—February 17, 1969
Breese, Lou—January 8, 1969
Cotton, Billy (69)—March 25, 1969
Elman, Ziggy (54)—June 25, 1968
Hawkins, Coleman (64)—May 19, 1969
Jefferson, Hilton (65)—November 14, 1968
Lewis, George (68)—December 31, 1968
Montgomery, Wes (45)—June 15, 1968
Pavageau, (Slow Drag) Alcide—January 19, 1969
Robinson, Willard (73)—June 24, 1968
Russell, Pee Wee (62)—February 15, 1969
Wettling, George (62)—June 6, 1968

OTHERS

Alber, David O. (59)—December 31, 1969
Public relations
Briscoe, Johnson (86)—February 16, 1969
Actors' agent and theater historian
Chandler, Thelma (64)—June 14, 1968
Stage manager
Coletti, Frank (68)—October 15, 1968
Stage manager
Cornell, John (55)—January 8, 1969
Stage manager
Craig, Hardin (93)—October 13, 1968
Shakespeare scholar and editor
Day, Cyrus L. (67)—July 5, 1968
Drama teacher
Downing, Russell (67)—June 28, 1968
President of Radio City Music Hall
Fitts, Dudley (65)—July 10, 1968
Translator of Aristophanes, Sophocles
Harris, John H. (70)—February 12, 1969
Showman
Hildreth, Albert (64)—January 14, 1969
Box office treasurer
Kay, Virginia (42)—April 8, 1969
Columnist
King, William A. (41)—October 3, 1968
Stage manager
Krakower, Arnold (53)—April 4, 1969
Theatrical lawyer
Lovell, Harold C. (82)—March 26, 1969
A founder of American Shakespeare Festival
Lowry, Philip W. (75)—February 13, 1969
Lawyer
Lyon, Herb (49)—August 6, 1968
Newspaper columnist
Maney, Richard (77)—July 1, 1968
Press agent
Mantle, Mrs. Burns (89)—December 25, 1968
Widow of drama critic
McLearn, Frank C. (67)—May 24, 1969
Pres., King Features
Menke, Captain Bill (88)—July 15, 1968
Owner of last Mississippi River showboat

Popper, Hermine I. (53)—November 18, 1968
  Ex-editor of Theater Arts
Rosenberg, George—May 10, 1969
  Agent
St. Denis, Ruth (88)—July 22, 1968
  Pioneer of modern dance
Strauss, Eduard (59)—April 5, 1969
  Great-grandson of Johann Strauss
Summers, Arthur (59)—March 22, 1969
  Agent
Totten, John J. (83)—May 3, 1969
  Vice pres., Carnegie Hall

Upton, LeRoy—May 2, 1969
  Second vice pres., I.A.T.S.E.
Varna, Henri (81)—April, 1969
  French showman
Weintraub, Milton (70)—November 17, 1968
  Secretary-treasurer A.T.A.M.
White, Jerome (78)—March 1, 1969
  Music arranger
Williams, Addie (75)—July 25, 1968
  Subscription manager
Young, Frank (56)—July 4, 1968
  Press Agent

INDEX

Bold face page numbers refer to pages where Cast of Characters may be found.

Gallery, James, 128
Galloway, Hunter, 479
Galman, Peter, 423
Galsworthy, John, 46, 148
Galton, Ray, 389
Galvin, Gene, 452
Gambler, The, 41, 458
Gamboa, Marcello, 398
Game of Adam and Eve, The, 117
Gammell, Robin, 398
Gammon, William, 403
Gampel, Morison, 414
Gandy, Irene, 440
Gano, David, 124
Ganshaw, Robert, and John Prescott, 413, 425, 439-440, 445-446, 448, 450, 452-453
Gantner, Carrillo, 115
Garcia, Louis, 393
Garcia, Nino, 415
Garcin, Henri, 166
Gardenia, Vincent, 443
Gardner, Ann, 404
Gardner, Claudette, 121
Gardner, Diane, 134
Gardner, Helen Louise, 479
Gardner, Herb, 9, 127, 396
Gardner, Jimmy, 146
Gardner, Rita, 442, 460
Garfield, John, Jr., 124
Garfield, Julie, 451
Garland, Geoff, 414
Garland, Patrick, 149
Garner, Jay, 7, 20, 403
Garnett, Katherine, 398
Garraud, Edith, 165
Garrett, Betty, 459, 462
Garrick, Beulah, 376
Garrivier, Victor, 167
Gary, Harold, 144, 151, 463
Gasc, Yves, 165
Gascon, Jean, 115, 133
Gaskill, William, 144
Gaskins, Deloris, 435
Gasper, Edd K., 382
Gasper, Eddie, 400
Gassell, Sylvia, 449, 453
Gates, Larry, 115
Gatti, Armand, 158, 160
Gaus, Robert, 410
Gaver, Jack, 471
Gavin, Gene, 417
Gavon, Igors, 412
Gay, John, 148
Gaynes, Edmund, 400
Geer, Ellen, 129-130
Geer, Faith, 377, 396, 408, 411, 413, 424, 443, 453
Geer, Will, 443
Geese, 26-27, 36, 443
Geist, Marie, 123
Gelber, Jack, 18, 34, 166, 377

Gelfer, Steven, 374
Gélin, Daniel, 166
Gence, Denise, 166
Genet, Jean, 119, 132
Geniat, Gilberte, 165
Gentleman Caller, The, 150
George, Nathan, 29, 474
George Dandin, 4, 21, 151, 374, **375**
George Freedley Memorial Award, 474
George Jean Nathan Award, 474
George M! 372, 460, 475-476
George Washington Slept Here, 58-59
Georgie-Porgie, 41, 455
Gerber, Alex, 480
Gero, Frank, 431
Gérome, Raymond, 167
Gerringer, Robert, 129-130
Gershwin, George, 33, 137, 150, 447, 455
Gershwin, Ira, 59, 447, 455
Gerstad, John, 411
Gersten, Bernard, 422
Gesner, Clark, 117, 420
Get Thee to Canterbury, 27, 31, **444,** 445
Ghelderode, Michel de, 372, 376
Ghost, The, 145
Ghosts, 126, 161
Giambri, Phillip, 448
Gianni Schicchi, 127, **407**
Giannini, A. Christina, 121, 452
Gibbens, Bill, 386
Gibbons, Jane, 119-120
Gibbs, Ann, 463
Gibbs, Matyelock, 145-147
Gibbs, Reedy, 125
Gibson, Clifford, 150
Gibson, Jeremy, 147
Gibson, Richard, 422
Gibson, Robert, 432, 445
Gibson, William, 18, 25, 391
Gide, André, 121
Gielgud, Sir John, 138, 144, 148
Gierasch, Stefan, 133, 462
Giffard, Wendy, 146
Gifford, Alan, 121
Gifford/Wallace, 430
Gift for Cathy, A, 114
Gil, Michael, 446
Gilbert, Barbara, 412
Gilbert, Lou, 380
Gilbert, Robert, 375
Gilbert, Ronni L., 378
Gilbert, W.S., 120, 390
Gilbert, Willie, 114

Gilbert Becaud Sings Love, 4, **382-383**
Giles, John Marlin, 429
Gilford, Madeline Lee, 408
Gillette, Anita, 459
Gillman, Jonathan, 399
Gilmore, Peter, 148
Gilroy, Frank D., 35, 372
Gingham Dog, The, 4, 10, 18, 110, 134, **413**
Gingrich, Susan, 440
Ginzburg, Natalia, 139, 151, 160
Giorda, 165
Giovanni, Paul, 460
Girard, Donald, 382
Girard, Louis, 123
Giraudoux, Jean, 59, 119, 125, 129
Girl of the Golden West, The, 120
Girl from Stockholm, The, 167
Girven, Howard, 412, 427
Gish, Dorothy, 479
Gisle, Anna, 128-129
Giunta, Aldo, 453
Giveaway, The, 141, 147
Gizmo Does the Audition, 456
Glanville, Maxwell, 385, 409
Glasgow, Carol, 135
Glasier, Gerry, 130, 463
Glaspell, Susan, 54
Glass, Katherine, 389
Glass, Ron, 398
Glass Menagerie, The, 127, 132, **166**
Glasshouse Productions, 378, 475
Glassman, Stephen, 411
Glassman, William, 411
Gleason, John, 115, 377, 382, 386, 391-393, 406-407, 412, 414, 438-439
Glenn, Cynda, 479
Glenn, James, 127
Glennon, John, 435
Glenn-Smith, Michael, 402
Glenville, Shaun, 479
Glick, Dennis, 402
Gloria and Esperanza, 474
Glory! Hallelujah! 130
Glover, William, 115, 413
Glover, William ·H., 471
Goat, The, 135
Goat Island, 167
Goble, Diana, 436
Goblet Game, The, 146
God Bless, 139, 144, 150
God Bless You, Harold Fineberg, 27, 449
"God Is a (Guess What?)," 27, 32, 15, 440